VOICES
OF AMERICA

VOICES OF AMERICA

The Nation's Story in
Slogans, Sayings, and Songs

Thomas A. Bailey

WITH THE ASSISTANCE OF
STEPHEN M. DOBBS

THE FREE PRESS
A Division of Macmillan Publishing Co., Inc.
NEW YORK

Collier Macmillan Publishers
LONDON

The Free Press
A Division of Macmillan Publishing Co., Inc.
866 Third Avenue, New York, N.Y. 10022

Collier Macmillan Canada, Ltd.

Library of Congress Catalog Card Number: 76–8143

Printed in the United States of America

printing number

1 2 3 4 5 6 7 8 9 10

Library of Congress Cataloging in Publication Data

Bailey, Thomas Andrew
    Voices of America.

    Bibliography: p.
    Includes index.
    1. United States--History. 2. Quotations,
American. 3. Slogans. 4. Songs, American--Texts.
I. Title.   1-20-77
E179.B16   973   76-8143
ISBN 0-02-901260-0

Contents

Foreword

As a kind of hobby I have been collecting the slogans of American history for more than fifty years. I finally decided to incorporate the more striking and significant of these, together with selected popular sayings and segments of song, in a general overview of the nation's story.

A more prosaic but perhaps more exact title than the one chosen would be "Words that Moved America." In short, this narrative presents in a historical framework popular utterances that were generally designed to produce some kind of result: to get people to vote, to give, to lend, to save, to fight, to avenge, or whatever. To this end I have utilized the most memorable catchwords, catchphrases, toasts, songs, familiar sayings, mottoes, and sobriquets. Most of the nicknames, often themselves slogans, help to form a negative or positive image of the cast of characters, ranging from "Old Hickory" Jackson to "Give 'em Hell" Harry Truman. I have also included many of the more moving statements of elected leaders, who often expressed in an important way a popular mood or an attempt to shape the public mind. We all remember Franklin Roosevelt's call to arms against the Depression, "The only thing we have to fear is fear itself."

I have naturally been selective because of the abundance of riches, and for obvious reasons I have deliberately excluded merchandising slogans, such as the florists' appeal, "Say It with Flowers." In general I have chosen items that focused on significant public issues and best illustrate what involved masses of people at a particular time. Many of the campaign slogans and songs are simplistic, even nonsensical, but they usually reflect what was regarded as important in winning elections. A few of the sayings are no doubt apocryphal (the tape-recorder is a recent invention) but they still have significance as instruments in shaping the public mind.

Slogans are comforting shorthand for thinking, which is usually avoided as hard work, and for this reason they are open to criticism. Even so, they are an essential part of the nation's history. They serve to highlight the main issues, provide colorful pegs on which to hang facts, and add life to what all too often is made unnecessarily dull.

My associate, Dr. Stephen M. Dobbs of San Francisco State University, helped to gather essential data; prepared first drafts of Chapters XXXII, XXXIII, and XXXIV; provided a masterly critique of the entire manuscript; and in various other ways served most usefully in shepherding the book through press.

THOMAS A. BAILEY
Department of History
Stanford University
Stanford, California

I

Planting a People

... For I shall yet live to see it [Virginia] an Inglishe nation.

Sir Walter Raleigh, 1602

THE SEEDS OF AN EMPIRE

Sloganeering on a large scale is a relatively modern development, although stirring appeals and rallying cries were known to antiquity. Prior to the third and last war between Carthage and Rome, 149–146 B.C., the Roman Cato the Elder harped monotonously and successfully on the one demand "Carthage must be destroyed" (Delenda est Carthago). Early Roman historians record that in 49 B.C. Julius Caesar proclaimed, "The die is cast," when he entered Italy against Pompey by crossing the Rubicon River. Two years later, at the Battle of Zela in Asia Minor, he further immortalized his victory with a dispatch to Rome, "I came, I saw, I conquered." Constantine the Great, the Roman Emperor, on the eve of his crucial battle near Rome (A.D. 312), allegedly saw a flaming cross in the heavens bearing the words "In this sign shalt thou conquer." He adopted the cross, routed his adversary, and brought about a turning point in the history of Christianity. King John III of Poland, after repulsing the invading Turks near Vienna in 1683, reported to the Pope, "I came, I saw, God conquered."

Early America was moved to some degree by slogans and other memorable sayings. The peopling of Virginia, founded at Jamestown in 1607, involved the solicitation of settlers and the advertisement of sailings but

1

produced few noteworthy catchwords. One rough woodcut, designed to attract young and procreative colonists, showed a couple engaged in amorous kissing, with the printed encouragement "Increase and Multiply." John Smith, who emerged as the savior of the Virginia colony in its early "starving time," reports in his *General Historie* the stern regulations that he laid down for idle and shiftless fellows: "You must obey this, now, for a law—that 'he that will not work shall not eat.' " This "law" finally took the popular form "He who will not work shall not eat."

Autocracy continued to hold sway in Virginia. In 1671, on the eve of Bacon's Rebellion, the irascible Governor Berkeley reported to his superiors, "But, I thank God, there are no free schools nor printing, and I hope we shall not have [them] these hundred years. For learning has brought disobedience, and heresy, and sects into the world, and printing has divulged them, and libels against the best government. God keep us from both!"

Notably different was the enlightened atmosphere of Pennsylvania ("Penn's Woodland"), which William Penn, a convert to Quakerism, launched so auspiciously in 1681 for his fellow "Broadbrims," as the Indians and others nicknamed them. Designing his outpost for persecuted Quakers (Friends), he called the colony a "Holy Experiment." The chief town was Philadelphia, a name appropriately taken from the Greek, meaning "brotherly love." Penn advertised widely and successfully for sturdy settlers, for whom he devised a famous Frame of Government. Its preface contained some memorable observations, such as "Governments, like clocks, go from the motion that men give them. . . ." "Let men be good," Penn sagely observed, "and the government cannot be bad; if it be ill, they will cure it."

PILGRIM FATHERS—AND MOTHERS

Pious Pilgrims, debarking at Plymouth in 1620, earned the honor of having planted the first substantial English settlement in New England, although they followed the first Jamestown experiment by thirteen years. This lonely colony of Separatists in Massachusetts proved more significant as an example of what dedicated men and women could do in establishing an outpost in the wilderness than for physical accomplishments. Begun as a small outpost, it remained one.

Inspirational words from this tiny colony echoed later, especially after the firsthand account by William Bradford appeared posthumously in 1669 as *Of Plymouth Plantation*. "They knew they were pilgrims," he recorded, and from this observation evidently came the honored title "Pilgrim Fathers." Bradford further relates that before sailing "they committed themselves to the will of God and resolved to proceed," despite predictions of hardship and danger. "Being thus arrived in a good harbor, and brought safe to land," he continues, "they fell upon their knees and blessed the God of Heaven who had brought them over the vast and

furious ocean, and delivered them from all the perils and miseries. . . ."
The famous quip of later days, especially popular in the anti-Yankee
South, was that the "Pious Pilgrims" first fell upon their knees and then
upon the aborigines. Actually the earliest relations of the Pilgrims with
the Indians were conspicuously good.

Cold, hunger, and disease soon took their ghastly toll at Plymouth.
The Pilgrim leader, Bradford, recorded that "it pleased God to visit us
then with death daily, and with so general a disease that the living were
scarce able to bury the dead." This chronicler's vision of the future led
him to conclude, "Thus out of small beginnings greater things have been
produced by His hand . . . ; and, as one small candle may light a thousand, so the light here kindled hath shone unto many, yea in some sort
to our whole nation."

Poor in soil but rich in courage and dedication, the Plymouth Pilgrims
inspired orators and poets of later generations, both in America and
abroad. Wendell Phillips declaimed at Plymouth in 1855, "Neither do I
acknowledge the right of Plymouth to the whole rock. No, the rock
underlies all America: it only crops out here." The English poetess Felicia
Hemans thrilled generations of American school children and others with
her poem of praise "The Landing of the Pilgrim Fathers," written about
1820:

> Ay, call it holy ground,
>   The soil where first they trod!
> They have left unstained what there they found—
>   Freedom to worship God.

Somewhat less elegantly, but no less pointedly, an anonymous poet
wrote:

> Oh, we are weary pilgrims; to this wilderness we bring
> A church without a bishop, a state without a king.

PURITANICAL PREACHMENTS

Unlike the Pilgrim Separatists at Plymouth, the settlers who landed at
Massachusetts Bay, the key New England colony, were Puritans. They
sought to purge the established Church of England of its "Romish practices," not abandon it. John Winthrop, one of their gifted leaders, declared in a sermon delivered on board his ship, the *Arbella*, "For we must
consider that we shall be a city upon a hill. The eyes of all people are
upon us, so that if we shall deal falsely with our God in this work we
have undertaken, and so cause Him to withdraw His present help from
us, we shall be made a story and a byword through the world."

Massachusetts Bay, unlike many other English colonies, embraced an
unusually high percentage of well-educated and propertied gentry. Colonists in those days were usually emigrants seeking their fortune, not risk-
ing it. As the old saying goes, "Dukes don't emigrate"—except when

fleeing the guillotine. Massachusetts Bay also exuded a feeling of superiority that grew out of possessing the true faith, as well as more than an ordinary amount of wealth and college education. "God sifted a whole Nation that he might send Choice Grain into this Wilderness," asserted William Stoughton of Boston in a famous sermon.

A belief that these "Saints" or "elect of the Lord" were God's chosen people promoted a degree of self-righteousness, even arrogance. Later generations acclaimed Boston as "a state of mind" and as "the Hub of the Universe"—spiritually and intellectually, if not physically.

Straight-laced Puritans in New England embraced Calvinist theology, which held that certain people, even dead infants, were destined for an eternity of hellfire, regardless of their good works. As Lorenzo Dow later declared (1836), "You will be damned if you do. And you will be damned if you don't." An immensely popular poem in New England came from the pen of the Congregational clergyman Michael Wigglesworth—"Day of Doom" (1662). It depicted the fate of the damned:

> They cry, they roar for anguish sore,
>   and gnaw their tongues for horrour.
> But get away without delay,
>   Christ pitties not your cry:
> Depart to Hell, there may you yell,
>   and roar Eternally.

Such burning faith led the Puritans to pass harsh "Blue Laws" for the regulation of personal conduct, as well as statutes prescribing the flogging or banishment of Quakers and other dissenters. Christmas celebrations were frowned upon by these early Puritans as reminiscent of "Popery"; indeed "Yuletide is fooltide" became a common saying. More than a grain of truth lay in the later barb of Artemus Ward (1866), "The Puritans nobly fled from a land of despotism to a land of freedim, where they could not only enjoy their own religion, but could prevent everybody else from enjoyin *his*." H. L. Mencken, the bad-boy journalist of the 1920s, defined Puritanism as "the haunting fear that someone, somewhere, may be happy." Less elegantly he wrote, "Show me a Puritan and I'll show you a son of a bitch."

Oppressive, theocratic practices in the "Bible Commonwealth," otherwise known as Massachusetts Bay, led to the ouster of religious dissenters such as Roger Williams and Anne Hutchinson, both of whom were forced to flee to Rhode Island. Back in Boston the Puritan bigwigs referred scornfully to "Rogues' Island" as "that sewer" which welcomed "the Lord's debris." For good reasons Rhode Island ("Little Rhody") came to be known as "the traditional home of the otherwise minded."

Compact New England naturally became the seed bed of town-meeting democracy, but the early leaders of Massachusetts Bay distrusted the common people. The Reverend John Cotton asked rhetorically, "If the people be governors, who shall be governed?" John Winthrop feared the "commons" as the "meaner sort," and held democracy to be the "meanest and worst" of all forms of government.

Distinctive sectional traits were bound to be the by-products of frigid winters, hot summers, hellfire theology, and rocky soil. About 1700, "Deeds, not words" became a common admonition among these thrifty people, and Connecticut honestly earned the title, "The Land of Steady Habits." A common New England maxim emerged:

> Use it up, wear it out;
> Make it do, or do without.

Frugality often undermined the Puritanical New England conscience to produce traditionally "sharp" Yankee traders, including Connecticut peddlers who palmed off wooden nutmegs. Hence the nickname "Nutmeg State" for Connecticut. Ebenezer Rockwood Hoar, an eminent nineteenth century Massachusetts jurist, declared that the three stages of the enterprising Yankee were "to get on, to get honour, to get honest."

Ranking in importance with the "Sacred Book" (the Bible) in shaping the youthful mind stood *The New England Primer,* first compiled in the 1680s and ultimately selling some 5 million copies. In addition to letters of the alphabet, illustrated with crude woodcuts, the booklet contained rhymes and moral admonitions derived from the Old and New Testaments. Beside a rough picture of the Bible appeared this couplet:

> Thy Life to Mend
> This Book Attend.

Calvinism hammered home the belief that

> In Adam's fall
> We sinned all.

and

> Our days begin with trouble here,
> Our life is but a span,
> And cruel death is always near,
> So frail a thing is man.

For good measure, *The Primer* encouraged attentiveness:

> The Idle Fool
> Is whipt at School.

FRUITS OF A FREE PRESS

Freedom of the press emerged as the burning issue in the New York trial (1734–35) of John Peter Zenger, a poor but courageous newspaper printer. Accused of having exposed the corruption of the colonial governor, he was brought before the bar of so-called "justice" on charges of seditious libel. Zenger received unexpected but outstanding support from an aged Philadelphia lawyer, Andrew Hamilton. In his moving conclusion the orator affirmed, "The question before the court and you, gentle-men of the jury, is not of small nor private concern. It is not the cause of a poor printer, nor of New York alone, which you are now trying. No! It may, in its consequence, affect every freeman that lives under a British government on the main [land] of America. It is the best cause. It is the cause of liberty."

Swayed by Hamilton's eloquence, the jury retired and returned with a verdict of "Not guilty." This was a daring decision, because all that the jurors could legally do was to pass upon the mere publication of the libel, whether true or not. Zenger was plainly guilty of this offense, because the maxim of that era, ascribed to Lord Mansfield (1704–1793), was "The greater the truth, the greater the libel." Yet freedom of the press gained only a temporary victory in the Zenger verdict. Many years were to pass before the principle was firmly established that truth could be a proper defense in certain libel suits.

Currents of liberalism that surged through the American colonies in the early 1700s weakened fears of eternal damnation implanted by Cal-vinism and its *New England Primer.* This reformist trend was temporarily reversed by "The Great Awakening," beginning about 1730. The move-ment featured a series of hellfire revival meetings, notably those held by Jonathan Edwards, an eloquent Congregational minister who preached that hell was "paved with the skulls of unbaptized children." Best known for his sermon "Sinners in the Hands of an Angry God," preached at Enfield, Connecticut, this "Artist of Damnation" described in sulphurous detail how the Almighty roasted poor wretches over the fires of hell for an eternity that wore out the moon and the stars.

On a more earthy level, most famous of the colonial almanacs was *Poor Richard's Almanac,* issued in Philadelphia by Benjamin Franklin from 1733 to 1758. It contained numerous homely sayings, many culled or adapted from the wisdom of ancient and European thinkers. Most of them related to the conduct of private life rather than public affairs, but a large number were hortatory in the manner of the conventional slogan. A reader finds commentaries on industry ("Never leave till tomorrow which you can do today"); on greed ("He does not possess wealth; it possesses him"); on gluttony ("Eat to live, and not live to eat"); on ex-perience ("Experience keeps a dear school, yet fools will learn in no other"); on religion ("A good example is the best sermon"); on vice ("What maintains one vice would bring up two children"); on marriage ("Keep your eyes wide open before marriage, half shut afterwards"); on drinking ("Drink does not drown care, but waters it and makes it grow faster"); and on self-help ("God helps them that help themselves").

THE FATE OF A CONTINENT

Friction in the international theater of events had meanwhile continued to build. A titanic struggle for control of most of North America finally began in 1689 with King William's War; it ended three wars later in 1763 with the Seven Years' War and the expulsion of a defeated France. In 1735, on the eve of the second of these clashes, the Anglican Bishop George Berkeley, after a two-year stay in the American colonies, published a memorable poem. It reflected his enthusiasm for settlement in America and caught a vision of future greatness:

> Westward the course of empire takes its way;
> The four first acts already past,
> A fifth shall close the drama with the day;
> Time's noblest offspring is the last.

Benjamin Franklin, worried by the threat of a fourth and final showdown with the French in 1754, was especially concerned over the necessity for colonial unity. He published in his *Pennsylvania Gazette* (May 9, 1754) what is regarded as the first American cartoon. A snake representing the colonies had broken into eight pieces, properly marked with the initials of New England, New York, New Jersey, Pennsylvania, Maryland, Virginia, North Carolina, and South Carolina. The drawing bore the famous caption "Join or Die." Delegates from the colonies gathered the next month in Albany, but failed either to join or die when their Albany Plan of Union, tentatively adopted, was rejected by the colonies and also by the mother country.

Some three weeks before the Albany Congress met, a small force under Colonel George Washington defeated a weaker French detachment in the wilds of the Ohio Valley. The victorious young commander wrote to his mother, "I heard the bullets whistle; and believe me, there is something charming in the sound." A month later he was cornered by a larger detachment and forced to surrender his entire command to the French, by which time the "charm" had worn off.

Fighting in the Ohio wilderness led to the French and Indian War, so called in America, and it dragged on from 1754 to 1763. The two most memorable battles were General Braddock's defeat near present Pittsburgh and General Wolfe's victory (and death) at Quebec. General Braddock, unaccustomed to behind-the-bush fighting with Indians, was fortunate in having as his aide Colonel George Washington, plus some "buckskin militia." Tradition has Braddock saying, "These are high times when a British general is to take counsel of a Virginia buckskin." Trapped, though hardly ambushed, Braddock met his death on the battlefield, while Washington miraculously escaped the hail of bullets. Braddock's last reported words were "We shall know better how to do it next time."

After initial setbacks, victory crowned British arms when William Pitt the elder, the masterful "Organizer of Victory," became head of a coalition ministry in 1757 and energized the complex military operations. He later told the House of Commons, "America has been conquered in Germany." This was clearly a tribute to Britain's allies on the European continent, including Frederick the Great of Prussia, who had diverted so much of France's strength to the Old World as to make possible Pitt's triumphs in the New World.

STAMPING OUT THE STAMP ACT

Laurel-bedecked Britain emerged from the Seven Years' War in 1763 with a huge new empire but, less agreeably, with a huge national debt incurred in acquiring it. Parliament's clumsy attempts to force the American colonials to pay what London regarded as a fair share of their upkeep led by stages to the revolutionary outburst. It was preceded by America's first outpouring of slogans, catch phrases, toasts, songs of protest, and other manifestations of discontent or outrage.

Most eloquent of the colonials who early protested was James Otis of Massachusetts, whose personal motto proclaimed, "Where liberty is, there is my country." Until his brain was damaged in 1769 by a savage beating administered by a British officer, he was probably the most impassioned and effective of those patriots struggling for what they regarded as their fundamental rights. In 1761 he argued vehemently in court against the issuance of general search warrants to apprehend colonial smugglers. On this occasion he erupted, in the words of John Adams, as "a flame of fire."

Many years later Adams reconstructed from his notes several imperishable passages by Otis, including "A man's house is his castle; and whilst he is quiet, he is as well guarded as a prince in his castle." More electrifying was "An act against the [British] Constitution is void; an act against national equity is void; and if an act of Parliament should be made . . . it would be void." Adams attributed to Otis the seductive slogan "Taxation without representation is tyranny," even though taxation was not relevant to the search warrants being debated. At all events this catch phrase became one of the great rallying cries of the colonies in the decade before the shooting began on the green at Lexington.

A short-sighted Parliament undertook in 1764 to raise additional revenue from the colonies when it passed the hated Sugar Act. James Otis responded with a vigorous pamphlet, *The Rights of the British Colonies Asserted and Proved.* He thus gave further currency to the cry "No taxation without representation." Actually the aroused colonials wanted neither taxation by nor representation in a Parliament in which they would be heavily and lawfully outvoted. They much preferred the existing system of taxation by their own representative assemblies.

Mounting pressures of the next year, eventful 1765, prompted Parliament to stir up a new hornet's nest. Hitherto the taxes imposed on the colonials had been collected at the customs houses; the new tax, involving stamps and stamped paper, went far beyond the customs house into the individual's house. Riotous disturbances, including burnings in effigy

The Colonies Reduced. A famous cartoon "invented" by Benjamin Franklin and published in the *Political Register,* London, 1768. It foresaw that Britain's policies would cause her to become dismembered, much as the famous Roman general Belisarius was ultimately defeated and allegedly reduced to blind beggary. "Give a penny to Belisarius" is the Latin inscription. Boston Public Library.

ensued, to the accompaniment of cries of "Liberty, property, and no stamps." Orating before the Virginia House of Burgesses, Patrick Henry, "The Forest Born Demosthenes," passionately vented dangerous sentiments: "Caesar had his Brutus; Charles the First his Cromwell; and George the Third ["Treason!" cried the Speaker] may profit by their example. If this be treason, make the most of it." A visiting Frenchman noted in his diary that Henry later apologized to the House for his outburst—a backdown little noted in later patriotic textbooks.

"The Sons of Liberty" or "Liberty Boys," supported by "The Daughters of Liberty," figured prominently in the violent outbursts against the Stamp Act and particularly against the unpopular agents appointed to sell the stamps. All of these frightened officials resigned under duress, as the protesters erected "Liberty Poles" or "Liberty Pillars" often bearing effigies of British officials. Loyal subjects of the King regarded the "Liberty Poles" as "Anarchy Poles."

Such furious mob scenes jarred open the eyes of Parliament and resulted in a grudging repeal of the stamp tax in 1766, the year after its passage. Great was the exultation in America. Even in England William Pitt the elder, also known as "The Great Commoner," had startled the House of Commons by declaiming, "I rejoice that America has resisted.

Three millions of people, so dead to all the feelings of liberty, as voluntarily to submit to be slaves, would have been fit instruments to make slaves of the rest."

TAX TROUBLES AGAIN

Colonial newspapers proved to be potent vehicles of propaganda during and after the upheaval over the Stamp Act. Several of them, from South Carolina to Boston, used the same patriotic caption: "The United Voice of His Majesty's *free* and *loyal* Subjects in AMERICA,—LIBERTY and PROPERTY, and NO STAMPS." By 1769 the Newport, Rhode Island, *Mercury* was defiantly proclaiming, "Undaunted by TYRANTS,—We'll DIE or be FREE."

Poets and song writers contributed to the popular outburst. In 1766 a nameless American set to the tune of David Garrick's "Heart of Oak" these stirring sentiments:

> With Loyalty, LIBERTY let us entwine,
> Our blood shall for both, flow as free as our wine.
> Let us set an example, what all men should be,
> And a toast give the world, Here's to those [who] dare to be free.

A new "Liberty Song," written in Boston and addressed to the Sons of Liberty, proclaimed:

> Come jolly Sons of LIBERTY—
> Come ALL with Hearts UNITED
> Our Motto is "WE DARE BE FREE,"
> Not easily affrighted!

British overlords in London, stubborn to the end, learned little or nothing from the Stamp Act uproar. In 1767 Parliament levied new taxes, which were relatively light and indirect, collectible at the customs houses. John Dickinson of Pennsylvania, one of the premier pamphleteers of the Revolution, responded with his own "Liberty Song":

> Then join hand in hand, brave Americans all,—
> By uniting we stand, by dividing we fall.

Dickinson also published his widely distributed and highly influential "Farmer's Letters," which set forth various arguments against British overlordship. "Let these truths be indelibly impressed on our minds," he warned, "that we cannot be happy without being free—that we cannot be free without being secure in our property—that we cannot be secure in our property if without our consent others may as by right take it away. . . ." He regarded taxation by the British Parliament as deprivation of property without consent. A popular sentiment often quoted during these troubled days was "Whoever would give up essential liberty to purchase a little temporary safety deserves neither liberty nor safety."

One ominous result of the new Townshend taxes was an upsurge of colonial smuggling, abetted by rioters who overbore the customs officials. In response to their pleas for help the British government landed two red-coated regiments of infantry at Boston to uphold law and order. The townsfolk jeered at the Redcoats as "Bloody Backs" and "Lobster Backs," as friction intensified. On the evening of March 5, 1770, a mob of some sixty civilians gathered to curse the soldiers, while throwing sticks and stones at them. In the confusion, some unidentified person evidently cried "Fire," whereupon the tormented troops fired into the crowd and killed or wounded more than a dozen "innocent" citizens. Boston was mightily aroused, and an outraged popular demand for the removal of the troops led to the cry "Both regiments or none." The soldiers were withdrawn.

Such was the "Boston Massacre"—a descriptive phrase which in itself was an anti-British slogan. The affair might better have been called the "Boston Brawl." "Massacre Day" was observed annually in Massachusetts until 1783, when the more glorious Fourth of July provided an appropriate substitute. Attorneys John Adams and Josiah Quincy courageously put their careers on the line when they defended the accused soldiers. Only two of these were convicted of manslaughter, and then they were let off with only a branding on one hand.

PARLIAMENT LEGISLATES A REBELLION

In 1773 a purblind British Parliament, in an attempt to force the colonials to pay a light tax on tea, passed an act granting a monopoly of the prized leaf to the monopolistic East India Company. A cry of outrage again shook America. Radical leaders fed the fire, conspicuously Samuel Adams of Massachusetts, who rightfully earned such sobriquets as "Man of the Town Meeting," "The Colossus of Independence," "The Machiavelli of Massachusetts," "The Grand Incendiary," "The Father of Democracy," "The Father of the Revolution," "The Engineer of Revolution," and "The Penman of the Revolution."

None of the "cursed weed" shipped to America under the new act reached the lawful consignees. At Boston, on the night of December 16, 1773, the leaves landed in the water when a band of townspeople disguised as Indians tossed overboard the cargo of three ships—an obvious breakdown of law and order. The famed "Boston Tea Party," at which the tea was brewed for the fish, found its counterpart elsewhere, spectacularly in Annapolis, Maryland. There the "patriots" rode into town in broad daylight, without masks and wearing on their hatbands the motto "Liberty and Independence or Death in Pursuit of It." The demonstration resulted not only in the destruction of the tea but also in the burning of the *Peggy Stewart* in the "Peggy Stewart Tea Party"—little known to history, partly because New Englanders wrote most of the early chronicles. The Boston outburst inspired a lively ballad, one of whose stanzas ran:

> Overboard she goes, my boys,
> Heave ho where darkling waters roar;
> We love our cup of tea full well,
> But love our freedom more.

Wanton destruction of private property, combined with an overawing of the authorities by mobs, provided an exhibition of lawlessness that no self-respecting government could ignore. Over a period of months, Parliament responded to the Boston Tea Party and related disorders by passing a series of "Coercive Acts" or "Repressive Acts." The rebellious colonials for their part used the terms "Intolerable Acts" and "The Massacre of American Liberty." First among these measures was the closing of the port of Boston, the windpipe of Massachusetts, until the offending colony should pay proper compensation. Josiah Quincy of Massachusetts, who had joined John Adams in defending the accused in the "Boston Massacre," responded by publishing in May 1774 his *Observations on the Boston Port-Bill*. He breathed defiance: "Blandishments will not fascinate us, nor will threats of a halter [noose] intimidate. For, under God, we are determined that wheresoever, whensoever, or howsoever we shall be called to make our exit, we will die free men."

Eloquent Patrick Henry also sprang to the ramparts. Speaking before the officially disbanded Virginia Assembly in Richmond in March 1775, he cried, "I know not what course others may take; but as for me, give me liberty or give me death." The precise words of his speech, reconstructed by auditors some forty years later, may be questioned, but no one could doubt his sentiments. This time he did not apologize to the Assembly for his outburst, and so "Liberty or Death" became one of the unforgettable slogans of the Revolution. In May 1775 Virginia militiamen displayed a yellow banner proclaiming "Liberty or Death" and depicting a coiled rattlesnake with the pointed warning "Don't Tread on Me." On a different front, wise old Benjamin Franklin, whose many talents did not include oratory or poesy, expressed his views of British overlordship in verse:

> We have an old mother that peevish is grown;
> She snubs us like children that scarce walk alone;
> She forgets we're grown up and have sense of our own.

THE CLASH OF ARMS

Force often produces counterforce. Increased colonial resistance led to the dispatch of a British detachment to Lexington under orders to seize arms and rebel ringleaders. The famed silversmith-horseman Paul Revere rode out to alert the countryside colonials with the cry, as traditionally recorded, "The Redcoats are coming." They came the next morning to

Lexington, where a tiny force of homespun "Minute Men"—ready at a minute's notice—was drawn up with loaded muskets. Captain John Parker, their leader, encouraged his men: "Stand your ground. Don't fire unless fired upon, but if they mean to have a war let it begin here." The commander of the much larger force of Redcoats reportedly cried, "Disperse, you villains." The "villains" were about to disperse when someone fired a shot, although no one knows who to this day. The British followed with a volley, and the colonials, responding with a few scattered shots, lost nearly a score killed and wounded. In a sense this was the "Lexington massacre."

Emboldened by their easy victory, the Redcoats pushed on to Concord. There the swarming Minute Men turned them back and forced them to retreat with heavy losses to the sanctuary of Boston, which then came under siege. "Remember Lexington and Concord" became a watchword during the subsequent struggle for independence—one of the first in a long series of "Remember" slogans.

Blood in quantity for the first time had baptized the struggle for coveted rights. Many years later Ralph Waldo Emerson, "The Sage of Concord," wrote the hymn to be sung at the dedication of the battle monument on July 4, 1837:

> By the rude bridge that arched the flood
> Their flag to April's breeze unfurled,
> Here once the embattled farmers stood,
> And fired the shot heard round the world.

It was truly a "shot heard round the world." Few democratic upheavals since that time have been unaffected, either directly or indirectly, by the example of the American Revolution.

In 1849 James Russell Lowell, the famed poet-journalist, provided the inscription for the graves of two unknown British soldiers who had died at Concord:

> They came three thousand miles, and died,
> To keep the Past upon its throne;
> Unheard, beyond the ocean tide,
> Their English mother made her moan.

These Redcoats were not the last soldiers to die thousands of miles from home in a strange and inhospitable country for a cause they did not fully understand.

II

The Birth
of the Republic

> The community hath an indubitable, inalienable, and
> indefeasible right to reform, alter or abolish govern-
> ment, in such manner as shall be by that community
> judged most conducive to the public weal.
>
> Pennsylvania Declaration of Rights, 1776

REBELS IN ARMS

During the grave disturbances of 1775–76 in and around Boston, "Yankee
Doodle" emerged as the most popular song of the Revolutionary War. Its
origins remain unknown; its countless stanzas are the work of anonymous
authors. At first the air was used by the British and Tories in deriding
the country-bumpkin colonials, as in the verse that appeared about 1775:

> Yankee Doodle came to town
> Riding on a pony
> Stuck a feather in his cap
> And called it [him] macaroni.

"Macaroni" was currently descriptive of a fop or a dandy.

When John Hancock, the merchant-smuggler-revolutionist, was the
bane of the British, the following antipatriot stanza appeared about 1775:

> Yankee Doodle came to town
> For to buy a firelock:
> We will tar and feather him
> And so we will John Hancock.

British soldiers would gather outside New England churches and bawl such verses while the faithful inside were intoning psalms. But after the rout at Concord, the colonials turned the tables by using the song to taunt their enemy. Lines popular after the shooting began were:

> Father and I went down to camp, along with Captain Good'in,
> And there we saw the men and boys as thick as hasty puddin'.

Also:

> And there was Captain Washington upon a strapping stallion,
> A-giving orders to his men; I guess there was a million.

Adaptable to fife and drum, "Yankee Doodle" was presumably the lively tune the artist had in mind when he painted the famous marching trio in "The Spirit of '76."

On the heels of the opening clashes at Lexington and Concord, the British troops were bottled up in Boston by the colonial militia, soon to be commanded by General George Washington. In May 1775, the month after "the shot heard round the world," a rebel force jointly commanded by Ethan Allen, of the Vermont "Green Mountain Boys," and Benedict Arnold, of Connecticut, surprised and captured the key British fort of Ticonderoga in upper New York. The cannon thus seized proved essential for the continuing siege of Boston. The astounded British commander at Ticonderoga, demanding by what authority he was being called upon to surrender, reportedly received the lofty reply from Ethan Allen, "In the name of the Great Jehovah and the Continental Congress."

Kill-joy historians have cast much doubt on Allen's declaration. First of all, the Second Continental Congress was convening that very day in Philadelphia, and certainly could not have sent instructions by horseback in time. Second, Allen was a notorious atheist, hardly in close communion with the Almighty. One prominent historian, aware of Allen's penchant for profanity, guessed that he more probably shouted something like "Come out of there you damned old rat!"

Elsewhere the British, seeking to break the siege of Boston, rashly launched a frontal attack on the entrenched American marksmen at the Battle of Bunker Hill, June 17, 1775. "Don't fire till you see the whites of their eyes" was the command given to the defenders and attributed to both Colonel William Prescott and General Israel ("Old Put") Putnam. The first two assaults were driven back with frightful losses to the attackers. Finally, after the colonials had run out of ammunition, they yielded the hill in considerable disorder to the final attack of the Redcoats. The British won their immediate objective at a terrible cost, but the Americans gained much prestige—and a valuable slogan.

Slain at Bunker Hill was a leading Massachusetts patriot, the physician-soldier Joseph Warren. His most enduring monument was the song, "Free America," which he had set to the tune of "The British Grenadiers" and which proved to be one of the great inspirations of the American

Revolution. After beginning with a reminder that the glories of Athens and Rome were gone, the lyric continued:

> Then guard your rights Americans,
> Nor stoop to lawless sway,
> Oppose, oppose, oppose,
> For North Americay [as it was then pronounced].

Some five months later John Paul Jones, destined to become the premier naval hero of the Revolution, raised the first American flag of the war on his ship the *Alfred*, December 3, 1775. The design depicted a pine tree, at the foot of which a rattlesnake lay coiled to strike; the banner itself bore the memorable motto "Don't Tread on Me." The budding American naval tradition gained another watchword in May 1776, when Captain James Mugford of the schooner *Franklin* reportedly uttered these dying words during a British attack in Boston Harbor: "Don't give up the ship! You will beat them off!" Thus was foreshadowed the last order of Captain James Lawrence of the ill-starred *Chesapeake* in 1813.

COMMON SENSE PREVAILS

Oddly enough, relatively few colonials yearned for independence during the year or so after Lexington and Concord; as "loyal" subjects they sought not only redress of their grievances but also reconciliation with their "beloved" King. Conspicuous among those leaders who began to agitate for a complete and permanent break stood Thomas Paine. Born in England to the Quaker faith, and a onetime corset maker, he emigrated to America in 1774. The next year he published a song, "The Liberty Tree" (July 1775):

> From the east to the west blow the trumpet to arms!
> Through the land let the sound of it flee;
> Let the far and the near all unite, with a cheer,
> In defense of our Liberty Tree.

Paine was increasingly disturbed, especially after bloody Bunker Hill, by colonial inconsistency in fighting with the olive branch in the right hand and the sword in the left. Such conduct ran contrary to all reason. In January, 1776, he published his powerful pamphlet *Common Sense*, which ran up an amazing sale and did much to prod the public toward independence.* The title in itself was a slogan, and passages like the following proved immensely appealing: "O! ye that love mankind! Ye that dare oppose not only the tyranny but the tyrant, stand forth! Every spot of the Old World is overrun with oppression. Freedom hath been hunted round the globe. Asia and Africa have long expelled her. Europe regards her as a stranger and England hath given her warning to depart.

---

* Paine's contributions were later dimmed by his identification with religious free thinking. In 1888 Theodore Roosevelt referred to him as "that filthy little atheist."

O! receive the fugitive and prepare in time an asylum for mankind." After reading Paine's impassioned appeal, increasing numbers of patriots were prepared to cry "God save the Congress" in place of "God save the King."

America's Declaration of Independence, since then dubbed "the world's greatest editorial," could claim numerous antecedents. In particular there was the action of the Second Continental Congress, on July 6, 1775, in adopting the "Declaration of the Causes of Taking Up Arms." Prepared jointly by John Dickinson of Pennsylvania and Thomas Jefferson of Virginia, it proclaimed near its conclusion, "Our cause is just. Our Union is perfect. Our internal resources are great, and, if necessary, foreign assistance is undoubtedly obtainable. . . . The arms we have been compelled by our enemies to assume, we will, in defiance of every hazard, with unabating firmness and perserverance, employ for the preservation of our liberties; being with one mind resolved to die freemen, rather than to live slaves."

But the "Union" was not "perfect," even though the "cause" may have been "just." The colonials were being pushed, with great reluctance, to the brink. In May 1776 Rhode Island declared itself free of British control, as patriots cried "God save the United Colonies." The next month, on June 7, 1776, Richard Henry ("Light-Horse Harry") Lee of Virginia presented his memorable motion to the Continental Congress: "That these United Colonies are, and of right ought to be, free and independent states; that they are absolved from all allegiance to the British Crown; and that all political connection between them and the State of Great Britain is, and ought to be, totally dissolved." After considerable debate Lee's motion passed on July 2, 1776, and on that day, not July 4, America formally declared its independence.

A DECLARATION FOR ALL PEOPLE

So momentous a step as formally seceding from the British Empire required an explanation to the outside world—"a decent respect to the opinions of mankind." The task of drafting the Explanation of Independence, much better known as the Declaration of Independence, fell to a committee whose most gifted penman, Thomas Jefferson, was chosen as chief draftsman.

A more powerful appeal than the Declaration of Independence never came from an American deliberative body. Resounding down through the ages is the preamble: "We hold these truths to be self-evident: that all men are created equal [Jefferson was a slaveholder]; that they are endowed by their Creator with certain unalienable rights; that among these are life, liberty, and the pursuit of happiness; that, to secure these rights, Governments are instituted among Men, deriving their just powers from the consent of the governed; that whenever any Form of Government becomes destructive of these ends, it is the Right of the People to alter or abolish it, and to institute new Government. . . ."

Then came a long and rapid-fire list of grievances against the King, as though he were in the hands of a prosecuting attorney. The conclusion was embodied in a magnificent peroration ending with these stirring words: "And for the support of this declaration, with a firm reliance on the Protection of Divine Providence, we mutually pledge to each other our Lives, our Fortunes, and our sacred Honor."

Jefferson's Declaration of Independence, which *advertised* rather than *declared* independence, has profoundly moved generations of Americans. It gave classic form to the popular war cry, commonly voiced in America at the time, "We will be free!" As a veritable "shout heard round the world," it has influenced countless revolutionary currents since that day in all corners of the globe, including that in Vietnam.

Shortly before signing the Declaration, John Hancock, the presiding officer, delivered an address from which this warning has survived: "It is too late to pull different ways; the members of the Continental Congress must hang together." Just prior to appending his own signature, ageing Benjamin Franklin reportedly remarked with grim humor, "Yes, we must, indeed, all hang together, or, most assuredly, we shall all hang separately." Upon signing the document first, with the largest letters by far of any of the signatories, Hancock is supposed to have said, "There, I guess King George will be able to read that"—presumably without his glasses. The implication of this daring remark is that the King had already placed John Hancock, a prominent revolutionist, high on his "must hang" list. All of the signers were doubtless aware, given the fate of unsuccessful Irish rebels of the era, that they were thrusting their necks into a noose.*

One indestructible legend holds that the Liberty Bell of Philadelphia was cracked while proclaiming independence. Actually, it had suffered damage earlier and was to be fatally cracked later, but not in proclaiming independence; indeed, it did not celebrate independence at all on that fateful July day, though it bears the patriotic inscription, "Proclaim Liberty Throughout All the Land Unto All the Inhabitants Thereof."

Liberty Bell or not, the unity of the thirteen squabbling states was far from perfect. Yet a committee of the Congress, in August 1776, formally proposed "E Pluribus Unum" (One from Many) for the seal of the United States. Adopted in 1781, the motto was used on certain coins as early as 1796.

GEORGE WASHINGTON AT BAY

British troops evacuated Boston on March 17, 1776, thereby establishing "Evacuation Day," which is still observed there annually. The London

---

* The expression "Put your John Hancock there" subsequently became a common way of asking a person to sign a document.

government next proceeded to amass an army and fleet for a concentrated assault on the critical New York area and its environs. General Washington, aware that a crisis was at hand, prepared a solemn address to the Continental Army before the Battle of Long Island on August 27, 1776: "The fate of unborn millions will now depend, under God, on the courage and conduct of this army. Our cruel and unrelenting enemy leaves us only the choice of brave resistance, or the most abject submissions. We have, therefore, to resolve to conquer or die."

General Washington did not conquer, but many of his men did die. Outmanned and outgeneraled, he was forced into a dispirited, crestfallen retreat across New Jersey. But this dismal campaign did provide one heroic episode. A young school teacher, Nathan Hale, had volunteered for needed duty as a spy, saying, "Every kind of service, necessary to the public good, becomes honorable by being necessary." Caught within enemy lines, he was condemned to die on the gallows, where his last words have come down to us as "I only regret that I have but one life to lose for my country."

Propagandist Thomas Paine, author of the best-selling *Common Sense*, enlisted in the patriot army as a common soldier and took part in the humiliating retreat across New Jersey. Yet he found time to write the first of his *Crisis* papers, which appeared late in December 1776, first in a Pennsylvania newspaper and then in a pamphlet. "These are the times that try men's souls," he began. "The summer soldier and the sunshine patriot, will, in this crisis, shrink from the service of his country; but he that stands it *now* deserves the love and thanks of man and woman. Tyranny, like hell, is not easily conquered; yet we have this consolation with us, that the harder the conflict, the more glorious the triumph."

Paine's inspirational words helped boost the army's morale and probably had something to do with Washington's subsequent success. The American leader crossed the ice-clogged Delaware River on the night of December 25–26, and then fell upon the drink-befuddled Hessians at Trenton, there to win a complete and cheaply won victory. A week later he defeated three British regiments at Princeton, and then went into winter quarters at chilly Morristown, New Jersey. Washington's tactics of retreating and then launching surprise counterattacks deservedly won for him the sobriquets "The Old Fox" and "The American Fabius," after the Roman general who used similar Fabian tactics in fighting Hannibal.

Early in 1777 Joseph Hopkinson, the talented and patriotic Pennsylvanian, lifted the flagging spirits of his countrymen with his "Camp Ballad," two stanzas of which follow:

> To arms, then to arms!   — 't is fair freedom invites us;
> The trumpet, shrill sounding, to battle excites us;
> The banners of virtue unfurled shall wave o'er us,
> Our heroes lead on, and the foe fly before us.
>
> On Heaven and Washington placing reliance,
> We'll meet the bold Briton, and bid him defiance;

Our cause we'll support, for 't is just and 't is glorious—
When men fight for freedom, they must be victorious.

MUSKETS AND TOMAHAWKS

As General Washington prepared for the spring and summer campaigns of 1777, he issued a circular letter of April 30 to regimental commanders regarding recruits for his personal bodyguard. He stipulated, "You will therefore send me none but natives"—that is, men born in the colonies. A short time earlier a deserter from the British Army who had tried to poison Washington had been hanged for his pains. As so often happens, others have made Washington's order more pointed by rewriting it to read, "Put none but Americans on guard tonight." In later years anti-foreign groups in the United States used this admonition to strengthen their argument that foreigners, whether naturalized or not, could not be trusted to behave like true Americans.

British plans for 1777 featured a massive invasion from Canada through upper New York under General ("Gentleman Johnny") Burgoyne. Learning that rebel supplies were piling up at Bennington, Vermont, he detached a hireling German-Hessian force of some 700 men to seize them. The invaders, later known as "Hessian flies," met a larger but untrained force under General John Stark. The commonest version of what he told his troops reads, "There, my boys, are your enemies, red-coats and Tories. You must beat them—or Molly Stark is a widow to-night." The Americans won a smashing victory—one of the few triumphs of militia over regulars in this war. Burgoyne was finally trapped and forced to surrender his entire army at Saratoga, October 17, 1777, and in the aftermath the French signed a military alliance with America in 1778 which did much to assure victory.

"Chester," a popular song later described as "the Marseillaise of the Revolutionary War," came from the pen of William Billings, a prominent Boston singing master, during the critical year 1778. It began:

Let tyrants shake their iron rod,
And slavery clank her galling chains;
We fear them not; we trust in God—
New England's God forever reigns.

.   .   .

The foe comes on with haughty stride;
Our troops advance with martial noise;
Their veterans flee before our youth,
And generals yield to beardless boys.

Played by fifers and sung lustily by soldiers, the song proved to be a great morale booster.

British-led Indian raids into the Wyoming Valley of Pennsylvania resulted in frightful massacres, several of which virtually wiped out the large and well-known Harding family. In preparing to defend a key fort in July 1778, the colonial Colonel Butler urged his men to fight desperately. His words have passed down to us in this form: "Your own fate, as well as that of your women, your children and your homes, is in your hands. Remember the fate of the Hardings, and make sure work. Victory is safety! Defeat is death!" The slogan "Remember the Hardings" was not enough; the fort fell and another massacre ensued. Yet this battle cry is one of the earliest of the many sloganized "Remembers" of the nation's history.

In this same summer of 1778, British-supplied Indians were on the warpath in the Northwest, and their depredations reached as far south as "The Dark and Bloody Ground" of Kentucky. The British commander at Detroit was reputed to be paying bounties for the scalps of Americans of both sexes and all ages, with the result that he won the epithet "hair buyer." An intrepid Virginian, Colonel George Rogers Clark, launched a successful incursion into the southern part of the Illinois country that lessened Indian attacks southward.

PRELUDE TO YORKTOWN

Most famous of the ship duels of the war, and the one that inspired its most memorable battle slogan, was a clash off the English coast on September 23, 1779. John Paul Jones, the naval hero, had secured from the French a reconditioned warship, renamed the *Bonhomme Richard* after Benjamin Franklin's *Poor Richard's Almanac*. Jones tackled a British frigate, the *Serapis*, a newer, faster, and more heavily gunned vessel. Early in the bloody duel some of Jones's most powerful cannon exploded, leaving him in wretched shape. The British commander, Captain Pearson, reportedly called out, "Do you surrender?" or "Has your ship struck?" Jones is supposed to have shouted back, "I have not yet begun to fight." Doubt exists as to precisely what he cried out in the heat of battle. Some have speculated that it may have been "Hell no," in the nautical tradition. At all events Jones's guns spoke louder than words, for the British captain was forced to surrender. The victorious American ship soon sank, but sagging spirits in America received a much-needed lift and the nation inherited one of its most cherished slogans. It was embodied in a lengthy song, one stanza of which reads:

> The battle rolled on, till bold Pearson cried:
> "Have you yet struck your colors? then come alongside!"
> But so far from thinking that the battle was won,
> Brave Paul Jones replied, "I'VE NOT YET BEGUN!" Hurrah!

A minor skirmish at Springfield, New Jersey, on June 23, 1780, resulted in the coining of a catch phrase by a militantly propatriot clergyman, James Caldwell, whose wife had recently been killed by a random British bullet. During the battle the Americans exhausted the paper wadding for their firearms, and Caldwell urged them to use hymn books from the neighboring church. Some of the songs had doubtless been written by Isaac Watts, and the preacher encouraged the soldiers by reportedly shouting, "Put Watts into 'em boys. Give 'em Watts!"*

Slumping American morale received a staggering blow late in 1780 with the last-minute exposure of General Benedict Arnold. This traitor had proved to be one of the bravest and most effective of the American commanders, yet for various reasons, including pressure for money, he had plotted to sell out the fort at West Point for a monetary reward and a commission in the British Army. The scheme was exposed in September 1780, and the defector fled to British lines, from which he operated viciously against his fellow countrymen. He died in England twenty years later, and one legend reports his deathbed remarks: "Let me die in my old uniform. God forgive me for ever putting on any other!" The words are unverified but they certainly stirred patriotic pulses.

In the dying years of the war the thirteen disunited states of America were in deplorable shape. Paper money printed by the Continental Congress withered in purchasing power to virtual nothingness—"Not worth a Continental" was the scornful phrase. Such powers as a weak Congress dared exercise met with jealous resistance by the states, and "King Congress" and "King Cong" became derisive nicknames for that much-abused body. The British shifted their major military efforts to the South, where they could count on ardent support from Loyalists. Partisan warfare waxed increasingly bitter, and when the nephew of General Marion ("The Swamp Fox") was butchered after being captured by the British, Marion's men adopted as their war cry the slogan "No quarter for Tories!"

Britain's General Cornwallis, after conducting rather fruitless operations in the South, withdrew with some 7,000 troops to the Yorktown peninsula of Virginia, confidently counting on support from the British fleet. But at this critical juncture Britain temporarily lost control of the sea to the French. A joint Franco-American force cut off and mouse-trapped Cornwallis, who was forced to surrender his entire command on October 19, 1781. As the Redcoats laid down their arms, their band appropriately struck up the popular song "The World Turn'd Upside Down":

> If buttercups buzzed after the bee,
> If boats were on land, churches on sea,
> If ponies rode men, and if grass ate the cows,
> And cats should be chased into holes by the mouse;
> If the mamas sold their babies to gypsies for half a crown,
> If summer were spring, and the other way 'round,
> Then all the world would be upside down.

---

* Thus was foreshadowed the cry of the navy chaplain at Pearl Harbor in 1941, "Praise the Lord and pass the ammunition."

THE FOUNDERS FRAME A NEW CHARTER

Not surprisingly, the troubled half dozen years after the peace treaty with Britain in 1783 caused many Americans to question Benjamin Franklin's sage observation in 1783, "There never was a good war or a bad peace." Vexations at home and abroad continued to be so burdensome that the historian John Fiske later published a book about this era, *The Critical Period of American History, 1783–1789* (1888), which still provides the lasting stereotype of this era. In more recent decades historians have doubted that the picture was as somber as once painted, but times were unquestionably difficult. Mob uprisings, notably Captain Shays' rebellion in Massachusetts (1786–87), sought to close the courts and ease the burdens of debtors.

Thomas Jefferson, then serving as Minister to France, regarded the outbursts in Massachusetts as an encouraging manifestation of democracy at work. Writing to James Madison early in 1787, he declared, "I hold it, that a little rebellion, now and then, is a good thing, and as necessary in the political world as storms in the physical." Later that same year he admonished another correspondent, "The tree of liberty must be refreshed from time to time with the blood of patriots and tyrants. It is its natural manure." (Both of these Jeffersonisms were widely quoted by later generations.) The more conservative ex-rebel George Washington deplored outbreaks like Shays'. "Good God!" he wrote privately, "who, besides a Tory, could have foreseen, or a Briton have predicted them?"

Under the Articles of Confederation (1781), the nation's first written constitution, Congress wielded only feeble powers. But this palsied body did manage to enact two landmark laws for administering and governing the Western lands, those vast expanses of territory between the Appalachian Mountains and the Mississippi River. The first of the red-letter measures was the Land Ordinance of 1785, which avoided much confusion by requiring formal survey before settlement. The second statute was the Northwest Ordinance of 1787, which provided for the orderly governance of an area that subsequently embraced five states of the Old Northwest, from Ohio to Michigan.

Especially memorable was Article 3 of the Northwest Ordinance, which asserted, "Religion, morality and knowledge, being necessary to good government and the happiness of mankind, schools and the means of education shall forever be encouraged." No less important for human freedom was the stipulation in Article 6: "There shall be neither slavery nor involuntary servitude in the said territory, otherwise than in the punishment of crimes whereof the party shall have been duly convicted. . . ."

Stark necessity meanwhile had brought about a determined move to strengthen the Articles of Confederation. The upshot was the Constitutional Convention of 1787, attended in Philadelphia by fifty-five state-appointed delegates, whom Thomas Jefferson called a collection of

The Reconciliation Between Britannia and Her Daughter America. America (represented by an Indian) is invited to buss (kiss) her mother. Detail from an English cartoon. New York Public Library.

"demi-gods." Rhode Island, alone of the thirteen, refused to send representatives and hence was again derisively referred to as "Rogues' Island." Strong but generally silent George Washington, "The Sword of the Revolution" and "The Atlas of America," was drafted as presiding officer. In his opening remarks he urged, "Let us raise a standard to which the wise and honest can repair; the rest is in the hands of God."

Prolonged debates during that humid summer in Philadelphia often waxed bitter, and hence were kept secret. States' rights proved to be the giant hurdle. Few citizens wanted to be lorded over by a powerful central government, and the small states were highly suspicious of their larger sisters. But the spirit of compromise finally prevailed, and the delegates adopted a series of checks and balances among the three branches of government to restrain possible tyranny. States' righters, fearful of this three-pronged mechanism, often referred to the Constitution as "The Triple-headed Monster."

Stubby James Madison of Virginia, "The Father of the Constitution," won distinction as one of the chief architects of the new instrument. He also kept the most detailed and valuable record of the proceedings. Elderly Benjamin Franklin, who had little to say, contributed wisdom and ballast. Youthful Alexander Hamilton from New York, despite his eloquence and brilliance, made only a slight impression. He weakened his influence by going overboard for a potent central government designed to restrain the masses. Born in the British West Indies and an extravagant admirer of things English, he declared on the floor of the convention, "I believe the British government forms the best model the world ever produced. . . ."

A zealous Hamilton laid bare his basic aristocratic ideas when he insisted, "All communities divide themselves into the few and the many. The first are the rich and well-born, the other the mass of the people. . . . The people are turbulent and changing; they seldom judge or determine right. Give therefore to the first class a distinct, permanent share in the government. They will check the unsteadiness of the second. . . ." This basic philosophy later came to roost in Hamilton's Federalist party, which openly distrusted "democratic babblers."

Benevolent old Dr. Franklin, a well known freethinker in religion, was so disturbed by the heat of the debate as to move that the sessions be opened with prayer. He reminisced, "I have lived, Sir, a long time, and the longer I live the more convincing proofs I see of this truth: that God governs in the affairs of men. And if a sparrow cannot fall to the ground without His notice, is it probable that an empire can rise without his aid?" After the Constitution was completed, one delegate recorded that a woman approached Franklin to ask, "Well, Doctor, what have we got, a Republic or a monarchy?" "A republic," he replied, "if you can keep it."

A CONSTITUTIONAL LANDMARK

While the Constitution was awaiting ratification by the state conventions, a popular song appeared entitled "The New Roof (A New Song for Federal Mechanics)." Written by Francis Hopkinson, it was sung to the tune of an old English drinking song, "To Anacreon in Heaven" (later used for "The Star-Spangled Banner"). After describing in detail how the rafters and other components of the roof of state were raised by the mechanics, the song concludes:

> The sons of Columbia shall view with delight
> Its pillars and arches and towering height.
> Our roof is now raised, and our song still shall be
> A Federal head, o'er a people still free
>
> Huzza! my brave boys, our work is complete,
> The world shall admire Columbia's fair seat;
> Its strength against tempests and time shall be proof,

And thousands shall come to dwell under our roof.
Whilst we drain the deep bowl, our toast still shall be,
Our government firm, and our citizens free.

Less poetically, "The New Roof" was also miscalled "The New Breeches," and this nickname gave some support to the false impression that the Fathers had tailored something entirely novel.

As expected, the Constitution drafted by the Founding Fathers encountered vehement opposition in some of the state ratifying conventions, largely on the grounds that the rights of the states and of individuals were not adequately protected. Several of the conventions grudgingly gave their approval with the understanding that a safeguarding Bill of Rights would be added by amendment. Friends of the Constitution accused these critics of being "Amendment-mongers," but a ten-amendment Bill of Rights was added to the Constitution by the new Congress and the states in 1791. Especially cherished was the First Amendment: "Congress shall make no law respecting an establishment of religion, or prohibiting the free exercise thereof; or abridging the freedom of speech, or of the press; or the right of the people peaceably to assemble, and to petition the government for a redress of grievances."

Beyond challenge, the Constitution has proved to be an outstanding success, despite one shattering civil war, and a "Constitution Cult" ultimately developed. Among the paeans of praise that have been showered upon the document, the accolade bestowed in 1878 by the British statesman W. E. Gladstone has perhaps been most flattering. He wrote that "the American Constitution is . . . the most wonderful work ever struck off at a given time by the brain and purpose of man." The achievement was indeed remarkable, but as the product of long years of gestation it was hardly instantaneous. What the Constitution actually aimed to do is best stated in the preamble, once memorized by countless school children: "We the people of the United States, in order to form a more perfect union, establish justice, insure domestic tranquility, provide for the common defense, promote the general welfare, and secure the blessings of liberty to ourselves and our posterity, do ordain and establish this Constitution for the United States of America."

Regrettably, the republic has not achieved all of these goals to the satisfaction of everyone, but they remain the guiding stars of a free people.

III

Federalist
Foundations

He [Hamilton] smote the rock of the national resources, and abundant streams of revenue gushed
forth. He touched the dead corpse of Public Credit,
and it sprung upon its feet.

Daniel Webster, speech on Hamilton, 1831

LAUNCHING THE NEW SHIP OF STATE

About four months before the required number of states had ratified the
Constitution, a Pennsylvania newspaper published a song stressing the
theme of unity under able leadership:

Great Washington shall rule the land,
While Franklin's counsel aids his hand.

Agitation for Washington as the indispensable man for President was
hardly new, for many citizens assumed that he alone could be trusted to
wield the awesome powers vested in the new Chief Executive. The year
before the memorable Constitutional Convention met, a Philadelphia
newspaper had published the song "God Save Great Washington," sung
to the tune of "God Save the King."

Under the freshly ratified Constitution the Electoral College unanimously drafted for the Presidency war hero George Washington, now
hailed as "The Saviour of America" and "The Deliverer of America." He
would not run for the Presidency; yet he could not run from it. To John
Adams, the able but crusty New Englander, fell the Vice Presidency.
This second-fiddle title, suggested Franklin, could well be "His Superfluous Excellency."

Impressive inauguration ceremonies were scheduled for March 4, 1789, in New York City, the temporary capital before moving to Philadelphia, also a temporary location. Various delays caused the swearing in to be postponed until April 30, a period during which the United States literally had no government. Commemorative medals struck off at the time bore the inscription "Remember March Fourth," "March the Fourth 1789 Memorable Era," and "Unity, Prosperity & Independence." Other verbal bouquets for the occasion were the Latin "Pater patriae" (Father of the country) and "Long live the President." The latter was no doubt a variation of the English acclamation "Long live the King" or "Long live our noble King."

Washington's northward journey from Mount Vernon, in Virginia, to New York City was one long triumphal procession. Included were breakfasts and banquets, pealing bells and booming cannon, flower-festooned bridges, petal-covered streets, and singing children. The songs "Yankee Doodle" and "Welcome Mighty Chief" graced the occasion. Philip Freneau, "The Poet of the Revolution," greeted the conquering hero in Philadelphia with

> O Washington! thrice glorious name,
>   What due rewards can man decree—
> Empires are far below thy aims,
>   And sceptres have no charms for thee.

These words had obvious import, for General Washington had spurned quasi-dictatorial powers and returned to tranquil Mount Vernon at war's end. He came to be known as "The Sage of Mount Vernon" or "The Hero of Mount Vernon." When "The Farmer President" heeded the call of duty, he received added acclaim as "The Cincinnatus of the West." Citizens who knew their ancient history remembered the Roman general Cincinnatus. When the state was in danger from within and without, he was induced, according to legend, to leave his plow in the field and temporarily assume dictatorial powers. In 1783, veteran officers of the Revolution had formed the long-lived Society of the Cincinnati, with Washington as their president and with eligibility for membership passing on to their eldest male descendants or collateral descendants. Criticized by contemporaries as aristocratic, the society nevertheless has continued to live on rather feebly into present times.

GEORGE WASHINGTON REPLACES KING GEORGE

As Washington's horseback cavalcade entered Trenton, New Jersey, it paraded under a flower-bedecked arch that bore the inscription "The Hero Who Defended the Mothers Will Protect the Daughters." An old lithograph portrays not only the inscription but the floral offerings of the numerous and excited young ladies.

Washington's party finally reached New York, where the gallery of Federal Hall opened onto the street. There, facing the crowd below, the hero took the oath of office as administered by Robert Livingston, who proclaimed in a loud voice, "Long live George Washington, President of the United States!" Moving on to the Senate chamber, Washington read his inaugural address in a barely audible voice. Keenly aware that the eyes of the world were upon him and his radical new government, he declared that "the preservation of the sacred fire of liberty," as well as "the destiny of the republican model of government," was "finally staked on the experiment" now in the hands of the American people.

Patriotic Americans were evidently satisfied with their champion. "Freedom's Favorite Son" came to be a popular sobriquet, and one Pennsylvania journal voiced the sentiment "The Father of his Country— We Celebrate Washington!" Actually the designation "Father of his Country" had been coined as early as 1778, two years after the proclamation of independence.

Yet shifting from monarchy to republic, from King to President, inevitably involved much awkwardness. Contemporary prints displayed the likeness of George Washington with the aristocratic inscription "His Excellency, General Washington," and that of Martha Washington with the inscription, "Lady Washington." An early question was what should Washington be officially called? Congress seriously debated "His Highness," "His Excellency," and "High Mightiness." A committee of the Senate gave solemn consideration to "His Highness, the President of the United States of America, and Protector of their Liberties." Fortunately this pompous honorific was dropped, and the Chief Executive enjoys the impressive enough title, "The President of the United States."

Disputes over titles served to remind the anti-Federalists how short they had fallen in their attempt to implement fully the ideals of the Revolution. Back in 1775 the cry was "Vox populi, vox dei" (The voice of the people is the voice of God). Now citizens were warned that democracy was a "volcano." In 1775 the colonials heard of "the natural equality of mankind"; now the emphasis was on "the well-born." In 1775 the patriots were "Sons of Liberty"; now they were "state demagogues." In 1775 men praised "our excellent state constitutions"; now the country had "the monster with thirteen heads." In 1775 people spoke of "the free and United States of America"; now the focus had shifted to "the national government."

HAMILTON CLASHES WITH JEFFERSON

A luminous figure in Washington's tiny Cabinet was Secretary of the Treasury Alexander Hamilton, the youthful financier born out of wedlock in the British West Indies. ("The bastard brat of a Scotch peddler" is the sneer attributed to John Adams.) In line with Hamiltonian views expressed in the Philadelphia Convention, the dynamic Secretary undertook to build up a strong central government favorable to the upper classes, which in turn would prop it up. He firmly embraced the aristocratic view attributed to men of his ilk, "Those who own the country ought to govern it." He believed that the government would succeed only if it established its credit by "funding" or redeeming the nation's depreciated currency at face value. He also favored tightening federal control by assuming the debts of the individual states, despite the heavy financial burden involved. "A national debt, if it is not excessive, will be to us a national blessing," he had written to Robert Morris in 1781. Hamilton naturally came to be known as "Father of the National Debt," as well as "Father of the Funding System."

As the capstone of his elaborate financial structure, Hamilton arranged for the creation of a powerful Bank of the United States. So great was popular support for this venture that its publicly offered stock rapidly sold out amid wild scenes of "Scriptomania" or "Scriptophobia."

A dynamic Hamilton, with his aristocratic leanings, encountered a formidable adversary in Secretary of State Thomas Jefferson, popularly known as "Man of the People" and "The Philosopher of Democracy." The tradition is that Hamilton, during a heated Cabinet meeting, burst out, "Your people, sir, is a great beast." These words, whether uttered or not, ring true. Hamilton believed in expanding the powers of the central government by a "loose construction" of the Constitution and its "implied powers"; Jefferson believed in curbing the powers of central government by a "strict construction" of the Constitution. Hence the Hamiltonian "loose constructionists" versus the Jeffersonian "strict constructionists."

Bitter clashes between Hamilton and Jefferson over fiscal policy, foreign affairs, and constitutional interpretation brought forth strange fruit. The first two political parties emerged about 1793: the Jeffersonian Republicans (or Democratic-Republicans) and the Hamiltonian Federalists. Hamilton received the nickname "King of the Feds," and his more aristocratic Federalists were branded "High-Flying Federalists."

One essential prop of Hamilton's financial edifice was an excise tax, which proved especially obnoxious to the whiskey distillers of western Pennsylvania as class legislation. So widespread was their product that on occasion even preachers were paid in "old Monongahela rye." Riotous demonstrations came on the heels of the hated tax, as "Whiskey Men" or "Whiskey Boys" roughly handled the federal agents in scenes reminiscent of the Stamp Act riots of 1765. The motto of the whiskeyites was "Liberty and No Excise," which seems to have been derived from the "Liberty, Property, and No Excise" used in England in the 1730s. The whiskey rebels, also known as "Tom the Tinker's Men," hoisted streamers bearing the message "United we stand, divided we fall." As in the days before the American Revolution, the dissidents erected "Liberty Poles" or "Whiskey Poles," which opponents branded "Sedition Poles" or "Anarchy Poles." Attached thereto were banners with such appeals as "An Equal Tax, and No Excise," "No Asylum for Cowards and Traitors," and "Liberty and No Excise, O Whiskey!" A common and somewhat belligerent challenge was, "Are You for Congress or for Liberty?"

Riotous defiance of the federal government by the whiskeyites finally persuaded President Washington, in response to the urgings of Hamilton, to dispatch an army of some 13,000 men to western Pennsylvania. So powerful was this force that when the soldiers reached their destination, the rebellion had evaporated. In his next message to Congress President Washington blamed the outbursts on "certain self-created societies," such as those spawned by the French Revolution. Critics were quick to point out that "self-created societies" had once engineered the revolution which Washington had headed.

THE FRENCH FRENZY

General Washington had occupied his high office for scarcely ten weeks when the French Revolution erupted with the storming of the Bastille in Paris by an angry mob. The American people, remembering their own uprising, greeted the outburst with an enthusiasm criticized as "Bastille fever" or "the love frenzy for France." In New England one orator proclaimed, "It was a spark from the altar flame of liberty on this side of the Atlantic, which alighted on the pinnacle of despotism in France and reduced the immense fabric to ashes in the twinkling of an eye."

Reactions to the upheaval in France took some strange twists in America. The names of streets that suggested monarchy were quickly changed. In Boston, Royal Exchange Alley became Équality Lane; in New York, Queen Street became Pearl Street and Crown Street became Liberty Street. When the revolutionists in France abolished titles and assumed the title of "citizen," sympathetic Americans called one another "citizen" or "citess."

Two powerful slogans swept across the Atlantic from France: "Liberté, Egalité, Fraternité" (Liberty, Equality, Fraternity) and "Ça ira, ça tien-

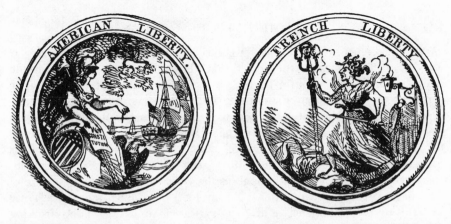

The Contrast. Adaptation of an English cartoon. C. C. Coffin, *Building a Nation*, 1882.

dra" (That will go, that will last). Both of these catch phrases were said
to have been suggested earlier by Franklin when he was an envoy in
France. "Ça ira" was set to music and widely sung by admiring Francophiles in America, along with the more stirring "Marseillaise."

Disorders abroad assumed a new complexion when the European
monarchs, assisted by exiled nobles, invaded France to restore Louis XVI
to his throne. With the Duke of Brunswick in command, the aristocrats
were hurled back at Valmy in September 1792. Enthusiasm for the
French defenders expressed itself in "Civic Feasts," especially one in
Boston, where a fat ox was sacrificed as an offering to "Liberty and Equality and the Rights of Man." School children were given small "civic
cakes," each stamped with the words "Liberty and Equality." A troop of
boys held aloft a banner inscribed:

> Brunswick's old Duke, with ninety thousand men,
> *March'd* into France, and then *run out* again.

Conservatives in America had greeted the French Revolution in its
early stages with lukewarm sympathy, while liberals of the Jeffersonian
stripe displayed high enthusiasm. But the upheaval took on an uglier
complexion in 1793, when the guillotine began to clang, and the "Reign
of Terror" followed. In 1793 Louis XVI and then his frivolous queen,
Marie Antoinette, lost their heads. One Jeffersonian newspaper gloated,
"Louis Capet has lost his caput," while various gatherings guillotined the
unfortunate monarch in effigy. American conservatives, feeling their
tender white necks, were shocked beyond measure. They feared that this
"moral influenza," more to be dreaded than "a thousand yellow fevers,"
might spread to America. An epidemic of yellow fever in Philadelphia,
according to John Adams, was indeed all that kept the frenzied multitude
from overthrowing the government and precipitating war against Britain
in support of France.

ANGLOMEN VERSUS JACOBINS

After the beheading of Louis XVI early in 1793, France declared war
on Great Britain, with the result that the initial shots of the French
Revolution widened into a titanic struggle for control of the seas. The
pro-British Hamiltonian Federalists, believing that only "Britain's fast-
anchored isle" stood between them and anarchy, naturally supported the
mother country. Pro-French Jeffersonian Republicans branded their rivals
as "British bootlickers," "Anglomen," and "Monarchists." The Federalists
disparaged the Jeffersonians as "filthy Jacobins" (after the French revolutionary Jacobin Clubs). Additional insults were "a despicable mobocracy,"
"Disorganizers," "Incendiaries," "Anarchists," "Gallic Jackals," "lying
dogs," "tools of baboons," and "frog-eating, man-eating, blood-drinking
cannibals." Editor William Cobbett warned the Jeffersonian Republicans,
those friends of France, "I say, beware, ye under-strapping cut-throats

who walk in rags and sleep amidst filth and vermin; for if once the halter gets around your flea-bitten necks, howling and confessing will come too late."

One burning question was on many American lips: Would the United States remain neutral during the death struggle between Britain and France—a France which had fought Britain for American independence and to which the United States was still bound "forever" by the alliance of 1778 to help the French defend their West Indies? Despite the clamor of the Jeffersonian Francophiles, a level-headed Washington concluded that since France had started this war, America could properly stand on the sidelines. After painful reflection he issued a proclamation of neutrality (1793), which was an act of statesmanship but which was condemned by the more ardent Francophiles.

From Paris the revolutionary government had sent to America a hot-headed young envoy, Citizen Genêt. He was outraged to hear of the proclamation of neutrality, all the more so because he was greeted with wild enthusiasm by the pro-French element. A French warship in the Delaware River exhibited warning banners: "Enemies of Equality, Reform or Tremble," "We Are Armed To Defend the Rights of Man," and "Freemen, Behold, We Are Your Friends and Brethren." Citizen Genêt grossly overreached himself when he threatened to appeal over the head of "old Washington" to the sovereign people, and as a result he was replaced by a better-balanced diplomatist.

Amid all the uproar, Americans sympathetic to the French Revolution enthusiastically drank toasts to "Thomas Paine, the clarion of freedom," "George Washington, the father of freedom," and "Lafayette, freedom's darling son." When General Lafayette, seeking to quiet the violence of the French masses, fell into disfavor and was subsequently imprisoned, the toasts took on a different tone. These included "The unfortunate but patriotic Lafayette! May he outlive his enemies and return in triumph to the arms of his enraptured and enlightened countrymen," and "The Marquis de la Fayette! May the gloom of a despot's prison be soon exchanged for the embraces of his father Washington, in the land of freedom."

THE DAMNATION OF "SIR" JOHN JAY

Armed conflict between Britain and France inevitably led the British Navy to seize scores of American merchant ships that were supplying the beleaguered French West Indies. The fury of outraged Americans knew no bounds as they cried out against George III, that "prince of land and sea-robbers." War seemed inevitable, even desirable. To quiet the uproar, President Washington dispatched John Jay, a prominent Federalist, as a special diplomatic emissary to England in the last-ditch hope of patching up a peace.

So notoriously pro-British was Jay that his appointment touched off a wild outcry from the anti-British Jeffersonian Republicans against "Jay birds." The envoy did his diplomatic best, even though he held weak cards. In the end Jay's Treaty salved some running sores but fell far short of expectations, particularly in failing to acknowledge American rights.

In America scores of bonfires burned effigies of "that damned arch-traitor, Sir John Jay." In Philadelphia, the City of Brotherly Love, an Irish orator declaimed, "What a damned treaty! I make a motion that every good citizen in this assembly kick this damned treaty to hell." An insulting effigy showed Jay holding scales with an attached placard that said, "Come up to my price, and I will sell you my country." On one fence were chalked the words "Damn John Jay! damn every one that won't damn John Jay!! damn every one that won't put lights in his windows and sit up all night damning John Jay!!"

Despite the uproar, ratification of Jay's unpopular treaty seemed imperative if the weak and disunited republic hoped to avoid war with Great Britain. President Washington, in an agonizing decision, threw his weight behind the pact and it barely scraped through the Senate. His courageous action brought down on his honored head the condemnation of rabid Jeffersonian Francophiles. One Virginia toast ran, "A speedy death to General Washington." John Randolph of Virginia cried in a public toast, "George Washington—may he be damned if he signs Jay's Treaty." Thomas Jefferson wrote privately, "Curse on his virtues; they have undone the country." Remembering Samson and Delilah of Biblical times, he placed Washington among those "who have had their heads shorn by the harlot England." This indiscretion leaked out and caused the author grave embarrassment.

Jay's foes held one last card after the Senate narrowly voted approval: the House of Representatives would have to appropriate the necessary funds to carry out the treaty. The issue hung in doubt until Fisher Ames of Massachusetts, the premier Federalist orator, rose from his sickbed to make an impassioned plea. Noting that "a treaty is the promise of a nation," he declaimed that in the event of war "the wounds yet unhealed" would "be torn open again; the [Indian] war whoop shall waken the sleep of the cradle." Moved by this superlative pleading, the House grudgingly voted the essential funds and the Jay Treaty survived.

WASHINGTON BOWS OUT

A harassed Washington, nearing the end of his second four-year term, was not only physically tired but weary of abuse from ungrateful countrymen. Common epithets were "The American Caesar," "Stepfather of His Country," "Monocrat," and "Anglomaniac." He had complained to Jefferson that he was the butt of such "indecent terms" as one could hardly apply to "a Nero—a notorious defaulter—or even a common pickpocket." On the other hand, the cry "Stand by Washington" often came from the lips of the President's supporters, as did the song "God Save Great Washington."

Washington's famed Farewell Address, as given to the press in September 1796, served not only as a formal announcement of retirement but as a treasury of advice from "The Father of His Country" to his excitable children. Remembering the recent uproar by pro-French and pro-British citizens, he urged his countrymen to avoid "the insidious wiles of foreign influence. . . ." An ocean separated young America from the broils of Europe, so "Why quit our own to stand upon foreign ground?" The "true policy" of the young republic was to "steer clear of permanent alliances" with other nations. Yet in "extraordinary emergencies" Americans might place their trust in "temporary alliances," always remembering that "there can be no greater error than to expect or calculate upon real favors from nation to nation."

Washington's formal retirement created joy among many Jeffersonian Republicans. Notorious among them was Benjamin Franklin Bache, an outspoken grandson of "Old Ben" known as "Lightning Rod, Junior." Editorializing in the Philadelphia *Aurora,* he rejoiced that this iniquitous President would lose his power "to multiply evils" by being reduced to the status of a private citizen. "Every heart . . . ought to beat high with exultation that the name of Washington, from this day, ceases to give a currency to political iniquity and to legalize corruption."

The shocking sentiments of Bache, who died the next year of yellow fever, were fortunately not shared by many, and Washington lived quietly at Mount Vernon for most of his remaining days, nearly three years. When the end came in 1799, Federalist newspapers published the sad news with wide black borders; the Jeffersonians used narrow black borders. Countless commemorative services were held throughout the land. The superb memorial resolution presented to Congress by Richard Henry Lee read, "To the memory of the Man first in war, first in peace, and first in the hearts of his countrymen."

Rancors gradually cooled and Washington underwent virtual deification. The famous "Father of His Country," so generations of youth were solemnly informed, "never told a lie." A major influence in both his deification and purification was Mason L. ("Parson") Weems, who about 1800 published his highly popular biography of Washington. Not until the fifth edition (1806) did the author evidently discover or invent the implausible story of the ruined cherry tree. There stands six-year-old George with his sharp new hatchet; out in the garden stands the cherry tree "terribly" barked; in front of the youth towers an irate father, who sternly asks if his son knows who "killed" the tree. Young George, who could not easily lie out of that damning situation, bravely cried out, "I can't tell a lie, Pa; you know I can't tell a lie. I did it with my hatchet." The father then joyously embraced his son for this "act of heroism."

FRICTION WITH FRANCE

Before Washington formally bowed out, the young republic experienced its first partisan presidential election, that of 1796. Vice President John Adams, a dyed-in-the-wool Federalist, clashed with Thomas Jefferson, standard bearer of the Democratic-Republican party. One Jeffersonian slogan proclaimed, "Liberty, Equality, and No King," evidently a slap at the allegedly monarchical George Washington. Worry over possible monarchy led to pamphlets and handbills which asserted, "Thomas Jefferson is a firm republican—John Adams is an avowed monarchist." In Pennsylvania the voters were urged to support Thomas Jefferson, "the uniform advocate of equal rights among citizens," and spurn John Adams, "the champion of rank, titles, and hereditary distinctions."

Adams narrowly triumphed over Jefferson by a margin of only three electoral votes. As a consequence, the victor was sneeringly referred to as "the President by three votes"—a characterization that hurt his pride, which was well developed. As one of the ablest of the Founding Fathers, he had honestly earned the sobriquets "The Atlas of Independence," "The Colossus of Debate," "The Colossus of Independence," and "The Partisan of Independence." Yet as a rather stiff, ungracious, and overweight personality, he was less flatteringly known as "His Rotundity" and "The Duke of Braintree," after his home in Massachusetts.

President Adams inherited a nasty quarrel with France that had grown largely out of America's favorable concessions to Britain in Jay's Treaty. In an effort to patch up relations, President Adams sent three prominent emissaries to Paris, who later appeared anonymously in the printed dispatches as X, Y, and Z. The trio was met by agents from the Foreign Minister, the slippery Talleyrand, who attempted to secure a bribe as a prerequisite to negotiations. Bribes, then as now, were common instruments of diplomacy, but the Americans recoiled from the magnitude of the proposed sum. They replied, according to their official dispatch, "No, no, not a sixpence."

When news of France's insulting proposition reached America, a wave of anger swept the young republic, especially "the British faction." President Adams piled fuel on the flames when he sent the XYZ documents to Congress. The slogan of the hour became "Millions for defense but not 1 cent for tribute." This ringing declaration was credited to Charles C. Pinckney, one of the three angered envoys, who was supposed to have uttered it when rejecting the bribe offer. Throughout his life he denied authorship, but after his death it was inscribed on a tablet to his memory in his native Charleston.

Patriotic frenzy against France vented itself in poetry and toasts. One favorite line was "May the American Eagle pluck out the Gills of the Gallic Cock." When President Adams appeared in public, bands struck up "The President's March," and countless throats bawled the words of

"Adams and Liberty" and "Washington and the Constitution." New stanzas blossomed for "Yankee Doodle":

> Bold Adams did in Seventy-Six,
> Our Independence sign, sir,
> And he will not give up a jot,
> Tho' all the world combine, sir.

Those few bold Francophiles who tried to respond with the French song "Ça Ira" or "The Marseillaise" were hooted down. Joseph Hopkinson composed his blood-tingling "Hail Columbia," which was set to the tune of the popular "President's March." Overnight it became the song of the hour. The chorus promised:

> Firm, united, let us be,
> Rallying round our Liberty;
> As a band of brothers join'd,
> Peace and safety we shall find.

President Adams, somewhat surprisingly, at first encouraged the popular outcry. He declared in a stirring message to Congress, "I will never send another minister to France without assurances that he will be received, respected, and honored as the representative of a great, free, powerful, and independent nation." Congress authorized the construction of the tiny but efficient fleet, and John Adams earned the title "Father of the American Navy." The ensuing undeclared war with France was waged on the sea for more than two years. Popular toasts were "The Wooden Walls of Columbia" and "The Rising Navy of America." In a pro-French phrase American seamen were "John Adams's Jackasses," and they in turn responded by singing lustily:

> Now let each jolly tar, with one heart and one voice,
> Drink a can of good grog to the man of our choice;
> Under John, the State pilot, and George's command,
> There's a fig for the French and the sly Talleyrand.

After earlier skating near the brink of a full-fledged war, Adams belatedly remembered Washington's advice to keep out of foreign quarrels, especially while the nation was still in its adolescence. When a break occurred in the European clouds, Adams perceived that Talleyrand probably would receive new American representatives with dignity, and he dispatched three envoys, much to the distress of the war-bent wing of his own Federalist party.

Adams's bold act required considerable political courage, though probably less than is traditionally supposed. His three envoys succeeded in negotiating the Treaty of 1800, which ended hostilities and released America from its entangling alliance of 1778. Adams was defeated for reelection in 1800, possibly though not certainly as a result of his having averted war. Yet he viewed his course with quiet satisfaction. He wrote to a correspondent in 1815, "I desire no other inscription over my grave-stone than: 'Here lies John Adams, who took upon himself the responsi-bility of the peace with France in the year 1800.' "

THE AMERICAN REIGN OF TERROR

Hostilities with France, which proved embarrassing to the pro-French Jeffersonians, enabled the anti-French Federalists in Congress to inaugu-rate their own "Reign of Terror." They passed the Alien and Sedition Acts, designed to shut off the influx of French and Irish revolutionists ("wild Irishmen") from abroad while stifling dissent at home. Specifically, the Sedition Act imposed penalties on those persons convicted of pub-lishing "any false, scandalous and malicious writing" that brought the federal government, including the President, into disrepute. Angered Jeffersonian Republicans branded the Sedition Act "the little monster" that choked off free speech with "Lock Jaw Federalism."

About twenty-five citizens suffered prosecution by the Federalist "mon-archists" under the sedition laws, ten of them Republican editors and printers. Such cases were actively pressed by Secretary of State Timothy Pickering, commonly called "The Scourge of Jacobinism." Conspicuous among the victims was Matthew Lyon, "The Beast of Vermont," "King of the Beasts," and "The Spitting Lyon [lion]." He earned these epithets by spitting in the face of a fellow Congressman during a heated verbal exchange. He was ultimately convicted under the Sedition Act for having declared that in President Adams's administration "every consideration of the public welfare was swallowed up in a continual grasp for power, in an unbounded thirst for ridiculous pomp, foolish adulation, and selfish avarice." This expression of free speech, though embodied in a private letter, found its way into an unfriendly newspaper. "The Spitting Lyon" was finally sentenced to four months in jail and assessed a fine of $1,000.

Aroused Jeffersonians refused to take these encroachments on funda-mental freedoms lying down. They hoisted anew the "Liberty Poles," which exhibited such sentiments as "No British Alliance" and "No Sedi-tion Bill." Jeffersonians also displayed "Liberty Caps," which their op-ponents denounced as "emblems of sedition." Federalists branded Vice President Jefferson, the head of the "French Faction" and "The Great Democratic Chief of America," as "The High Priest of Jacobinism."

Fearing persecution under the Sedition Act, Vice President Jefferson collaborated secretly with James Madison of Virginia in drafting the Virginia and Kentucky resolutions of 1798–99. These documents main-tained that the Alien and Sedition Acts were unconstitutional because through them the federal government had usurped powers not expressly delegated to it under the constitutional "compact" or "contract" with the states. Madison bluntly declared in his Virginia resolutions that in such cases the states "have the right and are in duty bound to interpose for arresting the progress of the evil." Jefferson went a giant step further in his second set of Kentucky resolutions when he proclaimed that in such instances "a nullification" by the states of all unconstitutional acts was "the rightful remedy" under the Constitution. Thus appeared the most conspicuous early usage of the ugly word "nullification."

THE GLADIATORS OF 1800

As the crucial election of 1800 approached, pitting Federalist President John Adams against the Democratic-Republican Vice President Thomas Jefferson, the issues were sharply drawn. The harsh Alien and Sedition Acts, aimed by the Federalists at their opponents, had aroused nation-wide condemnation. On the other hand, the Virginia and Kentucky resolutions, with their dangerous doctrine of nullification, seemed to many people to have gone too far in the opposite direction.

The Francophile Jeffersonian "Jacobins," who represented the "swinish multitude," continued their refusal to submit quietly to the Federalist "monarchists" and "Anglomen," who now abhorred all thoughts of revolution. Specifically, pro-French Jeffersonians assailed Adams for having taken too bellicose a stance toward France at the time of the XYZ crisis, and for having partially raised a large army and an unnecessary navy (to protect Federalist shippers). These heavy defense expenditures had required direct taxes, which in Pennsylvania had resulted in the Fries Rebellion, popularly known as "The Hot Water War" or "The Hot Water Rebellion." Embattled housewives poured scalding water from their windows onto the tax assessors. "Is it not High Time for a Change?" demanded a Republican leaflet addressed to the voters of New Jersey. Sneering at John Adams's alleged monarchical ways, Jeffersonians sang to the tune of "Yankee Doodle" a stanza devised in 1798:

> See Johnny at the helm of State,
> Head itching for a crowny,
> He longs to be, like Georgy [Washington], great,
> And pull Tom Jeffer downy.

Personalities, as much as issues, influenced the outcome of the clash between Adams and Jefferson. The fussy New Englander found the most damaging enemies within his own camp, notably Alexander Hamilton. Embittered because Adams had denied him the glory of a war with France, in which he had expected to shine as a military hero, he secretly circulated a back-stabbing pamphlet among leading Federalists condemning the President in the harshest terms. Hamilton branded him as "eccentric" and lacking in "sound judgment" while possessing "vanity without bounds" and "a jealousy capable of discoloring every object." The indiscreet pamphlet promptly leaked out and fell into the hands of Republicans, who gleefully reprinted it and spread it broadcast.

As for Jefferson, the philosopher-farmer, he believed that men who labored in the fields possessed a nobler nature than the workmen crowded into stinking urban slums. In his *Notes on the State of Virginia,* published in the 1780s, he had written that as long as there was "land to labor, let us never wish to see our citizens occupied at a work bench. . . . Let our workshops remain in Europe. . . . The mobs of great cities add just so much to the support of pure government as sores do to the strength of the human body." Federalist spokesmen seized upon these aspersions. The Boston *Centinel* published a pointed appeal during the campaign of 1800 entitled "Mechanics of Boston"; it reminded carpenters, masons, and other manual workers of Jefferson's unflattering views.

Fearful Federalists attacked Jefferson's morals in one of the nation's earliest whispering campaigns—only it was more like a shouting campaign. Among miscellaneous misdeeds, the Virginian was accused of having fathered numerous mulatto children by his own slave women. More damaging in an orthodox America was the charge of atheism, although as a deist Jefferson believed in God. A passage in his *Notes on the State of Virginia* was repeatedly thrown back in his face: "But it does me no injury for my neighbor to say there are twenty gods, or no God. It neither picks my pocket nor breaks my leg."

Heated debate over Jefferson's religious tolerance seems strange to a later generation. Old ladies of the Federalist faith hid their Bibles, fearing confiscation if Jefferson triumphed. *The Gazette of the United States* (Philadelphia) stated "The Grand Question":

> Shall I continue allegiance to
> GOD—AND A RELIGIOUS PRESIDENT;
> Or impiously declare for
> JEFFERSON—AND NO GOD!!!

One pamphlet, *Short Address to the Voters of Delaware* (1800), warned, "Remember that the reign of anarchy may create more evil in a year, than the order of government can eradicate in a century." This blast predicted, if Jefferson should be elected, assassination, seduction, rape, plunder, and irreligion. The Reverend Timothy Dwight, president of Yale College, prophesized that "the Bible would be cast into a bonfire, our holy worship changed into a dance of Jacobin phrensy, our wives and daughters dishonored, our sons converted into the disciples of [the atheist] Voltaire and the dragoons of Marat [a leader involved in the French Revolution massacres]."

Nothing daunted, Democratic-Republicans raised banners applauding "Jefferson, the Friend of the People," while a favorite toast extolled "Jefferson, the Mammoth of Democracy." Exultingly the Jeffersonians could sing:

> Lord! how the Federalists will stare
> At Jefferson in Adams' chair!

On a loftier note many hoarse-throated Democratic-Republicans bawled "Jefferson and Liberty":

The gloomy night before us flies,
The reign of terror now is o'er;
Its gangs, inquisitors and spies,
Its herds of harpies are no more.

Chorus:

Rejoice, Columbia's sons, rejoice;
To tyrants never bend the knee
But join with heart and soul and voice
For Jefferson and liberty.

"Long Tom" Jefferson triumphed by a narrow margin, to the dismay of the "Feds," who feared "the atheists" and "the levelers." On the other hand, the Republican Philadelphia *Aurora* rejoiced over the ousting of the "Anglomen" ("British bootlickers") and the "Monarchists." It proclaimed, "Now the Revolution of 1776 is complete." Jefferson himself, with his weakness for exaggeration, hailed the outcome as "The Revolution of 1800." Disillusioning events would prove that the election was much less of an upheaval than the winner anticipated.

IV

Jeffersonian
and Madisonian Democracy

> Sometimes it is said that man cannot be trusted with
> the government of himself. Can he, then, be trusted
> with the government of others? Or have we found
> angels in the forms of kings to govern him?
>
> Thomas Jefferson, first inaugural address, 1801

BOLD JEFFERSONIAN BEGINNINGS

Lanky Thomas Jefferson, with his graying reddish hair, came naturally
by the nicknames "Long Tom" and "The Red Fox." His most significant
literary achievement had won him the sobriquets "Father of the Declaration of Independence," "Pen of the Revolution," and "Scribe of the Revolution." Even the mottoes that he approved were much quoted, partly
because they embodied principles that he earnestly sought to follow, although not always consistently. Among them were "The world is governed too much" and "Rebellion to tyrants is obedience to God." The
year before becoming President he wrote, "I have sworn upon the altar
of God eternal hostility against every form of tyranny over the mind of
man."

Spurning the pomp and ceremony of a horse-drawn coach, Jefferson,
the newly elected "Man of the People," ambled over from his boarding
house to the scene of the inauguration ceremonies on March 4, 1801. His
much-quoted address on this occasion was designed to allay the fears of
the recently ousted Federalists, who, bitter from the heated electoral con-

test, feared reprisals. "But," he declared, "every difference of opinion is not a difference of principle. . . . We are all Republicans, we are all Federalists." Then came a ringing declaration of tolerance: "If there be any among us who would wish to dissolve this Union or to change its republican form, let them stand undisturbed as monuments of the safety with which error of opinion may be tolerated where reason is left free to combat it."

As for foreign countries, Jefferson voiced the simple prescription of "peace, commerce, and honest friendship with all nations, entangling alliances with none. . . ." This firm assertion was clearly prompted by recent difficulties with France over the "forever" alliance, formally terminated in 1800. The phrase "No entangling alliances" is incorrectly ascribed to Washington's Farewell Address, which avowed the same policy in less striking language.

Less than three weeks before Jefferson's administration began, the expiring Federalist Congress had passed a law creating sixteen urgently needed new federal judgeships. Lame-duck President Adams, acting like a true partisan, appointed only Federalists to the new posts, even though the Jefferson Republicans had recently won the Presidency. The legend rapidly took root that Adams spent his last day in office until the stroke of midnight signing the "deathbed" commissions of these new officials, soon known as "The Midnight Judges." Actually he signed only three judicial commissions during his last day in office, and he wound up his work at about 9 o'clock, before retiring to his "Dukedom" at Braintree, in Massachusetts. The new Republican Congress repealed the obnoxious Judiciary Act, thus sweeping the benches from under the sixteen Federalist judges.

As beneficiary of the first party overturn in American history, Jefferson could hardly be expected to leave all the opposition Federalists in office. Some were violent partisans; others were senile or otherwise incompetent. Although not usually blamed for installing the "spoils system" (Jackson is), Jefferson managed to remove proportionately about as many officeholders as Jackson. In a letter to a committee of New Haven merchants in 1801, the Virginian penned these famous words: "If a due participation of office is a matter of right, how are vacancies to be obtained? Those by death are few: by resignation, none." In popular shorthand, this complaint became "Few die and none resign."

To his great annoyance, Jefferson could not summarily remove from the Federal bench those partisan judges who had already used their high station to berate the Jeffersonian Republicans. Intolerably offensive was Justice Samuel Chase of the Supreme Court, who had made himself infamous by bullying, insulting, browbeating, and sentencing those Republican "martyrs" unfortunate enough to be haled before his Court. He was dubbed "The Wicked Judge" and "The American Jeffreys" (after an English hanging judge). Irate citizens named vicious dogs after Chase and berated him in barbed puns and epigrams. The Philadelphia *Aurora* vented its wrath:

> Cursed of thy father, scum of all that's base,
> Thy sight is odious, and thy name is . . . [Chase].

Jefferson, the champion of free speech, finally urged that formal charges be brought against Chase, who was impeached by the House and tried by the Senate in 1805. The accused had obviously been guilty of obnoxious speech, but had fallen so far short of "high crimes and misdemeanors" as specified by the Constitution that he was acquitted by a comfortable margin. Ironically, in this case, Jefferson favored free speech that was not too free.

THE LOUISIANA WINDFALL

Stirring events were meanwhile unfolding in foreign affairs. During 1801 and 1802 well-founded rumors began to circulate in America that Spain had agreed to transfer to France all of the vast domain known as Louisiana, stretching magnificently from the Mississippi River to the Rocky Mountains. Jefferson expressed deep concern, for he realized that a powerful France entrenched at the mouth of the river would pose grave dangers. In April 1802 he wrote to the American Minister in Paris that from the day France took possession of New Orleans, "we must marry ourselves to the British fleet and nation."

Anticipating the transfer of Louisiana, the Spanish authorities at New Orleans formally withdrew from downstream American shippers the right to deposit produce on land at the mouth of the river. "The Men of the Western Waters," fearing strangulation, rose in righteous wrath. One Kentuckian went overboard when he advocated an independent West or one allied with France. He was tried for sedition and burned in effigy while the crowd shouted, "Perpetuity to the Union!" "Confidence in Government," and "Free Navigation of the Mississippi!"

Eager to quiet the uproar in the West and hoping to acquire New Orleans, Jefferson dispatched James Monroe as a special envoy to Paris, where he found Minister Livingston well along with unauthorized negotiations for the purchase of all Louisiana. Napoleon's war plans were such that he could not hold the vast territory in the face of the British fleet. After signing the necessary treaties, Minister Livingston solemnly declared, "We have lived long, but this is the noblest work of our whole lives. . . . From this day the United States take their place among the powers of the first rank. . . ." Thus the republic purchased the western half of "The Valley of Democracy."

Jefferson was taken aback by the purchase treaties. He had authorized negotiations for the tail of the bear—New Orleans and some territory to the east—but his envoys had bought the whole bear. Although privately coveting all of Louisiana, he wrote that the purchase was "an act beyond the constitution" yet he hoped that Congress would overlook "metaphysical subtleties." Jefferson regarded himself as a "guardian" purchasing "adjacent territory" for a minor ward, who could later repudiate him when coming of age. But the bargain was simply too fantastic to be aborted by legalistic quibbling.

STRUGGLING FOR SAILORS' RIGHTS

Penny-pinching Jefferson, who favored strict economy in government, disliked the infant navy, and he recoiled from any thought of war. "Peace is our passion," he declared. Yet in 1801, early in the new administration, the piratical Pasha of Tripoli, dissatisfied with the protection money being paid for American shipping in the Mediterranean Sea, declared war. Jefferson, not only an antinavy zealot but an ardent peacelover, had no choice but to retaliate with heroic naval action. The blackmailing Pasha of Tripoli was finally glad to accept a less favorable treaty in 1805; it required the United States to pay the bargain price of $60,000 for the release of American prisoners and the end of annual tribute. Perhaps the most enduring memory of this martial episode is enshrined in the song of the United States Marines (formally organized in 1798):

> From the Halls of Montezuma,
> To the shores of Tripoli,
> We fight our country's battles
> On the land as on the sea.

Fighting with Tripoli produced curious consequences. During operations in Mediterranean waters a fleet of small gunboats was deemed useful, and Jefferson, with his cheese-paring budget, decided to pin his faith to these tiny craft for defense of American shores. Mounting one or two unwieldy guns, these unseaworthy boats were often more menacing to their crew than to the enemy; during the subsequent War of 1812 they proved virtually useless. They evoked much ridicule, especially from hostile Federalists, who regarded these "Jeffs" as making up "The Mosquito Fleet." For their part Jeffersonians referred to the expensive regular navy as "The Great Beast with the Great Belly."

A ferocious hurricane in 1804, one of the worst of the century, struck Savannah, Georgia, and hurled the one-gunned Gunboat Number One eight miles inland into a cornfield. Foes of Jefferson made merry with jeers about the new type of scarecrow. Among the toasts at a Boston dinner under Federalist auspices was "Gunboat Number One: if our gunboats are of no use upon the water, may they at least be the best upon earth." Another toast jeered, "Our farmers on the seacoast: may their cornfields be defended against Gunboat Number Three."

Ridicule of this sort made up part of the campaign against President Jefferson's reelection, but to no avail. He overwhelmingly defeated his Federalist rival, Charles C. Pinckney.

Jefferson had substantially federalized his Republican party by adopting such Federalist principles as a strong central government and a loose interpretation of the Constitution, notably in the purchase of Louisiana. There was added irony in his inaugural pronouncement four years earlier, "We are all Republicans, we are all Federalists."

Uneasy peace between England and France, enabling America to pick up Louisiana, was ruptured by Bonaparte in 1803. The new republic again found itself caught between the two rivals in their death struggle for control of the sea. Desperately needing sailors to man its fleet, Britain increasingly trod on American toes by its practice of impressing British subjects from Yankee ships. This crude method of conscription, which England had used for hundreds of years, was based on the belief that in time of peril every loyal British subject was duty bound to support his country. He could not seek refuge in foreign naturalization, for Britannia held doggedly to the principle "Once an Englishman, always an Englishman."

Some English sailors secured naturalization papers and joined the flourishing American merchant marine, where the pay was much better— "Dollars for shillings," the saying went. But British press gangs, when boarding American merchant ships on the high seas, waved aside naturalization papers, even though legitimately secured. Some of the impressees were native-born British subjects, others were deserters from Britain's "floating hells," and still others were *bona fide* American citizens —perhaps 11,000 all told. Short-handed British captains, branded "piratical man-stealers," were not disposed to be too particular in dealing with Yankee "dollar grubbers."

Despite the need for seamen, Britain never claimed the right to impress its own subjects from foreign warships, which might shoot back. Yet in 1807 the captain of the British *Leopard* approached the unsuspecting United States frigate *Chesapeake* on the high seas and demanded the return of four alleged deserters. Upon receiving a refusal from the American captain, the British warship poured in three broadsides at close range, killing three men and wounding eighteen. Hopelessly unprepared, the battered American vessel surrendered, and a British boarding party seized the four alleged deserters, one of them a *bona fide* English subject.

Outraged by the *Chesapeake* incident, America united in an outburst of anger unparalleled in the thirty-one-year history of the republic. General Andrew Jackson, referring also to a current treason trial, proclaimed to a crowd from the steps of the Tennessee state house, "Millions to persecute an American; not a cent to resist England!" An indignation meeting in New York denounced "the dastardly and unprovoked attack." A gathering in Boston, in the heart of Federalist territory, pledged cheerful cooperation "in any measures, however serious," that the administration might adopt. But Jefferson, recognizing the futility of war, was determined to secure amends from Great Britain through the quiet channels of diplomacy.

Bloodshed on the decks of the *Chesapeake* unleashed a flood of pamphlets. One, by "a Yankee farmer" who evidently was a Federalist, appeared in Boston in 1807 under the title *Peace without Dishonor—War without Hope. Being a Calm and Dispassionate Enquiry into the Question of the* Chesapeake *and the Necessity and Expediency of War.* Farther south, in the more Jeffersonian territory of Charleston, arose a belligerent plea in pamphlet form, *The Tocsin; or, The Call to Arms! An Essay Being an Enquiry into the Late Proceedings of Great Britain on her Unjustifiable Attack upon the Liberty and Independence of the United States of America.* But President Jefferson, ever the peacelover, rejected as futile any warlike measures against the "Mistress of the Seas." Diplomatic negotiations dragged on from 1807 to 1811, when London formally disavowed the attack and returned the two of the four prisoners who had survived.

THE EMBARGO BLIGHT

As the conflict in Europe waxed hotter, Jefferson desperately sought some substitute for war that would compel the belligerents to respect American rights. The scheme that he finally hit upon was the embargo, which a compliant Congress of "Embargoroons" adopted in 1807. It flatly forbade Americans to export foodstuffs and other supplies to foreign shores, even though urgently needed by the warring powers.

Withering depression gradually laid its skeleton hand on once busy ports and agricultural areas, while opposition to the embargo mounted, especially in Federalist strongholds. The very term "embargo" lent itself ideally to ridicule. One writer declared that the name ought to be "Dambargo." Spelled backward, it produced "O-grab-me," which federal agents tried to do to numerous violators. "Go-bar-em" was what was happening to once profitable American exports. If this odious law continued, the people would be goaded to "Mob-rage."

Federalists in New England, heavily dependent on overseas commerce, cried out that "Mad Tom" Jefferson's embargo was like "cutting one's throat to cure the nosebleed." Passed by the "Virginia Lordlings," they complained, it employed "Quaker-gun" or "wooden-gun diplomacy." It awakened memories of China's isolation behind its Great Wall—hence "the Chinese policy." Jefferson's method of fighting a war also reminded Federalists of the terrapin, which, like other turtles, retreats into its shell when foes approach. Hence "The Terrapin War." Washington's Birthday in 1808 was observed by hostile New Englanders as "Embargo Day." Numerous verses, some of them set to music, were written for the occasion, including one song entitled "The Terrapin Era." At Salem, Massachusetts, one musical effort was less bitter than others:

> Oh, dear, what can the matter be?
> Dear, dear, what can the matter be?

> Oh, dear, what can the matter be?
> Th' Embargo don't answer its end.

Economic losses resulting from Jefferson's "Chinese policy" and "Quaker-gun diplomacy" were especially galling to Federalist New England, from which flowed an immense illicit traffic to Canada. A New Hampshire poet vented his indignation in song:

> Our ships all in motion,
> Once whiten'd the ocean;
>   They sail'd and return'd with a Cargo;
> Now doom'd to decay
> They are fallen a prey,
> To Jefferson, worms, and EMBARGO.

But Jefferson found some defenders even in Federalist New England, where a Boston newspaper published a defense by a loyal Jerseyman:

> Should Hessian fly our wheat destroy,
>   Or granaries crawl with weevil,
> The Embargo's curst in language worst,
>   As source of all the evil.
>
>   .   .   .
>
> Do vermin bold on trees lay hold
>   And make their limbs quite bare go,
> 'Tis ten to one the mischief done
>   Is saddled on *the Embargo.*

Loyal Jeffersonians, for their part, stoutly defended the unpopular embargo. To them it was not a docile "terrapin" but a "snapping-turtle."

Condemnation of the embargo was principally aimed at Jefferson, "the philosopher," who was known to have diverse talents and interests. At the time of the Louisiana Purchase, he had demonstrated a deep curiosity about the area's animal life and vegetation and had solemnly reported to Congress the alleged presence of a salt mountain 45 miles wide and 180 miles long. Scandalous rumor also related that Jefferson had begotten a half dozen mulatto children by his black slave Sally. This malicious gossip gained greater currency when New Englander William Cullen Bryant, the precocious poet, published in Boston at age thirteen a remarkable poem of some 500 lines entitled "The Embargo: or Sketches of the Times, a Satire; by a Youth of Thirteen." It assailed Jefferson as an unpatriotic American, a tool of the French, a dabbler in science, and a hypocrite in morals:

> Go, wretch, resign the presidential chair,
> Disclose thy secret measures, foul or fair.
> Go, search with curious eye, for horned frogs,
> Mid the wild wastes of Louisianian bogs;
> Or, where Ohio rolls his turbid stream,

OGRABME, or, the American Snapping-turtle. The New York Historical Society, New York City.

> Dig for huge bones, thy glory and thy theme.
> Go, scan, Philosophist, thy [Sally's] charms
> And sink supinely in her sable arms;
> But quit to abler hands the helm of state,
> Nor image ruin on thy country's fate!

The poem sold well, and the next year it was published with several other pieces in a pamphlet under the youthful versifier's name. Bryant, who later became one of the nation's great poets, never included in his collected writings any of these items, which he dismissed as "stuff."

THE EXIT OF JEFFERSON

Resistance to the embargo finally became so violent that Jefferson could write in later years, "I felt the foundation of the government shaken under my feet by the New England townships." He overlooked his earlier maxim that "no more good must be attempted than the nation can bear." Congress, bowing to public opinion, formally repealed the hated restrictions early in 1809. Shortly thereafter it substituted a limited embargo in the form of the Non-Intercourse Act, which denied trade with only England and France. To the bitter end, Jefferson was able to commit his nation to limited economic warfare, which did succeed in bringing considerable pressure on the belligerents. He bowed out as President in

1809, after backing the election of his friend and neighbor, James Madison, who continued the "Virginia Dynasty" in power.

A much-abused Jefferson was only sixty-five years of age when he left Washington in 1809, at a time when the Constitution did not limit the number of terms that might be served. (That restriction came in 1951 with the Twenty-second Amendment.) But Jefferson, who had long feared the nightmare of a dictatorship, had made up his mind at least as early as 1805. He then wrote to a friend, in words that were later much quoted by supporters of a constitutional amendment, "General Washington set the example of voluntary retirement after eight years. I shall follow it, and a few more precedents will oppose the obstacle of habit to anyone after a while who shall endeavor to extend his term. Perhaps it may beget a disposition to establish it by an amendment of the Constitution." Jefferson did not really enjoy what he had described in 1797 as the "splendid misery" of the Presidency.

As "The Noble Agrarian," Jefferson retired to his plantation at Monticello to become "The Sage of Monticello" and "The Hero of Monticello" (in Democratic-Republican eyes) or "The Moonshine Philosopher of Monticello" (in Federalist eyes). His most noteworthy activity in retirement was designing and subsequently supervising the construction of the University of Virginia at Charlottesville, a short distance from his stately hilltop home. There can be no doubt that he fully merited the additional designation "Father of the University of Virginia."

During his sunset years Jefferson, the third President, revived his broken friendship with Federalist John Adams, the second President. The two men exchanged a voluminous and revealing correspondence on various subjects. By an extraordinary coincidence Jefferson, the chief author of the Declaration of Independence, died on July 4, 1826, fifty years to the day after the Continental Congress formally adopted his revised draft. His last words were reported to be "Is this the Fourth?" Upon receiving an affirmative reply, he expired peacefully, seventeen years after leaving the White House. By a no less extraordinary coincidence, John Adams died the same day. His last words were "Thomas Jefferson still survives." Actually Jefferson had died several hours earlier.

Man of many achievements, Jefferson rests at his beloved Monticello, beneath a tombstone whose inscription he had composed:

> Here was buried
> Thomas Jefferson
> Author of the Declaration of American Indepen-
> dence Of the Statute of Virginia for Religious
> Freedom and Father of the University of Virginia.

The Louisiana Purchase, of which Jefferson was not conspicuously proud, is notably missing from the list. He was habitually more concerned with things of the mind and spirit.

THE WAR HAWKS TAKE WING

Unimpressive-appearing James Madison, shortest of all the Presidents at five feet four inches, did not look like a dynamic leader and did not prove to be one. He had enjoyed a distinguished career as a legislator, a diplomatist, and a constitutionalist. In the last-named capacity he had deservedly earned the title "Father of the Constitution." Yet political foes sneered at "Little Jemmy" or "Master Jemmy"; and Washington Irving wrote a famous satire about a "withered little applejohn."

On taking office Madison inherited the limited Non-Intercourse Act of 1809, passed in the dying days of the Jefferson administration. When the British Minister in Washington gave unauthorized assurances that London would revoke its restrictions on American commerce, Madison promptly ended nonintercourse with Britain. "Great and Glorious News," proclaimed a broadside "extra" of the New Hampshire *Patriot:* "Our Differences with Great Britain Amicably Settled." But the British Minister had exceeded his instructions, and a crestfallen President Madison restored nonintercourse.

London replaced the errant Minister with a man of sterner stuff, Francis Jackson. The newcomer was nicknamed "Copenhagen Jackson" because in 1807 he had delivered the ultimatum preceding the brutal bombardment of the Danish fleet and capital, Copenhagen. Americans were determined to resist all attempts to "Copenhagen us." As the British envoy became increasingly overbearing, one irate Kentuckian ran afoul of the state profanity law when he shouted, "God damn Mr. Jackson; the President ought to . . . have kicked him from town to town until he is kicked out of the country. God damn him!"

Aroused Indians in the Northwest, using arms secured from British officials in Canada, were meanwhile butchering American pioneers on the Ohio frontier. The red men were allegedly being paid generous bounties for scalps, and this charge, although unproved, caused anger to boil anew against "the British hairbuyers." At the bloody Battle of Tippecanoe in 1811, near the Wabash River in present-day Indiana, General William Henry Harrison beat off attacks by the Indians, some of whom left behind newly marked firearms supplied from Canada. Andrew Jackson of Tennessee burst out, "The blood of our murdered heroes must be revenged," while the Lexington, Kentucky, *Reporter* charged, "The War on the Wabash is purely British. The British scalping knife has filled many habitations both in this state as well as in the Indiana Territory with widows and orphans." From the frontier to the East spread the cry "Look to the Wabash. Look to the impressed seamen!"

Agitation for fighting Britain swelled as the Twelfth Congress convened in November 1811. In the recent elections to that body a number of "senile submission men" had lost their seats to younger, superpatriotic "War Hawks." Many of these novices were Westerners, whom Easterners branded "pepper pot politicians," "buckskin politicians," "the boys," or "the liberty boys."

Among the most vocal "War Hawks" was Speaker Henry Clay of Kentucky, then known as "The Cock of Kentucky," "Harry of the West," and "The Mill Boy of the Slashes," as a result of his humble upbringing in a "slashed-over" or deforested area of Virginia. In 1810 he had declaimed in Congress, "No man in the nation wants peace more than I; but I prefer the troubled ocean of war, demanded by the honor and independence of the country, with all its calamities and desolation, to the tranquil and putrescent pool of ignominious peace."

Clay's views found an echo in a Fourth of July toast at Frankfort, Kentucky, in 1811: "Embargoes, nonintercourse, and negotiations, are but illy calculated to secure our rights. . . . Let us now try old Roman policy, and maintain them with the sword." Representative Felix Grundy of Tennessee, three of his brothers already butchered by the Indian "hell hounds," declared in Congress, "We shall drive the British from our continent—they will no longer have an opportunity of intriguing with our Indian neighbors, and setting on the ruthless savage to tomahawk our women and children." As for invading British Canada, Henry Clay boasted that the militia of Kentucky alone could accomplish this feat with ridiculous ease, while former President Thomas Jefferson, the man of peace, was confident that the invasion was "a mere matter of marching."

FREE SEAS OR FREE LAND

War Hawk cries of "On to Canada" on behalf of "free trade and seamen's rights" proved puzzling to many Easterners. "The Men of the Western Waters" sailed no ships on the ocean and had lost few or no seamen to impressment gangs, but they did grow agricultural surpluses to load into the ships. Moreover, Canada beckoned as the only place where Britain was "getatable." A northern conquest would remove Indian supply bases, add to American fur trade, and open up more acreage for pioneer axes. But to a Virginian like John Randolph the cry of "On to Canada" seemed like a hypocritical way to uphold maritime rights. He argued that if the War Hawks were sincere, their cry should be "On to Halifax," where the British maintained their greatest naval base in North American waters and from which the offending British warships routinely sallied.

A popular war song, "Yet Parliaments of England," reflected the cockiness with which Americans declared war:

> Ye Parliaments of England,
> Ye lords and commons, too,
> Consider well what you're about,
> And what you're goin' to do;
> You're now at war with Yankees,
> And I'm sure you'll rue the day

> Ye roused the sons of liberty,
> In North Americay.

The song then went on to list grievances:

> You first confined our commerce,
> You said our ships shan't trade,
> And then impressed our seaman,
> And used them as your slaves;
> You then insulted Rodgers,*
> While sailing on the main,
> And had we not declared war,
> You'd done it o'er again.

Pro-British Federalists vehemently opposed war with England, "that fast-anchored isle." They insisted with considerable plausibility that the republic, if determined to fight anyone, should tackle France, headed by the "Corsican butcher," the "anti-Christ of the age." Napoleon, while insincerely declaring, "His Majesty loves the Americans," had seized American ships and seamen on about as large a scale as the British, although he had no need to impress sailors as the British had done. One poet in Federalist Massachusetts declared:

> If England look askance, we boil with rage;
> And blood, blood only, can the wound assuage;
> Yet, whipt, robbed, kicked, and spit upon, by France,
> We treat her with the greater complaisance.

On the other hand, another versifier wrote of the Federalists that they were determined

> To rule the nation if they could,
> But see it damned if others should.

Pure logic dictated a declaration of war against both powers—"both or none." Nathaniel Macon of North Carolina complained, "The Devil himself could not tell which government, England or France, is the most wicked." But France was the ancient friend, the so-called "French connection," and Britain the ancient foe. More alluring, the conquest of Canada was "a mere matter of marching," and the prize could more than compensate Americans for the cost of the conflict. National honor demanded war; besides, it would pay. Britain, observed Niles' *Weekly Register* of Baltimore, was "tangible in her tenderest points."

A bellicose Congress, led by fight-thirsty War Hawks, pushed the nation into a conflict which Federalist New England bitterly opposed as "Mr. Madison's War." One errant Representative from Massachusetts who voted for it was kicked through the streets of Plymouth upon his

---

* Captain John Rodgers, commanding the frigate *President*, in 1811 fired upon the smaller British sloop *Little Belt* and cut it up badly.

return. New England Federalists could still drink to Timothy Pickering's famous toast "The world's last hope—Britain's fast-anchored isle."

IRON MEN IN WOODEN SHIPS

"On to Canada" lost much of its allure as the ill-coordinated, three-pronged American invasions to the north all collapsed in 1812. In January 1813, at the Raisin River on the Northwest frontier, a combined force of British and Indians defeated a small American army and captured several hundred soldiers. Many more, too badly wounded to escape, were butchered and scalped by the red men. "Remember the River Raisin" became a war cry to encourage greater vigilance and to arouse vengeful resistance against the enemy.

On the sea the Americans squeezed out what scant glory they could claim during the early months of the war. The triumphs proved all the sweeter because the British press in 1812 had sneered at the "piece of striped bunting flying at the mast-heads of a few fir-built frigates, manned by a handful of bastards and outlaws." The British frigate *Guerrière,* which had made itself especially obnoxious to American shipping, tangled with the *Constitution,* a United States frigate considerably superior in dimensions, oaken sides, firepower, and size of crew. In a bloody half hour on August 19, 1812, the enemy vessel was dismasted and forced to surrender—something that had not happened to a frigate of the British Navy in a single-ship engagement with a French counterpart for many a year. Tradition has it that one American seaman shouted during the engagement, "Huzza, her sides are made of iron!" The victory caused widespread rejoicing, and the *Constitution* won its nickname "Old Ironsides." The duel also gave birth to a famous ballad, "The Constitution and the Guerrière," which began:

> Oftimes it has been told that the British seamen bold
> Could flout the tars of France so neat and handy, oh!
> But they never found their match
> Till the Yankees they did catch,
> Oh the Yankee boys for fighting are the dandy, oh!

A few New England Federalists who had long favored a stronger navy to protect their commerce began to raise glasses again in the familiar toast "The Wooden Walls of Columbia."

Renewed invasions of Canada in 1813 all failed again, and from then on the American armies were generally on the defensive. At Fort Stephenson, in northern Ohio, twenty-one-year-old Captain George Croghan, with only one cannon and 160 men, successfully fought with great gallantry against an overwhelming force of British and Indians. His defiant response to the British General Proctor was "We give up the fort when there's not a man left to defend it." Captain Croghan's words so thrilled America that he was tardily awarded a gold medal by Congress.

An uninterrupted string of Yankee frigate victories ended abruptly when the crack British frigate *Shannon* captured the jinxed frigate *Chesapeake* off Boston Harbor, in June 1813. The luckless American commander, Captain James Lawrence, with a green crew but a presumably stronger ship, rashly responded to a challenge from the British Captain Broke, who had trained his gun crews to perfection. The dying American commander was reported to have ordered, "Don't give up the ship; blow her up," or something to that effect. Whatever the truth, Captain Lawrence's name became imperishably connected with this slogan. One variant was "Tell the men to fire faster and not to give up the ship; fight her till she sinks." "Fire faster" became a popular battle cry among American seamen during their subsequent engagements with British men-of-war.

America's wilting naval laurels perked up when, in September 1813, Master Commandant Oliver Hazard Perry, won control of Lake Erie in a memorable battle. His tiny fleet, with its flagship displaying the blue-bannered slogan "Don't Give Up the Ship," entirely destroyed or captured a somewhat inferior British fleet in a closely fought battle. A triumphant Perry reported to his superior officer, "We have met the enemy and they are ours—two ships, two brigs, one schooner and one sloop." This sloganized dispatch, shortened and imbedded in patriotic American textbooks, earned Perry even greater immortality than he otherwise would have attained. A popular victory song celebrated the heartwarming victory:

> The tenth of September
> Let us all remember,
> As long as the world on its axis goes round;
> Our tars and marines
> On Lake Erie were seen
> To make the proud flag of Great Britain come down.

Perry's triumph and other American successes on the Great Lakes gave further point to the popular song "Ye Parliaments of England." Its author evidently believed that the Yankees could still conquer Canada, for he confidently laid down terms of peace:

> Grant us free trade and commerce,
> And don't impress our men,
> Give up all claim to Canada,
> Then we'll make peace again.
> Then, England, we'll respect you,
> And treat you as a friend.
> Respect our flag and citizens,
> Then all these wars will end.

THE BANNER STILL WAVES

Gloomy 1814 turned out to be the climactic year of the war; America was desperately beating off invaders rather than invading. The salt-water

Yankee fleet, wiped out or driven off the high seas, virtually ceased to exist. One of the last of the American frigates was the *Essex*. Seeking refuge in a neutral Chilean harbor, it was unlawfully attacked by two British warships and forced to surrender. Captain David Porter, defiant to the end, reported, "We have been unfortunate, but not disgraced." In a desperate engagement on Lake Champlain the hastily gathered fleet of Commodore Thomas Macdonough wiped out a superior British flotilla. It was providing naval support for an invading army, which in turn beat a hasty retreat. The battle flag of the victorious Macdonough bore the clarion call "Impressed Seamen Call On Every Man To Do His Duty."

Critical encounters on land likewise gave birth to stirring slogans. At Lundy's Lane, on the Canadian frontier, the brigade of General Winfield Scott ("The Hero of Lundy's Lane") advanced with such gallantry under heavy fire as to wring from the British General Riall the cry "By God, these are Regulars." In the Chesapeake Bay area invading enemy forces, after routing the raw militia at the "Bladensburg Races," burned much of Washington, including the "Yankee Palace," or White House. But the Redcoats were subsequently beaten off at Baltimore. There an anxious Francis Scott Key, detained on a British warship during the bombardment of Fort McHenry, was inspired to write "The Star-Spangled Banner." The familiar first stanza ends with the familiar but inspirational query:

> Oh, say does that star-spangled banner yet wave
> O'er the land of the free and the home of the brave?

Loyal Philadelphians, fearing Redcoat raids on the Chesapeake Bay area, belatedly busied themselves digging protective earthworks. "Patriotic Diggers," a popular song for the occasion, gave notice to the British enemy:

> To protect our rights 'gainst your flint and triggers,
> See on yonder heights our patriotic diggers,
> Men of ev'ry age, color, rank, profession,
> Ardently engaged, labor in succession.

At Newark, New Jersey, a thousand volunteers sallied forth to work on the local defenses wearing labels bearing the slogan "Don't Give Up the Soil."

As the British blockade tightened along the Atlantic coast, caravans of freight wagons increasingly succored the hemmed-in cities. Pennants of the wagoners bore such battle cries as "No Impressment," "Free Trade and Teamsters' Rights," and "Free Trade and Oxen's Rights." The last two gave a different twist to the popular slogan of the War of 1812, "Free Trade and Sailors' Rights."

Britain's last major thrust came against New Orleans. Its defender was General Andrew Jackson, fresh from grueling Indian campaigns in the South that had won him the nicknames "Old Hickory," "Sharp Knife," and "Pointed Arrow." He managed to whip together a nondescript American army whose watchword was "Victory or death." Firing from behind breastworks on the advancing Redcoats, the outnumbered Americans won a smashing victory that conferred on their leader the enduring sobriquet "the Hero of New Orleans." The exhilarating engagement also inspired a popular song, "Hunters of Kentucky," one stanza of which boasted:

> But Jackson, he was wide awake,
> And was not scar'd o' trifles,
> Full well he knew what aim we take
> With our Kentucky rifles.
> He led us down the cypress swamp,
> The ground was low and mucky;
> There stood John Bull in martial pomp,
> And here was old Kentucky.

Actually most of the slaughter was caused by American artillery, not Kentucky rifles, and most of the militiamen were not "alligator horses" from Kentucky, as the song alleged.

PEACE WITH HONOR

During the dying phases of the war, Federalist New England revealed an increasingly ugly mood. The Madisonian Republicans had rejoiced over Napoleon's invasion of Russia, Britain's ally. But when the Russians turned the tables and virtually wiped out Napoleon's army, the Federalists celebrated with numerous "Cossack Festivals." Such bitter partisans seemed not to realize that France's defeat would make more likely America's defeat. Even worse, rumors persisted that "Blue Light Federalists" flashed blue signals at night from the shores of New London, Connecticut, to alert the blockading British squadron to the imminent departure of American warships.

Red-coated British invaders, using veterans from the Napoleonic wars, were expected to conquer vast stretches of Yankee territory by assaulting strategic New Orleans. When the news of Jackson's victory arrived, followed shortly thereafter by the stalemate Peace of Ghent, the nation burst into rejoicing. "A peace, a peace," was the cry on countless lips—that is, peace with honor. Niles' *Weekly Register* proclaimed:

> GLORIOUS NEWS!
> *Orleans saved and peace concluded.*
> "The star spangled banner in triumph shall wave
> O'er the land of the free and the home of the brave!" . . .
> *Who would not be an American? Long live the republic!*
> *All hail! last asylum of oppressed humanity!*

The ironical slogan of the hour, far from the boastful "On to Canada," became "Not one inch of territory ceded or lost."

From the Revolutionary War had emerged the term "Brother Jonathan" as a synonym for America. "We must consult Brother Jonathan," General Washington had frequently remarked, referring to his secretary, Colonel Jonathan Trumbull of Connecticut. The War of 1812 gave birth to two additional stereotypes, "Uncle Sam" for America and "John Bull" for England. An editorial in the Troy, New York, *Post* of September 7, 1813, remarked, "No ill luck stirring but what lights upon Uncle Sam's shoulders." The *Columbian Centinel* (Boston) in December 1814 referred to "Uncle Sam and John Bull." The nationalistic nickname "Uncle Sam," that delight of cartoonists, remains one of the curious by-products of this strange little conflict.

Another fruit of the War of 1812 was that overconfident Britons ended their sneering references to "striped bunting" flying over "American cockboats." And one contemporary Yankee war song, "Johnny Bull" made this point:

> But if again he should be vain
> Or dare to be uncivil,
> We'll let him know his rebel foe
> Can thrash him like the D - - - -.

If a nation is going to win only one smashing victory on land in a war —specifically that at New Orleans—the legend of overall triumph receives a mighty boost if that glorious success happens to be the last big one of the conflict.

V

Postwar Nationalism and Jacksonian Democracy

> National honor is national property of the highest value.
>
> James Monroe, first inaugural address, 1817

THE ERA OF FEVERISH FEELINGS

General Jackson's sensational victory at New Orleans in 1815 ended the war on an unexpectedly high note and caused a surge of patriotic fervor to sweep the nation. Defeatism and disunionism stood rebuked; a new and heady spirit of nationalism suffused the republic. American pride further swelled when, later in 1815, war hero Stephen Decatur, commanding a small fleet of warships, soundly thrashed piratical Algiers. To the Algerian commissioners he declared "If you insist upon receiving powder as tribute, you must expect to receive balls with it." The subsequent treaty ended the imprisonment and ransoming of American citizens, while opening the door for similarly satisfactory settlements with Tunis and Tripoli.

Decatur, "Champion of Christendom," returned to a hero's welcome. At a dinner in his honor at Norfolk, Virginia, in April 1816, he proposed the immortal toast "Our country! In her intercourse with foreign nations may she always be in the right; but our country right or wrong!" Such ardent patriotism ultimately drew from the British writer G. K. Chesterton the rejoinder that "My country right or wrong" is like saying "My mother, drunk or sober." Carl Schurz, the distinguished German-American who opposed America's acquisition of the Philippines in 1899, concluded more rationally before a Chicago audience, "Our country, right or wrong. When right, to be kept right; when wrong, to be put right."

When the shooting stopped in 1815, the British blockade ended and American merchant ships again put to sea. Many owners had placed empty tar barrels over the tips of the masts for protection against the elements, and these "Madison Nightcaps" came down with a great clatter. Yankee sails again whitened the seas, as the bustling citizens of seaports drank to "peace and plenty" and "peace, commerce, and prosperity."

In such an atmosphere mild-mannered James Monroe of Virginia, the fourth and last of the "Virginia Dynasty," and also "The Last of the Cocked Hats," was elected President in 1816 in the face of only weak opposition from the expiring Federalists. Tainted with disunion and reaction, they were so much a casualty of the recent War of 1812 as not to nominate a presidential candidate in 1820, when Monroe was reelected with one vote short of complete unanimity in the Electoral College. Four months after the victor first took office in 1817 the Boston *Columbian Centinel* hailed the new administration as "The Era of Good Feelings." The name has stuck despite the presence of many inflamed feelings over slavery, finance, the tariff, internal improvements, and other burning issues.

Much of the remaining "good feeling" went sour in 1819–20. First came the cyclical panic of 1819, with accompanying unemployment, hunger, and general distress. Alexander Hamilton's darling, the Bank of the United States, although allowed to expire in 1811, had received a new charter from Congress in 1816 in response to the resurgent spirit of nationalism. The Bank's conservative financial policies were loudly condemned by debtors during the panic months, and this powerful institution, soon to become the football of politics, was widely assailed as "The Monopoly of Chestnut Street" and "The Monster."

A frightening uproar convulsed the country in 1820 when Missouri sought admission to the union as a slave state. The former War Hawk Henry Clay, now emerging as "The Great Pacificator" and "The Peace Maker," arranged for a compromise under which Missouri would be admitted with slavery. The delicate balance between North and South was to be continued by the admission of Maine as a free state, with the further stipulation that there should be no more slavery north of the line (36° 30′) traversing the southern border of Missouri. Representative John Randolph of Virginia branded those Northerners as "doughfaces" who had compromised their principles by sanctioning slavery in Missouri. (This metaphor presumably referred to the making of a cookielike gingerbread man, whose doughlike face could be shaped as desired before it was put in the oven to be baked.) Thomas Jefferson, who gravely feared that the harsh words over slavery in Missouri foreshadowed a disruption of the union, wrote that the sudden arousal of the issue came to him "like a firebell in the night."

THE JOHN MARSHALL COURT

While mounting tensions over slavery in the territories were straining the bonds of union, the nationalistic decisions of the Supreme Court under Chief Justice John Marshall were strengthening the central government. A lame-duck appointee of the Federalist John Adams, the Federalist Marshall served about thirty days under a Federalist President and thirty-four years under non-Federalist Presidents. He grew increasingly objectionable to the Jeffersonian Republicans. Jefferson himself, a distant cousin, wrote privately of the "crafty chief judge," whose "twistifications" of the law showed his hatred of "the government of his country."

An inflexible Marshall nevertheless continued to hand down ringing decisions that upheld the sanctity of private contracts and federally supported private institutions. One memorable case was McCulloch *v.* Maryland, in March, 1819. The quasi-public Bank of the United States naturally proved unpopular with competing state banks, and the legislature of Maryland undertook to tax the notes issued by its Baltimore branch. The Marshall Court flatly denied the right of a state to tax an instrumentality of the federal government, thus striking down the encroaching hands of the states' righters. Few informed men could challenge the memorable dicta that "the power to tax involves the power to destroy" and that "a power to create implies a power to preserve." In the case of Cohens *v.* Virginia (1821) the Supreme Court declared, "The people made the Constitution, and the people can unmake it. It is the creature of their own will, and lives only by their will."

Dartmouth College *v.* Woodward (1819) is especially noteworthy among Marshall's decisions because it involved Senator Daniel Webster, a Dartmouth alumnus and a peerless orator, who often argued federalistic principles before the sympathetic Chief Justice. The case involved New Hampshire, which had undertaken to change the ancient charter of Dartmouth College. Spokesmen for the institution, arguing that a charter was a contract and could not be changed by statute, appealed the case to the Supreme Court. Arguing passionately for his alma mater, Webster reportedly proclaimed before the Supreme Court, "It is, sir, as I have said, a small college. And yet there are those that love it." Such a flight of eloquence was probably not needed, for the Marshall Court ran true to its usual federalistic bias in striking down the state's pretensions. Marshall would have approved an off-the-bench remark later attributed to Chief Justice Charles E. Hughes, "The Constitution is what the judges say it is."

Daniel Webster, "Defender of the Constitution," also came to be known as "Expounder of the Constitution." Too young to be a Founding Father, he was an "Expounding Father" whose federalistic philosophy often complemented and supplemented that of John Marshall in shaping the Constitution along nationalistic lines, often at the expense of states' rights. Webster proved to be a mighty force for the ideal of union, notably when he declaimed in 1825, at the laying of the cornerstone of the Bunker Hill monument, "Let our object be our country, our whole country, and nothing but our country."

MONROE'S DOCTRINE AND THE AMERICAN SYSTEM

Monroe's honored name is most imperishably associated with the Monroe Doctrine, which became a shibboleth mouthed by countless thousands of Americans, including those who did not know what it meant. The post-Napoleonic concert of European monarchs, led by Czar Alexander of Russia, and often erroneously called "The Holy Alliance," had grown increasingly disturbed over revolutionary outbursts in Europe and also in Latin America. The rumor factory reported that the crowned heads were about to join hands and reimpose Spanish tyranny on the Spanish-American revolutionists who had recently established new republics. President Monroe, working closely and harmoniously with his Secretary of State, John Quincy Adams, included in his annual message to Congress of 1823 several passages that proclaimed the hands-off-America policy of his famed doctrine.

Monroe's opening blast served notice that "the American continents . . . are henceforth not to be considered as subjects for future colonization by any European powers." This was a warning directly aimed at the presumed designs of the Russian bear on territory south of Alaska. Second, the United States would not involve itself in the wars of Europe. Third, the crowned heads of Europe were not to extend their autocratic system to the Americas because the United States would regard such action as "dangerous to our peace and safety." Finally, the Monroe administration would regard any attempt to restore monarchical control to revolted colonies in the Americas as "a manifestation of an unfriendly disposition towards the United States."

Monroe's bold defiance, though grossly disproportionate to the negligible naval strength of the United States, touched off an outburst of approval in the American press. A "lick all creation" spirit prevailed during the nationalistic years before the Civil War, and the Monroe Doctrine gave it further support.

By 1824, as Monroe's second term neared its end, pressure was mounting for an increase in the protective tariff. The inpouring of dammed-up British goods at the end of the War of 1812 had provoked loud outcries from such "infant industries" as had sprouted behind the wall of America embargo and British blockade. One result was the useful but only mildly protective tariff of 1816. The inadequacy of this so-called protection had become so glaring that in 1824 a riotous band of weavers broke up an antitariff meeting in New York's City Hall with cries of "No British goods!" "Tariff, tariff!" "American manufacturers!" and "Protection to domestic industries!"

In fighting for an increased tariff in 1824, Henry Clay delivered an impressive speech outlining what he called "a genuine American system." Behind an adequate tariff wall American factories would flourish; Americans would buy American manufactured products; the factory workers in turn would buy American agricultural produce. Federal revenue from higher tariffs would make possible the building of more roads and canals, and these would facilitate the flow of manufactured and agricultural products to the expanding internal market. This house-that-Jack-built proposal became so popular that Henry Clay honestly earned the label "The Father of the American System."

FRUITS OF THE CORRUPT BARGAIN

As Monroe neared the end of his two terms, the presidential campaign of 1824 began to gather momentum. The Federalist party had virtually died out at the national level, and for a brief period the country could not claim a two-party system. National nominating conventions were unknown until the 1830s, for the earlier practice was to nominate by Congressional caucus, that is, by the members in Congress of a particular party. This closed-door scheme seemed undemocratic, especially to those who lost out. Widespread opposition developed against the tyranny of "King Caucus," and the election of 1824 was the last one in which such a secretive method was used for nominating presidential candidates. In New York State the political atmosphere echoed with cries of "No more Congressional caucuses!" "No more legislative nominations!" and "The people must be heard!"

Four candidates finally emerged from the pack in what has become known as "The Scrub Race for the Presidency." They were Andrew Jackson of Tennessee ("The Hero of New Orleans" and "The Land Hero of 1812"); John Quincy Adams, son of John Adams and then Secretary of State; Speaker of the House Henry Clay of Kentucky ("The Gallant Harry of the West"); and William H. Crawford of Georgia, the nominee of "King Caucus." All four rivals were believed to be sympathetic to the strong nationalistic principles of the one-party Democratic-Republican party.

"Hickory Boys" noisily extolled the virtues of "Old Hickory," the nickname that the general had earned in his tough-as-hickory campaigning against the Indians of the Southeast. In Philadelphia "Hickory Clubs" were formed, with members donning vests stamped with portraits of "The Old Hero." Medals were struck off bearing the likeness of Jackson and such appeals as "The Nation's Good" and "The Nation's Pride." Also stressed was the fact that rough-hewn Jackson, unlike Adams, was not of "the dynasty of the Secretaries of State."

Partisan "Adamites" played up the nonmartial, statesmanlike achievements of Secretary John Quincy Adams, their colorless standard bearer. In the South especially some support had developed for a surefire ticket consisting of Adams for President and Jackson for Vice President. The scheme was extolled in simple doggerel:

John Quincy Adams,
Who can write,
And Andrew Jackson,
Who can fight.

A contemporary medal reveals a likeness of Adams on one side and "Science Gives Peace" on the reverse, evidently in an attempt to stress Adams's intellectual interests and attainments.

When the shouting died away, Jackson emerged with the most popular votes, with Adams second, but none of the four candidates received a majority. Under the constitutional provisions then existing, the choice had to be made by the House of Representatives, with Speaker Henry Clay, who had run last, being eliminated. After some parleying with Adams, Clay threw his influence behind the doughty New Englander, who was declared the winner.

A few days later a shocking announcement revealed that Clay would become Secretary of State—a conventional runway to the Presidency. He probably would have supported the New Englander in any event, for Adams's views were compatible with his, while those of Jackson ("The Military Chieftain") were not. But the obvious deal with "The Judas of the West" forthwith evoked outraged cries from the Jacksonians of "Unholy coalition," "Usurpation," "Corrupt bargain," and "Bargain and fraud," all of which had thwarted "the will of the people." Representative John Randolph of Virginia let fly more than his usual venom when he publicly upbraided the "coalition of the Puritan [Adams] with the blackleg [Clay]" and denounced Clay as "a man of splendid abilities, but utterly corrupt. He shines and stinks like rotten mackerel by moonlight." An outraged Clay challenged his adversary to a duel, which happily turned out to be bloodless when the pistol bullets of both failed to hit their targets.

His title thus tainted, Adams was destined for an unhappy four years. A Puritan of the Puritans, he smarted under charges of "usurpation" and "corruption." The Jacksonites, determined to undo the "corrupt bargain," began their campaign for their "Old Hero" some three years early and never ceased to beat the drums. As if other handicaps were not enough, Adams incurred further unpopularity by not doling out the loaves and fishes of political office. An ardent nationalist, he found himself a stranded fish on the beach of nationalism after the nationalistic upsurge following the War of 1812 had receded. In his first annual message he recommended such costly ventures as improved transportation, a national university, and a national astronomical observatory. Jacksonites ridiculed what Adams had termed "lighthouses of the skies."

A higher protective tariff than that of 1824 had the vocal support of Northern manufacturers, but political jockeying boosted the tariff in 1828 to unexpected and undesired heights. John Randolph of Virginia cynically remarked that the only manufacture the new law related to was "the manufacture of a President." Southern hotheads promptly branded it the "Black Tariff" or the "Tariff of Abominations." "Let the *New* England beware how she imitates the *old!*" cried C. C. Pinckney, an eloquent South Carolinian who remembered 1776. Congressman George McDuffie of Georgia called the Stamp Act of 1765 and the tariff of 1828 "kindred acts of despotism." One pro-Jackson toast in Virginia ran:

> The Tariff is a dirty thing;
> It injures all it touches;
> I'll good success to Hickory sing,
> If standing on my crutches.

ALL HAIL TO OLD HICKORY

Determined efforts by Jacksonites to unseat President Adams actually began with the revelation of the "corrupt bargain" in 1825. As the crusade neared its climax, it reached a new peak in froth and fury. The "Hurrah Boys" or "Huzzah Boys" gave vent to the cries "Hurrah for Jackson" and "Huzzah for Jackson." One surviving campaign poster featured the words "Huzzah for Gen. Jackson! Down with the Yankees," with evident reference to the protective "Tariff of Abominations" engineered by the self-serving Northerners. One of the milder pro-Jackson songs rejoiced:

> Though Adams now misrules the land,
> And strives t'oppress the free,
> He soon must yield his high command
> Unto "Old Hickory."

Jackson's heated campaign was also known as the "Hickory Pole Canvass." Many of the hickory poles or trees stuck into the earth or planted during the campaign still stood at streetside in Southern towns as late as 1845—seventeen years later. One Maryland newspaper taunted Adams and Secretary Clay for never having risked their lives in battle for their country, and ended its appeal with a poetical outburst:

> Freemen! cheer the HICKORY TREE
> In Storms its boughs Protected YE!

For their part, "Adamites" adopted the sturdy oak to symbolize the oaken independence of their candidate.

Voters were not permitted to forget "Old Hickory's" martial deeds. One of the more conspicuous medals of the campaign bore the stirring message "General Jackson the Gallant and Successful Defender of New Orleans. . . ." The Jacksonians, as champions of the poor people, also made much of the total sum that Adams had (honestly) earned during many years in the government service. To the tune of "The Hickory Tree" they sang:

> While Jonny [Adams] was lounging on crimson and down,
> And stuffing both pockets with pelf,
> Brave Andrew was pulling John Bull's colors down,
> And paying his army himself.

Jackson's magic name has often been associated with the emergence of the new manhood-suffrage democracy or the ballot for all adult white males. Beyond any doubt his following in 1828 stressed his role as "the candidate of the people" or "the man of the people." A current saying was that "every man is as good as his neighbor," and the Jacksonite newspapers sounded the clarion cry "To the polls" in their desire to bring out the masses. Jackson medals proclaimed, "Democracy Prevails Throughout the Union" and saluted Jackson as "The Advocate of the American System." Another Jacksonite appeal was "Jackson and Reform," which seems odd in view of the candidate's imperishable association with the spoils system. Evidently Jackson's concept of cleaning house was to sweep out the untrustworthy "Adamite" officeholders and fill the vacancies with his own loyal following. "Hickoryites" tauntingly brandished hickory brooms as tokens of the forthcoming "clean sweep." One minor contribution to this campaign was a new version of "Hail Columbia":

> Firm, united, let us be,
> Rallying round Old Hickory'
> As a band of brothers join'd
> Clay and Adams foes shall find.

Not content merely to extoll "The Old Hero's" virtues, "Heroites" and "Hurrah Boys" assailed the "corrupt bargain" which had subverted and perverted "the will of the people."

AN ORGY OF SCANDALMONGERING

Critics of President Adams viciously attacked his "royal extravagances," especially his having stocked the White House with "gaming tables and gambling furniture." This was a reference to Adams's purchase of a billiard table and some ivory chessmen, evidently with his own money. The President was further charged with having had premarital relations with the woman he married, and with having procured an American servant girl for the lust of the Russian Czar while a diplomat in Russia. One can hardly imagine this straight-laced Puritan in the role of a pimp.

In slinging mud the anti-Jackson people fully held their own. They stressed "Mischievous Andy's" youthful years, when he had turned to gambling, cock fighting, gun fighting, and dueling. In 1815, shortly after his victory at New Orleans, he had ordered six militiamen tried by court martial for desertion, although at least some of them claimed that their terms of enlistment had expired and that they were legally entitled to go home. They were all condemned to be hanged, and Jackson, the stern disciplinarian, executed the verdict.

Such devotion to military duty inspired a widely distributed "Coffin Handbill," headlined with "Some Account of Some of the Bloody Deeds of General Jackson." Black coffins were conspicuously displayed to represent the supposedly innocent lives that the general had snuffed out. Additional handbills were issued with black coffins in the borders, and these doleful boxes ranged in number from six to an exaggerated eighteen.

Jackson's foes employed still other dirty tricks. A published poem of six stanzas which stressed the general's inhumanity ended with these lines:

> All six militia men were shot;
>   And O! it seems to me
> A dreadful deed—a bloody act
>   Of needless cruelty.

A frightening cartoon showed the general using a rope to hang a cowering citizen on the limb of a tree. It bore the message "Jackson is to be President and You Will be hanged."

By degrees the noisy campaign sank even deeper into the gutter. Jackson had married a divorced woman (so he thought), but some two years later the couple discovered to their dismay that because of a technicality the divorce had not been legally granted. As soon as possible they were remarried, this time legally. Political foes branded Jackson a "bigamist" and "adulterer," and his beloved Rachel an "adulteress." "Shall we have a whore in the White House?" crudely asked his more outspoken foes. Not content with attacking Jackson's wife, his enemies besmirched his mother. One propaganda piece declared, "General Jackson's mother was a COMMON PROSTITUTE, brought to this country by the British soldiers! She afterwards married a Mulatto Man, with whom she had several children, of which number GENERAL JACKSON IS ONE!!"

Despite such low blows, the clarion call throughout the nation seemed to be "Let the people rule!" When the ballots were counted, the roaring response evidently was "The people shall rule!" The so-called "Revolution of 1828" swept the scholarly Adams out of office and ensconced a militant military man.

MORE VICTORS THAN SPOILS

War hero Jackson, elevated to office by an impressive popular majority, was triumphantly hailed as "the people's President." Iron-willed, he took firm stands, especially against his political enemies, and by any standard must be ranked as a strong President, perhaps overstrong. An aphorism commonly attributed to him is "One man with courage makes a majority."

At the height of his power, when he was crushing the monopolistic Bank of the United States and defying the South Carolina nullifiers, he was branded "Saint Andrew" and "King Andrew the First." A famous cartoon portrayed him as a crowned monarch, scepter in one hand, a veto message in the other, trampling under foot the Constitution and the judiciary.

On inauguration day an enormous crowd poured into Washington to see "the man of the people" inaugurated—and perhaps to pick up a public office. For the first time in history the White House was thrown open to everybody—nabobs and nobodys, the upper crust and the one-suspender men. Jackson was almost crushed to death as "the great unwashed" pushed and shoved, whether to see their champion or to get at the refreshments. Aristocratic conservatives, recalling the opening scenes of the French Revolution in 1789, recoiled in horror from "King Mob" and the excesses of the inaugural brawl.

Jackson's name is imperishably associated with "the spoils system," although it was not generally called by that term in 1829. Jacksonites advocated the principle of "rotation in office," which was a more delicate version of the later "Throw the rascals out." In simple terms "rotation" meant "Turn about is fair play"—a concept that helped Abraham Lincoln win a seat in Congress in the 1840s. In a democracy, where everyone was "equally better," many citizens believed that no one person should have a lifelong grip on public office—less delicately known as "the hog trough" or "the federal trough."

President Jefferson had displaced a number of Federalist incumbents when he came to the White House, and in this sense he established the precedent followed by Jackson. Although the latter eliminated about the same percentage of officeholders as Jefferson, the number newly axed was much larger in absolute terms because the Washington government had grown. The term "spoils system" appears to have come into general use after 1832, when Senator William L. Marcy of New York described in Congress the current philosophy of politicians as "To the victor belong the spoils of the enemy. . . ."

Patronage problems or "spoils" have bedeviled all subsequent Presidents. Civil service reform has gradually come to safeguard the great bulk of federal offices, yet over the years the scramble to the "gravy trough" or "pie counter" has been notorious. John C. Calhoun aptly referred to the "cohesive power of public plunder." Various Presidents have learned that an appointment often means many a disappointment, that for every selection there may be one ingrate and twenty or so enemies. "The victor belongs to the spoils," wrote F. Scott Fitzgerald in 1922.

Most notorious of all Jackson's bad choices was Samuel Swartwout, a notorious speculator. The President was amply warned yet he persisted in going ahead with this appointment to one of the most lucrative public offices in his gift, Collector of the Port of New York. After some eight years in office and some unfortunate private speculations, Swartwout fled to England leaving his accounts over a million dollars in arrears. He earned two unenviable distinctions. He was the first man (regrettably not the last) to steal a million dollars from the federal government, and he gave to the English language a new verb, "to Swartwout," meaning to misappropriate money and then abscond. Disillusioned citizens spoke cynically of "Swartwouters" and of officials who "Swartwouted" with funds.

JACKSONISM AND STATES' RIGHTS

Independent-minded to the end, Jackson supplemented his regular Cabinet of six members with an informal group of advisers numbering about thirteen. His numerous political enemies derisively dubbed this clique the "Lower Cabinet" or the "Kitchen Cabinet." Actually these cronies did not meet in the White House kitchen, they did not replace the official Cabinet, and they did give valuable counsel.

Unfortunately the regular Cabinet was stricken in 1831 by a malady known as "The Eaton Malaria." Jackson's Secretary of War, John H. Eaton, had married "Pothouse Peggy" O'Neill, the barmaid daughter of a local tavern keeper. Her reputation for premarital chastity was so dubious that she suffered complete ostracism by high society in Washington. Jackson's own wife had been the victim of scandalmongers, and when he failed in his determined attempt to have "this helpless and virtuous female" accepted socially by his official family, he revamped his regular Cabinet. Henceforth it took on greater significance.

Congress meanwhile had come to grips with a vexatious problem when, in 1830, it passed a law authorizing the removal of various Eastern Indian tribes to new hunting grounds beyond the Mississippi River. Problems had multiplied with the increasing encroachments of the rapidly growing white population on the Indians' Eastern lands. "Big Knife" Jackson, though a fierce foe of Indians on the battlefield, felt that removal was the most humane alternative. Tragically, the transplanting of the Eastern tribes by the "Great White Father" in Washington led to incredible hardships on "The Trail of Tears" that took the lives of thousands of the uprooted Native Americans.

A complication arose when the state of Georgia defied the Supreme Court, notably over a decision in March 1832, by insisting on jurisdiction over its Cherokee Indians. In ordinary circumstances this challenge to the national government by states' righters would have caused the hot-tempered Jackson to explode. For reasons not altogether clear, he quietly acquiesced in Georgia's defiance, remarking, according to tradition, "John Marshall has made his decision; now let him enforce it." Obviously the berobed Chief Justice had no army or navy to add teeth to his judgments.

After Jackson had "reigned" for less than a year, the nation was treated to a magnificent display of oratorical fireworks in Congress, January, 1831. Senator Daniel ("Black Dan") Webster of Massachusetts tangled with Senator Robert Y. Hayne of South Carolina over the nature of the union. Webster, after an earlier flirtation with states' rights, had become a burning nationalist and unionist. But Senator Hayne's South Carolina, increasingly unhappy over the "Yankee Tariff of Abominations," was voicing the Calhounite doctrine of nullification—that is, the right of a state to nullify an act of Congress that it found objectionable.

Webster bluntly challenged Hayne by declaring that a union in which each state could negate the national laws as it pleased was no longer a union, but a rope of sand. Denying that the Constitution was a "compact" made by thirteen sovereign states, he declaimed, "It is, sir, the people's Constitution, the people's government, made for the people, made by the people, and answerable to the people." At the end of several days of debate and rejoinder Webster concluded his soaring peroration with immortal words. Rejecting the states'-rights folly of "liberty first and union afterward," he came out foursquare for "liberty *and* union, now and forever, one and inseparable!"

"Godlike Daniel" Webster emerged from his encounter with Senator Hayne as more than ever "Defender of the Constitution," "The Great Expounder," and "Expounder of the Constitution." More conspicuously than anyone else, he held aloft the ideal of union at a time when nullification was spreading its pernicious roots. In that same year William Driver formally named the Stars and Stripes "Old Glory."

A hot-tempered Jackson had meanwhile not committed himself emphatically on this burning issue of nullification. The Southern extremists schemed to smoke him out on April 13, 1830, at a Jefferson birthday banquet where the tenor of the toasts would favor states' rights. At the appointed moment Jackson arose and, reportedly looking straight at Calhoun, flung a challenge into the teeth of the nullifiers when he emphatically declared, "Our union: it must be preserved." This was subsequently strengthened to read, "Our federal union—It must and shall be preserved." Vice President Calhoun, reflecting the sentiments of many South Carolinians present at the dinner, defiantly responded, "The union, next to our *liberty*, most dear." There could now be no doubt where either Jackson or Calhoun stood—on opposite sides of the fence.

THE "NULLIES" OF SOUTH CAROLINA

Bitterness over the "Yankee" tariff continued to mount in South Carolina. At a dinner attended by prominent South Carolinians in April 1831, the guests drank to "the tariff—a thing too detestable to have been contrived except by Yankees . . . or to be endured except by 'the submission men' of the South." At a dinner in Charleston a month later, one toast ran, "The general government—not for what it is, the parent of oppression, but for what it ought to be, the preserver of liberty." Another was "Nullification—the only rightful remedy of an injured state. In itself, peaceful and constitutional. It can never lead to disunion or civil war, unless an unjust government should grow so bold in usurpation as to seal its tyranny with blood."

"Nullify! Nullify!" was the watchword in South Carolina by 1832. Medals were struck off in the state in honor of John C. Calhoun bearing the words "First President of the Southern Confederacy." At a public dinner Judge Clayton proposed the toast (also attributed to George McDuffie), "The late Tariff Act [of 1832]. It is now a plain case—liberty or submission! He that dallies is a dastard. He that doubts is damned." A free-trade and states'-rights gathering at Charleston issued this statement: "The question is now distinctly put—Will you submit to the unjust oppression and unconstitutional taxation of a reckless majority in Congress, or apply the remedy? To us the choice is slavery or freedom."

A spirited electoral battle in South Carolina next occurred between the "Submission Men" or "Submissionists," on the one hand, and the "Nullies" or "Nullifiers," on the other. The states'-rights extremists won by a wide margin. Assembling in a convention late in 1832, they formally passed an Ordinance of Nullification which declared the tariff acts of 1828 and 1832 "null, void, and no law." A wrathful President Jackson responded with a ringing proclamation to the people of South Carolina. "I consider," he declared, "the power to annul a law of the United States incompatible with the existence of the Union, contradicted expressly by the letter of the Constitution, and destructive of the great objects for which it was formed. To say that any State may at pleasure secede from the Union is to say that the United States are not a nation."

Thoroughly aroused, Jackson and the "Nullies" both began active military preparations, and a clash seemed inevitable. But South Carolina found itself standing alone, and Henry Clay stepped forward to resume his role as "The Great Pacificator." A compromise emerged, under the terms of which the South was appeased by the lowered tariff of 1833. At the same time Congress passed the "Force Bill," known in South Carolina as the "Bloody Bill," which authorized the President to use armed force to collect the federal tariff revenues if force should be needed. The South Carolina convention thereupon met and rescinded its nullification of the tariff legislation. It then formally nullified the Force Bill (an unnecessary act of nose thumbing) and permanently adjourned.

"I met nullification at its threshold," Jackson boasted. But South Carolina was unrepentant, and its "fire-eaters" or extremists would be heard from again. At a public dinner John C. Calhoun (now U.S. Senator) insisted that the Constitution was only a compact among the states, and that the struggle for their rights had just begun. During a grand review of the Charleston militia the marchers displayed a standard on which appeared a palmetto tree and a coiled rattlesnake with the motto "Liberty—It must be preserved." The Stars and Stripes—only recently named "Old Glory"—were noticeably absent at a ball given by the volunteers. But conspicuous were such mottoes as "Nullification the Rightful Remedy," "Millions for Defence, but Not a Cent for Tribute," "Paramount Allegiance to the State," "Resistance to Tyranny is Obedience to God," and "The ballot box, the jury box, the cartouch [cartridge] box."

Defiant South Carolina, the first state to secede in 1860, came to be known in later years as "The Cradle of Secession." Some critics of Jackson later felt that if he had not appeased South Carolina in 1833, but had strangled the serpent of secession in the cradle, there might have been no Civil War.

BADGERING BIDDLE'S BANK

Nullification in South Carolina came to a boil concurrently with the "Bank War" and Jackson's reelection as President in 1832. An enlarged Bank of the United States (B.U.S.), having won a new charter in 1816, was not due for recharter until 1836, twenty years later. The federal government owned a substantial block of B.U.S. stock and used the institution as a depository for surplus funds. Yet the bank was essentially a private though extremely powerful institution, with its center in Philadelphia and some twenty-five radiating branches. For many years it functioned under the capable leadership of aristocratic and autocratic Nicholas Biddle, known derisively to many Jacksonites as "Nick Biddle" or "Czar Nicholas the First."

"Biddle's Bank" proved profanely unpopular with the poorer classes, especially the debtors, and particularly those in the West. Pioneers had their own "Wildcat Banks," where bank notes could not readily be redeemed with hard money, if backed by any at all. When the B.U.S., with its sound bank notes ("Old Nick's Money"), clamped down on such unsound finance, the debtors complained bitterly of paying "tribute" to the "Moneyed Monster" in Philadelphia. Even the better state banks viewed the big bank with hostility.

As Biddle's "Monster" grew wealthier and more powerful, it became correspondingly arrogant. It even went so far as to corrupt Congress, which was empowered to renew its charter, by making many obligating loans to members on highly favorable terms. Little wonder that much popular resentment welled up against "Emperor Nick of the Bribery Bank," who was said to head a "monster monopoly" that was no more than a many-headed "Hydra of Corruption," to use Jackson's phrase.

By 1832—a landmark date—the two-party system had reestablished itself. President Jackson, as head of the Democratic party, met his chief challenger in Henry Clay, eloquent leader of the National Republicans. Not fully aware of the Bank's unpopularity, the colorful Clay hoped to make its renewal the leading issue in the forthcoming presidential campaign of 1832. To this end he managed to secure premature passage through Congress of a bill rechartering the "Monster," although its charter had four more years to run. Angered by this transparent electioneering ploy, Jackson told Martin Van Buren, "The bank, Mr. Van Buren, is trying to kill me, but I will kill it."

BORN TO COMMAND

OF VETO MEMORY

HAD I BEEN CONSULTED

KING ANDREW THE FIRST.

Jackson assailed as a tyrant who tramples underfoot the Constitution, the courts, and domestic welfare. Houghton Library, Harvard.

The President's public response was a fiery veto message, of which Biddle complained to Clay, "It has all the fury of a chained panther biting the bars of his cage. It is really a manifesto of anarchy." Jackson's verbal thunderbolt to Congress argued that there was no place in a free society for a powerful, arrogant, monopolistic, and plutocratic institution, particularly one that granted special favors to the rich while grinding down the poor. The Bank, in Jackson's view, was unconstitutional, and although the Supreme Court had sustained it, he would interpret the

Constitution as he, not Justice Marshall, read it. A small anti-Jackson medal paraphrased Jackson's statement to read, "The Constitution as I Understand It."

JACKSON ROUTS CLAY AND THE BANK

Scandal and froth, which had marred the electoral clash of 1828, were notably lacking from the Clay-Jackson contest of 1832. This time the Bank provided a solid issue. But the "Hickoryites," still huzzaing for "Old Andy," employed such shouts as "Jackson forever—go the whole hog!" Through toasts, medals, and other devices, the people were constantly reminded of "The Gallant & Successful Defender of New Orleans" and of "The Old Hero's" stand against nullification. Especially popular was his ultimatum to Calhoun, "The union must and shall be preserved."

Nicholas Biddle continued to be abused as "Old Nick"—a well-known synonym for Satan. Jacksonites also expressed much concern over "foreign influence" among the stockholders of the B.U.S., especially British "lords and noblemen." The Bank itself, plutocratic to the end, contributed about $100,000 to Clay's campaign chest, thus giving further point to anti-Clay medals declaring "The Bank Must Perish."

Enthusiastic Whigs again hailed "The Great Peacemaker" Henry Clay as "The Champion of Republicanism and the American System." "Freedom and Clay" was clearly a protest against Jackson's dictatorial ways. One pro-Clay newspaper headline blared, "THE KING UPON THE THRONE: The People in the Dust!!!"

All these blasts availed Clay nothing. Jackson, with the anti-plutocratic masses on his side, swept to a convincing victory. The gallant and gamy Clay found himself "up Salt River"—a colorful expression which allegedly had some basis in fact. During the recent campaign he had accepted a speaking engagement at Louisville and had hired a boatman to row him up the Ohio River. Through accident or design, the oarsman took him up the tributary Salt River and consequently disappointed Clay's audience.

Jackson, his dander up, was not one to let the B.U.S. die quietly four years later. He arranged to have the federal funds that were ordinarily deposited in the B.U.S. placed in state banks, commonly called "Pet Banks" or "Jackson's Pets." Biddle, hoping to force a reconsideration of the U.S. charter, called in loans with unnecessary severity, thus promoting hard times that were known as "Biddle's Panic." The much-battered B.U.S. ceased to exist in 1836, and the stage was set for the great national panic of 1837.

OLD HICKORY BOWS OUT

In contrast with his handling of financial affairs, war hero Jackson showed unexpected moderation in dealing with foreign affairs. His general instructions to his first Minister to England were capsuled to read, "Ask nothing but what is right; submit to nothing that is wrong." With such an even-handed approach Old Hickory managed to secure a reopening of trade with the British West Indies, which had been closed to American shippers since the War of Independence. The *United States Telegraph*, a sympathetic Washington newspaper, printed "extras" proclaiming "Honor to the President of the People's Choice."

Financial claims against France, growing out of Napoleon's earlier seizures of American ships, proved to be a more difficult nut to crack. In 1831 France agreed by treaty to pay a substantial indemnity in six annual payments. But the French legislative body in Paris failed to vote the money, and after two payments were defaulted Jackson sent an un-diplomatic message to Congress. He specifically asked for authority to "seize" French property in the United States if the funds were not forth-coming from Paris. Whig critics raised the cry of "legalized piracy," and the French Chambers, deeply offended, refused to vote the money until the language of the President's message was satisfactorily explained. Jackson reportedly roared, "Apologize! I'd see the whole race roasting in hell first."

Popular excitement ran high in the United States, and the slogans of the hour were "Hurrah for Jackson!" "No explanations!" and "No apologies!" Both nations suspended diplomatic relations. Jackson yielded some ground when he publicly "explained" his previous words, but he was quick to add, "The honor of my country shall never be stained by an apology from me for the statement of truth and the performance of duty. . . ." Thanks to the friendly mediation of the British, the French reread Jackson's words and found in them sufficient apology. They paid the money in 1836 despite the President's protestations that he had not apologized.

Jackson's Democratic-Republicans had become simply Democrats by 1834, and Henry Clay's rival National Republicans had adopted the name "Whigs." The label "Whig" had the merit of reviving memories of the American Revolution, when the Whigs or "Patriots" had united against the "tyranny" of George III. Now they were reacting against the execu-tive tyranny of "King Andrew the First." The Whigs of Henry Clay's time acquired the nickname "Coons," after the raccoons that were painted on banners or carried alive in processions. These furry creatures were symbolic forerunners of the Democratic donkey and the Republican elephant.

Congressional elections in 1834 reflected some of the enthusiasm whipped up in the Presidential election of 1832 over the "Bank War." Pro-Whig slogans, many minted as "Hard Times Tokens," declared "For the Constitution Hurra!" "Flourish Commerce, Flourish Industry," and "Fellow Citizens, Save Your Constitution." Whig sneers directed at Jack-son ran, "The Constitution as I Understand It," and "I Take the Responsi-bility" (for crushing the B.U.S.). Jacksonian Democrats rather weakly responded with "We Commemorate the Glorious Victories of Our Hero in War & in Peace."

Presidential hopefuls seeking to succeed Jackson in 1836 were bound to be less colorful—his performance was a hard act to follow—and they managed to generate little enthusiasm. The controversial general was retiring, and factions in the ranks of the newly formed Whig party were so badly divided that they could not agree on a single candidate. A discouraged Henry Clay soon dropped out of the race, but evidently not until an admirer had struck off a medal bearing his likeness and the words "Equal & Full Protection to American Industry." Three prominent Whigs announced themselves as candidates, hoping to split the vote and force a choice by the House of Representatives. By far the best vote getter of the three was General William H. Harrison, the hero of Tippecanoe in 1811, who had received a decoration from Congress for his victory at the Thames River in Canada in 1813. One surviving campaign medal bears his likeness with the words "Resolution of Congress: Battle of Thames."

Vice President Martin Van Buren of New York, whom Jackson handpicked as his yes-man successor, emerged as the Democratic nominee, and he won an easy victory under the rather uninspiring banner of "Young Hickory." Best-known as a loyal machine Democrat and a wirepulling New York politician, he was dubbed "The Little Magician." He was not remembered for striking statements, and the few Van Buren medals of this campaign bear such platitudes as "Democracy and our Country," "The Principles & Prudence of Our Forefathers," and [the man] "Who Can Justly Appreciate Liberty and Equality."

A weary and sickly General Jackson retired to his Tennessee plantation, "The Hermitage," where he became "The Sage of the Hermitage." He died there eight years later and was laid beside his beloved Rachel. The general's old "body servant" Alfred would show the graves to visitors, one of whom asked if Jackson would go to heaven on Judgment Day. Alfred is said to have replied, "If Gen'l Jackson takes it into his head to git to heaven, who's gwine to keep him out?"

VI

Social and Economic Currents

I tremble for my country [over slavery] when I reflect that God is just.
Thomas Jefferson, *Notes on the State of Virginia*, 1782

PIONEERS ALL

From pioneering days the men and women who settled in what is now
the United States had to be a tough and self-reliant people. Surmounting
numerous obstacles, they endlessly pursued the American dream of finding a better life at the end of the transatlantic rainbow. A meaningful
saying told the story: "The cowards never started; the weak died on the
way." Unlike their deep-rooted fathers in the "Old Country" ("Ould sod,"
for the Irish), the newcomers were men and women on the move. The
novelist Charles Dickens, visiting the United States in the 1840s, observed that the watchword of the Americans was "Go Ahead," while that
of the Englishman was "All Right." Indeed the motto of Davy Crockett,
the fabulous bear-shooting rifleman who perished at the Alamo, was "Be
Sure You're Right, Then Go Ahead."

A virgin continent offered so much, from furs to gold, that time could
not be wasted on four o'clock tea. America was a nation in motion, generally westward. "Go West, young man, and grow up with the country,"
counseled the famed newspaper editor Horace Greeley in 1850.

"Root hog or die" became a popular expression early in the nineteenth
century; that is, one must work hard or suffer undesirable consequences.
"The Almighty Dollar" was the only object of worship, declared a Phila-

delphia newspaper in 1836—one of the earliest uses of this famous but unflattering phrase.

Ambition was often mixed with greed, which no doubt helped to inspire the saying attributed to the famous nineteenth-century showman P.T. Barnum, "There's a sucker born every minute." "The Prince of Humbug," as Barnum was dubbed, believed that the American people loved to be "humbugged," and he built a fortune on that principle, including such freaks as bearded ladies in his shows. Nor was individual greed unmixed with optimism. Americans lived for the future; pessimism about the country was a mild form of treason; "knockers" were not wanted.

Social and economic democracy, as though mingled in a mixing bowl, enriched American life. The tolerant "Land of the Free" tolerated little rigid social stratification. Especially on the frontier a traveler heard, "Each man is as good as any other man, maybe a little better." Everywhere one found elbow-rubbing equality, especially in the great evangelical camp meetings, or "religious fairs." A popular song appealed bluntly to worshippers with these words:

> Come hungry, come thirsty, come ragged, come bare,
> Come filthy, come lousy, come just as you are.

Boastfully proud of their democracy, Americans applauded when monarchical thrones in Europe and elsewhere toppled. Mark Twain had Huck Finn remark, "Sometimes I wish we could hear of a country that's out of kings." This endemic hostility to monarchy or tyranny has led to the sardonic observation that the Americans have heartily approved every great democratic revolution—except their own Civil War.

THE PLIGHT OF THE TOILERS

America's industrialization in the nineteenth century was one of the near miracles of the age. The secrets of textile technology were smuggled into New England in the 1790s by Samuel Slater, an emigré English mechanic, ultimately known as "The Father of the Factory System." This budding industrialization was both hurt and helped by economic crosscurrents, notably Jefferson's embargo and "Mr. Madison's War." When peace finally came, the outcry from the "infant industries" for protection resulted in the nation's first avowedly protective tariff, that of 1816. The new law strengthened the campaign to "Buy American" and "Wear American."

Behind the protective tariff wall factories sprouted with astonishing speed, especially in New England. Flourishing "spindle cities" employed large numbers of "wage slaves," male and female, from tots to totterers. Some of these establishments, notably the one at Lowell, Massachusetts, provided comparatively decent working conditions, but many did not. The "Song of the Manchester Factory Girl" painted much too roseate a picture:

> She tends the loom, she watches the spindle,
>   And cheerfully talketh away;
> Mid the din of wheels, how her bright eyes kindle!
>   And her bosom is ever gay.

Many "gay" New England girls were hauled from their distant homes in long, low, black wagons known as "slavers." Lured by the "commanders" of these vehicles with promises of earning silk gowns and other luxuries, the young ladies were often obliged to work for as long as fourteen hours a day for the pittance of $1 a week and board.

In the dreary era of the 1830s and 1840s the plight of the ordinary laborer was not enviable, whether male or female. Hours were so long that an increasingly popular slogan, "Ten Hour Day," became the ideal of many workers. Wages remained pitifully low. Strikes for whatever purpose were routinely branded "illegal conspiracies" by the courts until 1842, when the Supreme Court of Massachusetts partially opened the door to tactics that were "honorable and peaceful." Attempts to strike repeatedly collapsed when employers imported "scabs," or "rats," many of them professional thugs.

From across the Atlantic in 1848 came the crusading Communist Manifesto of Karl Marx and Friedrich Engels. They proclaimed, "The workers have nothing to lose but their chains. They have a world to win. Workers of the world, unite!" American laborers spurned communism, but they continued the battle for shorter hours, better pay, and improved working conditions—a ceaseless struggle that would drag on far into the late twentieth century.

THE TRANSFORMATION OF TRANSPORTATION

Improved transportation, the handmaiden of industry, was a prime goal of many Americans after the War of 1812. The aborted invasions of Canada, during which wagon wheels sank hub deep in mud, had taught a costly lesson. The famed Erie Canal across New York, although not completed until 1825, was begun by sections in 1817. The promoter-in-chief of this grandiose project was Governor DeWitt Clinton, whose vision of a "Big Ditch" from Lake Erie to the Hudson River evoked the ridicule commonly showered upon such forward-looking men. "Clinton's Ditch," also known as "The Governor's Gutter," called forth this wretched doggerel:

> Oh a ditch he would dig, from the lakes to the sea,
> The eighth of the world's matchless wonders to be.
> Good land—how absurd—but why should you grin?
> It will do to bury its mad author in.

In 1825 a bedecked canal boat left Buffalo, the western terminus, with Governor Clinton and his party. Gliding quietly eastward and then southward, it finally reached New York Harbor. There the governor poured a kegful of water from Lake Erie into the Atlantic Ocean, thus solemnizing the "Marriage of the Waters" and the baptism of a newly prosperous "Empire State."

Travel on the Erie Canal was sure but slow, and involved much ducking of heads when the boat came to bridges for the highways that crossed over it. The popular song "Erie Canal" captured some of the atmosphere:

> I've got a mule, her name is Sal,
> Fifteen miles on the Erie Canal.
> She's a good old worker and a good old pal,
> Fifteen miles on the Erie Canal.
> We've hauled some barges in our day,
> Filled with lumber, coal, and hay,
> And we know every inch of the way
> From Albany to Buffalo.
> *Chorus:*
> Low bridge, everybody down!
> Low bridge, for we're going through a town;
> And you'll always know your neighbor, you'll always know your pal,
> If you ever navigated on the Erie Canal.

Spectacular success with "Clinton's Ditch" spurred a "canal craze" or "canal fever," which resulted in a complex network of waterways that helped to bind the union closer together. Robert Fulton's *Clermont,* the nation's first commercially usable steamboat, belched its way up the Hudson River on a historic day in 1807. In a sense this inventor reversed the navigability of every navigable river in the nation, although his initial efforts had received the scornful name "Fulton's Folly." One old Negro, watching a steamboat churn upstream against the current, cried out, "By golly, the Mississippi has got her massa now!"

Steamboating on the large interior rivers, notably the Mississippi, led to reckless rivalry and senseless races. A number of frightful accidents resulted from overtaxed boilers as the passengers urged the captain to pile on the wood or coal. The song "Steamboat Bill" told the story of just another fatal explosion:

> Down the Mississippi steamed the *Whipperwill*
> Commanded by the pilot, Mister Steamboat Bill.
> The owners gave him orders on the strict q.t. [quiet]
> To try and beat the record of the *Robert E. Lee.*
>
> "Just feed up your fires, let the old smoke roll,
> Burn up your cargo if you run out of coal."
> "If we don't beat that record," Billy told the mate,
> "Send my mail in care of Peter to the Golden Gate."

The song then describes the blowup and the elevation of Steamboat Bill to the position of "a pilot on a ferry in that Promised Land."

Amazing developments in transportation and communication continued elsewhere. Canal boats and steamboats frequently competed with the "Iron Horse" or "Iron Monster," as the railroad locomotive was dubbed after its introduction in the late 1820s. Facilitating land transportation and communication was the electric telegraph, whose "talking wires" were perfected by Samuel F. B. Morse in 1844. His first long-distance message, from Baltimore to Washington, was "What hath God wrought!" Cyrus W. Field, "the greatest wirepuller of modern times," laid the Atlantic cable in 1866, after four complete failures and one brief success in the 1850s.

IMMIGRATION AND CATHOLICISM

From earliest days a steady trickle of immigration had left Europe for the land of plenty, but by the 1840s and 1850s the stream had become a flood. The Irish potato famine of the 1840s ("the Black Forties") drove tens of thousands of starving and destitute souls to America, where the promised land all too often turned out to be a smelly slum. Seeking employment, they encountered "NINA" signs hung over shops—"No Irish Need Apply." A ballad with this title reflected the resulting bitterness:

> I'm a decent boy just landed from the town of Ballyfad,
> I want a situation, and I want it very bad.
> I have seen employment advertised—"Tis just the thing," says I.
> But the dirty spalpeen [rascal] ended with "No Irish Need Apply."

Many sturdy Irishmen were forced to take pick-and-shovel jobs on the canals and railroads, where Hibernian brawn united with Yankee ingenuity to spur American economic expansion. An Irishman lay "buried under every railway tie" was the exaggerated observation. A cruel saying that entered American folklore about 1850 jibed that the wheelbarrow was the "greatest of human inventions" because "it taught the Irish to walk upon their hind legs." Traditionally Irishmen drowned their sorrows with the bottle. A contemporary song recounted how "Paddy Works on the Erie [Railway]":

> In eighteen hundred and forty-eight,
> I learned to take my whisky straight,
> 'Tis an illygant drink and can't be bate,
> For working on the railway.

Blaming England for their woes, the Irish-Americans became the most vocal and influential anti-British element in the country. Concentrated as large voting blocs in such key Northern cities as Boston and New York, they wielded considerable political influence. Observers noted that on the eve of presidential elections the politicians in Washington were prone to take a belligerent stand toward Britain, a process vulgarly known as "twisting the British lion's tail."

Displaced Germans, arriving in droves after the unsuccessful revolutions of 1848 in Europe, were commonly labeled "Forty-eighters." Many came because they despaired of democratizing Germany and hoped to improve their lot economically. Even though they generally were not destitute and went out to farms in the Middle West (unlike the penniless and slum-dwelling Irish), they encountered much hostility as "damned Dutchmen." Especially objectionable were their strange language, their clannishness, and their Old World habits.

Irish immigrants were preponderantly Roman Catholics, but only a minority of the Germans embraced the ancient faith. America, initially founded in large part by "anti-Papists" against "Popery" and "Popish idols," was still predominantly Protestant. In the early decades of the nineteenth century suspicions aroused by the presence of the Catholic Church festered into bitterness, especially as the tide of Irish immigrants swelled. Such feelings were further inflamed by a deluge of anti-Catholic propaganda, some of it imported from abroad, with such suggestive titles as *Master Key to Popery, Female Convents: Secrets of Nunneries Disclosed,* and *Jesuit Juggling: Forty Popish Frauds Detected and Disclosed.* All this was part of the "nativist" or "Native American" movement of the 1830s and later—a crusade promoted by "pure-blooded" Protestants whose forebears had come on earlier ships. One sloganized retort of the scorned newcomers—Americans by choice and not chance—was "Down with the Nativists."

POPERY AND PROTESTANTISM

Lurid tales of unchaste doings in Catholic convents ("Popish brothels") inflamed passions at Charlestown, near Boston, in July 1834, following the alleged escape of a nun from a convent there. Street placards blossomed forth:

> To Arms!   To Arms!
> Ye brave and free, the Avenging Sword uphold!
> Leave no stone upon another of that Accursed Nunnery
> That prostitutes female virtue and liberty under the garb of
>   holy religion.
> When Bonaparte opened the nunneries of Europe, he found cords
>   of Infant Skulls! ! ! ! ! ! ! !

A nativist mob at Charlestown gave vent to such cries as "No Popery," "Down with the cross," "Down with the convent," and "Away with the nuns." Before the night ended the rioters had burned the hated building. The supposed memoirs of the "escaped nun," Rebecca Reed, were subsequently published early in 1835 as *Six Months in a Convent,* and they enjoyed a whirlwind sale that reportedly ran into several hundred thousand copies.

Capitalizing on pornographic interest in nunneries, an enterprising publisher brought out the next year Maria Monk's *Awful Disclosures of the Hotel Dieu Nunnery of Montreal.* Shocking tales appeared in this book about babies who were born behind the sacred walls and then put to death after being hastily but properly baptized. This scandalous attack, which sold more than 300,000 copies, has sometimes been called the *Uncle Tom's Cabin* of the anti-Catholic crusade during the pre-Civil War years. The *Awful Disclosures* provoked a lengthy book of rebuttal by angered Catholics, and the claims and counterclaims continued to mount for many years. Passers-by saw on the walls of churches and lecture halls many posters advertising such shocking themes as

CELIBACY OF PRIESTS AND NUNS EXPOSED
THE GHOSTLY TYRANNY
MONASTERIES, NUNNERIES, AND NATIONS
CONVERTED INTO ONE VAST BROTHEL
PROOFS! HISTORICAL FACTS!

All this uproar was ammunition for the Know-Nothings and other anti-Catholic groups whose bigotry peaked in the 1850s against "The Mother of Abominations," as the Church of Rome was called.

Antipapist "Native Americans" again became involved in riotous disturbances in 1854, when the Pope sent an emissary to New York to settle a dispute over some church property. In various demonstrations inscribed transparencies* proclaimed, "No Popery," "No Priests," "No Tyranny." Excitement also flared up among "Native Americans" in Baltimore when thousands of them assembled to display such printed sentiments as "Young America, Assert Your Rights," "We Ought to be More Americanized," and "Eternal Separation of Church and State." Some Catholic pupils had refused to read the Protestant King James version of the Bible, and paraders demanded, "The Bible in our public schools." In various cities other marchers chanted a parody of the poem-song "Woodman, Spare That Tree," substituting:

> Roman, spare that Book,
> Keep off thy bloody hand.

Orthodox religion in America had meanwhile encountered a formidable foe in Thomas Paine, the pamphleteer hero of the American Revolution, who in 1794 published his *The Age of Reason.* As a freethinker and deist, he proclaimed, "My own mind is my own church." His impact was not great, but a sharp reaction against irreligion set in about 1801, when another "Great Awakening" in the form of "The Great Revival" rocked the nation. Huge camp meetings reveled in the preaching of hellfire gospel. One hymn breathed brimstone:

> My thoughts on awful subjects roll,
> Damnation and the dead;

---

* Transparencies were made of transparent material which, when elevated and lighted from within, showed the inscriptions on the sides.

> What horrors seize a guilty soul
> Upon a dying bed!

Many sinners "got religion," to the accompaniment of "the jerks" and "the holy laugh," but in a relatively short time many of the "saved" had "backslid."

Out west the more formalized Episcopal and Presbyterian churches were less popular than the more emotional Baptist and Methodist faiths. One frontier jingle ran:

> The Devil hates the Methodist
> Because they sing and shout the best.

LITERACY AND LITERATURE

In the midst of all this ferment the first half of the nineteenth century witnessed a nationwide acceptance of the tax-supported public school. The curriculum, without frills, consisted of the "three R's: readin', 'ritin', and 'rithmetic,'" all taught to the tune of a hickory stick. In this way "lickin'" provided much of the inspiration for "larnin'."

Several educational giants stood out, all of whom embraced the philosophy of the ancient adage "There is no royal road to learning." Horace Mann, who made his mark in reforming the educational system of Massachusetts, urged strict application to one's work with the aphorism "Lost, yesterday, somewhere between sunrise and sunset, two golden hours, each set with sixty diamond minutes. No reward is offered, for they are gone forever." "The Common School," Mann insisted, "is the greatest discovery ever made by man"; and "Schoolhouses are the republican line of fortifications." In 1859 he advised the graduating class at newly established Antioch College, of which he was president, "Be ashamed to die until you have won some victory for humanity."

Noah Webster, compiler of America's first great dictionary, sold millions of his famous "reading lessons" and spellers. They earned him the title "Schoolmaster of the Republic." Even more successful in marketing his grade-school readers was William H. McGuffey, who hammered home enduring object lessons in morality, patriotism, and American idealism. One copy exercise in his *Second Reader* declared:

> Beautiful hands are they that do
> Deeds that are noble good and true;
> Beautiful feet are they that go
> Swiftly to lighten another's woe.

During the generations between the American Revolution and the Civil War, New England stood proudly secure as the literary capital of the United States, and Boston was the self-proclaimed "Athens of America" or "Modern Athens." Oliver Wendell Holmes wrote in *The Autocrat of the Breakfast Table* (1858), "That's all I claim for Boston—that it is the thinking center of the continent, and therefore of the planet." The oft-repeated boast that Boston was "The Hub of the World" or "The Hub of the Universe" or "The HUB OF THE SOLAR SYSTEM" (as Holmes put it) led to the remark, attributed to Mark Twain, that "Boston is a state of mind." Satirizing the snobbishness of the upper-crust aristocracy, a latter-day versifier sneered:

> And this is the good old Boston,
>   The home of the bean and the cod,
> Where the Lowells talk to the Cabots,
>   And the Cabots talk only to God.

Holmes enjoys the unique distinction of having written a poem that saved a ship. The frigate *Constitution,* now the rotting "Old Ironsides" of the War of 1812, was about to be scrapped in 1830. Young Holmes, then unknown to fame, impetuously took pencil in hand and wrote on a piece of paper a poetical protest which was published in a local Boston newspaper. From there it spread like wildfire in the press and on handbills:

> O, better that her shattered hulk
>   Should sink beneath the wave;
> Her thunders shook the mighty deep,
>   And there should be her grave;
> Nail to the mast her holy flag,
>   Set every threadbare sail,
> And give her to the god of storms,
>   The lightning and the gale!

Among the other stellar figures of the New England literary scene loomed the transcendentalist philosopher and poet Ralph Waldo Emerson. He not only wrote prolifically but lectured widely. Possibly reacting to Sydney Smith's British sneer, "Who reads an American book?" he blazed across the intellectual firmament in 1837 with his Phi Beta Kappa address at Harvard, "The American Scholar." Oliver Wendell Holmes called it "Our Intellectual Declaration of Independence." Emerson urged Americans not to copy European culture slavishly. "We will walk on our own feet," he declared; "we will work with our own hands; we will speak our own minds." Other familiar Emersonisms are "That government is best which governs not at all," "Every burned book enlightens the world," "Shallow men believe in luck," "To be great is to be misunderstood," "Hitch your wagon to a star," "God offers to every mind its choice between truth and repose," "A foolish consistency is the hobgoblin of little minds," and "Every hero becomes a bore at last."

Emerson's close friend and fellow philosopher was Henry David Thoreau, who is most famous for his *Walden: Or Life in the Woods* (1854). The book describes his hermitlike experiences during two years of inhabiting a self-built hut. Thoreau was also an advocate and exemplar of civil disobedience, and in this regard his book exerted great influence abroad, as did his essay "On the Duty of Civil Disobedience." Practicing what he preached, he refused to pay his poll tax to a state that supported slavery, and consequently was jailed for a night. Over his protests his friends bailed him out. Legend has it that Emerson visited him and asked, "Why are you here?" Thoreau allegedly replied, "Why are you not here?" At all events, Thoreau did write, "Under a government which imprisons any unjustly, the true place for a just man is also a prison."

Among other well-known Thoreauisms are "I would rather sit on a pumpkin, and have it all to myself, than to be crowded on a velvet cushion"; "If a man does not keep pace with his companions, perhaps it is because he hears a different drummer"; "Aim above morality. Be not simply good; be good for something"; "The mass of men lead lives of quiet desperation"; and "Nothing is so much to be feared as fear."*

A different stripe of crusader appeared in the person of the Quaker abolitionist poet John G. Whittier, also a New Englander. He cried aloud against inhumanity, injustice, and intolerance:

> The outworn rite, the old abuse,
> The pious fraud transparent grown.

Immensely popular, but not a militant crusader, was the Cambridge poet, Professor Henry W. Longfellow of Harvard College. He inspired the nation with poems of uplift, as in "A Psalm of Life" (1839), which affirmed:

> Lives of great men all remind us
> We can make our lives sublime,
> And, departing, leave behind us
> Footprints on the sands of time.

And Longfellow then advised:

> Let us, then, be up and doing,
> With a heart for any fate;
> Still achieving, still pursuing,
> Learn to labor and to wait.

Highly prolific, Longfellow wrote some memorable poems designed to quicken patriotic pulses, notably "Paul Revere's Ride." With some historical inaccuracy, the poet had the thundering horseman warn the villagers at midnight that the Redcoats were coming. The concluding lines struck a solemn note:

> Through the gloom and the light,
> The fate of a nation was riding that night.

Most unconventional of the pre-Civil War poets was Brooklyn's Walt

---

* Compare this with Franklin D. Roosevelt's inaugural warning in 1933, "The only thing we have to fear is fear itself."

Whitman, who caught the exuberant spirit of an America on the move so successfully as to be named "The Poet Laureate of Democracy." With what he called a "barbaric yawp," he let loose his collection of poems *Leaves of Grass* (1855) and received a hail of brickbats from critics and ultimately praise from the "Whitmaniacs." Catching the spirit of a bustling republic that had turned its back on the Old World, he exulted:

> All the Past we leave behind;
> We debouch upon a newer, mightier world, varied world;
> Fresh and strong the world we seize—world of labor and the
>   march—
> Pioneers!   O Pioneers!

ALCOHOLISM AND FEMINISM

With drunkenness rampant, one of the most imperative needs of the nineteenth century was to bring about moderation in drinking alcohol. The American Temperance Society was born in Boston in 1826, and within a few years about a thousand local organizations had blossomed forth. Many of their zealots were advocating total abstinence, "teetotalism," rather than simple temperance. A motto current in 1826 warned, "Temperate drinking is the downhill road to intemperance." One of the leaders of the movement asserted, "Temperate drinkers are the parents of all the drunkards who dishonor and afflict the country."

As the antialcohol crusade gathered momentum, tens of thousands of earnest people signed temperance pledges, and children enrolled in clubs collectively known as "The Cold Water Armies." One popular song of the movement reminisced:

> We've done with our days of carousing,
> Our nights, too, of frolicsome glee;
> For now with our sober minds choosing,
> We've pledged ourselves never to spree.

The pledge of "The Cold Water Armies" was in rhyme but not poetry:

> We do not think
> We'll ever drink
>   Whiskey or Gin,
>   Brandy or Rum,
>   Or anything
>   That'll make drunk come.

Slightly better doggerel for the youth appeared in McGuffey's *New Eclectic Speaker* (1858):

> O, water for me! bright water for me,
> And wine for the tremulous debauchee. . . .

A juvenile singing group of the 1840s treated its audiences to such songs as "Drink Nothing, Boys, but Water," "Father, Bring Home Your Money

Tonight," "Lament of the Widowed Inebriate," and "Ridden by the Rum Power," which could be rendered as "Ridden by the Slave Power" for abolitionist audiences.

Lecturers on temperance filled the air with denunciations of "Demon Rum." Most conspicuous of the orators was an imported Englishman, John B. Gough, who had risen from the drunkard's gutter and who began a long career of public speaking in the 1840s. In all he secured tens of thousands of temperance pledges, largely as a result of delivering some 9,600 lectures to more than 9 million people. One of his favorite object lessons involved a drunkard who fell into a pig sty. As the hogs grunted in alarm, he muttered, "Hold your tongues; I'm as good as any of you."

The *Uncle Tom's Cabin* of the temperance movement was T. S. Arthur's melodramatic *Ten Nights in a Barroom and What I Saw There* (1854). This best-selling book described in shocking detail how a once prosperous village was ruined by Sam Slade's tavern. When later adapted to the stage, the sad tale incorporated a tear-inducing song, "Come Home Father," in which a small girl pleads with her drunken parent to leave Sam Slade's saloon and comfort his dying boy. It begins:

> Father, dear Father, come home with me now!
> The clock in the steeple strikes one.

First among the states to adopt outright prohibition was Maine, where Neal S. Dow, the so-called "Father of Prohibition," pushed through the "Maine Law." Many citizens hailed it as "the law of heaven Americanized," and Dow himself regarded prohibition as "Christ's work . . . a holy war, and every true soldier of the Cross will fight in it." Opponents of the Maine law received the nickname "Rummies," while proponents could sing "The Maine Law Banner":

> King Alcohol is quaking,
> His throne is crumbling fast,
> And all his petty princes
> With terror stand aghast!

All told, about a dozen states had passed various prohibitory laws by 1857. But Dr. Oliver Wendell Holmes, speaking to a New York audience, correctly prophesied, "The law of Maine will hardly take effect while the law of fermentation stands unrepealed on the pages of heaven's statute book."

Another significant reform movement of the pre-Civil War years involved women's rights. As the nineteenth century dawned, the American female, though generally better treated than her sisters in Europe, still could not vote, could not retain title to her property after her marriage, and could be legally beaten by her husband "with a reasonable instrument." In 1835 a popular song appeared, the first stanza of which ran:

> I'll be no submissive wife
> No, not I; no, not I

I'll not be a slave for life
No, not I; no, not I.

As the century neared its midpoint, a militant brigade of feminists emerged, clamoring for women's rights. Among the more conspicuous figures was Mrs. Lucy Stone, who retained her maiden name after marriage and hence gave birth to the "Lucy Stoners." Mrs. Amelia Bloomer, who revolted against the current "street-sweeping" long dresses, adopted "bloomers," a "bifurcated costume" in the manner of full Turkish trousers. Much ribald male laughter greeted "Bloomerism" and "loose habits." A jeering rhyme declared:

> Gibbey, gibbey gab
> The women had a confab
> And demanded the rights
> To wear the tights
> Gibbey, gibbey gab.

Newspaper writers also poked much fun at "The Amazons" by using such headings as "The Reign of Petticoats," "Office-seeking Women," and "Insurrection among the Women."

A red-letter event for the frustrated feminists came with the Woman's Rights Convention of 1848 at Seneca Falls, New York. It formally issued a "Declaration of Sentiments," which, in the manner of the Declaration of Independence, proclaimed that "all men *and women* are created equal. . . ." Further, "The history of mankind is a history of repeated injuries and usurpations on the part of man toward women. . . ." The goals of the embattled ladies were well encapsuled in the epigram of one of their most distinguished leaders, Susan B. Anthony, "The true Republic: men, their rights and nothing more; women, their rights and nothing less."

Rights for females, though grudgingly granted, made some slight progress before the Civil War. Some of the states, beginning with Mississippi in 1839, granted the gentler sex the right to own property after marriage. But "votes for women" on a national basis lay some eight decades in the future, while complete legal equality was still a distant dream.

SLAVERY AND THE SOUTH

Intimately connected with the movements for temperance and woman's rights, but overshadowing both, loomed the abolition of slavery. It led directly to the abyss of war.

British and New England slave traders had brought tens of thousands of enchained black slaves to America before the United States emerged as a nation in 1776. Untold thousands of blacks died and were fed to the sharks during the horrible "Middle Passage" from Africa. Jefferson, in the Declaration of Independence, could write that "all men are created equal," but he did not state, as a large Virginia slaveholder, that they were "free and equal." Like a few other far-sighted men, he could fear for the future as he contemplated the terrible moral cancer imported from the "Dark Continent."

Congress finally choked off the legal importation of African slaves, beginning in 1808. But a considerable amount of illicit "blackbirding" or trade in "black ivory" continued, and no effective limits were placed on interstate traffic, including those luckless souls "sold down the [Mississippi] River" for heavy gang labor in the lower South. A revolutionary change came in 1793, when a Yankee schoolmaster, Eli Whitney, invented an effective cotton gin (short for engine), and the large-scale production of cotton became highly profitable. One unfortunate result was that "the peculiar institution" (a softer term for slavery) fixed itself on the backs of the Southern "slavocracy" or "slave oligarchy." By supplying Northern mill owners with avalanches of the fluffy fiber, the Southern "slavocrats" entered into a lucrative alliance—that between "the lords of the loom" and "the lords of the lash."

Thrown on the defensive, the Southern "cottonocracy," some of whom became violent proslavery "fire-eaters," lashed back. They resented attempts by the Northern "dollar grubbers" and "codfish aristocracy" to interfere with their "peculiar institution" or with their prosperity under it. They especially deplored the protective tariff, which caused them to sell cheap in an unprotected market and buy dear in a protected market.

Cotton overshadowed all other Southern products, and in the 1850s took high rank as the most valuable export crop of the nation. The textile mills of France and particularly England became fatally dependent on the whitened Southern fields. Many planters felt certain that if war should erupt between North and South, the desperate British would have to break any blockade with their powerful navy in order to release the coveted fiber.

Not surprisingly, a book by David Christy published in 1855 bore the title *Cotton Is King: or Slavery in the Light of Political Economy.* The most memorable statement of this concept came three years later in a speech "to fire the Southern heart" by Senator James H. ("Mudsill") Hammond of South Carolina. In a famous proslavery speech in March 1858, he boasted, "You dare not make war on cotton. Cotton is king!" He then went on to tell fellow Senators that "in all social systems there must be a ["mudsill"] class to do the mean duties, to perform the drudgery of life."

THE ABOLITIONIST CRUSADE

Conscience-troubled, a few antislaveryites had spoken up in the colonial era, but not until about the 1830s did the abolitionists as a zealous group command national attention. In 1831 William Lloyd Garrison, "The Massachusetts Madman," heralded the new year with his incendiary

Contemporary Antislavery Propaganda

weekly newspaper, *The Liberator*. It soon became the most outspoken of
the abolitionist journals, though not the one with the largest circulation.
The motto of this paper was "Our Country is the World—Our Countrymen are all Mankind."

Garrison's initial blast heralded his uncompromising determination to
achieve complete abolition of slavery. "I will be as harsh as truth, and as
uncompromising as justice," he insisted. He then went on to declare, "I
am in earnest—I will not equivocate—I will not excuse—I will not retreat
a single inch—AND I WILL BE HEARD." Later he publicly burned a
copy of the Constitution because it protected slavery, denouncing it as a
"covenant with death and an agreement with hell." Favorite slogans of
Garrison and other extremists were "No Union with Slaveholders" and

"All Hail Dis-Union." But no one ever satisfactorily explained how a peaceful withdrawal of the South would cause Southerners to abolish slavery. Little wonder that in the South the abolitionists were called "nigger worshippers" and "nigger lovers."

In addition to newspapers, pamphlets, leaflets, and songs, the abolitionists used small metal tokens to proclaim their sentiments. One of these depicts a black female kneeling in her chains and saying, "Am I not a Woman & a Sister?" Published abolitionist songs of the 1840s offered such titles as "Oppression Shall Not Always Reign," "The Trumpets of Freedom," and "Arouse, New England's Sons."

If Garrison was the most strident voice of the abolitionists, the foremost orator was Wendell Phillips, a "proper Bostonian" known as "abolition's golden trumpet." In public addresses in the 1850s he proclaimed, "Eternal vigilance is the price of liberty" and "One on God's side is a majority." This last epigram chimed in with a motto adopted in 1847 by a faction of the Liberty party, "Duty is Ours, Results are God's."

Other zealous abolitionists contributed memorable words. In 1864 Senator Charles Sumner of Massachusetts declared, "Where slavery is, there liberty cannot be; and where liberty is, there slavery cannot be." Negro abolitionists also appeared in the North, the most conspicuous of whom was the remarkable ex-slave Frederick Douglass. One of his most appealing observations was "I know of no rights of race superior to the rights of humanity." He shocked a Pennsylvania audience in 1852 by saying, "My motto is extermination. . . . The slaveholders not only forfeit their right to liberty, but to life itself."

A potent ally of the extreme abolitionists, although she was not one of them, proved to be Mrs. Harriet Beecher Stowe. In 1852 she published her best-selling phenomenon *Uncle Tom's Cabin; or, Life Among the Lowly,* in which slavery appeared in unlovely hues. Read and wept over by hundreds of thousands of Northerners, the book through its very title became a powerful instrument in arousing emotions against the baleful institution in the South. Many Southerners reacted violently to "the vile wretch in petticoats."

Abolitionists and some less militant antislavery zealots had a conspicuous hand in operating what came to be known as the "Underground Railroad"—the name given to a chain of farmhouses, barns, and other sanctuaries reaching from the Ohio River to Canada. Antislavery "conductors" spirited their "passengers" from these various "stations" to the free-soil haven in the north. This risky operation continued, to the anger of the slaveowners, despite Southern "slavecatchers" and the "Personal Liberty Laws" in the Northern states designed to hamper recoveries authorized by the Fugitive Slave Act of 1850. The success of the clandestine "railroad" engineers was evidently exaggerated as the years passed, particularly by aged participants. But there can be no doubt that some kind of rough underground network did exist and did succeed in effecting the escape of some slaves, though few when compared to the millions left behind.

Fugitives heading toward Canada were guided north by the gourdlike Big Dipper, with its seven bright stars. A famous escape song stressed this theme:

> Where the great big [Ohio?] river meets the little river,
> Follow the drinkin' gourd,
> The old man is a-waitin' for to carry you to freedom,
> If you follow the drinkin' gourd.

Engineers on the Underground Railroad employed ingenious devices, including specially constructed woodpiles in the rear of houses. From this practice apparently came the expression "nigger in the woodpile," meaning that something suspicious might be going on.

Bitterness deepened among Southerners, especially slaveowners, over the attempts, whether successful or not, to spirit away their valuable "servants." Slavery could legitimately claim protection under federal statute and the Constitution, and many people in the South wondered how long they could live with neighbors under a government which permitted such infuriating abuses of their property rights.

Even in Yankeeland the extreme abolitionists encountered bitter hostility. Garrison himself, a rope around his neck, narrowly escaped lynching by a Boston mob in 1835. The Yankee "Lords of the Loom" in particular wanted a cheap and dependable supply of slave-grown cotton, as well as security for their investments in Dixieland. In addition, scorned Irish wage earners, crying "down with the nagurs," feared competition in the job market with blacks, who in turned called them "white niggers." As the Boston *Pilot* warned in 1859:

> When the negroes shall be free
> To cut the throats of all they see,
> Then this dear land will come to be
> The den of foul rascality.

No soothsayer with a crystal ball was needed to foretell that sectional confrontation and national disaster lay ahead.

VII

Little Van, Tyler, and Texas

Man and woman were not more formed for union, by the hand of God, than Texas and the United States are formed for union by the hand of nature.

Dollar Globe, August 29, 1844

PANIC DAYS WITH VAN BUREN

Little Martin Van Buren (five feet six inches), Jackson's handpicked successor, had promised to "tread generally" in the footsteps of his "illustrious predecessor." Such a me-too posture led to the witticism that Jackson was the first President to serve three terms—his own and that of Van Buren, who was dubiously dubbed "Young Hickory."

Though never regarded as a great President, "Matty" Van Buren accumulated more nicknames than any of his predecessors and most of his successors. His renown as a political wire-puller has overshadowed his more substantial merits. John Randolph remarked, "He rowed to his object with muffled oars." His cleverness as a politician won him such sobriquets as "The Little Magician," "The Red Fox of Kinderhook" (his New York home), "The Wizard of Kinderhook," "The American Talleyrand," and "Wizard of the Albany Regency" (a pioneer political machine). As the creature of "King Andrew I," Van Buren logically came to be called "King Mat" and "King Martin the First."

"Little Magician" Van Buren had occupied office scarcely three months when the devastating financial panic of 1837 burst, thus providing a new nickname, "Martin Van Ruin." Bankruptcy, unemployment, high prices, and food riots cursed the land. Even before inauguration day "bread

94

riots" had erupted in New York City. The Anti-Monopoly or Equal Rights party decorated walls and fences with a handbill calling for a mass meeting:

> Bread, Meat, Rent, Fuel.
> Their Prices Must Come Down!
> The Voice of the People Shall be Heard and Must Prevail!

Mobs broke loose and raided warehouses containing barrels of flour and sacks of wheat.

At another and quieter demonstration a few weeks later a crowd assembled with banners inscribed, "No Rag Money—Give Us Gold and Silver," "Down with Chartered Monopolies!" and "We go for Principle. No Monopolies!" Also exhibited were "Equal Rights must and Shall be Preserved!" and "We Will Enjoy Our Liberties or Die in the Last Ditch."

Confronted with the money crisis, Van Buren proposed a plan in 1837 to establish independent subtreasuries for government money, in place of the collapsible "pet" state banks. His "Independent Treasury" scheme was not adopted by Congress until 1840, but meanwhile it evoked much criticism from the Whigs, who clamored for a recharter of the B.U.S. "Hard Times Tokens," small copper tokens with imprinted designs and slogans, gained wide circulation. One anti-Democratic coin scorned the subtreasury scheme as "Executive Experiment"; on the reverse side ap-

A Hard Road to Hoe! Jackson urges Van Buren toward the White House over a road littered with log cabins and hard cider. Van Buren, handicapped also by his unpopular sub-treasury policy, would evidently prefer the smoother road back to his Kinderhook home. Note the early use of OK. A campaign cartoon of 1840. Library of Congress.

peared a donkey with the words "I [Van Buren] follow in the Steps of My Illustrious [anti-Bank] Predecessor."

As if frenzied finances were not troublesome enough, slavery raised its hideous head in every session of Congress from 1836 to 1844. The burning issue was the constitutional right of American citizens to petition against Negro bondage. In 1836 the House of Representatives, after a flood of petitions, passed a resolution requiring all such protests relating to slavery to be tabled without further debate. Ex-President John Quincy Adams, who had consented to serve in Congress after leaving the White House, sprang into the breach. He fought this "gag" resolution with all his eloquence—he honestly earned the sobriquet "Old Man Eloquent"—and finally succeeded in securing its repeal in 1844.

Ambitious Henry Clay, in an effort to curry favor with both Northern and Southern conservatives, condemned the abolitionist agitators in a Senate speech of February 7, 1839. When a colleague suggested that he might hurt himself politically with the Northern Whigs, Clay delivered the immortal reply, "I trust the sentiments and opinions are correct; I had rather be right than be President."

Northward, an unsuccessful Canadian insurrection in 1837 ran parallel to the panic of 1837. True to their antimonarchical instincts, the Americans south of the border generated much enthusiasm for the rebels struggling to throw off the "British yoke." Interest focused on the *Caroline*, a small American steamer unneutrally engaged in carrying arms across the Niagara River. A British-Canadian party rowed over to the vessel, then in American waters, killed one American in the struggle to board it, set fire to the ship, and let it drift out into the current and sink before it reached the famous falls.

Excitement rose to a fever pitch. Vengeful Yankees, crying "Remember the *Caroline*," boarded and burned a Canadian ship plying United States waters. Thousands of Americans organized "Hunters Lodges," whose announced purpose was "to emancipate the British Colonies from British Thraldom." To his credit, President Van Buren attempted to prosecute violators of the neutrality laws; yet for this lack of sympathy the "Hunters" never forgave him. Their cry "Woe to Martin Van Buren" doubtless contributed to his defeat for reelection in 1840.

THE HERO OF TIPPECANOE

Van Buren Democrats, hampered by hard times and other handicaps, faced serious difficulties as the presidential election of 1840 neared. The aristocratic Whigs, soliciting support from "the greasy mechanics," cold-shouldered such eminent statesmen as Daniel Webster and Henry Clay. Instead, they turned for their standard bearer to General William Henry Harrison of Ohio. To "balance the ticket," they nominated for the Vice Presidency, John Tyler of Virginia, a prominent member of the states'-rights Southern wing of the Whig party. This strategy, which later backfired badly, found expression in a campaign banner, "The Union of Whigs for the Sake of the Union."

Scornful Democrats labeled General Harrison, then an elderly gentleman of sixty-eight, "Old Granny." He had served as a member of both houses of Congress, as Minister to Colombia (where he bungled affairs), and as governor of Indiana Territory. In this capacity he had enjoyed much success in inducing the Indians to sign treaties that ceded away their land. He had gained a rather dubious victory over the red men at the Battle of Tippecanoe (1811) in present Indiana, where he lost about one-fourth of his army. The Democrats branded him a "sham hero," but the Whigs acclaimed "The Hero of Tippecanoe," "Old Tippecanoe," "Old Tip," and "Tip and Ty" (for Tyler).

Harrison had also gained fame as "The Hero of the Thames," because at this battle in Canada (1813) he had defeated a British-Indian army. Among the dead lay the gifted chieftain Tecumseh. But even this victory was not completely satisfying. Colonel Richard M. Johnson, the incumbent Democratic Vice President, had fought at the Thames with conspicuous gallantry and reputedly had slain Tecumseh with his own hands. A Democratic jingle, supporting "the Tecumseh killer," claimed that "Rumpsey, Dumpsey, Colonel Johnson Shot Tecumpsey."

One sentimental stanza of the Whig campaign song "Old Tippecanoe" touched on a theme that has often recurred when military men have heard the siren call of Presidential office:

> The country still loves her old soldiers,
> And soon will her gratitude show,
> By choosing as chief of her council,
> The Hero of Tippecanoe.

Another Whig campaign song bore the title "Should Brave Old Soldiers Be Forgot," and the "sailor vote" received a passing nod in "Tippecanoe and Jackets of Blue."

Opposing Democrats naturally strove to belittle "Old Tip's warlike achievements." One of their campaign songs, "Bullet Proof (or The Hero Who Never Lost a Battle)," explained:

> Oh, no, he never lost a fight!
> He's even bullet proof!
> For why? When e'er the battle raged,
> He always kept aloof!

THE DUEL OF THE SONGSTERS

Gathering in Baltimore, the dutiful Democrats renominated their rather colorless incumbent, the not so young "Young Hickory" Van Buren. Unlike their Whig adversaries, who evidently feared to alienate voters, they published a platform, and it stressed solid issues that were obscured by the nonsense of the ensuing campaign. The assembled Democrats not only opposed a rechartering of the Bank of the United States but also continued agitation over slavery. At the same time they favored hard money and the Independent Treasury System. Medals and slogans conveyed such appeals as "A Uniform & Sound Currency: The Sub Treasury," "Sub Treasury and Democracy," and "Martin Van Buren, The People's Choice, Subtreasury & Democracy."

All hope of a sober debate over national issues vanished after a correspondent of a Baltimore newspaper wrote of Harrison's nomination, "Give him a barrel of Hard Cider, and settle a pension of $2,000 a year on him, and my word for it, he will sit the remainder of his days in his Log Cabin, by the side of a 'sea-coal' fire and study moral philosophy." Seldom has a sneer boomeranged so disastrously, for it gave birth to a log-cabin, hard-cider campaign. The Whigs, in their attempt to create a real "man of the people" who would defeat the successor of Andrew Jackson, manufactured a myth. They turned Harrison into a rough-hewn, impoverished hillbilly who inhabited a log cabin, drank cheap hard cider (unable to afford expensive wines), and plowed his own fields with his own hands.

Far from being a hillbilly, Harrison was a college-educated statesman descended from one of the F.F.V.s ("First Families of Virginia"). His father belonged to the elite group of rebels that had signed the Declaration of Independence. "The Hero of Tippecanoe" did not swill great quantities of hard cider, for he evidently preferred whiskey. He did not live in a log cabin, but in a sixteen-room mansion built around the original cabin. His farm consisted of 3,000 acres at North Bend, and he did not plow them himself. He was not impoverished, for his income as clerk of a county court netted him a reputed $6,000 a year—a handsome sum in the days before the income tax and inflation.

Despite these sober facts, log cabins soon appeared on wheels in parades and without wheels elsewhere. The latch strings dangled out, offering Western hospitality, and a cider barrel beckoned the thirsty. One Whig song aptly summed up the new image of a mythical Harrison:

> . . . he lives in a cabin of logs,
> Drinks nothing but hard cider too,
> He plows his own ground, feeds his own hogs,
> This fellow of Tippecanoe.

Hard cider continued to loom large in the frenzied campaign of slogans and songs. A Philadelphia distiller of whiskey, E. G. Booz, bottled his whiskey in cabin-shaped containers for the campaign—a gimmick that evidently helped to popularize the word "booze." A Democratic newspaper, the *Albany Argus,* sneeringly proposed the following lullaby in "honor" of Harrison the "Tip-ler":

> Hush-a-by-baby,
> Daddy's a Whig,

> Before he comes home
>   Hard cider he'll swig.
> Then he'll be tipsy
>   And over he'll fall,
> Down will come daddy,
>   Tip, Tyler and all.

"Tip and Ty" supporters were clever enough to issue two-faced campaign buttons, one with the hard-cider barrel and one without it (for the temperance zealots).

Farming still dominated the American economy, and politicians could no more ignore the "farmer vote" than they could overlook the "soldier vote." "Old Tip" received acclaim in slogan and song, then and later, as "The Farmer of North Bend," "The Hero of North Bend," "The Farmer President," "Our Hero Farmer," and "The Farmer of Tippecanoe."

Even more appealing was the picture of Harrison at the plow, holding with his own honest and horny hands the oaken handles. He could not claim to be a day laborer who sallied out into the field to grasp the "north end" of the plow, especially at age sixty-eight. But the imaginative Whig songsters queried:

> What though the hero's hard "huge paws"
> Were wont to plow and sow?
> Does that disgrace our sacred cause?
> Does that degrade him? No!

Pictures of "The Hero Plowman" leaving his fields to heed the call of duty reminded citizens of the Roman Cincinnatus and also of George Washington, who had earned the sobriquet "Cincinnatus of the West." The aging Ohioan now also received that appellation, plus "The Second Cincinnatus" and "The Washington of the West," which added to his appeal.

NONSENSE ENTHRONED

The "Tippecanoe and Tyler too" campaign greatly surpassed all predecessors and most successors in froth, fervor, furor, and frenzy. Turnouts of "The Ciderites" were huge. Processions involved miles of marchers; convocations attracted "acres of people"—60,000 was the estimate of one assemblage. Untold hundreds of haranguing orators or "slangwangers" mounted the stump, while "Tippecanoe Clubs" rallied against "Hickory Clubs." Whig promoters published dozens of songsters or small pocket books, such as *The Log Cabin Song Book*. By contrast the relatively few tunes that the Democrats turned out lacked the punch of those sung by their opponents. Even the Whigs sometimes fell flat, as when someone mindlessly wrote:

> Without a why or a wherefore
> We'll go for Harrison therefore.

In truth this hoopla campaign was about as bad a setback for good poetry as it turned out to be for good government. One ingenious Whig, responding to the cry "Huzzah for Harrison," pointed out that the word "Harrison" spelled backward read "Nosirrah!"—a flat negative for the Ohioan's ambitions.

One of the favorite devices of the Tippecanoe crowds was to secure a large, inflated, balloonlike ball, paint slogans and mottoes on it, and then roll it from town to town. Although it sometimes went flat, it supposedly symbolized the majority rolling up for "Tippecanoe and Tyler too." Especially popular with the ball rollers was the song "Tip and Ty," which began:

> What's the cause of this commotion, motion, motion,
> Our country through?
> It is the ball a rolling on,
> For Tippecanoe and Tyler too,
> For Tippecanoe and Tyler too.
> And with them we'll beat little Van, Van, Van,
> Van is a used up man.

Less elegant was the sloganized threat "With Tip and Tyler We'll Bust Van's Biler." Also popular with the ciderized marchers were the stanzas:

> With heart and soul
> This ball we roll.
> May times improve
> As on we move.
>
> Farewell, dear Van,
> You're not our man;
> To guide the ship,
> We'll try old Tip.

Not content with extolling Harrison, the Whigs attacked the "Vanocracy" of "Martin the First: King of North America," or "King Mat" for short. "Down with Van Burenism" was one ringing battle cry. Memories of the depression remained fresh, for one Whig appeal to workingmen ran, "Matty's Policy, 12-½ Cents a Day and French Soup; Our Policy, 2 dollars a day and Roast Beef." The "Ciderite" song "Harrison" declared:

> His cabin's fit and snug and neat,
> And full and free his larder,
> And though his cider may be hard,
> The times are vastly harder.

Van Buren, "The Flying Dutchman," suffered many brickbats for aspiring to a second term, for many voters clung to the "unwritten law" of one-term rule or "rotation in office." One paraded Whig transparency—that is, letters on an illuminated box—urged "Democracy, Reform, and One Presidential Term."

Long notorious as a superslick wire-puller, the President was assailed as "Slippery Elm" Van Buren. A vicious Whig song harked back to his school days, when he allegedly was a great cheater. Chanting the praises of their war hero "Old Tippecanoe," Whigs also pointed to Van Buren's having dodged military duty:

> While Harrison marched to the border,
> Sly Van stayed at home as you know,
> Afraid of the smell of gun-powder—
> Then hurrah for Old Tippecanoe!

If the Whig propagandists managed to create in Harrison a poor, hog-slopping, cider-guzzling, log-cabin dweller, they also created an equally false picture of Van Buren. Charles Ogle, a Pennsylvania Congressman, delivered a lengthy speech attacking "Little Van" as a simpering, foppish, perfumed, corseted dandy, who ate gourmet food with silver service from solid gold plate and primped before massive French mirrors. Sinking even lower, the "Log Cabinites" jeered:

> Ole Tip, he wears a homespun shirt,
> He has no ruffled shirt, wirt, wirt.
> But Matt, he has the golden plate,
> And he's a little squirt, wirt, wirt.

This last line was punctuated by spitting through the teeth with noisy contempt.

Congressman Ogle's slanderous speech received wide distribution as a pamphlet entitled *The Royal Splendor of the President's Palace*. "Sweet Sandy Whiskers" became yet another sobriquet for Van Buren, who was also dubbed "Whiskey Van," presumably because of his distaste for hard cider. Whig songsters made merry with the image of the French fop in the White House, where he allegedly had gone so far as to install a bath-tub:

> Let Van from his coolers of silver drink wine,
> And lounge on his cushioned settee,
> Our man on a buckeye bench can recline,
> Content with hard cider is he.

A visitor from Mars might have thought that the Whig campaigners were calling for "Tippecanoe and Cider too." To the last gulp the Whigs obscured the real issues by irrelevant slogans and nonsensical rhymes. Yet many campaign medals and a few broadsides or leaflets exist bearing the slogan "Harrison and Reform." The overblown hero was the first presidential candidate to make even a few serious speeches, though the Democrats assailed him as "General Mum" and "The Mum Candidate."

Victory for the Whigs came by a relatively narrow margin, not at all proportionate to their greater skill in noise making. As one Democratic newspaper lamented, "We have been sung down, lied down, drunk down." Seemingly Harrison was swept into the White House on a tidal wave of hard cider, while Van Buren was washed out. Politicians thus created a most unfortunate precedent for froth and folderol. In a complex democracy hard cider is no substitute for hard thinking.

TYLER AND TROUBLED TIMES

"Old Tippecanoe" Harrison died of pneumonia after only one month in office, and his afterthought running mate donned the Presidential toga. "Tyler too" may have rhymed with "Tippecanoe," but there most of the harmony ended, for John Tyler was a stiff-backed Virginian of the states'-rights school. He represented the minority wing of the Whig party which conflicted with the majority objectives of its outstanding leaders, notably Senator Henry Clay and Secretary of State Daniel Webster.

A Whig Congress, responding to Senator Clay's eloquent leadership, passed a bill abolishing the Van Burenite Independent Treasury. President Tyler, surprisingly acquiescent, signed it. Congress next hammered out a bill establishing a new Bank of the United States, which, to avoid bad memories of the old B.U.S., was called a "Fiscal Bank." President Tyler, whose hostility to the scheme was notorious, vetoed the bill. A drunken mob insultingly serenaded the White House late at night with shouts of "Huzzah for Clay!" "A Bank!" and "Down with the veto."

Henry Clay, famed as a compromiser, probably should have been more deferential to the uncompromising Tyler. But the best that the Kentuckian could do was to come up with a revamped bill designed to establish a "Fiscal Corporation," not a "Fiscal Bank." An undeceived Tyler killed it with his veto pen, and that ended the last best chance for a new "Monster."

By this time John Tyler, "His Accidency" or "The Accidental President," had lost all influence with the Whig party, which bitterly resented his attempt to "Tylerize" it. His entire Cabinet resigned in a body, except Secretary of State Daniel Webster, then engaged in delicate negotiations with Britain. Only a so-called "Corporal's Guard" of close adherents remained conspicuously loyal. Tyler's popularity sagged even lower in 1842, when he twice vetoed a tariff bill before Congress passed one that he could reluctantly sign. The unpopular President was now commonly called "The Executive Ass," and a wave of influenza sweeping the country received the unflattering name "Tyler Grippe." Disgruntled Whigs changed their tune to "Tippecanoe—but not Tyler too!" while admirers of Henry Clay sang:

> Do you know a traitor viler, viler, viler
> Than Tyler.

Depression continued to bedevil the country in 1842, as mills and factories closed their doors. Cynical Democrats charged that instead of the promised "2 dollars a day and Roast Beef" the masses were getting only "10 cents a day and Bean Soup." Partial relief had come from Congress in the summer of 1841 when that body passed "The Log Cabin Bill" legalizing preemption—that is, settlement on public land before formal acquisition.

Economic distress also triggered a political upheaval in Rhode Island, one of the few states not yet enjoying universal manhood suffrage. "Little Rhody" still functioned under its colonial charter of 1663, which required the (male) voter to own land worth at least $134. Town dwellers and factory workers chafed under this inequality; and, led by Thomas Dorr, these "Suffragists" generated popular pressure for a new state constitution.

Some 3,000 Dorrites, adopting the tactics of the recent log-cabin campaign, paraded through the streets of Providence in April 1841. Armed with banners and badges, they proclaimed "Worth makes the Man; but Sand and Gravel [land ownership] Make the Voter" and "Virtue, Patriotism, and Intelligence Versus One Hundred and Thirty-four Dollars' Worth of Dirt." Also used were "Liberty Shall be Restored to the People" and "Peaceably If We Can, Forcibly If We Must." "Dorr's Rebellion" thus led by degrees to an armed confrontation between the "Suffrage Party" and the "Law and Order Party." The latter consisted chiefly of conservative Whigs, who assailed the "Suffragists" as "Destructives," "Levellers," and "Anarchists."

Protesting Dorrites were finally crushed by the state authorities in 1842, but the uprising resulted in a new constitution the next year which greatly liberalized voting requirements. This localized struggle for greater democracy attracted much interest elsewhere. In Philadelphia a printed call for a public meeting exhibited the heading "Rhode Island and Liberty! Free Suffrage and No Charter Government of a British Monarch."

BICKERINGS WITH BRITAIN

These feisty forties also experienced the "Third War with England," the "War of the Quarterlies." Luckily only ink was shed as British and American magazines lambasted their transatlantic rivals. Many complaints kept grievances green, among them the defaulting on bonds issued by various states and purchased by trusting British investors—those "bloated British bondholders." A British parody of "Yankee Doodle" touched a sensitive nerve:

> Yankee Doodle borrows cash,
> Yankee Doodle spends it,
>   And then he snaps his fingers at
> The jolly flat [simpleton] who lends it.

A more ominous dispute involved a forested area claimed by both Maine and Canada, and including the Aroostook River. In 1839 Canadian lumberjacks began operations in this wilderness, where they seized United States agents in the so-called "Aroostook War." Angry talk of armed hostilities mounted on both sides, as tough-fisted American lumberjacks moved into this no-man's-land singing more heartily than poetically:

> Britannia shall not rule the Maine,
>   Nor shall she rule the water;
> They've sung that song full long enough,
>   Much longer than they oughter.

With such irritants threatening a war, the London government farsightedly dispatched Lord Ashburton, a prominent financier, to iron out differences with Secretary of State Webster. The "Godlike Daniel" quickly established harmonious relations with the visitor, and in this task he received strong backing from the tormented President Tyler. A partial apology from Lord Ashburton patched up the long-festering *Caroline* affair, with its ugly memories of ship burning near Niagara Falls. American unwillingness to permit British men-of-war to search slave ships flying the Stars and Stripes led to an ineffective compromise: the establishment of joint cruising squadrons off the African coast to suppress the nefarious trade in "black ivory." The two negotiators also reached an agreement regarding the mutual extradition of criminals, but not including embezzlers. This explains why for many years "Gone to Canada" served as the stock explanation that followed an absconding American bank clerk.

Conspicuous among the concrete results of the Webster-Ashburton negotiations was a compromise settlement of the explosive Maine boundary dispute. In broad terms the negotiators agreed to a rough splitting of the difference, with 7,000 square miles of the disputed area going to the United States and 5,000 to Great Britain (Canada). Senator Benton of Missouri regarded the surrender of American soil as the fruit of a "solemn bamboozlement," while British critics assailed their negotiator for the "Ashburton capitulation." The cartographic data that each party invoked during the negotiations supported its maximum claim, while secretly each side possessed a seemingly more authentic map validating the claims of the other—the so-called "Battle of the Maps." Historians since then have discovered that the Americans could properly have demanded the entire area in dispute on the basis of an original map secretly withheld by the British.

THE TEXAN BRIDE

Late in 1844, during the dying months of "Traitor Tyler's" tempestuous administration, the issues of Texas and Oregon came to a boil.

Interest in Texas went back to the 1820s, when hundreds of Americans, at the invitation of Mexico, entered this largely unpeopled expanse. Most of them sought cheap land, but others changed countries to escape the clutches of the law or perchance the shotgun of a reluctantly expectant grandfather. "G.T.T." became current slang for "Gone to Texas." One

American newspaper, recalling the famous Australian penal colony, referred to the vast area in the Southwest as the "Botany Bay" of the United States. Other newcomers were foot-loose adventurers, including frontiersmen Sam Houston and Davy Crockett, (the fabulous Tennessee bear shooter and wit). Also present was James Bowie, (the reputed inventor of the murderous eighteen-inch knife popularly known as the "genuine Arkansas toothpick"). Men of this stamp would never bow their necks to what they called the "greaser [Mexican] yoke." In 1835 the restless Texan-Americans rose in revolt.

General Santa Anna, the Mexican dictator, swarmed into Texas with an overwhelming force. A band of nearly 200 Texans, determined to delay the invaders and exact a heavy toll, permitted themselves to be trapped in the Alamo, a former church converted into a fort. Their commander, Colonel William B. Travis, when called upon to yield, replied, "I shall never surrender nor retreat. . . . Victory or death!" The embattled Texas-Americans repelled some 5,000 attackers for twelve days, and then were slain to a man, including Jim Bowie and the wounded Davy Crockett. The proud Texans had reportedly written on the inner walls of their battered tomb, "Thermopylae had its messenger of defeat. The Alamo had none." (The reference was to the wiping out of the Greeks by the invading Persians, 480 B.C.) Later that month the Mexicans massacred as "pirates" about 400 Anglo-Americans who, expecting quarter, had laid down their arms at Goliad, Texas.

Pushing northeast to crush General Sam Houston's tiny Texan army, the overconfident Mexicans reportedly cried, "Exterminate to the Sabine [River]." But at San Jacinto, caught napping during their siesta hour, the invaders suffered a surprise attack by Houston's men, who shouted, "Remember the Alamo," "Remember Goliad," and "Death to Santa Anna." The invading Mexicans were completely dispersed or wiped out, and Santa Anna fell into the clutches of the vengeful Texans. He finally won release after signing, under duress, documents designed to establish an independent Texas Republic.

Cries of "Remember the Alamo," "Remember Goliad," and "Victory or death" swept up across the border. Aroused brothers, nephews, cousins, and other red-blooded Americans responded. Many of them rushed to Texas under the banner "Texas and Liberty" to serve with General Sam Houston. Without such belated assistance independence might not have been won. Popular songs in the United States were "The Death of Crockett" and "Remember the Alamo," which was to be sung, according to the printed instructions, "freely, with strong emotion." Two stanzas stood out:

> Heed not the Spanish battle yell,
>   Let every stroke we give them tell,
> And let them fall as Crockett fell.
>   Remember the Alamo!

> For every wound and every thrust,
>   On prisoners dealt by hand accurst
> A Mexican shall bite the dust.
>   Remember the Alamo!

"The Lone Star Republic" of Texas now sought annexation to the United States—the mother country. But Jackson, though a friend of Sam Houston, held back. The Texans owned black slaves at a time when the slavery issue was becoming increasingly disruptive; the annexation of Texas might result in the annexation of a war with Mexico. Not until a year after the crushing victory at San Jacinto, and one day before Jackson's handpicked "Matty" Van Buren was inaugurated President in 1837, did "Old Hickory" even go so far as to recognize the independence of Texas. Annexation lay in the lap of the future.

A willing Texas bride, although adorned for the nuptials, continued to be kept waiting for about nine years. During this period she openly flirted with both Britain and France in the hope of ensuring her existence as "The Lone Star Republic," while prodding her prospective bridegroom into wedlock. Fortunately for the expansionists, the "renegade" and "apostate" "Traitor Tyler" was a Virginian. Though "a man without a party" and supported only by "The Corporal's Guard" of followers, he favored the annexation of another slave state. Southern "fire-eaters" were crying, "Texas or disunion" and "Now or never." Aware of such pro-Texas slogans as "Tyler and Texas" and "Reannexation of Texas—Postponement is Rejection," the discredited President finally submitted a treaty of annexation to the Senate in April 1844. It failed by a wide margin to win the necessary two-thirds vote, and the Texas bride was again left at the altar.

MANIFEST DESTINY IN FLOWER

On the other side of the continent stretched the vast wilderness of the Oregon Country. Sprawling magnificently all the way north to 54°40′, the southern tip of the present Alaska panhandle, Oregon was claimed by both Britain and the United States. Each rival alleged prior discovery and exploration, and such credentials just about balanced one another. In 1818 the two nations agreed to what is popularly called "joint occupation," which really meant that the citizens or subjects of both countries could trade and settle in the entire region.

By the 1840s a contagious "Oregon fever" infected many Americans. Caravans of canvas-covered wagons, some with "For Oregon" painted on their sides, whitened the famed Oregon Trail. Most of the new arrivals settled south of the Columbia River, and optimists could conclude that before many years, with the help of "the American multiplication table," the newcomers would outbreed and overwhelm the few hundred British traders and settlers north of the river. As the pressure increased, the twin issues of "reannexing Texas" and "reoccupying Oregon" were tossed into the dusty arena of the Clay-Polk presidential election of 1844.

Increasing hunger for the lands of Texas and Oregon continued to reveal itself in a strange agitation that swept the country through the 1840s and 1850s—a malady that subsided only after the tragic blood-letting of the Civil War. This affliction, sometimes called "The Great American Disease," was popularly known as "Manifest Destiny," for it more than hinted at a high degree of divine inevitability. At an early stage in the history of the republic men of vision insisted that God Almighty, in His infinite wisdom, had "manifestly" or obviously "destined" His chosen people to continue to spread their ennobling democratic institutions over most of the North American continent, perhaps all of it, and possibly the South American continent as well. The concept represented a kind of intoxication with territorial expansion, commercial gain, national pride, do-goodism, and a sense of civilizing mission. While seizing other people's territory, the Americans could justify strong-arm measures by arguing that the "benighted" Indians, Mexican peons, and other "greasers" would benefit from superior Yankee talents, government, democratic institutions, and culture. The youthfulness of this expansionist outlook often found expression in the 1840s and 1850s in the slogan "Young America."

In a few minds "Manifest Destiny" doubtless antedated the formation of the republic, but evidently the first clear-cut expression of the phrase appeared in a national magazine in 1845. Its editor, John L. O'Sullivan, wrote, "Our manifest destiny is to overspread the continent allotted by providence for the free development of our yearly multiplying millions." James G. Bennett, editor of the New York *Herald*, reflected this lick-all-creation spirit when he wrote in 1865, "It is our manifest destiny to lead and rule all other nations."

As orators "made the buffalo bellow" and "the eagle scream," they boasted of "the universal Yankee nation" as "an ocean-bound Republic." Historian John Fiske records a toast allegedly proposed by a true-blooded American during the Civil War at a Paris banquet: "I give you the United States—bounded on the north by the Aurora Borealis, on the south by the precession of the equinoxes, on the east by the primeval chaos, and on the west by the Day of Judgment."

CLEARING THE WAY FOR HENRY CLAY

On the eve of the presidential campaign of 1844 the Whigs, disillusioned by their frustration over "Tippecanoe and Tyler too," turned again to "Glorious Henry Clay." An immensely popular figure, he had vainly sought the office for some twenty years. His old nicknames were dusted off or new ones were coined as voters heard of "Gallant Henry Clay," "The People's Choice," "The Man of the People," and "The Star of the

West." As if to atone for the 1840 snubs in favor of "Old Tip," a poster-picture of Clay called for "Justice to Harry of the West." He was built up as "Harry the Honest and True," who was an upright (plantation) farmer hailing from the West. Typical additional nicknames were "The Farmer of Kentucky," "Honest Farmer Harry," and "The Farmer President."

Clay's platform completely ignored the burning issues of annexing Texas and acquiring Oregon. As in the hard-fought hard-cider campaign of 1840, the voters were subjected to much froth and to such empty cries as "Hooray for Clay" and "Henry Clay Will Carry the Day." One medal bore the inscriptions "A Halo Shines as Bright as Day Around the Head of Henry Clay" and "Protection to the Working Class is an Assurance of Success." Clay had long championed "The American System," which would provide a protective tariff. The revenues from it would theoretically support the construction of roads, canals, and other internal improvements. A campaign picture of a factory over a stream carried the message, "Henry Clay for His Country Feels but Polk Would Stop Our Water Wheels."

Clay's conspicuous espousal of the tariff provided inspiration for such slogans as "Protector of Home Industry," "The Noble and Patriotic Supporter of Protection," "Let us Encourage Our Own Manufacturers," and "A Tariff for Reform." Additional appeals reminded voters of Clay's "American System": "The Champion of Internal Improvements" and "The Noble & Patriotic Supporter of the People's Rights."

Coonskins had symbolized the Whigs' campaign of 1840, along with log cabins and hard cider. Not surprisingly the raccoon had now come to be the emblem of the Whig party. Whig enthusiasts in 1844 composed songs praising Clay as "That Same Old Coon" and "The Same Brave Old Coon." They also parodied some of the most popular songs of the log-cabin campaign, notably with "Clear the Way for Harry Clay!" It began:

> What has caused this agitation,
> 'Tation, 'tation, our foes betray?
> It is the ball a rolling on,
> To clear the way for Henry Clay,
> To clear the way for Henry Clay,
> For with him we can beat any man, man,
> Man, of the Buren clan;
> For with him we can beat any man.

POLKING THE WHIGS

Whig politicians expected their rivals to nominate ex-President Martin Van Buren, who in fact proved to be the front runner when the Democrats met in their Baltimore convention. One of the early Whig campaign songs, "The Little Red Fox," warned in its chorus:

Get out of the way, you're quite too late—
You little Red Fox of the Empire State.

Smarting from the log-cabin nonsense, the Democrats in their platform understandably decried "factitious symbols" and "appeals insulting to the judgment and subversive of the intellect of the people." They came out emphatically against a high tariff, a new Bank of the United States, and the abolition of slavery. On the issue of expansion this platform did not straddle when it declared that "our title to the whole of the Territory of Oregon is clear and unquestionable" and that the nation should speedily achieve "the re-occupation of Oregon and the re-annexation of Texas." This phrase became a slogan, together with such variants as "The Northwest and the Southwest" and "All of Oregon or none." The well-known "Fifty-four Forty or Fight," legend to the contrary, did not come into general use until two years later, at the time of the crisis with Britain over dividing Oregon.

Van Buren lost out at Baltimore largely because of his lack of enthusiasm for slaveholding Texas. Hopelessly deadlocked, the Democratic delegates finally stampeded to James K. Polk of Tennessee, who was the first "dark horse" presidential candidate in the nation's history and thus acquired the nickname "Dark Horse" Polk.

Polk's nomination—"a pig in a Polk"—proved to be such a surprise that the Whigs, with their magnetic Henry Clay, repeatedly jeered, "Who is James K. Polk?" Democrats reportedly cried, "Hurrah for Polk," and then quietly inquired, "Who in the devil is he?" The truth is that Polk, while clearly a dark horse, was not an unknown horse. He had served as governor of Tennessee and Speaker of the national House of Representatives, both positions of high responsibility. He had gained fame as "Handy Jim of Tennessee" and "Tennessee Polk," while his gifts as a stump speaker had won him the sobriquet "Napoleon of the Stump," at a time when back-country orators actually stood on stumps in the partially cleared forest.

Polk's connection with Tennessee won for him the strong backing of "Old Hickory" Jackson, then a year from the grave, and the recent nominee (like Van Buren) came to be called "Young Hickory" and "Little Hickory." His supporters sang "The Young Hickory Tree" and "A Song of Hickories." The pokeberry inspired clumsy puns about Polk (pronounced by many "Poke"), and faithful Democrats stained their banners with the dark purple juice of this fruit.

Loyal Democrats vigorously supported their low-protection tariff law of 1842, and they backed it with slogans, including "Polk and the Democratic Tariff of 1842." Democrats who were especially bold regarding the tariff would add, "WE DARE THE WHIGS TO REPEAL IT."

Sometimes the tariff appeared side by side with expansion, especially in such appeals as "Polk, Dallas, Texas, Oregon, and the Tariff of '42" and "Polk, Dallas, and Texas." The latter also became the title of a song in which the political trinity was shifted around:

> Whigs clear the way,
> Whigs give way,
> Whigs give way for freedom becks us,
> On for Dallas, Polk and Texas.

One attractive Democratic medal carried the inscription "Press Onward—Enlarge the Boundaries of Freedom—Young Hickory."

Other Democratic songs claimed such titles as "Reform Is the Democrats' Cry" and "Two Dollars a Day," which reminded voters that the Whigs had not fulfilled their promises of higher wages. The "coon" motif inspired a dozen or so opposition songs, such as "The Coon Hunters." In one of them Clay received jeers as "That Cheating Old Coon." The coon hunt always ended disastrously for Clay, whose fate inspired "The Coon's Lament," "Burial of the Old Coon," and "Poor Coony Clay." The Whig candidate's views on the protective tariff prompted a variant of the "Coony Clay" theme:

> Oh, coony, coony Clay,
> The rich man is your god—
> You raise the Manufacturer,
> But doom the poor to plod.

CLAY COMPROMISES AWAY VICTORY

The Whig party, which attracted the bulk of well-to-do Americans, had grown increasingly unfriendly to the swelling influx of immigrants from Europe, partly because most of the newcomers joined the Democratic party. Especially distrusted were Irish Catholics, reputedly the advance agents of "Popery." Associated in spirit with the Whigs and favoring them was a nativist, anti-Catholic group known as "American Republicans," who voiced to the slogan "Elect none but natives to office." They aired their prejudices in an official song:

> Then strike up 'Hail Columbia' boys, our free and happy land,
> We'll startle knavish partisans and break the Jesuit's band.
> We'll snap the reins, spurn party chains and priestly politics
> We swear it by our father's grave—our sires of Seventy Six!

American Republican medals for the campaign of 1844, some with the features of Clay imprinted, bore such messages as "American Republicans! Beware of Foreign Influence!! Our Country First." Antiforeignism or "nativism" was to attain much greater momentum with the Know-Nothing party during the next decade.

On the explosive issue of Texas the Democrats came out flat-footedly for annexation with such slogans as "Polk and Texas; Clay and no Texas." Southern militants were heard to cry, "Texas or disunion." The Whig nominee, Henry Clay, hoping to antagonize neither the proslavery South nor the antislavery elements in the North, wrote a series of letters in which he tried to carry water on both shoulders. For his pains he succeeded in antagonizing Southerners and Northerners alike. Polk, the dark horse, outraced his rival by a nose; Clay apparently lost out by failing to take a firm stand on Texas. A Democratic editor in Missouri jeered at Clay's squirmings in verse:

> He wires in and wires out,
> And leaves the people still in doubt,
> Whether the snake that made the track,
> Was going South, or coming back.

Even so, Clay was obviously more opposed than Polk to annexing Texas and its slaves. As a result, much of the antislavery vote of the North swung to the famed compromiser, Henry Clay, who ironically compromised away his chances of victory. Cassius Clay, the fiery Kentucky abolitionist, declared that the overshadowing issue of the campaign was "Polk, Slavery, and Texas" versus "Clay, Union, and Liberty."

Antislavery zealots had formed their own tiny Liberty party, and in this heated campaign of 1844 they nominated James G. Birney for the Presidency. One of their songs, entitled "Get Off the Track," evidently drew its inspiration from the newly introduced "Iron Horse":

> Railroads to Emancipation
> Cannot rest on *Clay* foundation.
> And the road that *Polk* erects us
> Leads to slavery and to Texas!

Some of the songs in a collection called *The Liberty Minstrel* expressed concern for the slave through such titles as "O Pity the Slave Mother," "The Blind Slave Boy," "Our Countrymen in Chains," "Negro Boy Sold for a Watch," and "Stolen We Were [from Africa]." Other titles were calls to action, such as "Rouse Up, New England," "Strike for Liberty," "Wake, Sons of the Pilgrims," and "Come, Join the Abolitionists."

Clay, a three-time loser, failed of election when he lost New York State by about 5,000 votes out of nearly 500,000 cast. Birney, the abolitionist heading the Liberty party, polled nearly 16,000 votes in the same state, most of which would doubtless have gone to Clay if this puny third party had not nominated a candidate. Ironically, the antislaveryites defeated their own ends regarding Texas by entering the race.

Three long months had to pass before the victorious Polk would take over the reins from a lame-duck Tyler, now eager to do something about annexing Texas. A treaty, such as the Senate had rejected in 1844, required a two-thirds vote; a joint resolution of both houses of Congress would need only a simple majority. President Tyler, interpreting the close and confused election of Polk as a mandate to annex the rebuffed republic, arranged for a joint resolution. It passed Congress and received

Tyler's signature three days before he left the White House, in March 1845. "Diabolism triumphant," cried William L. Garrison, militant editor of the most conspicuous abolitionist journal. Yet Tyler ended his troubled years on a high note as the Lone Star of Texas mingled with the galaxy of twenty-seven companion stars in the folds of Old Glory.

VIII

Polk and the Fruits of Expansion

There is not an American on earth but what loves land.

Sam Houston, 1848

FIFTY-FOUR FORTY AND NO FIGHT

Newly elected and sworn in, "Young Hickory" Polk was not one to turn a deaf ear to the siren call of "Manifest Destiny." Remembering the nation's zeal for expansion during the campaign of 1844, he proclaimed in his inaugural address that "our title to the country of the Oregon is 'clear and unquestionable,' and already are our people preparing to perfect that title. . . ." In truth the American claim was anything but clear, and as a result the British press reacted angrily to this "Yankee bluster." Nine months later, in his first annual message to Congress, Polk bluntly proposed to end the decades-old "joint occupation" arrangement with Britain. For good measure he ringingly resurrected the almost forgotten Monroe Doctrine by declaring that "no future European colony or dominion shall with our consent be planted or established on any part of the North American continent."

Polk's bellicose language intensified a fighting mood in America. Senator Edward Hannegan of Indiana proposed this toast at a Philadelphia banquet: "Oregon—every foot or not an inch; fifty-four degrees and forty minutes or delenda est Britannia" (Britain must be destroyed). During ensuing months the country echoed with cries of "All of Oregon or none," "The whole or none," "All or none, now or never," and "Every foot or not an inch." The famous "Fifty-four forty or fight," evidently not born until 1846, was attributed to Senator William Allen of Ohio, whose booming voice caused him to be known as "The Ohio Gong," "Earthquake Allen," and "Foghorn Allen." Covered wagons headed west flaunted on their canvas sides the boastful words "Oregon, 54°40′, all or none." The craze went so far that babies were reputedly named, "Fifty-Four Forty," and the letters "P.P.P.P." stood for "Phifty-Phour Phorty or Phight."

Tough-talking Polk, with his tiny navy, was plainly trying to bluff the mighty "Mistress of the Seas," but he held a few high cards. Among them were the on-rolling covered wagons, plus "the American multiplication table," and the arrival in Oregon of "border ruffians" armed with the new-fangled "revolving pistol." All these factors made clear that in time the Americans would take possession of Oregon—and possession was still nine points of the law, especially in the West. The London government, faced with problems and pressures at home, was in a mood to compromise, and in 1846 Polk rather reluctantly accepted a rough split-the-difference adjustment along the present boundary of 49°.

Finally America got neither 54°40′ nor a fight, but something better, a reasonable compromise without bloodshed. Yet die-hard "manifest destinarians" voiced discontent as protesting Congressmen raised the cry "Fifty-four forty forever." Senator Benton of Missouri assailed Polk on the floor of the Senate: "And this is the end of that great line! All gone—vanished—evaporated into thin air—and the place where it was, not to be found. Oh! mountain that was delivered of a mouse, thy name shall henceforth be fifty-four forty!"

POLK PROVOKES MEXICO

Luck was with Polk when a formal settlement of the Oregon boundary came about six weeks after fighting had broken out with Mexico. The President thus escaped the dilemma of waging a two-front, two-ocean war.

Roots of conflict between the two neighbors were complex. The Mexicans bitterly resented the Yankee annexation of Texas in 1845; they had failed to pay claims for damages to American property incurred during Mexico's internal struggles; and they had flatly refused to sell California, which Polk was eager to acquire by paying $25 million. The smouldering Texas issue was doubly sensitive. Resentful Mexicans not only refused to acknowledge the loss of Texas to the United States but flatly rejected an ill-founded territorial claim of Texas. Texans continued to insist that their southwest boundary was not the Sabine River but the Rio Grande, about 100 miles farther south. "Uncle Sam and Mexico," a song popular in the United States, breathed defiance:

> They're kickin' up gunpowderation,
> About the Texas annexation.
> Since Mexico makes such ado,
> We'll flog her, and annex her too!

"Polk the Purposeful" was evidently determined to have California at any cost. Mexico would not sell, and so the only way to gain the golden prize was to provoke a war and seize it. As soon as the last negotiations collapsed, an impatient Polk ordered General Zachary Taylor's small army to proceed from the Sabine River (at Corpus Christi) to the Rio Grande. There he built a fort that blockaded the river—in itself an act of war. Mexican authorities, regarding this incursion as an intolerable invasion of their soil, fell upon one of General Taylor's detachments, killing or wounding sixteen men. Polk, eager to fight for other reasons, evidently welcomed this border incident and sent a rousing war message to Congress. In it he flatly declared that Mexico "has invaded our territory and shed American blood upon the American soil." He added that "war exists, and notwithstanding all our efforts to avoid it, exists by the act of Mexico herself. . . ."

"Old Glory" had suffered insult, and a Democratic Congress overwhelmingly passed the war resolution. Even the Whig opposition, at least temporarily, lent support to Polk. The patriotic spirit infusing the land inspired a popular soldier song:

> The Mexican bandits have crossed to our shore,
> Our soil has been dyed with our countrymen's gore.
> The murderers' triumph was theirs for a day,
> Our triumph is coming, so fire, fire away!

Yet Whig voices of protest gradually grew shriller. One abolitionist Congressman, suspecting a plot to annex more slave territory, denounced the conflict as "unholy, unrighteous, and damnable." Senator Thomas Corwin, the gifted orator from Ohio, hurt his political career when he declared in a shocking speech on the eve of hostilities, "If I were a Mexican, I would tell you, 'Have you not enough room in your own country to bury your dead men? If you come into mine I will greet you with bloody hands and welcome you to hospitable graves.'"

Homespun Abraham Lincoln of Illinois entered the House of Representatives as a Whig some ten months after the war erupted. Not anticipating his own future Presidency, he embarrassed the Polk administration by introducing his "spot resolutions." They probingly sought the precise spot "upon the American soil" where American blood had first been shed. The young Illinoisan pushed these resolutions with such persistence that he came to be known as "the spotty Mr. Lincoln" and "a second Benedict Arnold." Whigs like Lincoln who opposed the war were commonly said to be "Mexican Whigs" who would die of "spotted fever." James Russell Lowell wrote in his *Biglow Papers,* in Yankee dialect:

> Ez fer war, I call it murder,—
>   There you hev it plain an' flat;
> I don't want to go no furder
>   Than my Testyment fer that.

During the war antislavery men in Congress tried to pass the "Wilmot Proviso," designed to ban slavery from any territory that should be acquired from Mexico. They failed, but the Proviso did point up the issue, and it did inspire such watchwords as "No Compromise: No More Slave Territory."

MUTILATED MEXICO

Despite formidable obstacles, Polk prosecuted the war with remarkable success. Untrained volunteers sprang to the colors in response to such calls as "On to the halls of the Montezumas" and "Ho! for the halls of the Montezumas." General Zachary Taylor, affectionately known as "Old Rough and Ready" because of his informal attire, pushed across the Rio Grande into northern Mexico, capturing Monterrey on the way. At Buena Vista his force of nearly 5,000 men clashed with about 15,000 Mexicans, many of them exhausted from prolonged marching, and a bloody battle ensued.

When the foe called upon General Taylor to hoist the white flag, an aide responded, "General Taylor never surrenders"—a defiant response that soon became a campaign slogan. Possibly the less elegant response was "Tell him to go to hell." As the battle waxed hotter, "Old Zack" Taylor is supposed to have coolly remarked to an artillerist, "A little more grape [shot], Captain Bragg." When the Second Kentucky Regiment rallied, he is said to have cried, "Hurrah for Old Kentuck! That's the way to do it. Give 'em hell, damn 'em."

Badly bloodied, the Mexicans finally withdrew at Buena Vista, taking with them some captured flags and the claim that they had beaten the "gringoes." But "Old Rough and Ready's" bruised army had stood its ground, and Buena Vista became the most heralded battle of the war. It made two Presidents: Zachary Taylor of the U.S.A. and Jefferson Davis of the C.S.A. (Confederate States of America). Davis, a West Pointer commanding the Tennessee Rifles, had brilliantly checked the onrushing Mexicans by marshaling his men in a "V" formation. From that day onward he seems to have suffered a fixation about the "V" and his own military genius. During the Civil War the cynical remark was heard in the South that if the Confederacy collapsed, it would "die of the V."

The most decisive campaign of the Mexican War, as well as the most brilliant, was that conducted by General Winfield Scott from Vera Cruz to Mexico City. Probably the best military mind produced in America from the Revolution to the Civil War (he served in three major wars), he proved to be a man of statesmanlike talents whose nickname imposed a severe handicap. A strict disciplinarian and conventionally uniformed, he became known as "Old Fuss and Feathers," quite in contrast to informally dressed "Old Rough and Ready" Zachary Taylor. Scott's conquest of the heart of Mexico opened the door for peace terms that ceded

PLUCKED:

THE MEXICAN EAGLE BEFORE THE WAR! THE MEXICAN EAGLE AFTER THE WAR!

Yankee bumptiousness in the forties. *Yankee Doodle*, 1847.

the vast Mexican cession territory to the United States. The acquisition added about one-third again to the nation's expanse.

Under the spell of "Manifest Destiny," a considerable body of American opinion vainly supported the "All of Mexico Movement." One New York newspaper cried out against turning over "this beautiful country to the custody of the ignorant cowards and profligate ruffians who have ruled it for the last twenty-five years." As events turned out, speedy ratification of the peace treaty as submitted to the Senate ended such irresponsible agitation.

GENERAL TAYLOR'S ELECTORAL TRIUMPH

Hostilities with Mexico formally ended when the peace treaty was proclaimed on the Fourth of July, 1848. By this time, with President Polk about to bow out, the electoral campaign had officially got under way. The Whigs had a ready-made candidate in General Taylor, the most exciting hero of the recent conflict. After the news of his glorious victory at Buena Vista in 1847, a boom started for him that caused one enthusiast to remark that this man on horseback would be elected by "spontaneous combustion."

"Old Rough and Ready" further caught the public eye by often wearing an old straw hat and sitting sideways on his horse, "Old Whitey," when he could have appeared in proper uniform. He was "rough" if not altogether "ready" in his spelling and grammar; he was totally without experience in politics and had never voted in a presidential election. Domiciled in Louisiana, he owned scores of slaves, and hence was offensive to the antislavery "Conscience Whigs" of his party but quite acceptable to the conservative "Cotton Whigs," who did not want to arouse sleeping dogs in the South.

Office-starved Whigs, assembling in Philadelphia, felt that they now had a winner. They elbowed aside shopworn Henry Clay in favor of their new war hero, whose chief asset was the sweet scent of victory. Horace Greeley, the outspoken editor of the New York *Tribune,* called the convention that snubbed Clay and nominated Taylor "The Philadelphia Slaughterhouse . . . of Whig principles."

If the Whigs were divided into "Conscience Whigs" and "Cotton Whigs," the Democrats were split into antislavery and proslavery elements. In New York State an antislavery faction of the Democratic party had earned the nickname "Barnburners," after the fabled Dutch farmer who supposedly burned down his barn to get rid of the rats. At the national nominating convention of the Democrats in Baltimore, the proslavery conservatives prevailed and nominated General Lewis Cass, who was proslavery to the extent of endorsing "Squatter Sovereignty" or "Popular Sovereignty." These catchwords encapsuled the democratic concept that the settlers or "squatters" in a territory, when formally organizing a government, could themselves decide by a majority vote whether they wanted black bondage or not. The Democrats thus succeeded in partially sidetracking the bothersome issue.

General Cass, a worthy veteran of the War of 1812, was an eminently respectable candidate. But his name, as the cartoonists and song writers soon discovered, unfortunately rhymed with "ass" and "gas" ("General Gass"). He had held high office as a state legislator in Ohio, as a member of President Jackson's Cabinet, as Minister to France, and as a United States Senator. While envoy to Paris he had published a vigorous pamphlet against Britain's encroachments on freedom of the seas while seeking out slave ships flying the Stars and Stripes. His resolute stand won him warm support at home from the numerous Britain haters. A Democratic song of the campaign appealed to Irish-American "dimmicrats" and other foes of England:

> He bore our glorious banner through
> The battle and the breeze;
> He would not yield to England now
> THE FREEDOM OF THE SEAS.

Pro-Cass medals declared for "The Constitution and the Freedom of the Seas," "Principles, Not Men," and "Liberty, Equality & Fraternity, the Cardinal Principles of True Democracy." For good measure there appeared a rousing statement attributed to Cass during the War of 1812, "While I am Able to Move I will Do My Duty."

Opposing Whigs were not overjoyed by Cass's record as Minister to France. One of their songs, "Old Zack upon the Track," poked fun at Cass's Old World dandyism:

> Oh, Lewis Cass, he went to France,
> King Philippe showed him how to dance,
> He dressed him up in clothes so fine,
> Then let him come with him to dine.

Musically inclined Whigs enjoyed an advantage of some two years in the song department because they had issued their *Rough and Ready Songster* in 1846. Other offerings of 1847 and 1848 acclaimed "The Bold Soger Boy" and "Rough and Ready." Various pro-Taylor slogans, whether on broadsides, buttons, or medals included, "Rough and Ready: The Hero of Monterrey," "The Hero of Buena Vista," "Gen. Taylor the People's Choice," "Untrammelled with Party Obligations," and "I Ask No Favors & I Shrink From No Responsibility." Conspicuously featured were such well-known Taylorisms as "A little more grape, Captain Bragg," and "General Taylor never surrenders." This resolute affirmation was even versified in

> Clear the track if your toes are tender,
> For honest Zack can never surrender!

Militant antislaveryites, joined by some of the "Conscience Whigs" and Democratic "Barnburners," organized as the Free-Soil party in Buffalo and nominated ex-President Van Buren as standard bearer. Their platform forthrightly demanded, "No More Slave States and No More Slave Territory," and it proclaimed as the official party slogan "FREE SOIL, FREE SPEECH, FREE LABOR, AND FREE MEN." Another sloganized aphorism in the platform declared, "Congress has no more power to make a SLAVE than to make a KING." During the succeeding campaign the voters also heard the appeals "Free soil to a free people" and "Vote the land free." These earnest Free-Soilers not only coined meaningful slogans but also composed memorable songs. One tune, "Martin Van of Kinderhook," took a slap at both rival candidates:

> Come, ye hardy sons of toil,
> And cast your ballots for Free Soil;
> He who'd vote for Zacky Taylor,
> Needs a keeper or a jailer.
> And he who still for Cass can be,
> He is a Cass without the C;
> The Man on whom we love to look,
> Is Martin Van of Kinderhook.

Antislavery Free-Soilers—"Night Soilers" was the name given by pro-slavery critics—were distressed by "Old Zack's" ownership of slaves. In the same song they expressed their displeasure:

> When the Whigs they preach and pray,
> For the old man of Monterrey,
> I shake my head as up I figures
> The price of his two hundred niggers.

"Vote Early and Often," a slogan coming into usage at the time, was credited to John Van Buren, son of Free-Soil candidate Martin Van Buren. But not enough antislaveryites voted for "The Wizard of Kinderhook," whether early or often, to give more than 10 percent of the popular vote to "Van, the used-up man." He evidently siphoned enough strength away from the grade B war hero, General Cass, to throw the election to the grade A war hero, General Taylor, the slaveowner from Louisiana.

NEW TERRITORY, NEW TRIBULATIONS

Momentous problems were meanwhile sprouting in the spacious domain recently acquired from Mexico. First came the westward movement of the Mormons, hounded by their neighbors in the Middle West, into the inhospitable area now known as Utah, then called "Deseret." The advance guard arrived in 1847, while the Mexican War was still in progress and while the fugitives could hope that they would be free from American jurisdiction. The big crowd came the next year, 1848, after incredible hardships in crossing the plains and deserts. Drooping spirits were revived as the Mormons sang on the march, "Come, Come, Ye Saints." These "Saints," more commonly called "Latter-Day Saints," became the "Busy Bees of Deseret" when they used the miracle of irrigation to transform the desert into a new Eden.

West of Utah lay fabulous California, much in the public eye. Greed for this sun-bathed expanse had served as one of the major precipitants of the Mexican War, and provided a major bone of contention once the conflict had started. Many Whigs and Free-Soilers feared that Polk, under the influence of the Southern "slavocracy," was trying to narrow the frontiers of freedom. James Russell Lowell wrote in Yankee dialect (*Biglow Papers*):

> They jest want this Californy
> So's to lug new slave-states in
> To abuse ye, an' to scorn ye,
> An' to plunder ye like sin.

Even before news of the outbreak of war with Mexico had reached remote California, the Anglo-Americans there had acted. Restive under Mexican rule, they launched the miniscule "Bear Flag Revolt" and established the short-lived "Bear Flag Republic." Incoming American military and naval forces soon took over and brought California under the protecting wings of the American eagle.

Earlier but minor discoveries of gold had occurred in California, but in January 1848 James W. Marshall picked up some shiny metal in the American River above Sacramento, and soon the cry of "Gold, gold, gold" resounded through the territory—and later the country. Nine days after the discovery Mexico, unaware of the exciting news, signed the treaty in Mexico City that ceded all of California to the conquering Yankees. A tremendous inrush of gold seekers began, as thousands of adventurers thronged to "see the elephant," as a phenomenon of this magnitude was called. The great theme song of the gold crusaders, who were known as "Argonauts" and "Forty-Niners," was Stephen C. Foster's immensely popular "Oh! Susanna," to which they added impromptu stanzas of their own, such as

> Oh, Susanna, you're the gal for me,
> I'm off to Sacramento with my washbowl on my knee.

The primary use of the washbowl was to pan gold, not to ensure cleanliness in an occupation that involved much sweat and grime.

This sudden inpouring of avid fortune seekers inevitably attracted much lawless scum, people who "jumped" claims, robbed, and murdered. A contemporary song jibed:

> Oh what was your name in the States?
> Was it Thompson or Johnson or Bates?
> Did you murder your wife,
> And fly for your life?
> Say, what was your name in the States?

Decent citizens, including the few who "struck it rich" at the "diggings," were outraged by the prevalence of violent crime, especially after the arrival of the lawless "Sydney Ducks" of Australia. In 1851 the Vigilance Committee of San Francisco brought crime under control when the "Vigilantes," operating under home-made justice, strung up some of the worst malefactors and banished others.

A suggestion of the quality of the newly spawned population appeared in a jingle now firmly embedded in folklore:

> The miners came in forty-nine,
> The whores in 'fifty-one,
> And when they got together
> They produced the Native Son.

The brutal truth is that the ladies of purchasable virtue were not that tardy in arriving.

THE COMPROMISERS OF 1850

Early in 1850 boom-town California began hammering on the doors of Congress for admission as a free state. The lineup was then fifteen slave and fifteen free states, and this new threat to the delicate balance led to furious opposition from the "slavocracy" of the South. Ageing Henry Clay, "The Great Compromiser," had recently returned to the Senate to head off the disaster of disunion. Again he eloquently appeared in his familiar role: "I go for honorable compromise wherever it can be made." Senator John C. Calhoun of South Carolina, dying of tuberculosis, arranged for his pro-South speech to be read by a colleague; it was a defiant plea to safeguard the minority rights of his section and its "peculiar institution." He died before the month was out, and his last reported words were "The South! The poor South! God knows what will become of her." On a monument erected to his memory in Charleston appeared the words "Truth, Justice and the Constitution."

Rising to the challenge in the Senate, "Godlike Daniel" Webster pleaded in his famed Seventh of March speech, 1850, for sweet reasonableness and compromise. He believed that nature, through climate, soil, and topography, had already decreed that slavery on a large scale could not profitably exist in much of the new Mexican cession. His memorable address began, "I wish to speak today, not as a Massachusetts man, nor as a Northern man, but as an American. . . . I speak today for the preservation of the Union. Hear me for my cause." Webster was never an abolitionist, though some of the antislavery extremists thought he was and forthwith regarded him as an "apostate." The poet Whittier penned these cruel words in "Ichabod":

> So fallen! so lost! the light withdrawn
> which once he wore!
> The glory from his gray hairs gone
> Forevermore!

"Webster," declared the eminent educator Horace Mann, "is a fallen star! Lucifer descending from Heaven!" The Reverend Theodore Parker, an outspoken Massachusetts clergyman, avowed, "I know of no deed in American history done by a son of New England to which I can compare this, but the act of Benedict Arnold."

As the debate ground on in Congress, husky-throated Senator William H. Seward of New York represented the younger radicals who were weary of compromising on the slavery issue. He classified "all legislative compromises as radically wrong and essentially vicious." He further insisted that "there is a higher law than the Constitution" when the nation was confronted with the necessity of curbing slavery. Conservative citizens were shocked by this dangerous doctrine, which helped to bar Seward from the Presidency. But he evidently had in mind strengthening, not subverting, the Constitution. Those skeptics who spurned the idea of a "higher law" came to be known as "lower law" men.

At last the windy debate ended and the famous but battered Compromise of 1850 emerged from Congress. Its most significant provisions called for the admission of California as a free state, offset by the passing of a new Fugitive Slave Law designed to enable slave catchers to pursue their prey more effectively. Many of the escaped slaves living in the North became frantic. A mass meeting of blacks in New York City posted handbills proclaiming, "The Fugitive Slave Bill! The Panting Slave! Freemen to be Made Slaves."

Antislaveryites in general reacted angrily to the new statute, which they branded "The Bloodhound Law." "Disobedience to the act is obedience to God" was the cry arising from one Ohio mass meeting. Various Northern states passed "Personal Liberty Laws," some of which denied their jails to the "manstealers," and these restrictions greatly impeded the ugly work of the bloodhound men.

Distasteful though the epochal Compromise of 1850 was to both North and South, it definitely strengthened the ideal of union and possibly postponed the armed clash for a decade. Delay meant greater support for the concept of unity, and to this end the popular poet Longfellow contributed immeasurably with his poem "The Building of the Ship" (1849):

> Sail on, O Ship of State!
> Sail on, O Union, strong and great!
> Humanity with all its fears,
> With all the hopes of future years,
> Is hanging breathless on thy fate!

GENERAL SCOTT VERSUS GENERAL PIERCE

President Taylor, still the obedience-demanding old general, disapproved of truckling to the South in the Compromise of 1850 and was fully prepared to wield the Presidential veto and to string up Southern disunionists. Fortunately for conciliation, he died unexpectedly, and Millard Fillmore, "The Accidental President" or "His Accidency," stepped into his military boots. A rather inconspicuous New York lawyer, Fillmore had come up from humble beginnings ("The Wool-Carder President"), and he carried on as a moderate Whig ("The Last of the Whigs"). In this capacity he backed the union-saving Compromise of 1850, which proved to be the outstanding domestic achievement of his curtailed administration.

The Whig nominating convention of 1852 at Baltimore, unable to agree on either Millard Fillmore or Daniel Webster, turned to "Old Fuss and Feathers," General Winfield Scott. He was venerated as a hero of the War of 1812, notably for the battles at Chippewa and Lundy's Lane on the Canadian frontier, where he was severely wounded. Voters more vividly remembered his role in the Mexican War, especially the successive and successful engagements at Vera Cruz, Cerro Gordo, Contreras, Churubusco, and Chapultepec. The Whigs had won the Presidency only with war heroes "Old Tippecanoe" Harrison and "Zack" Taylor, so they not illogically chose the remaining top-drawer military hero. Their platform frankly supported the "finality" of the controversial Compromise of 1850, including the slave-catching Fugitive Slave Act. Angered antislavery Whigs in the North breathed defiance: "We accept the candidate but we spit upon the platform." The proslavery Whigs in the South—sometimes called "Finality Men"—doubted Scott's loyalty to this slave-catching commitment. In effect they accepted the platform but spat on the candidate. After Scott's seemingly inevitable defeat, the saying was circulated that the Whig party "died of an attempt to swallow the Fugitive Slave Law."

General Scott, though a brilliant military man and a skilled diplomatist, lacked an appealing public image. "Old Fuss and Feathers," his sobriquet, conjured up the true image of a man who was overweight, haughty, pompous, vain, and quarrelsome. Democrats made merry with some of his offhand but innocent remarks. Early during the Mexican War he had explained a brief absence from his office in Washington by saying that he had stepped out to take "a hasty plate of soup." As a Whig general who feared sabotage by the Democratic Polk administration, Scott reluctantly took the command at Vera Cruz, for, as he observed, "soldiers had a far greater dread of fire upon the rear than of the most formidable enemy in front." Democratic critics jeered at "a hasty plate of soup" and "fire upon the rear," which ran counter to the saying that "a good soldier never looks behind." Despite Scott's well-known anti-foreignism, he went out on the stump and stooped so low as to tell heckling crowds of Germans and Irish how much he loved "the sweet German accent" and "the rich Irish brogue."

Whigs countered sneers at the fussy general with such songs as "Old Chippewa," "The Battle of Niagara," and "The Men of Churubusco." Scott's supporters also strove to make an asset of his liabilities, especially in the song "Fuss and Feathers,"

> Since Fuss and Feathers is the cry,
>   Let us the fuss begin,
> And we will show them, by and by,
>   How fuss and feathers win.

Ingenious Whigs even tried to make a virtue of "hasty soup" in a tune by that name and in "Scott Soup for the Millions," the chorus of which concluded, "Our new Scott soup is just the thing." The soup bowl, like the log cabin of 1840, became a symbol of the campaign.

"Hasty soup" aside, various Whig medals advertised such solid sentiments as "Gen. Winfield Scott—First in War, First in Peace," "Scott & Graham [for Vice President], Union & Constitution," and the shopworn "United We Stand, Divided We Fall." Beneath all the personal sneers, jeers, and soupy silliness of the campaign, the nation clearly felt a deep concern for the preservation of the union.

As for their own nominee, the Democrats at Baltimore turned away from "Old Fogies" such as General Cass and finally stampeded to Franklin ("Handsome Frank") Pierce of New Hampshire, "The Young Hickory of the Granite Hills." He was the second dark-horse candidate of a major

American political party. A lawyer who had served in both houses of Congress, "The Forgotten President" was not well known outside his native state, and the Whigs tried to jeer him back into relative obscurity with the query "Who is Frank Pierce?" Undaunted by taunts, the Democrats formed "Granite Clubs" and raised "Hickory Poles" in honor of their new "Young Hickory," the same nickname that had served them well under Polk. Punsters clumsily exulted, "We Polked 'em in '44; we'll Pierce 'em in '52."

Pierce could boast a creditable military record, for he had risen to the rank of brigadier general of the volunteers in the Mexican War. But his martial laurels came nowhere near matching those of General Scott. Pierce, to his regret, had a well-known fondness for the bottle, and he had suffered an excruciating groin injury in Mexico that caused him to fall off his horse. Whigs sneered at him as "The Fainting General" and as the hero of "many a well-fought bottle."

Brigadier General Pierce won by a handsome margin in the Electoral College, routing his former chief, Major General Winfield Scott. "Handsome Frank" received especially strong support from the "Finality Men," who backed the Compromise of 1850, especially its Fugitive Slave Act, and also from the expansionist zealots of the "Young America" movement. The nation could anticipate an aggressive proslavery foreign policy.

IX

Slavery and the Rise of Republicanism

We must get rid of slavery or we must get rid of freedom.

Ralph Waldo Emerson, 1856

COVETING CUBA

Scooping up California and Oregon during the Mexican War caused America to become a power in the Pacific as well as in the Atlantic. With widened domain came widened horizons. The democracy-loving American people took a keen interest in the antimonarchical outbursts in Europe during 1848–1849, and expressed outrage when the Czar of Russia intervened to help Austria crush the abortive Hungarian revolution, led by fiery Louis Kossuth. When the Austrian government unwisely protested against America's meddlesome interference, it received a knuckle-rapping reply from Secretary of State Daniel Webster (1850): "The power of this republic at the present moment is spread over a region one of the richest and most fertile on the globe, and of an extent in comparison with which the possessions of the House of Hapsburg [Austria] are but a patch on the earth's surface."

In the aftermath of the Hungarian revolt the "Illustrious Kossuth" visited the United States, which greeted the "Noble Magyar" with unrestrained enthusiasm. Americans were showing the "effete monarchs" of the Old World that "the Universal Yankee nation" was "some pumpkins."

Simultaneously, America was casting covetous eyes on the sugar-rich island of Cuba, known as "The Pearl of the Antilles" and "The Ever-Faithful Isle," primarily because it had not broken away from Spain.

Southerners were especially interested in annexing this island jewel. They needed more slave territory from which to carve new slave states to balance the North, and they also feared that the Cuban blacks might break out of control. If Cuba should become "Africanized," an incendiary example of "Haitianization" would arise some ninety miles off the shores of the United States. American slaves might well be tempted to follow suit.

Adventurers known as "filibusters" added further spice to the feverish fifties in America. They organized small bands of soldiers of fortune to grab desirable territory and to "regenerate" backward peoples. Most successful of this colorful lot was William Walker, the wispy "Grey-eyed Man of Destiny," who seized temporary control of Nicaragua before he finally fell before a firing squad.

More alarming were two filibustering forays from the United States into Cuba in 1850 and 1851, both headed by the Venezuelan General Narciso López and designed to hasten the annexation of the island to the United States. The first incursion, consisting of several hundred men, collapsed. The second started with more fanfare, including posters in Washington bearing such messages as "Ho for Cuba" and "Huzzah for López!" Illusions that the oppressed inhabitants of the island would rise to welcome their Yankee deliverers proved fatal in 1851, as they did later in 1961 at the Bay of Pigs. López and fifty of his followers—"The Gallant Fifty-one"—were put to death, though mob scenes of protest flared up in the United States. Colonel William Crittenden, when ordered to kneel before being shot, defiantly responded, "An American kneels only to his God."

Cuba continued to mesmerize Americans, especially the expansionist Democrats who had elected Pierce in 1852. The slavery-oriented wing of the party was grimly determined to wrest the island from Spain by fair means or foul. A Democratic victory parade in New York City displayed transparencies which read, "The Acquisition of Cuba by Purchase." At a gathering of the Democrats in Albany popular toasts came to the point: "Cuba and the Sandwich Isles [Hawaii]—may they soon be added to the galaxy of states"; "The fruits of the late democratic victory—Pierce and Cuba"; and "May the Queen of the Antilles be added to our glorious confederacy under the prosperous administration of Pierce."

"Handsome Frank" Pierce, strongly under the influence of the Southern slaveholders, declared boldly in his inaugural address, "The policy of my administration will not be controlled by any timid forebodings of evil from expansion." His most audacious grab for Cuba came in 1854, when the Secretary of State instructed the United States Ministers to Spain, Britain, and France to meet and prepare appropriate recommendations. The trio emerged with what came to be called "The Ostend Manifesto" or more correctly the secret Aix-la-Chapelle dispatch to the Secretary of State. It urged the administration to offer Spain as much as $125 million for Cuba, and then if the offer was refused and Spanish control of the

Master Jonathan Tries to Smoke a Cuba, but It Doesn't Agree with Him! English chortle over America's Cuban debacle. *Punch*, 1850.

island seemed dangerous to the United States," by every law, human and divine, we shall be justified in wresting it from Spain."

This "Manifesto of Brigands," as it was labeled by a hostile American press when it leaked out, caused an uproar in the antislavery North. Greatly embarrassed, the Pierce administration rejected the recommendations of "The Three Wise Men of Ostend," and the ripening plum of Cuba never did fall permanently into the American basket.

BLEEDING KANSAS

Pierce's tempestuous administration was even more sorely vexed by the issue of slavery in Kansas. The pot came to a boil in 1854, when Senator Stephen Arnold Douglas of Illinois, the eloquent and dynamic "Little Giant," engineered the passage of the Kansas-Nebraska Bill. As for slavery, it threw open these two territories to the workings of "popular sovereignty" or "squatter sovereignty," as the will of the voters was called. Yet both areas lay north of the 36°30′ freedom line established in 1820 by the Missouri Compromise, which the new legislation expressly repealed. Free-soil men of the North, mightily aroused, branded as "Nebraskals" the supporters of the Kansas-Nebraska Bill.

Senator Douglas, a Chicago real estate investor, was evidently motivated in part by a desire to open up the West to settlers and railroads. He suspected that his bill would kick up a "hell of a storm," and in truth his worst fears were realized. Angry crowds branded him a "Judas" and a

"Traitor," while giving "three groans for Doug." He was repeatedly hanged in effigy. One of these dummies, exhibited on the Boston Common, flaunted the message "Stephen A. Douglas, the Author of the Infamous Nebraska Bill; the Benedict Arnold of 1854." Another was inscribed "Stephen Arnold Douglas, Hung for Treason." (Douglas's middle name evoked association with the arch traitor of the American Revolution.) Effigies of the Senator were not only hanged but burned. After the passage of the controversial measure Douglas declared, "I could travel from Boston to Chicago by the light of my own effigies." Ralph Waldo Emerson stated for publication, "The Fugitive [Slave] Law did much to unglue the eyes of men, and now the Nebraska Bill leaves us staring."

Backers of the Kansas-Nebraska Bill had rather generally assumed that the territory of Nebraska, adjoining free-soil Iowa to the east, would be voted free, while Kansas, adjoining slave-soil Missouri to the east, would be voted slave. Thus the "sacred balance" in the Senate between North and South would be preserved. But as events turned out, each side tried to "pack" Kansas with its partisans, while each condemned the other for rigging the game. The antislavery Massachusetts Emigrant Aid Society supported the arrival of a small body of free-soilers, some of them armed with "Beecher's Bibles." This was the name popularly given to their rifles in recognition of the prominent Brooklyn clergyman, Henry Ward Beecher, who arranged for the arms to be shipped in boxes labeled "Bibles." Shouting "Ho for Kansas," many of the marching emigrants sang the famous lines of the abolitionist poet, John G. Whittier:

> We cross the prairie as of old
> The Pilgrims crossed the sea,
> To make the West, as they the East,
> The homestead of the free!

Southerners strove to offset this assisted emigration from the North by such organizations as "Sons of the South," "The Friends Society," "Blue Lodges," and "Social Bands." All of these bore considerable resemblance to the Ku Klux Klan later spawned by the Civil War. Not surprisingly, one of the groups started from the South carrying a banner proclaiming, "The Supremacy of the White Race." These new arrivals joined forces with the "Border Ruffians" from Missouri, whose practice was to cross the border on election day, "vote early and often," and then return. Armed bands of proslavery irregulars, known by such names as "Kickapoo Rangers," carried banners proclaiming:

> Let Yankees tremble, abolitionists fall;
> Our motto is, Give Southern Rights to All.

But the South was fighting a losing game, largely because few slaveowners would take their valuable human cattle into an area where the bullets were flying, as they were soon to be in Kansas.

John Brown, a fanatical Northern abolitionist, did much to increase the flow of blood in "Bleeding Kansas." Angered when the slavery men sacked the free-soil town of Lawrence in 1856, "Old Brown" of Osawatomie, Kansas, led a small vengeful band which literally hacked to pieces in cold blood five alleged proslaveryites in May 1856.

Blood even flowed on the floor of the United States Senate after Charles Sumner, less than a week earlier, delivered a heated harangue entitled "The Crime against Kansas." With highly questionable taste, he flayed the proslavery men as "hirelings picked from the drunken spew and vomit of an uneasy civilization." He especially directed his venom at Senator Butler of South Carolina, whose cousin, Congressman Brooks of the same state, decided to give Sumner a sound caning, as one would beat an unruly dog. A dazed and bleeding Sumner fell to the Senate floor, suffering head injuries that incapacitated him for more than three years. Overnight "Bully Brooks" became a villain to much of the North but a hero to much of the South.

A Massachusetts colleague of Sumner, Representative Anson Burlingame, assailed Brooks in a House speech, after which Brooks challenged him to a duel. Burlingame accepted and named the Canadian side of the Niagara Falls as the spot, for many state laws in the North had already outlawed dueling. But "Bully" Brooks evidently concluded, with good reason, that he could not safely travel that far north. In the forthcoming campaign Republican songsters turned out tunes entitled "The Artful Dodger" and "Brooks' Canadian Song." Another musical satire jeered:

> O! my name is BULLY BROOKS,
>   Bully Brooks, Brooks, Brooks;
> O! my name is Bully Brooks,
>   Ha-ha! ha-ha!
> I've strength, if not good looks,
> Know bludgeons if not books,
> And am the dirtiest of the Brooks,
>   By far—by far.

Sumner's speech "The Crime against Kansas," was issued as a Republican campaign document and reached tens of thousands of voters. Thus the antislaveryites could couple bleeding Kansas with bleeding Sumner.

BACHELOR JAMES BUCHANAN

Rival political parties in 1856 staged an unprecedented musical extravaganza. This time, for a welcome change, the issues were not frivolous "hard cider" and "hasty soup," but such crucial concepts as free soil and the preservation of the union. A new crusading zeal enlivened American politics with the mushroom rise of the new Republican party. It sprang into being virtually overnight in the Middle West in angry protest against the gains of slavery, chiefly through the popular sovereignty provided by the Kansas-Nebraska Act of 1854. Two years later, almost incredibly, the youthful party mounted a formidable campaign for the Presidency.

Democratic delegates, assembling in Cincinnati, chose for their presidential standard bearer a confirmed and malleable "Doughface," James Buchanan of Pennsylvania, clearly a Northern man with Southern principles. His pro-Dixie bias inspired such Republican songs as "The Dirge of the Doughface" and "Old Buck, or the Living Automaton"—that is, puppet of the Southern slaveholders. But Buchanan's age counted against him; he would be nearly sixty-six if and when inaugurated. Republicans referred to him in song and printed sneers as "The Old Fogy," "The Old Fossil," and "Poor Old Buck." His name was pronounced "Buch-anan" in many parts of the country, and he was widely cartooned as a horned buck. Republicans cried, "We are Buck hunting," while one ingenious Democratic campaign button displayed a buck leaping over a cannon—meaning "Buckanon." "Buck and Breck" were paired in slogan after John Breckinridge won the nomination for the Vice Presidency.

Buchanan suffered from other unusual handicaps. He had reportedly remarked that 10 cents a day was wage enough for a workingman, and this penny-pinching view led to such Republican songs as "Get Out of the Way, Ten Cent Jimmy." Colorful floats in Republican parades showed underfed toilers under a tattered banner labeled "Buchanan's Workshop: Ten Cents a Day."

"Old Buck" was also vulnerable to witticisms and criticisms as "The Bachelor Candidate." He was the only President never to marry, evidently because a youthful broken engagement may have contributed to the early death of his betrothed. In one Republican parade a young woman lifted a banner inscribed with the words "Opposition to Old Bachelors." A current jingle ran:

> Who ever heard in all his life,
> Of a candidate without a wife?

One Republican slogan affirmed, "The White House No Place for an Old Bachelor," and a clever tune asserted:

> Old Bachelors are low in rate,
> They'll never populate a state.
> The White House parties must not drag,
> And what could Bucks be but a Stag!

Buchanan could counter these criticisms with some important assets. Aside from being acceptable to the South and much of the North, he had the advantage of being "Kansasless." He had served abroad as Minister to Great Britain when the debate over the incendiary Kansas-Nebraska Bill raged. He had also performed creditably in various offices, and hence came to be known as "Old Public Functionary" (O.P.F. for short), a label that he later conferred on himself in a message to Congress.

To Buchanan's advantage, especially in the South, the platform on which he ran fully endorsed popular sovereignty in the territories. In short, slave expansion would result if the local voters so chose, over the opposition of those whom one Democratic song branded "the crazy Nigger Worshipers." Supporters of "Old Buck," known as "Buchaneers" or "Buchaniers," claimed with considerable justification that his election would be less disruptive than a victory for the "nigger-loving" Republicans. Inscriptions on various medals advertised such appeals as "James Buchanan—No Sectionalism," "Constitution and Union," and "The Union One and Indivisable [sic]—The Crisis Demands his Election." A pro-Buchanan poster in Connecticut said it all, "No North, No South, One Country, One Destiny—The Union Forever."

Ever since the days of Thomas Jefferson the Democratic party had made a special appeal to the downtrodden. Despite the rising tide of antiforeignism is the 1850s, the Democrats were shrewd enough to woo the vote of incoming immigrants, especially the flood arriving from Ireland and Germany. The Democratic platform of 1856 eloquently and idealistically acclaimed America as "the land of liberty and the asylum of the oppressed of every nation."

THE FRÉMONT CRUSADE

Victory-scenting Republicans, though a newly born party, turned away from such a high-caliber man as "Higher Law" Seward, who had aroused too many enemies. At their Philadelphia convention they nominated instead the erratic, dashing, adventuresome explorer Colonel John C. Frémont. Despite his youthful forty-three years, he was known as "Old Pathfinder," "Pathfinder of the Rockies," and "The Pathfinder of Empire." One Republican song hailed "Frémont, the Mountaineer." Actually many of the paths that he "discovered" he merely publicized, especially those in the Rockies, where unnamed "mountain men" had already ventured. Allan Nevins, Frémont's best-known biographer, ultimately renamed him "Pathmarker of the West." His adoring wife, Jessie Benton Frémont, wrote with exaggeration, "From the ashes of his campfires have sprung cities."

Frémont's lowly birth became an ugly issue in the campaign. He had first greeted the light of day in Savannah, Georgia, as an illegitimate baby, for his young mother had abandoned her elderly husband in Virginia and run off with a young French adventurer. (The voters had their choice in this election between a bachelor and a bastard, whom, in this case, Southerners especially resented.) John C. Frémont, on attaining the age of twenty-eight, had eloped with the fifteen-year-old Jessie Benton, much to the temporary displeasure of her father, the influential Senator Thomas Hart Benton of Missouri. Jessie was a remarkable woman who enjoyed the unique distinction of having a half dozen or so presidential campaign songs written in her honor, notably "We'll Give 'Em Jessie" and "O, Jessie Is a Sweet, Bright Lady." The same admiration was expressed in slogans such as "Give 'Em Jessie" and "John and Jessie Forever! Hurrah!" One punning slogan ran, "Jessie Bent-on Being Free." A foreign visitor might have concluded that Jessie was John's vice presidential running mate.

As for black bondage in the territories, the Republicans bluntly rejected popular sovereignty; they would have no compromise on the extension of slavery. Their platform lashed out against "those twin relics of barbarism—Polygamy [in Utah] and Slavery." One Republican banner cynically averred, "Hurrah for the Kansas-Nebraska Bill—It Introduces Polygamy and Slavery." More jolting was the slogan "We Shall be Redeemed from the Rule of Nigger Drivers." A pro-Frémont campaign song, to the tune of "Yankee Doodle," was blunt:

> Yankee Doodle keep it up,
> It's all as clear as figgers,
> Buchanan is the candidate
> To raise the price of niggers.

Frémont's name proved to be a great asset in that it rhymed in various ways with freedom, the overshadowing theme of the campaign. A rousing Republican slogan was "Free soil, free men, free speech, and Fré-mont." In addition, partisans sang "Freemen Win Where Frémont Lives." This same motif predominated in the stirring song "Frémont and Victory," sung by Republican glee clubs to the tune of the French "Marseillaise."

> Arise, arise, ye brave!
> And let your war-cry be,
> Free speech, free press, free soil, free men,
> Fré-mont and victory!

And "free love," sneered the "Buchaneers," with a snide allusion to Frémont's tainted birth.

Other Republican Frémont songs declared for "Frémont and Freedom" and "Frémont and Liberty." "Song for the People" resurrected the tune of "Tippecanoe and Tyler, Too":

> Have you heard of one Frémont, mont, mont,
> So honest and true?
> He's just the man that'll do all he can
> For liberty here and in Kansas too!
> For liberty here and in Kansas too!
> And with him we'll beat old Buck, Buck, Buck,
> and his slavery Crew!

FREE SOIL AND OTHER FREEDOMS

Bleeding Kansas naturally received major attention in Republican songs. The basic issue of slavery versus free soil found expression in such titles as "A Warning to the South," "The Southern Serpent," and "The Times That Try Men's Souls." As for the bloodied territory, Republicans sang

"The Kansas Wail," "Kansas and Liberty," and "A Plea for Kansas." Related titles were "How the South Overreached Itself" and "The Nebraskaites Think"—that is, they think they will do well under "Old Buck" Buchanan.

Colorful Republican glee clubs and other organizations, with heavy emphasis on singing, adopted such names as "Rocky Mountain Clubs," "Pioneers' Clubs," and "Frémont and Freedom Clubs." Processions of "Young Pioneers" carried transparencies trumpeting, "We'll Take the Buck by the Horns" and "Free Labor, Free Speech, Free Men, Free Kansas, Frémont." During one giant parade in Indianapolis a German contingent (erroneously called Dutch) displayed in German such appeals as "Free Men in the Republic," "No Man Is the Property of Another," "Freedom in a Free State," "Let a Man Be a Man," and "Let the Slave Be Free."

A solid issue of the campaign of 1856, often overlooked, was set forth in the Republican platform and also dramatized in a popular song. It was the proposed railroad to the Pacific by the northern route, favored by the Republicans but disfavored by the Southerners. Frémont, the great "Pathfinder of the West," was clearly the ideal man to build the great iron pathway, at least according to the song "Huzza For the Railroad!":

> We'll bind the Union firmer, by the modern iron rail,
> For Frémont, our young candidate, knows no such word as fail;
> Then fling our banner to the breeze, and on its folds inscribe,
> "The Great Pacific Railroad!" upon which we'll take a ride.

In Indiana the voters heard "Hoosiers will go for the Pacific Railroad," while general support for internal improvements came in "Improvement to rivers and harbors."

Despite an occasional note of levity in Republican songs, surviving medals and other mementos attest to the deadly seriousness of the singers. One banner for Frémont proclaimed, "Protection to American Industry— And No Extension of Slave Power." Republican medals asserted "Free Soil, Free Speech, Free Labor and Eternal Progression," "Free Kansas— and the Union," and "No More Slave States."

Such an inspirational crusade for the various freedoms inevitably took on spiritual overtones. The *Independent,* a foremost religious journal of the era, saw in Frémont's leadership "the good hand of God." As election day neared it thundered, "Fellow-Christians! Remember it is for Christ, for the nation, and for the world that you vote at this election! Vote as you pray! Pray as you vote!"

KNOW-NOTHING NATIVISM

Complications arose during the spirited Frémont-Buchanan clash as the result of a nativist anti-Catholic, third-party ticket, the American party, popularly known as the Know-Nothing party. Begun as a secret patriotic society in 1849, it had evolved from the Supreme Order of the Star-Spangled Banner (S.S.S.B.). It acquired its name from the response of members as to its aims and practices: they normally replied with the words "I know nothing." Some of them reportedly spoke not even this much, but would close one eye and then place the thumb and forefinger shaped into an "O" over the nose. The result was "Eye nose nothing," meaning "I know nothing." Critics sarcastically proposed the creation of societies of "Owe-Nothings," "Say-Nothings," and "Do-Nothings."

Despite the veil of secrecy, word soon leaked out that the Know-Nothing party was more than anti-Catholic. It was also anti-immigrant, antiforeign, and pledged to vote only for "native Americans"—that is, white, native-born Protestants. A contemporary medal still warns, "Beware of Foreign Influence."

As the presidential campaign of 1856 got under way, Know-Nothing delegates met at Philadelphia. Basically a "no-Popery" party, they published a platform that headlined the slogan, "Americans Must Rule America." The convention then formally nominated for Chief Executive ex-President Fillmore, whose subsequent campaign stressed the dangers of sectionalism and the priceless boon of the union. Not surprisingly, those Know-Nothings who opposed slavery deserted the new party. They assembled in their own convention in New York and there nominated the free-soil Republican candidate, Frémont, rather than Fillmore, The seceders were dubbed "North Americans," while the stand-pat Know-Nothings were called "South Americans," obviously in reference to the South.

Remnants of the dying Whig party, sometimes called the "Old Grays," met in a last-gasp convention in Baltimore and formally endorsed Fillmore. But they adopted a separate platform which stressed the union, rather than Know-Nothing antiforeignism. One pro-Fillmore slogan advocated "Peace at Any Price. Peace and Union." Fillmore medals emphasized differing goals. One proclaimed "The Union Now, the Union Forever"; another declared "Americans Shall Rule America." Still other medals conveyed such elevated sentiments as "No North, No South, but the Whole Country," "Millard Fillmore for the Whole Country," and "Be Vigilant and Watchful that Internal Dissensions Destroy Not Your Prosperity."

Mudslingers in this Frémont-Buchanan contest of 1856, especially the Know-Nothings, accused Frémont of being a Catholic, although he was in fact an Episcopalian. This charge, though difficult to refute, seems not to have had a decisive effect on the outcome of the election. Yet two pamphlets appeared with these titles: *The Romish Intrigue: Frémont a Catholic* and *Frémont's Romanism Established: Colonel Frémont's Religious History—The Authentic Account—Papist or Protestant—Which?*

AN ELECTORAL VICTORY FOR UNION

Threats by the Southern slaveholders that they would break up the union, should their "doughface" Buchanan lose, evidently did not greatly bother confirmed Know-Nothings. They were annoyed that so many Irish Catholics were going to vote for "Ould Buchanan," and even more distressed by the presence of Catholics in the electorate. Popular Know-Nothing songs flaunted such titles as "Papal Bulls," "No Priestly Rule," and "Papal Foemen." One hymn of hate urged:

> Then gird on your strength, and the priests bid defiance,
> Let every one strike for his fireside and home,
> In the sons of Columbia place every reliance,
> But beware of the snares of the vile Church of Rome.

"Pathfinder" Frémont's newly sprouted "Black Republican" party—as it was called in the semiblack South—clearly outsang "Old Buck" and the Democrats, but Buchanan won by some 1,839,000 votes to 1,340,000 for Frémont. Fillmore, the Know-nothing entry, carried only one state, although he garnered about 850,000 votes. While the Whig party died, the Republicans made a remarkable showing, especially for a two-year-old organization. The abolitionist poet John G. Whittier found comfort in the outcome:

> Then sound again the bugles,
>   Call the muster-roll anew;
> If months have well-nigh won the field
>   What may not four years do?

At the rate they were expanding, the Republicans would have more votes than voters in 1860, at least on paper.

Gnawing fears that the South would secede, should victory crown the base-born "Black Republican" Frémont, undoubtedly had a crucial impact on the outcome of the contest. Southern "fire-eaters" made no bones about their intentions, even though many Northern supporters of "Buck and Breck" raised the cry "Save the union." On the Fourth of July, 1856, in Georgia, this toast was drunk: "The union—may it speedily be dissolved and the Honorable P. S. Brooks [Senator Sumner's assailant] be the first President of the Southern Republic." A flood of pamphlets and handbills reflected deep anxiety, especially those with such titles as "Will the South Dissolve the Union?" and "The Federal Union, Must It be Preserved?"

Frémont's defeat and Buchanan's victory may have saved the union and preserved the uneasy equipoise over the burning issue of slavery for a little more than four years.

X

The Eve
of the Breakup

I believe this government cannot endure permanently
half slave and half free.

Abraham Lincoln, 1858

THE SLAVERY CRISIS DEEPENS

"Old Fogey" James Buchanan, "The Bachelor President," came out four-square for "popular sovereignty" in the territories in his inaugural address on March 4, 1857. But the Presidential "honeymoon," normally several months in length, lasted only four days. An abrupt end came when the Supreme Court tore open old wounds with its explosive Dred Scott decision.

Dred Scott, a Negro slave, had sued for his freedom, alleging that his owner had taken him to live on free soil in the North for some five years. In a confused and confusing decision the Supreme Court, headed by Chief Justice Roger B. Taney, ruled that Scott, being a slave and hence not a citizen, could not lawfully sue in the federal courts. His prolonged residence on free soil, the Court held, had not changed his status as a bondsman. Further, the Missouri Compromise of 1820, forbidding slavery north of the line of 36°30′ (except for Missouri) had been unconstitutional all along. This ruling meant that popular sovereignty was meaningless because the sovereign people in the territories north of the Missouri line could not vote out slavery even if they desired.

Taney's Dred Scott decision stunned and angered the free-soilers of the North, especially the Republicans. Pointing to the Southern members on the Court, with their presumed antiblack bias, the anti-slaveryites con-

demned the "Dred Scottites" and "Dred Scottism." Such critics cried that
the justices had "sullied the ermine," and that their views deserved no
more respect than those of "a Southern debating society." Especially
objectionable was Justice Taney's historically sound but offensive dictum
"For more than a century before the Declaration of Independence, the
negroes had been regarded as beings of an inferior order . . . so far
inferior that they had no rights which a white man was bound to respect." Henceforth Taney was unfairly condemned for saying and believing that "Negroes enjoyed no rights that needed to be respected by
whites."

As if the Dred Scott decision were not depressing enough, a paralyzing
panic descended in 1857. Numerous banks collapsed; others refused to
redeem paper money with gold and silver. In Philadelphia popular opposition to legalizing the suspension of specie payments led to a mass meeting in Independence Square. Various translucent transparencies conveyed
pointed messages: "Expansion or Bankruptcy—Contraction Closes Our
Workshops," "The People, Not the Banks, Want Legislative Aid," "Gold
and Silver Currency—a Sure Basis for Honest Trade," and "Banks—the
Hydra that Feeds upon the Industrious Poor." Crowds at hunger meetings
in the larger cities shouted such slogans as "Bread or death" or waved
banners inscribed, "We Want Work," "We Want Bread," or simply
"Work-Arbeit"—an appeal from and to Germans.

In this panic year 1857, Hinton R. Helper, one of the poorer whites of
North Carolina, published a book in the North (the South would not allow it to be published) called *The Impending Crisis of the South: How
to Meet It*. He despised Negroes, who in his view worsened the lot of the
poor whites, yet he advocated free labor. The "hated Helper's" book, with
its "dirty allusions," was banned in the South, while the antislaveryites of
the North inflamed sectional bitterness by endorsing it.

LINCOLN'S EMERGENCE AND REPUBLICAN GAINS

One of the ablest Illinois lawyers, "Honest Abe" Lincoln, was meanwhile
gaining greater visibility. As a member of the recently born Republican
party, he had declared in a speech in Peoria, Illinois, on October 16, 1854,
"No man is good enough to govern another man without that other's consent." More striking was his famous address at the Republican state convention, in Springfield, Illinois, June 16, 1858, when Lincoln was forty-nine.
He solemnly declared, "A house divided against itself cannot stand. I
believe this government cannot endure permanently half slave and half
free. I do not expect the union to be dissolved—I do not expect the house
to fall—but I do expect it will cease to be divided. It will become all one
thing, or all the other." This was strong medicine, and one is surprised
that Lincoln's foes in the proslavery camp did not assail him more
vigorously.

Later in the summer of 1858 "Old Abe" Lincoln, so known in both affection and derision, ran unsuccessfully for the United States Senate. As chance decreed, the seat was then occupied by Stephen A. Douglas, the "Little Giant," notorious for sponsoring the Kansas-Nebraska Bill. Lincoln boldly challenged his opponent, a formidable air-pawing orator, to a series of seven joint debates, which were held during the summer and early autumn of 1858.

Lincoln, despite his ungainly appearance, showed to better advantage than might have been expected and gained a national audience. He scored a major point when at Freeport, Illinois, he prodded Douglas into enunciating the "Freeport Doctrine." This formula held that slavery could not exist in the territories, even where legally sanctioned by the voters, in the absence of "local police regulations." At Quincy, Illinois, Lincoln branded slavery "a moral, a social, and a political wrong." Between the second and third debates Lincoln supposedly said, "You can fool all of the people some of the time, and some of the people all of the time, but you cannot fool all of the people all the time." At Galesburg, Illinois, a banner displayed by the crowd bore the strange words "Small Fisted Farmers, Mud-sills of Society, Greasy Mechanics, For A. Lincoln."

Fires of sectional conflict were already crackling ominously when Senator William H. Seward, the foremost figure in the new Republican party, delivered a startling speech on the slavery issue in Rochester, New York, October 25, 1858. "It is," he declared, "an irrepressible conflict between opposing and enduring forces, and it means that the United States must and will, sooner or later, become either entirely a slaveholding nation or entirely a free-labor nation." His message was essentially that of Lincoln's "House-divided Speech" some three months earlier. But the phrase "irrepressible conflict" attracted much more notoriety, branded Seward a radical, and may have cost him the presidential nomination in 1860. Ominously for the incumbent Democrats, the snowballing Republicans won a plurality of the seats in the House of Representatives in the autumn elections of 1858. President Buchanan, although never conspicuous for wit, aptly paraphrased Oliver Hazard Perry, the victor on Lake Erie in 1813, in cynically remarking, "We have met the enemy and we are theirs."

JOHN BROWN'S BODY

In the following autumn of 1859 "Old Osawatomie" Brown, already notorious for his butcheries in "Bleeding Kansas," burst upon the stage of history. On October 16, 1859, "God's Angry Man" led an attack with about a score of armed men, including five blacks, on the federal arsenal at Harper's Ferry, Virginia. He evidently hoped to secure weapons for an insurrection by the nearby slaves, none of whom sprang to his arms. His tiny band was quickly wiped out, and the "Old Puritan," severely wounded, was captured after spurning all chances to escape. "If God be for us," he declared, "who can be against us?" Accused of being a "madman," he was clever enough to perceive his great value as a martyr for the abolitionists. From prison he wrote to his brother, "I am quite cheerful in view of my approaching end, being fully persuaded that I am worth inconceivably more to hang than for any other purpose."

"Old Brown" was speedily tried by the state of Virginia for treason against the commonwealth and for criminal conspiracy to incite slave insurrection. Found guilty, he declared in his well-publicized last speech to the court, "Had I interfered in the manner which I admit . . . in behalf of the rich, the powerful, the intelligent . . . it would have been all right, and every man in this court would have deemed it an act worthy of reward rather than punishment." On the day of his hanging he wrote, "I, John Brown, am now quite certain that the crimes of this guilty land will never be purged away but with Blood." On his way to the scaffold an incident supposedly occurred (it is a myth) that the condemned man stooped to kiss a Negro child. The episode has been preserved on canvas and in poetry, notably the verse of the "Poet Laureate of Abolitionism," John G. Whittier:

> John Brown of Osawatomie, they led him out to die;
> And lo! a poor slave-mother with her little child pressed nigh.
> Then the bold, blue eye grew tender, and the old harsh face grew mild,
> As he stooped between the jeering ranks and kissed the negro's child!

After a nerve-racking wait of ten minutes, the trap was sprung. As Brown dangled into eternal fame, the officer on duty cried out, "So perish all such enemies of Virginia! All such enemies of the union! All such foes of the human race!"

Aroused Southerners, unwilling to be "done to a Brown," voiced outrage at the attempt of the "nigger-stealing Black Republicans" and abolitionists "to Brown us." Most Republicans, not favoring servile insurrection, tried to dissociate themselves from the bloody episode and shake off the epithet "John Brown Republicans." But the more extreme antislavery men, especially the abolitionists, cheered their new martyr. Medals struck off honoring Brown bore such preachments as "Slavery the Sum of All Villainies" and "Resistance to Tyranny is Obedience to God." In the North men referred to "St. John" Brown. Ralph Waldo Emerson won an enthusiastic response from an audience in Boston when, bracketing the convicted felon with Jesus, he declared that "the new saint awaiting his martyrdom . . . will make the gallows glorious like the cross. . . ."

Grass grows more quickly over the battlefield than over the scaffold, and the poet E. C. Stedman wrote prophetic words:

> And Old Brown,
> Osawatomie Brown,
> May trouble you more than ever, when you've nailed his coffin down!

One of the most poignant ironies of history is that this once obscure and hunted man became, next to Jesus Christ, perhaps the most sung-about figure in history. One of the great marching songs of the Civil War declared:

> John Brown's body lies a-mould-ring in the grave,
> His soul is marching on.

Oddly enough, the original John Brown song was written to taunt a relatively unknown Massachusetts soldier by that name. But the "Boys in Blue" who sang it during the Civil War knew whom they had in mind.

Southerners had a less flattering song, entitled "Old John Brown," the chorus of which ran:

> Old Osawattomie [*sic*] Brown! old Osawattomie Brown!
> That will never pay,
> Trying to come away down South,
> And run the niggers away.

DEMOCRATS AND OLD FOGEYS

As the clouds of sectional conflict darkened, the Democratic National Convention met in Charleston, South Carolina, in April, 1860. The chairman announced in his address that the motto of the assembly would be the words inscribed on the memorial to John C. Calhoun in this same city, "Truth, Justice, and the Constitution." Stephen A. Douglas, the controversial "Squatter [popular sovereignty] King," loomed as the premier leader of the party and its logical nominee. But because he and his followers favored popular sovereignty in the territories, as modified by the Dred Scott decision, the "fire-eaters" of the South hopelessly deadlocked the convention and then bolted from it. The remaining rump was unable to agree on a nominee. Exultant Southerners sang an adaptation of an old nursery rhyme:

> For when the vote was opened
> The South began to sing,
> "You little Squatter Sovereign
> Shan't be our King!"

Two anxious months later the divided Democrats gathered again, this time in separate conventions in Baltimore. Douglas, the "Little Giant," won the nomination of the regular Democrats on a platform that came out foursquare for upholding the Supreme Court and the Constitution, particularly in relation to Dred Scott and slavery. Yet the delegates were sufficiently proslavery to favor the acquisition of slaveholding Cuba "on such terms as shall be honorable to ourselves and just to Spain."

Slave-oriented Southern Democrats, known to their opponents as practitioners of "sham Democracy," chose as their standard bearer the incumbent Vice President, John C. Breckinridge of Kentucky, though he was a moderate on the slavery issue. They declared firmly and flatly for the protection of slavery in the states and territories, as well as for the acquisition of slave-inhabited Cuba. The ardent sentiments of the bolting Breckinridge Democrats were expressed in such ·watchwords as "No Submission to the North" and "Our Country and Our Rights."

Alarmed over the split in the Democratic party and the dire prospect of disunion, remnants of the Whig party and the American (Know-Nothing) party converged on Baltimore in May 1860. This curious marriage produced the Constitutional Union party, sneered at as the "Do-Nothing party" and the "Old Gentleman's party." Branded also as "Old Fogies" and a "Gathering of the Graybeards," these earnest mavericks were admittedly an elderly, conservative group, desperately determined to preserve the union.

From this Constitutional Union convention came an exceptionally brief platform—a half page long. In no uncertain words it recognized "no political principle other than THE CONSTITUTION OF THE COUNTRY, THE UNION OF THE STATES, AND THE ENFORCEMENT OF THE LAWS." In sloganized form this sentiment became "The Constitution, the Union, and the Laws." The nominee for President was John Bell, a unionist from the border state of Tennessee; his running mate was Edward Everett, a brilliant orator from Massachusetts. The vice presidential tail of the ticket (Everett) was regarded as so much stronger than the head (Bell) that scoffers dubbed it "The Kangaroo Ticket"—a phrase that was commonly used where applicable in later elections.

"Old Fogey" Constitutional Unionists loyally supported the union and condemned "sectional parties," while their foes branded them appeasers and "Union Savers" or "Union Shriekers." Yet their sincerity could hardly be doubted. One of their banners proclaimed, "No North, No South, No East, No West, Nothing but the Union," thus paraphrasing a famous affirmation of Henry Clay. Medals supporting the "Kangaroo" candidates spread abroad such sentiments as "Union Forever, Freedom to All," "Liberty Union and Equality," and "The Union Must and Shall be Preserved." Also popular were "Union of States," "John Bell, Union, Constitution & Enforcement of the Laws," and "Our Rights, The Constitution and the Union."

Similar ideals found expression in the titles of songs in the Bell and Everett *Songster:* "The Union—Whole Hog or None," "We'll Stand by the Union Forever," "Our Union, Right or Wrong," and "The Flag of Our Union." One stanza of "Union Dixie" avowed:

> Of platforms let 'em make a fuss,
> But our Constitution's enough for us,
>
> .   .   .
>
> For Bell and Everett, let's give three cheers,
> And the Union's safe for the next four years.

A RAILSPLITTER CANDIDATE

Expectant Republicans met with bubbling enthusiasm in Chicago's "Wigwam," an enormous boxlike structure of flammable wood. Large portraits of "Old Irrepressible" Seward, the front runner, reminded delegates that the New York Senator was the premier figure in the party. But he had irreparably alienated middle-of-the-roaders by his "irrepressible conflict" speech in 1858, not to mention his "higher law than the Constitution" indiscretion in 1850. "Success rather than Seward," insisted his numerous foes. Even though the New Yorker led the field on the first two ballots, "Honest Abe" Lincoln of Illinois, "The Great Railsplitter of the West," overtook him and won the nomination. The Illinoisan's Cooper Institute speech of February 1860, in New York City, had proved a smashing success. "Let us have faith," he had declared on that occasion, "that right makes might." Ironically, "Old Uncle Abe," the cadaverous Kentuckian resident in Illinois, proved to be the most "available" candidate, though widely regarded as "Mr. Second Best."

Lincoln's promising Republican platform appealed powerfully to the needy and the greedy alike. It opposed the extension of slavery into the territories; it urged the construction of a railroad to the Pacific; it advocated general internal improvements, all the more so since President Buchanan had recently vetoed such a bill. "River and harbor improvements" became one of the battle cries of the ensuing campaign. Wage earners and manufacturers were assured of a higher tariff. Supportive medals called for "Protection to American Industry," "Protection to Honest Industry," "Protection to All at Home and Abroad."

Seductive indeed was the Republican plank that demanded free homesteads from the public land—but only for legitimate settlers. Frustration mounted when, about a month after Lincoln's nomination, lame-duck President Buchanan vetoed a Homestead Act that would have permitted the purchase of such virgin land at 25 cents an acre. Possibly the most effective single catch phrase in a slogan-rich campaign was the appealing "Vote yourself a farm." Associated battle cries were "Land for the landless," "Homesteads for all actual settlers," "Free homes for the homeless," and "Lincoln and free homesteads." Also heard were "Pass the Homestead Bill and that will settle the slavery question," "That 160 acres we must have," and "The United States is rich enough to give us all a farm."

Deeply rooted in free land was the issue of free soil. Relevant pro-Republican slogans demanded "Free Land, Free Speech, & Free Men," and "Free Homes for Free Men—No More Slave Territory."

THE GLADIATORS OF 1860

As excitement mounted, the crucial canvass of 1860, with four substantial parties contending, reached a new crescendo in slogan, song, color, and enthusiasm. Disunion or union were riding perilously on the result.

Republican campaigners clearly outsang and probably outmarched their three opponents, who had less rosy prospects of victory. "Old Abe the Railsplitter" had split some rails for wooden fences as a young man, and this rugged pioneer occupation caught the public's fancy. Young Republicans organized "Rail Splitter Clubs" and "Wide Awakes," who marched, sang, and cheered in colorful parades, often at night as oilskins protected their clothes from pitch-dripping torches. The exultant marchers extolled Lincoln, "The Little Giant Killer," and groaned dismally for the "Poor Little Dougs," as the supporters of Douglas were dubbed.

For their part, the Douglas partisans called themselves "Little Giants," "Douglas Guards," "Ever Readys," and "Invincibles." They shouted, "We want a statesman, not a railsplitter, as President." Republican retorts, including those imprinted on medals, were "The Great Railsplitter of the West Must & Shall Be our Next President" and, illogically, "The Man that Can Split Rails Can Guide the Ship of State." Slavery-expansion Democrats proclaimed, "Democracy [the Democratic party] is Good Enough for All," "Cuba must be ours," and "We Want None but White Men at the Helm."

Despite all the mindless clamor about fence rails, the menacing constitutional crisis loomed as the overshadowing issue. One all-purpose slogan, which appeared on medals bearing the likenesses of Lincoln, Douglas, or Bell, supported "Our Rights, the Constitution, and the Union." A separate Lincoln medal bore as its inscription "The Constitution & Union Forever."

A battling Douglas courageously supported the union in opposition to the Breckinridge Democrats, who attracted most of the Southern secessionists. Douglas medals flaunted the defiant Jackson ultimatum "The Union Must and Shall be Preserved" and added "Our Rights, the Constitution and the Union." Other medallic slogans for Douglas read, "Support 'the Little Giant' Who Has Proved Himself the Greatest Statesman of the Age," "Union and Equality," and "Liberty, Union, and Equality."

A popular sentiment advertised by both Douglas Democrats and Lincoln Republicans was "Intervention is disunion." (In this context "intervention" meant "interposition": the action of a state in opposing the federal government.) Nor did the medalists overlook Douglas's long-term advocacy of the right of settlers to determine their own institutions, for one engraved slogan acclaimed "The Champion of Popular Sovereignty."

In addition to union preservation the issue of slavery, inseparable from that of union, received much sloganized attention. No one could mistake the significance of such Republican slogans as "Freedom to All." Lincoln's own contributions were "A House Divided Against Itself Cannot Stand" and "Slavery is a Moral, Social, and Political Wrong." Other Republican appeals were "Millions for Freedom—Not One Cent for Slavery," "No More Slave Territory," "Free Territory for a Free People," and "Let Liberty be National & Slavery Sectional."

When Republican "Wide Awakes" marched at night, their lighted transparencies held aloft such views as "The Territories Must be Free To the People" and "We Do Care Whether Slavery Is Voted Up or Voted Down." (This was a sardonic response to Douglas's speech regarding Kansas in which he had declared, "I care not whether it is voted down or voted up.")

THE SOUND OF MUSIC

Lively campaign songs of 1860 stressed the candidates more than the issues. A new composition for the union was not especially needed, for the poet George Pope Morris had already contributed the stirring and highly popular "The Flag of Our Union (1851)." Sung throughout the 1850s and during the Civil War, it further enshrined a slogan:

> A song for our banner, the watch-word recall,
>   Which gave the Republic her station,
> 'United we stand, divided we fall';
>   It made and preserved us a nation.
>
> *Chorus:*
> The union of lakes, the union of lands,
>   The union of States none can sever!
> The union of hearts, the union of hands,
>   The flag of our Union forever.

Aside from songs about the union, the issue of slavery received top billing in the heated canvass of 1860. Notable among Republican songs were "Hope for the Slave," "Down with Slavery's Minions," "Freedom's Battle Cry," and "Freedom and Reform." The same theme appeared in "Lincoln and Liberty," one stanza of which declared:

> They'll find what by felling [trees] and mauling [rails],
> Our rail-maker statesman can do;
> For the people are everywhere calling
> For Lincoln and Liberty, too.

A Republican song writer directed a special appeal to free men in "Come, Freemen, Come Rally." With "Bleeding Kansas" still a red-hot issue, one is not surprised to find that there were songs such as "Ho! For Kansas," "The Song of the Kansas Emigrants," and "The Neb-rascality." And for good measure came the tune "Free Homesteads."

Douglas Democrats were quite capable of vigorous responses. One of their songs, "Stand by the Flag," sung to the tune of "The Star-Spangled Banner," condemned both Northern Republicans and Southern Democrats:

> Come freemen, then rally, to the flag let's be true,
> 'Gainst the treason of Lincoln, and Breckinridge too.
> "And conquer we must, for our cause it is just,
> And this be our motto *"In God is our Trust."*

Abraham Lincoln, his personality and background, unleashed a flood of Republican songs, including "Hurrah for Old Abe" and "Honest Old Abe," as well as the whimsical "That Old Man 'bout Fifty-two." His towering height invariably attracted much attention, as recorded in the songs "The Taller Man Well Skilled," "High Old Abe Shall Win," and "The Short and Long of It." The last-named title contrasted Lincoln's six feet four with "Little Giant" Douglas's alleged five feet one.

Lincoln appealed to the still-vibrant pioneering spirit of many voters because of his birth in Kentucky ("Son of Kentucky") and his upbringing in Indiana and Illinois, all of them Western states. Falsely suggesting that a dark horse had rather suddenly emerged, Republicans bawled, "Old Abe Lincoln Came Out of the Wilderness," to the tune of "The Old Gray Mare." In contrast with the star arisen in the east when Christ was born, a Republican song hailed "Western Star! Give it Three Cheers," as well as "Lincoln of the West" and "Abe of the West and Victory." Lincoln's reputation as an upright citizen and lawyer was musically refined in the songs "Honest Abe of the West" and "The Gallant Son of the West." One song, "Honest Abe, the Flatboatman," referred to Lincoln's early experience in twice floating down the Mississippi River to New Orleans.

A youthful Lincoln had split some rails, or rather had split the logs from which he made fence rails. Just as log cabins were the symbol of the hard cider campaign of 1840, fence rails, exhibited gleefully in parades, became the symbol of the 1860 canvass. Lincolnites sang:

> Then bring out the music and banners,
> The "fence rails" and orators too,
> And we'll teach Loco-focos [Democrats] good manners
> As we did with "Old Tippecanoe."

To embellish the Lincoln legend, Republican songs bore the titles "Rail Lyrics," "The Rail Song," "Old Abe, the Rail Splitter," "The Woodchopper of the West," and "Then Put Away the Wedges and the Maul." Obviously none of the songs bothered to explain how a muscular man experienced in splitting rails would prevent the union from splitting.

Gaunt and awkward "Old Abe," afflicted with sallow and wrinkled cheeks, never won a beauty contest. Widely regarded as an unusually homely man, he came to be known in unfriendly circles as "The Illinois Baboon" and "The Gorilla." Republican tunesmiths naturally ignored his homeliness to extol his honesty, but the Douglas Democrats were less considerate. One of their ditties jibed:

> Any lie you tell, we'll swallow—
> Swallow any kind of mixture;
> But, oh don't, we beg and pray you—
> Don't, for land's sake, show his picture!

Douglas, as the standard bearer of the Northern Democrats, did not escape the sting of Republican song writers. They devised "Poor Little Dug," "Old Abe and Little Dug," and "Get Out de Way, You Little Giant." One anti-Douglas song sank so low as to make an ungrammatical issue of the "Little Giant's" drinking habits:

> [His] legs was short, but his speeches was long,
> And nothin' but hisself could he see,
> His principles was weak, but his spirits was strong,
> For a thirsty little soul was he.

When the shouting died down, "High Old Abe" bested Douglas and his two other rivals at the polls. A curious combination of circumstances enabled him to parlay a 39 percent plurality of the popular vote into a 59 percent majority of the Electoral College. Condemned by the losers as a "Sectional President," Lincoln was hailed by one Republican medal maker as "The Right Man in the Right Place"—fence rails and all. As events turned out, the election of the railsplitter split the union.

THE SECESSION PARADE STARTS

Militant South Carolina had served notice that if the "Baboon" Lincoln and his "Black Republicans" won, it would leave the union. Widespread drilling of armed "Minute Men," named after the "Minute Men" of the Revolution, gave ominous point to this threat. Senator Hammond of South Carolina, famous for his "Cotton is King" speech in 1858, had recently predicted that "The North without us would be a motherless calf, bleating about, and die of mange and starvation." In such a spirit, "Don't trade with the North" became a common admonition in the South. Upon the election of "the Black Republican nominee and his fanatical diabolical Republican Party," a special convention assembled in Charleston some six weeks after Lincoln's election. Appealing to the "God of Justice" and the "God of Hosts," it passed an ordinance of secession, 169 to 0. The presiding officer then cried out, "I proclaim the State of South Carolina an independent commonwealth."

Despite this remarkable show of unanimity, more than a sprinkling of South Carolinians remained attached to the union, in the face of such taunts as "union shriekers," "dirt eaters," and "submissionists." Prominent among these dissenters stood James L. Petigru, an eminent jurist and political leader. When asked by a stranger in December 1860 where the insane asylum in Columbia was located, he pointed to the Baptist Church, in which the secession convention had gathered before adjourning to Charleston, adding, "It looks like a church, but it is now a lunatic asylum; go right there and you will find one hundred and sixty-four maniacs within." A short time later, when the fire-alarm bells heralded secession, he exclaimed, "I tell you there is a fire; they have this day set a blazing torch to the temple of constitutional liberty, and please God, we shall have no more peace forever." During the course of the war Petigru died an unhappy man, and his daughter had a memorable epitaph engraved on his tombstone in Charleston. It reads in part:

> Unawed by Opinion,
> Unseduced by Flattery,
> Undismayed by Disaster,
> He confronted Life with antique Courage
>   And Death with Christian hope. . . .
> In the great Civil War
> He withstood his People for his Country. . . .

Defiant South Carolina, leading the secessionist parade, left the union in a holiday spirit of rejoicing. But all of the other six Southern states that seceded before the firing on Fort Sumter, April 1861, exhibited much hesitation and outright opposition. The critical border states of Missouri, Kentucky, and Maryland, all of which maintained slavery, remained in the union to the very end, although at times they teetered on the edge. Loyal Kentuckians in particular made good use of the slogan "Secession Is a Remedy for No Evil." Disunionist sentiment also proved dangerously strong in Maryland, where a popular slogan proclaimed, "Marylanders Know Their Rights, and Knowing, Dare Maintain Them." To add point, this jingle was imprinted on envelopes:

> The North Shall Feel
> Old Maryland Steel.

War hero Winfield Scott, the eminent but ageing general, was quoted on envelopes as wishfully saying, "The Loyal States Will Have No Compromise with Traitors, Treason, or Treachery."

"OLD BUCK" AND THE SECEDERS

Before the shooting actually started, many Northerners believed that the principles of the Declaration of Independence applied also to the South. Horace Greeley, the influential editor of the New York *Tribune*, rejected the prospect of having one section "pinned to the residue by bayonets," and he actively promoted the appeal "Let Them Go." In the same spirit, Virginia-born Winfield Scott seriously considered the alternative of saying to the seceded states, "Wayward sisters, depart in peace."

"Old Buck" Buchanan—never dynamic, now seventy, and a legally constitutional lawyer—deplored the breakup of the union. Yet shackled he pointed out, quite properly, that the Constitution gave him no specific power to drag sovereign states back by force. He tried conciliation and negotiation, as Lincoln later did until the shooting started, but to no avail. Two-fisted Northerners, incorrectly believing that "Old Hickory" had crushed a comparable uprising in South Carolina in 1832, prayed, "Oh, for one hour of Jackson!" Unionists further reminded people of the "Old Hero" with such slogans as "By the Eternal the Union Must and Shall

Wretched Condition of the Old Party at the White House. Buchanan is hard pressed between Southern threats of violence and Northern reminders of his obligation to uphold the Constitution. *Harper's Weekly*, 1861.

be Preserved" and "We chastised them in 1832, and will Finish the Punishment in 1861." "St. Jackson's Day" was celebrated in New York on January 8, 1861, the anniversary of the "Old Hero's" victory at New Orleans. Cheers for Jackson mingled with those for Major Anderson, then precariously maintaining a small Union garrison at Fort Sumter at Charleston. "Trusting in God, we must succeed" was a remark widely attributed to him.

Early in February 1861, a month before President Lincoln took the inaugural oath, representatives of a half dozen states formed a provisional government at Montgomery, Alabama. They chose ex-Senator Jefferson Davis of Mississippi as President and the wispy Alexander H. Stephens of Georgia as Vice President. In his inaugural address Davis correctly paraphrased the Declaration of Independence when he stated, in reference to the new regime, "It illustrates the American idea that governments rest on the consent of the governed, and that it is the right of the people to alter or abolish them at will whenever they become destructive of the ends for which they were established." More than a month later (March 21, 1861) Vice President Stephens proved embarrassingly blunt in his famous "Cornerstone Speech" in Savannah, Georgia. Referring to secession he avowed, "Its foundations are laid, its cornerstone rests, upon the great truth that the Negro is not equal to the white man; that slavery

—subordination to the superior race—is his natural and normal condition." "Let us alone" became a watchword of Jefferson Davis and many other Confederates.

Confederate soldiers had meanwhile seized federal arsenals, post offices, customs houses, and other national establishments within their grasp. Secretary of the Treasury John A. Dix contributed a stirring war cry to the North when he telegraphed a Treasury official in New Orleans, "If anyone attempts to haul down the American flag, shoot him on the spot." This rousing sentiment was widely imprinted on envelopes.

By far the most important Union holdout was Fort Sumter, which commanded Charleston Harbor, itself the leading Atlantic seaport of the entire Confederacy. Such a bastion, flaunting the Stars and Stripes, further aroused the hot-blooded South Carolinians. A widely voiced slogan, "We Must Have the Forts," evidently originated in the secession convention of December 20, 1860.

During the crucial four months between the presidential election and Lincoln's inauguration, lame duck Buchanan helplessly and hopelessly served out his time. President-elect Lincoln meanwhile was powerless to do anything except through words. On February 11, 1861, "Old Abe" took affectionate leave of his neighbors in Springfield with a moving little address, "not knowing when or whether I ever may return [he returned in a coffin], with a task before me greater than that which rested upon Washington." His speeches en route added little to his stature as a statesman; in Pittsburgh, for example, he questionably remarked, "There is no crisis but an artificial one." Such utterances strengthened criticism, in the North and South, that he was a "Simple Susan." But at Philadelphia he delivered a statesmanlike address, foreshadowing his inaugural effort, in which he insisted, "There will be no bloodshed unless it is forced on the government."

A CONTESTED DIVORCE

Lincoln's first inaugural address, March 4, 1861, delivered against the symbolic background of a nakedly unfinished capitol dome, bristled with memorable passages. Toward the seceding South the new President was both firm and conciliatory. He had no right or purpose to "interfere with the institution of slavery in the states where it exists." On the other hand, he would not tolerate secession, for "the union is much older than the Constitution," which was "perpetual." "The rule of a minority" would bring only "anarchy or despotism." As for a breakup of the union, "Physically speaking, we can not separate," for there were too many ancient ties. With regard to revolution, "This country, with its institutions, belongs to the people who inhabit it. Whenever they shall grow weary of the existing government, they can exercise their *constitutional* right of amending it or their *revolutionary* right to dismember or overthrow it."

Lincoln preferred amendment. But he did not add that only a successful revolution could establish revolutionary rights.

The final passages of the new President's address burned themselves into memory: "In *your* hands, my dissatisfied fellow countrymen, not in *mine,* is the momentous issue of civil war. The government will not assail *you.* You can have no conflict without being yourselves the aggressors. . . . We are not enemies, but friends. We must not be enemies."

Lincoln would neither surrender Fort Sumter nor strengthen its garrison. But he would take the middle road of provisioning it, and he so notified the Confederates. Unable to wring from him a satisfactory pledge of withdrawal, they brashly opened fire on the stronghold on April 12, 1861, and the next day forced the tiny garrison to surrender. With "Old Glory" thus desecrated, the North rose in righteous anger. "Glory to God," cried out one antislavery leader, and throughout the North one heard the cries "Remember Fort Sumter" and "Save the union." Letter envelopes depicted the old flag over Fort Sumter with the inscription "Our Flag shall wave and none other," and, referring to Jackson in 1833, "Fort Sumter as it was and shall be; By the Eternal!" One medal, bearing the likeness of Lincoln, echoed the popular sentiment "We Will Not Interfere with the Constitutional Rights of Any State—The Fall of Sumpter [*sic*] Will be Avenged and the Rebellion Crushed and the Honor and Integrity of the United States Shall be Maintained."

The seven original seceding states were gradually joined over a period of nearly two months by four reluctant sisters—Virginia, Arkansas, North Carolina, and Tennessee. A unionist element expressed dissent in all of them. In Raleigh, North Carolina, a song appeared entitled "North Carolina: A Call to Arms!!!" The first stanza urged:

> Ye sons of Carolina! awake from your dreaming!
> The Minions of Lincoln upon us are streaming!
> Oh! wait not for argument, call or persuasion,
> To meet at the outset this treach'rous invasion!

North Carolina heeded the call, as did foot-dragging Tennessee, and a full-fledged Confederacy presented its eleven-starred flag to the world.

Next to "Dixie," the most popular Southern song of the Civil War, entitled "The Bonnie Blue Flag," spells out how the one state of secession, South Carolina, became eleven states:

> We are a band of brothers, and native to the soil,
> Fighting for the property we gained by honest toil;
> And when our rights were threatened, the cry rose near and far,
> Hurrah for the Bonnie Blue Flag that bears a Single Star.

The last stanza triumphantly recounts:

> Then cheer, boys, cheer, raise the joyous shout,
> For Arkansas and North Carolina now have both gone out;

And let another rousing cheer for Tennessee be given—
The Single Star of the Bonnie Blue Flag has grown to be Eleven.

So it came to pass that the abscess of sectionalism burst and two nations, one destined to die in four years, grew where only one had grown before.

XI

The War
for the Union

Let us keep our eyes and our hearts steadily fixed
upon the old flag of our fathers. . . . It has a star for
every state. Let us resolve that there shall be a state
for every star!

Robert C. Winthrop, Boston speech, August 22, 1862

THE BATTLE CRY OF UNION

Whatever the real motives for secession, few observers can doubt the
determination of the Southerners under President Jefferson Davis to bring
forth on this continent a new nation, conceived in liberty (for whites)
and dedicated to the proposition that all men (except nonwhites) are
created equal. The Confederate States of America (C.S.A.) drew up a
constitution, established a government, elected a president, formed a
cabinet, assembled a Congress, and raised armies for the defense of what
they regarded as their rights. Above all these operations floated a new
flag, the Stars and Bars—condemned by loyal Northerners as "the rebel
rag."

In Yankeeland the supreme goal was the restoration and preservation
of the Union. Freeing the slaves gradually became an additional and
secondary aim that finally received Lincoln's official sanction late in 1862,
more than a year and a half after belching guns spoke the language of
secession at Fort Sumter. A flood of popular Northern slogans and songs
extolled the concept of union. Common catchwords were "Liberty and
Union," "Our Whole Nation," "Whole or None," and "For the Union
We'll Die." In a similar vein appeared "The Union Forever," "What God
Hath Joined Together Let No Man Put Asunder," and "So Let it be to
Tyrants Who Would Destroy our Union." Still other widely heralded war

cries were "United We Stand," "The Union: It Cannot be Improved," "The Union Must be Preserved," and "Unity of Government is the Main Pillar of Independence."

Enthusiasm for the Union was implicit in such slogans as "The Constitution of Our Fathers" and "We Are All Brothers under the Constitution." As a waving symbol of union, the Stars and Stripes received numerous sloganized tributes, such as "Our Union! Our Constitution! and our Flag!" and "One Flag for the Whole Country." Rebellion found no comfort in "We Must Keep All the Stars" and "One Flag and One Government." Some assertions were less specific in referring to the Union, such as "We'll Prove True to the Red, White, and Blue" and "Up, Up with the Flag, Let it Float o'er the Free." Similar injunctions appeared in "Stand by Your Flag," "Stand by the Red, White, and Blue," and "The Flag of Our Country: To be Defended at Home or Despised Abroad." Especially biting was "The Star-Spangled Banner Shall Ever Float Above the Filthy Rag of Disunion."

Confederate or pro-Southern war cries were imprinted on countless envelopes and broadsides, which showed pictures of the Confederate Stars and Bars with "We Will Defend It with Our Lives and Fortunes," "Despots Dread," and "The Flag of the Oppressed." Southern defiance found further outlet in "We are in the Field and the [Stars and Bars] are up" and "We Have Nailed our Colors to the Mast. The People Rule!"

TYRANTS VERSUS TRAITORS

Embattled Southerners believed that they had ratified the federal Constitution in 1787–1789 with the understanding that their rights as states would be reserved and preserved. Secessionists now felt that the North had breached this compact or contract, and that they had every right to withdraw peacefully, just as they had entered the Union peacefully. On the official shield of the Confederate government appeared this motto (in Latin): "No country, no fatherland that does not keep faith."

Quite realistically, the favorite name in the South for the Civil War was "The War between the States." "Southrons" naturally looked upon the "damn Yankees" as the aggressors; and one of the less common names they gave "The War between the States" was "The War of Yankee Aggression." In an early message to the Confederate Congress President Davis stated simply, "All we ask is to be let alone. . . ." Another name sometimes applied by rebels to the conflict, especially in later years, was "The War for Southern Independence." Less lofty in tone were "The Abe Lincoln War," "The Abolition War," "The War for the Blacks," and "The Nigger War."

Confederate concern over states' rights found expression in the watchword "Southern rights: Let Us Alone." Related appeals were "Right Must Prevail," "The South and Equal Rights," and "Southern Rights and Southern Institutions." Defiance shone through in "Stand Up for the Right,"

"Don't Tread on Us" (with the usual snake), and "Southern Rights will be Defended by Southern Men." Memories of the earlier and happier days in 1776 and 1798 were invoked by "Southern Independence: We Will Defend it with our Lives and Fortunes," "Millions for Defense," and "For Our Altars and Firesides."

Rights naturally involved honor, a subject on which Southerners were traditionally sensitive. Revealing slogans were "Death before Dishonor," "We Will Maintain Our Honour," and "Ever Ready with our Lives and Fortunes." Regard for "Southern Rights" and a belief that "Truth is Mighty" led to such statements of conviction as "Tyranny is Dead" and "Thus It Will Ever be with Tyrants." Confederates were also reminded of "The End of Black Republicanism" and of the alleged malevolence of Lincoln in such watchwords as "Let Lincoln Blush for Shame" and "No Quarter Given to Lincolnites." One finds defiance mixed with bitterness in "No Favors Asked of Ungrateful Yankee Scoundrels" and "Onward! [Yankee] Fratricides, Do Your Dirty Work!"

If Southerners thought they were resisting tyrants, Northerners were no less convinced that they were fighting traitors. On the imprinted envelopes of 1861 one can commonly find such sentiments as "The Day of Compromise with Treason Has Irrevocably Passed" and "Send It Abroad that the Loyal States Will Have No compromise with Traitors, Treason, or Treachery." More menacing were "Beware of Traitors," "Death to Treason and Traitors," and "Annihilation to Traitors."

One ingenious Yankee envelope displayed the picture of a rope, with the words "Good Noose [news] for Traitors." Another representation was a coiled rope in the form of a skull labeled a Jeff Davis "neck-tie." Anti-Confederate medals ominously showed President Davis dangling from the gallows and partially surrounded by the inscription "Victory to Union, Down with Treason and Rebellion; A Decisive War Can Only Restore Peace and Prosperity."

Oddly enough, the "traitors" and the "tyrants" were both fighting for liberty, for the secessionists were seeking liberty from Yankee oppression and the Yankees ultimately sought liberty for the oppressed slaves. One Northern broadside called for black volunteers with the appeal "Men of Color, to Arms!" Numerous envelopes carried "Liberty or Death" (with the U.S. flag), "Union and Liberty, Onward to Victory," and, with memories of Daniel Webster, "Liberty and Union! Now and Forever, One & Inseparable."

At a time when Robert E. Lee had seceded with his native Virginia, George Washington, another distinguished Virginian, was claimed by both sides. One Northern envelope presented a picture of the revered father of his country with the words "A Southern Man with Union Principles." No less aptly a Confederate envelope displayed a likeness of Washington with the reminder "One of the Rebels."

"Our cause is just" was a Northern slogan, but it could well have been voiced by a Southerner. Both sides prayed to the same God for victory, although one finds few Confederate references to divine providence in slogans. Northern envelopes carried such sentiments as "God Save the Union," "God and Our Native Land," "God and Our Country," and "God Bless our Country!"

AN UNCIVIL CIVIL WAR

The clash between the two sections was undeniably a civil war: Americans fought Americans and brothers fought brothers. "Johnny Reb" and "Billy Yank," as they familiarly called each other, dueled to the death. Thousands of Southern Unionists, especially the "mountain whites," refused to fight for their section. Many of them regarded the bloodbath as "the rich man's war but the poor man's fight." Seceding "Southrons" branded these dissenters "Yankee lovers," "traitors," and "Tories." In the North, Unionists who favored the South were likewise called "Tories." Among the most vehement Southern opponents of the Confederate cause was a Tennessee clergyman named W. G. Brownlow, who honestly earned the nickname "The Fighting Parson." To staunch Unionists of the North the secessionists of the South were "rebels" or even "traitors." A name commonly given to the Civil War at the time by Yankees was "The War of the Rebellion" or simply "The Rebellion."

Enthusiasm by the so-called "Union Savers" for preserving the Union at any price was far from unanimous in the North. Slaveholding continued in the critical border states of Missouri, Kentucky, and Maryland, where the owners naturally feared the loss of their valuable human cattle. Elsewhere many Northern citizens, especially Democrats, asked why the nation should be shedding buckets of blood over "a passel of niggers." Democrats who supported Lincoln's unionist efforts were called "War Democrats"; those who wished "the wayward sisters" to "depart in peace" were condemned as "Peace Democrats" or members of the "White Feather party."

Notorious among the Northern opponents of the war stood the "Copperheads," a numerous and noisy faction. Doubt enshrouds the origin of the name, but a probable source was the poisonous copperhead snake, which strikes treacherously without a warning rattle. The leading Copperhead organization in the Ohio Valley was the "Knights of the Golden Circle," which ironically grew out of a secret, semimilitary organization formed in Alabama in 1855. Opposed by the "Union League," this band was known as the "Order of American Knights" in 1863 and in 1864 as the "Sons of Liberty"—a throwback to Revolutionary days. The opposing Union League, loyal to the core, issued medals inscribed with such sentiments as "Avoid the Extremes of Party Spirit" (paraphrasing George Washington) and "Union League Death to Traitors."

Towering among the Copperheads stood Clement L. Vallandigham, whose followers were dubbed "Vallandighammers." Defying "King Lincoln," he was tried for his antiwar utterances, found guilty, and then

The Copperhead Party, in Favor of a Vigorous Prosecution of Peace. *Harper's Weekly*, 1863.

banished behind the Confederate lines. He worked his way back to the United States through Canada, and his bizarre career may have inspired Edward Everett Hale to write in 1863 his classic story "The Man without a Country"—in itself a virtual slogan. The fictional hero was a gallant young army officer named Philip Nolan who became involved in the Burr conspiracy in 1805. In the story Nolan, tried and found guilty by a court martial, impetuously cried out, "Damn the United States! I wish I may never hear of the United States again." The shocked court condemned him to spend the rest of his life—some fifty-eight years—on U.S. Navy ships, all the while being denied the privilege of seeing or hearing of his country. The sentimental tale was published in 1863, shortly after Nolan's supposed death, and made a profound impression. It inspired love for the Union in the North, and it has lived in prose and on the screen to the present day.

In addition to the vexatious Vallandigham, numerous Copperheads were arrested, imprisoned, or suppressed by the Lincoln administration under a strained interpretation of the war powers conferred by the Constitution. Not surprisingly, a favorite slogan with the "Vallandighammers" was "The Constitution as it is and the Union as it was." Copperheads also ascribed to the Lincoln Republicans the savage sentiment "War to the Knife and the Knife to the Hilt."

Also rocking the Northern boat were the extreme abolitionists, many of them Republicans. Their leading spokesman was William Lloyd Garrison, "The Massachusetts Mad Man." Demanding disunion and hence supporting secession, these militant antislaveryites had already raised the war cry, "No Union with Slaveholders." By constantly clamoring for the emancipation of all slaves, such "Union haters" proved to be a source of great vexation to President Lincoln, especially when he was desperately trying to persuade the slaveholding Border States to remain in the Union. When these waverers were more secure in late 1862 Lincoln came out foursquare for the abolition of slavery in the states that had seceded—but not in the Border States.

GRAFTED INTO THE ARMY

As for the fighting front, Southern men were in some respects better material for soldiering than their Yankee brothers because they were more accustomed to using firearms and handling horses. Superb cavalry leaders emerged on the Confederate side, including J. E. B. Stuart and Nathan Bedford Forrest, who reportedly gave as his formula for success "I git thar fustest with the mostest men."* The Northern boys evidently had less faith in their own cavalry, to which they often shouted, "Dismount and grab a root," meaning "do your part." The "rebels" not only fought with great dash but exaggerated their ferocity with the famous "rebel yell." It was supposed to implant fear in the hearts of the green Yankee recruits, who were sneered at in Southern circles as "fresh fish," "clod-hoppers," and "shopkeepers."

Both sides relied solely on volunteers at first but ultimately supplemented such enlistments with conscription. The South, handicapped by a smaller pool of manpower, resorted to the draft first, in 1862. Exemptions were granted to men involved in essential industries, and this practice led to the "Fifteen Nigger Law," which excused from military service overseers or plantation owners with fifteen or more slaves under their jurisdiction. As a result, bitterness festered in the South over "the rich man's war but the poor man's fight." Those young conscripts who were "grafted" into the army, as the saying went, represented a robbing of both "the cradle and the grave."

Yankee conscription arrived in 1863 and likewise involved inequities. The most notorious loophole enabled the draftee to hire a substitute for $300 to go in his place—"the $300 men." Moneyless victims of the draft complained that it demanded, "$300 or your life." Inevitably the procurement of such substitutes fell into the hands of "bounty brokers" or "substitute brokers," who charged a commission for this service. The "bounty boys" proved to be a slippery lot. Many would pocket their $300, desert from the army, and repeat the process as "bounty jumpers" under different names. One enterprising substitute reportedly "jumped" thirty-two times.

But would-be draft evaders did not always succeed. The last stanza of

---

* This colloquial statement indicates an illiterate man, which Forrest was not.

a Northern song, "Come in out of the Draft," related the sad plight of one reluctant hero:

> I've tried to get a wife, I've tried to get a "sub,"
> But what I next shall do now, really, is the "rub."
> My money's almost gone, and I am nearly daft;
> Will some one tell me what to do to get out of the draft.

Even those lucky enough to hire a substitute were supposed to be suffering from uneasy consciences. A satirical song made this point:

> How are you Conscript, you thought it mighty clever,
> To pay three hundred dollars, and to go to war no never.

FILLING THE RANKS

Fierce opposition to the draft in the North resulted in an outburst of mobbings, burnings, and lynchings, principally in New York City, July 13–16, 1863, ten days after the Battle of Gettysburg. About a thousand persons were injured or killed. The victims of mob wrath were principally Negroes ("Nagurs") and Irishmen—the Negroes because they were thought to have caused the war, and the Irish because they were allegedly dodging the draft. Frenzied demonstrators shouted, "Down with Lincoln" and "Down with the draft," for they too were convinced that this was a rich man's war but a poor man's fight.

Despite the grimness of the subject, Henry Clay Work, who later wrote the rollicking "Marching through Georgia," published a popular song (1862) entitled "Grafted into the Army," which featured amusing Irish dialect. The first stanza and chorus follow:

> Our Jimmy has gone for to live in a tent,
> They have grafted him into the army;
> He finally pucker'd up courage and went,
> When they grafted him into the army.
> I told them the child was too young, alas!
> At the captain's forequarters they said he would pass.
> They'd train him up well in the infantry class,
> So they grafted him into the army.
> *Chorus:*
> O Jimmy, farewell! your brothers fell
> Way down in Alabarmy;
> I tho't they would spare a lone widder's heir,
> But they grafted him into the army.

Depressing antidraft songs in the North were offset by inspirational calls to duty, including "I Want to Be a Soldier":

> I want to be a soldier
>   And go to Dixie's Land,

> A knapsack on my shoulder
> And a gun in my hand.

Loyal Confederates naturally resented the North's enlisting of pro-Union Southerners ("Tories") and foreign dregs. Indignation shone through in "The Stars and Bars," sung to the tune of "The Star Spangled Banner":

> Oh! say has the star-spangled banner become
> The flag of the Tory and vile Northern Scum?

Southerners especially deplored the successful attempts of the North to arm ex-slaves against their former masters. All told, about 180,000 blacks served under Union colors and rendered valuable service. One song ("The Patriotic Contraband") written in Negro dialect by a man supposedly black, offered this chorus:

> O darkies, I'se a gwine
> To make de cannon roar,
> O come and jine de Union army,
> And end dis cruel war.

A folk song among Negroes during the war reflected a common sentiment:

> If de Debble do not ketch
> Jeff Davis, dat infernal wretch,
> An' roast and frigazee dat rebble,
> What is de use of any Debble?

Noteworthy among the black volunteers was the Massachusetts 54th infantry, commanded by a youthful white officer, Colonel Robert Gould Shaw. Leading his men against murderous Confederate fire at Fort Wagner, Charleston Harbor, he cried, "We shall take the fort or die there. Forward, fifty-fourth." He died there, together with many of his men. He failed to attain his objective but he gave to the North and the blacks an inspiring example of gallantry.

Yankee recruiters, not content with a heavy manpower advantage over the South, induced tens of thousands of Irish and German immigrants to enlist, often with generous outpourings of whiskey plus attractive monetary bounties. The "bounty brokers" even went abroad for their prey. Southerners regarded this practice as unfair, and they often referred to such foreign-born enlistees, whether naturalized Americans or not, as "vassals," "Hessians," "Hessians of the North," or "Hessian Yankees." Once more German "mercenaries" were fighting on American soil to crush American liberties, as the hired Hessians had done during the Revolutionary War. Entire regiments in the Northern armies were manned solely by Germans, whose German-speaking officers issued commands in their native tongue. Perhaps the ablest of these leaders was General Franz Sigel. A common expression of pride by German-American soldiers in the Union army was "I fights mit Sigel," and a popular song bore the title

"I'm Going to Fight Mit Sigel." General Carl Schurz, a prominent expatriate from Germany, suffered a sharp reverse in battle that was not entirely his fault, and the saying took root, "I fights mit Sigel and I runs mit Schurz."

A CIVILIAN COMMANDER

President Lincoln, though self-trained as a lawyer, held the constitutional rank of commander-in-chief of the Northern armies. He had no experience with military affairs, except for a few weeks of service in the Black Hawk Indian war, fought in Illinois and Wisconsin in 1832. But he learned a good deal about overall strategy as he patiently experimented with one incompetent commander after another, until at long last he found General Grant. Among Union soldiers and Republican supporters Lincoln was rather affectionately known as "Old Abe" or "Uncle Abe" and, after late 1862, as "The Great Emancipator." In July 1862 Lincoln issued a call for 300,000 more volunteers, and a rousing marching song, "We Are Coming, Father Abra'am," flowed from the pen of a Quaker abolitionist, James S. Gibbons:

> We are coming, father Abra'am, three hundred thousand more,
> From Mississippi's winding stream and from New England's shore,
> We leave our plows and work shops, our wives and children dear,
> With hearts too full for utterance, with but a silent tear.

The chorus sounded forth:

> We are coming, we are coming,
> Our Union to restore;
> We are coming, Father Abra'am,
> With three hundred thousand more.

A jeering Southern parody had the Negroes singing:

> We're coming Fodder Abrahan,
> To do, de best we can
> To make de Nigger just as good
> As any odder man.

"Father Abraham" was an appellation that gained great currency in the North. Southerners used less flattering terms to describe Lincoln, as did many antiwar Democrats and Copperheads. They employed such pejoratives as "Caesar," "Blackguard," "Buffoon," "Illinois Baboon," "Jester," "Sectional President," and "Simple Susan Tyrant." Lincoln's high-strung wife was branded "The She-Wolf." One venomous critic of Lincoln, evidently a Copperhead, responded to the "Father Abraham" appeal with "The Serenade of the 300,000 Federal Ghosts," which was "respectfully dedicated to Old Black Abe."

One of the many ironies of this desperate conflict is that Lincoln informally offered the principal command of the Union armies to Robert E. Lee, then a colonel in the United States Army. If Lee had accepted, the war probably would have been shorter. But the courtly "Marse Robert," torn by conflicting loyalties, finally decided to go with his native Virginia. As he said when resigning his commission in the United States Army after the firing on Fort Sumter, "I have been unable to make up my mind to raise my hand against my native state, my relatives, my children, and my home." His residence was the stately mansion that overlooks the Potomac River and the present national cemetery at Arlington, Virginia. Beneath his bust in the Hall of Fame in New York are inscribed these words: "Duty is the sublimest word in our language. Do your duty in all things. You cannot do more. You should never wish to do less."

After the war, fortunately for the South, General Lee deemed it his duty to drink with good grace from the bitter cup of defeat. In him his Southern countrymen found the embodiment of their noblest ideals.

XII

War Becomes Hell

There is many a boy here today who looks on war
as all glory, but, boys, it is all hell. You can bear this
warning voice to generations yet to come. I look upon
war with horror.

General William T. Sherman's speech
to war veterans, 1880

THE RUNNERS OF BULL RUN

A common delusion at the beginning of great wars is that the fighting
will end before the leaves fall—or at least before Christmas. After the surrender of Fort Sumter a popular slogan ran, "Let it be short, sharp, and
decisive." General Winfield Scott, the hero of two wars and then the foremost commander, had different expectations. He predicted that the North
would need about three years (it required four), as well as a huge army
and navy that could encircle and crush the South like a giant anaconda
snake. Armchair strategists, some of them newspaper editors, had great
fun deriding "Scott's anaconda." They laughed off the famous general as
an old fogey who was suffering from senility brought on by his seventy-
five years.

An ill-trained army of some 30,000 Union recruits gradually assembled
near Washington under General Irvin McDowell. Impatient newspaper
editors, as well as other self-commissioned generals, raised the cries "On
to Richmond" and "Forward to Richmond." In lower key, some Confederates responded with "On to Washington." Public pressures in the North
became so great that the raw recruits were ordered to push ahead in
what turned out to be a disorganized military picnic.

Advancing Union troops encountered a smaller Confederate force at
Manassas Junction, better known as Bull Run, on July 21, 1861. In the

early phases of this furious battle the Union forces were making some progress, but were checked when General Thomas J. Jackson and his force held firm. The Confederate General Bee rallied his troops with the cry "There is Jackson, standing like a stone wall," or words to that effect. Curiously, the most mobile of the Confederate infantry generals, whose "foot cavalry" became a legend, was thus tagged with the nickname "Stonewall."

As the humid afternoon of Bull Run lengthened, the Yankees inexplicably panicked and fled in wild disorder toward the capital. Fortunately for the North, the Confederates were too exhausted to follow up their advantage. Many of them left for home with their trophies, thinking that the war was over and joking that the Yankees had replaced "On to Richmond" with "Off for Washington." Slogans used both earlier and later in the North gained greater relevance: "The Capital is in Danger" and "Save the Capital." Such fears were expanded to "Drill and Organize," while some citizens anticipated a sentiment expressed widely later in the year, "Down with Lincoln."

Bull Run inspired a boastful, morale-building Southern folk song by that name. New lines were obviously added to it by the year:

> In eighteen hundred and sixty-one
> We whipped the Yankees at old Bull Run.
>
> .   .   .
>
> In eighteen hundred and sixty-two
> The rebels put the Yankees through.
>
> .   .   .
>
> In eighteen hundred and sixty-three,
> You ought to see them Yankees flee.
>
> .   .   .
>
> In eighteen hundred and sixty-four,
> The Yankees cried, "We want no more."
>
> .   .   .
>
> In eighteen hundred and sixty-five,
> We all thanked God that we were alive.

"TARDY GEORGE" McCLELLAN

Active command of the principal Union army defending Washington, the Army of the Potomac, fell to one of the most controversial generals of the war, George B. McClellan. Only thirty-five years of age and relatively short, like Napoleon, this stocky graduate of West Point had served in the Mexican War and had observed the Crimean War in Russia at close hand. Early in the Civil War he had gained some modest success against Confederate forces in West Virginia, and with it came the sobriquet

"Young Napoleon." Yellowing envelopes of the time bear the inscriptions "Maj. Gen'l McClellan: Our Napoleon," "McClellan: The Napoleon of America," and "The Liberator of West Virginia." Confederates called him "The Bag of Wind."

Arrogance and pride were serious defects in McClellan's character; he privately referred to Lincoln, as did many other Democrats, as "the baboon." His fatal weakness as a commander was excessive caution. He seemed not to realize that no army is ever ready to march with every button in place, and that battles between evenly matched forces are not won without taking some risks. Yet he was a master organizer and drill master: the Army of the Potomac under him and a succession of other generals suffered an incredible series of beatings and still maintained high morale. His men idolized "Little Mac," partly because he did not regard them as completely expendable in rash assaults.

Yet the Army of the Potomac was designed to fight, not drill. Lincoln tried to prod McClellan into movement but concluded that he had "the slows." The President, in a rare display of sarcasm, even went so far as to suggest that he would "borrow" McClellan's army if the general himself was not going to use it. Cynics sneered at McClellan's "masterly inactivity," and critics jeered at "Mac the Unready" and "The Little Corporal of Unfought Fields." (Napoleon was known as "The Little Corporal.") Popular songs vented Northern impatience, including the sardonic "Tardy George":

> What are you waiting for, George, I pray?
> To scour your cross-belts with fresh pipe-clay?
> To burnish your buttons, to brighten your guns;
> Or wait you for May-day and warm spring suns?

On a more somber note was the song "All Quiet along the Potomac," which began with appealing pathos:

> "All quiet along the Potomac," they say,
> "Except now and then a stray picket
> Is shot, as he walks on his beat, to and fro,
> By a rifleman hid in the thicket.
> 'Tis nothing: a private or two now and then
> Will not count in news of the battle;
> Not an officer lost, only one of the men
> Moaning out all alone the death-rattle."

In March 1862 McClellan was finally prodded into an advance on Richmond, a roundabout movement from Chesapeake Bay between the York and James rivers. This ultracautious advance enabled General Lee to strengthen his defenses, while "Stonewall" Jackson and his "foot cavalry" created alarming diversions on the flank of the Washington defenses. After a series of bloody battles, McClellan retraced his steps and achieved the near miracle of extricating his badly mauled army. His rear had almost been cut off by the improvised Confederate ironclad *Merri-*

mack, which, fortunately for him, was halted in a drawn battle with the pioneer Yankee ironclad *Monitor.* A queer-looking craft with a single revolving turret, it was dubbed by Confederates the "Yankee Cheese-box on a Raft."

FROM NEW ORLEANS TO ANTIETAM

McClellan's failure in the spring of 1862 was partially offset by the concurrent capture of New Orleans, "Queen of the South," by a Union naval force under David Farragut. The loss of this key city, which commanded the mouth of the Mississippi, came as a staggering blow to the Confederacy. General Benjamin Franklin Butler, subsequently branded "Beast Butler," was outraged by the behavior of the spirited Southern ladies, who spat upon or otherwise expressed contempt for the occupying Yankee officers. He responded by issuing an internationally infamous order in which he declared that "hereafter when any female shall, by word, gesture, or movement, insult or show contempt for any officer or soldier of the United States, she shall be regarded and held liable to be treated as a woman of the town plying her avocation."

Butler's order seemed like an invitation to rape, or at least to imprison respectable ladies with prostitutes. He was denounced as a fiend in the Confederacy and in British official circles. What he had in mind, so he later wrote, was that the spitting females were to be regarded as prostitutes—that is, ignored. His order, despite the uproar, worked like a charm. The ladies did not want to be thought prostitutes (any more than the prostitutes wanted to be regarded as ladies, at least when plying their trade).

Following McClellan's spectacular failure, the main Northern army defending Washington was placed under General John Pope, who had fought with some success in the Missouri-Arkansas theater. He issued an order tactlessly stating, "I have come to you from the West where we have always seen the backs of our enemies. . . ." He was quoted as having added that "henceforth my headquarters will be in the saddle," thus inspiring a ribald joke about a more fitting place for his hindquarters. At all events, he got a front view of Lee's army at the Second Battle of Bull Run in August 1862, where he suffered a crushing defeat. The discredited General McClellan, whom Lee had never conquered, now looked much better. He was reinstated, as popular support for him found expression in song:

> Give us Back Little Mac
> Our Old Commander.

McClellan's men cheered, tossed their caps, and hugged his horse as he again took command.

General Lee now launched a bold and climactic invasion of Maryland. This slaveholding border state was thought to be needing only a push to go over the edge of secession, and the invading Confederates sang, seductively and hopefully, "Maryland, My Maryland," a song written the previous year by James R. Randall, a professor of English literature in Louisiana. The final stanza ran:

> I hear the distant thunder-hum,
>   Maryland!
> The "Old Line's" bugle, fife, and drum,
>   Maryland!
> She is not dead, nor deaf, nor dumb;
> Huzza! she spurns the Northern scum—
>   She'll come!
> Maryland, my Maryland!

But she did not come. The Marylanders, noting the shabby uniforms and worn-out shoes of the invading men in gray, had sober second thoughts, whatever their hearts may have told them.

General Lee's daring invaders occupied the Maryland town of Frederick, thus providing inspiration for a famous poem, "Barbara Frietchie," published in 1864 by the abolitionist poet John G. Whittier. The ninety-six-year-old heroine defiantly waved from her window a tattered Union flag which Confederate bullets had just riddled.

> "Shoot, if you must, this old gray head,
> But spare your country's flag," she said.

General "Stonewall" Jackson gallantly countermanded the order to fire by shouting:

> "Who touches a hair of yon gray head
> Dies like a dog! March on!" he said.

Brave old Barbara Frietchie's heroics were evidently a creation of the poet's imagination, and the incident may never have happened to any other woman. But the poem is a fact, and it undoubtedly did something to promote the ideal of union. Certainly it aroused patriotic sentiments in the hearts of countless school children for decades after the war.

EMANCIPATION BY PROCLAMATION

Gray-clad Confederates invading Maryland finally clashed with the reinstated General McClellan at Antietam Creek, where occurred one of the most decisive indecisive battles in history. Militarily the bloody engagement was essentially a draw, but in the aftermath Lee abandoned his offensive and retired across the Potomac River. "Tardy George" McClellan, as usual, failed to follow up his slight advantage, and this time Lincoln removed him permanently from command. But the inconclusive battle proved to be of immense significance. It cooled off a serious proposal then before the British government to intervene in some fashion, and such intervention might have meant war with Great Britain. Antietam also proved to be the springboard "victory" that Lincoln needed for issuing his preliminary Emancipation Proclamation.

From the outset of the shooting, the abolitionists in the North had clamored for the prompt emancipation of all slaves. These zealots naturally included those blacks enslaved in the teetering border states, which had to be kept in the Union at all costs. But Lincoln wisely bided his time, while extreme abolitionists like Wendell Phillips denounced him as a "first-rate-second-rate man." The President had hoped to issue his Emancipation Proclamation some time in 1862, but these were dreary months of defeat and retreat. Southerners and foreigners alike would have regarded such a manifesto as a confession of weakness—as a last-ditch attempt to stir up a slave insurrection behind enemy lines. Secretary of State Seward criticized such a premature pronouncement as "the last shriek upon the retreat."

Late in August 1862, the month before bloody Antietam, the influential Horace Greeley of the New York *Tribune* publicly addressed to Lincoln "The Prayer of Twenty Millions." Arrogantly presuming to speak for that many people, he demanded that the President definitely commit the

Abe Lincoln's Last Card: or, Rouge-et-Noir. The London *Punch*, 1862, regards the preliminary Emancipation Proclamation as an act of desperation. Jefferson Davis watches smugly while Lincoln plays his ace of spades (note Negro face on card) in the game of rouge-et-noir (red and black).

nation to emancipation. Lincoln's reply was patient but pointed. He wrote in part, "If I could save the Union without freeing any slave, I would do it; and if I could save it by freeing all the slaves, I would do it; and if I could do it by freeing some and leaving others alone, I would also do that."

On September 23, 1862, only six days after the hard-fought Battle of Antietam, Lincoln issued his preliminary Emancipation Proclamation. In it he promised that on January 1 of the next year he would promulgate the final Emancipation Proclamation, and he kept his word when he declared "henceforward" and "forever free" all slaves then held within *enemy* jurisdiction. But he plainly excluded some 800,000 slaves held in the loyal border states. Where his authority ran, he realistically declined to emancipate; where it did not run, he decreed emancipation. In short, where he could, he would not, and where he would, he could not. Technically, the Emancipation Proclamation emancipated nobody, if we except those footloose blacks who engaged in self-emancipation by fleeing to the advancing Northern armies. Complete emancipation was not legally established until the Thirteenth Amendment was ratified in 1865.

Despite being less than a half loaf, the Emancipation Proclamation was greeted with cries of delight by many Northerners. They would be carrying a more exalted moral banner if they could be avowedly fighting for human freedom, as well as for the abstract ideal of union. "God bless Abraham Lincoln!" rejoiced the once critical editor Horace Greeley. A song emerged in the North:

> And of all the Generals, high or low, that help to save the nation,
> There's none that strikes a harder blow than *General Emancipation!*

But the extreme abolitionists were acutely unhappy because Lincoln had not gone "the whole hog," while Northern Democrats drank the toast:

> Damn the goose
> Which grew the quill
> That wrote the Proclamation
> Of Emancipation.

A broadside of the period even raised doubts as to "Honest Abe's" honesty:

> Honest old Abe, when the war first began,
> Denied abolition was part of his plan;
> Honest old Abe has since made a decree,
> The war must go on till the slaves are all free.
> As both can't be honest, will someone tell how,
> If honest Abe then, is he honest Abe now?

Many an enlistee in the Northern armies, having volunteered to fight for the Union, was dismayed, as he put it, to have to sacrifice his life for a "passel of niggers." The desertion rate increased sharply.

Southern bitterness mounted, as could be expected, against this attempt by the Yankee President to stir up the "hellish passions" of a slave
insurrection. Unable to defeat the Confederates honorably with the
sword, he was resorting instead to a diabolical pen. Lincoln, "The Illinois
Ape," suddenly became "Lincoln the Fiend" in the eyes of many Southerners.

"UNCONDITIONAL SURRENDER" GRANT

Scrubby-appearing General Ulysses S. Grant provides one of the most
incredible success stories in the nation's history. A West Pointer who had
served in the Mexican War, he had subsequently suffered so acutely from
boredom and loneliness at remote army posts as to drink himself out of
the army. After failing in business, he was working in his father's leather
store in Galena, Illinois, when the Civil War erupted. Grant's association
with the leather industry subsequently earned for him the nicknames
"Galena Tanner," "The Tanner's Son," "The Fighting Tanner," and the
"Tanner President."

Trained officers were in short supply when the guns first boomed, and
after Grant applied for a commission he ultimately received a colonelcy.
From there on, his rise to the top was rapid. After some sharp fighting,
he forced the surrender of Fort Henry and Fort Donelson, which commanded the Tennessee and Cumberland rivers, respectively. The Confederate commander at Fort Donelson, General S. B. Buckner, asked for
terms of surrender. Grant's immortal reply was "No terms except an unconditional and immediate surrender can be accepted. I propose to move
immediately upon your works." General Buckner, a West Point classmate
from whom Grant had earlier borrowed money, thought the terms un-
generous, but he was forced to accept them. The phrase "unconditional
surrender" caught the popular fancy in the North and lived on to figure
conspicuously under Franklin Roosevelt in World War II.

U. S. Grant's initials lent themselves to all kinds of nicknames and
catchwords, most of which helped the general's image. Many Northerners
thought that U. S. providentially denoted United States, rather than
Ulysses Simpson. Others suggested that the initials should stand for
"Uncle Sam," "Unconditional Surrender," "Union Safeguard," "Unprecedented Strategist," or "Unquestionably Skilled." But the name Ulysses on
unfriendly tongues became "Useless."

Yesterday's "Hero of Fort Donelson" became less heroic at the bloody
two-day Battle of Shiloh, in Tennessee, where he was caught by surprise
and almost wiped out April 6 and 7, 1862. Yet Lincoln, perhaps thinking
of McClellan, stuck by Grant, writing, "I can't spare this man, he fights."
Then and later rumormongers spread stories about Grant's drinking
problem, but the record does not show that his private habits ever seriously interfered with his military operations. When tale bearers came to
Lincoln to say that Grant consumed too much whiskey, the President

supposedly replied, "Get me the brand, and I'll send a barrel to my other generals."

Grant's next campaign, generally regarded as the most brilliant of his career, was directed against the Confederate bastion at Vicksburg, Mississippi. New Orleans had already fallen to the Yankees in 1862, and Vicksburg was the most important Southern outpost still holding on to the Mississippi River. Responding to the popular cries "On to Vicksburg" and "Vicksburg must be taken," Grant forced the fortress to surrender despite the heavy odds against him. Four days later, after Port Hudson in Louisiana fell, Lincoln wrote quaintly, "The Father of Waters again goes unvexed to the sea."

"Bulldog" Grant was next transferred to the East Tennessee theater, where his troops won several desperate engagements near Chattanooga late in 1863. Most spectacular was the victory at Lookout Mountain in "The Battle above the Clouds." In the fighting at Chickamauga Creek, General George H. Thomas, a Virginia-born Union soldier, stood firm against violent Confederate assaults and fully earned the sobriquet "The Rock of Chickamauga." Retiring unmolested to nearby Chattanooga, his men were reduced to half rations of hard bread and beef "dried on the hoof"—that is, half starved cattle. In response to a telegram from Grant that the town had to be held "at all hazards," "Old Reliable" Thomas sent the heartening reply, "We will hold the town till we starve." He did hold it and he did not starve.

THE ROAD TO GETTYSBURG

Massive Yankee forces protecting Washington had meanwhile suffered a dreary series of defeats. In December 1862, at Fredericksburg, Virginia, the replacement for McClellan, General Ambrose E. Burnside, frontally assaulted Lee, then in an impregnable position. Union losses were so heavy that the gory field was dubbed "Burnside's slaughter pen." To an associate, a saddened General Lee is said to have remarked, "It is well that war is so terrible—we should grow too fond of it." Some six months later, at the Battle of Gettysburg, Yankee troops used the single word "Fredericksburg" as a vengeful rallying cry.

General Burnside, after thus failing dismally, was replaced by "Fighting Joe" Hooker, whom Lincoln suspected of having dictatorial ambitions. The President wrote a curious letter warning him, "Only those generals who gain successes can set up dictators. What I now ask of you is military success, and I will risk dictatorship." Hooker, dazed by a near hit from a cannon ball, suffered a crushing defeat at Chancellorsville (May 2–4, 1863). General Lee's victory was dearly bought, because in the gathering darkness of the first day, "Stonewall" Jackson was mistakenly shot to death by his own men. "I have lost my right arm," lamented a saddened Lee. During the second and third days of the same battle aroused Confederate troops cried, "Charge!" and "Remember Jackson!" Southern folklore relates that when the daring general reached heaven he outflanked the angels.

In the early summer of 1863, General Lee seized the offensive with a thrust to the north, partly designed to stimulate the "peace Democrats" and encourage foreign intervention. The Confederate invaders and the Union defenders, under General George Meade, clashed in the titanic three-day Battle of Gettysburg, in Pennsylvania, July 1–3, 1863. On the second day the gunners of the First Pennsylvania Light Artillery, fighting hand to hand with pikes, pistols, and cannon rammers, rallied to the cry "Death rather than surrender our guns on our own soil."

At a critical moment on the third day, General George E. Pickett with his massed Virginians received orders to make what became a suicidal frontal assault across an open field in the teeth of murderous fire. Pickett's command at the beginning of the charge was "Up, men, and to your posts! Don't forget today that you are from Old Virginia." The desperate attack was narrowly driven back, and a worsted Lee retired from the gory field of Gettysburg across the Potomac. In the West, Vicksburg surrendered the day after the battle, and the Confederacy was doomed to the slow death of a cut flower.

Late that gloomy autumn of 1863, while the graves were still fresh, Lincoln journeyed to Gettysburg to dedicate the cemetery on the field where some 7,000 men, both Union and Confederate, had died. His two-minute speech, which followed a two-hour effort by the orator of the day, ended before the standing crowd had completely settled down.

Lincoln began by recalling that the Founding Fathers had created "a new nation, conceived in liberty and dedicated to the proposition that all men are created equal." He here expressed a theoretical truth that was not in fact honored by the Founding Fathers; otherwise there probably would have been no quarrel over slavery to trigger the Civil War. Lincoln concluded his brief remarks by expressing the hope that from this terrible conflict the nation would experience a "new birth of freedom, and that government of the people, by the people, for the people, shall not perish from the earth."

Lincoln's soaring conclusion, be it noted, was not altogether original with him. In years past various public figures had expressed the same thought in almost the same phrases. But nothing could have been more appropriate, in time and place, than the classic combination of words and ideas known as Lincoln's Gettysburg Address.

Lincoln himself felt that his remarks had fallen flat. A few newspaper men recognized the merit of the address, but unfriendly Copperhead journalists and others branded it as "dishwatery" and "ludicrous," or sneered at his "silly remarks" and "exceeding bad taste." One commentator thought that "Lincoln acted the clown," and another complained of the "sallies" that were "dull and commonplace." Only with the passage of time did critics fully appreciate the beauty of this magnificent psalm to democracy.

SHERMAN THE BRUTE

After hard-driving General Grant had assumed the chief field command in the East, the main Union force that had invaded Tennessee was turned over to red-bearded General William Tecumseh Sherman, better known to many of his soldiers as "Old Tecumseh." Early in his career he had won the reputation of being dangerously erratic, and he was later quoted as saying, "Grant stood by me when I was crazy, and I stood by him when he was drunk, and now we stand by each other."

Pushing southeastward into Georgia, the invading Yankees fought a bitter but losing battle at Kennesaw Mountain. At one critical point Sherman sent to a hard-pressed subordinate a message which was later slightly changed to read, "Hold the fort, for I am coming!" (These timely words of encouragement became the title of a popular gospel hymn in 1870.)

Sherman next plunged deeper into Georgia, thus responding to Northern cries of "On to Atlanta" and "Delenda est Atlanta" (Atlanta must be destroyed). After fierce fighting, he captured the city amid fearful scenes of destruction and then telegraphed Lincoln, "Atlanta is ours and fairly won."

Stony-hearted General Sherman had earlier lived in the South and was on friendly terms with many Southerners. As the reverse of Lee, he had been offered a high command in the Confederate armies early in the war, but had decided to go with the Union. He firmly believed that the essence of war is violence and that a merciful general should end the misery of combat quickly by ruthless means, not exempting private property. After the fighting had ended, he was quoted as saying in public "War is hell," and he certainly practiced what he preached as an early devotee of total war.

Sherman's iron-toothed philosophy was to "make Georgia howl," humble Southern pride, and bring back the Confederates from the fighting front to protect their homes. "Fear," he later said, "is the beginning of wisdom." With such aims in view, he daringly severed himself from his base of supplies and cut a sixty-mile-wide swath of destruction for some 300 miles in his famous "March to the Sea," all the way from Atlanta to the Atlantic seaport of Savannah. Yankee invaders burned homes, leaving only the brick chimneys—"Sherman's Sentinels." They tore up the iron rails of the railroads, heated them red hot in bonfires, and then twisted them into "Sherman's hairpins" or "Jeff Davis neckties," thus ensuring that they would never be laid again. Reaching Savannah on December 22, 1864, Sherman sent an encouraging dispatch to President Lincoln: "I beg to present you as a Christmas gift the city of Savannah."

Much of the damage done by Sherman's "Blue Bellies" was inflicted by an unsavory crowd of stragglers and looters known as "bummers," black and white, who accompanied the army. A curious atmosphere of vengefulness and revelry prevailed, as if the invading soldiers were off on a prolonged holiday picnic. Henry Clay Work, a Connecticut Yankee, caught the spirit in his rousing song "Marching through Georgia," which quickly became immensely popular in the North but extremely unpopular in the South, especially Georgia:

> Bring the good old bugle, boys, we'll sing another song,
> Sing it with a spirit that will start the world along,
> Sing it as we used to sing it fifty thousand strong,
>   While we were marching through Georgia.
> Hurrah! hurrah! We bring the jubilee!
> Hurrah! hurrah! The flag that makes you free!
> So we sang the chorus from Atlanta to the sea,
>   While we were marching through Georgia!

The sprightly song then recounted how the "darkies shouted" joyful greetings to "Sherman's dashing Yankee Boys," how the turkeys and sweet potatoes gladly readied themselves for eating, how Southern Unionists wept and cheered as they "saw the honored flag they had not seen for years," how the "saucy rebels" had boasted that Sherman would "never reach the coast," and how "treason fled before us, for resistance was in vain."

"Sherman the Brute," as he was branded in the South, next pushed north into South Carolina and North Carolina, where mounting resistance halted him. The invading Yankees vented their bitterness in South Carolina, "The Cradle of Secession." Its capital city Columbia, known to the Union troops as the "hell-hole of secession," caught fire and burned. Probably the Yankee invaders applied the torch, although responsibility for the great conflagration cannot be firmly established.

THE DECISION AT APPOMATTOX COURTHOUSE

After cautious General Meade failed to pursue Lee following the Confederate defeat at Gettysburg, General Grant was brought in from the Tennessee theater to take command of the main army in the Virginia area. Lincoln at last had found a general who could do the job, a commander whose basic strategy was to keep moving, pressing, fighting. Grant's personal motto was "When in doubt, fight." President Lincoln sent him a telegram in August 1864: "Hold on with a bulldog grip, and chew and choke as much as possible."

Grant mercilessly fought a war of attrition. Realizing that his manpower pool was much larger than Lee's, he reasoned that he could lose men on a two-to-one basis and still come out ahead. In the major concluding campaigns in Virginia, Grant's men suffered some 50,000 casualties, or about as many men as Lee commanded at the beginning of this offensive. Shocked critics assailed "Grant the Butcher," and some people concluded that he had gone mad. Yet Grant reported to Washington, "I propose to fight it out on this line if it takes all summer." The crushing of Lee took not just all summer, but all autumn, all winter, and a part of the spring of 1865.

In the bleak February of 1865, much too late in the game, the desperate Confederates took steps to induct slaves into their armies. The adverse reaction in the North was predictable, and the song "Jeff Davis on Arming the Nigger" emerged:

> But Jeff, you must go to the regions below,
>   Our country you never can sever;
> And the blood you have shed shall be on your vile head,
>   And damn you forever and ever!

A retreating Lee was finally cornered at Appomattox Court House in Virginia on April 9, 1865. Stubble-bearded Grant offered the courtly Lee generous terms of surrender, including the right of his men to retain their horses for spring plowing. "Lee's Ragamuffins" wept. The Yankee soldiers began to cheer, but the victorious Grant reportedly checked them with the curt words, "The war is over; the rebels are our countrymen again." Regrettably, this noble sentiment was not shared by all Northerners in the troubled years that lay ahead.

XIII

Behind
the Lines

I do not allow myself to suppose that . . . I am
either the greatest or best man in America, but . . .
that it is not best to swap horses while crossing the
river. . . .

President Lincoln, June 9, 1864

RIVAL SONGSMITHS

A hoary saying, fully applicable to the Civil War, assures us that God is
always on the side of the big battalions. He also seems to be on the side
of the bigger populations, smokestacks, banks, ships, and railroads. He
likewise appears to favor the adversary that produces the best songs—at
least this was evidently true during the Civil War. Fate was so unkind to
the South as to remind one of the lament, ascribed to a clergyman, that
the Devil has all of the good tunes. The North had not only better music
but more of it. If we may judge by the sheaf of Civil War songs preserved in the Library of Congress, the Yankees outnumbered the Confederates about three to one in the number of compositions produced.

A dissection of the tunes on both sides is revealing, including those deservedly forgotten. As in its slogans, the North expressed much concern
for the Union and the flag in its music. Relevant titles were "The Flag
of Our Union," "Old Glory," and "The Old Union Wagon." Liberty for
slaves and freedom for all found support in "The Rally Cry of Freedom"
and "John Brown's Soul," which of course kept marching on. Conscription and army life inspired "I Am Sick, Don't Draft Me!" and "Camp
Gals," about purchasable females who managed to rob the poor soldier.
War heroes, including those whose glamour dimmed, won their share of

acclaim, including General McClellan in "Star of the North, or Potomac's Young Hero" and General Hooker in "Gallant Fighting Joe."

Many of the Northern songs stressed the negative and hence were rather depressing. President Jefferson Davis took his lumps in popular tunes like "We'll Hang Jeff Davis." The despised Copperheads received brickbats in "The Soldier's Song—Unionism vs. Copperheadism!" Even the depreciating greenbacks came under attack in "How Are You, Green Backs?" a satire on financing the war by the printing press. Even more dismal was the attention to the lethal prison camps and war weariness, especially in songs like "The Prison's Release," "When This Cruel War Is Over," and "I Wish the War Was O'er!" Sentimental references to mother loomed large, especially in "Mother Kissed Me in My Dream," "Dear Mother, I've Come Home to Die," and "Who Will Care for Mother Now?" These tunes, though popular, could hardly be classified as potent morale builders.

Confederate songs featured variants of the famous "Dixie" and salutes to the new banner in such tunes as "The Bonnie Blue Flag" and "Rally around the Stars and Bars." Liberty from Northern bondage, rather than liberty for the black bondsman, found expression in the "Southern Song of Liberty." The Almighty, whose name appeared in few Confederate slogans, was besought in "God Save the South."

Many Southerners evidently reposed less faith in the King of Kings than in their own King Cotton. One illustrated Southern envelope carried the slogan "The Cotton Plant—King of the South," a sentiment that the songwriters varied in "Cotton Is King" and "King Cotton." Musical appeals to the border states to join hands under the "Bonnie Blue Flag," especially Maryland, inspired a number of songs. Kentucky was honored with "God Help Kentucky," and "Kentuckians to Arms!"

Victorious Southern generals, such as P.G.T. Beauregard and "Stonewall" Jackson, received homage in song. Southern soldiers, alive and dead, inspired such airs as "The Southern Men," "Southrons to Arms!" and "The Southrons Are Coming," which also suggested "The Campbells Are Coming." On the other hand, the invading "Blue Bellies" were greeted with "Root Yank or Die," a variant of the proverbial "Root Hog or Die," and "Old Abe" Lincoln was generously abused by Southern singers.

INSPIRITING SOUTHERN SONGS

From the mass of musical mediocrity in the South there emerged an especially noteworthy Southern song, the popular and electrifying "Dixie" or "Dixie's Land." Ironically, the words and music were composed in 1859 by an Ohioan, Dan Emmett. On a rainy day in New York City he dashed off the song for a blackface minstrel show in which he was involved. The original, which appeared in Negro dialect, was more a walk-on comic tune than a "Marseillaise." Some of it related to an "Old Missus" who had been seduced by a "gay deceber" (deceiver). The first few lines awakened nostalgia:

> I wish I was in de land ob cotton,
> Old times dar am not forgotten.
> Look away, look away,
> Look away, Dixie Land.

The last two lines aroused enthusiasm for the yet unfought war:

> In Dixie's land, we'll took our stand,
> To lib an' die in Dixie!

"Dixie" was honored by numerous adaptations and versions in the South, notably the version by Confederate Brigadier General Albert Pike. The concluding lines quickened Southern pulses:

> For Dixie's land we take our stand,
> And live or die for Dixie!
> To arms! to arms!
> And conquer peace for Dixie!
> To arms! to arms!
> And conquer peace for Dixie!

As for the inspirational power of "Dixie," we have only to note that at the Battle of Gettysburg Confederate General Pickett ordered the band to play it so as to sustain the morale of his troops just before their suicidal charge. After the South surrendered at Appomattox, President Lincoln ordered the band outside the White House to strike up the tune. Liking the song, he remarked half humorously that the victorious Union had acquired "Dixie" as the spoils of war.

Bracketed with "Dixie" in popularity was "The Bonnie Blue Flag," which provided a stirring salute to the Southern cause. Introduced in 1861 in New Orleans, it quickly became a favorite with Confederate soldiers by enshrining the concept for which they were fighting. "The Southern Girl," which borrowed the tune of "The Bonnie Blue Flag," gave voice to the determination of the Confederate ladies. Although the Yankee blockade denied them the jewels and gowns that their Northern sisters wore, they would bear this deprivation cheerfully. The chorus ran:

> So hurrah! hurrah! For Southern Rights, hurrah!
> Hurrah! for the homespun dress the Southern ladies wear.

FOR UNION AND FREEDOM

As for the musical repertoire of the Yankees, they enjoyed from the start George Pope Morris's "The Flag of Our Union." They also developed various versions of "John Brown's Body," which was adapted to the tune of a Southern camp-meeting song and which repeated "Glory, glory hallelujah!" One variant began the first stanza with "John Brown's body lies mouldering in the grave" and started the third with "He's gone to be a soldier in the army of the Lord!" Another more poetic variation by Edna Dean Proctor rejoiced:

> John Brown died on the scaffold for the slave;
> Dark was the hour when we dug his hallowed grave;
> Now God avenges the life he gladly gave,
>   Freedom reigns to-day!
>   Glory, glory hallelujah,
>   Glory, glory hallelujah,
>   Glory, glory hallelujah,
> Freedom reigns to-day!

Outclassing all other Northern songs as poetry, though set to the tune of the earlier "John Brown's Body," was Julia Ward Howe's magnificent "Battle Hymn of the Republic," which continues to be popular to this day. About Christmastime 1861 Mrs. Howe had just witnessed a skirmish between two opposing forces near Washington, and from it she received her inspiration. She dashed off her poem in the spirit of an Old Testament prophet whose vengeful Lord was trampling out "the grapes of wrath" and loosening the "fatal lightning of his terrible swift sword." The last stanza ended the poem-song on a loftier note, which gave a nobler purpose to the horrible war:

> In the beauty of the lilies Christ was born across the sea,
> With a glory in his bosom that transfigures you and me;
> As he died to make men holy, let us die to make men free,
> While God is marching on.

The greatest writer of martial airs was probably a New England musician and music publisher, George F. Root. His "The Battle Cry of Freedom," published in 1863, stressed the theme recently heralded by Lincoln's long-delayed stand for emancipation:

> Yes, we'll rally round the flag, boys, we'll rally once again,
> Shouting the battle cry of Freedom,
> We'll rally from the hillside, we'll gather from the plain,
> Shouting the battle cry of Freedom!
> The Union forever, hurrah! boys, hurrah!
> Down with the traitor, up with the star,
> While we rally round the flag, boys, rally once again,
> Shouting the battle cry of Freedom!

Root had other bugle calls to sound. His "Just Before the Battle, Mother," published in 1863, reputedly sold over a million copies of sheet music. The young soldier hero, in a farewell to his mother, lashed out at the Copperheads and other defeatists:

> Tell the traitors all around you
>   That their cruel words, we know,

> In ev'ry battle kill our soldiers
> By the help they give the foe.

The song concludes on a more exalted note:

> Hark! I hear the bugles sounding,
>   'Tis the signal for the fight,
> Now may God protect us, mother,
>   As He ever does the right.
> Hear the "Battle Cry of Freedom,"
>   How it swells upon the air,
> Oh, yes, we'll rally round the standard,
>   Or we'll perish nobly there.

Also immensely popular was another of Root's compositions, "Tramp, Tramp, Tramp" (or "The Prisoner's Hope"), published in 1864. A superb marching song sung by the tramping "Boys in Blue," it was designed to give hope to the hopeless thousands of prisoners rotting in Confederate prisons or prison camps:

> In the prison cell I sit,
> Thinking, mother dear, of you,
> And our bright and happy home so far away,
>   And the tears they fill my eyes,
>   Spite of all that I can do,
> Tho' I try to cheer my comrades and be gay.
> *Chorus:*
> Tramp, tramp, tramp, the boys are marching,
>   Oh, cheer up, comrades, they will come,
> And beneath the starry flag we shall breathe the air again,
> Of freedom in our own beloved home.

After "The Battle Cry of Freedom" had taken hold, President Lincoln wrote to composer Root, "You have done more than a hundred generals and a thousand orators. If you could not shoulder a musket in defense of your country, you certainly have served her through songs."

Another tenaciously popular war song was Walter Kittredge's "Tenting on the Old Camp Ground." A New Hampshire boy, the composer was drafted into the army in 1863 but was rejected on medical grounds. In a moment of depression he wrote his memorable song, which sold hundreds of thousands of copies in sheet music. Its theme was rather depressing, yet it was a beautiful song, and it lent itself so well to choral singing that it was a favorite of the soldiers. The first stanza ran:

> We're tenting tonight on the old camp-ground;
>   Give us a song to cheer
> Our weary hearts, a song of home
>   And friends we love so dear.

The concluding stanza, found in some versions, ended on a melancholy note:

> Many are the hearts that are weary to-night
>   Wishing for the war to cease;
> Many are the hearts looking for the light,
>   To see the dawn of peace!
> Dying tonight, dying tonight;
>   Dying on the old camp-ground.

Less doleful and hence more inspiriting was "When Johnny Comes Marching Home Again," a marching song believed to be the composition of the famous Irish-American military bandmaster Patrick S. Gilmore. The piece was popular with both civilians and soldiers, for it stressed the theme of an uproarious homecoming. The first stanza contained the same cheerful note as the rest of the song:

> When Johnny comes marching home again,
> Hurrah! Hurrah!
> We'll give him a hearty welcome then,
> Hurrah! Hurrah!
> The men will cheer, the boys will shout,
> The ladies, they will all turn out,
> And we'll all feel gay,
> When Johnny comes marching home.

KING COTTON AND JOHN BULL

Southerners seceded from the Union with high hopes of establishing a new nation on a permanent basis. Many of them, for convincing reasons, did not believe that the "damn Yankees" would fight over such an abstract issue as secession. Before the shooting started, one Southern orator flourished his pocket handkerchief and promised his audience to wipe up every drop of blood shed over disunion. When the Unionists surprised their fellow countrymen by resisting, the Confederates were confident that the North had neither the means nor the will to conquer the fighting breed reared in the South.

Dixieland's dreams of success rested heavily on the "King Cotton" complex. For a decade or so Southern orators and statesmen had boasted that "Cotton is King"—an intoxicating slogan repeated so often that many Southerners came to believe it. On paper, King Cotton should have triumphed, for the textile factories of Europe, especially Britain's, were heavily dependent on the fiber grown in the South. If the supply were shut off, one of the Old World's major industries would be prostrated, with accompanying mass unemployment and misery. Hungry and riotous English workers would presumably force the powerful British Navy to break the Yankee blockade and release the cotton. In this event the Southerners, with Britain on their side, seemed bound to win. So sure were the Confederates of the coercive power of King Cotton that they supplemented the Yankee blockade by burning great quantities of their own bales. The cry "Burn the cotton" resounded throughout the land.

Unhappily for the South, cotton proved to be no "King," largely because Europe had a heavy oversupply on hand when war erupted. British and European manufacturers were able to combine this backlog with alternate sources of the fiber, notably in Egypt and India. At the same time, advancing Union armies were able to seize and ship out unburned bales of cotton.

To the further discomfiture of "King Cotton," "King Wheat" and "King Corn" were crowned heads to be reckoned with. Workshop England was heavily dependent on the North for grain, which the Yankees produced in overflowing abundance, thanks to the McCormick reaper. Indeed, the British needed grain more than they did the cotton, and they were led to believe that they could not get food in sufficient supply elsewhere. If they quarreled with their granary, they might well go hungry. So "King Cotton" lost his scepter. One Northern magazine exulted late in 1862:

> Wave the stars and stripes high o'er us,
> Let every freeman sing,

> •   •   •

> Old King Cotton's dead and buried: brave young Corn is King.

Even so, Northern relations with Great Britain remained vexed during much of the Civil War. England was the South's chief foreign supplier of war materiel, and in addition the hereditary aristocracy of England supposedly had much in common with the cotton aristocracy of the South. A grave crisis developed in November 1861, when a Union cruiser seized from the British *Trent* on the high seas two prominent Confederate commissioners headed for Europe, James M. Mason and John Slidell. The British lion roared in anger, even though England had seized sailors from American decks during the impressment days before the War of 1812. The North rejoiced to see Britain receive a dose of its own quarterdeck medicine. But Lincoln feared that he had a pair of "white elephants" on his hands, and he averted war when he released the prisoners. He cleverly sweetened the pill for the public with a diplomatic note from his Secretary of State that in effect congratulated Britain for having finally accepted free sea principles for which America had fought in the War of 1812. But bitterness lingered in the North, and James Russell Lowell had one of his homespun characters say:

> It don't seem hardly right, John,
> When both my hands was full,
> To stump me to a fight, John—
> Your cousin, tu, John Bull!

In the North the resentful song "Secessia Land" reflected unhappiness over the release of Mason and "slick old Slidell":

> Where is blustering Mason,
> Where now is blustering Mason,

> Where now is blustering Mason,
> Safe with the English snobs.

More irritating to Northerners was the construction in England of Confederate commerce raiders which sallied forth and ravaged the Union merchant marine. Yankees branded such vessels "British pirates." The most famous of them all, the *Alabama,* was finally sunk by a Union warship in the English Channel, off the French coast, in 1864. A picture of this "pirate" cruiser that sold widely in the North bore the inscription "Built of English oak, in an English yard, armed with English guns, manned by an English crew, and sunk in the English Channel." Not until the days of President Grant in 1871 were the British willing to submit to arbitration and subsequently pay damages.

Even more alarming than the raids of commerce destroyers was the prospect that two ironclad ships with powerful rams, then being built in Great Britain for the Confederate navy, would smash the Yankee blockade and cause the North to invade Britain's Canada in anger. At a critical moment in the negotiations in 1863, the British government decided to avert a showdown by incorporating the two rams in its own navy. As the climax approached, the American Minister in London, Charles Francis Adams, wrote these memorable words to the Foreign Office, "It would be superfluous in me to point out to your Lordship that this is war."

GREENBACKS VERSUS BLUEBACKS

While the South slowly shriveled as a result of the blockade and the destructiveness of war, the economy of the North prospered feverishly. Not only did the growing of grain prove lucrative, but industry flourished as well. Factories mushroomed forth in unexpected places as war profiteers and "shoddy millionaires" waxed fat. These gentry would sell reprocessed wool or shoddy wool for uniforms, which would disintegrate in the first heavy rain. Oil was discovered in Pennsylvania in 1859, and a new breed of rich "coal oil Johnnies" joined the new plutocracy of "shoddy aristocrats."

Financing the war proved to be a major problem to both adversaries. With gold in short supply, each side issued paper money—"greenbacks" in the North and "bluebacks" in the South. In both cases the printing-press money depreciated in value, in the North moderately, in the South hopelessly. The "greenbacks" and "bluebacks" were supplemented by paper money in units below a dollar. In the North such fractional currency was contemptuously called "shinplasters," evidently after the practice of using brown paper saturated with vinegar as a plaster on leg sores.

Censorious Copperheads did not relish the financial state of the Union, and their *Copperhead Minstrel* of 1864 (second edition) published "Nursery Rhymes":

> Sing a song of Greenbacks,
> Pockets full of trash,

Nightmare of a War Profiteer. A dead soldier forces on him the same poisonous food and drink with which he supplied the army. *Vanity Fair,* 1861.

> Over head and ears in debt,
> And out of ready cash;
> Heaps of Tax Collectors
> As busy as a bee,
> Ain't we in a pretty fix,
> With Gold at fifty-three.*

North and South alike prayed to the same God for victory, but not even the Almighty could please both at the same time, as Lincoln pointed out in his second inaugural address. In 1864, the third year of the war and with the monetary outlook gloomy, the Treasury responded to pressures from pious people and first imprinted on United States coins the motto "In God We Trust." It was chosen in preference to "God Our Trust" and "God and Our Country."

---

* Fifty-three cents in gold would purchase a one dollar greenback.

"OLD ABE" AGAIN

Presidential elections in the United States come by the calendar, not by the crisis, and Lincoln was required to run again for his office in 1864 or bow out. As fate would have it, the war was going badly for the North in the middle of that year, and "Old Abe" was widely regarded as a failure. Especially disheartening was the lack of progress by "Grant the Butcher" in his duel to the death with General Lee in Virginia. Lincoln's leadership had not brought victory, and there was also growing dissatisfaction with burdensome taxes, grafting "shoddy millionaires," repeated calls for volunteers, the inequitable draft, the emaciated prisoners, the mounting casualty lists. Additional criticism involved Lincoln's arbitrary rule (including the denial of habeas corpus), the "nigger proclamation" of emancipation, and the ill-timed stories of "Abraham the Joker," that "Prince of Jesters." The peace-at-any-price men were becoming increasingly vocal.

Agitation mounted among Republican politicians to bypass or "dump" Lincoln, who was to be the victim of the so-called "Jonah Movement," with its allusion to throwing the Biblical Jonah overboard to the whale. In May of 1864 a group of hard-line "Radicals" in the Republican Party assembled in Cleveland, Ohio, and nominated for the Presidency General John C. Frémont, the first Republican nominee for this high office in 1856. He had already served without particular distinction in the Civil War, and had gained notoriety by prematurely emancipating the Missouri slaves in 1861. For reasons of high policy, Lincoln had forced withdrawal of his hasty declaration of emancipation and had removed Frémont from his command in St. Louis, thus offending many antislavery men.

Surviving medals attest to the kind of support that Frémont received. One read, "Elect me President—Freedom and the Reunion of States Shall be Permanently Established." Another revamped a familiar campaign slogan of 1856: "Free Speech, Free Press, Frémont." Still another hailed "Major General John C. Frémont the Coming Man," and enumerated his heroic deeds, including explorations in the Rockies and his rousing run for the presidency in 1856.

Frémont's candidacy quickly fizzled out. The intrepid "Pathfinder of the West" finally had to withdraw, though only after Lincoln made a deal with Frémont's backers which involved dismissing a Cabinet member distasteful to them. The Republicans, meeting in Baltimore, further solidified their front. They regrouped in the National Union party, which coalesced the Republicans and those "war Democrats" who cared enough about preserving the Union to support Lincoln. "Old Abe" was then named the official standard bearer of the new coalition, which really lasted for only one presidential election. Andrew Johnson, the Tennessee tailor and former U.S. Senator, although previously a Democrat, was picked as vice presidential nominee. This was a transparent attempt to seduce the "war Democrats" and sew up the election.

Little known is the fact that some sentiment developed for Grant as a presidential candidate to oppose Lincoln in 1864, even though the general had not yet won his great victory over Lee. At least two campaign songs in the Library of Congress attest to this boomlet: "Grant's the Man" and "Here's to the Tanner's Son." The latter was especially bitter:

> Abraham Lincoln and his faction Abolition
> Are up in convention for re-nomination;
> But put him down, for U. S. Grant is on the Slate
> As the Soldiers' and the People's candidate.
> We want no Bastilles, nor Fort Lafayettes [a prison camp],
> No Military Necessity Arrests,
> For United States Grant is our man
> For the next four years in the chair of Washington.

"TARDY GEORGE" CHALLENGES LINCOLN

Grant was passed over for four years, and by one of the strangest ironies of American politics the Democratic party undertook to oust Lincoln by nominating and electing General ("Tardy George") McClellan. This nominee was the very man whom Lincoln had removed from his command after a long series of disappointments. So-called Democratic "traitors" with "Copperhead" leanings forced into the platform of the party a statement denouncing Lincoln's "experiment of war" as a "failure" and proposing the restoration of the Union by a negotiated peace—as though that were feasible. But McClellan, unable to face his former comrades-in-arms on such a basis, repudiated the defeatist Democratic plank and made clear that he favored a prosecution of the war and the preservation of the Union.

Despite their candidate's disclaimer, "McClellan Minute Men" rallied smartly behind their usually slow-moving hero. With their hatred of "Old Abe" and their determination to elevate "Little Mac," they carried transparencies in scores of torchlight parades exhibiting such slogans as "Old Abe Removed McClellan—We'll Now Remove Old Abe," "Time to Swap Horses, November 8th," "The Constitution as It Is, the Union as It Was," "We Demand the *Habeas Corpus*," and "No Emancipation, No Miscegenation, No Confiscation, No Subjugation." Lincoln's penchant for telling amusing stories at inopportune times inspired the critical song:

> Hey! Uncle Abe, are you joking yet,
> Or have you taken a serious fit,
> And wisely set to pack up your kit,
> To be up and off in the morning?

Pro-McClellan campaign songs bore titles trumpeting such sentiments as "Mac Will Win the Union Back," "The Cry Is, 'Mac, My Darling,'" and "McClellan the Brave." In addition, there were "Union and Peace," "Traitors, Clear the Track," "Little Mac upon the Track," and "Our Captive Soldiers"—a reminder of the thousands of Yankee prisoners dying in

Southern prison camps. In slogan and song alike, the Democrats made a determined attempt to steal from the Republicans (Union party) the supreme goal of union, as in the McClellan campaign song:

> Hurrah for the Union, hurrah for the Union.
> Hurrah for the Union, and the gallant little Mac.

"Copperheaded" Democrats naturally supported McClellan, and the second edition of their *Copperhead Minstrel* vented their extreme bitterness in a parody of "We are Coming Father Abraham":

> We are coming, Abraham Lincoln,
>   From mountain, wood, and glen;
> We are coming, Abraham Lincoln,
>   With the ghosts of murdered men.
> Yes! we're coming, Abraham Lincoln,
>   With curses loud and deep,
> That will haunt you in your waking,
>   And disturb you in your sleep.

The official *McClellan and Pendleton Songster* was no less vicious, with such songs as "Abe the Dictator," "The Colored Cuss from Africa," and "Nigger Doodle Dandy."

Many violently antiwar Democrats and Copperheads believed that the crime of the century was to permit the loss of hundreds of thousands of lives and rivers of blood to free the lowly slaves. Ugly overtones of racism against "Lincoln and his niggerheads" were evident in a transparency carried in Illinois with the slogan "McClellan for President and White Men for Husbands." A banner in Philadelphia heralded these sentiments: "No Tyranny; No Niggers; White Men are as Good as Niggers When they Behave Themselves." One especially malicious song in the *Copperhead Minstrel* jeered:

> Fight for the nigger,
> The sweet-scented nigger,
> The wooly-headed nigger,
> And the Abolition crew.

Surprising numbers of McClellan medals have survived, among them one with an unflattering reference to the lethargic general as "The Great American Hesitator." Others reveal busts of McClellan with such sentiments as "The People's Choice for President" and "Little Mac for President—Spades are Trumps" (evidently a reference to his penchant for digging trenches rather than marching). The peace-at-any-price faction of the Democratic party found comfort in "Horrors of War—Blessings of Peace." McClellanites who wanted to fight on to some kind of victory supported "The Constitution as It Is the Hope of the Union," "No Compromise with Armed Rebels," and "One Flag and One Union Now and Forever." In addition to these medallic messages, one McClellan banner carried the battle cry "Peace! Union! and Victory!" All such affirmations gave point to the conclusion that both McClellan and Lincoln favored union, but McClellan less convincingly.

HUZZAHING FOR ABE AND ANDY

"Uncle Abe and Andy," for their part, did not lack formidable sloganized support. Especially effective was "Don't Swap Horses in the Middle of the Stream," which gained wide currency at this time from a remark by Lincoln that has roots deep in American political lore. The message was that while a war was being prosecuted by Lincoln, the voters should not undercut him by changing commanders-in-chief. Another slogan, designed to weaken veteran support for McClellan, was "Vote as You Shot," which was to become a shopworn Republican appeal during the next decade. "Peace with Dishonor" was clearly an appeal to citizens who favored McClellan, the nominee of the antiwar Democrats and Copperheads. The Republican (National Union) war cry "Lincoln and Liberty" found a powerful echo in the epigrammatic statement of Senator Sumner to the New York Young Men's Republican Union, "Where slavery is, there liberty cannot be; and where liberty is, there slavery cannot be."

Pro-Lincoln campaign songs, though rousing, lacked the punch of the better pro-Lincoln slogans. Among the titles in the printed songsters one finds many laudatory references to "Abe." They included "Abe of Illinois," "Brave Old Abe," "Uncle Abe and Andy," and "Rally for Old Abe." In a less familiar tone were "Shout Aloud for Lincoln," "Give Us Noble Leaders," and "Hurrah! For Lincoln and Johnson!" Lincolnites also devised an adaptation of the stirring song of 1862, "We are Coming Father Abraham, 600,000 More," as well as "Preserve the Union," "Let Traitors Despair," and "Ridden by Slave Power." So-called "traitors" in the North received a slap with "To Ye Copperhead—No Thanks to You." But perhaps the most effective pro-Lincoln campaign song was "Rally round the Cause Boys," sung to the tune of "The Battle Cry of Freedom." The chorus left no doubt:

> For Lincoln and Johnson huzza! boys, huzza!
> Down with rebellion, on with the war;
> While we rally round the cause, boys, rally in our might,
> Singing the holy cause of freemen.

Numerous Lincoln medals emphasized the virtues and objectives of the candidates. "The Railsplitter's" name figured in such sentiments as "Abraham Lincoln an Honest Man—The Crisis Demands his Reelection in 1864," "Lincoln and Liberty—Good for Another Heat [in the political race]," and "Abraham Lincoln: Freedom, Justice, Truth." More pointed were "Freedom to All Men—War for the Union," and (with echoes of the Liberty Bell) "Proclaim Liberty Throughout the Land." Nor did the medalists overlook such barbs as "No Compromise with Traitors" and "No Compromise with Armed Rebels—May the Union Flourish." Reinforcing the medals, Union party posters and banners upheld "The Union Forever," and "Liberty, Union, and Victory."

A BALLOT-BOX SETBACK FOR SECESSION

Harassed President Lincoln, shortly before the nomination of his rival, gave way to despondency, and if he had died then he probably would have gone down in history as a failure. Fearing defeat at the polls, he prepared a memorandum looking toward the orderly transfer of government, in March 1865, to those who would negotiate terms with the Confederacy. But in late August and early September 1864 came a dramatic turn in the tide. Admiral Farragut forced his way into Mobile Harbor, despite the lethal mines planted there, and closed the port to blockade runners. His reported cry was "Damn the torpedoes—go ahead!" With various variations in wording, this stirring appeal enlivens the pages of American history. Early in September General Sherman occupied Atlanta, and then he launched out on his devastating march to the sea, cutting a locustlike swath through the Confederacy. General Philip ("Little Phil") Sheridan won a noteworthy victory in the Shenandoah Valley of Virginia and laid waste that fertile expanse. He reportedly remarked, with exaggeration, that "if a crow wants to fly down the Shenandoah, he must carry his provisions with him."

Leaving nothing to chance, Lincoln's Union party arranged to have soldiers at the fighting front vote "the way they shot" and to furlough others home so that they could cast ballots for Lincoln. One Pennsylvania boy in blue reportedly voted for himself and the forty-nine absent members of the company. One election song, to the tune of "Yankee Doodle," had dishonest overtones, perhaps unintended:

> Yankee Doodle, keep it up—
> Yankee Doodle Dandy,
> This is the way we soldiers vote,
> For Honest Abe and Andy.

As events turned out, Lincoln did not need the "bayonet vote." A giant parade in Washington on the eve of the election featured marchers with torches, lanterns, banners, and other displays. One transparency was moved by five ambulances and forty-five soldiers, each of whom had suffered the loss of an arm or a leg. The illuminated message brought cheer: "We have lost our legs and arms but not our patriotism." Another slogan proclaimed, "We are coming, Father Abraham, 2,000,000 voters more."

Banners and transparencies in various cities flaunted such pro-McClellan sentiments as "Abolish Old Abe and Restore the Union" and "Abe Lincoln, First in War and First in the Pockets of His Countrymen." Copperheadish prejudices shone through in "Lincoln Demands Blood, the People Demand Peace" and "Blessed are the Peacemakers: God and McClellan are the Only Hope of Our Severed Union."

Some of the Democratic campaign parodies struck unseemly blows at Lincoln. A tune current in Connecticut, named the "White Soldier's Song" and adapted to the tune of "John Brown's Body," contained this unhappy thought:

> Tell Abe Lincoln on Antietam's bloody dell,
> Tell Abe Lincoln where a thousand heroes fell,
> Tell Abe Lincoln and his gang to go to h - - -,
> And we'll go marching *home*.

Lincoln's talent for telling earthy stories, allegedly in the wrong place at the wrong time, dropped him to the level, in Democratic eyes, of a "smutty joker" and a "filthy storyteller." One slogan urged "No More Vulgar Jokes," and a song, to the tune of "Yankee Doodle," drew a sharp contrast:

> Our "Little Mac" is just the man
>   To restore the nation's glories;
> He never will on the battle-field
>   Indulge in smutty stories.

Briefer and more pointed electioneering barbs against Lincoln were "Usurper," "Despot," "Ghoul," "Ignoramus Abe," "Swindler," "Monster," "Gorilla," and "Old Scoundrel." One of the greatest ironies in American history is that the man most generally judged to have been the greatest of the Presidents was the victim of the greatest personal abuse. "To be great is to be misunderstood," Emerson had written in 1841.

LINCOLN'S TRIUMPH AND TRAGEDY

"Little Mac" ran a surprisingly strong race, despite the spectacular and timely victories of Farragut, Sherman, and Sheridan. He carried only three states and 21 electoral votes to Lincoln's 212, but attracted 45 percent of the popular vote, as compared with the meager 40 percent for the triumphant Lincoln four years earlier. Woodrow Wilson in 1912 and Richard M. Nixon in 1968 were both elected to the Presidency with a smaller proportion of the popular vote than McClellan's. The South was pulling hard for the Democrats, and Confederate soldiers were heard to shout, "Hurrah for McClellan," because a negotiated peace or a prolonged cease-fire could spell success for Southern secession. The shooting might not be started up again. Lincoln's victory at the polls was one of the most disheartening defeats of the war for the Confederacy.

Much-abused Abraham Lincoln was inaugurated President for the second time on March 4, 1865. His address, which foreshadowed a lenient reconstruction of the wayward South, embodied one of the noblest passages in American political literature: "With malice toward none; with charity for all; with firmness in the right as God gives us to see the right, let us strive on to finish the work we are in."

On Good Friday, April 14, 1865, a weary Lincoln relaxed by attending a play at Ford's Theater. A fanatically pro-Southern actor, James Wilkes Booth, slipped into his box and shot him in the head. As the assassin fled he shouted "The South is avenged" and "Sic Semper Tyrannis" (Thus Always to Tyrants), a sentiment on the seal of Virginia and on some twenty different medals and buttons during the Civil War. Pursued into the nearby countryside, Booth himself was shot. His dying words were reported to be "Tell Mother—tell Mother—I died for my country."

Instantly the North was shocked, angered, stunned. Over Lincoln's dying body, Secretary of War Edwin Stanton remarked, "Now he belongs to the ages," which was probably the noblest thing Stanton ever said. Congressman James A. Garfield, later President, helped to calm a New York crowd when he proclaimed, "Fellow citizens! God reigns, and the government at Washington still lives!"

Thus it befell that Lincoln, whose numerous foes had called him "The Tyrant" or worse, overnight became "The Martyr President."

XIV

The Ordeal
of Reconstruction

The future condition of the conquered power [the
Confederacy] depends on the will of the conqueror.
Representative Thaddeus Stevens, December 18, 1865

A TAILOR IN THE WHITE HOUSE

In its shooting phase the Civil War had ended, at least openly, but the
piper's bill had to be paid. Staggering problems confronted the once
divided nation now that the war-weary sections were pinned together
with bayonets. Agonizingly difficult were the tasks of adjusting several
million blacks to their new status of freedom and restoring the rebellious
whites to their old status under the Stars and Stripes. Problems cried
aloud for statesmanship of the highest order, especially since a statesman
of the highest order had just fallen victim to Booth's bullet.

Luck was not with the republic, for a misfit Vice President inherited
the Presidential mantle. "Old Andy" Johnson, a Tennessee Unionist, suffered from an even more sterile educational background than Lincoln.
An orphan boy, he had never attended school for a day in his life, in
common with many of the South's "poor white trash." Endowed with considerable native intelligence, he taught himself to read, and after his
marriage his wife taught him to write. After serving a youthful appren-
ticeship to a tailor, he set himself up in his own shop in the "hillbilly"
country of eastern Tennessee, and subsequently came to be known as
"The Tennessee Tailor."

Eventually plunging into local politics, Johnson ascended the political ladder to become governor of Tennessee, and then served for ten years as a member of Congress, in both House and Senate. As a determined battler for the poor and as an inflexible foe of the South's slave-based plantation system, he deservedly earned the sobriquet "Father of the Homestead Act." As a once impoverished "poor white" who resented the "Cotton Lords" and their disruptive secession, he was drafted by President Lincoln in 1862 to be military governor of recently occupied Tennessee. He thus became a prime example of a "galvanized Yankee" or a Southern War Democrat with Northern sentiments.

Such a man seemed to be needed as a running mate for Lincoln in 1864, for the strategy was to use Johnson to attract pro-Southern votes. Not many Republicans seem to have feared that Lincoln would be shot and replaced by this War Democrat. So it was that "The Great Commoner," as Johnson was dubbed, entered the White House as another "His Accidency."

Vengeful toward the Southern secessionists, the new President at first breathed fire and hemp when he talked of these "traitors." But he soon sobered under the weight of responsibility, and before long adopted essentially Lincoln's "soft" or "rosewater" scheme for readmitting the Southern states without forcing them to drink the dregs of humiliation. As a New Hampshire versifier optimistically exulted:

> With Andy we'll weather the storm,
> He's the man who can pilot us through;
> For his heart, it is honest and warm,
> And his head, it is steady and true.

Unhappily for them, the ex-rebels were counting too heavily on the North's willingness to let bygones be bygones. During the war a popular song had boasted, "We'll hang Jeff Davis to a sour apple tree," to the tune of "John Brown's Body," and even small children lisped it. Davis was not hanged, but he was imprisoned for two years, a part of the time in irons. The North was many years removed from extending a warm handshake across the "bloody chasm." Yet Johnson, beginning the month after his accession, issued limited pardons and amnesty to thousands of Southerners. Northern critics complained bitterly about "damnesty," "whitewashed rebels," and the "softness" of Johnson—"The Great Accident" who had now become "The Great Pardoner."

JOHNSON CLASHES WITH THE RADICALS

"Old Andy's" thinking about reunion found expression in the aphorism "Once a state, always a state," and he acted accordingly. Between April and December 4, 1865, the date when Congress was scheduled to meet, he arranged for a revamping of the Southern states by the ruling whites under new constitutions that acknowledged the emancipation of the slaves. When Congress assembled in December, an unrepentant group of "whitewashed rebels" was present waiting to take their old seats—and more. This contingent consisted of assorted members of the "treasonable" Confederate Congress and Cabinet, plus a number of generals, colonels, and other former Confederate officers, plus the Vice President of the defunct Confederacy.

Radical Republicans, conspicuously Representative Thaddeus Stevens and Senator Charles Sumner, promptly seized control of Congress and forthwith excluded this entire contingent of "rebel brigadiers." Stevens regarded the seceded states as "conquered provinces"; Sumner argued that these wayward sisters had "committed suicide." The motives of the Radical Republicans as a group were a curious mixture. Some of them sought to punish the South radically. Others wanted to ensure the continued supremacy of the Republican party because the Southern states would surely vote Democratic and endeavor to scuttle Republican programs. Still others, like Senator Sumner, fought the new state governments to ensure maximum protection for the newly freed ex-slave and to guarantee him a vote for his own defense—and to guarantee the supremacy of the Republican party. Southern whites were unpleasantly reminded of a Negro song of the Civil War:

> De bottom rail's on de top
> An we's gwine to keep it dar.

Freedom for the blacks was clearly a major concern of many Radicals. The Thirteenth Amendment, legally implementing the "forever free" Emancipation Proclamations of 1862 and 1863, was formally ratified by enough states late in 1865. Yet actually the great mass of the former slaves were free only to straggle, struggle, suffer, and starve. The grapevine promise of "ten acres and a mule" or "forty acres and a mule" had sparked exaggerated hope among the tens of thousands of expectant blacks, but it continued to be only pie in the sky. Lucky indeed was the ex-slave who received "three acres and a cow."

Many Negroes, regarding themselves as "free as a bird" or "free as a fool," took off from "Old Massa's" plantation, often to die of illness, exposure, or malnutrition. Such footloose and pillaging vagrants were a menace to themselves and also to the whites. To control these mindless migrations and to ensure a desperately needed labor supply, the Southern legislatures passed "Black Codes," designed to keep the former slave down on the plantation. The Black Codes were harshest in the "Black Belt"—so called from the dark soil of Alabama and Mississippi and the heavy concentration there of former slaves. An inadequate attempt to grapple with the plight of the freedmen and the abandoned lands was the Freedmen's Bureau, established by federal legislation shortly before Lincoln's death. Fully developed, it generated extreme hostility among the ex-Confederates. At one time a newspaper in Mississippi carried on its masthead these shocking words:

Breathes there a man with soul so dead,
Who never to himself hath said,
G - d d - - n the Freedmen's Bureau.

Early in 1866 Congress passed a bill greatly enlarging the authority of the Freedmen's Bureau, and President Johnson vainly vetoed it on constitutional grounds. This setback was but one of a series of overridden vetoes that earned for him the nicknames "Veto President," "Andy Veto," "Old Veto," "Sir Veto," "King Andrew," and "King Andy the First." The last label overlooked "King Andrew" Jackson, who was no novice with the veto pen.

YANKEE BAYONET RECONSTRUCTION

A Radical-controlled Congress in June 1866 finally approved the Fourteenth Amendment, which conferred citizenship on the blacks and granted them civil rights. Ratification of this guarantee by a seceded ex-Confederate state was made a precondition for the restoration of its representation in Congress. Except for Tennessee, all of the "sinful eleven" defiantly and short-sightedly rejected these relatively lenient terms. The "wayward sisters" were hoping that in the crucial Congressional elections of November 1866, the voters would repudiate the unpalatable Radical program.

Unwisely, President Johnson decided to deliver a series of speeches while traveling on a circular route to and from Chicago, where he was scheduled to grace the dedication of a monument to the late Stephen A. Douglas. "We are swinging around the circle," he declared in one of his harangues; hence the stock phrase "Swing around the circle." As commander-in-chief he took with him several prominent figures, including war heroes General Grant and Admiral Farragut. En route he not only made ill-tempered and inflammatory speeches but exchanged unseemly epithets with Republican hecklers in the crowds, notably when he defended "my policy" against "Northern traitors," especially those in Congress.

The high point, or rather low point, appears to have come in Cleveland. There Johnson castigated "the subsidized gang of hirelings and traducers" (probably meaning Congressmen who opposed his policy toward the South.) He pledged that the "powers of hell and [Representative] Thad Stevens and his gang" would not turn him from his purpose. From the audience certain hecklers cried, "Is this dignified?" The response was "I care not for dignity." Cries arose of "You be damned," "Hang Jeff Davis," "Don't get mad, Andy," "Traitor," and "Three cheers for Congress." General Grant reportedly remarked that he was "disgusted at hearing a man make speeches on the way to his own funeral." The President's oratory, critics said, sank to the level of that of "the commonest slangwanger."

Johnson as a Parrot. *Harper's Weekly.*

Voters naturally suspected that Johnson, in campaigning for Congressional support, was preparing the path for election in his own right two years later. An anti-Johnson campaign song, to the tune of "Just Before the Battle, Mother," expressed distaste for such a scheme:

> You have swung around the circle
> That you ought to swing [hang] 'tis true;
> Oh, you tried to veto Congress,
> But, I guess, we'll veto you!

Seldom has a speaking tour been so successful in winning votes—for the opposition. The Republicans triumphed with a two-thirds, veto-proof majority in Congress. Johnson's intemperate speeches alienated many former supporters, who were now proclaiming, "Stand by the Congress" against "The Tailor of the Potomac." Negro voters in the North were especially apprehensive of Johnson's soft-on-the-South policy. Many of them remembered the slogan that had developed among abolitionists in the early stages of civil war, "The Republican Party Is the Ship; All Else Is the Sea." A distinguished black leader, Frederick Douglass, paraphrased this rallying cry to read, "For the Negro the Republican Party is the deck; all else is the sea." The few blacks who shifted over to the Democratic party were said to have "crossed Jordan"—after the river in the New Testament.

Triumphant Republicans now went ahead with their plans to reconstruct the defiant ex-Confederates with bayonets. All this was achieved in the teeth of outspoken but futile opposition from President Johnson, "the dead dog in the White House." The South was sliced into five military districts with a Yankee general in command of each, and the Radical Republicans pressed ahead with their schemes to "Republicanize" the seceded states and turn the ex-slave into a reliable Republican voter. The outcome was a number of "Black and Tan" Southern legislatures, which generally consisted of white men and a substantial minority of blacks. In Southern politics the "Black and Tans" came to be opposed by the "Lily Whites," or Southerners opposed to any Negro participation in government.

Speculators and other adventurers from the North descended upon the troubled South, eager to make hay while the sun of bayonet reconstruction shone. Some were respectable citizens with investment capital, grudgingly acceptable to the Southern whites, but many were so-called "carpetbaggers." This damnatory term, still applied to late-arriving politicians in the United States generally, had gained currency in the frontier West before the Civil War to denote a "capitalist" who arrived with just enough currency in his carpetbag or handbag to open a "wild cat" bank. A satirical song, "The Carpet-Bagger," jeered at these gentry:

> Now I got no eddication;
>   Of brains I does not brag,
> But I owns a big plantation
>   All in my carpet bag.
>
> *Chorus:*
> I'm a gay old Carper-Bagger!
>   O! can't you understand?
> 'Mong the color'd folks I swagger
>   Down in the cotton land.

"Carpetbaggers," who brought mostly greed with them, won the hatred of the white Southerners, who also aimed their venom at the "scalawags." These were whites, including a few leading citizens who, for one reason or another, acquiesced in or gave support to the military regime imposed from Washington. Loyal Southerners roundly cursed the "damnyankees" and their "blue-bellied" vassals, as the Northern soldier boys in blue were called.

Southern bitterness against Yankee reconstruction reached its peak under military reconstruction. A widely sung song of hate, "The Good Old Rebel," faithfully reflected and probably prolonged the defiance of many ex-rebels. Various versions exist, including the one here partially reproduced in the dialect of an ill-educated "poor white":

> Oh, I'm a good old Rebel,
>   Now that's just what I am;
> For this "fair land of Freedom"
>   I do not care a dam.
> I'm glad I fit [fought] against it—
>   I only wish we'd won.
> And I don't want no pardon
>   For anything I've done.

BESHEETED NIGHTRIDERS

In such a hotbed of hate, underground vigilante organizations inevitably mushroomed. They were all dedicated to "keeping the Negro in his place" —which was down—and resisting the rule that the Radical Republicans were attempting, with success, to impose on the South. These spontaneous organizations bore such names as "Pale Faces," "Constitutional Guards," "The White Brotherhood," "The Council of Safety," "The Men of Justice," "The Society of the White Rose," "The '76 Association," "The Knights of the Rising Sun," "The Sons of Washington," and "The Knights of the White Camellia" (the largest of all). But by far the most notorious and long-lived was the Ku Klux Klan, founded as a prank in Pulaski, Tennessee, in 1866, by some young ex-Confederate soldiers. They had formed a club or "circle," which they found to be "kuklos" in Greek, and the alliterative Ku Klux Klan was born.

Prospective members of the K.K.K. were asked, among various questions, if they belonged to "The Grand Army of the Republic" (Northern veterans), "The Radical Republican Party," or "The Loyal League," which was formed by pro-Northern Southerners. Applicants were also asked if they favored "a white man's government," together with the "re-enfranchisement and emancipation" of the white people of the South. The Ku Klux Klan organization, often called "The Invisible Empire," was headed by the "Grand Wizard," with various inferior gradations of "Hydras," "Furies," "Goblins," and similar spooky characters. Among other exploits, nightriding and besheeted Ku Kluxers flogged, mutilated, and murdered Negroes so as to persuade them to keep in their "place," which often meant away from the polling place.

Fears implanted in the superstitious ex-slave by "Ku-Kluxery" were deepened by crude placards ornamented with drawings of coffins and other horrendous objects. They warned, "The Dark and Dismal Hour

Draws Nigh," "Unholy Blacks, Cursed of God, Take Warning," "Twice Hath the Sacred Serpent Hissed," and "To be Executed by the Grand White Death and the Rattling Skeleton." Further fear was implanted by the chilling words "When the Black Cat is Gliding under the Shadows of Darkness and the Death Watch Ticks at the One Hour of Midnight, then We Pale Riders are Abroad" and "When the Finger of the White Skeleton Points to the New Made Grave, Brothers Strike! Spare None."

Ghoulish activities of the Ku Klux Klan and similar organizations slackened after Congress curbed Ku Klux Klanism with iron-toothed legislation in 1870–1871. But the ghoulish brotherhood had done much of its work in "Ku-Kluxing" luckless blacks, carpetbaggers, and scalawags. Protective groups such as the Loyal Leagues and the Lincoln Brotherhood were but straws in the storm.

JOHNSON WALKS THE IMPEACHMENT PLANK

Radical Republicans in Congress had meanwhile grown thoroughly tired of the obstructive tactics of "Judas Johnson," and in 1868 decided to make him walk the impeachment plank. The main charge against him was that he had violated the Tenure of Office Act, already passed over his veto, by removing an inherited Cabinet member whom he found uncooperative. Johnson wanted to test the constitutionality of this act—a law that was ultimately and indirectly declared unconstitutional by the Supreme Court in 1926. The House formally impeached the President by a majority vote, and the Senate then undertook to try him on the specified charges and to remove him by the required two-thirds majority. The Radicals had lined up as his successor the President pro tempore of the Senate, Senator "Buff Ben" Wade. The parody of a popular song ran:

> Old Andy's gone, ha, ha!
> And Old Ben's come, ho, ho!
> It must be de kingdom am a-comin'
> In de year of jubilo.

Prosecution in the Senate for trumped-up "high crimes and misdemeanors" ran its appointed course, and Johnson, fortunately for him, had the good sense to hold his tongue. When the tense moment came for the crucial voting, close observers realized that everything depended on the attitude of seven doubtful Republicans, all of whom finally followed their consciences and refused to convict Johnson. He escaped without a single vote to spare. The "Seven Recusants" or "Recreant Seven" were denounced by partisan Republicans as "renegades" and "Copperjohnsons" (Copperheads for Johnson). But America's constitutional system was spared the shock of removing on purely partisan grounds a President whose chief fault was to uphold the Constitution as he interpreted it. "The country is going to the Devil," cried the ailing Representative Thaddeus Stevens as he was carried away from the chamber.

If Johnson's narrow escape brought new respect for the Constitution, the amending process brought new strength. The Fourteenth Amendment, seeking to protect the Negro and ratified in 1868, decreed that no "person" shall be deprived of "life, liberty, or property, without due process of law. . . ." To the delight of later corporate businesses, the word "person" was interpreted by the courts to mean business aggregations as well as human beings. In the same year that the Fourteenth Amendment was ratified, Chief Justice Salmon P. Chase of the Supreme Court, in Texas *v.* White, drove a final nail into the coffin of secession with his memorable dictum "The Constitution, in all its provisions, looks to an indestructible Union composed of indestructible States." Mr. Justice Chase merely put in legal language the policy that Johnson had followed throughout the years of his troubled Presidency, "Once a state, always a state."

Seven years after the futile impeachment proceedings, Johnson was triumphantly reelected to the same Senate that had narrowly failed to remove him, and there he faced some of his former accusers. He delivered one memorable speech to a crowded chamber in which he criticized the continuing Radical Republican reconstruction, and ended with his old battle cry "God save the Constitution!"

GRANT BATTLES SEYMOUR

In May of 1868, less than a week after the end of President Johnson's impeachment trial, the Republican national nominating convention jammed into Chicago. Discarding the wartime Union party label adopted four years earlier, the assembled delegates adopted the label "National Republican Party." "Unconditional Surrender" Grant, the "Man from Appomattox" who had ground down General Lee, was the overwhelming choice of the convention. The band played "Hail to the Chief," and a portrait of the hero with the slogan-motto "Match Him" was spectacularly unveiled amid prolonged cheering. Grant's letter of acceptance, which caught the popular mood regarding the conquered South, declared with his usual economy of words, "Let us have peace."

Noisy Democratic politicians gathered in New York City for their convention early in July 1868. Many delegates, especially those from the Middle West, championed the "Ohio Idea" or paying off part of the national debt in greenbacks. During the recent war the wealthier investors had bought many U.S. government bonds with depreciated greenbacks ("rag money"), and such investors were now demanding that they be paid off in gold coin. Opponents of such an unfair scheme supported the "Ohio Idea." They forced their formula into the Democratic platform with the ringing declaration "One currency for the government and people, the laborer and the officeholder, the pensioner and the soldier, the producer and the bondholder." In simpler terms, this appealing statement became the slogan "The same currency for the bondholder and the plowholder." On tongues of well-to-do Republicans, such an even-handed prescription became repudiation of an honest obligation; indeed, one Republican slogan of the ensuing campaign urged, "Repudiate the Repudiators."

By an odd twist, the deadlocked Democratic convention ultimately stampeded to the presiding officer, Horatio Seymour, a former New York governor somewhat tinged with Copperheadism. "May God bless you for your kindness, but your candidate I cannot be," vainly protested the personable chairman five times. But the pressures on him became so great that he finally caved in and accepted, thereby becoming, on unfriendly tongues, "The Great Decliner." He probably would have persisted in his refusal if he could have foreseen the popularity of war hero Grant.

Ulysses S. Grant had worked in the family leather store in Galena, Illinois, and he became in the mouths of symbol-seeking politicians "The Tanner of Galena" and "The Great American Tanner." Mock tanneries sprouted throughout the land, in the manner of the log-cabin campaign of 1840, and praises showered upon "Ulysses the Tanner," the man who had tanned the hides of General Lee and other Confederates. Monster parades featured "Tanners' Clubs," "Grant Invincibles," and "Boys in Blue" who had served in the Union armies. As they marched, they advertised their sentiments on illuminated, bobbling transparencies.

Grant's "Let us have peace," frequently displayed as a slogan, carried a potent appeal to the war-weary, but the General's record in the recent blood-letting was not forgotten. Especially on medals and buttons one found such war-born Grantisms as "I Propose to Move Immediately on Your Works" [at Fort Donelson], "I Intend to Fight it out on this Line if it Takes All Summer," "The Men Will Need their Horses to Plow With" [to Lee at Appomattox], and "First in the Hearts of his Soldiers."

Catchy Republican songs such as "The Sword of Ulysses" glorified Grant as the man who had rescued the republic. The general's valor was acclaimed in "Brave U.S.G." and in "Grant, the Daring, the Lion-hearted." Similar themes were voiced in "The Man Who Saved the Nation," "For Grant and the Union," and "The Union Right or Wrong." Grant's qualities of leadership were hailed in "General Grant's the Man" and "The Soldier's Chief, the Nation's Chief." Nor was the veteran vote overlooked in "Grant and the Boys in Blue" and "A Call to the Boys in Blue." For good measure, popular Grantisms found expression in "The Grant Pill; or 'Unconditional Surrender'" and "We'll Fight It Out Here, on the Old Union Line."

Grant's fame as a cigar smoker had spread, and the quiet, contemplative man of peace inspired the Republican campaign song "Grant and His Segar." The chorus advised:

> Puff away, Ulysses,
> Puff away, Ulysses,
> Puff away, Ulysses,
> And think with all your might!

Another appreciative Republican ballad came out "For President, Ulysses Grant, A-Smoking His Cigar," and the general's odoriferous habit was often portrayed by cartoonists as they created the image of a supposedly reflective general.

In contrast to this rather whimsical treatment of Grant, bitterness in an extreme form colored some of the Republican campaign songs. Suggestive titles were "The Loyal Blue and the Traitor Gray," "Traitors in Council—Traitors in War," and "The Copperhead," which condemned

> A draft-evading Copperhead;
> A rebel-aiding Copperhead;
> A growling, slandering
> Scowling, pandering,
> Vicious States' Rights Copperhead.

Through medallic inscriptions, as well as other slogans, Republican voters were not permitted to forget that numerous Democrats in the North had been Copperheads and that the ex-Confederates who had forced war on the Union were preponderantly Democratic. Common sloganized appeals by the Republicans advertised such sentiments as "Vote as You Shot," "Scratch a Democrat and You'll Find a Rebel under His Skin," "The Party that Saved the Union Must Rule It," and "Loyalty Shall Govern What Loyalty Has Preserved." Popular inscriptions of a general nature read "The Will of the People Is the Law of the Land" and "The People's Choice for President."

A GENERAL CAPTURES THE WHITE HOUSE

Embattled Democrats fell far short of matching the Republicans in rhymed enthusiasm. Their candidate, Horatio Seymour, was no war hero, not even a warrior, and he suffered much abuse for his pro-Confederate sympathies during the recent conflict. Republicans jeered "A peace man in war, a war man in peace." Democratic slogans contained little punch, aside from "The Same Currency for the Bondholder as the Plowholder" and "Reduce Taxation before Taxation Reduces Us." One Democratic "victory" banner proclaimed the noble sentiment "Peace, Union, and Constitutional Government." As if to atone for past sympathy for the Confederacy, Democratic medals and buttons carried such sentiments as "Union and Constitution—Preservation of the Rights of the People" and "No North—No South—The Union Inseparable." One also finds "General Amnesty—Uniform Currency—Equal Taxes and Equal Rights," as well as "White Men to Govern the Restoration of Constitutional Liberty."

In sharp contrast to the great songs inspired by the war, those of 1868 fell flat. Early that year, when some voters feared that the discredited President Johnson would be a candidate on the Democratic ticket, two tunes appeared. One was entitled "Andy Never Was the Man He Used to Be," and another was "Ye Tailor-Man" ("Respectfully inscribed to Ye 'Dead Dog' of Ye White House").

Whatever the reason, Democratic campaign songs were comparatively few. Among them were "Union and Justice," "The Irish Volunteers" (an appeal to the Irishmen who had fought for the Union), and "Hiram Ulysses [Grant], Come Home." The last included a call from Grant's father in Galena to return and haul wood.

Suggestive Democratic tunes included "The White Man's Banner," which, with unabashed racism, urged that the white man's government be restored to the seceded South. One song title told its own story: "The White Man's Flag with Every State a Star." Others touched on Grant's alleged fondness for the bottle, as in the line "I smoke my weed and drink my gin." The song with this jeer was "Captain Grant of the Black Marines," which began:

> I am Captain Grant of the Black [Negro] Marines,
> The stupidist man that ever was seen.

Democratic marchers in a torchlight parade in Nashville, Tennessee, held up signs reading "Grant the Drunkard," "Grant the Butcher," "Grant the Speculator," and "Grant Talks Peace But Makes War."

Newspapers echoed and reechoed the slogans and songs of the hustings. For many consecutive days the Republican New York *Tribune* headed its political news with

> So, boys! a final bumper
> While we all in chorus chant,
> For next President we nominate
> Our own Ulysses Grant;
> And if asked what state he hails from,
> This, our sole reply shall be,
> From near Appomattox Court House,
> With its famous apple tree.

U. S. Grant, the conquering warrior, swept to victory in November 1868 by a margin of some 300,000 popular votes. But since about 500,000 ex-slaves had probably voted Republican, the "white man's candidate," Seymour, may well have won a majority of the white votes. This statistic meant that the Republicans would increase their efforts to enfranchise the ex-slave, as indeed they did two years later with the Fifteenth Amendment to the federal Constitution.

Radical Republican newspapers heralded the victory with such headlines as "Repudiation Repudiated," "Peace! Peace! Peace!" and "The Second Rebellion Closed," The old war issue appeared anew in such published rejoicing as "The Union Men of the South Rescued," "The Union Ballot Like the Union Bullet Invincible" and "The Men Who Saved Shall Rule the Republic."

FENIAN FORAYS AND "SEWARD'S FOLLY"

Domestic issues undoubtedly dominated the election of 1868, but several dramatic happenings in the area of foreign affairs played a minor role in the electioneering.

Thousands of Irish-Americans who had enlisted in the Union armies hoped that when the war was over they could march north, seize British Canada, and extort the independence of Ireland from British overlordship. A Northern marching song, set to the tune of "Yankee Doodle" and popular with the Irish, boasted:

> Secession first he would put down,
> Wholly and forever,
> And afterwards from Britain's crown
> He Canada would sever.

Many of the Irish Yankees belonged to the secret organization of Fenians, whose wartime marching song announced:

> We are the Fenian Brotherhood, skilled in the art of war,
> And we're going to fight for Ireland, the land that we adore.
> Many battles we have won along with the boys in blue,
> And we'll go and capture Canada, for we've nothing else to do.

In 1866 and again in 1870, tiny Fenian "armies" of a few hundred men each invaded Canada, but these incursions all collapsed and Ireland remained unredeemed. One song of 1867, "Strike Fenians, Strike!" did not generate significant support. Failure of the invasions was due in part to the vigilance of the Washington authorities and United States troops in attempting to preserve neutrality, and for their pains the federal government was roundly cursed in rich Irish brogue.

Especially noteworthy among the achievements of the harassed Johnson administration in the field of foreign affairs was the purchase of Alaska from Russia in 1867 for the bargain price of $7.2 million. Secretary of State Seward was an ardent expansionist, and the Russian Czar was committed to a policy of retrenchment. After initial feelers from Russia, Seward jumped at the bargain. But America did not urgently need more land, and Alaska was enshrouded in the icy fogs of ignorance. The press hooted at this "egregious blunder and bad bargain" palmed off by the "shrewd Russians." To such critics Alaska was a land of "short rations and long twilights," "a barren, worthless, God-forsaken region," "a hyperborean solitude" consisting of "walrus-covered icebergs." Scoffers sneered at "Walrussia," "Johnson's Polar Bear Garden," "Frigidia," "A National Icehouse," "Seward's Icebox," "Seward's Snow Farm," and "Seward's Folly."

Quite appropriately, the name of the main purchaser is now attached to the town of Seward, as well as to the Seward peninsula in Alaska. "Seward's Folly"—one of the most far-sighted follies of history—panned out infinitely better in furs, gold, fish, and oil than expected. The one-sided transaction might better be branded "Czar Alexander's folly."

By an odd coincidence, the flag of French monarchy left Mexico (and North America) the same year (1867) as the flag of Russian monarchy left Alaska (and North America). Behind the smoke screen of the Civil War, the Emperor Napoleon III had forcibly established his "archdupe," Archduke Maximilian of Austria, on the throne of Mexico in violation of the Monroe Doctrine. Two popular songs, "Maxy!" and "Get Out of Mexico," expressed American resentment in music. The latter announced:

> Uncle Sam has thirty million
> Loyal hearts, who want to know
> If the vagrant, Maximilian,
> Won't get out of Mexico.

The chorus concluded with

> For the Universal Nation says,
> "Get out of Mexico!"

So it was that Secretary of State Seward, backed by hundreds of thousands of veteran bayonets, gradually applied the diplomatic heat. In 1867 Napoleon III took "French leave" of his disillusioned puppet, who perished before a Mexican firing squad.

CLOSING THE BLOODY CHASM

"Waving the Bloody Shirt" continued to be a commonplace phase of the "outrage business" for several decades after the war, despite substantial progress in reconciling North and South. This stratagem was used by Republicans to combat the struggling efforts of the Democrats, especially the Southern Democrats, to regain political power. The origins of the expression are obscure, but one explanation is that a member of Congress, incensed by the murderous forays of the Ku Klux Klan, waved the bloody shirt of a badly beaten carpetbagger victim to highlight his harangue. Reactionary Republicans fought "Bourbons," as "unreconstructed" Democrats were called, especially those in the South. They were named after the famed royal family of France that allegedly could "learn nothing and forget nothing" when restored to power after the head-chopping French Revolution.

Southern "Redeemers" of the Democratic Party gradually regained control of their own state governments. The ex-Confederacy rapidly solidified as the "Solid South," and for about a half century could be confidently counted on to vote the Democratic ticket in presidential elections. Many of the diehards evidently believed that the South would "rise again," but most level-headed Southerners were persuaded that, on a military basis at least, "The Old Cause" was indeed "The Lost Cause."

Even so, Confederate flags were again defiantly displayed in the 1960s and 1970s during the struggle between the South and the federal government over desegregation of blacks.

Reconstruction—some have said "redestruction"—is generally thought of as the period from the end of the Civil War in 1865 to the withdrawal of federal troops from near the last two Southern capitols by President Hayes in 1877. But in a sense reconstruction has never ended and is still most sharply manifested in the readjustment of race relations made necessary by abolition during the Civil War. From one viewpoint, reconstruction was but the continuation of the "War between the States" by other means. Claude G. Bowers branded the troubled postwar years "The Tragic Era" and Vernon L. Parrington referred to them as "The Great Barbecue." Someone else coined the less elegant phrase "The Spitoon Decade." One basic problem was that the fighters, who had vented their bitterness in combat, did not do the reconstructing, but left it to those outraged civilians who had kept the home fires burning.

As the years passed, passions faded. Men on both sides sought to "bridge the bloody chasm," to forgive "the erring brethren," and to forget "the late unpleasantness." A memorable step in this direction came from the New York lawyer-poet Francis M. Finch, who in 1867 wrote his touching "The Blue and the Gray," which was later set to music. It was notably popular in the South. The last stanza ran:

> Under the sod and the dew,
> Waiting the judgment day;
> Love and tears for the Blue;
> Tears and love for the Gray.

A red-letter date came in 1881 with the first formal reunion in the South of ex-Yankee "boys" in blue and ex-Confederate men in gray. The gathering in New Orleans heralded a long succession in later years of friendly musters, some of them on former battlefields. On this occasion *Harper's Weekly* in New York published a full-page cartoon which featured the noble sentiment "No North! No South! But the Union."

XV

Eight Long Years of Grantism

A great soldier might be a baby politician.
Henry Adams on General Grant, 1918

CORRUPTION RAMPANT

Critics have branded President Grant's two terms as "eight long years of scandal." A babe in the woods politically, the dogged general had never held civilian office prior to coming to the White House. His own record is relatively clean, but he was so gullible that he attracted to himself or appointed to high office designing and corrupt men. Not without reason has the Grant era been dubbed "the era of good stealings."

Wars beget rogues as well as heroes, and the Civil War was no exception. Taking advantage of the nation's internal commotion, a shoddy millionaire class emerged, while business ethics sank to a new low point. There were railroad deals and railroad "steals," as foreign and domestic investors alike were liberally fleeced. Promoters sold railroad stock in abundance to provide paper ownership of "two streaks of rust and a right of way." Trusted public officials plundered treasuries of the taxpayers' money and then took refuge in the cynical principle of "addition, division, and silence."

Three of the most unscrupulous and successful millionaire manipulators were Daniel Drew, Jay Gould, and James Fisk, all of whom gambled with and wrecked railroads. Drew was reputed to be the author of the couplet:

> He who sells what isn't his'n,
> Must buy it back or go to prison.

In 1869 Fisk and Gould jointly attempted to corner the gold market, as each tried to doublecross the other and as honest businessmen went under during the ensuing financial panic known as "Black Friday" (September 24, 1869). Slippery Jim Fisk lost out during the excitement, but brazenly repudiated his commitments. When Congressional investigators asked what happened to the money, he replied elusively, "Gone where the woodbine twineth." He also reportedly quipped, "Nothing is lost save honor." Though a married man, he kept numerous mistresses, including a famous actress, and he was fatally shot by a jealous male rival in 1872. His death inspired a song that praised his good deeds:

> We all know he loved both women and wine,
> But his heart it was right I am sure;
> Though he lived like a prince in his palace so fine,
> Yet he never went back on the poor.

Grant had nothing to do with the notorious "Tweed Ring" in New York City, but it was symptomatic of the sickly times. By 1871 burly "Boss" Tweed, resorting to bribery, graft, and fraudulent elections, had managed to milk the city treasury of $100 million or so. His hands were strengthened by membership in the corrupt Democratic political organization, Tammany Hall, which was the target of a slogan of the *New York Sun,* "No King, No Clown to Rule This Town." One of Tweed's boasts was, "As long as I count the votes, what are you going to do about it?" The answer was, "Not much," as long as the ballots were bought and the courts cowed.

Tweed's downfall began in 1871 when the unbribable *New York Times* secured damaging evidence, and the gifted cartoonist for *Harper's Weekly,* Thomas Nast, supplemented these exposures with a series of cartoons that pilloried the arrogant boss. He reportedly remarked that he did not care about the printed exposures, but his illiterate constituency could not help seeing "them damned pictures." Among Nast's captions were "In Counting [ballots] there is Strength" and "Ain't I got the power? What are you going to do about it?"

A scandal involving the Crédit Mobilier occurred in the late 1860s, before Grant took office, but its exposure in 1872 further blackened a President already besmirched by corruption. The management of the Union Pacific Railroad had set up a construction company called the Crédit Mobilier, which paid itself excessive millions to lay the rails. Shares of the juicy inside operation were distributed to certain key Congressmen and to the Vice President of the United States, presumably to buy their silence. "I placed it where it would do the most good," wrote Oakes Ames, an official of the Crédit Mobilier, in a private letter that lost its privacy. Two Congressmen were formally censured, and another, the future President James A. Garfield, was cleared after inconclusive evidence had involved him to the extent of a trifling $329.

THE LIBERAL REPUBLICAN REVOLT

On the eve of the presidential campaign of 1872, disgust with the scandal-tainted Grant administration, combined with the severe reconstruction of the South, nauseated many voters. A swelling band of reformers took up the battle cries "Turn the rascals out" or "Throw the rascals out"—slogans that assailed voters' ears countless times during subsequent elections. Republicans deserted the ranks of the party in droves to organize or join the Liberal Republican party, whose members the "regulars" called "Copperheads" and "Soreheads."

Zealous Liberal Republicans met in a nominating convention in Cincinnati, where this "conclave of cranks" fell into the hands of political manipulators. Instead of nominating a statesman of repute, they handed the banner of leadership to "Old Horace" Greeley, the bizarre and eccentric editor of the influential New York *Tribune.*

Greeley formally emphasized his commitment to leniency and amnesty for the South in his letter of acceptance. He wrote, "I accept your nomination in the confident trust that the masses of our countrymen, North and South, are eager to clasp hands across the bloody chasm which has so long divided them." The term "bloody chasm," spurned by many hard-line Republicans, underscored the determination of the Liberal Republicans to achieve reform in Washington while ending reconstruction in the South. Two of their most popular slogans were "Universal Amnesty, Impartial Suffrage," and "Liberty, Equality, and Fraternity."

"Old Honest Horace" or "Our Uncle Horace" looked like a character from the pages of Charles Dickens. His innocent blue eyes set in a cherubic face peered out through steel-rimmed spectacles while he ambled along in a white coat ("Old White Coat") and a high white hat, clutching a green umbrella. His summer home was located on a farm at Chappaqua, New York, hence "The Chappaqua Farmer" and "The Sage of Chappaqua." For diversion he liked to cut wood, hence "The Old Tree Chopper" or "The Wood Chopper of Chappaqua." A powerful if eccentric editor, he was no fool, and although his judgments were sometimes unstable, he possessed a high degree of moral courage. Surprisingly, he proved to be a far better stump speaker than anyone would have expected by merely looking at him.

Songs churned up by the Grant-Greeley campaign matched many of the slogans in their emphasis on trivia. In the log-cabin and hard-cider campaign of 1840 the songsters had stressed symbols that reflected the spirit of the frontier. But the tunes of 1872 emphasized symbols that mirrored personal eccentricities, such as the white hat and the old white coat. Greeley's residence was also acclaimed, as though relevant, in "The Axman of Chappaqua" and "Chappaqua, Fair Chappaqua."

Additional campaign airs hailed "The Wise Man of the East," "The Old White Hat and Coat," and "The White Chapeau." A borrowing from the Civil War classic "We are Coming, Father Abraham," emerged as

"We are Coming, Father Greeley," with 2 million men marching for reform, freedom, and amnesty. A pro-Greeley song slapped at Hiram Ulysses Grant:

> Down with Grant, Useless Grant!
> Up with Greeley, good old Greeley!
> Down with Grant, Useless Grant!
> Hurrah for Greeley! Old White Hat.

Greeley, the ink-stained candidate, was clearly vulnerable on various counts. Critics pilloried him as a vegetarian, a brown-bread eater, an atheist, an advocate of free love, a Communist, and a near traitor. Along with a few other men he had courageously signed the bail bond that procured the release of President Jefferson Davis from prison. For this act of compassion he became the butt of the barb "Grant beat Davis—Greeley bailed him." One Republican song, to the tune of "John Brown's Body," reflected a common sentiment:

> We'll hang the "Lib-'ral" Greeley on a sour apple tree,
> Because he bailed Jeff Davis and he set the traitor free;
> He never can be president, as you can plainly see,
> As we go marching on.

GENERAL GRANT DEFEATS GREELEY

Frustrated Democrats who had no chance to win with a regular candidate opportunistically adopted the cry "Anything to beat Grant." Accordingly, they endorsed the nomination of Greeley, and in so doing provided one of the sorriest pictures on record of "eating crow." For years Greeley's acid editorial pen had castigated the Democrats, including Southerners, as scoundrels, slave whippers, and begetters of mulattoes. "I never said all Democrats were saloon keepers," he allegedly remarked. "What I said was that all saloon keepers were Democrats." Yet a quotation from Greeley's *Tribune* in January 1868 had charged, "Everyone who chooses to live by pugilism, or gambling, or harlotry, with nearly every keeper of a tippling house [saloon], is politically a Democrat." Unable to choke down Greeley, the remnants of the regular Democratic party, known as "Straight Outs," put up a lost-cause ticket that attracted only a few thousand votes.

Like other political spoilsmen of the age, Grant had engaged in "cronyism" and nepotism by appointing to federal office designing politicians and relatives, including in-laws of the Dent family. One anti-Grant song ran:

> When Useless [Ulysses Grant] came to Washington
> He wore a jaunty plume,
> The Dents and Murphys [Irish politicians] crowded in
> And drove him to his doom.

On the other hand, the Liberal Republicans could give assurances of

Horace and no relations
To fill the public stations.

Embarrassed Republicans, saddled with a willing incumbent, had no choice but to renominate the mud-spattered Grant. For the Vice Presidency they selected Henry Wilson, "The Natick Cobbler," who had worked his way up as a shoemaker from Natick, Massachusetts. Thrown on the defensive, the Republicans pleaded, "Grant us another term!" The "Bloody Shirt" was dusted off to do duty again, as the cry went forth to keep the party in power that had preserved the Union and not to lose at the polls what Grant had won on the battlefield. Yet the high enthusiasm of 1864 and 1868 was lacking, when the "Wide Awakes" and the "Tanners" had chanted their way down the streets. Democrats and Liberal Republicans alike stigmatized Grant as a "dictator," a "loafer," a "swindler," an "ignoramus," and an "utterly depraved horse jockey."

Thomas Nast, cartoonist extraordinary of the century, supported Grant and pilloried Greeley on the pages of *Harper's Weekly*. The pudgy form

Greeley and the Democrats "Swallow" Each Other. A Republican jibe at the forced alliance between these former foes. Thomas Nast, *Harper's Weekly*, 1872.

of a bespectacled and white-hatted Greeley repeatedly appeared with a book sticking out of a pocket of his long white coat. It was successively shown with such titles as "What I Know About Farming," "What I Know about Liars," "What I Know about Eating My Own Words," "What I Know about Reform," and "What I Know About Bolting" [my party].

Among the medals struck off for this campaign were such oddments as "Grant, Wilson & Prosperity," "On to Richmond," "The Natick Cobbler— the Galena Tanner—There's Nothing Like Leather." This was an obvious reference to the fact that the two running mates had at one time both engaged in the leather business. As for Greeley medals, one finds "The Honest Old Farmer of Chappaqua" and "Universal Amnesty [for ex-Confederates] and Impartial Suffrage [for blacks?]," "The Sage of Chappaqua H. Greeley," and "Greeley, Brown [for Vice President] and Amnesty." Greeley supporters carried medals endorsing "Reform," "Acts Not Words," and "The Pen is Mightier than the Sword," which reproduced in metal the candidate's editorial quill pen.

Clever Republican campaign songs extolled the battling hero of Appomattox. Among them were "We'll Fight on the Line" (if it takes all summer), "The Fighting Tanner," "The Tanners are Coming," and "Ulysses Tried and True." One of Grant's achievements was acclaimed in the "Ku Klux Song," for he had allegedly destroyed the Klan by enforcing the anti-Klan legislation of 1871.

Hostile Republican tunes sneered at "Old White Hat" Greeley and especially at the Liberal Republicans. Their cry was put into the title of a song, "Anything to Beat Grant," which continued, "the soreheads now rant." Other songs announced "With Greeley You Can't Fool Us," while jeering at "Goosey Greeley" and "Greedy or Greeley?" "Old Horace" received a blast for snuggling up to the Democrats in "To Our New Friend, the Old Democrat, H.G.," which was supposedly a greeting from the Tammany bosses of New York. A nonsensical Republican ballad, "Chap-Chap-Paw-Quaw," pilloried "The Farmer of Chappaqua" as a scarecrow:

> Chap, Chap, Chap, paw, quaw, quaw,
> An old white hat and a man o' straw.

Challenger Greeley made a gallant run of it, but was trampled down at the polls by Grant, "The Man on Horseback." When the dust settled, the loser wrote to a friend that he had not known whether he was "running for President or the Penitentiary." Within a month after election day "Old White Hat" had lost successively his wife, the election, his editorial job, his mind, and his life.

AN ORGY OF SCANDAL

In the stormy months following Grant's reelection, scandals bursting like popcorn continued to dominate the news. The Crédit Mobilier investigation, which shattered various reputations, went forward in Congress, and Congress itself became involved in the "Salary Grab." The calloused members voted to increase their salaries by 50 percent, retroactive for two years—hence a cash bonus of $5,000. A wave of public indignation forced a repeal.

If Grant himself was honest, he was distressingly loyal to dishonest subordinates. In 1875 the news leaked out that a gigantic "Whiskey Ring" was engaged in robbing the Treasury of millions of dollars in taxes. "Let no guilty man escape," insisted Grant in one of his high-sounding utterances. Yet when he found that his private secretary was deeply involved, he volunteered a favorable written statement for the jury. The guilty man did escape. Also criminal was the conduct of Secretary of War Belknap, who had accepted thousands of dollars in bribe money for lucrative contracts to supply (and-cheat) the Indians. The House unanimously voted to impeach him, but the Senate could not convict him because Grant made him a private citizen by accepting his resignation, shockingly "with great regret."

Dishonor during the Grant era, noxious though it was, did give a needed impetus to the halting movement toward civil service reform. Old-line politicians who had been buying votes and feathering their nests naturally scorned what they called "snivel service reform." In the 1870s citizens heard sneering references to "Sunday-school politics" and "goody-goody reformers." Senator Charles Sumner, orating in the Senate in 1872, declared with undue optimism, "The phrase 'public office is a public trust' has of late become common property."

Already besmirched, the Grant years lost even more of their respectability when the panic of 1873 descended like suffocating fog. One of the burning issues was "resumption," which grew out of the decision during the Civil War not to redeem paper currency in gold on the demand of the holder. "Greenbacks" consequently depreciated in value. Inflationists, known as "cheap money men" or "soft money men," preferred to have this "battle-born currency" retained or even expanded. But the "sound money redeemers" favored redeeming the paper money in gold on demand. Impatient with delay, they voiced the slogan "The way to resume is to resume," which grew out of a statement by ex-Secretary of the Treasury Chase in 1866. In 1875 Congress passed a partial resumption bill which provided for full redemption in specie of greenbacks presented on or after January 1, 1879. Not surprisingly, when people found that they could secure heavy gold for lightweight greenbacks at par value, they kept their more convenient paper currency.

America's hundredth birthday coincided with Grant's last full year in office. A Centennial Exposition honoring the event opened in Philadelphia in May 1876 and continued for six months. The typewriter and telephone were both introduced to the public, for in March of that same year Alexander Graham Bell, the Scottish-born Bostonian, had transmitted to his assistant in an adjoining room the first intelligible sentence ever to come over a telephonic wire, "Mr. Watson, come here. I want you."

Numerous other nations exhibited at Philadelphia the productions of their countries of which they were most proud. While the exposition was still in the planning stage, the poet James Russell Lowell wrote a biting satire:

> Columbia, puzzled what she should display
> Of true home make on her Centennial day,
> Was urged to exhibit scandals, graft, and rings,
> And challenge Europe to produce such things,
> She'll find it hard to hide her spiteful tears
> At such advance in one poor hundred years.

Yet so strong and lusty was the republic that it shook off such defects and annoyances and forged ahead, much like a rhinoceros plunging through a thick jungle oblivious to flies and ticks.

BLAINE OF MAINE AND HAYES OF OHIO

Opening rumbles of the presidential campaign of 1876 were confused by President Grant's disquieting desire for a third term, despite the sorry record of scandal. But the Democratic House of Representatives effectively spiked his guns by passing a resolution late in 1875 declaring that "any departure from this time-honored custom [two presidential terms] would be unwise, unpatriotic, and fraught with peril to our free institutions."

Glamorous James G. Blaine, "The Magnetic Statesman" from Maine, had clearly emerged as the front runner as the Republicans prepared to meet in their nominating convention in Cincinnati. A radiant personality and a spellbinder on the stump, Blaine was notorious for making political capital by baiting the British so as to win acclaim from the Irish-American voters. This provocative tactic continued to be a common ploy of politicians before or during important national elections.

More notorious was Blaine's penchant for winning acclaim from Northern voters by goading ex-Confederates with his vigorous waving of the "Bloody Shirt." A year before the Republican nominating convention met, he had delivered a fiery speech in the House of Representatives during which he resurrected memories of the thousands of boys in blue who had rotted and died in the Southern prison camps. He provoked angry responses in Congress, as he doubtless expected, from some of the dozens of Confederate veterans in the House. "The Magnetic Statesman" had never served in the war, and such absenteeism explains why one Democratic Congressman rejoined, "The dead smelt well to Blaine." Another critic referred to him as one of those men who are "invincible in peace and invisible in war."

Bolstered by the Bloody Shirt and the twisted British lion's tail, Blaine's candidacy was proceeding under full steam in the spring of 1876, when it struck a fatal reef. Damning evidence then leaked out that as Speaker of the House in 1869 the personable candidate had used his influence to save a land grant for a Southern railroad. Later he had sought and received financial favors from the same company—a situation that a later generation would call "conflict of interest." Thrown on the defensive, Blaine delivered a dramatic but self-serving speech to the House of Representatives during which he read from certain selected "Mulligan letters" that, in his judgment, proved him innocent of wrongdoing. But he steadfastly refused to permit probers to see the letters, and in these circumstances such a suppression of evidence seemed to be a confession of guilt.

Eight years later Blaine's Mulligan letters (now owned by James Mulligan) were published, and in one of them appeared the damaging statement "I do not feel that I shall prove a deadhead in the enterprise if I once embark in it. I see various channels in which I know I can be useful." At the end of one of the handwritten missives appeared the admonition "Burn this letter." The evidence in 1876 was strong that Blaine had adopted pre-Grant moral standards that were not acceptable to a post-Grant reformist generation, especially one determined to "throw the rascals out."

Controversial Robert G. Ingersoll, a superlative orator and the leading agnostic of the era, nominated Blaine at Cincinnati in a tremendous effort. He made dramatic reference to Blaine's Bloody Shirt speech before Congress, declaiming, "Like an armed warrior, like a plumed knight, James G. Blaine marched down the halls of the American Congress and threw his shining lance full and fair against the brazen forehead of every traitor to his country and every maligner of his [Blaine's] fair reputation. . . . In the name of those that perished in the skeleton clutch of famine at Andersonville and Libby, whose suffering he so vividly remembers [though never there], Illinois, Illinois nominates—James G. Blaine." Thus overnight "The Magnetic Statesman" became "The Plumed Knight," and was commonly cartooned with a huge feather in his headgear.

But when aroused by scandal in high places, American voters are inclined to rate honesty above glamour or even demonstrated statesmanship. As a consequence, in 1876 the deadlocked Republican convention finally turned from Blaine to Rutherford B. Hayes, whom unfriendly critics unfairly dubbed "The Great Unknown." He had in fact been elected governor of Ohio for three terms, but above all he had a reputation for sterling integrity. Joseph Pulitzer of the *New York World* wrote, "Hayes has never stolen. Good God, has it come to this?"

Yet "Brave Rutherford Hayes" enjoyed other assets. He could appeal to the soldier vote because he not only had risen to the rank of major general but had been wounded three times in action. An added plus proved to be his long residence in the state of Ohio, which was usually doubtful in close elections and which commanded a large electoral vote. A political saying of the 1870s paraphrasing Shakespeare ran:

> Some are born great,
> Some achieve greatness,
> And some are born in Ohio.

During most of the nineteenth century Virginia was known as "The Mother of Presidents"; Ohio was on the way to becoming "The Mother of Presidents"—mostly mediocre presidents or worse.

"SLIPPERY SAM" TILDEN

Meeting in St. Louis, the Democratic nominating convention picked a potential winner in Samuel J. Tilden, the multimillionaire bachelor governor of New York. He had established a national reputation by helping to smash the notorious (Democratic) Tweed Ring in New York City, but his image as a reform candidate was somewhat tarnished. He had gleaned most of his millions from a law practice that had involved him with some slimy characters, including the disreputable "Jubilee Jim" Fisk. Not for nothing was the lawyer-candidate called "The Great Forecloser." Nor was Tilden an impressive figure of a man, despite his undoubted shrewdness. Slightly built, sickly, nervous, and weak-voiced, he had acquired the nickname "Whispering Sammy" because he sounded secretive. He was also labeled "Slippery Sam" because he had formed unsavory connections with politically corrupt Tammany Hall in New York City. In addition "Thrifty Sam" had allegedly dodged much of his income tax during the Civil War. Yet despite his handicaps of wealth, health, and stealth, he looked like a winner to the Democratic wheelhorses. Drooling for the spoils of office, they condemned Republican scandals and held out the hope of civil service reform with their "reform" candidate.

As the centennial campaign of 1876 gathered steam, "Copperheadism" was again resurrected by the Republicans as they cried or sang "Avoid rebel rule," "Vote as you shot, boys," and "The boys in blue will see it through." Republicans were evidently content to rely on these time-tested but by now stale war cries, plus a few stereotypes like "Hurrah! for Hayes and honest ways" and "We'll vote for the Buckeye Boy" (Hayes of Ohio).

Vocal Democrats countered with "Turn the rascals out," "Tilden and reform," "Hayes, hard money and hard times," and "Grantism means poor people made poorer." The Tildenites also devised a jingle that was evidently contemptuous of the Republican nominee:

> Pa! Pa! please tell Ma
> Hayes is in the White House!
> Ha! Ha! Ha!

Among Democratic partisans, the house-cleaning motif surfaced in such slogans as "Reform is necessary in the civil service" and "Let us have a clean sweep." Economic regeneration was closely associated with political purity by the Democrats in such slogans as "Reform is necessary to establish a sound currency" and "We demand a rigorous frugality in every department of the government." The issue of a "tariff for revenue only" likewise made an early appearance in "We demand that our customhouse taxation shall be for revenue only."

Special medals carried both conventional and unconventional appeals. One ingenious Democratic device was shaped like a long-handled broom that could be worn as a pin with the word "reform" appearing on the handle and the names "Tilden" and "Hendricks" [vice presidential candidate] on the brush. A more standardized approach was "The Aggressive Leader of Reform Samuel J. Tilden," who was also called "Uncle Sam" Tilden and "The Sage of Greystone [his home]."

Republican medals endorsing Hayes emphasized such themes as "Honest Money, Honest Government," "Our Centennial President," and "The Centennial Candidates" (the two Republican candidates). One medal lashed out at "Shammy [Sammy] the Shameless—Cheats Uncle Sam on His Income Tax—The People will Never Condone it." Another pro-Hayes medal showed the face of "Shammy Tilden" surrounded by the words "Democratic Party Died of Tildenopathy, 1876, in the 60th Year of its Age" and "Let it R.I.P.," that is, rest in peace. The reference was evidently to Tilden's well-publicized ill health, for he had survived a stroke the year before and suffered from hypochondria. On the reverse of the same medal appeared the inscription below a coffin, "Gone To The Old 'World' To FIND A MOTHER-IN-LAW." This was a transparent dig at Tilden's bachelorhood.

Agonizing memories of the late war were kept green in 1876 by the printed Republican songsters, which contributed such titles as "Brave Rutherford Hayes," "An Empty Sleeve," "We'll Fight Traitors to the Death," "The Voice of the Nation's Dead," and "Hurrah! for the Army Blue." All of these were aimed at keeping aloft the flapping "Bloody Shirt." Sung by "Boys in Blue Clubs," such songs seethed with "treason," "rebellion," "Confederate thieves," "rebel traitor," and "Rebel Sam," which "Sammy" Tilden definitely was not.

In defense of the ticket, Democratic campaign songs sang the praises of "Honest Sam Tilden." One of them, "Hold the Fort for Tilden," hailed "Uncle Sam" as a leader under a "Reform Banner." The same song regarded Tilden's bachelorhood as a mantle of virtue, for with rather dubious logic it proclaimed:

> No seductive woman tempter,
> Can draw him aside,
> His loved wife is our whole country,
> She's his only bride.

THE "GREAT FRAUD" OF '76

Prolonged and nerve-shattering deadlock followed the voting in 1876. Three Southern states—Louisiana, South Carolina, and Florida—filed two sets of returns, one for Tilden and one for Hayes. The results filtered in so slowly as to give birth to the expression "Another county heard from." Both parties made haste to send "visiting statesmen" to all three disputed states to do what they could, corruptly or otherwise, to resolve the controversy in their favor—a process known as "stealing the election."

As for the Southern balloting just ended, dishonors were roughly even. Republican workers, whom their opponents called "Radical Rogues," doubtless miscounted many votes and spent money corruptly. The Democrats, for their part, no doubt "Ku-Kluxed" thousands of black voters or "bulldozed" them from the polls. Aroused Republicans adapted a nursery rhyme for the occasion:

> Sing a song of shotguns,
> Pocket full of knives
> Four-and-twenty black men,
> Running for their lives;
> When the polls are open,
> Shut the nigger's mouth,
> Isn't that a bully way
> To make a solid South?

Unwilling to be robbed of the White House, many Democratic hotheads cried, "On to Washington," "Tilden or fight," or "Tilden or blood." Aroused "Minute Men" began to drill in 1876 with the intention of seating their "victorious" leader. But one Civil War was enough, and sanity finally prevailed as an Electoral Commission was set up to decide between the two sets of returns. This extraconstitutional body, consisting of eight Republicans and seven Democrats, voted eight to seven on strict party lines to give all twenty disputed electoral votes to Hayes, who thus managed to scrape through by one electoral vote, 185 to 184. In a sense, the Democrats stole the election and the Republicans stole it back.

Immediately, and for years thereafter, the Democrats complained bitterly about "The Great Fraud" and "The Crime of '76." Yet, in Republican eyes Hayes was not the "Fraud" but the "Hero of '77." Charges of stealing the election died down appreciably after the publication in 1878 of the "Cipher Dispatches," which threw Democrats on the defensive. These coded telegrams related to the possible use of money to "buy" Florida and South Carolina for the Tilden ticket. Yet one fact is undisputed: Tilden polled some 265,000 more popular votes than Hayes, regardless of how they were obtained. Elected by a popular vote of the American people, he never took office.

XVI

The Republican Doldrums

He loves his country best who strives to make it best.

Robert G. Ingersoll, 1882

HONEST WAYS WITH RUTHERFORD HAYES

No President has ever reached the White House with such a cloud on his title as Rutherford ("Rutherfraud") B. Hayes. He was dubbed "Old 8 to 7" and "His Fraudulency"; he was branded "Boss Thief," "The Usurper," De Facto President," and "President De Facto"; he was cartooned with "Fraud" on his brow.

All this abuse cut Hayes to the quick, for he was a man of spotless integrity whom Republicans hailed as "His Honesty"—a kind of "Queen Victoria in breeches," it was said. His wife shared his straight-laced views on temperance, and "Lemonade Lucy," as she was called, served no alcohol during her husband's "cold water administration." One prominent guest at the White House, when asked how well the dinner had gone, reportedly remarked, "Excellently. The water flowed like wine."

Hayes shocked many supporters when, in fulfillment of a preelection bargain, he appointed to his Cabinet a Democrat who was, incidentally, an ex-Confederate general. Republicans felt that fellow Republicans should occupy the more prominent offices, if not all of them. One sour observation was that if Hayes were Pope, he would feel obliged to appoint a few Protestant cardinals.

Even more shocking, and also pursuant to a preelection bargain,

Hayes pulled out the federal troops that were sustaining Republican carpetbag governments in the last two "unredeemed" Southern states, South Carolina and Louisiana. Jubilant Democrats promptly seized control, and henceforth politicians could count on the Democratic solidarity of the Solid South. Corrupt Republican hangers-on were outraged at being deprived of "four more years of good stealing"; honest Republicans feared the rise of Democratic political strength in the South. But as Hayes had declared in his inaugural address, "He serves his party best who serves his country best"—the most remembered of his high-minded pronouncements.

Unlike many politicians, Hayes generally practiced what he preached. He deservedly earned the title "The Spokesman of Reunion" by resolutely ending federal reconstruction in the South and by snubbing many professional officeseekers. But disappointed politicians sneered at "Granny" Hayes and the "old woman policies" of the "Goody-Two-Shoes Reformer."

Hayes was further bedeviled by the lingering aftermath of the panic of 1873, for labor violence erupted during a prolonged period of depression and deflation. Wage earners and others with marginal incomes suffered acutely. Many of them veered away from demands for more green-backed paper money to hail silver, "the sacred white metal," as the inflationary cure for their financial woes. But in 1873, when silver had commanded a higher price in the open market than at the Treasury, the coinage of silver dollars was quietly dropped in what later came to be branded "The Crime of '73." Subsequently, when the Western silver miners began to pour out a surplus of silver, a persistent demand arose that the nation return to using the metallic "Dollar of our Daddies" instead of the hated greenback or "rag money." The ratio of undervalued silver to gold would thus be set at 16 to 1. Such a move would be inflationary, and hence the "hard money" or "sound money" supporters of gold and gold-backed greenbacks engaged in a prolonged battle against the "soft money" or "dishonest money" advocated by the silverites.

Agitation for more silver coinage subsided appreciably in 1878 when Congress passed the Bland-Allison Act, initially sponsored by Representative Richard ("Silver Dick") Bland. It provided that the Treasury would purchase 2 million to 4 million dollars' worth of silver bullion a month and coin it into dollars then worth only 93 cents intrinsically. This legislation was passed over the veto pen of President Hayes, a "sound money" man.

A clear-cut victory for sound money occurred on January 1, 1879, when, pursuant to the Redemption Act of 1875, the Treasury "resumed" the redemption of greenbacks with gold, thus making them "good as gold." On that historic day the great orator and agnostic Colonel Robert G. Ingersoll spoke from the steps of the subtreasury in Wall Street in Biblical terms, declaiming, "I am thankful I have lived to see the day when the greenback can raise its right hand and declare, 'I know that my Redeemer liveth.'"

A CANAL BOY VERSUS A WEST POINTER

Long before the deadline date President Hayes had announced that he would not be a candidate for a second term. This firm decision relieved the party bosses of the disagreeable task of "dumping" the annoyingly pure incumbent, plus "Lemonade Lucy." Craving what they regarded as "four more good years of stealing," the professional politicians yearned for a return of the "Old Man," ex-President Grant, who had meanwhile "broadened" himself by a much-publicized globe-girdling trip. The befuddled general, so lacking in good judgment as to show a willingness to be used, was persuaded that the no-third-term tradition applied to consecutive terms only. A Republican song, "Around the World with Grant My Boys," offered as its chorus:

> Hurrah for General Grant my boys,
>   Hurrah for General Grant;
> The country calls on him once more
>   To be her President.

But foes of the general again called for "Anyone to beat Grant" and "Anything to beat Grant."

Ranks of the Grand Old Party (G.O.P.), as the Republican party was immodestly beginning to call itself, were being swollen by the legions of the Grand Army of the Republic (G.A.R.). These were Union veterans who had organized themselves as a pressure group in 1866. Rival Democrats, not far from the mark, claimed that G.A.R. stood for "Generally All Republicans."

Meeting in their nominating convention in Chicago, the assembled Republicans were treated to a superlative speech nominating Grant. It was delivered by Roscoe Conkling of New York, the conservative Old Guard "Peacock Senator," whose imperious self-esteem had earlier provoked from Congressman James G. Blaine a costly sneer about his "turkey gobbler strut." (Thereafter Conkling was often cartooned as a turkey gobbler.) The Senator began his great effort for Grant with these stirring words:

> And if asked what state he hails from,
>   This our sole reply shall be,
> "From near Appomattox Court-house,
>   With its famous apple tree."

Then, among other promises, Conkling gave this assurance regarding Grant: "He will hew to the line of right, let the chips fly where they may."

Enheartened by Conkling's electrifying speech, Grant's Old Guard supporters remained loyal to the end—the immortal "Three Hundred and Six." Of them it was said, "The Old Guard dies, but never surrenders"—a reference to Napoleon's Imperial Guard that vainly made the last charge at Waterloo. With a total of 379 votes needed to make a choice, the convention fell into a deadlock. As a compromise candidate, it finally turned to James A. Garfield, a Congressman from Ohio who had made an impressive speech nominating a fellow Ohioan, "Honest John" Sherman.

As for the badly needed housecleaning, the Republican platform declared that "the reform of the civil service should be thorough, radical, and complete." This pledge was largely window dressing, for the office-holding Old Guard obviously did not have their hearts in it. A "spoilsman" leader of the Republican party in Texas blurted out an immortal remark, "What are we here for, except the offices?"

Vengeful Democrats assembled in Cincinnati still seething over "The Great Fraud" that had robbed "Old Sammy" Tilden of the Presidency to which he had been nominally elected by popular vote. They hoped to right this grievous wrong by running the decrepit Tilden again, but as he was four years older and sicker, he prudently bowed out. The Democrats then turned to General Winfield S. Hancock, a West Pointer, like Grant, who had served brilliantly during the war, notably at Gettysburg, where he was wounded. A dispatch from General McClellan had reported that "Hancock was superb"; hence the sobriquet "Hancock the Superb" and the inscription on a medal "A Superb Soldier—A Model President." The general was popular in the South, where he had been a lenient reconstruction commander, and his nomination would cleanse the Democratic party of some of the stain of Copperheadism and the "Bloody Shirt." The Democratic platform trumpeted its support for badly needed civil service reform and especially for a "tariff for revenue only."

After the unfortunate experience with West Pointer Grant, many voters were dubious about another professional soldier and the dangers of "Bonapartism." An eight-page Republican campaign pamphlet purporting to describe in detail Hancock's statesmanship turned out to have only blank pages. A common sneer growing out of an editorial in the *New York Sun* was "Winfield Scott Hancock is a good man weighing 250 pounds." When interviewed in New Jersey, the general seemed to display incredible ignorance when he remarked, "The tariff question is a local question." In truth, the tariff was indeed a local question because different localities produced different products that might or might not be helped by tariffs. Yet cartoonist Thomas Nast had Hancock stupidly ask, "Who is Tariff, and Why Is He for Revenue Only?"

BOOSTING BOATMAN JIM

Unawed by Hancock's splendid war record, the Republicans again unfurled the "Bloody Shirt" and, with good reason, cast doubts on Democratic sincerity for reform. As the event proved, the idea of reform embraced by the "outs" consisted mainly of ousting the incumbent politicians and installing their own. The journalist-poet Eugene Field put his boast in verse:

> Out on reformers such as these;
> By Freedom's sacred powers,

> We'll run the country as we please;
> We saved it, and it's ours.

Garfield, for his part, had all the appeal of a "rags to riches" American success story. Born in a log cabin and early deprived of his father, "The Buckeye Boy" in his youth had driven mules on the tow paths of the Ohio Canal—hence the nicknames "Our Boatman," "Boatman Jim," and "The Canal Boy President." One Republican medal proclaimed, "From the Tow Path to the White House," and a pro-Garfield campaign song ran:

> He early learned to paddle well his own forlorn canoe
> Upon Ohio's "grand canal," he held the helm so true;
> And now the people shout to him: "Lo! 'tis for you we wait,
> We want to see Jim Garfield guide our glorious ship of State."

At various times Garfield had done some teaching ("The Teacher President"), as well as some lay preaching ("The Preacher President"). Far more important in that era, he had risen to the rank of major general of the volunteers in the Civil War, thus offsetting General Hancock's appeal to the veteran vote. "They Saved the Flag" was a Republican song written in honor of both Garfield and his running mate, Chester A. Arthur.

Garfield's greatest personal liability was the persistent allegation, never conclusively proved, that he was corrupt. As a member of Congress he had become tainted by the Crédit Mobilier, the railroad-building scandal, to the extent of a $329 profit—a ridiculously small sum when one considers the large-scale graft of those years. Thus was born one of the great digital slogans of American history. The tell-tale figure not only appeared on countless transparencies in parades but was chalked on innumerable walls, buildings, and stones by gloating Democrats.

Busy Republican organizers outdid themselves in raising campaign funds or slush funds. They were eminently successful in "frying the fat" out of corporations anxious to fatten indefinitely on Republican protective tariffs. In particular, the state of Indiana was "drenched" with Republican money, now coming to be called "soap." It no doubt greased the cogs of the Republican political machine.

Republican campaign songs featured Garfield's boyhood hardships and his Ohio background. Typical were "The Plow Boy of Ohio," "Hurrah for the Buckeye Boy," and "Jim Garfield of the West." The voters were not allowed to forget his early experience as a canal boy. Such descriptive titles appeared as "Garfield's Canal Boat" and "The Tow-Boy Raised in the West," as though an experienced hand were needed to tow the scandal-riddled ship of state into port.

Nor was General Garfield's battle record overlooked in Republican booklets and songsters, which made available such offerings as "Brave Garfield Is Our Man," "With Garfield We'll Conquer Again," and "Jim

Garfield's at the Front."* A special musical appeal in both English and German was made for "The Veteran's Vote," especially the vote of those amputees with an "empty sleeve." Related titles were "Boys in Blue, Fall in Line" and "Still Fighting for the Union."

Pro-Republican song writers enthusiastically flapped the Bloody Shirt in an attempt to solidify "The Solid North" against "The Solid South." Appeals were channeled through "The Voice of the Nation's Dead," and through fear of what would happen "When the Johnnies Get into Power." These ex-rebels and "traitors" would surely reenslave "the darkeys" and replace the Union stars with Confederate bars.

Votes of the liberated slaves were openly courted by Republican composers. "Ef de Party Wins" was a blatant appeal in Negro dialect. The tingling tune of the Civil War song "The Battle Cry of Freedom" was pressed into satirical service, with one of the anti-Southern stanzas reading:

> 'Tis slavery forever, hurrah, boys, hurrah!
> Down with the Yankees, up with the bars;
> While we ostracize the loyal and murder thousands more,
> Shouting the battle cry of freedom.

Another bitter composition, "Six Thousand Millions Strong!" referred to the $6 billion debt that the seceded Southerners, mostly Democrats, had foisted onto the nation's taxpayers.

One amusing anti-Hancock song was a parody of the recently produced Gilbert and Sullivan operetta *H.M.S. Pinafore*. One of its stanzas ended with a reference to General Hancock's supposed political amateurishness:

> I [Hancock] knew so little that they rewarded me,
> By making me the leader of the Democracee.

For their part, the Democrats adapted Gilbert and Sullivan to the words of an anti-Garfield air ("Sir James' Song"), the first stanza of which read:

> When I was a boy, to keep me alive,
> A canal boat team I was driven to drive,
> I traveled on foot and the reins I did yank,
> And I held the mule's tail on the boat's gang plank,
> I clung to that tail with such fixed intent
> That now I'm a candidate for President.

SONGS OF THE ALSO-RANS

If we may judge from the relatively few Democratic songs, the Republicans outsang their rivals by a wide margin. The Democrats, boasting about General Hancock's "superb" war record, appealed for "The

---

* This was derived from a report that General Rosecrans reportedly sent from the Battle of Chickamauga, "Gen. Garfield Proceeded to the Front."

Soldier's Vote" in both English and German. They also stressed urgently needed political reform in the aftermath of the Grant scandals. "We Need a Change" is a song title that foreshadowed a long succession of "Time for a Change" slogans. The Whiskey Ring and other cesspools of corruption in Washington inspired a ballad, "No Ringsters Need Apply," which was an adaptation of the familiar posted notices warning Irish immigrants, "No Irish Need Apply." Democrats aimed one of their musical barbs directly at the "Stalwarts," the name given to hard-line and corrupt politicians in the Republican camp:

> Our Nation's laws we will obey,
> And bury the bloody shirt;
> Cement the Union North and South,
> Sweep out the Stalwart dirt.

Reflecting sensitivity to Republican shirt wavers, the Democrats came out with tunes entitled "The Old Bloody Shirt" and "The Bleached Shirt." Hancock was acclaimed the launderer-in-chief. For added measure, Democratic songs carried such titles as "The Glory of a Reunited Nation," "The Blue and Gray for Hancock," and "Once Again Our Old Commander." Bordering on sacrilege was "The Power of Hancock's Name," which parodied the popular gospel hymn "All Hail the Power of Jesus' Name".

Zealots of the Greenback party, representing a considerable number of "soft money" advocates from the South and West, added an emerald dash of color to the canvass of 1880. Initially favoring currency inflation with more greenbacks, the Greenbackers broadened their aims with the addition of various labor elements. Their newer platform included such objectives as shorter hours for workers, the exclusion of Chinese immigrants, and the granting of public lands to *bona fide* settlers. One of the more spirited of the songs in *The Complete Greenback and Labor Songster* unveiled "A New Yankee Doodle," the chorus of which jibed:

> Yankee doodle, banks and bonds!
> Yankee doodle dandy,
> Bounce the banks and burn the bonds,
> Oh, Yankee doodle dandy.

Other Greenback songs were entitled "Down with the Money King" and "Pay the Bonds with Greenbacks." All this netted little or nothing. The Greenbackers had made an impressive showing in the Congressional elections of 1878, but trailed the field lamely during the Garfield-Hancock sweepstakes of 1880.

"Boatman Jim" Garfield barely nosed his scandal-riddled Republican craft over the reefs of corruption and misrule to the quiet waters of victory. He won by only 9,464 popular votes out of nearly 9 million cast, although his margin in the Electoral College was a comfortable 214 to 155. The North was not yet ready to turn the management of the country over to General "Hancock the Superb" and his "whitewashed rebel brigadiers."

GARFIELD'S ASSASSINATION

"Boatman Jim" Garfield was a fine, upstanding, intelligent, kindly, Christian gentleman who turned and kissed his mother after taking the inaugural oath. His gravest weakness was that he hated to hurt people's feelings by saying "no"—an indispensable word for any politician who seeks to attain the status of statesman. In his inaugural address he declared, "It has been said that unsettled questions have no pity for the repose of nations," from which came the shortened "Unsettled questions have no pity."

Mad scrambling for political office—the usual role of the victors—overwhelmed President Garfield. He blurted out in private, "My God! What is there in this place that a man should ever want to get into it?" His party was badly split into two factions: on the one hand the pro-Grant, severe-on-the-South, "Stalwart" faction; on the other the anti-Grant, soft-on-the-South, "Half Breed" faction. Proud Senator Roscoe Conkling of New York, he of the "turkey-gobbler strut" in Blaine's barbed phrase, was a leader of the Stalwarts. James G. Blaine, the magnetic "Plumed Knight from Maine," was the leading Half Breed. He enjoyed the friendship and support of Half Breed President Garfield, who appointed him Secretary of State. Evidently working hand in glove with the ambitious Blaine, President Garfield removed a prominent Conklingite as Collector of the Port of New York—a high-salaried political plum.

A fearful row ensued. "Lord Roscoe" Conkling resigned from the Senate and went to Albany, where he lobbied for his reelection. (Before the Seventeenth Amendment in 1913, state legislatures elected Senators.) Junior Senator Thomas C. Platt, thereafter known as "Me too" Platt, had resigned in sympathy for Conkling and the "Battle of Albany" raged more furiously. Both men were defeated for reelection. Senator Conkling retired to private life, but "Me Too" Platt, who staged a comeback some seven years later, was long prominent in national and New York politics as the "Easy Boss."

During the bitter "Battle of Albany" Garfield was fatally shot while in the Washington railroad station. His assassin proved to be a disappointed and deranged officeseeker who, smoking pistol in hand, was said to have shouted, "I am a Stalwart. Arthur is now President of the United States." The appointment that Charles Guiteau received was not appointment to a political office, but a rendezvous with the hangman. Before the trap was sprung, the assassin shouted, "Glory, hallelujah! Glory!" Guiteau's abrupt end inspired at least one sad song and also a children's chant:

> One, two, three, four, five, six, seven;
> All good children go to Heaven;

All the rest go below
To keep company with Guiteau.

"CHET" ARTHUR IN COMMAND

Chester A. Arthur, as the vice-presidential nominee, had won a place on the Garfield-Arthur ticket as a balancing Stalwart. His selection was a vain attempt to appease the anger of the Stalwarts over the sidetracking of General Grant and the nomination of Half Breed "Boatman Jim" Garfield. Arthur had won some unpleasant notoriety as a New York spoilsman, and when word got out that Garfield had been shot, a common reaction was "My God, 'Chet' Arthur President of the United States!"

To the amazement of many skeptics, Arthur turned out to be a respectable President, mutton-chop whiskers and all. Perhaps the shock of the assassination awakened his better instincts; after his swearing in he remarked, "Men may die, but the fabrics of free institutions remain unshaken." He turned his back on the Stalwart politicians and threw his weight behind the passage of the Pendleton Civil Service Act of 1883, the "Magna Carta of civil service reform." Initially about 10 percent of civil service was to be classified, that is, removed from the uncertainties of political patronage. Many Democrats who clamored for this kind of reform turned against it because they expected to gain the Presidency in 1885 (as they did), and they did not want 10 percent of the federal offices "frozen" with Republican incumbents. This curious situation prompted cynics to reverse the Jacksonian adage "Unto the victors belong the spoils" and to substitute, "Unto the vanquished belong the spoils."

By a cruel twist of fate, the bullet that felled Garfield also killed Blaine's political hopes. As uncrowned king of the party, he had taken over the post of Secretary of State expecting to bask in the limelight while serving as a kind of prime minister for four years, possibly eight. But the Half Breed Blaine could not hit it off well with Stalwart President Arthur and he departed in bitterness less than three months later. He had enjoyed only limited opportunity under Arthur to conduct what he had hoped would be a "spirited foreign policy" or to engage in the kind of jingoism that won him the sobriquet "Jingo Jim" Blaine.

"Chet" Arthur, "Our Chet," did well enough as President to deserve nomination in his own right in 1884, even though he had earned the cynical titles "Friend of the Stalwarts," "Gentleman Boss," and the usual "His Accidency." Well-educated, urbane, and moderately courageous, he won fame as a fancy dresser. His wardrobe was reported to contain eighty pairs of trousers. The air of elegance surrounding him gave rise to such other sobriquets as "Prince Arthur," "America's First Gentleman," "First Gentleman of the Land," "Arthur the Gentleman," "Elegant Arthur," "The Dude," and "Dude President." He died of a cerebral hemorrhage the year after he left the White House, a sad finale suggesting that he would not have lasted a full four-year term if he had been nominated and elected for one.

REVOLT OF THE MUGWUMPS

Wind-swept Chicago welcomed the Republican delegates as they flocked there for the purpose of nominating their standard bearer in June 1884. Many of the faithful, shaken by events, recognized that after these long years of scandal and corruption the times demanded a man of un-questioned honesty. Hoping to wring one more military hero from the Bloody Shirt, they approached General William T. Sherman of "Marching through Georgia" fame or infamy, depending on one's feelings about the "Lost Cause." He effectively halted any attempt to draft him by firing off a telegram to the convention: "I will not accept if nominated and will not serve if elected." This emphatic declination has been changed to read, "If nominated I will not run; if elected I will not serve." In political parlance such an iron-clad refusal is known as a "Sherman statement," or "Pulling a Sherman," which is the extreme in unavailability. But the general's declination should have come as no great surprise, for his distaste was well known. Twenty years earlier he had written a friend, "If forced to choose between the penitentiary and the White House for four years, I would say the penitentiary, thank you."

The "Magnetic" Blaine: or, a Very Heavy "Load"-Stone (Magnet) for the Republican Party to Carry. Blaine's personal magnetism, which was famous, here attracts to himself assorted scandals of the Grant era, including his own involvement in the railroad bonds and the Mulligan letters. *Harper's Weekly,* 1880.

Regular Republicans favored the glamorous "Plumed Knight from Maine," James G. Blaine, whom they forced down the throats of the convention, feather and all. Reformist Republicans openly threatened to defect or desert if the "Magnetic Man" should be chosen, and these "Independents" or "Soreheads" were as good as their word. Since 1880 they had used the slogan "I carry my sovereignty under my hat," a shortened form of the expression "I am a Republican who carries his sovereignty under his own hat." Thousands of them either refused to campaign for Blaine, or supported a third-party candidate, or voted the Democratic ticket in the ensuing election. Theodore Roosevelt, a leading young reformist, regarded Blaine as tainted. Angered Stalwarts branded the defectors "Mugwumps," evidently after an Indian word meaning "big chief" or "holier than thou."

Republican regulars viewed the "bolting" Mugwumps with scorn, branding them "Dudes" and "Pharisees," after the self-righteous Jewish sect of Christ's day. Horace Porter, who had served President Grant as private secretary, declared during this campaign, "A mugwump is a person educated beyond his intellect." Wits have humorously described the Mugwump as a voter with "his mug on one side of the political fence and his wump on the other."

In reading the platitudinous platform hammered together by the Republicans in Chicago, an observer would correctly sense that the tariff would be a major issue in the campaign. But he could hardly have suspected that so much of the campaign oratory would involve the personal honesty of the "Plumed Knight." An early warning came when ex-Senator Roscoe Conkling, who could never forget the "turkey gobbler strut" that Blaine had pinned on him, was reportedly asked if he planned to campaign for the "Magnetic Man." He replied, "No, I do not engage in criminal practice."

THE CLEVELAND-BLAINE BATTLE SHAPES UP

In Chicago the frustrated Democrats turned for their "Man of Destiny" to Grover Cleveland, then governor of New York but two years earlier than that only the mayor of Buffalo. A lawyer and a bachelor, he was only forty-seven years old. He had earlier served as sheriff of Erie County in New York (1871–73), and as a conscientious upholder of the law, he had taken his official duties seriously; when called upon to do so, he hanged a couple of men with his own hands. He was thus known, then and later, as "The Buffalo Sheriff" and "The Hangman of Buffalo." When accepting the mayoralty of Buffalo in 1882, he unwittingly coined a slogan for his later presidential campaign when he declared, "A public office is a public trust." He practiced what he preached by freely wielding a veto pen, which earned him the label "Veto Mayor."

As a reform governor of New York, Cleveland continued the battle against corruptionists with his inky lance and was dubbed the "Veto Governor." The legislature of New York had reduced the streetcar fare in New York City to 5 cents. This measure was extremely popular with the strap-hanging masses, but it broke faith with the transit company that was hoping to operate the lines at a fair profit. During Cleveland's race for the Presidency his courageous veto of the legislation returned to haunt him, as masses of Republicans surged through the streets of New York chanting in cadence, "Five, five, five cent fare."

Embittered Democrats had long memories of the "Great Fraud" that had robbed Tilden of the Presidency in 1876, and they still smarted from the narrow defeat of General Hancock in 1880. When their nominating convention met in Chicago, many of the delegates were nursing past wrongs rather than looking to present or future rights. Congressman E. S. Bragg from Wisconsin struck a refreshing note when he placed the name of Grover Cleveland, the "Reform Governor," before the convention. He declared that he spoke for the young men of his state: "His name is upon their lips. His name is in their hearts. They love him, gentlemen, and respect him, and they love him and respect him not only for himself, for his character, for his integrity, for his iron will, but they love him most for the enemies he has made." This characterization was astute, for Cleveland had made enemies of corrupt interests and scheming politicians, notably those of Tammany Hall in New York City, who showed little love for "Grover the Good" during the ensuing campaign. Thus was born one of the great slogans of the nineteenth century. "We Love Him for the Enemies He has Made."

Democrats in their platform responded to the challenge of the protectionist Republicans on the tariff. Alarmed by the mounting surplus in the Treasury from customs duties, they raised the cry "Unnecessary taxation is unjust taxation." Cleveland, in his letter of acceptance, added a refreshing note when he wrote, "Honor lies in honest toil." Here spoke the "unowned candidate"—not owned by any of the powerful interests.

From the opening gun of the presidential race the Democrats hailed Grover Cleveland with high hopes. "Grover the Good" was spotlessly honest. The flashy Blaine, on the other hand, had much to answer for—and he had answered evasively. A famous cartoon in the humor magazine *Puck* branded him "The Tattooed Man." It showed Blaine before the Chicago convention-tribunal, clad in a loincloth, his body liberally tattooed with "Mulligan letters," "Bribery," and other scandals. The epithet "The Tattooed Man" stuck, and in addition chanting Democratic marchers gloatingly proclaimed, "Blaine, Blaine, James G. Blaine, monumental liar from the state of Maine."

In the heat of the campaign more "Mulligan letters" came to light which further indicated that Blaine had involved himself in some notorious railroad scandals. The recipient of one of these letters, a Bostonian named Warren Fisher, was warned at the end, "Burn this letter," along with "Kind regards to Mrs. Fisher." Exultant Democrats cried in unison as they paraded through the streets of the great cities:

> Burn, burn, oh burn this letter.
> Kind regards to Mrs. Fisher.

For their part, the Republicans were no amateurs as dirt diggers. At first they attacked Cleveland as a draft dodger, without pointing out that Blaine, "invincible in peace and invisible in war," had not gone to the fighting front either. Cleveland, who had to remain behind to support his mother and two sisters, hired a substitute for $300, although he did not have to do so. Blaine also legally hired a substitute. The Republicans additionally made much of the "Buffalo Hangman" incident, and they branded Cleveland a drunkard. The truth seems to be that during his carefree bachelor days in Buffalo he could on occasion hoist a mug of beer with his companions.

CLEVELAND'S BASTARD BOY

Cleveland's campaign was moving at full steam when suddenly the roof fell in on "Grover the Good." Scandalmongers broke the devastating story that bachelor Cleveland had sired a boy, now eight years old, whose mother, Maria Halpine, was a widow back in Buffalo. This scandalous information was correct, though hardly relevant to Cleveland's capacity to perform in the White House. He evidently had made no promise of marriage, and several other men had been attentive to the widow Halpine at the same time. Yet, possibly to protect a married man who also knew the widow, Cleveland had assumed financial responsibility for the support of the illegitimate child, who ultimately, under a different name, became a figure of some importance in the business world.

Flabbergasted, Democratic politicians besought Cleveland to "lie like a gentleman." But honest "Old Grover" flatly refused. "Tell the truth" was his forthright admonition, and he clung to it. On gloating Republican tongues "The Beast of Buffalo" became a "Self-confessed Adulterer," which he was not. By definition "adultery" is an affair in which one or both of the participants are married to others; this was simply a case of fornication. Eager Democrats came to Cleveland with countertales of Blaine's alleged premarital doings, but Cleveland is reported to have objected, "The other side can have a monopoly of all the dirt in this campaign."

A versifier by the name of H. H. Monroe seized the occasion to write some scornful lines:

> Ma! Ma! where's my Pa?
> Up in the White House, darling,
> Making the laws, working the cause,
> Up in the White House, dear.

Picking up this theme, jeering Republican paraders and embattled Democrats alike chanted:

> Ma, ma, where's my pa?
> Gone to the White House,
> Ha, ha, ha!

Sometimes gleeful Republicans would start to chant:

> Ma, ma, where's my pa?

and from embattled Democrats would come the antiphonal response:

> Gone to the White House
> Ha, ha, ha!

After the election defiant Democrats defended the Maria Halpine scandal with this triumphant rhyme:

> Hurrah for Maria,
> Hurrah for the kid
> I voted for Grover
> And am damn glad I did.

Alarming indeed was the health of American political life when the alleged paternity of a bastard boy of eight should claim headlines as a leading issue in a national campaign.

Blaine's public dishonesty, though practiced in private, clashed with Cleveland's private immorality, though admitted in public. To some degree, the offsetting sins of the rivals cancelled one another out. Yet in the eyes of most of the clergy and many churchgoers, Cleveland was a greater sinner than Blaine. The Bloody Shirt, now upstaged, faded to a shade of pink, all the more so since neither Blaine nor Cleveland had fought in the Civil War—and time has a way of healing all wounds. This presidential campaign was the only one from Polk's of 1844 to Wilson's in 1916 in which neither of the two major-party candidates could boast of a war record.

THE CLASH OF SONGS AND CATCHWORDS

The "balanced" Republican ticket of Blaine for President and Logan for Vice President did present a swarthy war hero, John A. ("Black Jack") Logan. Fighting with dashing distinction in the Civil War, he had twice suffered wounds in action, and had risen to the rank of major general of Northern volunteers. His nomination probably did more than anything else to keep the Bloody Shirt feebly alive. Republican songs appealing to the soldier vote concentrated on Logan, with Blaine in the background. "The Nation Loves Its Soldiers" was dedicated "to the gallant Gen. John A. Logan." Somewhat similar were "Hold the Fort for Blaine and Logan," "Give Blaine and Logan Three Times Three [cheers]," and "Shout the Slogan" (the chorus ran, "Shout the slogan, Blaine and Logan!").

Other songs of the same genre were "Blaine of Maine and Logan the Brave," "With Blaine and Jack We'll Clear the Track," and "The Plumed Knight [Blaine] and Black Eagle [Logan]." Reviving unpleasant memories of the Civil War, the Republicans produced such songs as "The Democratic Party and the War" and "When I Was a Reb," which told of a man who now voted Republican. Grim reminders were "Starved in [Confederate] Prison" and "We'll Fight It Out Here on the Old Union Line."

Glowing tributes to the gallant "Plumed Knight" appeared in dozens of other musical combinations. Among them were "Blaine the Knight of Maine," "March of the Plumed Knight," and "We'll Follow Where the White Plume Waves." All these references to the nonfighting "Plumed Knight," in slogan as well as song, doubtless helped to create in many sluggish minds the image of a gallant, armor-clad warrior who had ridden into battle with his shining lance and gorgeous white plume. No one seems to have realized that "showing the white feather" was a term used to denote cowardice.

Cooler-headed Democrats, with their Copperheaded background and their nonwarrior Cleveland, were wise not to get entangled in the folds of the Bloody Shirt. One Democratic song offered the title, "The Blue and Gray for Cleveland," which suggested hands across the "bloody chasm" in its appeal for the votes of Union veterans. The Democrats also issued a printed funeral announcement relating to the death of Blaine and the Republican party. The epitaph read, "Conceived in Sin, Matured in Tyranny, and Died of Chronic Disease of the Bloody Shirt."

Among the few substantive issues, tariff duties loomed large in the campaign of 1884, but even this controversy was badly fuzzed by the froth of campaign oratory, slogans, and songs. The Republicans had traditionally favored a protective tariff for their oversized "infant industries" as a barrier against goods fabricated by "cheap foreign labor." Republican campaign tracts exhibited such titles as "Blaine and Logan and Protection!" and "If General Jackson Was Alive He Would Be a Republican." (He had allegedly opposed "free trade.") Campaign broadsides warned, "A Vote for the Democratic candidate means free trade and reduction of wages." Voters were also urged to "Think! Think!! Think!!!" and "Vote for Blaine and Logan, and Maintain the Present Wages and Values." One medallic slogan advised, "No British Pauper Wages for Americans." Other slogans expressed a similar theme: "Preserve Home Industries" and "Labor is King."

The battling Democrats, more dedicated to "free enterprise," favored a "tariff for revenue only," not "free trade." They would raise enough funds at the customs houses to run the government adequately, for the federal income tax was not to be authorized by constitutional amendment until 1913. But the existing tariff schedules were piling up an embarrassing surplus, which reinforced the Democratic slogans "Unnecessary Taxation is Unjust Taxation" and "Workingmen, Don't Be Fooled." Also popular were "Workingmen: Turn the Republicans out! Vote for Cleveland!" and "If you want a change to better times, vote for Grover Cleveland."

Politicians are not prone to call a spade a spade; they are more inclined to call spades steam shovels. Republican strategists naturally hung the danger sign of "free traders" on the Democrats. There is a gulf between free trade and a moderate protective tariff. But nothing could keep the foes of a tariff for revenue only from crying "Down with Free Trade" and "No Free Trade." In the cities, marching legions of Republicans kept step to the chant "No, No, No, Free Trade."

Thrown on the defensive by so-called free trade, the Democrats in their songs stressed "Let's Have a Change," "Turn the Rascals Out," "An Honest Man for President," "Cleveland's the Man," and "Victory and Reform." Parodying a popular song, Democrats sang "Oh, Naughty Bosses!" as well as another favorite: "All They Want's an Office to Fill."

BLAINE'S FINAL BLUNDERINGS

As the mudsplattered campaign reached its final stretch (stench?), Blaine headed for New York State after a Western speaking tour during which he had not "set the prairies on fire." He could have kept on traveling east to his quiet home in Maine, but en route he made a fatal blunder. He decided to head south for New York's metropolis and the grand finale.

Blaine was so indiscreet as to attend the grand "shakedown" dinner of wealthy Republicans at Delmonico's famed restaurant. It quickly became known as "The Boodle Banquet" and "The Royal Feast of Belshazzar."* Additional money or "soap" was desired for the gears of the Republican political machine, and the dinner offered a chance to "fry the fat" out of what later came to be known as "fat cats." Millionaires were conspicuously present, including some of the most famous "robber barons," notably the notorious railroad manipulator Jay Gould. One of the most striking cartoons of the *New York World* showed a ragged and hungry trio—a man, his wife, and his child—out in the street begging for crumbs. They were peering through Delmonico's plate-glass window at the assembled diners, who had diamond pins in their cravats and gourmet food on their plates. "The Boodle Banquet" gave added fervor to the Democratic marching slogans "Soap! Soap! Blaine's only Hope!" and "Scalp, scalp, scalp Jim Blaine."

Jay Gould, the unscrupulous Republican speculator, received unwanted publicity not only from "Belshazzar's Feast" but also from another source. He now controlled the Western Union Telegraph Company, which he used to disseminate reports indicating Republican success as

---

* Belshazzar was an impious Babylonian prince who, according to the Bible, gave a great banquet at which mysterious handwriting appeared on the wall predicting that his days were "numbered."

the returns rolled in. Surging Democratic marchers chanted, "Blaine, Blaine, Jay Gould Blaine, continental liar from the state of Maine." For added measure, crowds in New York sang, to the tune of "The Battle Hymn of the Republic," "We'll Hang Jay Gould on a Sour Apple Tree." A variant ran:

> We'll hang Jim Blaine on a Sour Apple Tree,
> Glory, Glory, Grover Cleveland.

Blaine's blundering continued. On the eve of the balloting, the weary candidate met a delegation of about a thousand clergymen, most of whom did not condone Cleveland's "adultery." Blaine spoke briefly, pointing out that the Christian Republican party had freed the slaves and that with a Republican tariff it would provide "bread for the hungry" and "clothing for the naked." A response was delivered by the Reverend Samuel Burchard, a prominent New York Presbyterian, as the exhausted Blaine evidently permitted his mind to wander to other subjects. In one of the most devastating smear-sneers in political history, Burchard loudly declared, "We are Republicans, and we don't propose to leave our party and identify ourselves with the party whose antecedents have been rum, Romanism, and rebellion."

If Blaine had only had his wits about him, he might have interrupted the bigoted clergyman by crying out, "Stop! I repudiate that libel on the Catholic faith of my mother and sister and on the faith of countless Irish-American and German-American Catholics who are respected fellow citizens, both Republican and Democratic." But Blaine kept quiet, either because he was not listening or because he did not grasp the full import of the statement. His temporary silence seemed to give assent.

Alert to their opportunity, delighted Democrats plastered the country with placards hailing that great alliterative trinity "Rum, Romanism, and Rebellion," sometimes shortened to "R.R.R." Nothing, the proverb affirms, hurts like the truth; and there was a large measure of truth in this insult, which stung and clung. Most of the ex-rebels were Democrats, and most Catholics in America were Democrats, especially the Irish-Americans. The persecuted Irish, whose woes went back to Oliver Cromwell in the 1600s and further, were notorious for drowning their troubles in whiskey (not rum). Horace Greeley had charged that all saloon keepers were Democrats, and in later years the Democratic party was called "the saloon party." Undoubtedly, "Rum, Romanism, and Rebellion" alienated enough prospective Blaine voters to cost him the election in the pivotal state of New York.

As election day 1884 neared, the Blaineites worried about rain, especially in upstate New York, where many Republican voters lived. If it rained, as in fact it did, large numbers of them would not bother to hitch up old Dobbin and drive wearisome miles to the polling places and back. But Ohio had held its state election in October, and there the Republicans had scored a narrow success. Elated partisans, donning plumed helmets and carrying knightly battle-axes, paraded in New York city on the eve of the balloting. As they surged through the streets, they kept time to the rhythm of

> Blaine, Blaine, James G. Blaine
> We don't care a bit for the rain
> O-O-Ohio.

THE DAY OF RECKONING

Unlucky Blaine lost the election by a margin of 1,149 popular votes in New York out of more than 1,100,000 cast. If he could have picked up 575 votes from Cleveland's supporters, he presumably would have won. In this election, as in all closely contested national elections, various "ifs" or "might have beens" influenced the result. Among them was the rain on election day in upstate New York, as well as the presence on the ballot of Prohibition candidate John P. St. John. Recently governor of Kansas, he diverted over 25,000 votes in New York, many of them from the two major candidates. His campaign slogan was "He's All Right!" Even more damaging to Blaine were the defections of the "goody-goody" Republican Mugwumps (Independents) and the hostility of the Stalwart Conklingites.

When the smoke of battle had cleared away, a triumphant banner in a New York parade announced, with reference to local newspaper accounts:

> The *World* says the Independents [Mugwumps] did it.
> The *Tribune* says the Stalwarts [Conklingites] did it.
> The *Sun* says Burchard did it.
> Blaine says St. John did it.
> Roosevelt says the soft-soap dinner did it.
> We say Blaine's character did it.
> BUT WE DON'T CARE WHO DID IT: IT'S DONE.

When the votes were tallied, Blaine wrote, "I feel quite serene over the result. As the Lord sent upon us an Ass in the shape of a Preacher and a rainstorm to lessen our vote in New York, I am disposed to feel resigned to the dispensation of defeat which flowed directly from those agencies."

Such was the low level of the campaign that cost the "Plumed Knight" his chance and won for "Grover the Good" the uneasy Presidential chair. Much of the bitterness is preserved in a postelection medal. On one side is a buffalo (Beast of Buffalo?). Below it, in obvious reference to Cleveland's corpulence, were the words "BEEF TAKES THE PRESIDENTIAL CHAIR—March 4, 1885—R.R.R. [Rum, Romanism, and Rebellion] DID IT."

Unrestrained gloating by the victory-starved Democrats greeted the result. Jubilant paraders, chanting "Burn, burn, burn this letter," put matches to pieces of paper that they held aloft. Others shouted, "Grover,

Grover had a walkover," as well as "Blaine! Blaine! We gave him a pain, the con-ti-nent-al liar from the state of Maine." And to top it all off came the chorus of "Glory, Glory, Grover Cleveland."

Unscrupulous Democratic politicians in New York City had a well-earned reputation for using "repeaters" and for voting dead men "early and often." A completely honest counting of the ballots in 1884 might well have given the state (and the election) to Blaine. Yet a battle cry of the Democrats in '84 was "No More '76." In politics, as in other sports, the breaks tend to even out. If the Republicans robbed Tilden in 1876, the Democrats may have robbed Blaine in 1884.

XVII

Postwar Society
in Ferment

Our country has liberty without license and authority
without despotism.

Cardinal James Gibbons of Baltimore, 1887

UNREGULATED RAILROADING

Amazing westward expansion after the Civil War owed much to the extension of the railroad web, especially in the trans-Mississippi West. The "Iron Horse," as it was called, brought prosperity to those centers of population that it visited, while leaving the bypassed "instant cities" to wither away as "ghost towns." High drama accompanied the building of the first transcontinental line, as sweating gangs of the Union Pacific raced westward from Omaha, Nebraska, while the Central Pacific gangs raced eastward from Sacramento, California. Both were frantically seeking federal subventions for the mileage laid.

Tough and grimy construction gangs labored on the Union Pacific, with many of the workers Irishmen ("Paddies") and some of these Civil War veterans. They seemingly fought off marauding Indians with one hand while they laid track with the other. A favorite song was:

> Then drill, my Paddies, drill;
> Drill, my heroes, drill;
> Drill all day,
> No sugar in your tay [tea],
> Workin' on the U.P. Railway.

At the California end, the "Big Four," promoters of the Central Pacific, employed cheap Chinese laborers, many of whom lost their lives. The "wedding of the rails" was finally consummated in 1869 near Ogden, Utah, as two approaching locomotives softly kissed cowcatchers. The presidents of the two companies flashed a telegram to President Grant: "The last rail is laid, the last spike driven."

Responding to this dramatic breakthrough, railroad building continued elsewhere, but at a less frantic pace. A clever saying was "A locomotive is the only good motive for riding a man on a rail." Fortunes were made and lost, as unscrupulous manipulators resorted to "stock watering" —that is, selling bonds whose paper worth greatly exceeded the actual value of the railroad. A raw new aristocracy emerged in which the "Lords of the Rail" substantially replaced the prewar "Lords of the Lash" and "Lords of the Loom."

Few of the so-called "Railroad Barons" felt any obligation whatever to the public. Conceiving of their lines not as common carriers but as private preserves, they resented outside interference, complaining, "Can't I do what I want with my own?" Crusty old Cornelius Vanderbilt of the New York Central, when informed that the law stood in his way, reportedly burst out, "Law! What do I care about the law? Hain't I got the power?" On another occasion he is said to have written in wrath to some associates, "I won't sue you, for the law is too slow. I'll ruin you." Ironically, his deathbed words were reported to be "I'll never give up trust in Jesus. How could I let that go?"

Cornelius Vanderbilt's son William was a chip off the old family tree. In 1882 a newsman from the *New York Times* reported him as saying, "The railroads . . . are not run for the benefit of the dear public. That cry is all nonsense! They are built for men who invest their money and expect to get a fair percentage on the same." When asked later in the year about the discontinuance of a fast mail train, he allegedly snorted, "The public be damned." The deathbed message of this multimillionaire is supposed to have been "I have had no real gratification or enjoyment of any sort more than my neighbor on the next block who is worth only half a million."

Multiple evils arose from the "robber baronism" of the railroads, aside from "stock watering." "Pooling" profits after raising rates collusively enabled these gentry to keep the rates high. Operators would also charge more for a noncompetitive "short haul" than for a competitive "long haul," in accord with the general policy of charging "all that the traffic will bear."

MECHANIZATION AND TRUSTIFICATION

Railroad networks were but one phase of the miraculous mechanization of America in the post-Civil War years. "Millionaire" was a word not coined until the 1840s, but now vast accumulations of wealth were falling into the hands of a relatively few men, who achieved the American dream of "making it big." The rich were getting richer, while the poor were falling far short of reaching that fabled pot of gold at the end of the American rainbow. The Connecticut born poet Edward Rowland Sill (1841–1887) expressed an obvious truth in local dialect:

> Them ez aims, hits.
> Them ez hez, gits.

Edward N. Westcott, in his immensely popular *David Harum: A Story of American Life* (1898), has one of his characters remark, "The' ain't nothin' truer in the Bible 'n that sayin' thet them that has gits." Edward Eggleston, in his novel *The Hoosier Schoolmaster* (1871), was somewhat more affirmative: "Git a plenty while you're agittin'." This was not quite so brutal a philosophy as that expressed in *David Harum*, "Do unto the other feller the way he'd like to do unto you, an' do it fust."

Inventive genius played a key role during these postwar years in what is now known as "The Second American Industrial Revolution." In the cities the electric tramway came to replace the cars drawn by horses and mules, whose droppings attracted swarms of disease-carrying flies. A mass meeting in New Orleans proclaimed as its slogan:

> Lincoln Set the Negroes Free!
> Sprague Has Set the Mule Free!
> The Long-Eared Mule No More Shall Adorn Our Streets.

Especially noteworthy was Alexander Graham Bell's telephone, first made usable in 1876. The land of free speech gradually became a nation of "telephoniacs," as large numbers of "hello girls" or "number please girls" were engaged to operate the switchboards. The growing number of women in industry was being swollen by the invention of Christopher Sholes' typewriter or "literary piano," introduced on a considerable scale in the 1870s.

By far the most productive of all the inventors was Thomas A. Edison, known as "The Wizard of the Wires." His most memorable discovery was the electric light, which he perfected after experimenting with some 6,000 filaments. "Genius," he remarked, "is 1 percent inspiration and 99 percent perspiration." Less precisely he said, "There is no substitute for hard work."

Spurred by numerous inventions, a menacing fruit of the Second Industrial Revolution proved to be the trust titan. It involved the consolidation of a number of smaller competing enterprises into a giant trust, which served as trustee or manipulator and which had as its unwritten motto "Let us prey." Most notorious of the early trusts was Standard Oil, headed by John D. Rockefeller.

Oil production was a relatively new industry, for not until 1859, two years before the Civil War, did "Drake's Folly"—another misnamed "folly"

—spew forth its liquid "black gold" in Pennsylvania. Grasping John D. Rockefeller, operating "just to the windward of the law," drove lesser competitors to the wall by underselling and then outselling them. His harsh orders to his salesmen were clear: "Sell all the oil that is sold in your district." His son later observed that the American Beauty rose could be produced "only by sacrificing the early buds that grow up around it." His grandson, Nelson A. Rockefeller, who became Vice President of the United States in 1974, once remarked that his grandfather broke no laws but "a lot of laws were passed because of him." By 1877 Rockefeller controlled 95 percent of all the oil refineries in the country, and could raise or lower prices at will. As for his princely fortune, he observed piously, "God gave it to me."

Oil and steel, both giant industries, developed side by side. The heyday of steel dawned in the 1850s when a cheap method was devised to make the refined metal by blowing cold air on red-hot iron—a process producing what was first derided as "Kelly's fool steel" after inventor William Kelly—another successful "folly." Andrew Carnegie, a Scottish immigrant, emerged as the "Napoleon of the Smokestacks" and contributed to the making of some forty "Pittsburgh millionaires." In 1889 he published an essay in which he wrote, "Surplus wealth is a sacred trust which its possessor is bound to administer in his lifetime for the good of the community" and "The man who dies rich dies disgraced." Carnegie gave away during his lifetime about $350 million to support universities, libraries, and other worthy agencies, but he still died rich—by most standards. The numerous municipal library buildings that he donated bore the inscription "Let There Be Light."

Carnegie's mammoth steel operations constituted a multiple partnership, not a trust. But by this time the abuses of the giant monopolies had become so intolerable that Congress passed the Sherman Anti-Trust Act in 1890. The new law lacked real teeth, but it had real loopholes. "Trust busting" was not to crash into the headlines until early in the next century under big-sticking, two-fisted President Teddy Roosevelt.

Another industrial transformation of the postwar years was the slow emergence of the so-called "New South." Rising painfully from the rubble of war, the manufacture of cotton textiles boomed in the 1880s. The cry of Southerners was "Bring the mills to the cotton," rather than ship the fiber all the way to New England factories. This shift provided jobs in the new mills but did little or nothing to boost the price of cotton raised by the poor farmers and sharecroppers. A song popular among distressed Southern farmers complained:

> Huzzah—Huzzah
> 'Tis queer I do declare:
> We make the clothes for all the world,
> But few we have to wear.

STRUGGLING WAGE SLAVES

Public attitudes toward laboring folk in the nineteenth century were not conspicuously enlightened. The Reverend Henry Ward Beecher, brother of Harriet Beecher Stowe and probably the most famous clergyman of the post-Civil War era, made some revealing observations. "Is the great working class oppressed?" he asked. "Yes, undoubtedly it is. God has intended the great to be great and the little to be little." Beecher was not conspicuously friendly to organized labor: "The trade union, which originated under the European system, destroys liberty. I do not say a dollar a day is enough to support a working man, but it is enough to support a man. Not enough to support a man and five children if a man insists on smoking and drinking beer."

A distinguished professor of economics at Yale University, William Graham Sumner, delivered a lecture in 1883 on "The Forgotten Man," a phrase later revived by President Franklin D. Roosevelt. That "Forgotten Man," Sumner declared, "works, he votes, generally he prays—but his chief business in life is to pay"—that is, to pay for the support of his family, his church, his school, and his government, through the tax collector.

Callous-handed laboring men unfortunately were not receiving their fair slice of the industrial melon. A glutted labor market, overflowing with millions of immigrants from southern and eastern Europe in the 1880s and 1890s, led inevitably to unemployment, low employment, or low-paid employment. Unions were few, weak, and at a serious disadvantage in fighting the great corporations. Employers could employ strikebreakers ("scabs") or thugs to beat up labor organizers. Jay Gould reputedly boasted in 1886, "I can hire one-half of the working class to kill the other half."

Tough-fisted employers wielded still other weapons. They could lock the factory doors against the worker ("the lockout") and they could compel employees to sign "ironclad oaths" or "yellow dog contracts," both of which were solemn agreements not to join a labor union. Factory owners also circulated "blacklists" of so-called "agitators" among employees, who in turn would slam the door in the face of the blacklistee.

Reacting to such conditions, "The Noble Order of the Knights of Labor"—better known simply as the Knights of Labor—sprang into being in 1869 as a secret society. Their slogan was "An injury to one is the concern of all," and their aim was to include essentially all workers, skilled or unskilled, men or women, black or white, in "One Big Union." Shunning politics, the Knights broke lances for economic and social reform, in keeping with their cry "Labor is the only creator of values and capital." They favored arbitration rather than strikes, and the eight-hour day rather than the usual ten-hour stint. One of their favorite songs was:

> Hurrah, hurrah, for labor, it is mustering all its powers,
> And shall march along to victory with the banner of eight hours.

Disaster befell the Knights of Labor in May 1886, when about half of their May Day strikes failed. In Chicago, where a few foreign-born anarchists agitated, a meeting was held at Haymarket Square to protest police brutality and other grievances. Unexpectedly a dynamite bomb was hurled which killed or maimed several dozen people, including policemen. Eight so-called "anarchists," convicted of ill-supported charges of conspiracy in the "Haymarket Massacre," were either put to death or given stiff prison sentences. One of the condemned men wrote from his cell, "Monopoly triumphs! Labor in chains ascends the scaffold for having dared to cry out for liberty and right!" Some six years after the bombing, a German-born mayor of Chicago, John P. Altgeld, infuriated American conservatives when he pardoned the three survivors of the original eight. To liberals he was something of a hero, and the poet Vachel Lindsay immortalized him in a widely quoted poem, "The Eagle That Is Forgotten (1913)." "To live in mankind," wrote the bard, "is far more than to live in name."

As darkness fell upon the Knights, their place was partially filled by the American Federation of Labor, founded in 1886, the year of the Haymarket Square incident. The new organization, as its name implied, was a federation of local unions which embraced only skilled crafts. Its gifted leader was Samuel Gompers, a London-born Jewish cigar maker. He did not seek sweeping social or economic reform, only a bigger share of the cake. When asked what he wanted, he reportedly replied, "More." By that he meant more wages, more leisure, and more favorable working conditions. A favorite song of the A. F. of L. ran:

> Whether you work by the piece, or work by the day—
> Decreasing the hours, increases the pay.

A political slogan of the A. F. of L., used most effectively at the time of voting, urged "Reward your friends and punish your enemies."

A major goal of the federation was the "trade agreement" authorizing the "closed shop," that is, all-union labor in a specific establishment. Gompers's chief weapons were the walkout and the boycott, enforced by "We Don't Patronize" signs. By 1900 the A. F. of L. could boast 500,000 members, but those critics who dubbed it "The Labor Trust" were incorrect. The vast majority of America's workers were still unorganized. The age of big business had dawned, but that of big labor lay several decades in the future.

STRANGERS WITHIN THE GATES

A colorful and curiously clad wave of immigrants, arriving in hordes by the 1880s and 1890s, ushered in what came to be called the "New Immigration." It contrasted strikingly with the "Old Immigration," which had come largely from the British Isles and northern Europe. The newcomers flooded in from southern and eastern Europe, bringing strange languages and cultures, as well as living standards that were generally below those of their predecessors.

Attractions of the land of the free and the home of the strenuous had awakened a raging "America fever." It was fed by well-worn "America letters," written by earlier arrivals and passed from neighbor to neighbor. "We eat here every day," wrote one jubilant Pole, "what we get only for Easter in our [native] country." Mary Antin, who came to America from Russian Poland in 1894, when she was thirteen years of age, later wrote in *The Promised Land* (1912), "So at last I was going to America! Really, really going, at last! The boundaries burst. The arch of heaven soared. A million suns shone out for every star. The winds rushed in from outer space, roaring in my ears, 'America! America!'"

From colonial days, when Crèvecoeur had seen "the new man, the American," emerging from the melting amalgam, America had pursued a policy of the open door toward immigrants from the mother continent. The Democratic platform of 1856 had referred grandiloquently to the "asylum of the oppressed of every nation." William Cullen Bryant had put the concept in more colorful language several years earlier:

> There's freedom at thy gates and rest
> For Earth's down-trodden and oppressed,
> A shelter for the hunted head,
> For the starved laborer toil and bread.

A colossal tribute to freedom came in 1886 with the formal unveiling in New York Harbor of the Statue of Liberty, officially known as "Liberty Enlightening the World" with her uplifted torch. She was a gift from the people of France, whose own revolution in 1789 had found inspiration in that of America. A New York poet of Jewish immigrant stock, Emma Lazarus, wrote the moving poetical inscription, a part of which read:

> Give me your tired, your poor,
> Your huddled masses yearning to breathe free,
> The wretched refuse of your teeming shore,
> Send these, the homeless, tempest-tossed, to me:
> I lift my lamp beside the golden door.

As if to mock these noble words, much antiforeignism has always existed in the United States, conspicuously among those Americans whose parents had been fortunate enough to arrive on earlier ships. Such agitation was especially clamorous in the 1850s, at the time of the Know-Nothing movement. Later the flooding "New Immigration" from south Europe in the 1880s prompted America-born Americans to develop increasing opposition to "the wretched refuse" from Europe's "teeming shore." As "Little Italys" and "Little Polands" mushroomed in the larger cities, voices of protest rose more stridently against using America as the slug heap for cripples, paupers, idiots, anarchists, and others who could not be readily melted down into good Americans. "Refuse the refuse" became an implied slogan when the Democratic national platform of 1892 declared, "We heartily approve all legitimate efforts to prevent the United States from being used as the dumping ground for the known criminals and professional paupers of Europe."

Not until 1908 did the London playwright Israel Zangwill present his play *The Melting Pot*, in which a character declared, "America is God's Crucible, the great Melting Pot where all the races of Europe are melting and re-forming! . . . God is making the American." But the concept originated much earlier, for many old-line Americans thought a better comparison would be the stew kettle, in which the scum of Europe continued to bubble to the top. Fearful that the "pure" Anglo-Saxon types would be mongrelized by "inferior" south European blood, Thomas Bailey Aldrich, a son of New England, cried out in anguish:

> O Liberty, White goddess! is it well
> To leave the gates unguarded?

Conspicuous among the protesting organizations was the secret, anti-Papist American Protective Association (A.P.A.), founded in 1887 and destined to claim a million militant members in the 1890s. Such zealots were rabidly anti-Catholic, and they feared a "Jesuit plot" to destroy the nonparochial public schools. Among the various A.P.A. songs was one to the tune of "John Brown's Body":

> A throng of foreign paupers are swarming to our shore,
> Who seek to serve the Romish church and papacy restore;
> They must learn that in America his power can be no more.
>   Our country must be free.

Welcome or not, hundreds of thousands of the expectant immigrants, churned up from Europe's crowded cities, merely swapped slums. In some respects the new ghettoes were as bad as, if not worse than, those left behind. In New York, "The Shame of the Cities," later exposed by the "muckrakers," assailed both eye and nose. The metropolis was cursed with an infamous "Lung Block," where hundreds of immigrants coughed away their lives in the "Promised Land." "Flophouses" abounded where the impoverished and unemployed slept overnight on verminous mattresses or blankets. Crime bred rapidly in so lush a seed bed of filth.

THE HEATHEN CHINEE

Mounting pressures for stemming the foreign flood bore fruit in two epochal restrictive laws of 1882 regarding immigration. One lengthened the list of those who were undesirable, whether mentally, morally, or physically, while the other barred Chinese immigrants entirely.

Inpouring Chinese coolies, ultimately called the "yellow peril," aroused great anxiety on the Pacific coast, where increasing numbers of thrifty and industrious Chinese laborers were able to undercut white labor. In a popular poem, "Plain Language from Truthful James" (1870), Bret Harte had stereotyped the "Heathen Chinee." He relates how two white men tried to cheat one Ah Sin in a card game in which the supposed dupe managed to outcheat them. Bill Nye, crying "We are ruined by Chinese cheap labor," assaulted the "Heathen Chinee," who in the scuffle dropped two dozen concealed cards from his flowing sleeves. As Harte related in his poem:

> Which I wish to remark,
> And my language is plain,
> That for ways that are dark
> And for tricks that are vain
> The Heathen Chinee is peculiar
> Which the same I would rise to explain.

If a wronged Chinese managed to get to court, he did not have "a China-man's chance," but he usually did not get to court. He often came out on the short end—sometimes on the rope end of a lynching mob.

As the barometer of bigotry rose, especially in California, white men, including recent white immigrants, raised the cry "America for Ameri-cans," or as Irishmen put it, "Immeriky fur Immerikans, bejabers." Alarmed Californians sang:

> Oust the pagans, far and near,
> From your fields and homes so dear,
> Falter not, your duty's clear;
> They or you must go.

King of the San Francisco hoodlums was Denis Kearney, a recently naturalized Irish demagogue who headed a group of what he called the "horny-handed sons of toil." In the late 1870s they formed the Working-men's Party or the Sandlot Party, which decried "durrty furruners." The voluble Kearney, exhibiting as his platform four feet of noosed hemp, would cry to his angry following, "The Chinese must go" and "Four dol-lars a day and roast beef." A variant slogan was "The Chinese must go and a rat a day." An enterprising saloon keeper solicited trade with this verse:

> His drinks are A 1 and his prices are low
> His motto is always, "The Chinese Must Go!"
> So call on your friends, workingmen, if you please,
> Take a good solid drink and drive out the Chinese.

During the ensuing disorders dozens of Chinese were injured and killed. In 1879 Congress passed a restrictive immigration law which Presi-dent Hayes vetoed—and thus earned the title "Missey" Hayes in the West. The subsequent legislation of 1882, as extended in later years, paved the way for the effective exclusion of "cheap Chinese labor."

CURRENTS IN RELIGION AND EDUCATION

As the nineteenth century lengthened, America was obviously growing more materialistic in its worship of what philosopher William James called "the bitch-goddess success." The new gospel of wealth proclaimed that God prospered the righteous. Meanwhile orthodoxy had received a shattering blow from the revelations of the English scientist Charles Darwin, whose *The Origin of Species* (1859) set forth in book form the concept that man had evolved from a lower form of life. He called his basic principle "Natural Selection" but conceded that the expression "the Survival of the Fittest, is more accurate, and is sometimes equally convenient."

In the disunited United States of 1861–1865 the survival of the Union eclipsed the "Survival of the Fittest," but in the decades after the Civil War, many Protestant religious organizations split into two groups. One was the fundamentalists, who clung to the Bible as the inspired and infallible word of God. These earnest souls bitterly condemned Darwin's "bestial hypothesis" that (as they put it) "man sprang from a monkey." The modernists, parting company with the fundamentalists, rejected much of the Holy Scripture as neither accurate history nor recognizable science. An American poet, W. H. Carruth, reconciled the two approaches when he wrote that some called the deity "Evolution," while others called it "God."

The most reviled skeptic of the era was the orator and lecturer Colonel Robert G. Ingersoll (1833–1899), "The Great Agnostic." Perhaps his most memorable utterance was to reverse the famed epigram "An honest man is the noblest work of God" and say, "An honest God is the noblest work of man." His creed was:

> Justice is the only worship.
> Love is the only priest.
> Ignorance is the only slavery.
> Happiness is the only good.
> The time to be happy is now,
> The place to be happy is here,
> The way to be happy is to make others so.

A fleet-footed professional baseball player, William A. ("Billy") Sunday, turned evangelist in the 1890s, and his sensational antics and epithets attracted thousands of listeners. In 1908, nine years after Ingersoll's death, he asserted, "I have studied the Bible from Genesis to Revelation, I have read everything that Bob Ingersoll ever spouted from one end of the land to the other. . . . And if Bob Ingersoll isn't in hell, God is a liar and the Bible isn't worth the paper it is printed on."

Orthodox religion undoubtedly was further weakened by the expansion of colleges in the sunset decades of the nineteenth century. Existing institutions were expanding and important new ones were being founded, including the University of Chicago and Stanford University, both endowed by multimillionaire industrialists. In some respects the most remarkable achievement in education was that of a slave-born mulatto, Booker T. Washington, who in 1881 became head of the new Negro normal and industrial school at Tuskegee, Alabama, named the Tuskegee Institute. His primary goal was to teach Negroes useful trades so that they could gain self-respect and merit a position of economic equality, though not social equality, with the whites. He wrote in his autobiography, *Up From Slavery* (1901), "No race can prosper till it learns that there is as much dignity in tilling a field as in writing a poem." Willing to accept social separateness for blacks, he declared in a famous Atlanta address in 1895, "In all things that are purely social we can be as separate as the fingers, yet one as the hand in all things essential to mutual progress." All this was regarded by militant blacks as self-abasing before the lordly white man, and Booker Washington was labeled an "Uncle Tom" who practiced "Uncle Tomism" by toadying to rich white men. But he persisted in his efforts to elevate his race.

WOMEN AND DRUNKARDS

Reform in another arena featured women's rights, which chalked up some impressive gains in the second half of the nineteenth century. In response to the slogan, "Ballots for Both" and "Votes for Women," increasing numbers of females were being permitted to vote in local elections. In 1869 the territory of Wyoming, reflecting the higher regard in the West for the scarcer sex, granted unrestricted suffrage to women. Hence the later "Equality State." In that same year a popular song appeared in Toledo, Ohio, "We'll Show You When We Come to Vote," the chorus of which lamented:

> Oh, sad is the life of womankind,
> Trod under foot we've always been,
> But when we vote, you soon will find
> That we'll fix these "terrible men."

A leading postwar suffragist, Susan B. Anthony, proclaimed, "Men, their rights and nothing more; women, their rights and nothing less." More simply a lament displayed by children in a parade in the 1880's declared, "I Wish Ma Could Vote."

Females were clearly becoming more visible and voluble. Barriers were breaking down, even in the South, where the honeysuckle type of clinging vine had flourished. Gentlemen of the Old South would say, "A woman's name should appear in print but twice—when she marries and when she dies."

In the closing decade of the century Americans expressed much concern over the ambition of parents to marry off their daughters to wealth, and particularly to foreign titles. One song of the period, "A Bird in a Gilded Cage," carried the sentimental lines:

> Her beauty was sold for an old man's gold,
> She's a bird in a gilded cage.

Prostitution and the fate of "soiled doves" who had suffered "betrayal" gave birth to a tear-jerking ballad of the 1890s. As some carousing young bucks were jeering at a "fallen woman" at the next table, an old woman interceded:

> She is more to be pitied than censured,
> She is more to be helped than despised,
> She is only a lassie who ventured,
> On life's stormy path, ill-advised.
> Do not scorn her with words fierce and bitter,
> Do not laugh at her shame and downfall,
> For a moment just stop and consider,
> That a man was the cause of it all.

Respectable females, whose home life was often shattered by alcoholic husbands, played a leading role in the continuing campaign against "King Alcohol." A special target of their wrath was the corner saloon, often dignified by patrons as "the poor man's club" and "the nursery of democracy." The National Prohibition party emerged in 1869 and attracted a sprinkling of ballots in subsequent national elections. Favorite songs of the sober prohibitionists were "I'll Marry No Man if He Drinks," "Vote Down the Vile Traffic," and "The Drunkard's Doom." Typical was:

> Now, all young men, a warning take,
> And shun the poisoned bowl;
> 'Twill lead you down to hell's dark gate,
> And ruin your own soul.

Conspicuous among the ladies who joined hands in the battle against booze were those of the Women's Christian Temperance Union, organized in 1874. Their mottoes were "For God and Home and Humanity," "For God and Home and Native Land," and "For God and Home and Every Land." Their symbol was the white ribbon of purity, from which came the slogan "Wind the White Ribbon 'Round the World." A special object of female wrath was the seductive saloon. The militant Anti-Saloon League emerged in 1893, with its motto "Clean Up or Close Up." Among its favorite songs were "The Saloons Must Go" and "Vote for Cold Water, Boys." Other tunes of the prohibitionists before the turn of the century were "Save the Boy," "Shall Gin Rule?" and "Shall Rum Unchallenged Reign?" Favorites among women included "I'll Marry No Man if He Drinks" and "The Lips That Touch Liquor Must Never Touch Mine." This was parodied in the Southwest with "The lips that chew tobacco

Here They Come. Praying ladies about to descend on a saloon. *Harper's Weekly*, 1874.

shall never chew mine." Not unrelated was a temperance song of the late nineteenth century:

> We don't use tobacco
> Because we all think,
> That people who do so
> Are likely to drink.

INDIANS AND COWBOYS

Explosive expansion in the "Great West" was among the most amazing developments of the post-Civil War decades. Many of the Indian tribes had surrendered their ancestral lands to the grasping "palefaces" in return for promises of food, blankets, and other supplies from the "Great White Father" in Washington. Repeatedly cheated by government agents and driven to desperation, the Indians dug up the hatchet and for about two decades waged a series of losing campaigns against the encroaching whites. General Philip Sheridan, the Civil War hero who fought them, regarded them as "varmints," as did countless other whites. He was quoted in 1869 as saying, "The only good Indians I ever saw were dead." This cruel gibe was sharpened to become the motto of many white Westerners, "The only good Indian is a dead Indian." General W. T. ("War Is Hell") Sherman, who also had dealings with the Indians, concluded, "You can make an Injun of a white man but you can never make a white man of an Injun."

"Boy General" George A. Custer, "The White Chief with the Yellow Hair," rashly attacked a vastly superior force of Indians at the Little Big Horn River in Montana in 1876. He and his command were wiped out to the last man. But the Indians, confronted with the railroad ("bad medicine wagon") bringing in endless supplies and reinforcements, were finally crushed and pushed off into reservations known as "human zoos."

Shameful indeed is the story of the white man's treatment of the American Indian, who had occupied the land for centuries before the Europeans arrived with "lightning sticks." The sad saga is one of greed, rapacity, bad faith, brutality, and injustice by the newcomers—enough inequity to disturb the nation's collective conscience. In 1881 the poet-novelist Helen Hunt Jackson published her devastating historical account *A Century of Dishonor,* to be followed by a most disquieting supplementary novel, *Ramona* (1884), a love story unfolded against a background of wrongful treatment of the California aborigines.

Aside from "pacifying" the Indians, high rank must be accorded several factors in promoting the great Western boom, including mining, cattle raising, and homesteading.

"Pay dirt" was struck in California by the "Forty-Niners," and the Golden State continued to yield a yellow harvest for many years to come. In 1858 an electrifying "gold strike" convulsed Colorado, to which the "Fifty-Niners" rushed in greedy hordes. Many a goldgrubber, with "Pike's Peak or Bust" bedaubed on the canvas of his covered wagon, tried his luck, only to return with a revised version, "Busted by Gosh." "Fifty-Niners" also rushed feverishly into Nevada in 1859, after the famous Comstock lode had yielded its fabulous secret. It was mined by "The Kings of the Comstock," and as a result Nevada, "Child of the Comstock Lode," became a state in 1864. Smaller "lucky strikes" attracted eager prospectors to Montana and other Western territories. Gradually these "acreage states"—big in land but small in population—entered the indissoluble union.

Beef bonanzas in Texas added richly to the phenomenal expansion of the West. After the Civil War the grasslands of Texas supported countless thousands of long-horned cattle, but the railheads were far to the north, the nearest ones in Kansas. The answer proved to be the "Long Drive" over the grassy, unfenced range. The meaty beasts grazed as they moved north to "cow towns" like Dodge City, "The Bibulous Babylon of the Frontier," and Abilene, Kansas, where "Judge Colt" in the person of Marshal James B. ("Wild Bill") Hickok kept the lid in place. The Long Drive did not last beyond the 1880s because the sheepherders and the homesteaders, with barbed-wire fences, put an end to the northward exodus.

These were the colorful days when cowboyhood was in flower. Cowhands sustained their own morale, lulled the nervous cattle, and relieved the boredom of lonely hours by singing numerous folk songs as the bawling beasts moved slowly north. Highly popular among the songs of the Long Drive was "The Old Chisholm Trail," with numerous ad-lib stanzas:

> Come along boys, I'll tell you a tale,
> All about my troubles on the old Chisholm trail.

Another favorite of the Long Drive was "Git Along Little Dogies," in reference to the orphaned calves. One of the greatest and certainly the saddest of the cowboy songs was "Oh Bury Me Not on the Lone Prairie," the dying words of a sickly youth:

> Oh bury me not on the lone prairie
> Where the coyotes'll howl and growl o'er me.

THE HOMESTEAD HOAX

Still another major factor in the rapid taming of the West was the Homestead Act of 1862, under which a *bona fide* settler could acquire 160 acres of land by improving and living on it for five years. As events turned out, land-grabbing speculators, using various illicit devices, acquired more acreage than did the settlers. Such thievery ultimately aroused considerable public indignation. A broadside issued in New York in 1888 cried out, "Preserve the Public Domain" and "Restore the Land to Settlers."

In other respects the Homestead Act proved to be a hoax, particularly in those vast Western areas where rainfall was scanty or unreliable. "Pioneering," said Andrew Carnegie, "does not pay." A "claim" of 160 acres was generally too arid for successful farming or cattle grazing. Unfavorable conditions in Greer County, western Oklahoma, inspired a poignant folk song:

> Hurrah for Greer County! The land of the free,
> The land of bedbug, grasshopper, and flea;
> I'll sing of its praises, I'll tell of its fame,
> While starving to death on my government claim.

Prospects were less grim in those areas, such as parts of Utah, where irrigation was feasible and in those places where the techniques of dry farming or intensive cultivation could be employed. But these sons of the soil discovered that "dry farming succeeds best in wet years"—and many years were not wet. In the 1880s merciless drought seared huge areas in the trans-Mississippi West. Whole towns were abandoned, as observers saw chalked on the grimy sides of eastward-bound wagons, "Going Back to Our Wife's Folks" and "In God we Trusted, in Kansas we Busted." One discouraged rhymester complained:

> Fifty miles to water,
> A hundred miles to wood,
> To hell with this damned country,
> I'm going home for good.

Frontier life, far from proving to be a satisfactory "safety valve" for Eastern economic discontent, became the seed bed of agrarian bitterness. Such protest expressed itself most formidably in the late 1880s and early 1890s, when it crystallized in the Farmers' Alliance and in the People's (Populist) party. Members urged the sun-blistered sons of toil to raise less grain and more "Cain." They did.

XVIII

The Return of the
Democrats to Power

The Democratic Party is like a mule—without pride
of ancestry or hope of posterity.

Attributed to Emory Storrs, 1888

THE DEMOCRATS RECAPTURE THE CAPITAL

A dark cloud of misgiving hovered over the portly frame of Grover
Cleveland, "The People's President," in March 1885, as he took the Presidential oath. He enjoyed the distinction of being the first Democratic
President since Buchanan in 1857 had placed a hand on the Bible at the
swearing-in ceremony. Worried Republicans feared that the triumphant
Democrats, especially those from the Solid South, would attempt to turn
back the hands of the clock. The new "left wing of the Confederate
army," now advancing on Washington, would allegedly reenslave the
blacks and reverse the results of the Civil War, including the highly protective Republican tariff.

"Old Grover" attempted to calm Republican fears at the outset. "Your
every voter," he declared in his inaugural address, "as surely as your chief
magistrate, exercises a public trust." He later announced that his administration would be conducted behind "glass doors," which was another way
of saying in a kind of goldfish bowl. But such promises were less than
reassuring to resolute Republicans. Cleveland, as was his privilege, loaded
his Cabinet with Democrats, including two ex-Confederates. The Union
veterans of the Grand Army of the Republic (G.A.R.) protested bitterly
but vainly.

As a slave to conscience, Grover Cleveland favored some kind of merit system for officeholders, and this conviction squared with his ideal that "a public office is a public trust." In a circular letter to federal employees he warned against "pernicious activity" in support of any party. Yet he was overwhelmed by the flood of officeseekers who descended like vultures on Washington. He complained bitterly to a friend about the "damned everlasting clatter for offices," and concluded that "office-seeking is a disease. It is even catching." Democratic friends would recommend ex-prison stripers to him, and he was forced to respond privately, "A Democratic thief is as bad as a Republican one." When Cleveland refused to sign a bill on the grounds that it was unconstitutional, the political hack who prodded him replied, "What's the Constitution between friends?"

As hungry officeseekers descended like harpies by the thousands and the pressures on Cleveland mounted, he was appalled by what he called the "cohesive power of public plunder." Not even his granite will could withstand all the clamor, and he reluctantly turned over the task of "decapitating" Republican officeholders to the First Assistant Postmaster General, Adlai Stevenson.* "Adlai's Axe" chopped off the heads of some 40,000 incumbent postmasters. As for the tenure-of-office laws, of the kind that had harassed "Old Andy" Johnson, Cleveland sent a special message to Congress in 1886 protesting against their revival after "nearly twenty years of almost innocuous desuetude," an expression that aroused much derision. Cleveland, the lawyer, had a weakness for heavy and somewhat archaic language.

PENSION PERPLEXITIES AND TARIFF TRIBULATIONS

Pensions likewise bedeviled Cleveland, who announced, "I have considered the pension list of the republic as a roll of honor." In short, those who had bravely fought for the Union and had incurred disabilities which prevented them from earning a livelihood should be gratefully cared for from the nation's Treasury. But where there is honey there are flies, and where there is money there are fleecers. Seemingly the Union military units had disbanded and then had reorganized as the Grand Army of the Republic for repeated raids on the Treasury by Civil War "bounty jumpers," deserters, "bloodsuckers," malingerers, and other unsavory characters.

When the Pensions Bureau rejected an applicant, he could often persuade a compliant Congressmen from his district to introduce a private pension bill. Hundreds of such handouts were "log-rolled" through Congress by mutually cooperating members. High-principled Grover Cleveland, who read these grab-bag bills carefully before signing them, vetoed hundreds, often with a sarcastic pen, on the grounds of unworthiness.

---

* Grandfather of the Democratic presidential candidate of 1952 and 1956 who bore the same name.

Typical was a veto message which cuttingly referred to the applicant's "terrific encounter with the measles."

Cleveland's busy pen quickly earned for him the titles of "Old Veto" and "The Veto President," similar to sobriquets he had won as mayor of Buffalo and as governor of New York. His position was especially delicate because he had not fought in the war, and many veterans of the Grand Army of the Republic believed that this was no time, some twenty years after the bloody conflict, to be weighing the claims of ageing veterans with "apothecary's scales."

Cleveland's "Rebel Flag Order" plunged him deeper into hot water. Incorrectly judging that the war was really over, he signed an order to return to the South certain Confederate battle flags captured by Union troops. This gracious gesture toward further closing the "bloody chasm" unhappily turned out to be an idea whose time had not come. Cleveland had never fought for those flags, and his Democratic party was indelibly branded as "the party of the rebellion." A frightening uproar burst from the North, where the commander of the Grand Army of the Republic, Lucius Fairchild, a wounded veteran, cried out, "May God palsy the hand that wrote that order. May God palsy the brain that conceived it, and may God palsy the tongue that dictated it." Henceforth this critic was known to the press as "Fairchild of the three palsys." The New York *Tribune* erupted with such headlines as "The Old Slave Whip Cracking Again," "Now Pay the Rebel Debt," and "Slapping the Veterans in the Face." "Fire Alarm" Joe Foraker, governor of Ohio, broadcast the challenge "NO rebel flags will be surrendered while I am governor!" In the forthcoming presidential campaign defiant Republicans sang:

> We'll never, no, never give up the flags,
> We'll shout to the land of flowers [the South],
> We'll cling to the rags of the old tattered flags,
> The flags that we captured are ours.

When a crestfallen Cleveland belatedly discovered that only Congress had authority to return the "rebel" flags, he rescinded the order. Some eighteen years later a Republican hero of the Spanish-American War, President Theodore Roosevelt, returned the battle-stained banners without stirring up a furor.

Tariff reform, not pensions, became the burning issue in the last year or so of Cleveland's first administration. Customs duties were pouring unneeded surpluses into the federal Treasury, and Cleveland believed with his party's platform that "All unnecessary taxation is unjust taxation." He deplored the spectacle of "infant industries," many now bloated giants, still suckling at the bottle of protection. Further, a huge surplus was an irresistible temptation to Congress to squander the funds on pension legislation and "pork barrel" bills.

Late in 1887 Cleveland, ever high-minded, decided to arouse the country with a devastating annual message to Congress devoted solely to the tariff. Democratic politicians pleaded with him not to rock the boat by thrusting this major issue into Republican hands on the eve of a presidential election, in which Cleveland would presumably run again. But stubborn "Old Grover" would not budge, for he declared, "What is the use of being elected or reelected unless you stand for something?" More epigrammatically he said, "Party honesty is party expediency."

Cleveland's blockbusting message of 1887 laid the cards face up on the Congressional table. He demanded tariff reform as a means of reducing the surplus, for, as he said in one of his most striking epigrams, "It is a condition that confronts us—not a theory." He therefore urged tariff reduction, not free trade. Rejoicing naturally swept Republican ranks following this political godsend. Happy partisans hailed Cleveland's appeal as a "Free Trade Manifesto," while a frustrated James G. Blaine gloated, "There's one more President for us in [the issue of] protection."

"OLD GROVER" VERSUS "YOUNG BEN"

Dispirited Democrats, burdened with "Old Grover" and his bombshell tariff message, assembled for their quadrennial convocation in St. Louis early in June 1888 to renominate their headstrong leader. They had no one else anywhere near his stature. The completed ticket was considerably enlivened by the selection of a former United States Senator, Allen G. Thurman, referred to as "The Old Roman" and "The Noble Roman." In a literal sense he proved to be about the most colorful vice presidential candidate ever nominated. "Old Bandanna" Thurman reportedly took snuff and then blew his nose on a large red bandanna handkerchief, which quickly became the emblem of the crusading Democrats in 1888.

Given new life by Cleveland's sensational tariff message, the Republicans met in Chicago late in June, 1888, bubbling with enthusiasm. They were fully prepared to steal the Democratic slogan and shout, "Turn the rascals out!" The Blaine faction continued to trumpet the battle cry "Blaine or Bust," but they "busted." Their "Plumed Knight" finally bowed out when he realized that he could not win the nomination without a bitter fight that would again see him dragged through the gutter of the Mulligan letters and other scandals. As a compromise choice, the cheering delegates turned to United States Senator Benjamin Harrison and Levi P. Morton, a wealthy New York banker-politician.

"Young Ben" Harrison, despite his cold-fish personality and his strong claims to mediocrity, could boast several politically marketable assets. A prosperous corporation lawyer from the doubtful state of Indiana, he had risen to the rank of brigadier general in the Civil War. "Brave Ben of Indiana" or "Our Brave Ben" would appeal to the veterans, as well as to the wavers of the Bloody Shirt. But most important of all to the Republican shouters and singers was Harrison's blood relationship to a distinguished grandfather, President ("Old Tippecanoe") Harrison, the beneficiary of the frothy log-cabin and hard-cider campaign of 1840. The disappointed Blaineites comforted one another with the couplet:

> We'll vote this year for Tippecanoe,
> And for James G. Blaine in '92.

Such inanities as had featured the silly campaign of 1840 were largely repeated as Republican marchers displayed portable log cabins and raccoons in parades and torchlight processions. "Little Ben" Harrison (a stumpy five feet six inches) was hailed as "Son of His Grandfather," "Grandpa's Grandson," "Young Tip," "Our Tippecanoe," and "Young Tippecanoe." Slogan and song revived old memories with the words "Tippecanoe and Morton too." Dismayed Democrats, thrown on the defensive by this rattling of "Old Tip's" coffin, sneered in word and cartoon that "Little Ben," a "bewhiskered pigmy," was such a mediocre copy of "Old Tippecanoe" that he rattled around in his grandsire's tent-sized headgear. Some Republicans took to wearing hats of the style of 1840, and thus further proclaimed that they were trying to elect the "Old General's" ghost as much as his grandson. A well-remembered Republican campaign song ran:

> Yes, grandfather's hat fits Ben—fits Ben;
> He wears it with dignified grace, Oh yes!
> So rally again and we'll put Uncle Ben
> Right back in his grandfather's place.

A Democratic slogan even jeered, "Grandpa's Pants Won't Fit Benny."

"Old Roman" Thurman's flamboyant bandanna, a counterweight to "Grandfather's Hat," proved to be a bonanza to the Democrats. Loyal supporters of the Cleveland-Thurman ticket formed "bandanna clubs" and sported bandannas on their hats, while girls and ladies wore the flaming emblem around their necks or waists. Scornful Republicans produced campaign songs about the "Free-Trade Bandanna" and the "Confederate Banner." They hailed the American flag as the "Republican Bandanna," and chorused, "Up with the flag, down with the rag." For their part, the Democrats sang "The Old Red Bandanna" to the tune of "The Star-Spangled Banner," and they were confident that "The Old Bandanna's Bound to Win." Up-and-down movement characterized the confusion, as one side sang "Up with the Red Bandanna" and opponents responded with "Down with the Red Bandanna." Imaginative songsmiths sallied forth with such earthy contributions as "Down with the Free Trade Wipes," "Down with the Small-Pox [quarantine] Signal," "Snuff, Sneeze, Wipe," and "The Old Red Wipe." One of the more colorful Republican efforts advised the Democrats:

> Let them stick to their flag,
> Daddy Thurman's red rag,
> "Free trade" their exultant hosanna;

> But our Harrison true, with his red, white and blue
> Will down Thurman's flaunting bandanna.

A puzzled visitor from Latin America might have thought that Señor Red Bandaña was running for some high office, and that the American flag was imprinted on pocket handkerchiefs.

THE COLLISION OF CAMPAIGN SONGS

Bandanna frivolity aside, the campaign of 1888 attained a much higher level than that of the bastardized, "Where's my pa?" contest of 1884. Any successor could hardly have sunk lower. "Young Tip's" creditable war record prompted some flapping of the Bloody Shirt through reference to Cleveland's vetoes of pension legislation and his presumed sympathy for the South. Especially pointed were such Republican song titles as "The Soldier's Reason Why," "The South Is in the Saddle, Bob," and "Not Battle Flag Returning Time." Other tunes reminded voters of Cleveland's well-inked pen: "Grover's Veto," "Cleveland's Reward to Veterans," and "I'm the Monarch of Veto." Gray-haired "boys in blue" were reminded of the popular Civil War song which had announced, "We are coming father Abra'am, three hundred thousand more." The chorus of "We are Coming General Harrison" predicted:

> We are coming, we are coming,
> As we came in sixty-four;
> And we'll overwhelm the Johnnie [Reb]
> With five hundred thousand more.

A clever Republican song, "Grover's Veto," sung to the tune of "Tit Willow," pilloried "a fat man" who once sat in the White House "singing veto, veto, veto" as he rejected the private pension bills of allegedly worthy claimants:

> For said he, "Had they followed my excellent plan,
> And paid a small sum for a substitute man,
> These bills would have never come under the ban
> Of my veto, veto, veto."

Critical Republicans produced several musical compositions relating to "Sheriff Grover's" exploits as a "hangman" and to his lack of a war record. To the tune of "Yankee Doodle" the song "Hip, Hip, Hurrah, Harrison!" boasted that the "man from Indiana" clearly "did his part," and asked, "But where oh where was Grover?" Another ballad, "The Canada Reserves," to the tune of "Tramp, Tramp, Tramp," took dead aim at the Democratic crew of "Copperheads" marching in parades for Cleveland. The chorus, which also referred to these draft dodgers, jeered:

> Tramp, tramp, tramp, some folks are marching,
> Who have never marched before,

Who when men in blue and gray were engaged in deadly fray,
Slyly skulked away to Canada's safe shore.

The Republicans further puffed up their battle-active candidate with "There Are No Flies on Harrison." A listener gathered that "Young Tippecanoe" did not stand still long enough while fighting for "Old Glory" to offer flies a resting place:

There can be no comparison,
'Twixt a man who bravely goes,
For his native land to shoot,
And a man who skulks behind a substitute.

Nor, in reference to Cleveland's premature battle-flag order, could there be any comparison

'Twixt the man [Harrison] who captured flags in the battle's blazing track,
And the cringing craven who would give them back.

Bothersome surpluses that the Democrats were trying to eliminate by tariff reduction encountered the persuasive Republican rejoinder "A surplus is easier to handle than a deficit." This dreary subject, oddly enough, inspired at least two campaign songs: "Don't Worry about That Surplus" and "O! Where and O! Where Is That Blooming Surplus Gone?" The Democrats countered with a broadside slogan, "Stop All Unnecessary Taxation."

Beneath all the nonsense the tariff was clearly the major substantive issue. Both parties, seeking to "educate" the electorate, flooded the country with millions of pamphlets on the subject. Popular slogans included "Tippecanoe and Tariff, Too," "Protection for Home Industries," and "Protection and Prosperity."

The odd fact is that both sides were shadow boxing, albeit with vigor. The Democrats fought for a low tariff, not free trade. But the Republicans persisted in pinning the label "free trade" on their opponents in such slogans as "No Free Trade," "Protection to American Labor," "No Free Trade for Us," and "America for Americans—No Free Trade." A Republican lyric ran:

Protection, oh, Protection, the joyful sound proclaim
Till each remotest nation has heard the Tariff's name.

Ingenious Republicans seem to have had many more titles on their side in the singing and sloganizing battle over the tariff. A New York broadside came up with this appeal: "Reduce the Unjust Profits of Protected Monopolists." One Democratic ditty urged "Free Wool to Make Our Breeches." But the Republicans took the offensive with such ballads as "Free Trade Is Knocking," "The Free Trade Banner," "Under the Banner of Protection," "The Free Trade Fiend," and "Mary's Lamb Protected." There was also "Free-Trader's Body," which, like John Brown's, would soon be mouldering in the grave. A patronizing appeal to superstitious Negro voters warned, "Look Out for de Free Trade Ghost!"

THE BRITISH BOGEY

Campaigning Republicans were especially concerned over the prospective impoverishment of American wage earners by the low-paid workers of Europe. Relevant slogans were "Free Trade and Pauperized Labor," "No British Pauper Wages for Americans," "American Wages for American Workingmen," and "We are not Going to Vote Away our Wages." In a similar vein came such cries as "Our Home Markets for Home Producers" and "Cleveland Runs Well in England." To the tune of "Yankee Doodle," Republicans urged voters to guard "your country's tariff wall," for it "gives us all protection":

> John Bull is trying hard again
> To ruin this Yankee Nation,
> By forcing down our workingmen
> To foreign degradation.

A subtle reminder that the Siamese twins of Republicanism and high tariff were associated with the Union cause in the Civil War came in "Protection for American Labor!" to the tune of the nostalgic and inspiriting "Battle Cry of Freedom." The chorus trumpeted:

> Protection forever, and protection laws;
> Down with free-trade Demmies who oppose our cause,
> For we're marching to the fray, boys, to protect our rights,
> Shouting the battle-cry "Protection."

A nasty dispute with Great Britain over the Canadian fisheries unhappily came to a boil in the campaign year 1888. The British Minister in Washington, Sir Lionel Sackville-West, stupidly fell into a Republican trap. When asked in a private letter from a Republican inquirer whether or not Cleveland's election would best promote Britain's interests, he responded in effect that a vote for Cleveland would be a vote for England. Elated Republicans held back this damning indiscretion until the eve of the balloting, and then burst into the headlines with devastating force. A New York newspaper blared, "The British Lion's Paw Thrust Into American Politics to Help Cleveland." One journal demanded, "Bounce Him," while others favored "sacking" Sackville-West. As the crucial Irish vote in New York started to melt away from "the British candidate," President Cleveland, in one of his few exhibitions of weakness, bundled "the damned Englishman" off home. Gleeful Republican marchers in New York crowed, "Grover, Grover, your time is over," and "Sack, sack, Sackville-West." A variant of this was:

> West, West, Sackville-West,
> He didn't want to go home,
> But Cleveland thought it best.

The New York *Tribune* published a pointed jingle:

> Believe me that I made him go
> For nothing that he wrote,
> But just because, as well you know,
> I feared the Irish vote!

Hordes of Democratic paraders in New York, flourishing red bandannas and defying the rain, shouted in unison as they marched in the closing days of the campaign, "No, no, no Jim Blaine," "Grover, Grover, has a walkover," "Grover, Grover, he'll hold over," "Four, four, four years more," and, reassuringly, "Don't, don't, don't be afraid, tariff reform is not free trade."

BUYING THE ELECTION OF 1888

Powerful and grasping trusts were coming to be recognized as a menace by Cleveland and other Democrats, but Blaine in a campaign speech in 1888 blandly dismissed the issue when he said, "Trusts are largely private affairs." Republican campaign managers put the squeeze on various corporations in a highly successful effort to "fry the fat" out of them in the form of "protection money" for the continuance of a high tariff. In the belief that the Democrats had stolen victory from Blaine in 1884, the Republicans in Indiana left little to chance. Colonel W. W. Dudley, treasurer of the Republican National Committee, allegedly issued a directive to party workers stating, "The rebel crew can't steal this election from us as they did in 1884 without some one getting hurt." He therefore was quoted as commanding his lieutenants: "Divide the floaters [purchasable voters] into blocks of five and put a trusted man with the necessary funds in charge of these five and make him responsible that none get away and that all vote our ticket." Using the "fat" squeezed out of the rich to buy votes, the Republicans narrowly carried Indiana with these "slush fund" tactics.

Maine, the Pine Tree State, won further recognition as a weather vane in 1888 because it held its local elections several weeks in advance of the national canvass in November. As was normal during these years, it voted solidly Republican, and thus supported the saying "As Maine goes, so goes the nation."

Jubilant Republicans won a narrow triumph nationally in November 1888, as "Grandfather's Hat" beat "The Old Red Bandanna." "Young Tippecanoe" Harrison, though an unyouthful fifty-five, emerged the victor by carrying New York State, where a change of about 7,000 votes out of more than 1 million cast would have reversed the result. Yet while losing in the Electoral College, Cleveland won in the popular-vote column by more than 100,000 votes out of more than 11 million counted nationwide. The statistical evidence indicates that he had launched his tariff thunderbolt a little too late in the political game. Yet shortly after his defeat he remarked that he would rather have his name attached to his politically courageous tariff message than win reelection. "Perhaps I made a mistake from the party standpoint," he reflected, "but damn it, it was right."

On the night before Harrison's inauguration in 1889 as the centennial President (George Washington had taken the oath in 1789), a crowd of revelers gathered on the White House grounds. With some of them in high alcoholic spirits, they sang a favorite campaign ditty, to the tune of "Massa's In the Cold, Cold Ground":

> Down in the cornfield
> Hear that mournful sound;
> All the Democrats are weeping—
> Grover's in the cold, cold ground!

But the temporarily entombed Grover would rise from the political graveyard and gain the White House again.

HARRISON AND "CZAR" REED

"Little Ben" Harrison, with a heavy beard on his chest that suggested a pouter pigeon, impressed observers as cold and colorless. He was known as "His Hirsute Highness" and "The White House Ice Chest." Most of the glamour of his administration emanated from "Plumed Knight" Blaine, the uncrowned and frustrated king of the Republican party. Tradition demanded that he be appointed to the exalted position of Secretary of State, and in these circumstances the crowned king and his ambitious subordinate did not hit it off well. Harrison nevertheless ladled out the gravy of high office with the usual partisan hand, avowing that "honorable party service will certainly not be esteemed by me a disqualification for public office."

Out of power for four long years, the incoming Republican Congress had a formidable list of bills that it wanted to pass. Opposing Democrats, just barely a minority, were fully prepared to dig in with delaying tactics and stem the flow of undesired legislation. To the rescue lumbered the hulking form of the Speaker of the House, acid-tongued Thomas B. Reed of Maine, called "Great Thomas the Fat" by opposition newspapers. He honestly earned the title of "Czar" Reed by ignoring the parliamentary rule book and refusing to recognize obstructing Democrats who sought to gain the floor.

A dyed-in-the-wool partisan, Reed reputedly showed his contempt for the opposition by sneering, "The Democratic party is like a man riding backward in a railroad car; it never sees anything until it has got past it." His one-sided view of the two-party system came through pointedly when he remarked in the House, "The best system is to have one party govern and the other party watch." Ever quick with the quip, Reed demolished one member who declared that, like Henry Clay, he would rather be right than President. The Speaker's drawled reply was "The gentleman need not worry. He will never be either."

Regular Republicans, who did not believe that the Democratic minority in Congress should be allowed to defeat majority rule, were not altogether unhappy over the sobriquets "Czar" and "Tyrant" pinned on Reed. A song of the upcoming presidential campaign of 1892, "Tyrant Reed," voiced this praise:

> Hurrah for majority ruling,
>   The nation's right and need;
> Hurrah for the sense of the speaker,
>   Hurrah for the "Tyrant,"—Reed!

Under "Czar" Reed's tattooing gavel a flood of legislation flowed through the Fifty-first Congress, which came to be known as "the billion-dollar Congress." It was the first, but certainly not the last, to pass appropriations that totaled a billion dollars. When complaints arose about extravagance, one current response was "Well, isn't this a billion-dollar country?"

Bending to pressures from the Grand Army of the Republic, Congress showered pensions like confetti upon Civil War veterans, worthy and unworthy alike. Most open-handed of all was the Commissioner of Pensions, Corporal James Tanner, who had lost both legs at the Battle of Bull Run. He promised to drive a six-mule team through the Treasury and "to wring from the hearts of some the prayer, 'God Help the Surplus.'" The surplus has never been a real problem since his day.

This was the Republican Congress that, while busily spending money, found time belatedly to shake a warning finger at the rapidly multiplying industrial monopolies known as trusts. It passed the feeble Sherman Anti-Trust Act of 1890, which was later equipped with dentures by supplemental legislation designed to produce genuine "trust busting."

Landmark legislation of a different sort also ground through the "billion-dollar Congress" under Speaker Reed's watchful eye. Silver producers of the West, burdened with their "beloved white metal," demanded protection against sinking prices. Debtors and poor farmers, especially in the plains states, clamored for the coinage of more silver so as to inflate the currency, raise the prices of their products, and otherwise alleviate their distress. The "Gold Bug" East looked with horror on the unlimited coinage of silver but insisted on tariff protection for manufactured products. Mutual back-scratching accelerated the Congressional machinery. Silverites secured the Sherman Silver Purchase Act of 1890, which about doubled the amount of silver being purchased by the Treasury. Easterners obtained the highly protective tariff of 1890, known as the McKinley Bill after the Chairman of the House Ways and Means Committee, Representative William ("Bill") McKinley of Ohio. Hence the subsequent slogan "Bill McKinley and the McKinley Bill."

A towering protective tariff, by raising the price of manufactured

President Harrison in Grandfather's Hat Disposes of Surplus. *Puck,* 1892.

goods, aroused further discontent in the impoverished and price-depressed West. "Bill" McKinley lost his bid for reelection in 1892 when the Democrats cleverly "gerrymandered"* his district. But he emerged as governor of Ohio and successful presidential candidate in 1896.

THE POPULIST EXPLOSION

As the presidential derby of 1892 drew near, the newly formed People's party or Populist party claimed front-page attention. These new "Popocrats" embraced remnants of the old Greenbacker groups and the Farmers' Alliance, those calloused and gallused sons of toil, many of whom had sung "Toilers Unite" and "Where Will the Farmer Be?" By the early 1890s the Populists had churned up bewhiskered prophets

---

* The term "gerrymander" was coined in 1812 when a sprawling district in Massachusetts, reshaped roughly like a salamander, was created in the days of Governor Gerry to win votes for his party.

whom Easterners called "crackpots." Among them were bizarre characters like "Sockless Jerry" Simpson, the "Sockless Socrates of the Prairies,"
a candidate for Congress who had twitted his opponent ("Prince Hal")
for wearing silk socks. One song of 1892, "Jerry Simpson's Socks," announced that the "hayseed" hero, "devoid of fear" and "devoid of socks,"
would wear no hosiery while there was a tariff on wool.

In an era when women were supposed to look demure and not be
heard on the hustings, the queen of the "Calamity Howlers" proved to
be Mary Elizabeth ("Mary Yellin'") Lease, a tall, mannish woman known
as the "Kansas Pythoness" and a "Patrick Henry in Petticoats." She upbraided the Eastern plutocracy and condemned the government in
Washington as being "of Wall Street, by Wall Street, and for Wall
Street." She also reportedly cried that the people of Kansas "should raise
less corn and more hell." They did. Annoyed by these prairie "hayseeds,"
the New York *Evening Post* snarled, "We don't want any more states
until we can civilize Kansas."

Populist crusaders burst into full bloom at their presidential nominating convention in Omaha in 1892, regarded by conservatives as a
mass meeting of maniacs. Among various inspirational songs these malcontents gave vent to

> Bring out the good old ballot, boys,
> We'll *right* our every *wrong*.

Chosen as candidate of the Populists was an eloquent old Greenbacker
and veteran campaigner, General James B. Weaver. Their platform set
forth the bitter grievances of those unfortunate husbandmen and laborers
who were aroused by the drought, the low prices for farm crops and for
silver, the high mortgage rates, the high railroad rates, the high tariff
rates, and the high living of the millionaire class. The Populist platform
cried out that "tramps and millionaires" came from "the same prolific
womb of governmental injustice." The time was at hand "when the railroad corporations will either own the people or the people must own the
railroads." Little hope remained for the redress of these grievances and
numerous others, for "corruption dominates the ballot box, the legislatures, the Congress, and touches even the ermine of the bench."

Protesting Populist campaigners of 1892 and even earlier sang "Good-
bye Party Bosses" and "Goodbye, My Party, Goodbye." Such songs took
dead aim at Republicans and Democrats alike, for they had turned the
duped farmer into "a willing tool." A song called "The Kansas Fool"
complained, "But twelve-cent corn gives me alarm, and makes me want
to sell my farm." Another ballad, "The Hayseed," protested against the
"fraud and corruption" of railroad monopolies and "old party bosses":

> I once was a tool of oppression,
> And as green as a sucker could be,
> And monopolies banded together
> To beat a poor hayseed like me.

THE CLEVELAND-HARRISON RERUN

Converging Republican legions had meanwhile gathered in Minneapolis, in June 1892, to renominate "Brave Ben" Harrison. Though disliked by the party bosses, he was their only prospective winner. "Jingo Jim" Blaine, ageing and ailing, resigned dramatically but futilely three days before the convention met, as if to direct attention to his availability. Blaine men at the convention hailed him as "The People's Choice" and chanted:

> Blaine! Blaine! James G. Blaine!
> We had him once, we'll have him again!

Such pressures proved unavailing, and Harrison again won the nomination easily on a platform that stoutly upheld the protective tariff. Chosen as his running mate was a prominent New York journalist, Whitelaw ("Whitelie") Reid.

Discerning Democrats realized that their best bet was "Old Grover" Cleveland, who had failed of reelection four years earlier while winning the popular vote. Already hailed as "The Man of Destiny" because of his spectacular rise from sheriff to statesman, he was easily chosen again by the Democrats in Chicago. Honored by this third nomination for the Presidency, Cleveland provoked the Republican sneer "The Perpetual Candidate." Opponents also dubbed him "The Stuffed Prophet," presumably because he had allegedly stuffed the people with false prophecies about tariff reform.

True to tariff principles, the Democratic platform lashed out against the McKinley Tariff Act, while lambasting entrenched monopoly. As for civil service reform, one plank incorporated the lofty epigram "Public office is a public trust."

Personalities and issues received superficial and empty-headed attention in various jingles and slogans during the ensuing campaign. Republican stalwarts cried, "Grover, Grover, all is over." Democratic opponents, no doubt dreaming of fat political jobs, sang a jubilant chorus:

> Grover! Grover!
> Four years more for Grover!
> Out they go, in we go,
> Then we'll be in clover.

Republicans countered such nonsense with more nonsense:

> Harrison is a wise man,
>   Cleveland is a fool;
> Harrison rides a white horse
>   Cleveland rides a mule.

Harrisonites also came up in 1892 with a new chorus for "Grandfather's Hat," one of the big issues of the previous campaign:

> There's a head under grandfather's hat,
>   There's a head under grandfather's hat;
> O, it's plain to be seen, there's a thinking machine,
>   In the head under grandfather's hat.

Undaunted Democrats responded lustily with an ancient, all-purpose war cry always usable by a party of the "outs":

> We want a man for President,
> We'll turn the rascals out,
> We want a head and not a hat,
> We'll turn the rascals out.

Refreshingly, there was a solid issue, the tariff, though it was treated with the utmost superficiality. Republican singers chorused, "Good-Bye, Free Traders, Good-bye," "No Free Trade! No Competition with Foreign Pauper Labor," "Under the Flag of Protection," and "Hail Protection." The Democrats responded with such equally profound sentiments as "Free Wool to Make Our Breeches," to the tune of "Yankee Doodle," and "Drive the High-Tariff Tinkers to the Wall."

No postwar Republican presidential campaign would have been complete without at least a few feeble flaps of the Bloody Shirt. A handful of songs emerged, such as "Treason's Fate," "The Veterans' Hallelujah Chorus," and "When Harrison Heard the Bugle's Call." The grandson of "Old Tippecanoe" had fought bravely in the Civil War but Cleveland had stayed home. A rollicking reminder was "How Will the Soldier Vote?" The chorus appealed to Northern voters:

> Hurra for the Grand Old Party!
> Hurra for the G.A.R.'s!
> Down with the Cleveland outfit!
> Up with the Stripes and Stars!
> Up with the men who stood by The Country in her need!
> Hurra for the True Blue Ticket! For Harrison and Reid.

To the red-faced embarrassment of the Republicans, a crippling strike by low-paid steel workers near Pittsburgh erupted during the campaign, and it headlined the fact that the Republican protective tariff did not guarantee high wages. The laborers at Andrew Carnegie's Homestead plant were set upon by 300 armed Pinkerton detectives, whom Populists condemned as "a hireling standing army, unrecognized by our laws." When the smoke cleared away, ten persons were dead and sixty wounded.

With the McKinley tariff thus further discredited, Cleveland won handily. Noteworthy was the showing of the Populists, who, singing "Good-bye, Party Bosses," carried four states totaling twenty-two electoral votes. The "Popocrats" thus became one of the few third parties in American history to break into the electoral column.

Distressing by-products of the Harrison-Cleveland election of 1892 further burdened the blacks. During reconstruction they had received some protection against the white Ku Klux Klan by a series of "Force Acts" in the 1870s but they had not proved adequate. Various unsuccessful attempts to revive such legislation led to Southern cries in 1892 of "No Force Bill" and "No Negro Domination."

More importantly, until 1892 those blacks who were bold enough to vote often supported Democratic candidates, along with the white Democrats of the Solid South. But in the confusing national election of 1892 many Negroes crossed over and cast their ballots for Populist candidates. When the Southern whites discovered that they could not control the black voter, they proceeded to deprive him of the ballot for about seventy years, until the civil rights legislation of the 1960s in Lyndon Johnson's administration.

Whites finally achieved their goal of virtually complete disenfranchisement of the Negroes by a number of ingenious schemes. A good many Southern whites were illiterate, and if both blacks and whites were required to take the same literacy test, whites would also be subject to disqualification. The solution of the problem lay in tricky devices, including the "Grandfather Clause," which was written into a number of Southern constitutions. It exempted every adult white male from taking suffrage tests if he had been a voter prior to 1867 or could claim such a voter as a progenitor. Negroes were not voting before the Fifteenth Amendment (1870) and hence were automatically disqualified. Thus it came about that the Populists, in seeking to lighten their own economic burdens, inflicted new political burdens on the blacks.

XIX

Hard Times and Free Silver

The humblest citizen of all the land, when clad in the
armor of a righteous cause, is stronger than all the
hosts of error.

William J. Bryan, "Cross of Gold" speech, 1896

HAWAII AND EVIL DAYS

Grover Cleveland, no less corpulent but clearly more conservative, returned to the White House in 1893 as hard times increasingly gripped
the country. Like President Hoover after him, he resisted weakening the
national fiber by handing out federal benefactions to the poor and underprivileged. As he stated in his second inaugural address, "The lessons of
paternalism ought to be unlearned and the better lesson taught that
while the people should patriotically and cheerfully support their government, its functions do not include the support of the people."

An unwelcome baby lay bawling on the White House steps in the
shape of the infant Republic of Hawaii, which was seeking annexation
to the United States. Early in 1893 the white minority in the islands,
predominantly American, had revolted against the arbitrary rule of their
dusky Hawaiian ruler, Queen Liliuokalani. The rebels set up a republic
after securing unauthorized moral support from American troops stationed on a warship in the harbor, and then hurriedly drew up a treaty
designed to annex Hawaii to the United States. American public opinion
seemed favorable, as indicated by a somewhat childish jingle that quickly
swept the country:

> . . . Liliuokalani
> Give us your little brown hannie!

Cleveland viewed the rush-order treaty with deep suspicion, for he felt that the United States had not done right by "Queen Lil." Among other irregularities, the U.S. Minister in Honolulu, acting on his own, had authorized the landing of American troops to support the white revolutionists, who otherwise might have failed. Cleveland therefore withdrew the abortive treaty from the Senate, and then tried in vain to restore the deposed potentate to her throne. As fate would have it, the jilted Republic of Hawaii was forced to wait outside the gate until the Spanish-American War indicated a pressing need for the islands.

A much weightier problem was the cyclical panic of 1893, which burst with full fury in the middle of the year. Unemployment and related forms of misery cursed the land, as countless hoboes or tramps wandered through the country. Motley armies of the unemployed assembled for protest demonstrations, the most memorable of them headed by "General" Jacob S. Coxey. His "Commonweal army" of about 500 men marched from Massillon, Ohio, to Washington in the spring of 1894, although its wealthy leader rode in a carriage with his wife and infant son, appropriately named Legal Tender Coxey. One of the "general's" aims was to force the government to issue half a billion dollars in legal-tender paper money. The marchers substituted Cleveland for the "Father Abraham" of Civil War songs as they tramped along:

> We're coming, Grover Cleveland, 500,000 strong,
> We're marching on to Washington to right the nation's wrong.

This "petition in boots," reduced to about 350 marchers, finally straggled into Washington, where Coxey was arrested for staging an unauthorized demonstration and for walking on the grass.

To plug the hemorrhaging of the gold reserve in the Treasury, Cleveland was forced to engineer a repeal of the Sherman Silver Purchase Act of 1890—a backdown highly unpopular with the increasingly vocal "soft money" men. When this stopgap failed to plug the drain of the precious metal, Cleveland arranged a private bonds-for-gold deal with a Wall Street syndicate headed by J. P. ("Jupiter") Morgan. Cries arose of a "sellout" to Wall Street by "Morgan's errand boy," but Cleveland defiantly asserted, "Without shame and without repentance I confess my share of the guilt."

Discontent deepened in the spring of 1894 when the American Railway Union struck the Pullman Palace Car Company, whose operations centered near Chicago. Violence and the disruption of vital railroad lines naturally followed, while mail deliveries were interrupted. A federal injunction was issued against interfering with trains carrying U.S. mail, and when the strikers openly defied it, Cleveland sent in federal troops to crush the strike. Bitter cries of "government by injunction" burst from organized labor, but "Old Grover" resolutely responded, "If it takes the entire army and navy to deliver a postal card in Chicago, that card will be delivered." The President found a kindred spirit in one

Congressman who pointedly asked, "Shall law and order prevail or shall mobocracy triumph?"

Thanks to lavish spending, the bothersome surplus had by now vanished from the Treasury, and the Democrats in Congress undertook to pass a new tariff bill that would provide adequate revenue and also low-key protection. But the high-tariff lobbyists buttonholed key Congressmen, and the result of the "tariff tinkering" was a legislative monstrosity. Cleveland denounced it as the product of "party perfidy and party dishonor," much to the anger of many Democratic Congressmen. In a rare exhibition of indecisiveness, he finally permitted the resulting Wilson-Gorman Tariff Bill to become law without his signature.

Unusual interest attached to the midterm Congressional elections of 1894. There were Republican songs entitled "Bye O, Grover!" "Times Are Mighty Hard," and "The Soup House." One tune, "The 'Cuckoo' Song," was dedicated to "Tariff Tinkers" and "Free Traders," among others. Nor was Cleveland's spurning of Hawaii forgotten in the song "Lilikaloo," referring to Queen Liliuokalani. The demoralized Democrats, handicapped by the current panic and its ugly by-products, lost the House by a landslide and the Senate by a narrow margin. Among the senatorial victors was Benjamin Tillman of South Carolina, a violent anti-Negro racist and an extreme champion of Southern agrarianism. "Send me to Washington," he had shouted to cheering crowds, "and I'll stick my pitchfork into his [Cleveland's] old ribs." He soon became known as "Pitchfork Ben" Tillman.

BEARDING THE BRITISH LION

Hard times continued to bedevil the final two years of Cleveland's Presidency, and an added burden came in 1895–96 when a spectacular controversy with Britain threatened a diversionary war. Hereditary hatred of England continued virulent to the end of the century and beyond, for Americans had fought the English in two wars and the sires of the Irish-Americans had fought them in the days of Oliver Cromwell. Small boys chanted an adapted nursery rhyme on the Fourth of July:

> Fee, fi, fo, fum,
> I smell the blood of an Englishman;
> Dead or alive, I'll have some,
> Fee, fi, fo, fum.

Cleveland's Secretary of State Richard Olney, a pugnacious character, blundered into the long-simmering dispute between Great Britain and Venezuela over the precise boundary of British Guiana. In his eyes the presumed attempt of an Old World power to enlarge a boundary at the expense of an American neighbor was a violation of the Monroe Doctrine. In a lengthy and undiplomatic diplomatic note, Secretary Olney bluntly informed the London Foreign Office, "To-day the United States is practically sovereign on this continent, and its fiat is law upon the subjects to which it confines its interposition."

Downing Street, which had come to expect "tail-twisters" on the eve of elections, delayed its response unduly and then rebuffed American interference. Angered, Cleveland asked Congress to appropriate money for an investigating commission, which would decide where the line should be drawn. In brief, the United States would determine the boundary itself and, if need be, fight to maintain it. A headline in the *New York Sun* blared, "WAR IF NECESSARY." Fortunately for peace, the British finally consented to sign an arbitration treaty with Venezuela, after which the dispute was settled amicably—and substantially in Britain's favor.

Twisting the British lion's tail over the Venezuela boundary undoubtedly gave a sharp boost to Cleveland's popularity, and if he had been a candidate for reelection, he might have enjoyed some success in challenging the two-term tradition. In any event, Republican chances would presumably be improved if the voters were repeatedly reminded of his shortcomings as the Democratic leader. One tune, "Grover Did a Fishing Go" kept alive the tale that Cleveland, a nonveteran, went fishing on Decoration Day when he should have been laying flowers on the graves of Union veterans. Another song, "Grover's Veto!" was a pointed reminder that "Old Grover" was no friend of Civil War veterans seeking pensions.

A few Americans evidently warmed to the idea of having Cleveland run for a third elective term, despite his widespread unpopularity with debtor groups and other "soft money" men. A copyrighted song of 1896 bore the title "Grover Cleveland's Third Term Campaign Song," a part of which made reference to "Old Grover's" belligerent stance on Venezuela:

> Now Grover Cleveland is the man that stands by James Monroe
> And he says no part of our land shall be taken by a foe.

The chorus exulted:

> Then hurrah! boys hurrah for our glorious Yankee nation
> Then hurrah! boys hurrah for our Grover's nomination.

But no boom for "Old Grover" caught fire, and at the end of his four vexatious years he returned to Princeton, New Jersey, and seldom meddled in public affairs thereafter. Ex-Presidents are always something of a problem, especially energetic ones. What to do with them was a question which Henry Watterson, the acid-penned Kentucky journalist, reportedly answered by quipping, "Take them out and shoot them." But Cleveland is quoted as having said, "The best thing to do with ex-Presidents is to leave them alone to earn an honest living like other people." He died in 1908. His last words were "I have tried so hard to do right."

"BILL" McKINLEY AND SOUND MONEY

Silver, the "sacred white metal," was being warmed up to a white heat in anticipation of the presidential campaign of 1896. One of the most effective pamphlets in American history, entitled *Coin's Financial School* (1894), praised in word and woodcut the virtues of a monetary system based on silver, while denouncing the tyranny of gold. One lurid illustration portrayed the entrance to a ghoulish tomb labeled "Gold Standard," below which appeared the depressing admonition "All Ye Who Enter Here Leave Hope Behind." One of the most arresting statements in the pamphlet was "A war with [gold-standard] England would be the most popular ever waged on the face of the earth."

Preeminent among the Republican candidates stood Congressman William McKinley of Ohio, the "Bill" McKinley of the high-tariff McKinley Tariff Bill of 1890. Rather short in stature, like Napoleon, and bearing a striking facial resemblance to the French military genius, he received plaudits as "The Napoleon of Protection." Acclaimed also as "The Advance Agent of Prosperity," he brilliantly summarized discontent with Cleveland by declaring on the stump that the country was "tired of this tariff-tinkering, bond-issuing, debt-increasing, treasury-depleting, queen-restoring administration [a snide reference to Queen Liliuokalani]."

Good fortune had smiled on McKinley when a wealthy industrialist, Marcus Alonzo Hanna of Ohio, formed a warm attachment for him and arranged to organize and finance his campaign. Better known as Mark Hanna or "Dollar Mark" Hanna, he relished his role of President maker, and had earlier bailed McKinley out of a crushing debt of nearly $130,000. In the preconvention campaign McKinley had spread abroad the popular slogan "The People against the Bosses," and the irony is that he helped to create one of the most potent party bosses in American history in the person of Mark Hanna. Hanna was a "rich standpatter" who naturally supported the gold standard and the status quo, while wholeheartedly subscribing to the trickle-down theory—that is, the theory that prosperity trickles down from the prosperous to the poor.

Meeting in St. Louis, the Republican "gold bugs" were solidly in the saddle, as advocates of the existing gold standard were called. These "sound money" men did make a concession to the Republican silverites within their camp by proposing to adopt a bimetallic standard of both gold and silver, provided that the other nations of the world did, as they obviously were unwilling to do. A small band of about twenty discouraged and hissed-at silverites walked out of the convention amid derisive cries of "Go! Go! Go!" and "Go to Chicago," where the silver-crazed Democrats were about to meet. Ringing in the ears of the bolters was a popular convention ditty:

> Gold, gold, gold,
> I love to hear it jingle.

Gold, gold, gold,
Its power is untold
The women they adore it,
While the men try hard to store it.
There is not a better thing in life than
Gold, gold, gold.

BRYAN'S CROSS OF GOLD

When the Democrat politicos assembled in Chicago, President Cleveland was no longer the leader of his party. Branded "The Stuffed Prophet," he was undoubtedly the most unpopular man in the country. Bitter memories lingered, including those of the silver-purchase repeal, the crushing of the Pullman strike, and the backstairs Morgan bonds-for-gold deal. In an unprecedented rebuke the delegates voted nearly two to one not to endorse the administration of their own President.

At this roaring Chicago convention the silverites commanded an overwhelming majority. Their platform came directly to the point: "We demand the free and unlimited coinage of both silver and gold at the present legal ratio of 16 to 1 without waiting for the aid or consent of any other nation." Thus official sanction was given to the slogan "Sixteen to one," called a "heaven born ratio."

William Jennings Bryan, a former Congressman who had spoken widely and eloquently for silver, was not the front runner. But, given the right circumstances, he had better than an outside chance to capture the nomination. Then a youthful thirty-six, he was widely known as a spellbinding orator with Messianic powers of persuasion. Sincere and possessed of a quick intelligence, he was never esteemed as a deep thinker—his was a great heart rather than a great mind. Yet the man and the hour met to perfection as Bryan stood masterfully before the convention and, with his tremendous voice penetrating to all corners of the hall, swept the assemblage off its feet with his prosilver, antigold speech. He ended magnificently with "You shall not press down upon the brow of labor this crown of thorns, you shall not crucify mankind upon a cross of gold." The next day he was overwhelmingly nominated and thus became "The Peerless Leader" and "The Great Commoner," a sobriquet shared in American experience by Henry Clay and Thaddeus Stevens. Bryan continued to be called "The Boy Orator of the Platte," although cynics were prone to remark with obvious exaggeration that the Platte River in Nebraska was "six inches deep and a mile wide at the mouth." This quip was unfair to the river and also to Bryan's intellectual depth.

Anti-Semitism raised its unlovely head at the Democratic convention because many depressed farmers of the Middle West bore the burden of high-interest mortgages held by Eastern bankers, some of whom were Jews. At Chicago the Democratic silverites were heard to shout not only "Down with gold" but also "Down with the hook-nosed Shylocks of Wall

Street" and "Down with the Christ-killing gold bugs." The money of the
Jewish house of Rothschild in England was believed to have been
siphoned off into Wall Street, and consequently one silverite song of the
ensuing campaign explained "How It Happened (or the Jew of Lombard
Street)."

Gold-bug Democrats, who could not choke down Bryan's free-silver
heresy, bolted the party. At the nominating convention one observer remarked that "for the first time I can understand the scenes of the French
Revolution!" Senator David B. Hill of New York remarked after the
nomination of Bryan, "I am a Democrat, but not a revolutionist." When
asked if he was still a Democrat and would take part in the campaign,
he reportedly responded, "Yes, I am a Democrat still—*very* still." The
sound-money remnants of the old-liners, meeting in Indianapolis, nominated a lost-cause Democratic ticket of their own. A small reminder appears in a surviving campaign button, which reads, "I am a Democrat
but Will Vote for Gold Standard."

Unhappy Populists, who had made an impressive showing in the election four years earlier, soon discovered that the Democrats had robbed
them of their burning issue—free silver. Rather than suffer a victory by
the hard-money Republicans, the bulk of the bereft Populists wryfacedly
endorsed Bryan. Singing "The Jolly Silver Dollar of the Dads," they were
dubbed the "Demo-Pop" party.

THE FREE SILVER CRUSADE

Gold locked horns with silver in "The Battle of the Standards" as a
dynamic Bryan launched an unheard of whirlwind campaign across the
country. The "Silver Messiah" from the West even spoke in New York
near the canyons of gold-standard Wall Street. There he realistically, but
tactlessly, called the teeming metropolis "the enemy's country," as it undoubtedly was. The fervor of his silverite crusade suggested to many
critics that the issue was almost as much religious as financial. Fanatics
of finance even hailed Bryan as the Moses who would lead them out of
the wilderness of debt. Expressive of their mood was the song "We'll
All Have Our Pockets Lined with Silver," the chorus of which rejoiced:

> Hurrah, for Bryan! the boy that's bound to win!
> Hurrah, for Bryan! McKinley can't get in!
> We'll put Bryan in the White House and McKinley in the hole,
> And we'll all have our pockets lined with silver!

Far-flung Britannia was the foremost champion of the gold standard,
and the Bryanites could be expected to pillory the ancient foe. One song
declared:

> The Silver Dollar we'll coin again,
> No matter what Englishmen say.

"We'll Put 'Em In the Hole" was also sung, to the tune of "Massa's in de Cold, Cold Ground":

> Way down in Wall Street,
>   Hear that mournful wail!
> All the gold-bugs are a' weeping,
>   For England now they all must sail.

Still another political hymn, born of the uproarious Chicago convention, bore the title "No Crown of Thorns, No Cross of Gold." Its chorus captured the spirit of the campaign:

> "No crown of thorns; no cross of gold,"
> But freedom from the tyrant's hold,
> The cause for which we raise our voice
> When won, will make the world rejoice.

Clearly "free silver" and "sixteen to one" dominated the musical repertoire of the Democrats. Included were "Free Silver Battle Hymn," "Free Silver's Bugle Call," "The Honest Silver Dollar," "Give Us Silver—Jolly Silver," and "The Gold-Bug Now Must Fly or Die." The mortgage-crushed farmer found an outlet in the air "The Banks Are Running the Government," and the workingman lamented "If Labor Could Get What it Earned." The issue of protection received relatively little musical attention from the Democrats, although one satirical song was addressed to the tariff: "And Still the Old Thing Won't Protect."

"Sound money" Republicans, sporting "gold bug pins" and buttons proclaiming "Grand Old Party, Good as Gold," had as their unproclaimed slogan "In gold we trust." They circulated imitation dollars bearing a crude likeness of Bryan and the inscription "In God we Trust—with Bryan we Bust." Eastern conservatives branded "The Boy Orator" a "fanatic," a "madman," a "traitor," and a "murderer." Fearing anarchy, the more prosperous citizens backed the law-and-order appeal. Clergymen, supposedly less concerned with worldly goods, loudly condemned Bryan, who was a fine Christian gentleman. A New York cleric denounced Bryan from his pulpit as "a mouthing, slobbering demagogue whose patriotism is all in his jaw bone." A Methodist bishop castigated Bryan's "cross of gold" as blasphemous. The cross, so the argument ran, was "never intended to be the emblem of a political party or to be used to teach anarchistic doctrines. The crown of thorns was for the Savior's brow, and not for those who would overthrow the best government on earth."

Cynics said of Bryan that no other man had ever aroused more apprehension without actually taking human life. He was called a "dishonest dodger," a "daring adventurer," and a "political faker." Bankers and other investors feared that their dollars would be depreciated; manufacturers feared that the protective tariff would be lowered or lost; laborers feared that the factories would be closed. Many laborers were

"You Shall Not Press Down Upon the Brow of Labor *This* Crown." A parody of Bryan's famous crown-of-thorns speech, with Bryan pressing down the fifty-cent "bunco dollar." *Harper's Weekly,* 1896.

told not to come back to work the day after the election if Bryan won. So-called "Bryan clauses" were written into business contracts to invalidate the agreement in the event that the Nebraskan triumphed. One slogan ran "It's McKinley we trust to keep our machines free of rust."

Free silver caused the Bryanites to appear to be radicals assailing the foundations of the economy and the government, with the consequent fears of a "Democratic panic" and attendant anarchy. The Republican law-and-order men could appeal strongly to the "belly vote" with their prize slogan "McKinley and the Full Dinner Pail," or alternatively "Four More Years of the Full Dinner Pail." If Bryan burst into the White House with his "crazy" ideas about free silver and plunged the country back into the depths of depression, jobs and McKinley's "Full Dinner Pail" could both be kissed goodbye. Four lines of one song blared:

> Let fact'ry whistles shriek once more,
>   To labor's friend all hail.
> And shout the cry from door to door—
>   "McKinley's dinner pail."

Chilling fears of the "silver lunacy" enabled "Dollar Mark" Hanna, as chairman of the Republican National Committee, to stage the best-organized and best-financed political campaign thus far in the American experience. He fried the fat out of the plutocrats and the trusts. He piled up an enormous slush fund for his campaign of "education," which involved hundreds of thousands of leaflets, pamphlets, and other forms of political propaganda. With good reason Hanna was accused of buying the election, not by bribing the voters directly but by scaring them into voting Republican.

McKinley, who was no match for Bryan on the stump, conducted a quiet and dignified "front porch campaign" from his home in Ohio. At the same time a small army of gold-bug "spellbinders" swarmed out into cities, towns, and villages. The nation witnessed the free and unlimited coinage of words and catchwords, of epigrams and epithets. The humorist "Mr. Dooley" (F. P. Dunne) remarked saltily, "The whole currency question is a matter of lungs." Kim Hubbard, the Indiana quipster, observed, "Only one fellow in ten thousand understands the currency question, and we meet him every day."

Sloganizing citizens seemed not to realize that bimetallism—a joint gold and silver currency standard—is immensely complicated, and that only a handful of trained economists and financiers are capable of understanding it in all of its implications. Yet campaigners continued to mouth the slogan "Sixteen to one," when not one in sixteen knew what it really meant. One Republican button scoffed, "16 Parts Foam, 1 Part Beer."

SONGS OF CHEER AND FEAR

Most Republican songsmiths appear to have felt deep concern for free silver, as did the Democrats. But the menace of bimetallism was often joined like a Siamese twin to the protective tariff. One composition, "Sound Money and Protection," used the tune of "The Battle Cry of Freedom":

> Protection forever, hurrah! boys, hurrah!
> Down with "free silver," and stop Bryan's "jaw,"
> Then we'll rally 'round McKinley, we'll rally once again,
> Shouting sound money and protection.

Republican gold bugs expressed much distress over the "dishonesty" of free silver, for the coined dollar then contained metal worth only 53 cents in the open market. Relevant songs were "Fifty-three, Oh, Fifty-three," "One Hundred Cents—Not Fifty-three," "Sound Money and Honesty," and "Do You Want Honest Money?" Other tunes denounced "the silver craze" and gave firm assurances that "free silver won't save it," that is, the Democratic party.

Republican preoccupation with protection found vent in such airs as "Prosperity, Protection, and McKinley," "Protection Mac Is Coming," and "Gold and Protection Forever." Voters were again reminded of the earlier tariff statesmanship of McKinley in the tunes "The Great McKinley Bill" and "Billy and His Bill." In particular, Democratic "free traders" were scorned in "Bye, Free Traders, Good-Bye" and "Free Trade Farewell."

If the misguided voters rejected McKinleyesque protection and embraced Bryanite free silver, so Republicans darkly predicted, unemployment and poverty would surely follow. Suggestive songs were "Open Mills—Not Mints" and "Up with the Poor," who would rise to the top after Bryan ruined the rich. The popular song "Sixteen to One" warned:

> Free trade and free silver, free whiskey, free lunch,
> Free love and free speech is their cry,
> But when all our products are free as they wish,
> Of whom will our customers buy?

Citizens were also reminded in song of the bad old times that had descended under the Democratic President Cleveland. Memories were jogged with "A Thousand Dollars a Minute" (national deficit) and "The Little Tin Pail Is Empty" (the opposite of the "Full Dinner Pail"). But efforts were made to raise hopes with "There Are Better Days at Hand" (when McKinley beats Bryan).

"Billy Boy" McKinley won musical acclaim as "That Man from O-HI-O," "The Noblest of Them All," who would bring in "McKinley's [Full] Dinner Pail." There could be no doubt that "McKinley Is the Man"; indeed he was the "McKinley Cyclone." In addition came the tune "Hurrah for the Major," who had risen to the rank of major of the volunteers in the Civil War. (This was one of the last feeble attempts to capitalize on heroes of the "late unpleasantness.")

Republican composers lavished praise on themselves with "The Grand Old Party's Good as Gold" and on Mark Hanna with "What's the Matter with Hanna?" Of course, he was "all right." On the other hand, the Democratic nominee received no bouquets in "The Orator Boy," "Boy Bryan's Epitaph," and "The Crown of Thorns," which the poor would have to wear and bear. For added emphasis, the sensational "crucifixion" speech in Chicago received a black eye in "Bryan's Boomerang: The Crown of Glory and the Crown of Thorns."

The Populists or "Popocrats," as recent turncoats, also became the targets of Republican derision. Musical brickbats were hurled at "The Motley Horde of [Calamity] Howlers" and "The Demo-Pop Party." In the same vein the people were reminded that "The Popocrats are Coming Boys" with "The 'Popocratic' Circus." The composition "McKinley and Hobart Forever" castigated these so-called "crackpots":

> Hurrah! Hurrah! the fight we're bound to win!
> Hurrah! Hurrah! 'twould be an awful sin
>> To let the silver loonies and their followers get in
>> And keep out McKinley and protection.

"Dollar Mark" Hanna's brilliant and well-financed campaign of fear prevailed, although one cannot be sure that economic disaster would have struck the country if Bryan had won. McKinley's electoral vote was 271 to 176, although he polled only 51 percent of the popular vote. The "Peerless Leader," who had fought a good fight, did his best to alleviate the plight of the Western farmer and the underpaid laborers with modest inflation. Silver alone did not sink him; the depressed conditions of the previous four years also hurt. "I have borne the sins of Grover Cleveland," he lamented after the dismaying returns were tallied.

XX

The Siren Call of Empire

We want no war of conquest. . . . War should never
be entered upon until every agency of peace has
failed.

President McKinley, inaugural address, 1897

WIDENING HORIZONS

As the nineteenth century neared its sunset, potent new forces were
astir that finally prodded America onto the global stage as a major world
power. Isolationism had served the nation well during most of its forma-
tive years, for citizens remembered the warning in Washington's Farewell
Address against "permanent alliances" and Jefferson's counsel in 1801
against "entangling alliances." But the nation was filling up, and conditions were changing. In 1890—a red-letter year—the Superintendent of
the Census could announce that a frontier line could no longer be traced,
although there were still large undeveloped areas. Energies that had once
been funneled into reconstruction were now being diverted to the West
and to the great industrial centers of the East. By 1898 America, with
its bulging warehouses, was a major producer of steel and other manufactured goods that were crying for overseas markets. "Expand or explode" is a fundamental law of economic physics—and Americans would
not calmly choose explosion.

"Manifest Destiny" had suffered anemia on the bloody battlefields of
the Civil War. In the aftermath America had neither the desire nor the
surplus energy to embark on foreign adventures. But the "New Manifest
Destiny," already in evidence, was beginning to show feverish symptoms.
Not the least among the stimulants was the "spirited" foreign policy of

Secretary of State ("Jingo Jim") Blaine in the 1880s and early 1890s. American seals were being slaughtered in Alaskan waters by British poachers, and he looked the lion in the eye when he told the London government, "The law of the sea is not lawlessness." Blaine won a point when Britain accepted arbitration, but he lost when the award in 1893 proved unfavorable to the American position.

In 1889 the United States became involved in a dangerous scramble with Germany for the Samoan Islands in the faraway western Pacific, of all places. American shippers of pork were already angered by the German tariff and by sanitary restrictions against that "noble animal the American hog." The affronts to Old Glory by the Germans in Samoa raised American resentment to a perilous level, as the consuls of both nations schemed frantically in what was called "furor consularis." Three American and three German warships, with loaded guns, glowered at one another in Apia Harbor. But at a critical moment a terrific hurricane wrecked all three ships, cooled the atmosphere, and made possible an amicable division of the tiny islands. The one British ship in the harbor survived by heading out into the teeth of the wind past the reefs, and was lustily cheered by the stranded Americans. As a Canadian poet wrote:

> The memory of those cheers
> Shall thrill in English ears
> Where'er this English blood and speech extend.

Closer to home a group of Italians in New Orleans, allegedly members of the Mafia Black Hand Society, were jailed in 1891, accused, among other offenses, of killing the chief of police. Although formally acquitted, they were lynched in "a Mardi Gras of mob violence" by good citizens who shouted derisively, "Who killa da chief?" Ugly talk of war boiled up, but the rift thus caused was papered over when the Washington government voluntarily paid Italy an indemnity of $25,000 as a friendly act.

A brawl occurred during the same year in Valparaiso, Chile, when an infuriated mob set upon some drunken American sailors from the U.S. warship *Baltimore*. Two were killed and seventeen injured. Washington took a stern stance with Chile, as Captain "Fighting Bob" Evans arrived in a warship eager to "fill hell with garlic." Elongated Chile was finally forced to knuckle under, and proud Chileans have never forgotten the *Baltimore* affair. Frustrated American jingoes, like "Teddy" Roosevelt, were robbed of a "bully fight."

On the occasion of the overthrow of Hawaii's "Queen Lil" in 1893, the U.S. Minister reported "The Hawaiian pear is now fully ripe, and this is the golden hour for the United States to pluck it." When President Cleveland, refusing tainted fruit, tried to put the pear back on the tree, disappointed American imperialists could only express indignation.

Most alarming of all these diplomatic flareups before 1898 was the senseless row with John Bull over the Venezuela boundary in 1895–96. President Cleveland shaved close to the teeth of the British lion but emerged unscathed. American jingoes were again robbed of the fight for which they clamored because London went out of its way to avoid a blowup. Faced with the rising military might of Germany in the Old World, the British were about to abandon their century-long "splendid isolation," and in doing so they were looking for friends if not allies. Who was a more likely prospect than their "giant daughter in the west"? On the eve of the Spanish-American War in 1898, the era of "twisting the British lion's tail" by Washington gave way to one of "patting the eagle's head" by London. Increasing numbers of Britons were embracing the counsel of their own Tennyson:

> Be proud of those strong sons of thine
> Who wrench'd their rights from thee.

During nine yeasty years—1889 to 1898—the nation had engaged in furious debate over imperialist annexations in Samoa and Hawaii, and had seriously considered going to war with Germany, Italy, Chile, and Great Britain. As frustrations piled up, an explosion was seemingly inevitable. Enfeebled Spain had the misfortune to stand in the way.

"CUBA LIBRE" AND THE *MAINE*

Sugar-rich Cuba, long known as "The Pearl of the Antilles," was also acclaimed as "The Ever Faithful Isle" because it had not rebelled against Spain early in the century when most Latin American republics were born in blood. Enforced "faithfulness" was ensured by vulnerability to blockade by the Spanish Navy. But this uneasy allegiance wore thinner as the century grew longer, and the most serious revolt of all erupted in 1895 after the new American tariff of the previous year had brought additional economic distress. The rebels and the Spanish authorities alike resorted to harsh measures, as the Cubans dynamited trains and the Spaniards set up reconcentration camps to keep civilians from succoring the *insurrectos*. In the absence of adequate sanitation, the victims died like flies, and the Spanish General Weyler, in command of the herding, was branded "Butcher" Weyler in the American press.

Bloodshed in Cuba coincided with the flowering of "yellow journalism" in America—a name derived from the "Yellow Kid" comic strip in the *New York World*. Joseph Pulitzer of the *World* locked horns with newcoming William Randolph Hearst of the *New York Journal* in a frantic struggle for increased circulation. The nation was treated to an orgy of inflammatory headlines, invented atrocities, imagined interviews, faked evidence, and other deceptions not sanctioned by ethical journalism of that day or now. Hearst dispatched to Cuba a talented artist, Frederic Remington, with instructions to draw pictures of the atrocities. On arriving the visitor reported by telegram to the home office that conditions were not so bad as supposed. His employer allegedly flashed back,

"Please remain. You furnish the pictures and I'll furnish the war." Hearst was later reported to have boasted that it cost him $3 million to bring on the Spanish-American War. If he actually said this, he exaggerated his influence on a nation that already was near the boiling point.

"Butcher" Weyler was removed in 1897, and the next year the U.S. battleship *Maine* arrived in Havana Harbor on what was presumably a "friendly visit." Actually it had come to evacuate endangered American citizens, who feared for their lives should local disturbances get completely out of hand.

Two weeks after the visiting warship cast anchor, Hearst added fuel to the flames by publishing a stolen private letter of the Spanish Ambassador in Washington, Dupuy de Lôme. Writing to a friend in Cuba, this official not only confessed bad faith in dealing with the United States on pending commercial matters but added, "McKinley is weak and a bidder for the admiration of the crowd, besides being a would-be politician who tries to leave a door open behind himself while keeping on good terms with the jingoes of his party." This was a private barb, but it contained enough truth to hurt. After the American press angrily demanded that de Lôme be shown the open door, the Spanish government recalled the author of the indiscreet epistle.

On the calm night of February 15, 1898, six days after the publication of the de Lôme letter, came the climactic sensation. The *Maine* blew up in Havana Harbor with the loss of two officers and 258 men. To this day we do not know who or what caused the explosion, but after an official American investigation had reported an initial external explosion, the country broke loose.* Popular catch phrases were "Avenge the *Maine*" and "Death before Dishonor." "Remember the *Maine*" became the great slogan of the war, to which the more daring added "and to hell with Spain." The couplet made a rousing two-step marching slogan. Many songs entitled, "Remember the *Maine*" were written, and the composition "Onward for Cuba" also reflected the belligerent mood of the country:

> Your war cry resounding, "Remember the *Maine!*"
>   Think of our sailors brave
>   Who now lie beneath the wave.
> Onward for Cuba! Now vengeance on Spain!

An overheated public opinion, lashed by the yellow press, clamored for war to chastise Spain and free Cuba. But McKinley held back. He was denounced by the jingoes as "Wobbly Willy" and "Wobbly William," and Assistant Secretary of the Navy Theodore Roosevelt, himself on fire for a fight, reportedly denounced him as having the "backbone of a chocolate eclair." Roosevelt and others seemed unaware that the Presi-

---

* The current "line" in Communist Cuba is that the American officials blew up the ship themselves so as to have an excuse for a war that would bind the Cubans in the golden chains of Wall Street.

Another Old Woman Tries to Sweep Back the Sea. Public opinion in favor of war overwhelms McKinley. The New York *Journal*, 1898.

dent needed backbone to stay out of the war rather than plunge into it. Finally, after extorting significant concessions from Spain, an exhausted McKinley tossed the whole issue of peace or war into the laps of a war-mad Congress. He realized that the *insurrectos* would not accept any terms short of full independence, which Spain was unwilling to grant, and he seems to have feared the political harm of not yielding to what appeared to be the will of the people. He desired reelection in 1900, and his chances would be badly hurt if he handed the Democrats the twin issues of "free Cuba" and "free silver." Congress voted for war after knots of Congressmen in the lobbies sang "Hang General Weyler to a Sour Apple Tree as We Go Marching On."

A HOT TIME IN MANILA BAY

A badly unprepared United States, not having experienced a foreign war for about a half century, entered upon the clash with Spain in the spirit of school boys off for a picnic. Everywhere bands blasted "There'll Be a Hot Time in the Old Town Tonight," "Hail, Hail, the Gang's All Here," and Ta-Ra-Ra-Boom-De-Re," a "nonsense song" of the 1890s. On occasion foreign observers concluded that the "Hot Time" song was the national anthem. John Hay, soon to gain fame as the "Open Door" Secretary of

State, referred to the conflict as a "splendid little war." It was little all right, but to most of the sweating, nauseated, and fever-stricken soldiers in Cuba it was anything but "splendid." Anti-imperialist William James called it "our squalid war with Spain."

Spain happened to have an obsolete and nondescript fleet of so-called "warships" at Manila, in its Philippine possession, and an elementary rule of war is to hit the enemy where he is. To the surprise of many observers the war to free Cuba began with a spectacular naval battle in the far-away Philippines. Under orders from Washington, Commodore George Dewey, then at Hong Kong, descended on Manila and confronted the overmatched Spanish fleet on May Day, 1898. "You may fire when you are ready, Gridley," he ordered the captain of his flagship, and cannonading followed which resulted in the destruction of the entire Spanish fleet of some ten vessels. Casualties were heavy on the enemy side, but there was no loss of life on the American side. One spectator reported that the only medicine needed was cough drops for throats made hoarse by victory shouts.

Unrestrained rejoicing swept America. Commodore Dewey was not only promoted to admiral but further honored by having dogs, cats, and babies named after him. A well-known Kansas poet, Eugene Ware, gushed forth with priceless verse:

> Oh, dewy was the morning
> Upon the first of May,
> And Dewey was the Admiral,
> Down in Manila Bay.
> And dewy were the [Spanish] Regent's eyes
> Them orbs of royal blue,
> And dew we feel discouraged?
> I dew not think we dew!

War hero Dewey had won only a naval engagement, and strategic necessities forced him to remain in the harbor awaiting the arrival of troops from the United States. The Germans, then on the prowl for island possessions, committed the grave discourtesy of amassing a more powerful fleet than Dewey's and ignoring his proclaimed blockade regulations. Dewey finally blew up and in effect told the German officer acting as a go-between that if the German admiral wanted a fight he could have it "as soon as you like."

All this time, the ranking British naval officer in the bay was conspicuously friendly to Dewey, and this agreeable attitude helped to give currency to the myth that the British menacingly sailed their two warships between the Germans and Dewey at a critical time, thus causing the German admiral to abandon his diabolical plan to destroy Dewey. Pro-British sentiment grew in the United States, while antipathy deepened toward the colony-grabbing Germans and their saber-rattling

Kaiser. One of Dewey's captains, on returning to the United States in 1899, recited a satirical poem, "Hoch! Der Kaiser!" to the Union League Club in New York. It began:

> Der Kaiser of dis Faterland
> Und Gott on high all dings command.
> Ve two—ach! Don't you understand?
> Myself—und Gott.

After a formal protest by the German Ambassador in Washington, the Navy Department reprimanded the indiscreet captain, without undue severity. Not surprisingly, American sentiment was strongly pro-British and anti-German when world war exploded in 1914.

CAMPAIGNING IN CUBA

A victorious invasion of Spain's Cuba required cooperation with the local insurgents, one of whose leaders was General Calixto García. To this end the War Department dispatched Lieutenant Andrew S. Rowan to the island commander to secure and give information of mutual assistance. After severe hardships in the jungles and in open boats, he succeeded in delivering his unwritten message to García and bringing back an oral message from García. The phrase "a message to García" came into common use as a shortened description of delivering the goods in the face of almost impossible difficulties. In 1899 the popular writer Elbert Hubbard published an inspirational essay entitled "A Message to García, of which some 40 million copies had allegedly been printed by 1914. Special editions were published by industrialists to promote greater efficiency and loyalty among their employees.

Aside from Manila Bay, the only hot fighting of the war occurred in Cuba or in Cuban waters. Spain sent out a wretchedly prepared fleet, which was forced to duck into Santiago Harbor for coal and other supplies. A superior force of American warships gathered to prevent an exit, and Naval Constructor Richmond P. Hobson became an overnight hero when he and his men daringly sank a collier, the *Merrimac,* under heavy fire in a brilliant but futile attempt to bottle up the enemy. An exceptionally handsome figure, he was greeted on his triumphal return with grateful kisses from the young ladies. "Hobsonizing" became the slang term for bestowing such favors on a man, especially a reluctant one.

American army units next pressed an attack on Santiago from the rear in the hope of driving the Spanish fleet out to its destruction. Abundant manpower had sprung to the colors, including Colonel William Jennings Bryan, of the Nebraska volunteers, but this was a Republican war and there was no zeal in high quarters for making a war hero out of the "Boy Orator." He never saw Cuba, but he did experience in Florida the pestilential army camps, in which many recruits died of various diseases. Bryan himself contracted typhoid fever.

The American force of some 16,000 men that invaded Cuba was commanded by General William R. Shafter, an obese and ailing warrior. But the headlines were captured by the regiment of "Rough Riders," commanded by Colonel Leonard Wood, with Lieutenant Colonel Theodore ("Teddy") Roosevelt initially second in command. The "Rough Riders," also known as "Teddy's Terrors," were a crazy-quilt collection of bronco-riding cowboys and other tough characters, with a sprinkling of ex-polo players and ex-convicts. Roosevelt was in such a sweat to see action that his doughty horsemen arrived in Cuba without most of their mounts and hence became "Wood's Weary Walkers," many of them bowlegged. The bungling but successful prosecution of the war reminded critics of the cynical saying that "God looks after fools, drunkards, and the United States of America."

In some of the sharpest fighting of the war, near Santiago, Roosevelt recklessly exposed himself to enemy bullets as he charged on foot up a prominent hill at the head of his horseless Rough Riders. After the shooting ended with an armistice, he gained further notoriety by co-signing a "round robin" demanding that the authorities remove the sickly army from Cuba before it perished from malaria and yellow fever. Aside from diseases, the soldiers had to contend with "embalmed beef," as the improperly canned and spoiled meat was cynically called. Upon returning home, Roosevelt recorded his experiences in a book which he entitled *The Rough Riders* but which the humorist Finley P. Dunne ("Mr. Dooley") thought should be retitled *Alone in Cubia* [sic]. Such publicity caused Roosevelt to emerge as the one great and lasting hero of the war. Admiral Dewey and the much-kissed Hobson sank into relative obscurity.

One happy by-product of this spectacular little war was a further narrowing of the "bloody chasm" between North and South. Numerous Southern volunteers sprang to the Yankee colors and fought gallantly under the once hated Stars and Stripes. Conspicuous among them was the famous ex-Confederate cavalry officer "Fighting Joe" Wheeler, who participated aggressively in the Santiago campaign. One story, possibly apocryphal but certainly credible, was that he yelled to his advancing men on one occasion, "To hell with the Yankees! Dammit, I mean the Spaniards."

With Santiago thus assailed from the rear, the overmatched Spanish fleet upheld the honor of Spain by a suicidal attempt to escape from the trap. All four ships in the foul-bottomed squadron were run down and sunk or otherwise put out of action. One American was killed, in sharp contrast to about 500 Spaniards. "Don't cheer, boys," admonished Captain John W. Philip of the *Texas*, "the poor devils are dying"—or words to that effect. An ugly dispute soon arose over which of two commanders, Sampson or Schley, deserved credit for the victory. Schley's unoriginal remark was, "There's glory enough for all!"

In a hasty grab for more Spanish territory before the war ended, General Nelson A. Miles, a renowned Indian-fighter, invaded Puerto

Rico. He was showered with bouquets rather than bullets, as most of the populace greeted the invaders as conquering heroes who would lift the Spanish yoke. "Mr. Dooley" wrote whimsically of "Gin'ral Miles' Gran' Picnic an' Moonlight Excursion." In this way Uncle Sam shortsightedly acquired another overseas headache.

IMPERIAL PLUCKINGS

After the armistice with Spain was signed, in August 1898, the burning question remained: What should be done with the Philippines? To return the misgoverned and rebellious Filipinos to Spanish misrule would be unthinkable; to turn the islands loose meant that they probably would be seized by some imperialistic land grabber, probably Germany. Congress had promised Cuba its freedom before it was invaded, but the Filipinos had received no such pledge. As glowing reports came in about the islands' natural resources, "the little brown brothers" seemed more brown and less capable of governing themselves. The Philippines might yet prove profitable for American commercial interests. "If this be commercialism," Mark Hanna reportedly exclaimed, "for God's sake let us have commercialism!"

President McKinley supposedly informed his Methodist brethren somewhat later that he sought divine guidance on his knees. The revelation finally came to him that he should acquire the Philippines and "uplift and civilize and Christianize" the natives, "for whom Christ also died." Yet cynics rewrote the well-known adage to read, "God helps those who help themselves—to the Philippines." Other skeptics remarked that McKinley may have confused the inner voice of the Almighty with the outer voice of Mark Hanna. In any event, the President declared in a Chicago speech, "Duty determines destiny." As a consequence, the United States agreed in 1899 to pay Spain $20 million for the privilege of taking the Philippine white elephant off its hands. Ex-Speaker "Czar" Reed sneered that the United States had acquired millions of Malays at $3 a head, "in the bush."

White elephant or not, the Philippines could not be formally acquired until the treaty with Spain won approval in the Senate. The anti-imperialists contended that to acquire these islands would violate the "consent of the governed" philosophy proclaimed in the Declaration of Independence. "Despotism abroad" would doubtless beget "despotism at home." But the imperialists were thinking of honor, glory, and profits as they cried, "Don't dishonor the flag by hauling it down." Two-fisted Theodore Roosevelt was prepared to deal roughly with any "dastard" who would so demean "Old Glory." After prolonged debate the Senate finally approved the treaty.

Misery loves company, and the uncrowned poet laureate of British imperialism, Rudyard Kipling, cheered Americans along the slippery path to empire with "The White Man's Burden." His appeal became immensely popular in America:

> Take up the White Man's burden—
> Ye dare not stoop to less—
> Nor call too loud on Freedom
> To cloak your weariness.

In short, America should be not the world policeman, but the world's uplifter and profiteer.

Once the Philippines, Guam, and Puerto Rico had become legal liabilities of the United States, perplexing new questions arose. Did the Constitution "follow the flag," or was that flexible document unable to stretch in full force as far away as the Philippine Islands and other overseas windfalls? The Supreme Court in the Insular Cases finally ruled that the flag outran the Constitution. But it arrived at these decisions only after the presidential election of 1900, which brought to a new climax the old arguments for imperialism. "Mr. Dooley" quipped that whether the Constitution followed the flag or not, the Supreme Court evidently followed the "iliction returns."

Idyllic Hawaii must in a sense be regarded as among the insular spoils of the Spanish-American War. When hostilities broke out, the spurned republic had been waiting outside the gate for about four years, unwelcome at any price. Even big-navyites like Captain A. T. Mahan failed to carry decisive weight, although his world-famous book *The Influence of Sea Power upon History* had appeared in 1890. Then the May Day booming of Dewey's guns at Manila jarred the American people into action. Reinforcements must be rushed by a grateful people to an exposed Dewey, and a truly neutral Hawaii, "The Crossroads of the Pacific," might not be available as an all-important way station for the necessary shipping. An appreciative America simply could not permit Dewey to dangle on the end of a Far Eastern limb. "Bridge the Pacific," cried one Philadelphia newspaper in supporting Hawaiian annexation. During the debate in Congress one member argued, "Manifest Destiny says, 'Take them in.' The American people say, 'Take them in.'" Congress responded favorably, and President McKinley signed a joint resolution of annexation, remarking, "Annexation is not change; it is consummation." It was the consummation of a long period of Americanization by missionaries, whalers, traders, sugar planters, and imperialists.

SHOOTING FILIPINOS AND CHINESE

Less fortunate was the fate of the "uncivilized" Filipinos, who understandably felt deceived. But America did not believe that the natives were yet ready for freedom, especially since they had natural resources to exploit, and Congress refused to pass a resolution promising them liberty at any definite time in the future. In February 1899 fighting broke out between American troops and Filipino forces under Emilio Aguinaldo. This gifted leader, now crying betrayal, had previously cooperated with Admiral Dewey in forcing the Spaniards to surrender. To many Americans, McKinley's "mission" of "benevolent assimilation" now seemed like brutal annihilation.

Chasing Filipino insurgents through the jungles lasted about six times as long as the Spanish-American War and involved more soldiers, more casualties, more scandal, and little glory. Shooting Asiatics to save them from themselves was ugly business—and still is. The chorus of one self-serving American campaign song in 1900 rings rather hollow:

> Yes, we shed our blood to save them from oppression,
> And to free them from the cruel rule of Spain,
> And we couldn't let the tyrant Aguinaldo
> Curse the helpless Filipinos with his reign.

In all bitterly fought wars of any length there are always atrocities—on both sides. Dragged down by the barbarous methods of a primitive people, the patriotic American soldier boys found themselves administering the painful "water cure" and other tortures to extort military information. They adapted the famous Civil War song ' Tramp, Tramp, Tramp the Boys Are Marching" to jungle conditions:

> Damn, damn, damn the Filipinos!
> Cross-eyed kakiak ladrones! [thieves]
>   Underneath the starry flag
>   Civilize 'em with a Krag [rifle],
> And return us to our own beloved homes.

Brutal warfare in the Philippines spurred an official investigation, which bared much of the scandal for the world to see. Especially shocking was the retaliatory order issued by the American General Jake ("Hell Roaring") Smith to kill all males over ten years of age on the island of Samar. This command was not carried out, but the shock waves carried all the way around the world.

A desperate attempt to crush the insurrection involved herding civilians into concentration camps, which brought back disquieting memories of "Butcher" Weyler's similar tactics in Cuba. The noble ideal of beginning a war to free the Cubans was evidently ending in an attempt to shackle the Filipinos on the other side of the world. One New York newspaper published a reply to Rudyard Kipling's famous poem:

> We've taken up the white man's burden
>   Of ebony and brown;
> Now will you kindly tell us, Rudyard,
>   How we may put it down?

Aguinaldo was finally captured by an unsporting ruse in 1899, but sporadic jungle fighting dragged out well into 1902.

A special Philippine Commission was dispatched in 1899 and future

President William H. Taft ultimately became its head. He liked the Filipino people and got along well with them, calling them his "little brown brothers." But to sweaty American soldiers wearily beating the jungles for wraithlike Filipinos, there were less flattering names. As one versifier complained:

> He may be a brother of Big Bill Taft,
> But he ain't no brother of mine.

A generous America poured immense sums of money into the conquered Philippines for sanitation, education, and transportation. Teachers known as "pioneers of the blackboard" brought in English as the second language. But the Filipinos, not fully appreciative of all this do-goodism, pined like caged eagles for complete freedom. They finally won it on the Fourth of July, 1946, nearly a half century later.

By accidentally acquiring the vulnerable Philippines, a "heel of Achilles" as it was called, the United States definitely became a Far Eastern power. Its attention focused on the attempts of the European powers to extort from defenseless China leaseholds and other concessions which threatened to elbow out American commercial interests. In 1899 Secretary of State John Hay called upon the competing European powers to subscribe to the principle of the "Open Door"—that is, respect for the principle of fair competition in their leaseholds and spheres of interest. The acquisitive powers responded with restrained enthusiasm, but the colorful phrase "Open Door" caught on in America and added to the glamour of Secretary Hay. Actually the ideal, though not the phrase, was an old one in America's relations with China in the nineteenth century.

High drama came the next year, 1900, when Chinese nationalists reacted violently to the bullying and land-grabbing of the "foreign devils." Extremists known as "The Society of Patriotic Fists," or "Boxers" for short, broke loose shouting, "Kill the foreign devils." More than 200 Westerners were murdered, and the foreign legations in Peking were brought under siege. A multinational army was hastily assembled for their rescue, with the United States contributing some 2,500 troops. As the German contingent was sent off, the Kaiser urged his warriors to behave like the "Huns" of old in chastising the butchers—and he thus helped to fasten on Germans the epithet "Hun" of World War I. In the end the rebellious Chinese were crushed and forced to pay a huge indemnity to the victorious Western nations. The United States handed back an unneeded $18 million, and the appreciative Peking government set aside this "Boxer Indemnity" sum for the education of hundreds of Chinese students in America.

DEWEY AND BRYAN AS PRESIDENTIAL PROSPECTS

Anyone familiar with America's adoration of war heroes, from George Washington to Dwight Eisenhower, would expect Admiral Dewey to have been a prime candidate for the Presidency of the United States. He was the number one hero of the war—temporarily. His victory in Manila Bay was spectacular and overwhelming, and the enthusiasm it begot was heightened by premature news that he had been defeated. After the fighting ended, he returned to a grateful country to be greeted with low-grade poetical ecstacy:

> Admiral George Dewey
> Coming home, they say.
> Bring out the pyrotechnics,
> Let's have a holiday.

Dewey was approached by newsmen eager to know if he would be a candidate for the Presidency, but he expressed a strong disinterest. Yet in April 1900 he gave to a newspaper correspondent a signed statement in which he wrote that if the American people wanted him, he would "be only too willing to serve them." He went on: "Since studying this subject I am convinced that the office of the President is not such a very difficult one to fill, his duties being mainly to execute the laws of Congress. Should I be chosen for this exalted position I would execute the laws of Congress as faithfully as I have always executed the orders of my superiors."

This incredibly naive statement pricked Dewey's presidential bubble. He revealed himself to be what he was: a simple, competent naval officer who had no feel for politics and who had not completely mastered his high-school civics. In doing his plain duty, he had bequeathed to the American people a Philippine problem that was to endure for more than half a century. A local bard wrote for a Boston newspaper:

> O Dewey at Manila
> That fateful first of May,
> When you sank the Spanish squadron
> In almost bloodless fray,
> And gave your name to deathless fame;
> O glorious Dewey, say,
> Why didn't you weigh anchor
> And softly sail away?

After Dewey cut his own throat politically, the Democrats assembled in Kansas City, Missouri, on the Fourth of July, 1900, to nominate a candidate for the Presidency. Bryan, the free-silver Messiah, was still their hero, although not a war hero, unless one acclaims as such any soldier who had exposed himself to "embalmed beef" and typhoid fever in Florida. The Bryanites now had a new "burning issue"—imperialism— with which they hoped to rout the Republicans. Prosperity had recently returned with a rush following a dramatic increase in the world's supply of gold, and as an issue free silver was as dead as last year's bird's nest. But Bryan, a stubborn man of principle, insisted on forcing silver into the Democratic platform. This decision seems to have been a costly blunder, although one must add that the gold-bug voters would have hung "free silver" on him anyhow, as they soon did.

A huge banner displayed at the Democratic convention set the tone. It bore the slogans and mottoes "A Republic Can Have No Colonies"; "The Flag of a Republic Forever, of an Empire Never"; "The Constitution and the Flag, One and Inseparable, Now and Forever"; and "Governments Derive their Just Powers from the Consent of the Governed." Such watchwords found fuller expression in the Bryanite platform, which insisted, as did Bryan, that imperialism was the "paramount issue," although the bloated trusts and the high tariff wall appeared as secondary grievances. One plank intoned, "We assert that no nation can long endure half republic and half empire, and we warn the American people that imperialism abroad will lead quickly and inevitably to despotism at home." Hardly less striking was the formal declaration "We hold that the Constitution follows the flag, and denounce the doctrine that an Executive or Congress deriving their existence and their powers from the Constitution can exercise lawful authority beyond it, or in violation of it." The spirit of the platform found expression in a Democratic song:

> Say the Filipinos, "Give us Independence,
> This you promised us if we would help you fight,
> By the Declaration of your great Republic,
> It is ours to have by every sacred right."

Sympathy expressed by the Democrats and other anti-imperialists for the Filipinos undoubtedly encouraged the enemy to resist, as during the later Vietnam War. For this reason the Republicans loudly fastened the label of "traitor" on Democrats who criticized President McKinley's policy of "pacification" and "benevolent assimilation." One popular magazine published an ingenious front cover. Below a flap were the words "WHO IS BEHIND AGUINALDO?" A curious reader would lift the flap and be greeted by the hawklike features of candidate William Jennings Bryan.

McKINLEY AND THE DAMNED COWBOY

Exulting Republicans, capitalizing on a victorious war and booming prosperity, were happy to let well enough alone and run their winner again, President McKinley. He received renomination at Philadelphia, two weeks before Bryan's renomination. When McKinley's mentor, Mark Hanna, was asked by an inquiring reporter what the issue of the campaign would be, he reportedly said, "We'll stand pat"—a term deriving from draw poker and meaning that the player is content to bet on the hand dealt to him. The word "standpatter" came into wide use about 1900, and was often clung to by conservatives who were satisfied with the status quo and did not want to rock the boat with dangerous reforms.

Hanna himself again became something of an issue in this campaign as a glaring example of bossism in politics, particularly in raising slush funds. One Democratic song bore the title "When Hanna Fries the Fat." Another, "Hoch Der Hanna," parodied the anti-German satire "Hoch Der Kaiser". The first stanza ran:

> That Kaiser Bill across the sea
> Thinks he's a man of high degree,
> But "in it" he is not with me [Hanna]
> Myself and Major McKinley.
> I'm Kaiser from America land,
> And I and Mack all things command;
> We two, as one you understand,
> Myself and Major McKinley.

On a more American note, various Democratic songs assailed McKinley as "The Gold Bug Politician," while hailing Bryan as "The People's President" and "The Nebraska Lily." The chorus of "The Nebraska Lily" was an unusually inane musical tribute to the Nebraskan "Billy" Bryan:

> Billy, Billy, Billy, Billy,
> Oh! thou dear Nebraska lily,
> We will knock Mark Hanna silly
> And make his pals feel chilly
> In November, with our Billy.

McKinley's renomination in Philadelphia was a cut-and-dried process, but the selection of a Vice President produced real fireworks. "Teddy" Roosevelt, the heroic and self-advertising Rough Rider, had capitalized on his war fame by winning election as governor of New York. "Easy Boss" Platt, finding him headstrong, conspired to have him railroaded into the Vice Presidential "burying ground." The scheme worked to perfection, as the convention went wild with cries of "We want Teddy." Teddy did not really covet the Vice Presidency but he wanted to show that he could get it if he did want it. He received every vote except his own.

Mark Hanna, the archconservative, was profanely displeased by Roosevelt's nomination. He moaned about the "madman," that "damned cowboy," who would be only a single heartbeat away from the White House. But the Rough Rider plunged into the campaign with all the fury of a charge up San Juan Hill. "I am as strong as a bull moose and you can use me to the limit," he wrote consolingly to Mark Hanna. He continued to assail the "dastards" who would haul down "Old Glory," in keeping with his slogan "Don't Haul Down the Flag." One Republican ditty reinforced "Teddy's" assault on Bryan:

We cannot vote for Bryan, with his imperialistic fad,
Oh no, we cannot trust him, he would make our money bad.

No Protection, No Expansion, while he seeks his own renown,
On Uncle Sam's New Islands, he would pull Old Glory down.

A SPURIOUS MANDATE ON IMPERIALISM

A calm McKinley, as before, ran a sedate "front porch" campaign from his Ohio home. Voters were not allowed to forget that the candidate was a Middle Westerner, particularly in the song "Ohio Gives a Man of Fame." Bryan again embarked on a whirlwind campaign that featured the free and unlimited coinage of wordage. He insisted that the "paramount" issue was imperialism, which the McKinleyites disputed. "Liberty, Justice and Humanity" was a favorite Bryan slogan, and one of his speeches in 1900 was entitled "The War of Criminal Aggression." Democrats took an especially critical view of the proposed "benevolent assimilation" of the Filipinos. A Democratic song flaunting that title predicted:

When they're civilized and unified they'll know what panics are,
There'll be tramps and cramps and spasms everywhere.
They will have some thrifty sweat-shops, and soup houses for to feed,
This "benevolent assimilated" band.

One of the curious issues of this campaign was "What *is* the paramount issue?" Bryanites cried, "Imperialism"; McKinleyites replied, "Bryanism." Indeed the issue of imperialism was stale by 1900: it had been kicked around for more than two years. America already had the Philippine Islands and was reluctantly engaging in imperialism; the only real question was when the white elephant would be turned loose. "Bryanism" or what the Bryanites would do when they got into power with their "crackpot" schemes frightened countless voters. The Republicans especially feared that unsound money would blight prosperity. One warmed-over Democratic watchword was an eloquent reminder: "No Crown of Thorns, No Cross of Gold." Effective pro-McKinley slogans, some not new, were "The Full Dinner Pail," "Sound Money—Good Markets," "Employment for Labor," "Prosperity at Home, Prestige Abroad," and "One Country, One Flag."

Bryan tried desperately to make an additional issue of the monopolistic trusts, as voters heard the slogan "Equal Rights to all, special Privileges to None." More specifically, Democratic lapel buttons urged, "Down with the Beef Trust!" For the Democrats the issues were summarized on a clever button, "Democracy Stands for Bimetallism Not Monometalism, People Not Trusts, Republic not Empire."

Republicans enjoyed much success in countering the Democrats with the time-worn "protective tariff." Prosperity songs carried such titles as "Mary's Lamb," which related to the tariff on wool, "The Tin Tariff Man," an accolade to McKinley, and "The Workingman's Best Friend." Perhaps most memorable of this genre was "McKinley Protection":

> The voice of the nation went up with a shout;
>   "We want McKinley protection."
> McKinley went in and Bryan stayed out,
>   For we want McKinley protection.
> When you shut up our markets to the foreigner's will
>   And give to home labor a chance at the till,
> We brought back prosperity over the hill
>   When we got McKinley protection.

Until balloting day in 1900 the Republicans continued to sing and shout for "McKinley and Teddy too," "Mack and Teddy," "Hooray for Bill McKinley and that brave Rough Rider Ted," and "We are ready! Mac and Teddy." Bryan, though he put up a gallant fight, lost by a wider margin than in 1896. Many writers have assumed that the country thus gave McKinley a mandate for continued imperialism. But the electorate was never asked to decide whether to keep or not keep overseas possessions; that question had already been settled, at least for some time. A majority of the voters evidently voted against "Bryanism" and unsound money, while declaring their faith in "the three p's" of protection, gold-based prosperity, and the full dinner pail—that is, the status quo. One of the catchier Republican songs declared:

> Down with Silver Dollar Bryan, with his promises of wind,
> And his bill of fare so meagre and so stale,
> We're contented with our lot, and we want the man we've got,
> That's McKinley with the well-filled Dinner Pail.

Boat rockers like Bryan were not wanted. Triumphant Republicans branded the "Peerless Leader" the "Peerless Loser."

XXI

Rough Riderism and the Big Stick

There is a homely adage which runs, "Speak softly and carry a big stick; you will go far." If the American nation will speak softly and yet build and keep at a pitch of the highest training a thoroughly efficient navy, the Monroe Doctrine will go far.

Vice President Theodore Roosevelt,
Minnesota speech, 1901

A STRENUOUS PRESIDENT

Mark Hanna's nightmare about a single heartbeat separating President McKinley and the "damned cowboy," Vice President Theodore Roosevelt, came true. In September 1901, barely six months after taking the inaugural oath, McKinley became a "martyr President" when shot by a crazed anarchist. "Rough Rider" Colonel Roosevelt then charged into the White House and rode high in the saddle as an exemplar of what he called "the strenuous life."

William R. Hearst, the high priest of the yellow press, was promptly accused of having incited the anarchist to murder. The year before, in February 1900, one of his Washington correspondents had published these words in the New York *Evening Journal,* following the fatal shooting of the governor elect of Kentucky, William Goebel:

> The bullet that pierced Goebel's breast
> Cannot be found in all the West;
> Good reason, it is speeding here
> To stretch McKinley on his bier.

In April of 1901 Hearst's *Evening Journal* had editorialized, "If bad institutions and bad men can be got rid of only by killing, then the killing must be done." Proof that this newspaper had incited the assassination could not be produced, but Hearst had a hard time living down the accusation.

One of the many descriptive phrases that admiring Americans tried to pin on "Our Teddy" was "typical American." Nothing was more inappropriate; Roosevelt was typical of nothing. Born to a wealthy New York family, he built up his sickly body by a self-imposed program of exercise, and then went on to Harvard, where he developed some skill in boxing and writing. In pursuit of better health, he became a bespectacled cattle rancher in the Dakotas ("The Cowboy President"). Although dubbed "Four Eyes" out West, he won respect as a he-man, despite the Eastern accent of a "dude." After turning to politics in New York, he rose to the position of Assistant Secretary of the Navy, a post that he resigned to organize the Rough Riders. Soon thereafter the headline-catching cowboy burst into fame as "The Hero of San Juan Hill."

Ever restless, Roosevelt exuded energy. Henry Adams remarked that he was "pure act," and John Morley, a visiting Englishman, observed that the two phenomena in America that most impressed him were "Niagara Falls and Theodore Roosevelt." "The Rough Rider" believed that it was better to burn out than to rust out—and he burned out and died in his sixtieth year. While in the White House, he would put on the gloves with experienced boxers, one of whom blinded him in the left eye. He played strenuous tennis with cronies ("The Tennis Cabinet"); he rode 100 miles on horseback in one day (using several horses) to prove to portly cavalry officers that it could be done; and he energetically shot bears while on a restful vacation.

Roosevelt loved life, especially in the open air. The "Teddy Bear," a child's toy, was so named following one of Roosevelt's highly publicized bear hunts. His attachment to the out-of-doors was undoubtedly responsible for his becoming as President the greatest conservationist of his time. "Clean as a hound's tooth" was one of his favorite expressions. He especially deplored what he called "nature fakers"—that is, writers who caused animals to talk or engage in other unnatural acts. He also deplored birth control or what he called "race suicide"; in fact he practiced what he preached and begot six healthy children—all of them active.

To "Terrible Teddy" life was like a football game, within the rules of "fair play." He was simply "dee-lighted" with his role in the Presidential goldfish bowl, in which he had a "bully time" and on occasion enjoyed an "elegant row." The red-blooded advice that he gave, especially to boys, was "Don't flinch, don't foul, and hit the line hard." As for fighting, his philosophy was simple: "Don't hit at all if it is honorably possible to avoid hitting; but *never* hit soft." Determined to keep "the fighting edge," he spurned "soft living." His favorite song was "The Battle Hymn of the Republic," and his favorite dish was rare beefsteak.

"Our Teddy" had a glorious time in the White House practicing the "strenuous life" that he had long preached. He had no patience with "civilized softness," and no respect for "professional pacifists," "the peace-at-any-price people," and the "non-resistance, universal arbitration people." He believed that these "softies," "mollycoddles," and "flubdubs" would "Chinafy" the country—that is, turn it into a defenseless door mat.

T.R., as the Rough Rider was called, proved to be the cartoonists' delight. He often appeared with heavy mustache, magnificent mule teeth, pince-nez glasses, and wearing a cowboy hat, all the while shooting revolvers or flourishing a gigantic club. He was seldom depicted in repose. The "big stick" became his trademark, especially in dealing with foreign affairs. He enjoyed quoting what he called an African proverb, "Speak softly and carry a big stick; you will go far." If he had a powerful

Teddy and the Big Stick. The New York *Globe*.

navy to back him up, as he did, he could speak softly to other nations, especially the smaller ones, and work his will. He had a "bully time" thus bullying weaker nations.

THE BIG STICK ABROAD

War with Spain had demonstrated the need for an Isthmian canal that could shuttle the navy quickly from one ocean to another, and Roosevelt was determined "to make the dirt fly." (Various and unwanted kinds of dirt ultimately flew.) He arranged for the leasing of a canal zone at Panama, which then belonged to Colombia, in return for $10 million and an annuity. But the Colombian Senate at Bogotá blocked the treaty on the grounds that the payment was not large enough for one of their nation's most valuable natural resources. Roosevelt reacted angrily to this unexpected setback at the hands of "the blackmailers of Bogotá," those "corrupt" and "inefficient bandits." Eager to be elected "in his own right" in 1904 with the canal as a feather in his cap, he reportedly burst out privately, "Damn the law! I want the canal built."

In due time Roosevelt gave tacit encouragement to a revolution in Panama and also used the U.S. Navy to prevent Colombian troops from crushing it. He hastily recognized the infant new Republic of Panama and in 1903 concluded a treaty with it highly favorable to the United States. Roosevelt's methods had the merit of getting quick results, but critics, domestic and foreign, had much to say about America's "cowboy diplomacy."

Roosevelt heatedly defended himself by proclaiming that he had received a "mandate from civilization" to start the canal, and that trying to deal with "the blackmailers of Bogotá" was like "nailing currant jelly to the wall." As the debate went on, the construction of the canal did also, and General W. C. Gorgas, who had helped wipe out yellow fever ("yellow jack") in Havana, turned the fever-stricken canal zone into a place "as safe as a health resort." The opening of the waterway in 1914 gave point to the words of Lord Bryce that the project was "the greatest liberty that man has taken with nature."

Heart-balm compensation to Colombia was painfully slow in coming. It was helped along in 1911 by an indiscreet Roosevelt speech in Berkeley, California, in which he boasted, "I took Panama and let Congress debate." Ten years later "black gold" in the form of oil had been discovered in Colombia, and American promoters feared exclusion from the profits. Congress thereupon voted $25 million to the wronged republic, without adding an apology, but that amount of money is an apology in any language.

Elsewhere in the Caribbean, T.R. wielded the big stick with Rooseveltian flourishes. He made clear that he did not appreciate the use of naval force by Germany and Britain in 1902 to collect bad debts from Venezuela. While feeling that misbehaving "banana republics" could legitimately be "spanked," he feared that too strong and too permanent an armed intervention might lead to a violation of the Monroe Doctrine. He may have had some effect in persuading the British and Germans to arbitrate delinquent debts in 1902, when he stationed Admiral Dewey in the Caribbean within striking distance of La Guaira, a principal Venezuelan port. A Minneapolis newspaper expressed a patriotic sentiment in verse:

> Yankee Dewey's near La Guaira,
> Yankee Doodle Dandy.
> Maybe just as well to have our
> Yankee Dewey Handy.

A worried Roosevelt had come to the conclusion by 1904 that "spanking" by the European powers in the Caribbean was not the answer to what he called "chronic wrong doing." In a message to Congress he declared that in support of the Monroe Doctrine the United States might have to resort to "international police power." His subsequent "preventive intervention" came to be known as "The Roosevelt Corollary" to the Monroe Doctrine. To prevent the European powers from challenging the United States by intervening, T.R. would himself intervene and arrange for the collection of bad debts. This kind of big stickism operated most conspicuously in the Dominican Republic.

Rooseveltian waving of the big stick elsewhere managed to settle an Alaska boundary dispute with Canada much to the advantage of the United States. Though a foremost disciple of Mars, the Rough Rider won the Nobel Peace Prize by serving as an "honest broker" in arranging for a settlement of the Russo-Japanese War. In the aftermath, he encountered a problem with Japanese coolies coming from their crowded islands to the Pacific coast of the United States. Concerned Californians, remembering the Chinese "menace" of previous decades, feared that they would be inundated by the new "yellow peril." Hence they refashioned the old anti-Chinese cry to read, "The Japanese Must Go." Roosevelt resolutely interposed his big stick between California and Japan, thus managing to work out the "Gentleman's Agreement" of 1907–08. By its terms the Japanese government pledged itself to issue no passports to coolies seeking to emigrate to the mainland of the United States.

Two-fisted "Teddy" Roosevelt began to fear that the Japanese thought him afraid of them. As if to demonstrate that America then boasted the number two navy in the world and Japan only the number five navy, he decided to send the U.S. battleship fleet of sixteen ships all the way around the world in a grand flourish. In 1907 the "Great White Fleet" left Chesapeake Bay, so its commander remarked, ready for "a feast, a frolic, or a fight." The giant ships rounded South America, visited San Francisco and other Pacific ports, and then pushed on to New Zealand, Australia, and Japan. The greeting in Japan was overwhelmingly friendly. As a consequence, the uneasy atmosphere was greatly cleared, and a new era began in relations with that island empire. Americans who followed the fleet learned a good deal about world geography, as did the sailors who went along. "Join the Navy and See the World" became a potent recruiting slogan at the time of the Great White Fleet.

Not content with brandishing the big stick in the Caribbean and East Asia, Roosevelt flourished it in the direction of Morocco. An American citizen—or supposed citizen—by the Greek name of Perdicaris had fallen into the clutches of a notorious Moroccan bandit, Raisuli. Arrangements were made for the release of the captive, but Roosevelt wanted to electrify the Republican convention which was then meeting to nominate him in Chicago. He therefore arranged with Secretary of State Hay to send a cabled ultimatum which insisted that the United States have "Perdicaris alive or Raisuli dead." This electioneering ploy was completely unnecessary, but the nominating convention greeted a reading of the official telegram with a mighty outburst of approval.

BLOATED TRUSTS AND SHRINKING RESOURCES

In domestic as in foreign affairs, Roosevelt's ever-restless big stick captured the headlines. One of his favorite expressions, in public and private, was "The Square Deal"—for capital, labor, and society at large. This even-handed label attached itself to his administration, as did "The New Deal" to that of his distant cousin Franklin Roosevelt some thirty years later.

Both The Square Deal and the big stick received a severe test in 1902 when the overworked and underpaid anthracite coal miners of Pennsylvania struck for higher wages and better working conditions. A blunt spokesman for the operators, multimillionaire George F. Baer, reflected the insensitivity of the owners when he wrote that the workers would be cared for "not by the labor agitators, but by the Christian men to whom God in His infinite wisdom has given the control of the property interests of this country." The unwillingness of these "wooden-headed" gentry to make reasonable concessions angered T.R., who threatened to seize the closed mines and order the army to operate them, even though soldiers cannot dig coal with bayonets. The owners, responding slowly to government interference in the form of the big stick, grudgingly accepted a compromise settlement.

Other industrial giants, especially the trusts, were now claiming increasing attention. The Sherman Anti-Trust Act of 1890 from the outset had lacked adequate teeth, and successive Presidents had permitted it to sicken for lack of exercise. "Teddy the Trust Buster" proceeded to gain an inflated reputation by resurrecting the Sherman Act and launching a number of prosecutions against some of the most offensive giant monopolies. He vigorously and publicly scolded "the predatory rich," "the criminal rich," "the fool rich," and "certain malefactors of great wealth." Yet he conceded that there were "good trusts" as well as "bad trusts" and that bigness did not necessarily mean badness. He believed in policing rather than punishing. But the cry from an aroused public was "Smash the trusts."

Responding to the spurs of the Rough Rider, Congress passed loop-holed legislation designed to regulate the monopolistic railroads. Roosevelt himself launched a spectacular suit against the Northern Securities Company, which involved a merger of key Western railroads under such men as financier J. P. ("Jupiter") Morgan and "Empire Builder" James J. Hill, tycoon of the Great Northern Railroad. In 1904 the Supreme Court captured the headlines when it ruled that the Northern Securities Company violated the Sherman Anti-Trust Act and must be dissolved. The jolt to the financial world was unnerving.

Despite all Roosevelt's noise, bluster, and big-stickism, his reputation as a "trust buster" was greatly exaggerated. His mild-mannered successor, President Taft, actually "busted" more trusts during his four years than did the Rough Rider in seven. Roosevelt's most praiseworthy contribution in fighting the menace of monopoly was to raise the Sherman Act from the dead or the near dead. His willingness to draw a distinction between the "good" and the "bad" trusts prompted "Mr. Dooley" to have him say, "On wan hand I wud stamp thim undher fut; on th' other hand not so fast."

As a conservationist, the bear-shooting Roosevelt fought a gallant but uphill battle. Sons of American pioneers who had chopped down forests so as to plant crops were prone to remark, "Why preserve the wilderness when we've been fighting it for years?" While despoiling the land they also asked, "What has posterity ever done for us?" Undeterred, Roosevelt achieved substantial gains by securing remedial legislation or taking direct action to promote such objectives as flood control, irrigation (the Roosevelt Dam in Arizona), land reclamation, and forest preservation. Especially noteworthy was his setting aside as federal reserves millions of acres of forests and mineral lands. T.R. took conservation out of the conversation stage, and with a far-seeing eye to posterity and vanishing resources, he established himself as the number one conservationist of his generation, if not of his nation's history.

THE PARKER-ROOSEVELT MISMATCH

Resenting the time-worn sneer "His Accidency," Roosevelt was franti-cally eager to be nominated and elected "in his own right." His popularity with the masses was so overwhelming that the big-business New York *Sun* resignedly suggested as the Republican platform, six weeks before the delegates met in Chicago, "RESOLVED: That we emphatically endorse and affirm Theodore Roosevelt. Whatever Theodore Roosevelt thinks, says, does, or wants is right. Roosevelt and Stir 'em Up; Now and Forever: One and Inseparable!"

T.R.'s dream came true when he received the nomination by acclamation. Wealthy standpatters of the party still distrusted him, and as an antidote chose as his running mate a cold and conservative Indianan, Charles W. Fairbanks, who was dubbed "Icebanks." The G.O.P. platform affirmed conservative Republican principles by plumping for the tariff and the gold standard, while letting off the trusts, largely controlled by rich Republicans, with a verbal slap on the wrist.

Office-starved Democrats, meeting in St. Louis in July 1904, pined for a winner. Devoted Bryanites would have liked to run their "Peerless Leader" for a third time, but the conservative Eastern wing of the party was completely fed up with this two-time loser. It demanded and secured a "safe and sane" candidate in the person of Judge Alton B. Parker, a respectable New York lawyer with no sparkle and no claims to greatness. In comparison with Bryan the so-called "Parker the Silent" seemed unglamorous indeed. A noisy and self-promoted boom by William R. Hearst, the multimillionaire newspaper publisher from California, fell far short of success, although his claque intermittently cheered:

> Boom, boom, boom;
> First, first, first;
> California; California
> Hearst, Hearst, Hearst.

Authors of the Democratic platform naturally deplored Roosevelt's grandiose flourishes of the big stick at home and abroad, including his alleged encroachment on the legislative and judicial branches. This high-sounding document flayed the Rough Rider's stewardship as "spasmodic, erratic, sensational, spectacular, and arbitrary." No mention whatever was made of the dead issue of free silver, though Parker infuriated the Bryanites by telegraphing the convention that he still favored the gold standard. By this time the delegates were saddled with him, while probably aware of the indisputable political axiom "You can't beat somebody with nobody."

Off to a bad start, the presidential campaign of 1904 turned out to be the tamest in many decades. If the Democrats could not win with a colorful Bryan, they were not likely to do so with a colorless Parker pitted against the dynamic and headline-capturing T.R. Judge Parker, blasting Rough Riderism, called for a "government of law, not men." He probably was thinking of Roosevelt's radical "stewardship theory." It held that a president could take any action for the common good that was not specifically forbidden by the Constitution and the laws. As the poet Wallace Irwin noted:

> The Constitution rides behind
> And the Big Stick rides before,
> (Which is the rule of precedent
> In the reign of Theodore.)

Roosevelt was nothing if not a supreme egoist; his public utterances ran heavily to the perpendicular pronoun "I." His tiresome references to "my policies" provided excellent ammunition for cartoonists and other critics, who branded him not only an "imperialist" and a "militarist" but also a "usurper." In a sense, he reigned rather than ruled.

Lackluster Judge Parker finally injected some fireworks into an otherwise dull campaign when he bluntly accused the Rooseveltians of extorting large campaign contributions from corporations that expected favors from Washington in return. This kind of bribery had been and continued to be standard practice, conspicuously later in the Nixon years. Roosevelt cried, "Liar," but a subsequent Congressional investigation proved that the charge had substantial validity. The outspoken Rough Rider called so many people liars during his Presidency that those so designated were informally lumped into an "Ananias Club," after the greedy character in the New Testament who fell dead after lying to the apostle Peter.

A prominent New York journalist, Oswald Garrison Villard, relates in his memoirs how Roosevelt, seeking financial support for his campaign, summoned to the White House the wealthy railroad magnate Edward H. Harriman and the steel baron Henry Clay Frick. Between them they personally contributed $150,000, in the expectation of deferential treatment in the future. T.R. infuriated them after the election by intensifying his program for regulating big business, by condemning the "malefactors of great wealth," and by blasting juries for failing to impose jail sentences on "the criminal rich." The embittered Frick complained to Villard that Roosevelt "got down on his knees to us. We bought the son of a bitch and then he did not stay bought."

SINGING TO VICTORY

The actual existence of countless full dinner pails—that is real prosperity —added metallic luster and substance to the Republican crusade of 1904. But the overshadowing issue was T.R.'s big-stick personality—"Theodore Roosevelt, One and Indivisible." Slogans on Republican lapel buttons and elsewhere advertised "The Big Stick," "Stand Pat," "Win with Teddy," "Roosevelt and Protection," and "Sound Money, Expansion, Protection, Prosperity." A reminder that the telephone was still in its infancy is provided by a button saying, "Hello Central, Give us Teddy."

Republican songsmiths turned out a number of compositions, but the theme song of this campaign was clearly "There'll Be a Hot Time in the Old Town Tonight." It repeatedly reminded listeners that T.R. was the most durable hero of the Spanish-American War. His worshipful following also sang such contributions as "There Cheers for the Rough Rider," "The Hero of San Juan Hill," and "We Want Teddy for Four Years More." The chorus of the last-named ran:

> We want Teddy the brave our banner to wave,
> We want freedom from shore to shore.

> We want honor and right, and a man who can fight,
> We want Teddy for four years more.

Another song, "You're All Right, Teddy," acclaimed the hero for having "steered the country straight" and for having made it "great"— "In fact, you've put the country on the map." As for his specific deeds, when the country needed him to charge up San Juan Hill, "Teddy didn't balk, he didn't stop to talk." And as for taking the Canal Zone, this same tune ended with this preposterous stanza:

> When Europe raised a fuss,
> And tried to say to us:
> "What? Dig through Panama, you never shall!"
> Our Teddy said: "All Right!
> I'll think it over for a night."
> Next day we got the Panama Canal.

One pro-Republican writer, harking back to the days of 1844 and the jeering question "Who is James K. Polk?" composed a song entitled "Who Is Parker?" Additionally a Republican air reminded voters of previous hard times with the title, "When the Demmies Were in Power."

Democratic composers showed neither conspicuous originality nor ingenuity when they came up with "We Will Turn the Rascals Out," "Good-bye! Mr. Roosevelt," and "Judge Parker a Noble Man for Our Next President." Hardly less commonplace was the chorus of another song:

> Parker, Parker, the days are growing darker,
> Your country needs you badly in its hour of distress;
> Parker, Parker, you're not a side-show barker,
> You're the Moses who will lead us out of the wilderness.

To his credit, Roosevelt had spoken out against injustices to Negroes, allegedly in an attempt to win black votes in the North. There were relatively few Republican voters in the Democratic Solid South. He had assailed the atrocious series of current lynchings; he had invited the black educator Booker T. Washington to dinner at the White House; he had appointed at least two Negroes to federal office, including a post in Charleston, "the cradle of the Confederacy." The bitterness of racist Southern Democrats found vent in the air "Parker and Davis Jim Crow Quickstep".

Ironically, two years later Roosevelt damaged his pro-Negro record by intemperately discharging from the United States Army more than 100 black soldiers who had allegedly shot up the town of Brownsville, Texas. "Remember Brownsville," proclaimed a pro-Negro broadside of 1906.

In the Parker-Roosevelt campaign of 1904, T.R. was accused of having sneaked up and shot a Spaniard from behind—a charge that rasped the Rough Rider's instincts for fair play. One Democratic song, "Work! Vote! Watch!" related how "Teddy claims he won the war" and shot a Spaniard in the back. Another campaign ballad, to the air of "Marching through Georgia" (a strange tune for Southern Democrats), was "Marching with Parker." The chorus jubilated:

> Hurrah! Hurrah! we'll gain the victory!
> Hurrah! Hurrah! from Trust Rule we'll be free!
> And we'll have no government of warring monarchy
> When we go marching with Parker.

Despite these feeble efforts to unhorse the Rough Rider, T.R. won the presidential race of 1904 in a canter; the pedestrian Parker proved to be the worst-beaten major presidential candidate since "Old White Hat" Horace Greeley in 1872. The ebullient victor, no longer a "political accident," was simply "dee-lighted." Carried away by the heady wine of victory, he blurted out in words that came back to haunt him, "A wise custom which limits the President to two terms regards the substance and not the form, and under no circumstances will I be a candidate for or accept another nomination." Yet he later did, as a Bull Mooser in 1912.

T.R. AND THE MUCKRAKERS

A sharp and painful financial flurry, centering in Wall Street, shook the country in 1907. Known as "the rich man's panic," it resulted in a number of suicides and criminal indictments. The men whom Roosevelt called malefactors of great wealth promptly blamed "Theodore the Meddler" for the upheaval. They insisted that this "quack," "demagogue," and "crazy man" had brought on the acute distress known as "the Roosevelt panic." But the two-fisted President, never one to suffer criticism gladly, countercharged that the "criminal rich" had deliberately engineered the crisis so as to blunt T.R.'s attacks on the trusts.

Fortunately for the country, the panic proved relatively short. Reflecting the returning spirit of optimism, the powerful banker J. Pierpont Morgan, speaking in Chicago in 1908, paraphrased an earlier statement of his father, "Remember, my son, that any man who is a bear on the future of this country will go broke." In short, bullish investors were wanted who would not "sell America short."

Tidal waves of reform, with origins in the late nineteenth century, had meanwhile begun to crest during Roosevelt's second term. To all citizens who had eyes to see, "the promise of American life" (the title of a book by Herbert Croly in 1909) had proved a delusion. The poor and underprivileged were far too numerous. In 1890 a perceptive New York reporter, Jacob A. Riis, had published a book entitled *How the Other Half Lives*, which exposed the misery and degradation of the stinking slums. "The slum," he wrote, "is the measure of civilization."

Monopolistic big business was an object of growing concern. What were known as the "bloated trusts" and "dirty-handed millionaires" had already come under heavy fire, notably in Henry Demarest Lloyd's accusations against the monopolistic Standard Oil Company in *Wealth versus Commonwealth* (1894). In 1899 Dr. Thorstein Veblen brought out in book form his assault on "predatory wealth" and the "conspicuous consumption" of "gentlemen of leisure" in *The Theory of the Leisure Class*. A brilliant young novelist, Frank Norris, exposed the deadly grip of the railroads on the California wheat farmers in *The Octopus* (1901), and he subsequently pilloried the Chicago wheat speculators in *The Pit* (1903). In addition, swelling ranks of socialists, decrying "bloody capitalism," were transplanting to America ideas spawned by Karl Marx and other European radicals.

By 1902–03 the group of flaming young writers known as "muckrakers" began to emerge with a burning determination to cleanse American life by exposing its inequities. They got their name from a disapproving President Roosevelt, who was annoyed by their excess of zeal and by the evident determination of some of them to dig up dirt for dirt's sake. Speaking in Washington in 1906, he compared them to the man with the manure rake in *Pilgrim's Progress* who was so intent on the muck at his feet that he could not see the celestial crown suspended above him. "Men with the muckrake," he declared, "are often indispensable to the well-being of society, but only if they know when to stop raking muck."

A gifted muckraking reporter, Lincoln Steffens, wrote a series of articles in 1902 called "The Shame of the Cities." He nakedly exposed "the system" or the corrupt alliance between big business and government. Such "boss rule" was commonly called "invisible government," which was partly held together by "the cohesive power of public plunder."

Muckrakers also attacked the Standard Oil Company, the life insurance companies, the "Beef Trust," the "Money Trust," and other "financial buccaneers." One millionaire speculator, Thomas W. Lawson, laid bare the underhanded practices of his accomplices in a series of articles entitled "Frenzied Finance." In 1906–07 David G. Phillips shocked high-minded citizens with his series on "The Treason of the Senate," a body sometimes called the "American House of Lords." He pointed out that this "Millionaires' Club," the self-styled "greatest deliberative body in the world," consisted largely of members who did not represent the people but the railroads and trusts. Other muckrakers unmasked the "white slave traffic" in prostitutes, and John Spargo, in *The Bitter Cry of the Children* (1906) exposed the horrors of child abuse.

Militant muckrakers turned their attention to public health when they tackled the enormous traffic in patent medicines, which were found to be adulterated with alcohol, opium, and other drugs. Dr. H. W. Wiley, in the U.S. Department of Agriculture, created the "Poison Squad" and performed extensive experiments with food preservatives. Pure-food advocates found a powerful ally in Upton Sinclair, whose socialistic novel *The Jungle* (1906) aimed at public opinion with nauseous effect. The author focused on the loathsome stockyards of Chicago and the loathsome beef that poured out from them. An aroused Roosevelt appointed a special commission whose factual report outdid Sinclair's novel. It told how piles of poisoned rats, rope ends, splinters, and other debris found their way into cans as potted ham. A clever jingle made the point:

> Mary had a little lamb,
> And when she saw it sicken,
> She shipped it off to Packingtown,
> And now it's labeled chicken.

Novelist Sinclair himself complained, "I aimed at the public's heart and hit it in the stomach."

THE HEYDAY OF PROGRESSIVISM

Crusading Muckrakers, seeking all the filth fit to rake, were caught up in the Progressive movement, which roughly spanned the years from 1898 to 1914. It first bubbled up in certain politically aroused states, notably Wisconsin, in which the undersized but overengined Robert M. ("Fighting Bob") La Follette led the battle against "the interests." Reaching the governor's chair after a desperate battle, he was able to carry through a considerable part of his "Wisconsin idea." It embraced such features as regulatory commissions, child-labor legislation, safety regulations, workmen's compensation, and primary elections. Other states followed suit or worked in unison, notably California under Governor Hiram W. ("Holy Hiram") Johnson, who broke the stranglehold of the Southern Pacific Railroad Company on California politics and then, like La Follette, governed with his own machine.

As various states fell into step with current Progressivism, they enacted statutes against the entrenched "interests." These new laws set up the "initiative," which enabled voters to initiate legislation; the "referendum," which permitted them to have a whack at legislation already passed; and the "recall," which empowered them to unhorse officials corrupted by the bosses or bribed by lobbyists. To gain these ends, "the Australian ballot" or secret ballot was imported from abroad. The Seventeenth Amendment, adopted in 1913, authorized the voters to elect directly, rather than through state legislatures, the members of the then plutocratic United States Senate.

Political reformers, especially females, believed that "the petticoat vote" would purify the electorate and purge the government. The resulting ground swell finally brought the Nineteenth Amendment in 1920. The militant "suffragists" of the Progressive era, protesting against "taxation without representation," urged "votes for women," "equal suffrage for men and women," and "universal suffrage." Male chauvinists would reply, "Let the women suffer," and a cynical masculine definition of a suffragist was "One who has ceased to be a lady and has not yet become a gentleman."

As in earlier years, women were taking a leading role in the fight against "Demon Rum." "Booze interests" and the liquor lobby were intimately associated with such evils as the urban "red-light districts" (for prostitutes) and the blowsy political "boss." He allegedly counted poker chips by night and miscounted ballots by day, including "the cemetery vote." Through the processes of "local option," a number of localities and states had voted themselves "dry" by 1914, as contrasted with states that had remained "wet," alcoholically speaking.

Popular songs of the antibooze crusade were "We'll Rout John Barley-corn," "Working for Rum God's Doom," "Vote for Local Option," "Let 'No' Be Your Answer," and "Little White Ribboners"—in honor of the white-ribbon badge for purity of the Woman's Christian Temperance Union (W.C.T.U.). "Demon Rum" was in retreat, but he was not to be floored (temporarily) until the Eighteenth Amendment was adopted in 1919.

BILL TAFT BEATS BILLY BRYAN

At heart strenuous "Teddy" did not want to leave the exciting White House but he felt bound by the no-third-term pledge that he had impulsively made when intoxicated by victory in 1904. He looked around for a sympathetic successor who would carry out "my policies," and he finally selected his portly Secretary of War, William Howard ("Big Bill") Taft, who weighed about 350 pounds. A conservative lawyer and judge, Taft had occasionally "sat on the lid" while T.R. was absent on one of his numerous forays from Washington. The country received the impression that whenever the oversized Taft remained on the lid, the situation was under control.

T.R.'s restless big stick was much in evidence as the Republicans assembled in 1908 in Chicago. After lining up in advance enough pro-Taft delegates, Roosevelt controlled an irresistible "steam roller," which pushed through the nomination of his handpicked successor on the first ballot. The pro-Roosevelt platform, pointing with pride in all directions, praised the Republican record and declared against monopoly while favoring tariff revision and currency reform under the gold standard.

Hopeful Democrats met some three weeks later in mile-high Denver, deep in the heart of the silver country, although free silver as an issue was now as dead as an abandoned mine. The delegates, remembering their Waterloo under stodgy Judge Parker, opted for their two-time loser, that hardy quadrennial "Billy Boy" Bryan. His clarion call was "The Democratic party must be progressive." The resulting platform blasted the efforts of T.R. to establish a dynasty by ramming through the nomination of Taft; it deplored the stranglehold of "predatory wealth" on the nation's life; and it repeated the Jeffersonian maxim "Equal rights to all; special privileges to none." Finally, the platform heralded "Shall the people rule?" as "the overshadowing issue" of the campaign.

"Big Bill" Taft, a ponderous speaker, took to the stump, from which he read cut-and-dried speeches. For conservatives he stressed conservativism; for liberals he took on a more liberal coloration. Many Americans concluded that a vote for Taft was a vote for the departing Roosevelt, and to this extent the candidate cashed in on the Rough Rider's popularity. In essence the Republican platform was "We stand pat," with its emphasis on prosperity, even though some of the glitter on the full dinner pail had been smudged by the "Roosevelt panic" of 1907.

"Smiling Bill" Taft was acclaimed in slogans as "Safe and Sane" and as "The Man of the Hour." The more interestingly titled Republican songs carried their own message: "Vote for Billy Taft," "Taft's the Man to Lead the Band," "Big Bill for Me," "Our Good and Honest Taft," and "Big Bill Taft." Two additional tunes gave recognition to James S. Sherman of New York, Taft's vice presidential running mate: "Peaceful Bill and Sunny Jim" and "Smiling Bill and Sunny Jim." A blatant and patronizing appeal to the Negro vote in the North was "Taft Am Gwine to Be de Black Man's President."

The free and unlimited coinage of campaign songs had evidently passed with the McKinley-Hanna orgies of 1896 and 1900. Many of the colorless airs for 1908 were about as inspired as the "Huzza for Jackson" type of 1828. Some song writers and button designers worked both sides of the street, and they could "hip, hip, hooray" for either candidate by merely inserting the desired name. The name Taft rhymed with "raft," "craft," "aft," "abaft," "draft," and even "graft"; the songsmiths could take their choice. One popular paean to Taft, entitled "B–I–Double L–Bill," declared that his supporters sailed on a raft with Taft. The very thought of being on a crowded raft, especially a small one, with a man as corpulent as "Big Bill," must have given some voters a sinking feeling. The song "Get on the Raft with Taft" promised that "Smiling Bill" Taft would save the country from all kinds of ills, including "graft".

A balding Bryan, once "The Boy Orator," again toured the country, piling up mileage and wordage. His favorite battle cries were "Let the people rule" and "Shall the people rule?" and the latter became the title of a Democratic song. Another musical tribute to the great orator, much less original, was "Bryan, Bryan, Hallelujah!" set to the rousing tune of "John Brown's Body." Other compositions were "The Commoner," "Have You Heard the News from Denver?" (of Bryan's nomination), "Billy Bryan Is the Man for Me," "The People's Choice," "Star of the West" (Nebraska), and "Our Billy of the Platte."

One Democratic air poked fun at good-natured Taft in "The Merry Smile," which would disappear as soon as his defeat was announced. Another contribution, "Willie Taft," attempted to deflate the plump candidate by using his diminutive name.

Taft's victory could be confidently predicted, even without public opinion polls. A Democratic broadside had optimistically announced, "The Conscience of the Nation is Aroused," but evidently it was not.

Bryan, though he put up a gallant fight, polled fewer votes than he had in 1896, at a time when the country was less populous and less prosperous. When the silver-tongued orator called, "Let the people rule," he intended that they should do so under him rather than under "Smiling Bill" Taft. One Republican pin carried the cutting message, "Vote for Taft This Time—You Can Vote for Bryan Any Time."

After turning over the reins to Taft in March 1909, T.R. left for an extensive big-game hunt in East Africa. His numerous enemies, including the "malefactors of great wealth," clinked glasses in their plush clubs to the toast "Health to the Lions," but the noble beasts failed to "do their duty." The superactive huntsman came back with his trophies in time to don antlers as a "Bull Moose" in the presidential campaign of 1912.

In retrospect T.R. had proved that he was a progressive, but one "with the brakes on." Some of his battles, in which he had cried, "My spear knows no brother," had produced more noise and fury than concrete results. Yet on balance he had provided a great breath of fresh air by throwing himself into the reformist movement, battling for conservation, and leading the United States nearer the center of the world stage.

XXII

From the Square Deal to the New Freedom

> The masters of the government of the United States are the combined capitalists and manufacturers of the United States.
>
> Woodrow Wilson, campaign speech, 1912

TAFT THE MISFIT

"Smiling Bill" Taft was not cut out to be a spectacular success as President. Of judicial training and temperament, he yearned to serve on the Supreme Court, as he later did with distinction. "Politics makes me sick" is a refrain that runs through his correspondence. "Peaceful Bill" Taft, as he was also dubbed, was no fighter, no name caller, no brandisher of a big stick. In serving as Secretary of War and in other offices, he had acted only as a lieutenant, not as the leader. His talents, which he was often called on to use as a "trouble shooter," ran to conciliation and compromise. Virtually appointed to the Presidency by Theodore Roosevelt, "good old Will" would have fared better in quieter times. But he had the ill luck to follow the clatter and fury of a noisy Rough Rider who happened also to be a spectacular showman. Roosevelt's was a hard act to follow.

An eminent jurist, Taft was restrained from becoming an activist President by his respect, even reverence, for the Constitution. He would have recoiled in horror if he had heard T.R. explode, "Damn the law! I want the canal built." Taft's administration was heavily staffed with conservative standpatters, who seemed out of place to the rebellious liberals in the party, especially those who were forming the "insurgent" group in Congress. The Grand Old Party was crumbling into two factions, and the new President found himself caught in the middle, no longer smiling.

Taft quickly floundered into hot water over the tariff. The Republican platform, bending to the winds of change, had come out "unequivocally" for revised schedules. Most voters naturally assumed that the revision would be downward, not upward. But Republican conservatives in Congress, bending to pressures from a swarm of lobbyists for big business, boosted many of the schedules upward. Rather than wreck the party, Taft reluctantly signed the patchwork Payne-Aldrich Tariff Bill of 1909. More than that, he ventured out on the stump to defend it and then overdid the defense. At Winona, Minnesota, he insisted that the new law was "the best [tariff] bill the Republican party ever passed." This praise may have been defensible, if one bears in mind that the Republican party was historically committed to relatively high tariffs. But Taft left the wrong impression. Unhappily afflicted with a bad case of "foot-in-mouth disease," he made matters worse when he lamely explained to the press that he had dashed the speech off hurriedly between stations. One Congressman remarked that Taft was "a well-meaning man who was born with two left feet."

Dissatisfaction mounted among Republicans over the tariff and Taft's vulnerable stand on conservation. Discontent found a dramatic outlet in the "insurgent revolt" in the House of Representatives against the Speaker, cigar-chomping "Uncle Joe" Cannon—coarse, profane, and dictatorial. Republican reformers or "insurgents," combining with the Democrats in Congress, rebelled against "Cannonism" in 1910 and sheared the Speaker of much of his tyrannical power. By this time Taft's ineptitude had helped to split the Grand Old Party wide open, and Roosevelt worshipers longed for a return of their hero from his African safari with what he called "my policies." One popular rephrasing of a nursery rhyme voiced this yearning:

> Teddy, come home and blow your horn,
> The sheep's in the meadow, the cow's in the corn.
> The boy you left to tend the sheep
> Is under the haystack fast asleep.

DOLLAR DIPLOMACY IN FLOWER

Teddy Roosevelt's imminent return and his actual arrival inspired an awesome outpouring of songs, many more than in some presidential elections. Most of these efforts took the form of copyrighted sheet music designed to be played on the piano. Precisely how well they sold cannot be determined, but they clearly presented sentiments that the composers themselves hoped would catch fire as reflecting popular acclaim. If any doubt exists as to T.R.'s immense popularity, these compositions should prove persuasive.

Some of the songs related to the Rough Rider's African lion hunt, which resulted in such titles as "When Teddy Hit the Jungle" and "When Teddy Comes Home with His Gun." One air obviously referred to T.R.'s ebullient personality, for its title was the single characteristic word "Dee-lighted." Two tunes honored the war hero's past exploits: "Roosevelt and the Rough Riders" and "Welcome Home Comrade." Other melodies expressed concern over the insurgent movement that had developed within the Republican party: "Song of the Insurgents," "What Will Teddy Do Next?" "Teddy Come Home!" and "Mr. Roosevelt Our Country Calls for You." Still other titles rejoiced over T.R.'s imminent or actual return: "When Rough and Ready Teddy Dashes Home," "When Yankee Doodle Teddy Boy Comes Marching Home Again," and "Mr. Roosevelt, Our Country Welcomes You." Many of the songs expressed admiration, even adoration: "Our Teddy Is Ahead of Them All," "A Tribute to Our Teddy," "Oh You Teddy!" and "Ho! Ho! for Teddy!"

Still bursting with energy, a suspicious Teddy Roosevelt finally returned to New York in June 1910, where he received a hero's welcome. Tale-bearers advised him that Taft was carrying "my policies" out—on a stretcher. Unable to tolerate a quiet retirement, T.R. delivered a speech at Osawatomie, Kansas (John Brown's old stamping ground), that scandalized the Old Guard standpatters of his party. He proclaimed "The New Nationalism," that is, a large increase of federal power to correct social and political abuses—in short, a welfare state. Conservatives moaned about "the wild man from Oyster Bay" (a Roosevelt residence).

As a "trust buster," President Taft actually brought a number of successful actions against trusts, although some of these important proceedings were initiated under T.R. A noteworthy Taft triumph came in 1911 when the Supreme Court, invoking the Sherman Anti-Trust Act of 1890, ordered the dissolution of the Standard Oil Company. At the same time the berobed jurists handed down their memorable "rule of reason," which meant that the government should prosecute only those trusts or combinations suspected of an "unreasonable" restraint of trade. Taft himself dealt moderately with what was called "the curse of bigness," for he declared "Mere size is no sin against the law."

Wall Street "interests" received another severe jolt in 1912–13 when a committee of the House of Representatives launched a probe of the so-called "Money Trust." Dr. Woodrow Wilson of Princeton, a fast-rising star in New Jersey politics, charged that "the greatest monopoly in this country is the money monopoly."

Taft's forays into foreign affairs were neither so spectacular nor so fruitful as those of T.R. As befitted the spokesman for the party of big business, Taft adopted a course regarding foreign investments known cynically as "dollar diplomacy." He would use American foreign policy to protect dollars invested abroad, conspicuously by landing the Marines on the shores of the banana republics of Latin America, notably Nicaragua, to restore order. On the reverse side of dollar diplomacy, he would urge American bankers to pump their surplus funds abroad into strategically located countries, such as China and the republics of Latin America, so as to promote Washington's objective in those areas. As Taft told Congress in 1912, "This policy has been characterized as substituting dollars for bullets. It is one that appeals alike to idealistic humanitarian sentiments, to the dictates of sound policy and strategy, and to legitimate commercial aims." "The almighty dollar" thus came to supplant the big stick, but not with conspicuous success.

"Big Bill" Taft suffered a stinging reverse in his attempt to establish more friendly relations with Canada through a reciprocal lowering of tariff duties on both sides of the elongated border. High-tariff Republicans opposed the scheme, but Taft, for once a fighter, was able to ram his pet proposal through Congress. His chronic foot-in-mouth disease again betrayed him when he informed Congress (and the suspicious Canadians) that Canada (and Britain?) had come to "the parting of the ways." Viewing reciprocity as a step toward the ultimate annexation of Canada, Speaker Champ Clark declared, "I am for it, because I hope to see the day when the American flag will float over every square foot of the British North American possessions clear to the North Pole." Alarmed Canadians, feeling forced to choose the Union Jack or Old Glory, flocked to the polls and threw back into Taft's face the scheme that the President had painfully extorted from a bruised Congress.

TAFT CHALLENGED BY TWO OPPONENTS

As insurgency gathered momentum within the Republican party, the old rough-riding warhorse began to champ again at the bit. The more his handpicked Taft seemed to fall under the thumb of the Old Guard, the more concerned T.R. became about the fate of "my policies" and the less restrained he felt by his impetuous pledge of no third term. He reportedly remarked in private, "I would cut off my right hand here if I could recall that statement." His reasoning, despite his clear-cut promise in 1904, was that the third-term tradition applied only to three full consecutive terms. He declared that because a man once said he did not want a third cup of coffee for breakfast, he did not necessarily mean that he "was never going to take another cup of coffee." To newsmen T.R. finally exploded, in February 1912, "My hat's in the ring!" and "The fight is on and I am stripped to the buff!" *Harper's Weekly* sourly observed, "Hate, not hat, is in the ring."

Roosevelt then seized the banner of the rebellious liberal Republicans and charged into a number of the presidential primaries. He insulted his "dear Will" by saying, "Taft means well; but he means well feebly." The placid incumbent finally became aroused and branded Roosevelt's supporters as "emotionalists and neurotics." Again with foot in mouth, Taft reportedly complained, "Even a rat in a corner will fight." He thus left the impression with some voters that he would act like any other rat.

As the fury of battle increased, T.R. went overboard for popular control of government. He proposed the "recall" or removal of judges who might be "interest-controlled" by big corporations. Even more shocking, he urged the "recall of judicial decisions" at the state level subject to review by the U.S. Supreme Court. Increasing numbers of voters evidently began to wonder if the horsy ex-President had not fallen on his head too many times; a few seem to have thought that Roosevelt regarded himself as the new Messiah. The text of a famous poster, distributed by an unknown humorist on the eve of the Chicago nominating convention of the Republicans in 1912, recalled Jesus: "At three o'clock Thursday afternoon, Theodore Roosevelt will walk on the waters of Lake Michigan."

When the badly divided Republican delegates were all assembled, the Taft conservatives occupied the driver's seat of the "steam roller" that

Teddy Roosevelt Changes His Mind. K. K. Knecht, the *Evansville Courier*.
Reproduced with permission of the *Evansville Courier*.

T.R. had used so ruthlessly to push Taft into the White House. Roosevelt commanded the votes of most of those states that had held primaries, but Taft controlled the machine vote of those states, many of them in the South, that did not select their delegates by popular vote. As a result, the portly Ohioan crushed his former benefactor and new rival. The angered followers of Roosevelt, crying "fraud" and "naked theft," left the convention in a mood to launch a third-party crusade.

This fatal split in Republican ranks proved to be the godsend for which the Democrats had prayed. An old political maxim was borne out: "The party in power is seldom defeated; it splits into factions and defeats itself." The new Moses of the Democrats was Dr. Thomas Woodrow Wilson, formerly president of Princeton University and a noted political scientist. As "The Scholar in Politics" or "The Schoolmaster in Politics," he was elected in 1910 as governor of boss-ridden New Jersey, notorious as "The Mother of Trusts," including Standard Oil of New Jersey. Displaying forceful leadership and demanding "pitiless publicity" for the corporate "interests," he managed to ram through the legislature a sheaf of forward-looking measures—popularly known as "The Seven Sisters." Taken together, they turned the once reactionary state into a showcase of progressivism.

When the victory-starved Democratic convention met in Baltimore in 1912, Speaker Champ Clark of Missouri had emerged from the pack as the front runner. An experienced politician of the old school, he had not only shown moderately progressive tendencies but had supported Bryan's radical agrarian policies. Back-country Missourians typically kept one or more hounds, and Clark's following whipped up enthusiasm for their hero with the popular song "They Gotta Quit Kickin' My Dawg Aroun'." Clark himself got kicked around when he fell short of accumulating the then necessary two-thirds vote, and the prize fell to the chief challenger, Woodrow Wilson.

Wilson's running mate, Thomas R. Marshall, hailed from the Hoosier State of Indiana, where he had gained some repute as a homespun philosopher. He is perhaps best known as the author of the saying "What this country really needs is a good five-cent cigar." In those days the chief function of the Vice President was to hang around and be available if the President should die. Marshall wrote in his recollections, "Once there were two brothers. One ran away to sea, the other was elected Vice-President, and nothing was ever heard of either of them again."

THE BULL MOOSE EXTRAVAGANZA

Roosevelt's overheated Progressive followers met in Chicago in the humid August of 1912 to nominate their aroused Rough Rider for the Presidency. He brought down the house as he shouted in a fighting speech,

"We stand at Armageddon,* and we battle for the Lord." In the spirit of a revival meeting the delegates sang "Onward, Christian Soldiers" and "The Battle Hymn of the Republic," both of which became Progressive theme songs in the ensuing campaign. Another tune, less elevated, was "We're Ready for Teddy Again." William Allen White, the gifted Kansas journalist and a T.R. worshiper, later wrote, "Roosevelt bit me and I went mad."

Combining righteousness with high enthusiasm, the newly formed Progressive party, fresh from what one member called "the grass roots," proclaimed a platform that described itself a "Covenant with the People." It endorsed house-cleaning reform and lashed out at "invisible government." Roosevelt had earlier boasted that he felt "as strong as a bull moose," and thereafter the bull moose took its place with the donkey and the elephant in the American political zoo. One rhymester, probably with tongue in cheek, wrote:

> I want to be a Bull Moose,
> And with the Bull Moose stand
> With antlers on my forehead
> And a Big Stick in my hand.

Ring Lardner, the well-known humorist, confused his animals when he wrote a song in honor of "Bull Moose" Roosevelt. It was entitled, "Teddy, You're a Bear." And button makers promised "A Square Deal All Around," while assuring the voters, "Our Country Needs Roosevelt for Another Term."

With two angry rivals about to split the Republican vote and thus slit each other's throats, the outcome of the election seemed to be a foregone conclusion. The only question, remarked "Uncle Joe" Cannon, was which corpse "would get the more flowers." Taft, the "Peaceful President," and Roosevelt, the Rough Rider, tore into each other as only former friends could. "Death alone can take me now!" exclaimed the once placid Taft, who assailed T.R. as "a dangerous egotist," a "demagogue," and a "brawler." Roosevelt, fighting mad, branded Taft an "apostate" and a "fathead" with the brain of a "guinea pig" who was a party to a "barefaced fraud."

Further proof of Taft's lack of political appeal was the scarcity of pro-Taft slogans. One of the more pointed was "Washington Wouldn't! Grant Couldn't! Roosevelt Shan't! No Third Term!" One of the punchier buttons warned, "Good Republicans Don't Bolt the Party Ticket." Even the songs for Taft were rather scarce, including tunes of the preceding campaign. Among them one finds "Peaceful Bill," "Possum Bill," and "Tariff

---

* Armageddon, a word evidently derived from the last book of the New Testament, is the place where the final battle will supposedly be fought between the forces of good and evil.

'Bill.' " One tune satirized Roosevelt's evident grasping for power with "Teddy Must Be King," while another warned, "Taft is Too Much for You, Teddy." Tunesmiths for Taft Republicans and Wilson Democrats could quite agree that Roosevelt was "Teddy the Meddler" and "The Man on Horseback." "Get on the Raft with Taft" was revived from the previous campaign, although by now the raft was clearly sinking.

What Taft's supporters failed to produce in slogan and song was more than offset by the almost hysterical outpouring of adoring catchwords, slogans, and songs for T.R. After the election "Bull Moose" Roosevelt observed that "there is a lunatic fringe to every reform movement," including his. One lunatic, whether on the fringe or not, shot Roosevelt in the chest in the closing days of the campaigning. "It takes more than that to kill a bull moose," the grievously wounded Roosevelt reportedly remarked as he ended his oral harangues.

Some of the pro-Roosevelt songs of this campaign related to the pro-Taft tactics that had robbed the Rough Rider of the nomination, notably "Teddy and the Steam Roller." Many of the other airs referred to the cowboy hat T.R. had tossed into the fray, such as "My Hat Is in the Ring," "Teddy's Hat Is in the Ring," "Rally 'round the Hat, Boys," and "Don't Kick Our Teddy's Hat Aroun'."

Other Rooseveltian tunes recalled the rousing Progressive convention that had nominated "Bull Moose" Roosevelt. Among them were "We Stand at Armageddon" and "The Song of Armageddon." The antlered emblem loomed large in "The Bull Moose Song," "Teddy's Moose," "The Brave Young Moose," and "The Moose Is Loose."

On a less frivolous level were such airs as "Teddy's for the People" and "Teddy'll Swat the Bosses." In addition there were the usual "hurrah" appeals such as "Teddy the Tried and True," "Roosevelt for Me," "We Want Teddy," "Teddy, Teddy's in It Yet," "We Are with T.R.," "Go Ted, Go," and "Roosevelt, a Magical Name." In a different category, "Teddy da Roose" was a dialect song evidently designed to appeal to the Italian-American vote. Additionally, one of the most pointed Bull Moose slogans broadcast this happy thought: "Pass Prosperity Around."

THE TRIUMPH OF WOODROW WILSON

Cool, collected, and eloquent, Wilson wisely refused to get into the same bull-moose ring with his two wrathful opponents. A conservative in his earlier years, he could not claim to be the foremost champion of progressivism, only a progressive "with the brakes on." He chose as his campaign theme the forward-looking principles of what he called "The New Freedom," new opportunity under government regulation for free enterprise. He specifically pointed to the need to foster competition by reducing tariffs and curbing the bloated trusts—"that invisible empire of special interest." Bryan, the ageing "Boy Orator," loyally supported "The Scholar in Politics," although in 1907 Wilson had written privately of him, "Would that we could do something, at once dignified and effective, to knock Mr. Bryan once and for all into a cocked hat!" This indiscretion leaked out in 1911 while Wilson was governor of New Jersey, to the embarrassment of both men, but Bryan graciously accepted Wilson's apologies.

"The New Freedom," while a rather vague concept, must rank as an effective Democratic slogan, although many surviving campaign buttons display a rather obvious alliteration, "Win With Wilson." What appears to have been a popular Democratic campaign song was "Wilson—That's All." This title was adapted from a well-known whiskey advertisement.

"Woody" for "Woodrow," though proposed and occasionally used as a nickname, did not lend itself well to slogan or music. One Democratic song carried the title "Row, Row, Woodrow," and another "I'm a Woodrow Wilson Man." Others were "Welcome Wilson" and "Bust the Trusts." An interesting air was "Sit Down and Rock It Out with Me," a reference to Wilson's sitting down with visitors at his home at Sea Girt, New Jersey, and discussing problems while activating his rocking chair. Champ Clark's "houn dawg" song experienced a rousing revival, and also spawned such variants as "I Just Can't Help a-Humming That 'Houn Dawg' Tune" and "Bring Your Houn'." One Democratic booklet included such tunes as "Steam Roller," and, in an evident appeal to the black vote, "To Put Dat 'Steam Roller' Down" and "Want Yo', Wilson, 'Deed We Do!"

After this wearisome barrage of words and music, the voters trudged to the polls in November 1912. The final tally gave victory to Wilson by a wide margin in the Electoral College, although he had attracted only 42 percent of the total popular vote, the smallest percentage since Lincoln. "Bull Moose" Roosevelt outdistanced the torpid Taft, who carried only two states. T.R. was the lively corpse that got the bulk of the second-place ballot-box flowers. Yet progressivism was the most convincing victor because the combined votes of Roosevelt, Wilson, and Eugene V. Debs, the Socialist candidate, constituted a whopping majority. The Rough Rider's rough tactics had disrupted the Republican party, which was now destined to be the "outs" for eight long years. As William Allen White now concluded, perhaps T.R. had bitten himself and gone mad.

PROFESSORIAL BEGINNINGS

Thomas Woodrow Wilson, known as "Tommy" Wilson in his youth, was born in Virginia and reared in the post-Civil War South. There he witnessed at first hand the wreckage caused by the attempt of the Confederates to achieve "self-determination of peoples," a phrase that was to loom large in his thinking as a peacemaker in Europe in 1919. A stern Presbyterian, he became a leading moralist, "angry for the right," and a master of lofty epigrammatic prose—a so-called "phrase maker" or "phraseocrat." One critic remarked that Wilson was born halfway between the Bible and the dictionary and never got away from either. Following up his long training in theoretical government, he turned out to be an eminently successful practical politician. In 1908 he had written in a book, "The President is at liberty, both in law and conscience, to be as big a man as he can. His capacity will set the limit; and if Congress be overborne by him, it will be no fault of the Constitution."

Indisputably an intellectual, "The Professor in Politics" developed a degree of arrogance toward lesser intellects, particularly stupid Senators, whose "bungalow minds" made him "sick." For his own part, his powers of concentration were so highly developed, so he remarked in 1912, that "I have a single-track mind." Earlier he had written privately that his mind was "a one-track road and can run only one train of thought at a time." His sense of duty was so strong as to lead him into the paths of "moral imperialism" or "the imperialism of righteousness," notably in neighboring Mexico, where his interference seemed like "meddling and muddling."

Wilson's Cabinet presented a collection of mostly unknowns. Josephus Daniels, a North Carolina newspaper man, was chosen as Secretary of the Navy, or "managing editor of the navy," as he was called. He banned alcohol from American warships, thus earning in thirsty naval circles an unflattering sobriquet, "Joe Syphilis" Daniels. William Jennings Bryan, the uncrowned king of the party, was by tradition entitled to the premier position in the Cabinet, Secretary of State, and hence received the appointment. Wilson was not enthusiastic about the choice; he recognized Bryan's goodness of heart but thought less well of his head, which he thought lacked "a mental rudder." "The man has no brains," he had written to a friend privately in 1904. But as "Mr. Dooley" humorously remarked, Wilson would rather have Bryan "in his bosom than on his back."

Clean-living Bryan proved something of an embarrassment to Wilson. A prohibitionist, the new Secretary of State barred alcohol from official functions, and "grape-juice diplomacy" was a derisive phrase frequently heard. Some of the diplomats fortified themselves too well in advance of what they knew would be an arid affair. More bitterly criticized was an unfortunate phrase that Bryan used when he wrote to a Democratic official in 1913, "Can you let me know what positions you have at your disposal with which to reward deserving Democrats?" More than 6 million Democrats had voted for Bryan in three presidential elections, and "The Peerless Leader" had many debts to pay off. But the opposition party, which had been filling offices for many years with "resolute Republicans," jeered at this blatant exhibition of spoilsmanship by the "Prince of Job Hunters."

As an ardent champion of world peace, Bryan supplemented his income by lecturing on the Chautauqua circuit with an address entitled "Prince of Peace." Republican newspaper editors lambasted his "peace piffle" and "grape-juice guff." Yet Bryan persisted in negotiating a series of conciliation pacts, popularly known as "cooling off" or "wait a bit" treaties. They embodied the ancient maxim "When angry count fifty, when very angry count one hundred." These "scraps of paper" might have done substantial good if the Great War in Europe had not erupted in 1914.

Bryan also worked hard, but with limited success, to patch up a quarrel between California and Japan in 1913. Californians were determined to bar Japanese from owning land in the Golden State, where they were regarded as a wage-depressing menace. At one critical period, the Japanese Ambassador in Washington asked Bryan, "Is this final?" The Secretary's diplomatic reply became a byword: "There is nothing final between friends." Headstrong California passed the discriminatory land legislation anyhow, but did so by tactfully not mentioning the Japanese. The law barred only "aliens ineligible to citizenship," which meant Asians, including those from Japan.

Honoring his "New Freedom" pledge to provide new economic freedom for the masses, President Wilson launched a formidable assault on the "triple wall of privilege": the tariff, high finance, and the trusts. In his message urging tariff reform, he shattered precedent when he appeared before Congress in person—a practice abandoned by weak-voiced Thomas Jefferson in 1801. As Wilson rode away from Capitol Hill, he remarked to a companion in reference to the unconventional T.R., "I think we put one over on Teddy that time."

Tariff reform—ultimately the Underwood Tariff of 1914—encountered rough sledding in Congress, especially the Senate. That windy body contained many "tools" of the "special interests," whom Wilson had earlier branded as watchdogs of "predatory wealth." A locustlike swarm of lobbyists descended—the so-called "Third House of Congress"—determined to block or at least water down the proposed legislation. But Wilson, reverting to his habit of appealing over the heads of the legislators to the sovereign people, helped to thwart their sabotage by resorting to what he had earlier called "pitiless publicity."

Wilson next tackled head-on the "Money Trust" by pushing through Congress the Federal Reserve Act of 1913. It was designed to create a more flexible currency and to place greater financial power in the hands of the federal government. At one point in the battle a dejected Senator Carter Glass, a Democratic leader, spoke of resignation, but Wilson burst out, "Damn it, don't resign, old fellow, outvote them."

Bloated trusts provided the third bastion of the "triple wall of privilege." In 1914 Congress, under Wilson's determined prodding, passed the Federal Trade Commission Act, which was designed to halt harmful sales practices by using "cease and desist" orders. Next came the Clayton Anti-Trust Act of 1914, which attempted to add real teeth, without conspicuous success, to the gums of the aged Sherman Anti-Trust Act of 1890. Among other changes, it lifted labor from the category of "a commodity or article of commerce." Samuel Gompers, head of the American Federation of Labor, hailed the act with unwarranted enthusiasm as the "Magna Carta of Labor."

WATCHFUL WAITING SOUTH OF THE BORDER

In the tricky arena of foreign affairs, Wilson shocked diplomats by a sudden and spectacular attempt to reverse the "dollar diplomacy" of Taft. He bluntly announced at the outset that he was not interested in supporting any "special group of interests." This abrupt warning in the press—a classic example of "shirt sleeves" diplomacy—served notice on Americans who invested dollars abroad. The reluctant bankers, whom Taft had induced to enter a six-power financial consortium in China, concluded that they had better withdraw—and they did.

Wilson's efforts to disentangle the nation from dollar diplomacy in Latin America proved less successful, in part because the "insurrectionary habit" brought the Marines to Haiti and Santo Domingo in 1915 and 1916 respectively. During these years Franklin D. Roosevelt was Assistant Secretary of the Navy, and he later boasted in a campaign speech in 1920, "The facts are that I wrote Haiti's constitution myself, and, if I do say it, I think it a pretty good constitution."

An imminent wedding of the waters, scheduled at Panama in 1914, caused much agitation in the United States to exempt American ships engaged in coastwise trade from paying tolls. Competing maritime nations, notably Great Britain, cried "unfair" but most Americans evidently did not agree. As the Progressive platform of 1912 made clear, "The Panama Canal, built and paid for by the American people, must be used primarily for their benefit." Wilson's Democratic platform took the same position, but an embarrassing treaty with Great Britain prohibited the United States from discriminating in its own favor. National honor was involved, and Wilson took the honorable course when he told Congress that the nation was "too big, too powerful, too self-respecting" to reread treaties in its own favor "just because we have power enough to give us leave to read them as we please." By appealing to honor and idealism alike, he induced a balky Congress, after a bitter debate, to repeal the act discriminating in favor of American shipping.

Wilson's early months were bedeviled by the revolution in Mexico, which gravely endangered American lives and investments. For dreary decades the Mexican masses had endured exploitation by the upper classes, who worked hand in glove with foreign exploiters of oil and other natural resources. As Wilson confessed in 1914, "My ideal is an orderly and righteous government in Mexico; but my passion is for the submerged eighty-five percent of the people of that republic who are now struggling toward liberty."

Such idealism in the White House was challenged by the emergence of a dictatorial strongman in Mexico, President Victoriano Huerta. He would play ball with foreign exploiters, but he had attained power by plotting the murder of his predecessor. Wilson, who deplored "government by murder," stubbornly refused to grant Huerta recognition, and finally succeeded in driving him into exile. A fiery Republican journalist, George Harvey, demanded, "What legal or moral right has a President of the United States to say who shall or shall not be President of Mexico?"

Plainly alluding to Mexico, Wilson delivered a memorable address at Mobile, Alabama, in the autumn of 1913. "It is," he declared, "a very perilous thing to determine the foreign policy of a nation in the terms of material interest." As evidence of his good faith, he pledged that "the United States will never again seek one additional foot of territory by conquest."

After the Mobile assurances, Wilson pursued a policy of what he called "watchful waiting," which interventionist Republicans condemned as "deadly drifting." As American citizens continued to be killed during the Mexican turmoil, bellicose Theodore Roosevelt cried, "He kissed the blood-stained hand that slapped his face." A dance step then popular was called "the Wilson tango." It consisted of one step forward, two backward, a side step, and then a moment of hesitation. Yet Wilson was determined to allow the Mexicans to have their revolution and not be dominated by "a small group of Americans with vested interests in Mexico." The king of yellow journalism, William R. Hearst, owned a ranch in Mexico that was larger than Rhode Island, and his San Francisco *Examiner* jeered:

> Oh, say, can you see by the dawn's early light
> Any possible way of avoiding a fight?
> The Star-Spangled Banner, oh, long may it flap,
> While we're kicked by the Greaser and slapped by the Jap.

An armed clash between Mexico and "The Colossus of the North" finally grew out of a trivial incident at Tampico. A U.S. Navy boat, after landing several men routinely, was seized, and the crew suffered temporary arrest. The commanding American admiral, Henry T. Mayo, issued a twenty-four-hour ultimatum demanding disavowal, apology, and punishment, in addition to hoisting an American flag and saluting it with twenty-one guns. All this he required of a government that Washington then refused to recognize. When the Mexican officials refused to humble themselves to this degree over a slight misunderstanding, Wilson felt compelled by national honor to back the admiral's arbitrary demands. He ordered the seizure of Vera Cruz, at the cost of 19 Americans and about 125 Mexicans, not counting the wounded combatants and civilians on both sides.

As a full-fledged war with Mexico threatened, Wilson was taken off the hook by a mediation offer from the "A.B.C." powers, Argentina, Brazil, and Chile. The subsequent conference at Niagara Falls gave birth to a plan that the Mexican regime rejected, but in the aftermath the "unspeakable" Huerta, bending to Wilsonian pressures, went into voluntary exile in the summer of 1914. Wilson's "watchful waiting" was successful at least to the extent of avoiding a full-scale war. A contemporary campaign button read, "Watchful Waiting Wins."

Chaos unhappily continued under Huerta's successor, Venustiano Carranza. A foremost rival for his power was Pancho Villa, a combination of bandit and Robin Hood. Showing his contempt for both the Mexican government and Wilson, he invaded and shot up the town of Columbus, New Mexico, killing eighteen citizens of the United States. At last "American blood," to use President Polk's language of 1846, had been shed on indisputably "American soil."

Neither "watchful waiting" nor even "wrathful waiting" could endure longer in the face of the outburst of American indignation. Wilson ordered General John J. ("Black Jack"*) Pershing to pursue and break up the bandit band. President Carranza of Mexico acquiesced with great reluctance after receiving face-saving assurances of reciprocal privileges. The "perishing expedition," as it was dubbed, penetrated deep into Mexico with surprising speed, but failed to catch Villa. A frustrated Wilson withdrew the invading force early in 1917, on the eve of a vastly larger war with Germany. The Mexicans were left free to complete their revolution without hindrance from Wilson's "imperialism of righteousness."

---

* Earlier known as "Nigger Jack," Pershing had served as an officer with the crack Negro Tenth U.S. Cavalry.

XXIII

Keeping out of War

America cannot be an ostrich with its head in the
sand.

President Wilson, 1916

THE HUN ON THE LOOSE

Europe burst into flames in August 1914, and the long-dreaded, long-predicted world war had at last come. The British Foreign Secretary, Sir Edward Grey, himself going blind, remarked sadly, "The lamps are going out all over Europe; we shall not see them lit again in our lifetime."

Like a string of exploding firecrackers, one nation after another declared war on its foes. The flaming pistol of a Serbian nationalist had assassinated the heir to the throne of Austria-Hungary, which in turn had presented an intolerable ultimatum to Serbia. This small country in its turn caused Russia, a nation of fellow Slavs, to mobilize in the rear of Germany. The Germans in turn burst into Belgium in an effort to knock France out before the Russians could stab them in the back.

Germany was bound to respect the neutrality of Belgium under an ancient treaty of 1839, also ratified by the other major powers of Europe. But "necessity knows no law," and the Berlin government disregarded its solemn obligation, thereby ravaging "poor little Belgium" and creating a burning issue of the war. The British, fearful of a menacing German presence opposite their coast, entered the conflict on the side of France, Belgium, Serbia, and Russia. The British Ambassador in Berlin, referring to the neutrality treaty of 1839, reported that the aggrieved German

Chancellor had remarked, "Just for a word—'neutrality,' a word which in wartime has so often been disregarded, just for a scrap of paper—Great Britain is going to make war." The phrase "scrap of paper" became an immensely damaging anti-German slogan, especially in America, which had already made scraps of paper of countless Indian treaties.

Despite the presence of some 8 million German immigrants or German-descended Americans, many United States citizens disliked and distrusted the Berlin government under the theatrical Kaiser Wilhelm II. Elbowing for "a place in the sun," as the Kaiser put it, Germans had already come near clashing with American warships in Samoa and the Philippines. Superbly efficient German manufacturers, with their fearsome trademark "Made in Germany," had also provided unwelcome competition to American industry, at home and abroad.

In 1900, at the time of the Boxer Rebellion in China, the Kaiser had urged his departing troops to behave like the barbaric "Huns" of old, and the Hunnish practices of the Germans in Belgium, although exaggerated by British and French propaganda, pinned the label "Hun" on the Germanic invader. People were reminded of what Jacob Cats, a Dutch poet, had written about 1600:

> When the Hun is poor and down
> He's the humblest man in town;
> But once he climbs and holds the rod
> He smites his fellow-man—and God.

The blond Germans were not Attila's Asiatic Huns, but the name stuck, and in World War II Prime Minister Winston Churchill could quote the saying "The Hun is always either at your throat or at your feet."

So-called "German Huns," pleading necessity, undoubtedly destroyed libraries and churches during the course of their operations in Belgium. They also shot civilian snipers and hostages in accord with what they narrowly construed as military necessity and the rules of war. One of their worst blunders was to execute an English nurse, Edith Cavell, who had helped many convalescent Allied soldiers to escape. Technically her shooting could be justified, but the revulsion in civilized foreign countries further blackened the German cause. One of the most telling wartime moving pictures produced in America was "Edith Cavell, the Woman the Germans Shot."

PRO-ALLY NEUTRALITY

A pacifist at heart, President Wilson viewed the outbreak of war with deep concern. In August 1914, he issued an appeal to the American people in which he declared, "The United States must be neutral in fact as well as in name. . . . We must be impartial in thought, as well as in action. . . ."

Neutrality in action was possible, though not attained, but neutrality in thought was impossible. America was a so-called "menagerie of nationalities." German-Americans, Irish-Americans, Italian-Americans and all others with hyphens in their names could not be oblivious to the land of their birth and its stake in the war. The scornful term "hyphenated American," although not coined by Theodore Roosevelt, was widely used by him, notably when he declared in 1916, "The hyphenated American always hoists the American flag undermost." In a widely quoted speech in Saratoga, New York, he insisted, "There can be no fifty-fifty Americanism in this country. There is room here for only 100 percent Americanism, only for those who are Americans and nothing else."

President Wilson entertained similar thoughts. As he pointed out in a speech in May 1914, "Some Americans need hyphens in their names because only part of them has come over." Echoing the common travel slogan "See America First" rather than war-ravaged Europe, he publicly stated in April 1915, "Our whole duty for the present, at any rate, is summed up in the motto 'America First: Let us think of America before we think of Europe.'" "America First" became a common rallying cry.

Most Americans had lost their hyphens, for their ancestors had come over generations earlier. The great bulk of Wilson's countrymen spoke the English language and were indebted to Great Britain for much of their cultural heritage. Naturally their sympathies lay with the so-called "mother country." As for France, Americans remembered the invaluable aid they had received in the American Revolution, which in turn had helped to spark the French Revolution. From the pen of Robert Underwood Johnson, a New York editor, came:

> Forget us, God, if we forget
> The sacred sword of Lafayette.

But all this did not mean that Americans, whatever their sympathies, itched to get into the bloodbath. The Democratic textbook for the Congressional campaign in the autumn of 1914 proclaimed, "War in the East! Peace in the West! Thank God for Wilson." The President himself was pro-British—a great admirer of British institutions and statesmen. On one occasion he burst out in private, "England is fighting our fight." In public he pursued a pro-British neutrality which helped to drive Germany to the desperate expedient of unrestricted submarine warfare in 1917—and war with the United States. Yet he told Congress in December 1915, "We have stood apart, studiously neutral."

THE SUBMARINE EMERGES

America's chances of remaining out of the war suddenly took an ugly turn when the submarine emerged spectacularly. The German government, reacting to an illegal, long-range surface blockade by the British ("the hunger blockade"), proclaimed in February 1915 a retaliatory U-boat blockade of the British Isles. President Wilson went out on a limb when he sent a note of protest to Berlin insisting that Germany would be held to "a strict accountability" if American ships were attacked and American citizens suffered injury, presumably on American ships. The menacing phrase "a strict accountability" proved to be perhaps Wilson's most fateful. It led to an inflexible policy regarding the submarine that led inexorably to the nation's descent into the abyss.

In the early weeks of the U-boat campaign, four American lives were lost to German submarines, three of them on a torpedoed U.S. tanker, which did not sink. Then, on May 7, 1915, wholesale horror struck. A German U-boat torpedoed without warning the palatial British passenger liner the *Lusitania,* with the loss of nearly 1,200 lives, 128 of them American citizens. The civilized world was stunned; America was outraged.

Three days after the *Lusitania* tragedy, Wilson made an astonishing response in a public address in Philadelphia: "There is such a thing as a man being too proud to fight. There is such a thing as a nation being so right that it does not need to convince others by force that it is right." "Too proud to fight" was not the kind of response that red-blooded Americans like Theodore Roosevelt wanted to hear, and Wilson privately admitted that he had erred by speaking off the cuff. The ridicule and contempt poured on "too proud to fight," both in America and in Allied countries, proved embarrassing. But basically Wilson was on sound ground. When one nation defeats another on the battlefield over a question of right, nothing is proved except that one is stronger or luckier than the other—perhaps both. Might does not necessarily make right.

After further reflection Wilson decided to save face and stand behind his "strict accountability" challenge to Germany. In subsequent weeks he dispatched a series of three stern notes to Berlin on the *Lusitania* outrage. After some ten months of writing he wrested from the Germans a statement of regret and a promise of indemnity. But they flatly refused to admit the illegality of the *Lusitania* torpedoing. The memory of the horror remained, and some of the American soldiers subsequently sent abroad to fight Germany shouted, "Remember the *Lusitania*" as they charged into action. The slogan gained no real popularity; unlike the *Maine* and Spain of 1898, the *Lusitania* did not seem to rhyme with anything especially relevant; and besides, it was a British ship.

THE PUSH FOR PREPAREDNESS

A continuance of the bloodletting in Europe awakened many Americans to the desirability of greatly increasing the nation's military muscle. If a well-prepared republic should be drawn into the war, it would be able to make a substantial contribution relatively soon. Better yet, it might even restrain Germany from flouting American rights by having in hand a big stick formidable enough to command respect for basic rights.

Predictably the foremost champion of "preparedness" was the rough-riding apostle of the big stick, the retired but not retiring ex-President.

His gospel of national preparedness was capsuled in the title of a book that he published in 1916, *Fear God and Take Your Own Part*. The Rough Rider won support from his former commander, General Leonard Wood, who championed "the Plattsburg idea." It led to the inauguration of summer military-training camps in 1915 for business and professional men at Plattsburg, New York. Roosevelt continued to lash out at the "mollycoddles," while consistently berating all those who were using the slogan "Peace at any price." Much of his fire was directed at "Professor" Wilson, who enjoyed the backing of the "flubdubs" and the "flap-doodle pacifists."

"Broomstick preparedness," or the use of broomsticks by trainees in the absence of rifles, was but one criticized feature of the preparedness movement. William J. Bryan issued an incredible public statement, "The President knows that if this country needed a million men, and needed them in a day, the call would go out at sunrise and the sun would go down on a million men in arms." A potent piece of antipreparedness propaganda was the popular song, published in 1915, "I Didn't Raise My Boy to Be a Soldier." The cover of this sheet music showed a gray-haired woman protecting her son while shells burst around the twain. The pacifist title inevitably provoked some disapproving parodies, including "I Did Not Raise My Boy to Be a Coward" and "I Didn't Raise My Boy to Be a Soldier, but I'll Send My Girl to Be a Nurse."

A foot-dragging Wilson finally responded to public pressures and also to the logic of his "strict accountability" warning. In December 1915 he threw his weight behind a preparedness program. But Congress did not pass it in modified form until June and August of 1916, and when the crunch with Germany came early in 1917, Wilson had no big stick that could command respect for American rights. His program for a strong army and a "navy second to none" was too little, too late, or of the wrong kind.

In December 1915, concurrently with Wilson's call upon Congress to vote preparedness, Henry Ford, a peace zealot, made the headlines. This multimillionaire "automobile wizard" who had "put America on wheels," sailed for Europe in his "peace ship," the *Oscar II*. Transporting a curious collection of pacifists, he planned to sail to the neutral Scandinavian countries and persuade them to induce the belligerents to stop fighting. He was reported as having said to a newsman, "We'll get the boys out of the trenches and back to their homes by Christmas." The resulting jeers boded ill for the mission, which of course proved to be a farce.

TOO PROUD TO FIGHT

During the anxious weeks following the *Lusitania* disaster, several more critical incidents occurred involving German submarines. In September 1915, after torpedoing the British passenger liner *Arabic*, the Germans gave Washington the reassuring "*Arabic* pledge." No more unresisting enemy passenger liners would be sunk without warning and without adequate provision for the safety of those on board. But many Americans reasoned that the best way to avoid trouble was to forbid United States citizens to embark on belligerent steamers, especially those "floating arsenals" loaded with munitions for Germany's foes.

An idealist and humanitarian, Wilson was dead set against accepting any restrictions on so-called American "rights" to sail through blockades on belligerent merchant ships like the *Lusitania*. Actually United States citizens had a right to embark, but they had no legal right to claim immunity for their carrier against legitimate enemy attack—otherwise they would be "human shields." But Wilson put humanitarianism and honor above legal technicalities. In January 1916 he publicly avowed, "The nation's honor is dearer than the nation's comfort; yes, than the nation's life itself."

Congress finally took the bit in its teeth when it began serious consideration of two "scuttle resolutions" designed to warn American citizens not to embark on belligerent ships. But Wilson's fighting spirit was aroused. In the teeth of strong support in Congress for such a warning, he managed to sidetrack the objectionable legislation after sending an emphatic letter, in February 1916, to the Chairman of the Senate Committee on Foreign Relations. "For my own part," he insisted, "I cannot consent to any abridgement of the rights of American citizens in any respect. . . . Once accept a single abatement of a right, and many other humiliations would certainly follow, and the whole fine fabric of international law might crumble under our hands piece by piece." Wilson flatly refused to concede that much of international law had already crumbled under the impact of new weapons and modern conditions of warfare.

After Wilson had scuttled the "scuttle resolutions," American travelers continued to sail freely on belligerent liners into submarine-infested waters, even though neutral ships, including American, were plying the same routes. So the nation clung to a dubious right and finally found itself up to its ears in a deadly war.

A new crisis broke in March, 1916, when an unarmed French passenger ship, the *Sussex*, was torpedoed, though not sunk, by a German submarine in the English Channel. Heavy loss of life resulted, as well as serious injury to several Americans. Diplomatically this vessel was the most important merchant ship of the war, not even excluding the *Lusitania*. An aroused Wilson sent what amounted to an ultimatum to Berlin: "Unless the Imperial Government should now immediately declare and effect an abandonment of its present methods of submarine warfare against passenger and freight-carrying vessels, the Government of the United States can have no choice but to sever diplomatic relations."

Berlin's response was only partially satisfactory. The German government agreed to halt the sinking of unresisting merchant vessels without

"Stop!" Wilson tries to stop "Murder" with "Strict Accountability." The New York *World*.

warning and without humanitarian precautions. But the Berlin Foreign Office attached a "string." If Washington could not persuade Britain to respect "the laws of humanity" (that is, relax the "hunger blockade"), Berlin would reserve to itself complete "liberty of decision." Wilson accepted the concession but not the "string," and in this way he handed the Germans a blank check for war. Whenever they filled it in by completely unshackling the submarine, Wilson would have to sever diplomatic relations, as he had threatened. At that time and in that atmosphere such a break was almost equivalent to a declaration of war. Superficially, Wilson had won a diplomatic victory, but actually he was only postponing the evil day.

RESURGENT REPUBLICANS

Political pundits wondered aloud if Theodore Roosevelt would seek the Republican nomination in 1916. The question became more urgent as the delegates of the Republican party and those of the Progressive party prepared to meet on the same day in separate halls in Chicago, early in June 1916. Enthusiasm for the Rough Rider was overwhelming among Progressives, and it was substantial among the regular Republicans, whom he had deserted four years earlier. Songs composed with the election in view were "We Want Teddy for President," "Give us Teddy—the Spirit of America Incarnate," "Teddy You're a Bear," and "The Greatest of Americans Lives down at Oyster Bay."

Starry-eyed Progressives, those battle-scarred Christian soldiers, predictably nominated their hero by acclamation on the first ballot. But Roosevelt was a realist—at least this time. He realized that his only hope of ousting Wilson, the "pacifist professor" whom he despised, was for the Progressives to return to Republican ranks. He therefore "betrayed" his followers and the Progressive cause by declining the nomination. The journalist William Allen White lamented that the Progressives were "all dressed up, with nowhere to go."

A mile or so away in Chicago the Republican regulars gathered simultaneously, as numerous delegates and spectators in the gallery shouted, "Teddy, Teddy, everybody's for Teddy." But the Old Guard was not for Teddy. They trotted out Charles Evans Hughes, a former New York governor, who held moderately progressive views. At that time he was a Justice of the Supreme Court, and his hesitant acceptance of the nomination spawned the quip that he was leaving "the bench for the fence." As his subsequent career further demonstrated, this heavily bewhiskered statesman was a figure of the highest intelligence and integrity, but he gave the impression of having a cold-fish personality. Critics said he was an "animated feather duster"—but not too animated. "Teddy" Roosevelt disliked him, and sneeringly referred to him in private as a "bearded iceberg" and a "whiskered Wilson," adding that the only difference between the two men was "a shave."

Meeting in steamy St. Louis, the Democrats uproariously renominated their professorial Moses, Woodrow Wilson. The theme of the convention was Americanism, with all that this implied in peacefully upholding American rights in the teeth of Germany's submarine warfare. The keynote speaker, Governor Martin Glynn of New York, began to recite a rather boring list of ugly international incidents in American history that the government had managed to patch up without fighting. To his amazement the crowd caught fire and began to chant after each one, "What did we do? What did we do?" From the startled Governor Glynn each time came the response "We did not go to war." He was supported by Senator Ollie James, who shouted, while acclaiming Wilson's stern notes to Berlin on the *Lusitania* and the *Sussex,* "Without orphaning a single

American child, without widowing a single American mother, without firing a single gun or shedding a drop of blood, he wrung from the most militant spirit that ever brooded above a battlefield the concession of American demands and American rights." The delegates went wild.

From this St. Louis convention emerged the rousing slogan "He Kept Us Out of War." There is no evidence that President Wilson devised it or even approved of it. But it did appear in the final draft of the Democratic platform which commended "the splendid diplomatic victories of our great President, who has preserved the vital interests of our Government and its citizens, and *kept us out of war*." (Italics added.) Democratic campaign buttons picked up this theme with "Peace with Honor" and "He Proved the Pen Mightier than the Sword."

WILSON BATTLES FOR RE-ELECTION

A major goal of the Wilson campaign was to seduce the Roosevelt Progressives with the Wilsonian brand of progressivism. Obviously, if the bolters all returned to the Grand Old Party, the Democrats were doomed. The aggressive type of progressivism that Wilson now preached indicated that he was abandoning the more easygoing "New Freedom" for the active federal intervention of Theodore Roosevelt's "New Nationalism."

Peace proved to be a tricky issue for both candidates. Wilson was criticized for going too far or not going far enough in laying down the law to both Mexico and Germany. The German-Americans, who traditionally voted Republican, loomed large in political calculations. Wilson's policy of taking a stern position with Berlin, notably in the *Lusitania* and *Sussex* crises, had offended many German hyphenates.

Hughes also confronted a dilemma. "Awkwardly straddling the political fence, he indicated that he would uphold American rights vigorously without being too severe on Germany. Much of the time he resorted to such vague phrases as "America First" and "America Efficient," all of which caused critics to rename Charles Evans Hughes "Charles Evasive Hughes." On the other hand, Roosevelt no doubt hurt rather than helped Hughes by making "skin 'em alive" speeches denouncing Wilson, "that damned Presbyterian hypocrite," for not having made Germany crawl. He compared the President to Pontius Pilate, with apologies to the latter.

Wilson scored heavily when he received an insulting telegram from one Jeremiah A. O'Leary, president of the German-financed American Truth Society. The critic berated Wilson for truckling to the British, whose illegal blockade practices had hurt American markets in Western Europe. Far from backing down, Wilson fired back this blistering message to O'Leary: "Your telegram received. I would feel deeply mortified to have you or anybody like you vote for me. Since you have access to many disloyal Americans and I have not, I will ask you to convey this message to them."

Hughes hit hard at Wilson for his policy of appointing "deserving Democrats" and for not having handled the Mexican mess with firmer hands. But in general Wilson ignored his bewhiskered opponent. He believed that there was no point in murdering a man who was committing suicide.

"He Kept Us Out of War" was clearly the campaign slogan that overshadowed all others. Also effective was "War in the East! Peace in the West! Thank God for Wilson!" A journalistic blockbuster was a full-page advertisement that was published in the leading newspapers on the eve of the election by the Wilson Business Men's National League:

> You Are Working—*Not Fighting!*
> Alive and Happy;—*Not Cannon Fodder!*
> Wilson and Peace with Honor?
> or
> Hughes with Roosevelt and War?
>
> •   •   •
>
> The Lesson is Plain:
> If You Want WAR, vote for HUGHES!
> If You Want Peace with Honor
> VOTE FOR WILSON!
> And Continued Prosperity

Prominent among campaign buttons were "The Man of the Hour—Woodrow Wilson," "Wilson—8 Hours," and "Vote for Champions of the 8 Hour Law." The last two referred to Wilson's having signed the controversial Adamson Act of 1916, which granted the numerous railroad men in interstate commerce an eight-hour work day. Such an epochal interference with the management of big business subjected Wilson to caustic criticism from the Old Guard. But the President's capitulation averted a crippling nationwide tieup of the railroads and won him many votes from laboring men. As for the peace issue, one clever button read:

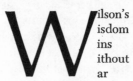

W ilson's
isdom
ins
ithout
ar

Prominent among the theme songs of the canvass, and in line with the peace issue, was "I Didn't Raise My Boy to Be a Soldier." Among special Democratic campaign tunes one heard "Never Swap Horses When You're Crossing a Stream," an adaptation of a slogan of the second Lincoln campaign. "Four More Years in the White House (Should Be the Nation's Gift to You)" honored Wilson's second marriage, to widow Edith B. Galt late in 1915. Other tunes included "Woodrow Wilson Four Years More," "The Man of the Hour (Wilson Is His Name)," and

"I Think We've Got Another Washington (and Wilson Is His Name)." Daring new dance steps left their mark in "We're Going to Celebrate the End of the War in Ragtime (Be Sure that Woodrow Wilson Leads the Band)." Still another song declared in its title, "Go Right Along, Mister Wilson (and We'll All Stand by You)."

Clearly the Republicans were outsloganed in the campaign of 1916. Possessing no battle cry remotely comparable in effectiveness to "He Kept Us Out of War," they pressed into service "America Always" and "America Efficient." "Fear God and Take Your Own Part," the title of a volume that Roosevelt published in 1916, did duty also as a slogan. The election was so close that greater equality in catchwords probably would have reversed the result.

Republican songs were likewise few and flat. One of the few worthy of notice was "Charles E. Hughes, the American." Other musical titles told their own story: "Prosperity and Hughes," "So Long, Mr. Wilson," "There Was a Man [Charles Hughes] from New York Town," and "The Dizzy Dem-erratic Donkey." One Republican answer to the Democratic theme song was "That's Why I Raised My Boy to Be a Soldier," although many peaceloving mothers doubtless still preferred the original and better known title.

THE WINNING OF THE WEST

As results poured in from the East that November night in 1916, Hughes seemed to have won by a landslide. Prominent New York newspapers conceded the election and issued "extras" displaying huge likenesses of "The President-Elect—Charles Evans Hughes." The "icy" candidate went to bed that night thinking that he probably was elected, and the apocryphal story spread that a newspaper reporter was turned away at the Hughes residence with the excuse "The President cannot be disturbed." The rebuffed newsman was said to have replied, "Tell him when he wakes up that he is no longer President."

Wilson's winning of the West guaranteed his narrow electoral triumph. He finally carried most of the trans-Mississippi states and pulled through by a breathlessly narrow margin in the Electoral College. A change of twelve electoral votes would have brought defeat by one vote, but Wilson managed to win California with its thirteen, although his plurality in that state was only 3,800 votes out of about 1 million cast. The hair-breadth result can be partly explained in terms of "the forgotten handshake." Hiram Johnson, ex-governor of California, was a fiery Progressive who had campaigned as Roosevelt's running mate in 1912. The Old Guard Republicans despised him as a renegade, and they managed to keep Hughes from meeting him, even though the two men stayed in the same hotel in Long Beach at the same time. Many of Johnson's devoted followers, resenting this snub, turned to Wilson, certainly enough of them to ensure his election. A song copyrighted nine days after the balloting bore the title "Be Good to California, Mr. Wilson (California Was Good to You)."

War or peace was clearly the issue uppermost in the public mind. Wilson received much of the "mother vote" in those states where women could now wield the ballot and where they had not raised their boys to be soldiers. On the other hand, there was much resentment against the President by women, whether they could vote or merely influence their husbands' votes, because of his conspicuous opposition to woman suffrage. One of the cleverest anti-Wilson slogans growing out of the campaign was "He Kept Us Out of Suffrage."

Had Wilson given a solemn pledge to the American people to keep out of the European bloodbath? As a statement of plain historical fact "He Kept Us Out of War" held water. It promised nothing for the future, but it implied that Wilson would continue to stay on the sidelines. Beyond doubt enough peace-loving citizens voted for him to ensure his victory. Wilson could not have been altogether happy with what seemed to be a mandate to stay out of war whatever the provocation. Earlier in the year, speaking in Cleveland, he had said, "You have laid upon me this double obligation: 'We are relying upon you, Mr. President, to keep us out of war, but we are relying upon you, Mr. President, to keep the honor of the nation unstained.'" The voters evidently favored peace but, as events were to demonstrate, not "peace at any price."

GERMANY THRUSTS WAR ON AMERICA

Wilson fully realized that the only sure guarantee of keeping out of war was to bring the one then raging to an end. He therefore donned the thankless mantle of mediator, but neither camp of belligerents welcomed his intrusion. Undaunted, he stood before the Senate on January 22, 1917, and delivered what many critics regard as his most statesmanlike speech. In an appeal to world opinion he declared with prophetic vision that there must be no "balance of power" but "a community of power," no "organized rivalries" but "an organized common peace." As for the immediate goal, "*It must be a peace without victory. . . .* Victory would mean peace forced upon the loser, a victor's terms imposed upon the vanquished. It would be accepted in humiliation, under duress, at an intolerable sacrifice, and would leave a sting, a resentment, a bitter memory upon which terms of peace would rest, not permanent, but only as upon quicksand. *Only a peace between equals can last* [italics added]." In these words Wilson unwittingly foretold the failure of the forthcoming Treaty of Versailles.

Germany's answer to Wilson's "peace without victory" appeal came with a smashing blow of the mailed fist. Nine days later, on January 31, 1917, Berlin announced, in an evident attempt to knock Britain out of the war, that German submarines would sink all ships, including neutral

American vessels (except one), entering the blockaded zone. In the *Sussex* ultimatum Wilson had threatened to sever diplomatic relations in such an eventuality, and the German warlords were now calling his hand. He had no choice but to send the German Ambassador packing, and this he did. Yet he still hoped that Berlin would not carry through its proclaimed all-out warfare, and announced that he would await the "actual overt acts" by German submarines before leading his people into the war. Meanwhile he would place guns with gun crews on American merchant ships, a kind of "armed neutrality" that was neither war nor peace until shooting started. His efforts to arm such vessels received a temporary setback in the Senate when about a dozen German-sympathizers and peace men conducted a successful filibuster. Wilson burst out angrily, "A little group of willful men, representing no opinion but their own, have rendered the great Government of the United States helpless and contemptible." Then, finding the authority in an almost forgotten law, he began arming American vessels defensively.

The long-dreaded "actual overt acts" came in mid-March 1917, when German submarines sank four unarmed American merchantmen on the high seas with a loss of thirty-six lives. Germany was now making open war on the United States. One Philadelphia newspaper remarked that the difference "between war and what we have now is that now we aren't fighting back."

Too proud by now not to fight back, a pale President Wilson stood before Congress on April 2, 1917, to ask for a declaration of war against Germany. Referring to the unrestricted submarine campaign now being waged, he insisted, "Property can be paid for; the lives of peaceful and innocent people cannot be. The present German submarine warfare against commerce is a warfare against mankind." He had tried arming American ships. "But armed neutrality, it now appears, is impracticable" and "ineffectual enough at best." Congress, he believed, must brand the submarine warfare of Germany as "nothing less than war against the government and people of the United States," which must therefore "formally accept the status of belligerent which has thus been *thrust upon it.* . . ." Wilson's use of "thrust" echoed President Polk's "thrust" in his request for a declaration of war against Mexico; this term also foreshadowed Franklin Roosevelt's use of "thrust" before Congress after Pearl Harbor in 1941.

As for Wilson's larger goals, his war message declared, "*the world must be made safe for democracy*" so that democratic institutions could live without fear of militaristic aggression. Referring to his own countrymen, Wilson promised, "We desire no conquest, no dominion. *We seek no indemnities.* . . ." In a moving peroration he conceded that "It is a fearful thing to lead this great peaceful people into war. . . . *But the right is more precious than peace*," and the nation would fight for democracy and other ideals that it held dear.

Congress overwhelmingly voted to accept the conflict that Germany had thus "thrust" upon the United States. But bitter opposition arose from a vocal minority, most of whom had numerous German-American constituents. Conspicuous among the dissenters was Senator Robert M. ("Fighting Bob") La Follette of Wisconsin, who cried, "I say Germany has been patient with us." What he evidently meant was that the United States had demanded the right to sail through the German submarine blockade on belligerent ships while acquiescing under protest in the mine-and-cruiser British blockade. La Follette's critics made much of the fact that the Germans sank American ships and took American lives while the British only searched and confiscated American ships. The Boston *Globe* concluded that one side was a "gang of thieves" but the other was "a gang of murderers. On the whole we prefer the thieves but only as the lesser of two evils."

As events shaped up, Germany appeared to be the mad-dog aggressor, and many Americans believed that if fellow citizens were not anti-German and pro-Ally, they were not "100 percent American." The possibility of a German victory raised grave fears of an ultimate invasion by the helmeted and goosestepping "Hun." At one time an American newspaper headline proclaimed, "England's Defeat our Defeat." When the crunch came, the American people concluded, in response to Wilson's leadership, that there were more important goals than simply keeping out of war.

XXIV

Winning the War and Losing the Peace

A general association of nations must be formed
under specific covenants . . . for great and small
states alike.

President Wilson, January 8, 1918,
the Fourteenth Point

WORK OR FIGHT

President Wilson, the flaming idealist, lifted America's participation in
World War I to the heights of a holy crusade. Two slogans that helped
to set the tone were "Make the World Safe for Democracy" (by getting
rid of German autocracy) and "The War to End War."* So inspiring did
these twin ideals prove to be that many men seemed eager to sacrifice
their lives, if necessary, in so noble a cause. Some of them expressed bitter disappointment when the shooting stopped before they could get into
action "over there."

At a Liberty Loan rally in Baltimore in April 1918, the President who
had pleaded "too proud to fight" in 1915 urged "force, force to the utmost, force without stint or limit, the righteous and triumphant force
which shall make peace the law of the world and cast every selfish
dominion down in the dust." Less elegant were the popular cries "Swat
the Hun," "Hang the Kaiser" and "To hell with the Hohenzollerns and
Hapsburgs" (the ruling houses of Germany and Austria-Hungary).

Europe's bloodbath had flashed a fiery warning for more than two

---

* A cynical British statesman, David Lloyd George, reportedly said, "This war,
like the next war, is a war to end war."

years, yet America the unready was wretchedly prepared for the fighting "across the pond." Its available military force was ridiculously small when compared with the gigantic task ahead—the republic's first all-out conflict. "It is not an army that we must train for war," Wilson declared in May 1917, "it is a nation." In 1919 he explained that the American army was raised so rapidly because the men were trained to go only one way—forward. This, of course, was risky in the extreme.

While recruits were being drafted, the civilian front slowly mobilized to the accompaniment of such slogans as "America, Wake Up" and "Let's Go." Highly paid executives of both parties volunteered their services in Washington as "dollar-a-year men." Bernard M. ("Barney") Baruch, a millionaire stock speculator who came to be known as "The Park-Bench Philosopher," served as the head of the War Industries Board. It fixed prices, established priorities, and reduced waste.

Women responded to the call of industry and also of farms, where they were known as "farmerettes." The hoary saying "A woman's place is in the home" became "A woman's place is in the war." One poster plea read, "This Girl is Doing War Work for Uncle Sam. Will You Rent Her a Room?"

About 11,000 women enlisted in the navy ("Yeomanettes"), and nearly 300 joined the Marines ("Marinettes"). A placard appeal showed a robust female recruiter pleading, "I Want You for the Navy." Women and girls at home also "did their bit" by knitting sweaters for servicemen, and additional posters urged, "Knit a Bit For Our First Line of Defense" (the navy).

Horny-handed laborers were urged, through posters and other appeals, to put their shoulders behind the war machine, spurred on by the slogans "On the Job for Victory," "Labor Will Win the War," and "We're Behind the Man Behind the Gun." Only two alternatives were offered by the War Department in 1918: "Work or Fight." "Stick to Your Job" was standard advice given to the itchy-footed, who were also counseled to "Keep Work Moving," with "Less Waste, More Production." Not just frantic motion, but quality production was wanted: "Wherever you are, whatever you do—You Help to Win the War by Doing Your Work Well."

Organized labor, on the whole, rolled up its sleeves and pitched in. It responded with enthusiasm to such published appeals as "Work with the Spirit of Patriotism," "Work! Every Lick Counts," "The Battle Line is Not Alone in France," and "Are You Idle Today? The Boys in the Trenches Are Not." More specific were "Boost and Smile" and, with a subtle appeal to Negroes, "Lift—Man!—Lift."

Sabotage of industry on a minor scale, especially lumbering, was engineered by the relatively few Industrial Workers of the World (I.W.W.s), popularly branded the "I Won't Works" or "Wobblies." Demanding "one big industrial union" and proclaiming "An injury to one is an injury to all," they took up the refrain:

The hours are long, the pay is small,
So take your time and buck them all.

During this war "to make the world safe for democracy," a considerable number of "Wobblies" were arrested, beaten up, or run out of town—in some cases all three misfortunes befell them. They could sing with more bitterness than usual the I.W.W. song:

You will eat bye and bye
In that glorious land above the sky;
Work and pray, live on hay,
You'll eat pie in the sky,
When you die.

THE BATTLE OF PRODUCTION

"Fuel Will Win the War" became a popular slogan under the Fuel Administration, which sponsored the watchword "Mine More Coal." Self-sacrificing citizens responded to such appeals as "heatless Mondays" and "lightless nights." "Daylight savings time" became an energy-conserving scheme spawned by the war, though earlier conceived by Benjamin Franklin. The need to conserve petroleum products for the conflict brought the voluntary acceptance of "gasless Sundays," without the ration books that were later necessary in the less idealistic World War II.

Producing and saving food also became a key objective, for America had to supply not only itself but its European allies. Herbert Hoover, the famed American engineer who had organized the feeding of the Belgians after the German invasion, headed the Food Administration. A letter addressed to him as "Miracle Man, Washington, D.C.," reached his desk promptly. Widely displayed pleas reminded citizens, "Food Will Win The War—Don't Waste It" and "To Farm Is as Necessary as to Arm." Patriotic Americans were urged "to use all leftovers," to embrace "the gospel of the clean plate," to practice "the patriotism of the lean garbage can," and when eating apples to be "patriotic to the core." "Full Garbage Pails," warned a popular slogan, "Mean Empty Dinner Pails." In broader terms all citizens were exhorted to "Make Saving Rather Than Spending Your Social Standard" and to "Eat Plenty, Wisely, and Without Waste, and Help Win the War."

Perspiring patriots spaded empty lots into vegetable plots known as "victory gardens," as they responded to the challenges "Help Feed Yourself" and "Work a Garden—Raise Chickens." Children enrolled in this open-air activity as they responded to posters showing two juveniles gardening and saying, "We Eat Because We Work—We Belong to the U.S. School Garden Army." Other appeals urged, "Produce Food, Conserve Food, Dry and Can Food" and "Can Vegetables, Fruit, and the Kaiser, Too." Additional posters addressed to housewives advised, "Fats are Fuel for Fighters" and "Boil, Bake, and Broil More—Fry Less." Still another pictorial warning declared, "Victory is a Question of Stamina. Send the Wheat, Meat, Fats, Sugar—the Fuel for Fighters." Even more pointed was "Feed a Fighter!"

America's European allies were accustomed to wheat rather than corn; many of them feared that corn meal caused impotence and sterility. The word went out in America to use as much corn as possible at home and ship as much wheat as possible abroad. Relevant slogans urged, "Eat More Corn, Less Wheat" and "Plant Corn—Corn Must Help Win the War." Also seen and heard were "Blood or Bread" and "Save a Loaf a Week—Help Win the War."

Throughout this gigantic campaign to conserve food the main emphasis was on thrift and self-sacrifice in the hope of supplying "the boys" at the fighting front. Especially pointed was the exhortation "You Are Helping the Country Fight When You Help Feed Its Fighting Men." Nor was the "Hunnish" enemy overlooked, as attested by "Save Food and Defeat Frightfulness."

Special poster appeals were aimed at immigrants, notably one slogan that referred to "Many Peoples—One Nation." A gorgeous poster, entitled "Americans All," listed an "Honor Roll" of servicemen whose names represented the blood of fourteen different nations. A placard, with the Statue of Liberty towering in the background, directed a special plea to newer arrivals: "Food will Win the War—You Came Here Seeking Freedom—You Must Now Help Preserve It." In this context "preserve" applied to food and freedom alike, perhaps unintentionally.

"To Hooverize" became a new verb for "to economize," as Herbert Hoover, "The Knight of the Lean Garbage Can," advised various abstentions and substitutions, including wheatless "victory bread." One "poet" complained:

> My Tuesdays are meatless,
> My Wednesdays are wheatless,
> I'm getting more eatless each day.
> My coffee is sweetless,
> My bed it is sheetless,
> All sent to the Y.M.C.A. [for servicemen].

THE DOLLAR JOINS THE BATTLE

Fantastic sums had to be raised to feed the gods of war. Four great "Liberty Loan" drives, followed by a "Victory Loan," netted over $21 billion. Support for these appeals, as well as for war savings stamps, came from orators, billboards, posters, buttons, and other media. Massive parades, with many marchers singing, gave point to such exhortations as "Buy Liberty Bonds" and "Have You Bought a Bond?" In a similar vein were "I Own a Liberty Bond" and "I Have Bought a Bond. Have You?"

No less direct were "Help Till It Hurts," "Are You 100 Per Cent American?" and "Fight or Buy Bonds." This last concept appeared in "They Also Serve Their Country Who Buy a Liberty Bond," "Strike Your First Blow! Buy a Liberty Bond To-day," and, more bluntly, "Win the War—Buy a Bond." The alternatives presented were "Bonds or Bondage."

Thrifty souls were doubtless attracted by "Invest in the Victory Liberty Loan" and "If You Can't Enlist—Invest!" More practical approaches were "A Liberty Loan Bond Is a Mortgage on the United States" and "Liberty Loan Bonds—Patriotic and Safe." The German aggressor was ever foremost in such reminders as "Halt the Hun," "Hun or Home," "Beat Back the Hun with Liberty Bonds," and "Help Uncle Sam Stamp Out the Kaiser." References to German-spawned tragedies of the war came in "Remember Belgium" and "Remember the *Lusitania* and Buy a Liberty Bond." One little-known song was entitled "Death to the Hun."

Wilsonian ideals found expression in "That Liberty Shall not Perish from the Earth—Buy Liberty Bonds" and "To Make the World a Decent Place to Live in—Do your part—Buy Government Bonds." Two memorable posters called out, "Ring it Again" (with the Liberty Bell conspicuously displayed) and "Do Your Bit to Keep it Lit" (the Statue of Liberty).

As for financing the war, memorable slogans were "Lend It to End It," "Remember! It's Cheaper to Win than to Lose," "Over the Top [of the trenches] with You" (used in the third Liberty Loan drive), and "Bring Them Back Victorious! Buy a Liberty Bond To-day." In "The Battle of the Fences" waged by posters, two especially colorful displays carried these messages: "You Buy a Bond Lest I Perish" (a frantic female speaking in the background) and "Provide the Sinews of War—Buy Liberty Bonds" (with ship construction as the backdrop).

Charitable agencies in private hands, such as the Red Cross and the Y.M.C.A., staged less massive drives of their own. They enjoyed the blessing of President Wilson, who announced, "I summon you to comradeship in the Red Cross." Among their most effective slogans were "Give Until It Hurts" and "Think What You Can Afford to Give—then Double It." The goal of the Red Cross was 10 million members by Christmas of 1917, and one effective poster urged "On Christmas Eve a Candle in Every Window and a Red Cross Member in Every Home." By 1918 this organization was proclaiming itself "The Greatest Mother in the World," and urging "In the Name of Mercy Give!" (poster showing a nurse bending over a wounded soldier).

Humanitarianism even extended to beasts of burden. One poster showed a soldier holding the head of a prostrate horse, with these words added: "Help the Horse to Save the Soldier—Please Join the American Red Star Animal Relief." Further concern for the soldier's comfort was expressed in the poster slogan "Sammy's S.O.S.—'Send Over Smokes.'" This was decades before the Surgeon General had determined that "Cigarette Smoking is Dangerous to Your Health."

TRANSPORTATION AND TROOPS

Capacious ships were desperately needed to replace the hundreds sunk by German submarines, as well as to transport American troops and their supplies to France. "Ships, Ships, and More Ships" was the desperate call of the Allies; Americans took up the cry "Ships Will Win the War." Urgently needed was a "Bridge of Boats" or a "Bridge of Ships" across the wide and stormy Atlantic. A gigantic program of construction was launched, to the accompaniment of such slogans as "Rivets Are Bayonets —Drive Them Home" and "The Ships Are Coming," which paralleled the war cry "The Yanks Are Coming." Posters added a spur with "Shoot Ships to Germany and Help America Win" and "Delay Means Danger— Are You Doing Your Bit?" The Emergency Fleet Corporation, heavily involved in numerous launchings, promoted the slogan "Another Ship— Another Victory."

America's far-flung railroad lines, which funneled cargo to the ships, were appropriated "for the duration" by the federal government. They were managed by the Secretary of the Treasury, William G. McAdoo, dubbed "The Crown Prince" because he had married one of the President's daughters. Under his direction the weblike lines were operated in response to such appeals as "The Nation is Counting on You." Yet snarls generated by the war caused the railways to be operated from Washington at a heavy loss, and the numerous opponents of government ownership could claim, rather unjustly, that the networks had been "Mc-Adoodled."

As war hysteria mounted, classical German music and even the German language fell under ridiculous bans. Sauerkraut became "liberty cabbage"; Hamburger steak became "liberty steak"; German measles became "liberty measles"; and dachshunds became "liberty pups," that is, if one dared to own them. Socialists, with their German Marxist background, fell into further disrepute for opposing what they regarded as a "capitalistic war." Their presence gave added punch to the poster warning, "Don't Talk—Spies are Listening."

First to get into action with the slogan "To Arms!" was the navy, the "first line of defense" and traditionally better prepared than the army. Primary responsibilities of "the boys in blue" were two: to sink the lurking German submarines and to transport American soldiers ("doughboys") "over there" to France. Popular slogans on navy recruiting posters were "Help Muzzle the Mad Dogs of the Sea" and "Stop Cheering and Enlist Now." At the same time, the navy conducted an active campaign for recruits, employing one poster in particular that had a sailor counseling a civilian, "The Navy Needs You! Don't Read American History— MAKE IT!"

Other pictorial proddings included "Those of You Who Are Not Making Steel, Make History, and Enlist in the Navy" and "Be a Submarine Chaser—Help Your Country." In yet another poster a sailor astride a torpedo is saying, "Join the Navy—the Service for Fighting Men." Stressing another theme was the appeal "They Kept the Sea Lanes Open." Especially effective was a poster by the artist James Montgomery Flagg, who had Uncle Sam pointing a finger at the viewer and saying "I Want You," with the added message "Uncle Sam is Calling You! Enlist in the Navy! Do it Now!" The same picture was used with modifications for army recruiting.

SONGS, CINEMAS, AND SLOGANS

Morale on the home front and abroad received a further boost from an amazing outburst of popular songs, old and new. These added immensely to the spirit of an idealistic crusade as their words rose enthusiastically from huge assemblies of servicemen and civilians under the rhythmic hands of song leaders. World War I was unquestionably the most musical of all American wars, not even excepting the Civil War. But the songs were generally less nostalgic and grim than before, even when hanging the Kaiser, and they were deliberately used by the Washington government to promote the overall war effort.

Immensely popular was George M. Cohan's stirring "Over There," which assured both friends and foes that the Americans planned to finish the war across the pond. Other tunes that focused on the doughboys, at home and abroad, included "Goodbye, Broadway, Hello, France!" and "I May Be Gone for a Long, Long Time," which suggested the melancholy of certain Civil War songs. Also popular were "Hello, Central, Give Me No Man's Land" (the area between the two lines of trenches), "Oh, How I Hate to Get Up in the Morning" (a recruit's complaint against the five o'clock bugler), and "Till We Meet Again." Favorite borrowings from Britain included the rollicking marching song "It's a Long, Long Way to Tipperary" (a county in Ireland) and "Pack Up Your Troubles in Your Old Kit Bag and Smile, Smile, Smile." The composition "Joan of Arc" was a salute to America's old-new French ally.

A few daring pacifists were bold enough to cling to their theme song, "I Didn't Raise My Boy to Be a Soldier," which inspired the cruel parody "I Didn't Raise My Dog to Be a Sausage." But sterling patriots overwhelmed the unwarlike with "I Didn't Raise My Boy to Be a Molly Coddle," "I Didn't Raise My Boy to Be a Slacker," and "I Didn't Raise My Boy to Be a Soldier but He'll Fight for the U.S.A." Lighter airs or nonsense songs of the war years were "K-K-K-Katy" (a stuttering ballad about a bucolic beauty), "Good Morning, Mr. Zip, Zip, Zip," "Hail, Hail, the Gang's All Here," and the best-selling "Smiles." A heavy dose of nostalgia came with "There's a Long, Long Trail" and a boost to flagging spirits with "Keep the Home Fires Burning," imported from England.

A potent propaganda machine, assembled in Washington and known as the Committee on Public Information, slipped into high gear under George Creel, a journalist from Missouri. Its domestic aim was to "sell" the country on the war; its global goal was to "sell" America and the world on Wilson's war aims, notably in millions of leaflets, pamphlets, and posters. Creel sent out thousands of orators known as "four-minute men," who deluged the country with much "patriotic pep." Artists also rallied to the colors and against the Hun as the country blossomed with posters.

Popular hang-the-Kaiser movies emerged or were carried over from the years before America declared war. They bore such titles as "The Kaiser the Beast of Berlin," "To Hell with the Kaiser," and "America's Answer to the Hun." Other titles were "The Common Cause," "Over the Top," "War Brides," and "Womanhood the Glory of Nations." The dominant themes were the generally accepted accusations that Germany had brought the holocaust on the world and violated Belgian neutrality and women with malice aforethought. "The Battle Cry of Peace" portrayed in cinematic colors what the Hun would do if he ever landed on American shores. Special movies, aimed at the acceptance of women workers and American Indians, claimed such titles as "A Girl's a Man for A' That" and "The American Indian Gets into the War Game." One cinema that related to the musical front was titled "Keep 'Em Singing and Nothing Can Lick Them."

Printed slides were prepared to prompt "four-minute singing" in the movie houses, and the announced slogan was "Let Us Get It Going with a Swing," that is with an expert arm swinger. The official list of the "four-minute songs" included old patriotic standbys such as "America" and "When Johnny Comes Marching Home," plus such newer entries as "There's A Long, Long Trail," "Keep the Home Fires Burning," "Pack Up Your Troubles," "When You Come Back," "Helping On," and "Saving Food."

JOHNNY GETS HIS GUN

When unprepared America declared war, the intention was to conduct only limited hostilities against German submarines. But when the Allies made clear that they were scraping the bottom of their manpower barrel, Congress lumbered into action with all deliberate speed. Six long weeks after the declaration of hostilities, a conscription bill that provided for "selective service" received Wilson's signature. Memories of the draft during the Civil War, plus hatred of German militarism, clogged the legislative machinery for a time. Speaker Champ Clark of Missouri shocked many people when he insisted that there was "precious little difference between a conscript and a convict."

"Selective service" meant that Washington would select the service for which the draftee would be most useful, whether manning a machine gun or a riveter. The official rule issued by the army was "Every man in the draft age must work or fight," from which came the peremptory order "Work or fight." As expected, "draft dodgers" and "slackers" created something of a problem, but on the whole conscription proved to be a success.

Volunteers were most welcome to the army, which found that the mechanism of the draft ground too slowly. Conspicuous among the recruiting posters plastered on walls were "The Regulars [regular army] are in France—Join Them Now!" "The Call to Duty—Join the Army For Home and Country," and "The Spirit of 1917—Old Glory Calls Americans —Join the Army!" But such patriotic appeals had only limited effectiveness, for the overwhelming bulk of the servicemen were draftees.

As selective service slipped into high gear, "Johnny Get Your Gun," taken from the first line of "Over There," emerged as a favorite war cry of the hour. The "rookies" were herded into hastily constructed wooden camps, where they received grueling doses of tough training. A popular song ran:

> They marched me twenty miles a day to fit me for the war—
> I didn't mind the first nineteen but the last one made me sore.

More earthy was another soldier song:

> You're in the army now,
> You're not behind the plow;
> You'll never get rich, you son of a bitch,
> You're in the army now.

Yet morale remained high, and it was boosted with popular songs of the war, conspicuously "Over There." After some six months of concentrated training, the doughboys could be shipped across "the big drink," singing "Good-Bye Broadway, Hello France."

Before the draftees were ready, the United States dispatched a token force to France, in July 1917, largely to bolster French morale. The American commander-in-chief was General John J. ("Black Jack") Pershing, fresh from his fruitless chase of Pancho Villa into Mexico. His small army of some 14,000 men paraded through the streets of Paris amid cheers of "Vive l'Amérique." At the tomb of Lafayette in Paris, Colonel Charles E. Stanton, Pershing's subordinate, tastefully declared, "Lafayette, we are here," implying that the Americans had come to repay their ancient debt to Lafayette, the French Revolutionary War hero. This eminently appropriate remark is often falsely ascribed to General Pershing, who was more a fighter than an orator.

As the green draftees of the A.E.F. (American Expeditionary Force) began to pour into France, they were first given further intensive training and then usually assigned quiet sectors. The newcomers made friends with the French girls, or tried to, and perhaps the most sung-about woman in American history was the mythical and completely promiscuous "Mademoiselle from Armentières." One of the more printable verses of this endlessly improvised song ran:

> She was true to me, she was true to you,
> She was true to the whole damned army, too.

Daring American airmen of the pioneering air force, so-called "Cavaliers of the Clouds," hung up an enviable record. Some of them became "aces" after downing five or more enemy craft, notably Captain Edward V. Rickenbacker, whose "kills" included twenty-two enemy airplanes. Seductive posters lured recruits with "Be an American Eagle" and "Give 'er the Guns," as aircraft and ground crew stood ready and eager to blast the Hun.

Cocky Marines, "The Soldiers of the Sea," stressed their tradition of toughness going back to the war with Tripoli (1801–1805) and that with Mexico. They energetically sought recruits with "Rally 'Round the Flag with the United States Marines." One of their most colorful posters said it all: "First to Fight—Democracy's Vanguard—U.S. Marine Corps—Join Now and Test Your Courage—Real Fighting with Real Fighters." Lean and mean, the Marines performed gallantly in 1918 during a relatively minor engagement in bloody Belleau Wood, France. Thereafter they could boast in posters, "First in France," "First in the Fight," "First to Fight in France for Freedom," and "First in Defense on Land or Sea." Many of these chesty fighting men, though relatively few in number, boasted that they won the war, to the annoyance of the army, the navy, and the Allies. Warriors in the rival services were more prone than ever to say disdainfully, "Tell that to the Marines"—a saying of ancient British origin.

WAR PLANS AND WAR AIMS

Latecoming American doughboys, though still few in numbers, helped to stem the high tide of the fearsome German drive in France during the spring of 1918. In an early baptism of fire, Gunnery Sergeant Daniel Daly, U.S. Marine Corps, reportedly urged his men to rush forward with the cry "Come on, you sons of bitches! Do you want to live forever?" He later wrote that what he really shouted was "For Christ's sake, men, come on! Do you want to live forever?" The stock answer to this brand of suicidal leadership became "No, only fifty more years." It parallels a standard saying among American doughboys in World War I, "The first hundred years are the hardest."

As the ranks of the inpouring American troops swelled, they joined in the general forward movement that ended with the gigantic Meuse-Argonne offensive. Overall command fell to the French Marshal Ferdinand Foch, whose axiom was "To make war is to attack." The "Yanks" suffered heavy casualties in charging the machine-gun nests of the enemy, but the German lines sagged on a wide front. In this last great offensive movement, Major Charles W. Whittlesey and his "Lost Battalion" were pinned down by heavy German fire in a ravine, where they suffered severe losses over a five-day period. The detachment was not really "lost"—its location was well known—but Whittlesey crumpled the written German demand for surrender and threw it to the ground. His recollection was that he muttered something like "They can go to hell." Help finally arrived and the Allied offensive ground forward as the German resistance faced collapse.

President Wilson made it clear that he would accept no deal with the "military masters" of Germany. Instead he encouraged the German people to overthrow their Kaiser, who fled to a permanent sanctuary in Holland on November 10, 1918. The American press, demanding "On to Berlin" and "Hang the Kaiser," wanted "unconditional surrender." But the enemy soldiers were capable of many months of last-ditch fighting, and if they could be disarmed by negotiations, so much the better. The Germans finally laid down their arms on Armistice Day—at eleven o'clock on the eleventh day of the eleventh month of 1918.

The prearmistice "contract" guaranteed that they would be granted a peace based on Wilson's idealistic "Fourteen Points," with the exception of a British modification of freedom of the seas and a French elucidation regarding monetary reparations for damage inflicted by the German invasion. Wilson's ideals, by one way of reckoning, had disarmed Germany by weakening its will to resist, including that of its Polish subjects and other minorities. In an address to Congress early in 1918, Wilson had encapsuled his idealistic war aims in the "Fourteen Points," although with subsequent additions they came to number about twenty-three points and principles. Leaflets containing these "Wilsonisms" had been showered over German lines and on German soil from airplanes, balloons, rockets, and shells. As anticipated, they had raised up in the fatherland revolutionary hopes of a better future if the Kaiser would only sue for peace.

An analysis of the "Fourteen Points" highlights their potency. The first one was "open covenants of peace, openly arrived at," which came to be reflected in the slogans "Open diplomacy" and "No secret treaties." Point Two was "absolute freedom of navigation upon the seas," or "freedom of the seas," an ancient and ill-defined principle for which America had fought several wars. Point Four could be summarized as "arms reduction," or what was popularly and misleadingly called "disarmament." Other Wilsonian points related to redistributing the numerous racial minorities in Europe so that each substantial group could live under a government of its own choosing. This principle came to be known as "self-determination" or "self-determination of peoples"—a devastatingly seductive catchword that since then has triggered many an uprising. Wilson's final Fourteenth Point called for "a general association of nations," which was born in 1919 and formally christened the League of Nations.

WILSON FIGHTS FOR PEACE

As the terrible war ground into its final spasm, Wilson towered at the height of his powers as a world leader. But at this critical point some of his sureness of touch deserted him. On the eve of the November Congressional elections in 1918, about two weeks before the armistice, he issued his controversial "October Appeal" for the election of Democrats. He believed that only his own party could give him the necessary support in negotiating the forthcoming peace.

Republicans let fly a barrage of criticism at "Kaiser Wilson" for having broken the nonpartisan truce that allegedly had prevailed during the war. Wilson, voters recalled, had solemnly declared, "Politics is adjourned." But politics had not been adjourned, for ex-President Roosevelt, among others, had kept up a volley of criticism at the President, who was condemned as "the drum major of civilization." Demanding "Win War Now," the Republicans carried both houses of Congress in the November elections, leaving the President with dubious support at home in his peacemaking endeavors.

Wilson further offended Congress by not placing a single Senator on his Peace Commission of five men, although the Senate was required to give its "advice and consent" when the final treaty draft emerged. The President had valid reasons for not choosing any of the Senators, among whom loomed his bitter political foe Senator Henry Cabot Lodge, a Ph.D. from Harvard, the so-called "Scholar in Politics" before Wilson arrived on the scene and became preeminent in that regard. In addition Wilson made no great secret of his low regard for the "pygmy-minded" Senators.

Reaching Europe late in December 1918, the new messiah risen in the West received uproarious acclaim from enormous and expectant crowds. He then settled down in Paris to the task of threshing out a peace treaty with the other three members of the Big Four, who represented France, Britain, and Italy. At the very outset the first of the Fourteen Points, "open covenants of peace, openly arrived at," was tossed out the window when the Big Four met in secret session.

After prolonged negotiations, Wilson won a signal victory when he managed to secure agreement on a preliminary draft of the League of Nations—the Fourteenth Point. More than that, he arranged to have this "covenant" engrafted into the final Treaty of Versailles as the first section. The idea of a League of Nations was not original with Wilson—various European thinkers had long worked on it—but it became increasingly unpopular at home with the Republican opposition, especially in the Senate. These politicians professed to fear an "entangling alliance," deplored by Thomas Jefferson, though Wilson used the term "disentangling alliance."

A hostile phalanx gradually formed in the Senate consisting mostly of a dozen or so Republicans, commonly called "irreconcilables," "bitter-enders," or "the battalion of death." To them the "League of Nations claptrap" would lead to a "League of Denationalized Nations," which would be either a weak "sewing circle" or an omnipotent "super-state." In March 1919, thirty-nine Republican Senators or Senators elect—enough to defeat any treaty—signed a "Round Robin" in which they served notice that they would reject the League of Nations in its existing imperfect form.

On returning briefly to the United States, the President struck back in a speech in New York when he declared that the League would be so intimately tied into the Treaty of Versailles that his brainchild could not be cut out without killing the whole document. "Dare we reject it," he asked, "and break the heart of the world?" The Senators accepted the grim challenge.

After reaching Paris to whip the treaty into final form, Wilson was forced to fight several battles for the self-determination of various national groups, notably Germans, Yugoslavs, and Chinese. At best he secured only unsatisfactory compromises. Premier Georges Clemenceau of France, one of the Big Four, reportedly remarked, "God gave us His Ten Commandments, and we broke them. Wilson gave us his Fourteen Points—we shall see." In the end, only four of Wilson's original Fourteen Points and his nine supplementary principles emerged intact in the Treaty of Versailles, despite the prearmistice pledge to Germany of a peace based on the unbroken Fourteen Points.

A weary Wilson returned from Paris in an uncompromising mood. Yet compromise was imperatively needed. The nation was suffering from the onset of a severe "slump in idealism"; it had keyed itself up too long for Wilsonian ideas, and people were vowing, "No more parades." Something had to give. The world was not "safe for democracy," for dictatorship was on the rise in Russia and elsewhere. Just after the "war to end war" a score or so of conflicts of varying dimensions were being fought in various corners of the globe.

BREAKING THE HEART OF THE WORLD

In America disillusionment kept pace with the slow-motion demobilization of the doughboys. Fed up with Europe and the gouging French shopkeepers, the restless "Yanks" were desperately eager to return to "God's country." In December 1918 a slogan took root among the homesick soldiers: "Heaven, hell, or Hoboken [New Jersey] by Christmas." Unhappiness bred such contemptuous remarks as "Let Europe stew in her own juice," and "Lafayette, we are still here." A popular song expressed this despair:

> We drove the Boche [German] across the Rhine,
> The Kaiser from his throne.
> Oh, Lafayette, we've paid our debt,
> For Christ's sake, send us home.

Yet not even home would completely relieve a feeling of restlessness, which found expression in the popular song entitled "How Ya Gonna Keep 'em Down on the Farm? (After They've Seen Paree [Paris])."

Superpatriots in America were girding for war against the new-fangled "League of Notions." Recalling the warnings (in garbled form) of Washington and Monroe, such critics cried that the flag of no superstate should ever fly above the glorious Stars and Stripes. One rhymester wrote a sneering parody of the hymn "America":

> Our foreign countries, thee,
> Lands of the chimpanzee, ·
> Thy names we love.

Hun-haters found the Treaty of Versailles too soft on the Germans; German-Americans and other hyphenates found it too severe.

When Wilson submitted to the Senate the Treaty of Versailles, with the League of Nations firmly riveted in, that Republican-dominated body was in no mood to move rapidly. Senator Lodge, as Chairman of the key Senate Committee on Foreign Relations, adopted the strategy of delay and amendment. Republicans had enjoyed no real part in framing the treaty; now was their opportunity to "Americanize," "Republicanize," and "Senatorialize" it. A common slogan in such partisan circles was "Down with Wilson."

Driven to desperate measures, the worn-out President reverted to his "appeal habit" and undertook to build a backfire behind the Senate with a transcontinental speaking tour. Two of the "irreconcilable" Senators trailed him like bloodhounds, orating in the same cities to crowds that shouted, "Impeach him, impeach him!" Yet the farther Wilson journeyed into the West, which had reelected him in 1916, the more enthusiasm he evoked. On the way back he delivered his last, impassioned speech at Pueblo, Colorado, after which he collapsed. Whisked back to Washington, he suffered a massive .stroke, which paralyzed one side of his body and thickened his speech. During the months of convalescence, Mrs. Wilson served as the shield between his sickbed and the outside world— "boudoir government," it was called. On one occasion a so-called "Smelling Committee" from the Senate visited the invalid to ascertain if his mental processes had been seriously affected.

At long last, in November 1919, the Senate prepared to vote on the Treaty of Versailles, with fourteen Lodge reservations attached. Most of them were relatively innocuous safeguards regarding the Monroe Doctrine and the Constitution. But Wilson, whose hatred of Lodge burned ever deeper, spurned them when he charged that they "emasculated" the entire treaty. To head off ratification with the Lodge reservations, he wrote a crucial letter to the Democrats in the Senate. He declared that such ratification would be "nullification" of the treaty, and that if the crippling Lodge reservations were rejected, "the door will probably then be open for a genuine resolution of ratification." "I trust," he concluded "that all true friends of the treaty will refuse to support the Lodge resolution." Loyal Democrats in the Senate blindly followed the bidding

Going to Talk to the Boss. Wilson appeals to public opinion. Reproduced with permission of the Chicago *Daily News*.

of their lamed leader, and the treaty failed to muster the necessary two-thirds vote.

Fate gave Wilson an unexpected second chance in March 1920, when the Senate again voted on the treaty. As before, he urged the Democrats to reject it with the unpalatable Lodge reservations tacked on. Enough of them did so to achieve a second rejection. Senator Henry Ashurst of Arizona, a Democrat, stated in the Senate, "As a friend of the President, as one who has loyally followed him, I solemnly declare to him this morning, 'If you want to kill your own child because the Senate straightens out its crooked limbs, you must take the responsibility and accept the verdict of history.'" Senator Ashurst perceived, as did most of the Senate, that the choice was either the treaty with the Lodge reservations or no treaty at all.

A secluded Wilson nursed the hope of appealing successfully to the country over the head of the Republican Senate in the upcoming Presidential election of 1920, which he referred to as a "great and solemn referendum." It failed, as did the Treaty of Versailles and its engrafted League of Nations. Thus "the war to end war" ended with a "peace to end peace." Enemies of Wilson remarked that far from "keeping us out of war," "he kept us out of peace" and contrived to bring only a temporary truce or "peace with dishonor."

Wilson died early in 1924, a broken and secluded man. One of his bitterest critics, the journalist William Allen White, softened a bit when he wrote:

> God gave him a great vision.
> The Devil gave him an imperious heart.
> The proud heart is still.
> The vision lives.

XXV

The Roaring Twenties

Prosperity is only an instrument to be used, not a deity to be worshiped.

Calvin Coolidge, June 11, 1928

THE UNSOLEMN REFERENDUM

The presidential campaign of 1920 was hardly the "great and solemn referendum" that Wilson had called for. The adjective "savage" fits it better. The President and his Democratic following were seriously discredited by the peace muddle; again critics raised the refrain "Down with Wilson." Republican stalwarts, rejoined by most of the wayward Bull Moosers, exuded jubilation. As in 1896, before they elected McKinley, they were saying that all they had to do was nominate "a rag baby or a yellow dog" and they would win.

When the Republican conventioneers met in Chicago, the several leading candidates killed one another off politically. Affable Senator Warren G. Harding of Ohio, a rank dark horse, emerged with the nomination. This astonishing result followed numerous informal sessions in "the smoke-filled room," Number 404 in the Hotel Blackstone, where journalist George Harvey held court with Senator Lodge and other leaders who wandered in and out. "Smoke-filled room" is a term which since then has carried sinister implications, although in truth smoke-filled rooms are common at all national nominating conventions. Shortly after receiving the surprise nomination, poker-playing Harding allegedly remarked to newsmen, "We drew to a pair of deuces and filled"—meaning that he drew three cards of a kind to make a "full house," despite the heavy odds against doing so.

Harding, whom Wilson had characterized as having a "disturbingly dull" mind, proved to be a glad-handing Ohio politician. The nation was settling back into its sober old ways after the recent debauch to make the world safe for democracy. America neither wanted nor needed an idealistic statesman calling for further sacrifices and moral overstrain. Republican politicians were saying that the times did not demand first-raters; hence they settled for a third-rater. One of Harding's strongest assets was a recent speech in which he had declared, "America's present need is not heroics but healing; not nostrums but normalcy; not revolution but restoration; . . . not surgery but serenity." "Normalcy" was not a word in common use, but the yearning was common. Hence the nostalgic, reactionary slogan of the ensuing campaign, "Back to Normalcy"—of course with Harding. Normalcy was equated with hard-to-beat prosperity on the lapel button "Harding and Prosperity."

The choice for vice presidential nominee, Calvin Coolidge, the dour Vermonter from Massachusetts, reflected the current atmosphere of fear. A spirit of antiradicalism permeated the country, for the Bolsheviks had taken over in Russia in 1917, and a few Communist agitators, known as "The Red Menace," were abroad in America. A recent strike by the Boston police force had unleashed an orgy of looting, and Governor Calvin Coolidge had burst into the headlines with the ringing declaration "There is no right to strike against the public safety by anybody, anywhere, any time." Ironically, the right words spoken at the right time proved to be the making of "Silent Cal" Coolidge. Actually the back of the strike had been broken before the taciturn governor appeared on the scene, but his law-and-order manifesto helped to sweep the Chicago convention off its feet and win for him the vice presidential nomination. In these troubled times the public wanted a stern disciplinarian.

Political platforms are traditionally fashioned to get into office on, not to stand on. The Republican manifesto of 1920 was a masterpiece of fence straddling, for it brought together progressives and conservatives, as well as nationalists and internationalists. It appealed alike to those who favored rejecting the League of Nations and to those who favored joining it. In these circumstances all hope of a "referendum" evaporated, "solemn" or otherwise.

For the first time in the history of national nominating conventions, windswept San Francisco played host to the gathering clans of bickering Democrats. President Wilson, sick and paralyzed though he was, desired and actually angled for a third nomination so that he could honor his commitment to the League of Nations. Nothing could better expose the extent of his detachment from reality. His son-in-law, "Crown Prince" William G. McAdoo, was a leading contender, but the nonsupport of his rival father-in-law helped to kill his chances. The convention wound up offsetting Harding, an Ohio newspaper man, with Governor James M. Cox, also an Ohio newspaper man of some standing. Franklin Delano Roosevelt, Wilson's young, handsome, and vibrant Assistant Secretary of the Navy, bolstered the ticket by providing geographic balance and the glamorous Roosevelt name.

Cox and Roosevelt supported the League of Nations with vigor, and in this sense the crippled Wilson, not the "Coxsure" Cox, was running. One sticker pleaded, "Keep Faith with our Sons—Bring America into the League of Nations—Vote for Cox and Roosevelt." Yet the League issue, as a Socialist newspaper put it, was as "vital as a dead cat in a gutter." Besides "Back to normalcy," Republicans voiced such sentiments as "Down with Wilson," "Steady America," "Think of America first," and "Let's be done with wiggle and wobble." Actually, the Republicans did most of the wobbling, specifically on the League issue. Harding's most consistent theme was that he would work for a vague "Association of Nations," not *the* League of Nations. In short, a league but not this League.

PAEANS OF VICTORY AND DEFEAT

Americans had sung themselves hoarse boosting the doughboys "over the top" to a victory that had proved frustrating and unsatisfying; now the peace settlement seemed shipwrecked on the rocks of controversy. One could hardly expect the campaign of 1920 to be a great singing crusade, and it definitely was not. The great musical campaigns lay back in the nineteenth century, and by 1920 the war generation was tired of vocalizing. Besides, much of their music was now "canned" on phonograph records.

Such special campaign songs as surfaced proved rather few and uninspiring. Republicans could claim "Harding, You're the Man for Us" and also "Mr. Harding (We're All For You)." Somewhat related was "The Little Snug Old White House in the Lane," which would be occupied by the Republican candidate. Evidence that the Republicans were now keenly aware of the "petticoat vote" came in "The Campaign Hymn of the Republic," sung to the tune of "John Brown's Body." It called upon daughters as well as sons to rise.

Other copyrighted pieces of sheet music in the dusty files of the Library of Congress carry assorted pro-Harding titles, including, "Rah! Rah! Rah! for Warren G. Harding," "The Man of the Hour," and "A Man and a Credit to the Nation." Harding's connection with Ohio, the mother of modern Presidents, received acclaim in "When the Country Needs a President, They Have to Get a Resident, of O-Hi-O." Additionally one finds "Ohio and Warren G." and "O-Hi-O: He's Every Inch a Man." Other Republican song titles concluded that "Eight Long Years of the Democratic Mule" had caused such revulsion that "The G.O.P. Looks Good to Me."

Harding's sleepy home town in Ohio, Marion, gained a new eminence. A marching song titled "Oh, Marion!" extolled Harding with words and music. The nominee honored his fellow townsfolk by delivering his speech of acceptance in their presence, at which time a glee club sang:

> We'll throw out Woodrow and his crew,
> They really don't know what to do.

Democratic campaign songs in 1920 were even fewer and flatter than those of the opposition, and the meager lot included "Jimmy Cox Will Win the Day" and "Gov-nor Cox You'll Surely Do." Several interesting musical relics favoring the Democrats may also be found in the archival dust bins. "Who Wrecked the League of Nations?" at least related to a current issue. Perhaps the only Democratic song that enjoyed a modest and transient popularity was "The Tie That Binds (or Jimmy [Cox] Is the Man for Us)."

All such vocalizing was wasted effort. So weary were the voters of Wilson and moral overstrain that Harding swamped Cox in the most tremendous outpouring of votes yet witnessed in America. Woman power added to the landslide, because the embattled ladies at long last had won the ballot nationwide by the Nineteenth Amendment, ratified in 1920. During the recent war, as a means of achieving greater unity, Wilson had abandoned his opposition and come out in favor of woman suffrage. But he did not win as much acclaim as he desired, for "He kept us out of suffrage" was a saying of 1916 repeated by frustrated females.

Wilson's "solemn referendum" thus turned out to be neither solemn nor a referendum. It was a senseless muddlement. The American people did not vote on the League, only for two undistinguished candidates, one of whom did not take a clear-cut position on the League. If the election was a referendum on anything, it was on "Back to Normalcy"—with Harding. As between Cox and Harding, a common cynical saying was "Thank God only one of them can be elected."

A possible third choice was the Socialist candidate, Eugene V. Debs, who was serving a ten-year sentence in a federal prison for having violated the Espionage Act by condemning the war. One campaign button showed a picture of the prisoner with the words "For President—Convict No. 9653." Although never a decisive factor in the race, he polled an astonishing 919,000 votes, which were a tribute to his long proclaimed slogan, "Workers of the World Unite."

PEACE AND PSEUDO-DISARMAMENT

Full-dress conservatism returned to Washington with the inauguration of Warren Harding; the Old Guard once more rode high in the saddle, with a vigilant eye to the interests of big business. The befuddled Harding, strong on affability but weak on intellectuality, had promised to gather around him "the best minds," as though conceding the obvious fact that his own was inferior. He partially redeemed his pledge when he included in his Cabinet Secretary of State Charles Evans Hughes and Secretary of Commerce Herbert C. Hoover, the famed wartime "Hoover-izer." But Harding offset these few "best minds" with some of the basest in the nation's history, including Secretary of the Interior Albert B. Fall, a key figure in the subsequent Teapot Dome scandal, and Attorney General Harry M. Daugherty, who became deeply involved in crime while ostensibly prosecuting it. He was a key member of "The Ohio Gang," or "The Poker Cabinet," labels attached to the designing, poker-playing cronies whose company Harding enjoyed. The President is supposed to have told William Allen White, "I have no trouble with my enemies. But my Goddam friends, White, they are the ones that keep me walking the floor nights."

Negotiating formal peace with the defeated enemy was one of the most pressing tasks facing Harding. The "irreconcilables" in the Senate still blocked a formal treaty; hence a joint resolution passed Congress in July 1921, declaring the war officially ended but formally claiming all of the rights and privileges (but none of the responsibilities) conferred by the unratified peace settlements. "Peace by resolution" was actually the title of a Democratic campaign song in 1920. In August 1921 Washington formally negotiated separate peace treaties with Germany, Austria, and Hungary, in which America again claimed all of the privileges with none of the responsibilities.

"Wobbly Warren" Harding quietly dropped his vaguely promised Association of Nations; he was awed by his recent avalanche of votes, which seemed evidence enough that Wilsonian idealism had faded. In one of his last speeches he pronounced the League of Nations issue "as dead as slavery." America would till its garden alone and "let Europe stew in its own juice," as the callous saying went. Yet Washington sent "unofficial observers" to Geneva, the seat of the League of Nations, to hang around and pick up information in the manner of detectives shadowing a criminal. In 1929 the novelist Thomas Wolfe could refer back to "making the world safe for hypocrisy."

As for 1918, Germany's surrender had come considerably sooner than anticipated, and the United States found itself building a "second-to-none" navy for which there seemed to be no use whatever in the years that lay ahead. All the victorious great powers had both feet in the arms race, whose very existence promoted warlike distrust, especially between America and Japan. During the recent conflict the Japanese had expanded their influence in the Pacific and China by taking over Germany's holdings, and the "yellow press" in the United States was again headlining the "yellow peril."

One serious bone of contention was the tiny Pacific island of Yap, which Japan had taken over from Germany and where the United States sought cable rights, ultimately secured in 1922. Using the title "Yap for the Yappers," one humorist wrote a parody of a popular war song:

Give us Yap! Give us Yap!
The Yanks have put it,
The Yanks have put it,
The Yanks have put it,
On the map!

In this tense atmosphere, Harding responded with dragging feet to the prodding of those anxious souls who feared that the international arms race would bring war. In the end he summoned to Washington in 1921 what was loosely called "The Washington Disarmament Conference," although the official title was "Conference on the Limitation of Armament." Even the word "limitation" proved illusory because only naval armaments were considered, and the only curb accepted related to big battleships and aircraft carriers. In capital-ship strength the United States, Britain, and Japan would have a ratio of 5-5-3, which the Japanese accepted with great reluctance and only after securing concessions restricting foreign naval bases in East Asia. The sensitive Japanese Ambassador complained that the formula 5-5-3 sounded too much like "Rolls-Royce, Rolls-Royce, Ford."

To achieve a scaling down to the 5-5-3 ratio in capital ships, the United States had to junk a number of powerful warships partially completed but needing additional sums of the taxpayer's money. This sacrifice led to the charge that the Americans, in resorting to "disarmament by example," scrapped fine big battleships while their rivals scrapped fine big blueprints. Actually the three leading powers all scrapped some ships, though, as the formula worked out, the United States scrapped the most.

Critics of the "disarmament by example" arrangements charged that Uncle Sam, the honest greenhorn at the poker table, had "scuttled the navy." A prominent American admiral moaned, "Anybody can spit on the Philippines and you can't stop them." Yet the partial arms limitation did temporarily ease tensions, and conscience-troubled Republicans could refer to the Washington conclave as "the peace conference." To them it provided a partial substitute for the aborted Treaty of Versailles. Yet the outcome seemed to give point to the observation by humorist Will Rogers, "The United States never lost a war or won a conference." This jibe, though widely believed, was open to serious question on both counts.

ROUSTING THE REDS

A bothersome legacy for Harding from the closing months of the Wilson administration was the aftermath of the "Big Red Scare" of 1919–20. Fear of bomb-and-whisker Bolsheviks grew out of the Communist revolution in Russia in 1917, as well as from the presence in America of a scattering of "fellow travelers," Communist sympathizers who did not formally belong to the party. Many of these hangers-on were accused of fomenting strikes, financed by "Moscow gold." A popular song captured the spirit of the hour: "If You Don't Like Your Uncle Sammy, Then Go Back to Your Home Over Seas." In popular phrase, this admonition became "Why don't you go back where you came from?"

Wilson's Attorney General, A. Mitchell Palmer, "the fighting Quaker," fell prey to the hysteria. Under his auspices about 250 undesirables were rounded up in 1919 and shipped out on a transport satirically known as the "Soviet Ark." Applauding what some others called the "deportation delerium," author-soldier Guy Empey wrote, "My motto for the Reds is S.O.S.—ship or shoot. I believe we should place them all on a ship of stone, with sails of lead, and that their first stopping place should be hell."

Such hysteria, generated by the recent war, had released much venom against the Socialists and other radicals opposed to fighting a holy war against Germany. Truth to tell, the Wilson administration had not distinguished itself for tenderness in dealing with dissenters. Many of the states in the aftermath of war had passed "criminal syndicalism laws," which were designed to make the mere advocacy of violence a crime. One of the most calming observations came from Mr. Justice Holmes, who, alluding also to recently adopted prohibition, declared, "With effervescing opinions, as with the not yet forgotten champagne, the quickest way to let them get flat is to let them get exposed to the air."

Another ugly phase of antiforeignism was the so-called "judicial lynching" of Nicola Sacco and Bartolomeo Vanzetti, Italian immigrants, accused of murder during a robbery in Massachusetts. The judge and jury were probably prejudiced against the defendants because they were Italians, atheists, anarchists, and draft dodgers. Convicted in 1921, the two foreign "martyrs" were executed in 1927, but only after these alleged victims of the "class struggle" had aroused international protest. As Sacco was strapped to the electric chair, he cried out in Italian, "Long live anarchy!" Several months earlier Vanzetti had told a reporter in his cell, "If it had not been for these thing . . . I might have die, unmarked, unknown, a failure. Now we are not a failure."

ABNORMAL NORMALCY

Harding's brand of normalcy was not so normal as one might suppose. Industry, including the railroads, had to be demobilized and put back on a peacetime footing, to the accompaniment of many strikes and other disorders. A severe business recession descended in 1921 and brought serious hardship. The veterans who had fought abroad for trifling soldiers' pay were distressed by the high wages that the "slackers" had been earning while the draftees were "over there" dying for democracy. A militant demand arose for lump-sum "adjusted compensation," that is, partial payment of what might have been earned in civilian life, popularly known as "the soldier's bonus." A bill to that end passed Congress, but President Harding vetoed it.

Collapsing prices of farm products, including wheat, brought new cries for relief from the farmers, as in the days of the Populists, especially in the Middle West and plains states. Malcontents formed a vocal "farm bloc" in Congress but made little progress. The "hicks in the sticks" received scant sympathy from well-to-do Easterners; Senator George Moses of New Hampshire in 1929 branded them "Sons of the Wild Jackass."

One of the most pressing problems facing Harding was the horde of impoverished Europeans poised to pour into the promised land from their war-torn and bankrupt continent. "Refuse the refuse" was the popular cry of Europe-descended nativists who cherished their "100 percent Americanism." Congress partially turned off the spigot by passing the Emergency Quota Act of 1921, which discriminated against newcomers from southern and eastern Europe, while favoring the "Nordic types" from northern and western Europe. Congress also discovered that cheap foreign goods were hardly less unpopular than the foreigners themselves. The most significant response was the Fordney-McCumber Tariff of 1922, which boosted the schedules of duties to a new high point.

Rampant antiforeignism sparked an astonishing revival of the Ku Klux Klan early in the 1920s throughout much of the country, especially the Middle West and the "Bible Belt" South. On the affirmative side the Klan was Protestant, pro-Anglo Saxon, and pro-native American; on the negative side it was antiforeign, anti-Catholic, anti-Negro, anti-Communist, antievolutionist, and anti-Jewish, not to mention other antis. Catering to the American love of secret ritual, the "Knights of the Invisible Empire" as of yore boasted "Imperial Wizards" and other horrendous "Kreatures" who in white sheets met in "konclaves" and worked up enthusiasm for their "Klandidates" for office. One K.K.K. slogan urged, "Kill the Kikes, Koons, and Katholics." Favorite trademarks were the fiery cross, the lash, and tar and feathers. Popular among the songs of the K.K.K. were "The Fiery Cross on High," "One Hundred Percent American," and "The Ku Klux Klan and the Pope" (against kissing the Pope's toe). Fortunately for sanity, the new orgy of hooded horror finally collapsed in the late 1920s; the cowardly robes had concealed a dues-collecting conspiracy by insiders.

Worried and ailing, Harding died unexpectedly in San Francisco in August 1923, just before the sensational exposure of a series of get-rich-quick scandals. A shocking case arose from the looting of the Veteran's Bureau by the President's appointee and friend, Colonel Charles R. Forbes, who was responsible for the loss of about $250 million. More spectacular was the Teapot Dome scandal, which involved the transfer of government oil reserves at Teapot Dome, Wyoming, and elsewhere by Secretary of the Interior Fall. The beneficiaries were oil tycoons Henry F. Sinclair and Edward L. Doheny, and the money changing hands amounted to several hundred thousand dollars. Secretary Fall, after resigning in disgrace, was convicted of bribe taking and sentenced to one year in jail. But the oil magnates were not punished for offering the bribes, and this miscarriage of justice gave further point to the sardonic saying "You can't put a million dollars in jail." The old saw, "Them that has gets," was thus cynically changed to "Them that has—gets off." A variant became, "In America everyone is assumed guilty until proved rich."

KEEPING COOL WITH COOLIDGE

"Silent Cal" Coolidge immediately succeeded the deceased Harding. Despite the stench of scandal, he moved slowly and cautiously in cleaning house and in arranging for the prosecution of those crooks who had been robbing the government. Aided by the rising tide of prosperity, he enjoyed unusual popularity for a man of such evident mediocrity—one who, it was remarked, "looks as if he had been weaned on a pickle."

Coolidge's thrifty New England upbringing no doubt prompted him to veto a "soldier's bonus" bill (repassed over his veto), but he could not bring himself to reject the Immigration Act of 1924. By denying Orientals a quota, it proved especially offensive to the undersized Japanese, who were highly sensitive to racial slights. The Japanese Ambassador in Washington, hoping to head off this explosive legislation, warned Secretary of State Hughes in a note that its passage in the form proposed would result in "grave consequences." This unfortunate phrase sounded like a threat of war, and Congress reared up and passed the offensive legislation by overwhelming majorities. No truer words were ever penned than "grave consequences"; the bitterness of the Japanese ultimately found a partial outlet in the flames that enveloped Pearl Harbor in 1941.

"Cautious Cal" Coolidge, who had restored respectability to his party, was inevitably nominated for President in his own right when the Republican convention met in Cleveland in 1924. As the ideal businessman's candidate, he ran on a platform that clucked contentedly over the new prosperity enriching the country, especially among those citizens who were the beneficiaries of what Democratic critics called "entrenched greed" or "entrenched wealth." The Republican vice presidential nominee was fiery "Hell 'n Maria" Charles Gates Dawes, a salty brigadier general and Chicago banker who had served on General Pershing's staff in France.

Nationwide prohibition of alcohol, later called "the noble experiment," had received constitutional sanction under the Eighteenth Amendment in 1919, but the country was seriously split over the issue. The Republican platform paid lip service to prohibition, but the Democrats were sharply divided between the "dry," "Bible Belt," Protestant South, on the one hand, and the "wet," immigrant, Catholic, urban centers of the North,

on the other. In particular, the Catholics in the Democratic party bitterly resented the anti-Catholic Ku Klux Klan, while many Southern Protestants approved the besheeted brotherhood.

Already badly divided, the Democrats of 1924 met in New York City
for the longest balloting marathon and roughhouse in American presidential campaigns—sixteen days. Governor Alfred E. Smith of New York
—a Catholic, an urbanite, and a "wet"—was nominated by the now paralyzed Franklin D. Roosevelt, who hailed his candidate as "The Happy
Warrior of the Political Battlefield." (The phrase "Happy Warrior" was
evidently borrowed from the English poet Wordsworth.) "Al" Smith's
chief rival was William G. McAdoo, President Wilson's "Crown Prince"
son-in-law and a "dry" Protestant. He had considerable backing by Ku
Klux Klan elements, which rejected Smith as a Catholic from "Jew York."
McAdoo, as an attorney, had become involved indirectly but only slightly
in the oil scandal, which inspired the campaign button for Al Smith reading "No Oil on Al." After the two contestants had endured deadlock for
102 ballots, the convention wearily and sweatily turned to a white-haired
New York corporation lawyer with Wall Street connections, John W.
Davis, who was no less conservative and cautious than Coolidge.

"Battling Bob" La Follette, adding spice to an otherwise rather dreary
campaign, headed a progressive grouping which appealed to the farmer-
labor groups. Among various schemes he advocated government ownership of railroads and relief for farmers. He made a respectable showing
by polling nearly a million votes, but his party died the next year when
he died.

RIVALRY IN SLOGANS AND SONG

Republican sloganeers hailed Coolidge as "A Man of Character" who
merited the three-C accolade of "Courage, Confidence, and Coolidge."
His personal motto was "Do the day's work." More conspicuous were
puns on "Cool" and "Coolidge," particularly in "Keep Cool with Coolidge" and "Keep Coolidge." Less alliterative but on the mark were "Safe
and Sane Cool-idge," "Deeds—Not Words," "Let Well Enough Alone,"
"Coolidge of Course," and "Coolidge and Prosperity." President McKinley's ghost appeared in "Coolidge and Dawes—Full Dinner Pail." Will
Rogers, the homespun rope-twirling "poet lariat" of the era, gave a hostile Democratic jab when he suggested, "Keep cool with Coolidge and
do Nothing." He was also quoted as saying that the country wanted
nothing done and Coolidge "done it."

Democratic sloganeers naturally exploited Republican shortcomings.
The Harding scandals were revived with "Remember Teapot Dome"
and "Honesty at Home—Honor Abroad," which suggested honorable col-
laboration with the spurned League of Nations. One button, which pictured Teapot Dome, predicted "Honest Days with Davis."

Republicans feared that La Follette would divert enough votes to throw the election into the confused House of Representatives, and hence the G.O.P. seized upon the slogan "Coolidge or Chaos." Adapting such reasoning to their own candidate, the Democrats proclaimed, "A vote for Coolidge is a vote for chaos."

On the musical front, the Democrats as before provided rather slim pickings. The preconvention campaigns produced at least one song for Al Smith ("Sure Al Is Meant for President") and one for McAdoo ("Mc A Doo Mc A-Did"), both of which faded into deserved obscurity. Among the more memorable Democratic tunes one finds "John W. Davis (Remember the Teapot Dome)," as well as "Tea Pot Dome" and "A Democrat Is Going to the White House."

One of the most popular Republican tunes was "Keep Cool and Keep Coolidge." Other Republican airs harped on the same theme: "Coolidge and Country," "Let Coolidge Carry On," "Coolidge and Dawes—for the Nation's Cause," and "Hurrah! for Coolidge and Dawes." Even less formal were "How Do You Do, Mr. Coolidge, How Are You?" "C-A-L" (for "Cal"), "Ride 'Em Cal!" (referring to the Republican elephant), and, with an allusion to Coolidge's New England background, "The Yankee Dood'l Do!"

Teapot Dome and other skullduggery normally would have fatally scalded the party in power, but these were not normal times. The scandals were now stale; cool Coolidgean prosperity was hard to beat. "Cautious Cal" and the oil-bespattered Republicans won in a walk. The slogan of the victors might well have been, as it inferentially became, "Don't swap horses in the middle of prosperity." Opponents of Coolidge grumbled that the only mandate the Republicans had received was one to keep on stealing. During the canvass the Democrats had pointedly sung a parody, in Negro dialect, of the popular song "It Ain't Gonna Rain No Mo' ":

> But how 'n the 'ell kin the country tell,
> You ain' gwine steal no mo'?

NONSENSE UNLIMITED

That delirious decade known as "The Golden Twenties" began with 1922, just after the sharp postwar recession lifted. "The Long Boom" continued until the fatal stock-market crash of 1929, thus spanning the Coolidge years. The period is also referred to as "The Era of Wonderful Nonsense" and "The Gin and Jazz Age." One of its early prophets was a visiting Frenchman, Emile Coué, whose formula for faith healing, "Every day in every way, I'm getting better and better," was widely repeated in 1923. On the other hand, the decade was one of heavy cynicism, as exemplified by the common retort "Oh, yeah?"

Feverish prosperity characterized these frenzied years. "My God, How the Money Rolls In," a tune that enjoyed wide popularity, seems to have been the theme song until 1929. But the inane "Yes, We Have No Bananas" was perhaps more representative of the current slaphappiness. Worship of "The Bitch Goddess Success" attained a new level of fervor, while a common sneer was that "only suckers work." The New York Stock Exchange became a veritable madhouse, for seemingly everybody was speculating in stocks and paying for the paper gains by buying on "margin," that is, borrowed money. Popular sayings, applicable to the stock market, urged, "Don't sell America short" and "Don't be a bear on the United States." Texas Guinan, a prominent night-club entertainer of the 1920s, hailed her fans with the salutation "Hello sucker" and popularized the saying "Never give a sucker an even break."

"Flaming youth" was having its fling, as rouged "flappers" displayed knee-high skirts and rolled stockings. With cigarettes dangling from reddened lips, the young folk further shocked their elders by dancing the "Charleston," the "Black Bottom," and other so-called inventions of the devil. Religion retreated before this onslaught of Satan; many churches even followed the principle "If you can't lick 'em, jine 'em." One house of worship in New York advertised its wares thus: "Come to Church: Christian Worship Increases Your Efficiency."

Middle-class materialism and morality created a stereotype in "Babbittry," after the prosperous real estate broker George F. Babbitt, the protagonist of Sinclair Lewis's novel *Babbitt* (1923). The word "debunking" was evidently coined in the same year by W. E. Woodward, who portrayed George Washington and other national heroes with warts instead of halos. Cynicism and brutal realism found expression in the theater, especially in *What Price Glory?* (1924), whose uncensored soldier talk featured the disillusionment of World War I. F. Scott Fitzgerald, an alcoholic novelist whose candle burned too soon, found "all Gods dead, all wars fought, all faiths in men shaken."

Materialistic America badly needed a hero to restore vanishing values. One flashed across the skies in 1927, when shy and boyish Charles A. Lindbergh, "The Flying Fool," completed a daring and grueling solo flight across the Atlantic to Paris in his *Spirit of St. Louis*. "Lucky Lindy" or "Plucky Lindy," a superb technician, received overwhelming adulation upon his return and attained the status of a demigod—to his great annoyance. A score or so of songs promptly appeared in his honor, many of them including his nicknames. One of Irving Berlin's less successful efforts was "Why Should He Fly at So Much a Week (When He Could Be the Shiek of Paree)?"

MONKEY BUSINESS AND MATERIALISM

"Progressive education," veering away from the routine discipline of the three R's in favor of more permissiveness, encountered regressive education in the famed "monkey trial" in Dayton, Tennessee, in 1925. The state legislature, reflecting a trend in the "Bible Belt" South, forbade the

Gathering Data for the Tennessee Trial. Bryan finds no proof of evolution in the zoo. The New York *World,* 1925.

teaching of Darwinian evolution in the public schools. Here the fundamentalist religionists ran headlong into the modernists. The faith-bottomed fundamentalists decried the "bestial hypothesis" that "man sprang from a monkey," while the modernists, who looked upon much of the Bible as allegorical, preferred to follow the rationalism of empirical science.

A young teacher of biology in Tennessee, John T. Scopes, challenged the law and was brought to trial. Clarence Darrow, a famed trial lawyer and a leading agnostic, appeared for the defense. As he explained to the court, "I do not consider it an insult but rather a compliment to be called an agnostic. I do not pretend to know where many ignorant men are sure—that is all that agnosticism means." He later remarked, "I don't believe in God because I don't believe in Mother Goose."

William J. Bryan, the three-time presidential reject, appeared as both a prosecutor and an expert witness for the prosecution. He stood staunchly by a literal interpretation of the Scriptures, testifying, "I will believe just what the Bible says," even that the great fish had swallowed and regurgitated Jonah. Darrow, in his persistent cross-examination, caused Bryan and "his fool religion" to look ridiculous to skeptics. The peerless orator and perennial candidate died in his sleep five days later.

Defendant Scopes lost his case, but the tide began to recede in the area of antievolution legislation and other shackles on teaching. The most strident cynic of the 1920s, Henry L. Mencken, editor of *The American Mercury* and known as "The Bad Boy of Baltimore," had a field day. He continued to excoriate the "boobs," the "booboise," and the "Boobus Americanus" of the "Bible Belt." In a similar vein he wrote, "No man ever went broke underestimating the intelligence of the American voter."

Materialism found further outlet in the amazing mechanization of America in the 1920s, particularly with the cheap automobile. The leading pioneer of mass production was Henry Ford, an ill-educated but mechanically brilliant technician, one of whose most enduring sayings was "History is more or less bunk." His assembly-line techniques were such that he was prepared to give the buyer any color of car he wanted, "as long as it was black." The claim that Ford "put America on wheels" is an exaggeration, but not by a great deal. By 1930 he had turned out 20 million "Tin Lizzies," the name given to this cheap but "rattling good car." Jokes about the Ford flivver were legion, but automobiles ceased to be derided as the horse and buggy were left in the dust. Motorists in stalled cars no longer heard the cry "Get a horse," as faithful old Dobbin trotted by a stalled automobile.

Permeating the alcoholic atmosphere of "The Gin and Jazz Age" was prohibition, or rather the absence of its effective enforcement. American experience amply demonstrated that a law which is not approved by large masses of the people inevitably spawns widespread lawlessness. "Speakeasies" sprang up like mushrooms. Illicit booze was sold as "just off the boat," which meant it was liquor smuggled in from some foreign source, often by speedy craft known as "rum runners." Nationwide one found a vast amount of "alky [alcohol] cooking," home-made "bathtub gin," and other kinds of "rotgut." Tragically, it often produced illness, sometimes blindness and death.

Illicit liquor proved to be a godsend to the gangsters, the most notorious of whom was Italian-born "Scarface Al" Capone, headquartered in Chicago. He made millions in the booze business, while his henchmen with chattering "typewriters" (machine guns) "rubbed out" their rivals in gang wars. Other gangsters "muscled in" on the "Capone mob" at their peril.

Capone was branded "Public Enemy Number One" by the Chicago Crime Commission, although he explained that he was merely rendering a public service by supplying good liquor for private consumption. He complained to a newsman, "Prohibition has made nothing but trouble." Open flouting of the law became so widespread and bred so many evils that the Eighteenth Amendment was repealed in 1933 in response to a tidal wave of protest. The federal government was never able to prove Capone guilty of dozens of murders, but in 1931 he was convicted of evading income taxes and sentenced to federal prison for eleven years.

ISOLATIONISM TRIUMPHANT

"Cautious Cal" Coolidge was a hard-fisted Yankee who believed in getting the maximum sap out of a maple-sugar tree. Wedded to old American values, especially the Almighty Dollar, he is known for such platitudes as "The business of America is business" and "Civilization and profits go hand in hand." His bill-collecting instincts came to the 'fore in connection with the debt of some ten billion dollars owed to the United States by about ten of its associates in the recent war for democracy. In response to arguments that this money had been fired away in a common cause, he turned a partially deaf ear. "Well, they hired the money, didn't they?" he is supposed to have twanged in 1925. In truth they had hired only the expendable materials of war. Most of the borrowed money was actually spent in the United States, incidentally for its own enrichment. Yet Coolidge believed that faith in international dealings would be undermined if America's former allies did not pay on the barrel head. "We went across, but they won't come across," insisted one prominent Ohio politician in the 1930s.

During the 1920s the reluctant allies were granted installment-plan terms, which with reduced interest rates amounted to a substantial cancellation of the war debts. But America's former comrades-in-arms resented even this considerable concession, and to former European allies Uncle Sam, once "Uncle Sam the Savior," became the hated "Uncle Shylock." In France, where bitterness mounted, "U.S." stood for "USurer"; in America, the wartime expression "Forty Million Frenchmen Can't Be Wrong" was changed to "Can't Be Wrung." When the Great Depression descended in the 1930s, the debtors all defaulted on their obligations, although "brave little Finland" continued to pay off a relatively small commercial (nonwar) debt. Many resentful Americans renamed Uncle Sam "Uncle Sap," or "Uncle Sucker."

Despite America's firm stand on war debts, the United States under Coolidge continued to edge rather cautiously toward the icy waters of international cooperation. President Harding in 1923 had bluntly asserted that America would not enter the League of Nations "by the side door, or the back door, or the cellar door." Yet the United States continued to send "unofficial observers" to the Geneva-based League of Nations, now branded by some critics as the "League of Hallucinations." From the 1920s to the 1930s all Republican Presidents urged that the United States join the World Court, the judicial arm of the League of Nations, but isolationists cried out against the "League Court" and the "League Trap." A suspicious Senate, spurred on by a yellow snowstorm of telegrams from isolationists, finally rejected membership in 1935.

In the mid-1920s the fear of another world-shattering conflict caused a tide of public opinion to well up in America in favor of a scheme known as "the outlawry of war"—that is, declaring war illegal by "outlawing" it. An international treaty, known as the Pact of Paris or the Kellogg-Briand Pact (after the American and French negotiators), emerged in 1928. Ultimately it won ratification by sixty-two nations, including all the major powers. As might have been anticipated, the outlawry of war proved to be about as ineffective as the concurrent outlawry of alcohol. One Senator scoffed at this "international kiss." The gaping loophole was that a nation could always legally fight in self-defense; and what scheming dictator was there who could not claim that he was in danger of attack?

Elsewhere in the global theater, Coolidge achieved a modest success. To protect American lives and property, Yankee troops had landed on the shores of the banana republics of the Caribbean under Democratic and Republican Presidents alike. In 1927, reacting to disorders spawned by civil disturbances, Coolidge was waging a "private war" in Nicaragua against the rebel "bandits (patriots?) with some 5,000 U.S. troops. Reacting to harsh criticism, he insisted, "We are not making war on Nicaragua any more than a policeman on the street is making war on passersby." Tension eased after Coolidge sent Colonel Henry L. Stimson (later Secretary of State and Secretary of War) to arrange for a special election under American supervision.

Strained relations with Mexico were nearing the breaking point in 1927 over the seizure of American-owned properties, chiefly in oil. Coolidge had the happy inspiration to send to this troubled land as Ambassador an Amherst College classmate, Dwight Morrow. He in turn invited "Lucky Lindy" Lindbergh and his airplane for a goodwill tour. This new "Ambassador of the Air" combined with the Ambassador of the United States to elevate relations with Mexico to a more favorable plateau. The episode received acclaim as one of the earliest phases of "Good Neighborism" or the so-called "Good Neighbor Policy" so widely acclaimed in the days of Franklin D. Roosevelt.

XXVI

Hoover and the Onset
of the Depression

Prosperity this winter is going to be enjoyed by everybody that is fortunate enough to get into the poorhouse.

Will Rogers, November 1929

PRESIDENTIAL HOPEFULS OF 1928

Poker-faced "Cal" Coolidge could have won renomination and almost
certainly election. But he startled the nation in August 1927 by issuing
the statement "I do not choose to run for President in 1928." This announcement, couched in quaint New England idiom, suggested that
although he did not want to run, he might do so if drafted. In any event,
"Cautious Cal" was taken at what seemed to be his word. At their
Kansas City convention the Republicans responded to the button slogan
"Draft Hoover" and turned overwhelmingly to Herbert Hoover. As
Coolidge's stellar Secretary of Commerce, he was even better known as
"The Great Humanitarian," who had saved millions of Europeans from
hunger and starvation. Not for nothing was this quiet Quaker also
called "The Man of Great Heart" and "The Friend of Helpless Children."

Hoover had first won acclaim as a "boy wonder" who had shot to the
top in the tradition of Horatio Alger. Orphaned in Iowa as a small lad, he
had enjoyed later success as a mining engineer, principally in foreign
lands, where he became a millionaire. The name Hoover had become a
household word as head of Belgian relief and with his "Hooverizing"
program as Food Administrator during World War I. Although not a
seasoned politician, he enjoyed impressive popular support from the
masses, whose sloganized query was "Who but Hoover?" He towered as

the embodiment of conservative Republican principles and hence as the high priest of prosperity—an overriding theme in the forthcoming campaign. Indeed the Republican platform on which he ran unabashedly took full credit for the jingling cash registers, while upholding the protective tariff and the nonprohibitive prohibition.

Jaunty, wisecracking Alfred ("Al") Smith, the able and liberal governor of New York, loomed as the odds-on choice of the Democrats as they gathered in a brand-new wooden structure in Houston, Texas. "The Old Gray Mare Ain't What She Used to Be" blared from the bands, suggesting that the Republican elephant wasn't what it used to be. Governor Smith's name was again eloquently presented by Franklin D. Roosevelt, who warmed over his four-year-old speech and lauded "The Happy Warrior," Alfred Emanuel Smith. Like Hoover, "Newsboy Al" Smith exemplified the Horatio Alger tradition, yet he had not worked his way up from a farm in Iowa but from the littered sidewalks of New York and the smelly Fulton Fish Market. A Democratic lapel button was frank: "Al Smith: Up from the street."

As a national candidate Smith suffered from numerous handicaps. He seemed less than "100 percent American," for although his parents were native New Yorkers, his grandparents were Irish immigrants. He professed the Catholic faith, yet the land of the free was not ready for a Catholic until John F. Kennedy came along in 1960. Protestant America, especially the Ku Klux Klanners, feared that through a Catholic President the Pope would rule the republic. Many people did not even regard Catholics as Christians, as indicated by the slogan "God would not permit a Roman Catholic to be President of the United States."

As if such drawbacks were not enough, Smith was "dripping wet." He unabashedly favored repeal of the prohibition amendment at a time when probably most Americans favored continuing "the noble experiment." Finally, the breezy, cigar-smoking, brown-derbied "Al (cohol)" Smith was an urbanite who enjoyed the support of the notoriously corrupt Tammany Hall in New York City. Altogether he was too much the "city slicker" for citizens in the "sticks," where most of the agrarian support of the Democrats could be found, especially in the Solid South.

After wet Al Smith won the nomination at Houston on a dry platform, with a dry running mate (Senator Joseph Robinson of Arkansas), he fired off a bombshell telegram to the convention. He declared that although he would enforce prohibition, he would work actively for watering it down, in accord with states' rights. One acute observer wrote, "The Democratic donkey with a wet head [Smith] and wagging a dry tail [Robinson] left Houston."

A QUAKER VERSUS A CATHOLIC

Radio had come to be a major weapon in presidential campaign strategy, and Hoover, with his double-breasted dignity and solemn monotony, came through better than his smiling, sparkling rival. Smith's New York accent betrayed a lack of higher education and refinement, and his pronunciation of "radio" as "radd-dee-o" grated on cultured ears. His long cigar and rakish brown derby further stereotyped him as a city slicker; indeed his hat, reproduced on pins, buttons, and posters, became one of the most conspicuous symbols of the campaign.

A forthright Hoover did not hesitate to make known his views. In his acceptance speech in the Stanford University football stadium—Stanford was his alma mater—he generously credited the Republican party with bringing prosperity. He went even further and frontally challenged the fates by declaring flatly, "The poorhouse is vanishing from among us." In ponderous campaign speeches he decried un-American "socialism" and preached individualism of the bootstrap-pulling variety. Late in the campaign Hoover declared in New York, "We are challenged with a peacetime choice between the American system of rugged individualism and a European philosophy of diametrically opposed doctrines—doctrines of paternalism and state socialism."

On various platforms candidate Hoover daringly made such statements as "The slogan of progress is changing from the full dinner pail to the full garage." From this evolved "A chicken in every pot," to which the Republican National Committee added, "A car in every garage." Even this roseate prospect became inflated to "A chicken in every pot and two cars in every garage." After the Great Depression had engulfed Hoover, cynical Democrats revamped the poultry slogan to read, "A chicken in every pot and two families in every garage."

Sloganizing Republicans bracketed their candidate with efficiency and prosperity in "Help Hoover Help Business" and "You Never Had It So Good." Other popular slogans were "Who but Hoover?" "Hoo but Hoover?" "Let's Keep What We've Got: Prosperity Didn't Just Happen," and "Hoover and Happiness or Smith and Soup Houses: Which Shall It Be?" Ironically, soup houses arrived in a few months under Hoover, not Smith.

Official Republican advertisements for newspapers advised readers, "Hard times always come when the Democrats try to run the nation. Ask dad—he knows! Take no chances! Vote a straight Republican ticket!" Another appeal warned, "*Is your bread buttered?* Remember hard times when we had a Democratic President! You can't eat promises. Play safe! Vote a straight Republican ticket!"

Religious bigotry raised its hideous head against "Newsboy Al." A whispering campaign darkly warned voters that "a vote for Smith is a vote for the Pope," and that the White House would become a branch of the Vatican, complete with "rum, Romanism, and ruin." Ku Klux Klan foes of Smith expressed their determination to "Keep the Pope out of the White House," while reviving the spirit of the favorite K.K.K. slogan "Kill Katholics, Koons, and Kikes." As in the anti-Catholic days of the pre-Civil War decades, some 10 million handbills, leaflets, and posters carried such familiar titles as "Popery in the Public Schools," "Crimes of the Pope," "Convent Horrors," and "Convent Life Unveiled." Nor were voters permitted to forget that Al Smith, though himself above reproach, was supported by the politically corrupt Democratic Tammany Hall. "No Contammanyation of the Nation" was one barb.

Al Smith, the now unhappy "Happy Warrior," staged a valiant speaking campaign in the face of enormous odds. "Let's look at the record" was a memorable admonition to his audiences that became one of his watchwords. As for prohibition, he made no bones about his determination to end the Eighteenth Amendment, despite the presence of a dry vice presidential running mate.

Normally the Democrats carried the Solid South, that "Bible Belt" bastion of 100 percent Americanism. They might have gagged down a Catholic, or a wet, or the grandson of Irish grandparents, or a wisecracking city slicker. But a mixture of Catholicism, wettism, foreignism, and liberalism brewed on the sidewalks of New York near the Fulton Fish Market was too bitter a dose for Southern stomachs. Smith's constantly blared theme song, "The Sidewalks of New York," was a rasping reminder that this asphalt candidate was not a "grassrootish" farm boy and hence not quite 100 percent American:

> East Side, West Side, all around the town,
> The tots sang "Ring-a-Rosie," "London Bridge is Falling Down."
> Boys and girls together, me and Mamie O'Rourk,
> Tripped the light fantastic on the sidewalks of New York.

Scornful Republicans changed "East Side, West Side" to "East Side, Wet Side."

HOOVERCRATS TRIUMPHANT

Strong emotions generated by this campaign should have produced some outstanding songs, but as in 1924 and earlier, the pickings were rather thin. Two of the most popular tunes were not new. The pro-Republican classic, "California, Here I Come," had been written in 1924, while Smith's song, "Sidewalks of New York," had first appeared in 1894. The paean to California reminded the hitherto slighted West that it was being honored, for Hoover, with his residence at Stanford University in the Golden State, was the first major party Presidential nominee ever chosen from West of the Mississippi.

Most of the copyrighted Republican compositions seem to have been of the "Hurrah for Hoover" type, reminiscent of "Huzzah for Jackson" 100 years earlier. Such offerings included "Hoover the Great," "Hoover Is the Man!" and "We Want Hoover." In a similar vein were "Big Chief Hoover" (he was called "Chief" by associates), "Who is Hoover?" "Hoover's Who," and "Hoover! We Want Hoover!" More specific were such tunes as "You Wonderful Californian," "The Happy Farmer Wants

Hoover," and (with a picture of an owl) "The Wise Old Bird Say, Hoo, Hoo, Hoo-Hoover." Musical slaps at the corrupt Democratic machine in New York appeared in "To Smith and Tammany" and "Good-bye to Tammany."

Rather surprisingly, the Democrats seem to have produced better tunes, partly because they had better composers. Among their songs were "Good-bye Cal—Hello Al!" " 'Al' for All and All for 'Al,' " "Alfred E. Smith 'The Happy Warrior,' " and "We Want Al Smith for the Presidential Chair." A standout among the catchiest original songs was one composed by the incomparable Irving Berlin, "(Good Times with Hoover) Better Times with Al." Little did the lyricist glimpse the dark clouds gathering on the horizon.

At last the shouting and singing died away and the voters—bigots and nonbigots alike—tramped to the polls. Hoover won in a landslide. "The Great Humanitarian" had too much going for him; "The Unhappy Warrior" had too much going against him. Tens of thousands of Southern Democrats from the Protestant, dry South deserted their party and voted for Hoover. Hence the nickname "Hoovercrats," one of whose slogans was "Principle above party." Yet Smith polled an impressive urban vote —the "sidewalk vote"—and in defeat amassed almost as much support as the winning Coolidge had polled in 1924.

Polio-crippled Franklin D. Roosevelt, at Al Smith's urging, had run in this same November election for the governorship of New York. To objections that Roosevelt was a polio cripple, Smith declared in a speech, "The governor of New York does not have to be an acrobat." Roosevelt won by a narrow margin while his sponsor was losing by a wide margin, and the governor-elect was well on his way toward the presidential nomination in 1932, that is if his good friend Al could be elbowed aside.

RUGGED TIMES FOR RUGGED INDIVIDUALISTS

Herbert Hoover, the high priest of Republican prosperity, exuded confidence as he took the Presidential oath in March 1929. He seems to have ignored Dwight Morrow's sage observation "Any party which takes credit for the rain must not be surprised if its opponents blame it for the drought." If Hoover had only been in the White House during the prosperous 1920s, when "Coolidge luck" held, he might have won an enduring place in history as one of the greatest Presidents.

At the outset there were few clouds in the sky, except for depressed prices in the farm belt and the mounting clamor over repealing prohibition. Hoover's Cabinet inspired confidence, especially the elderly Secretary of the Treasury, the aluminum multimillionaire Andrew W. Mellon. He had served under Harding and Coolidge and was often spoken of (before the stock-market crash caused his stock to fall) as the "greatest Secretary of the Treasury since Alexander Hamilton." He had gained fame by substantially reducing the national debt while lowering taxes, especially for the rich. The "Inner Cabinet" or "Medicine Ball Cabinet" consisted of a group of health-minded associates who exercised with Hoover by tossing around a heavy medicine ball.

As for the dry-throated demands of the wets for prohibiting prohibition, Hoover had stated in the campaign of 1928 that he did not favor repeal of the Eighteenth Amendment. He solemnly declared, "Our country has deliberately undertaken a great social and economic experiment, noble in motive, far-reaching in purpose." Hence the phrase, often used sneeringly, "the noble experiment." Hoover was keenly aware of the difficulties of enforcement, and in the early months of his administration appointed a commission of eleven prominent citizens to probe the problem. After two years they reported that prohibition was collapsing but that it ought to be continued—with modifications. One New York newspaper published a satirical version of the report:

> Prohibition is an awful flop,
>> We like it.
> It can't stop what it's meant to stop,
>> We like it.
> It's left a trail of graft and slime,
> It's filled our land with vice and crime,
> It don't prohibit worth a dime,
>> Nevertheless we're for it.

As agitation for repeal mounted, parched "wets" continued to sing dolefully, to the tune of a well-known gospel hymn:

> Nobody knows how dry I am,
> Nobody cares, don't give a damn.

But Senator Morris Sheppard of Texas told a newspaper interviewer in September 1930, "There is as much chance of repealing the Eighteenth Amendment as there is for a hummingbird to fly to the planet Mars with the Washington Monument tied to its tail." Three years later repeal was formally achieved and the noble experiment came to an ignoble end.

DEPRESSION HEADACHES

Late in October 1929 that enormous speculative bubble known as the New York stock market collapsed and wiped out thousands of investor-gamblers, many of whom had been speculating on margin. After "Black Tuesday" (October 29), Wall Street became a wailing wall. Bankruptcies and even suicides were the order of the day. A current sick joke had hotel clerks ask prospective guests when they registered, "For sleeping or jumping?"

"Wall Street Lays an Egg" ran a headline in *Variety* as the suffocating Great Depression gradually descended. Its causes were complex, and it was unlike other great panics in that it reflected the ills of overproduction and glutted markets. The term "Hoover Depression" was unfairly misleading; Hoover inherited rather than "caused" it. But whatever the causes the consequences were devastating. "We'll hold the distinction," remarked the rope-twirling Will Rogers in 1932, "of being the only nation in the history of the world that ever went to the poorhouse in an automobile." A theme song of the 1920's, titled "My God, How the Money Rolls In," yielded to the doleful tune "Brother, Can You Spare a Dime?" A popular jingle ran:

> Mellon pulled the whistle,
> Hoover rang the bell
> Wall Street gave the signal
> And the country went to hell.

A complicating factor in fighting the Great Depression proved to be the tariff. An amateurish politician, Hoover had unwisely promised in the recent presidential campaign to call Congress in special session to consider relief for farmers and to bring about "limited" changes in the tariff. Sleek, well-paid lobbyists got behind a huge log-rolling operation, which resulted in the highest protective duties in America's peacetime history—the Hawley-Smoot Tariff. It soon caused the name "Hawley-Smootism" to become a byword for excessive, scandal-ridden protection. Hoover reluctantly signed the bill in the hope that he could use the "flexible clause" to adjust schedules downward by as much as fifty percent upon recommendation of the Tariff Commission.

As the worldwide depression deepened in Europe in 1931, those nations that owed installments on their World War debt to America either could not or would not pay them. Hoover consequently initiated, and Congress later approved, a one-year moratorium on such payments. This so-called "Hoover holiday" gave promise of easing the global disaster, but cynics correctly predicted that the emphasis would soon be on the "more" in "moratorium." When another year rolled around the prophets were proved correct: six of the debtor nations defaulted outright, including France. "Honest little Finland" was the only country that paid promptly and in full. From then on the other debts were essentially dead, except for a few token payments.

With Europe and America mired down in depression, expansionist Japan decided to make hay while the "Rising Sun" shone. It staged a military coup in China's Manchuria in 1931 and seized this vast area, all in violation of solemn international treaty obligations and in defiance of the League of Nations. The peaceloving Quaker in the White House, perhaps wisely, would have nothing to do with military intervention or economic sanctions. Instead of "collective security" under the League of Nations, he resorted to collective indignation and words without weapons. The "Hoover-Stimson doctrine," proclaimed in January 1932, announced to the world that the Washington government would not recognize territorial changes brought about by force.

Nipponese militarists were neither awed nor deterred by Hoover's tap on the wrist with a paper pronouncement. Before the month was out they attacked and occupied Shanghai. President Hoover, seeking to halt this momentum toward global conflict, proposed to the World Disarmament Conference at Geneva that the nations of the world abandon all "offensive weapons," even though most "defensive weapons" could be used offensively. Then he urged that existing land armaments be reduced by approximately one-third. But mutual fears were too great to permit such wholesale disarmament.

Frustrated as an arms reducer, Hoover enjoyed some modest success with his policy toward the nations south of the border. Shortly after his election in 1928 he had embarked on a goodwill tour of Latin America (in a battleship), and in his speeches referred specifically to "neighbor" and "good neighbor." He followed through with several concessions pleasing to the unhappy Latins, who resented the overshadowing dominance of the "Colossus of the North." Noteworthy was his withdrawal of the U.S. Marines from Nicaragua, where they had been fighting a "bandit" named Sandino. He also made arrangements for a similar withdrawal from black Haiti. The much-praised "Good Neighbor Policy" of Franklin D. Roosevelt thus had promising beginnings in the gloomy days of "The Great Humanitarian."

HOOVER ON THE HOT SEAT

As a self-confessed "rugged individualist," Hoover was loath to have the government weaken the backbone of the people by doling out doles of any kind. Deploring an unbalanced budget and "deficit spending", he told the press in 1930, "Prosperity cannot be restored by raids upon the public treasury." He finally yielded grudgingly to demands for governmental assistance to hungry and footsore people who could not find nonexistent jobs. To the very end he resisted what came to be called the socialism of "a planned economy." "They are playing politics at the expense of human misery," he complained late in 1930 when Congress was debating bills for unemployment relief.

Still fearing with good reason that government handouts would undermine the character of the people, Hoover reluctantly agreed to useful public works such as the gigantic Hoover Dam (Boulder Dam) on the lower Colorado River. The funds would "trickle down" in the form of jobs for needy citizens. He belatedly and then with considerable enthusiasm endorsed the billion-dollar Reconstruction Finance Corporation, established by Congress in 1932. It extended "pump priming" loans to financial institutions and other corporations, from which the benefits would presumably "trickle down" to the destitute. Because the money went directly into the hands of wealthy corporations, the scheme was cynically dubbed "the millionaires' dole" and the "billion-dollar soup kitchen." Yet it proved to be the most successful large-scale and self-liquidating scheme of the 1930s, and it paved the way for the more grandiose outlays under the New Deal of Franklin Roosevelt.

Hoover never lost his commitment to rugged individualism. But during the Great Depression "rugged individualism" gradually became "ragged individualism" as millions of despairing workers heard, "Sorry, we're firing, not hiring." Pulling oneself up by one's bootstraps sounds resolute and heroic, but what should a man do when he had no bootstraps and often no boots? The tin-and-paper shantytowns erected by the destitute jobless were sarcastically dubbed "Hoovervilles," and the newspapers under which shivering men slept were called "Hoover blankets."

Through it all the harrassed Hoover opposed or reluctantly approved leaf-raking schemes and other projects that swelled the national debt. He vetoed the so-called "Muscle Shoals bill" that would have launched the Tennessee Valley Authority of the subsequent New Deal years; it was "socialism," he felt, to have the government competing with private business. Rebuffing the prophets of "gloom and doom," as a leader in his position had to do, he periodically issued cheery statements about prosperity hovering "just around the corner." "Hoovering around the corner," scoffers sneered. "Take it easy" meanwhile became the watchword of men who were "laboring" on make-work projects or who were about to finish a slow-motion job too soon.

In the last year of the Hoover ordeal, an incredible embarrassment developed in the form of the "Bonus Army" or the "Bonus Expeditionary Force." The hungry ex-doughboys, who had supposedly "saved America for democracy" in World War I when their country needed them, now needed their country. In 1924 Congress (over Coolidge's veto) had arranged that their "adjusted compensation" (bonus) be made payable in 1945, thousands of meals in the future. Raising the cries "We want our bonus" and "On to Washington," more than 10,000 of the saviors-become-suppliants converged on the capital. There they set up unsightly and unsanitary quarters in abandoned buildings or huts, particularly on marshy Anacostia Flat, where the hand-dug latrines were named "Hoover Villas." Congress, resisting this overt attempt at intimidation, voted down immediate payment, although it had earlier authorized limited loans against the principal.

Hoover was icily unsympathetic to this attempt to unbalance further the red-inked budget and to promote inflation. Yet he arranged to pay for the return fare of about 6,000 marchers; the residue, with a sprinkling of Communists in their number, refused to depart, though posing the threat of an epidemic of disease. Hoover then ordered the army to evacuate the uninvited guests, although he did not anticipate that extremely brutal measures would be used. General Douglas MacArthur, later to gain greater fame against well-armed opposition, ignored his specific orders and evicted the ex-heroes (now become bums) with bayonets, tear gas, and torch. A few of the "bonus boys" were injured when their pathetic shanties were burned in the inglorious "Battle of

Anacostia Flat." "A bad-looking mob animated by the spirit of revolution," reported General MacArthur.

All this did not help the image of "The Great Humanitarian" when he stood for reelection some three months later. He could not count too heavily on the veteran vote.

A PARALYTIC FOR PRESIDENT

As the presidential campaign of 1932 impended, the Hoover Republicans feared the worst. Seemingly the "chicken in every pot" had laid a discharge slip in every pay envelope. A down-at-the-mouth Hoover exuded defeatism, but the Republicans who swarmed into Chicago could not confess failure by dumping him in favor of a substitute. Their platform

1932's Soap Box. The Republicans shift ground from 1928 to 1932. *St. Louis Post-Dispatch*, 1932. Reproduced with permission of the *St. Louis Post-Dispatch*.

sang the praises of their President's (ineffective) anti-Depression policies, while half-heartedly pledging a repeal of prohibition and a return of liquor control to the states.

A rising star had appeared in the Democratic firmament in the person of glamorous, tooth-flashing Franklin D. Roosevelt, governor of New York and a fifth cousin of ex-President Theodore Roosevelt. Crippled by polio in 1921, F.D.R. had fought his way back to steel-brace mobility, remarking that after a person had tried for many months to wiggle a big toe, all else seemed easy. Handsome, wealthy, aristocratic, vibrant, and able to turn on charm as though from a faucet, he did not impress many observers as solid "presidential timber." Early in 1932 journalist-pundit Walter Lippmann wrote, in a classic miscalculation, that Roosevelt was "a pleasant man who, without any important qualifications for the office, would very much like to be President." Other critics branded him a lightweight "feather duster" and a devious "corkscrew candidate."

Roosevelt had proved to be an energetic if controversial Depression governor of New York. Believing that money rather than humanity was expendable, he advocated heavy spending for relief. In April 1932 he declared in a radio address that the "unhappy times" called for building "from the bottom up and not from the top down" in the interests of "the forgotten man at the bottom of the pyramid." From then on he won praise from the common people as a champion of "the forgotten man" and endured condemnation from the wealthy as a demagogue and "a traitor to his class."

At the exciting Democratic convention of 1932, also convened in Chicago, Roosevelt wrested the nomination from Al Smith, who thought that he deserved a second chance. But a beautiful friendship wilted after Roosevelt elbowed him aside, and the "Unhappy Warrior" ultimately "took a walk" into other camps.

Political carpenters, hammering out the Democratic platform in Chicago, produced a compact and devastating masterpiece of political cunning. They fashioned an antiprohibition plank for the thirsty. They denounced the "Hoover Depression," as well as the budgetary red ink produced by costly and fruitless experimentation. They promised to pass sweeping measures of social and economic reform, without hinting that these would result in expenditures that would make Hoover's look like small change indeed. "Throw the Spenders Out" was a Democratic campaign slogan that made ironic reading in view of the subsequent splurge of Roosevelt's New Deal years. Out on the stump the nominee himself cried, "Stop the deficits," little dreaming of the flood of red ink that would soon flow.

Defying precedent, nominee Roosevelt undertook a hazardous flight to Chicago to accept the Democratic nomination in person. To a roaring crowd he shouted with his magnificent voice, "I pledge you, I pledge myself, to a new deal for the American people." Thus was unveiled the phrase "New Deal," though it received little notice during the excitement of the convention.

In the bitter campaign that followed, Franklin Delano Roosevelt traveled thousands of miles to deliver his slashing attacks on Hoover and the "Old Dealers." He was eager to demonstrate his physical vigor ("Roosevelt is robust," ran the slogan) and thus prove that a politician did not have to be an acrobat to be President. He consistently preached a "new deal for the forgotten man," although he was annoyingly vague about the specifics of what he was going to do, primarily because he did not then know. But he warned that America could not endure "half boom and half broke." His numerous speeches, unlike those of the ponderous Hoover, were "ghost written" by the "brains trust," soon to be called the "brain trust." This intellectual group consisted largely of youngish college professors with liberal tendencies—especially with the taxpayer's money. Such was the glorified kitchen cabinet that proved to be the architect of many New Deal reforms and innovations designed "to make America over."

High spirits pervaded the Democratic camp, for not even a George Washington, much less a Hoover, had much of a chance in a nation befogged by depression. The anticipated joy of victory found expression in an ever-present theme song, "Happy Days Are Here Again." They were not actually here again, but the assumption was that the election of F.D.R. would bring them. Roosevelt, with his indestructible smile and jauntily angled cigarette holder, radiated undying optimism.

Grim-faced Herbert Hoover, conscience-chained to his desk in the White House, battled the overpowering Depression through short lunches and long hours. With the campaign for his reelection going badly, he responded to pressures to take to the stump, where he made a number of generally sensible but dull speeches. In the closing days of the campaign, he became somewhat hysterical in his defense of the towering Hawley-Smoot Tariff when he predicted, "The grass will grow in the streets of a hundred cities, a thousand towns; the weeds will overrun millions of farms if that protection is taken away." Democratic campaigners "simplified" this horrible picture to read that grass would grow in the streets if Hoover failed of reelection.

THE SOUND OF SLOGANS AND SONGS

Again suggesting that God seems to be on the side with the more effective and more numerous slogans and songs, the Democrats had the upper hand. Many of their battle cries were brutally anti-Hoover, as "In Hoover We Trusted, Now We Are Busted," "A Vote for Roosevelt Is a Vote against Hoover," and "Roosevelt or Ruin." In a similar vein were "Remember '29 and '33—We Don't Want Wall Street Again" and "Return the Country to the People." Some catch phrases were simply pro-Roosevelt, as "Roosevelt and Recovery," "Roosevelt—Friend of the People," "America Calls Another Roosevelt," and, with what became ironical, "Out of the Red with Roosevelt."

Republican sloganeers countered bravely with upbeat offerings, such as "Hoover and Happiness," "Help Hoover Help Business," "Bring Back Prosperity with a Republican Vote," "Play Safe with Hoover," and "Speed Recovery—Re-Elect Hoover." In a similar vein were "It Might Have Been Worse," "The Worst Is Past," "He Kept Us out of Worst," "Prosperity Is Just Around the Corner," "Don't Swap Horses—Stand by Hoover," and "Hold on to Hoover." One Republican journalist wrote that it was "dangerous to change parties in mid-Depression." *The New Republic* acidly observed that this advice was equivalent to saying, "Don't change barrels while going over Niagara." Democrats themselves contributed the urgent advice "Swap horses or drown." Even children in New York City chanted:

> We want Hoover, we want Hoover,
> With a rope around his neck!

As for campaign songs, the Democratic anthem "Happy Days Are Here Again" actually had been introduced two years earlier in the motion-picture musical *Chasing Rainbows* (1930). But the upbeat "Happy Days" bolstered flagging spirits, while holding out an implied promise and ignoring "Chasing Rainbows." Democratic Presidents from F.D.R. through Lyndon B. Johnson enjoyed the cheerful support of the rousing tune.

Other Democratic songs were "Everything Will Be Rosy with Roosevelt," "Row, Row, Row with Roosevelt (on the Good Ship U.S.A.)," and "On the Right Road with Roosevelt." Tunes with similar themes were "We Want a Man like Roosevelt," and "Kiss Yourself Goodby!"—that is, if foolish enough to vote for Hoover. Roosevelt, that magic name, received top billing in most of the Democratic campaign songs, which also included "Hip, Hip, Hooray for Roosevelt" and "We're All with You, Mister Roosevelt." Tunes that alluded to the Depression carried such titles as "No Hard Times with Franklin D.," "Bring Back Prosperity with Franklin D. Roosevelt," and "The Country's Calling Roosevelt." An appeal to the memory of Teddy Roosevelt found musical expression in "Here's to the Name of Roosevelt," and "T.R.'s Shoes Just the Fit" (for F.D.R.).

Republican campaign songs, for their part, gave what support they could to Hoover and the Republican cause. Among them were "Hail to Hoover," "Hoover for President: The Hope of Our Nation," and "We're Going to Keep Mr. Hoover in the White House Chair." Less personalized titles were "Battle Hymn of the Republican Party" (to the tune of "John Brown's Body") and "It's an Elephant's Job, You Bet It Is."

Intimately connected with the Hoover-Roosevelt campaign of 1932 was the concurrent battle between wets and drys over repealing or amending the Eighteenth Amendment. To drink one's way out of the Depression was the goal of many wets, for the legalizing of liquor would make jobs for more men (except bootleggers) and produce more taxes for the red-inked treasury. On the other hand, there were many musically inclined drys who found solace in such pro-Constitution pieces as "Defend—Not Amend" and "Booze Begone."

At Chicago the Republican platform had suggested a return to state option, while the Democratic platform more emphatically had favored outright repeal of the Eighteenth Amendment. Hence Hoover was regarded as more dry than Roosevelt. By association wet songs became pro-Roosevelt songs, although F.D.R. had campaigned for governor in 1930 with the slogan "Bread Not Booze."

An immediate goal of the wets, conspicuously Democrats, was the legalization of light wines and beer (achieved in March 1933) in advance of outright repeal. Relevant songs were "Okay Beer (and Better Times Will Soon Be Here)," "Beer by Easter," and "Give Us Back Our Beer, Uncle Sam." (The Eighteenth Amendment had won approval while many thirsty doughboys were overseas.) Other wet titles were "Goodbye Prohibition (Good Bye Blue Nose)," "Let's Drink Without Fear, or the Voice of Jefferson," and "Wake Up, America! A Toast to the Death Knell of Prohibition." Such appeals were well capsuled in the slogans "Roosevelt & Repeal" and "Repeal and Prosperity." Supplementary button slogans featured "Bye-Bye Mr. Dry—You're All Wet," "It Won't be Long Now," and "No Beer. No Work." Button manufacturers for the prohibitionists replied rather lamely with "I'm on the Water Wagon Now" and "Save America—Don't Save Beer and Wine."

Hard times, hard liquor, and hard work proved too much for Hoover. After having been swept into the White House four years earlier in one of the giant landslides in American history, he suffered the humiliation of being swept out by a landslide that in some respects was even greater. The sick economy had dragged him down in history—way down—and had left him a baffled and bedeviled ex-miracle man. Damming the Great Depression proved to be a task beyond the powers of the "Great Engineer." He was a "stationary engineer," critics jibed, who had "ditched, drained, and damned the country."

XXVII

Relief, Recovery, and Reform

I pledge you, I pledge myself, to a new deal for the American people.

Franklin D. Roosevelt, Chicago acceptance speech, July 2, 1932

THE DAWN OF THE NEW DEAL

On a dreary March 4, 1933, as banks were collapsing like tenpins, a self-confident Franklin Roosevelt braced himself on the inaugural platform and proclaimed, "The only thing we have to fear is fear itself." Denouncing the rich "money changers," the new President promised resolute action aimed at recovery and also a balanced budget.

Frantic action became normal. The day after inauguration Roosevelt closed all banks that had not already shut their doors, preparatory to re-opening them on a sounder basis. He also called Congress into special session—the "Hundred Days Congress" which actually met for 104 days—its primary task to enact what F.D.R. called "must legislation" to launch the "New Deal." A week later he turned to the radio to deliver the first of his famous "fireside chats" to the American people, which routinely began with the comforting, golden-voiced salutation "My friends." Re-assuring his audience of tens of millions, he asserted, "It is safer to keep your money in a reopened bank than under the mattress."

Green and panicky, the "Hundred Days Congress" rubber-stamped a paper avalanche of New Deal legislation, much of it cooked up by the liberal brain trusters whom Roosevelt had brought to Washington with him. The flood of emergency laws was designed to promote a triple-headed, forward-moving program of "Relief, Recovery, and Reform"—

the "three R's." Some of the more liberal-minded brain trusters, allegedly socialists, eagerly grasped this opportunity to remake American society into "a dictatorship of the do-gooders." But one unpleasant truth soon became clear: New Deal legislation, far from balancing the budget, floundered even deeper into a cesspool of red ink. Conservatives assailed "deficit spending," as they had in Hoover's day, but they now had a "spendocracy" on their hands that made the previous raids on the Treasury look like small change indeed.

Numerous "alphabet agencies" mushroomed as a result of Congressional and Presidential teamwork, then and later. Noteworthy among them were FERA (Federal Emergency Relief Act), HOLC (Home Owners' Loan Corporation), PWA (Public Works Administration), CWA (Civil Works Administration), FHA (Federal Housing Administration), WPA (Works Progress Administration), and USHA (U.S. Housing Authority). Critics, notably disgruntled Al Smith, were prone to jeer at "alphabet soup." But whatever called, the new agencies had one thing in common: they all cost millions of dollars. And few of them lived up to expectations. But deficit spending to combat depression was in line with the "new economics" of the brilliant British economist John M. Keynes. As Roosevelt explained to "My friends" in one of his earlier fireside chats, "I have no expectation of making a hit every time I come to bat." And he certainly did not.

Movement is not necessarily progress, but the country seemed ready to grasp at any straw that afforded the slightest prospect of hope. Prolonged inaction under Hoover had undermined national morale. While campaigning for the Presidency in 1932, Roosevelt had told an audience at Oglethorpe University in Atlanta, "The country needs and, unless I mistake its temper, the country demands bold, persistent experimentation. It is common sense to take a method and try it. If it fails, admit it frankly and try another. But above all, try something." This view squared with common American sayings "We don't know where we're going, but we're on our way" and "Try anything once." Roosevelt in fact regarded himself as a kind of quarterback whose next play depended on the success or failure of the preceding one. To change the metaphor, he seemed like the magician who was repeatedly pulling rabbits out of a tall silk hat—or trying to. Not for nothing was he nicknamed "The Houdini in the White House."

F.D.R.'s apparent happy-go-luckyism led to considerable embarrassment. In October 1935, during a slight upturn in the economy, he spoke in Charleston, South Carolina, boasting "We planned it that way." Critics were quick to point out that if he could plan the upward turns he must also have planned the downward dips. Another incautious remark emanated from the architects of the New Deal after Congress adjourned in 1935. The White House promised the country a "breathing spell" so that it could recover from the breathless pace of the legislation rammed through a rubber-stamp Congress.

Roosevelt and his fellow New Dealers had developed a strong dislike of "entrenched greed," a phrase already familiar in American politics. FDR did not really dislike rich men, his enemies said, he merely wanted to "skin them." One result was that taxes on the wealthy were ultimately increased, in line with a philosophy of "Soak the rich" or "Soak the Successful." The stock market became less of a gambling casino as safeguards were erected to protect the buyer against the misrepresentation of so-called "securities." The rule changed from "Let the buyer beware" to "Let the seller beware," especially after the passing of the Truth in Securities Act (Federal Securities Act of 1933). The worrisome era of failing banks, going back to the "wildcat banks" of Jackson's day, ended in 1933 when Congress created the Federal Deposit Insurance Corporation, which greatly increased its coverage in subsequent years.

Roosevelt also took the nation off the gold standard in 1933, determined as he was to prevent hoarding and protect the melting reserve. He reduced the gold content of the noncirculating dollar and in other ways inaugurated a "managed currency." Critics assailed the New Deal's "rubber dollars," while unhappy Al Smith wrote for publication, "I am for gold dollars against baloney dollars. I am for experience against experiment." But experiment continued with special pills for special ills.

BOONDOGGLING AND DEMOGOGUES

In an effort to ease unemployment, the New Dealers doled out immense sums of money directly to the jobless. This technique was known as "priming the pump" of recovery—a figure of speech suggested by the common practice on farms of pouring a little water into a pump to coax the beginning of a large outflow. The financial need was so great and the deficits were so large that cynics were reminded of throwing snowballs into a furnace to reduce the temperature.

One of the earliest and most laudable efforts of the Hundred Days Congress was the creation of the Civilian Conservation Corps (CCC). Unemployed young men would volunteer for wholesome out-of-door work involving such tasks as reforestation, flood control, and fire fighting —a so-called "investment in manhood." Young men and young trees both profited, but critics complained about "militarizing" "bums" and "loafers."

On a much vaster scale was the Works Progress Administration (WPA), established by Congress in 1935 and ultimately spending about $11 billion for such expensive projects as buildings, bridges, and public roads. Millions of persons received jobs. A popular jingle ran:

> We work all day
> For the WPA.
> Let the market crash,
> We collect our cash.

Shocked by these billion-dollar "giveaways," critics of such make-work schemes had a field day. They claimed that WPA meant "We Provide Alms." They complained about the slow-motion shirkers, not workers, who leaned on shovel handles all the livelong day. Cynics jeered that these "bums" had adopted the philosophy that "The only thing we have to fear is work itself," not appreciating that there was no point in hurrying to finish a job that might be the last job. The sneering word "boondoggle" came into common use, meaning unnecessary jobs or tasks of little permanent value, such as raking leaves. But Roosevelt was defiant. Speaking in Newark, New Jersey, early in 1936, he declared, "If we can boondoggle our way out of the Depression, that word is going to be enshrined in the hearts of the American people for years to come." Pickets in Washington clamoring for more WPA appropriations carried signs proclaiming, "The People Starve Amid Plenty," and (for veterans) "1918 [We] Died for Democracy—1938 [We] Died for Jobs and Food."

Joblessness and hunger in the midst of plenty inevitably gave birth to many prophets with pie-in-the-sky proposals. Some of these saviors were obviously crackpots who commanded little or no following. But several colorful figures headed formidable movements.

Self-designated "Kingfish" Huey Long of Louisiana, a rabble-rousing Dixie demagogue, lusted for power. Governor and then United States Senator, he headed a dictatorial political machine that virtually suspended the democratic processes in his state. At first a supporter of the New Deal, he turned violently against it with a "Soak the rich" program that found expression in a movement called "Share the Wealth" or "Share Our Wealth." One of his slogans was "Every Man a King, but No Man Wears a Crown," which was reflected in his book *Every Man a King* (1933). Himself a near fascist who was a threat as a potential president, he once stated that if fascism ever came to the United States, it would be clothed in the guise of "Americanism." Though surrounded by armed bodyguards, he was shot in the rotunda of his state capitol by an assassin who was immediately riddled with bullets. His last words were uttered as he lay in blood on the marble floor, "I wonder why he shot me."

Depression-cursed "senior citizens," obviously not enjoying their golden years, mobilized behind the Townsend Plan, launched by an elderly physician, Dr. Francis E. Townsend of California. Each citizen over sixty was to receive $200 every month, provided that it was spent within the month. The total annual cost of some $20 billion was to be raised by a national sales tax. A movement thus developed which spawned a great outpouring of low-quality parodies, poems, and songs. Among the tunes were "Our Castles in the Air" and "When Grandma Draws Her Townsend Pension."

A new movement, backing the Old Age Pension Plan of 1939, gathered steam under the slogan "Thirty Dollars Every Thursday." This so-called "crusade" was also known as the "ham and eggs" campaign, presumably in expectation of more nutritious and palatable breakfasts. Yet all of these schemes for senior citizens suffered a severe setback when Congress passed the epochal Social Security Act in the summer of 1935. Critics claimed that its aim was to provide security "from the cradle to the grave" and "from womb to tomb."

Conspicuous among the demagogues of the 1930's was Father C. E. Coughlin, a Catholic priest in Michigan who virtually hypnotized an enormous following on radio with his appeal for "Social Justice." This "microphone Messiah" at first supported the New Deal with cries of "Roosevelt or ruin" and with demands that the "money changers" be driven from the temple. He later turned savagely against the "brain trusters" and other minions of Roosevelt with such intemperance that he had to be silenced by his ecclesiastical superiors.

FROM BLUE EAGLE TO SICK CHICKEN

Most ballyhooed of all the New Deal measures was the National Recovery Administration (NRA), established by the Hundred Days Congress in 1933. Triple-barreled, it was supposed to help industry, labor, and the unemployed. It would increase employment by reducing hours and buttering thin existing work under codes of "fair competition." Minimum wages were established and ceilings were imposed on maximum wages. The hated "yellow dog" or no-union contract, favored by employers, was forbidden.

Self-denial by management and labor alike was required under NRA. To achieve such goals, a great propaganda campaign was whipped up in the manner of Liberty Loan drives of World War I. The "Blue Eagle," hatched by Congress, became the symbol of NRA and "We Do Our Part" emerged as the major slogan.

About 200 songs were written, few of them published, in support of the NRA's Blue Eagle. The writers hailed the sacred bird with such titles as "The Blue Eagle's Flying High," "NIRA and Her Eagle Blue," and "Good-bye Blue Eagle Blues." Other compositions were less feathery, such as "Hooray For the NRA," "Let's Go America," "Rosy with Roosevelt," and "Goodbye Old Man Depression, Hello Miss Prosperity."

In 1917–18 Americans had shown that they could "give until it hurts" in the war against Germany, but self-denial was more painful in a save-who-may war against depression in the 1930s. In an early fireside chat Roosevelt had asserted, "We cannot ballyhoo our way to prosperity"—and he was right. The old age of chivalry had long since passed, and people now witnessed a new age of "chiselry." America seemed to be turning into a nation of "chiselers." Critics jeered that NRA stood for "National Run Around," "Nuts Running America," "National Racketeers Arrangement," and "Never Roosevelt Again."

Noble bird though it was, the Blue Eagle was shot to earth by the Supreme Court in May 1935, in the memorable "sick chicken case" involving a New York poultry dealer. The learned justices held that this

Big Business Holds Line Against NRA. Knott, the Dallas *News,* 1933.
Reproduced with permission of the Dallas *News.*

fowl business was purely local, and not to be regarded as in interstate
commerce under the jurisdiction of Congress. Roosevelt complained
bitterly about the Court when he said, "We have been relegated to the
horse-and-buggy definition of interstate commerce." Worse criticism was
soon to be heard about the "mossbacks" on the Supreme Court.

An epochal constitutional change was meanwhile in the making as
prohibition, which had generated multitudinous evils, was being abandoned. Yet last-ditch prohibitionists were still raising such cries as "Dry

up, America" and "America cannot be preserved in alcohol." Pending the
official repeal late in 1933, the Hundred Days Congress made haste to
legalize beer and light wine with an alcoholic content of not more than
3.2 percent by weight, presumably nonintoxicating. New jobs would be
created, and the Treasury would profit from an added inflow of tax
revenue. Disgruntled drys assailed Roosevelt as a "3.2 percent American."

FROM DUST BOWL TO SIT-DOWN STRIKES

Farmers anticipated relief through the Agricultural Adjustment Administration (AAA), set up by the Hundred Days Congress in 1933. Washington would create "artificial scarcity" by paying the growers to reduce
or plow under their crop-producing acreage and thus eliminate profit-
killing surpluses. "Parity prices" for the growers, adjusted to pre-1914
purchasing power, were to be established for the scheduled crops. The
Supreme Court axed the first AAA Act, but a new and more limited one
rose in its place.

As if the farmer did not have troubles enough, a prolonged drought
scorched the trans-Mississippi plains states in 1933. Swirling winds
whipped up an enormous dust bowl. Burned and blown out, over
300,000 inhabitants of Oklahoma ("Okies") and Arkansas ("Arkies")
trekked to sunny but inhospitable California in "junkyards on wheels."
The hardships that they encountered en route, as well as the chilly
reception they received, found dramatic portrayal in John Steinbeck's
famous novel *The Grapes of Wrath* (1939). It included the memorable
description "Okie use' to mean you was from Oklahoma. Now it means
you're scum."

Depression songs were inherently depressing. Among them were "My
Oklahoma Home, It Blowed Away," as well as "There Is Mean Things
Happening in This Land." Perhaps the most famous theme song of the
Great Depression was "Brother, Can You Spare a Dime?" which told its
own sad tale.

From the standpoint of "planned economy" perhaps the most successful—certainly the most imposing—of the New Deal brainstorms was the
Tennessee Valley Authority or TVA. Bitterly opposed by Herbert
Hoover as a form of statism or collectivism, this "creeping socialism in
concrete" brought a majestic series of dams to the rivers and valleys of
a much-eroded Tennessee Valley. Aside from control of floods, erosion,
and navigation, the scheme was designed to generate an immense
amount of electric power. At the same time it would supposedly provide
an accurate "yardstick" to measure costs of production, so that the
charges imposed by private utilities could be brought into line.

"The TVA Song," a folk creation, related:

> The government begun it when I was but a child,
> But now they are in earnest and Tennessee's gone wild.

Power produced by the TVA aided enormously in promoting rural electrification; one poster showed a bolt of electricity darting out from a closed fist, with the message "TVA—Electricity for all."

Farm folk thus received many benefactions from "the handout state," but what about laboring men? The truth is that a new deal for labor did arrive with the New Deal, as F.D.R. quickly became "The Forgotten Man's Man." Democratic precinct workers were not backward in telling laborers, "Roosevelt wants you to join a union." The NRA Blue Eagles, with their call for collective bargaining, provided a godsend to organized labor. More important was the Wagner or National Labor Relations Act of 1935, which asserted the right of laborers to bargain collectively.

Noteworthy was the progress of unionization among unskilled workers, conspicuously under the leadership of crusty John L. Lewis, boss of the United Mine Workers. He succeeded in forming the Committee for Industrial Organization (CIO), later named the Congress of Industrial Organization. Significantly, Negro workers, the "last hired and the first fired" during a depression, were welcomed to its ranks.

A startling development came in 1936 when men at the General Motors plant at Flint, Michigan, resorted to the sit-down strike—a weapon already used in Europe and not completely unknown to America. Strikebreakers were prevented from entering the building, and the laborers finally won a resounding victory. The folk song "Sit Down" became widely popular:

> When the boss won't talk,
> Don't take a walk;
> Sit down, sit down.

"Labor, like Israel, has many sorrows," declared John L. Lewis during a funeral-toned radio speech in September 1937. This was all too true, especially when the Little Steel companies fought savagely against the unionization by the CIO of their employees. At the South Chicago plant of the Republic Steel Company in 1937 a bloody fracas erupted when police fired on pickets and workers, leaving the area strewn with several score of dead and wounded—the so-called "Memorial Day Massacre."

On the whole, Roosevelt's "coddling of labor" produced spectacular results among the workers, most of whom voted for him "again, and again, and again"—to use one of his favorite phrases. A campaign button of the New Deal years ran, "Labor for Roosevelt—Roosevelt for Labor." As one workingman put it, "Mr. Roosevelt is the only man we ever had in the White House who would understand that my boss is a son-of-a-bitch."

REPUBLICAN RIVALS OF 1936

As the Republicans gathered for their quadrennial convention in Cleveland, much-booed Herbert Hoover evidently wanted a second chance in what he regarded as "a holy crusade for liberty." Instead, the delegates turned to the mildly liberal Governor Alf Landon from the "Sunflower State" of Kansas, a wealthy oil man who enjoyed the distinction of having balanced his budget, as required by the state constitution. The keynote speaker delivered an impassioned indictment of the "three long years" of Roosevelt, a reference that inspired a band to strike up "Three Blind Mice." The Republican platform, though promising handouts that would cost billions, assailed the New Deal of Franklin "Deficit" Roosevelt, its confusion and "frightful waste." In the ensuing campaign Landon, "The Kansas Coolidge," stressed "deeds, not deficits," while his supporters served him up with various sunflower buttons, badges, and banners. On the other hand, pessimists pointed out that "sunflowers do not bloom in November," and one Democratic button quoted a "Disgusted Republican" as saying, "We Can't Eat Sunflowers—Let's Lose with Landon."

Renomination of Roosevelt, "The Champ," was regarded as automatic in 1936, and his new coronation took place at Philadelphia. The Democratic platform rested so heavily on the New Deal that a smashing victory in November would inevitably be regarded as a ringing endorsement of Roosevelt and all his works, including relief checks for hungry voters.

Alf Landon's name lent itself to a flood of alliterative words or strained puns. They included "Life, Liberty, and Landon," "Vote for Landon and Land a Job," "Land Landon with a Landslide," and "Let's Make It a Landon-slide." Other Republican sloganized appeals were "Up with Alf, Down with the Alphabet" (a reference to Roosevelt's "alphabet soup" agencies) and "Landon Knox Out Roosevelt" (Knox was Landon's running mate). A related slogan ran "Off the Rocks with Landon and Knox," which Democrats cleverly reversed to read, "Back on the Rocks with Landon and Knox." Less personal anti-Roosevelt barbs were "Defeat the New Deal and Its Reckless Spending" and, referring to playing cards, "Let's Get Another Deck." Telephone operators at the pro-Landon *Chicago Tribune* routinely answered calls with "Only [insert the proper digit] more days to save the American way of life."

Music-making Republican partisans generally reinforced these slogans, but their offerings were relatively few and undistinguished, for old-fashioned campaign songs were now losing their appeal. The official Republican campaign anthem was "Happy Landin' with Landon," although some merit could be found in "Landon, Oh, Landon." Other anti-New Deal song titles were "Have You Ever Tried to Count to a Billion?" "Humanity with Sanity," and "Three Long Years!"

Republicans received some support from the American Liberty League, a conservative organization that had surfaced to combat the "New Dealocrats" and their alleged excesses. Its aim, like Hoover's, was "a holy crusade for liberty." Consisting heavily of wealthy men, it could claim the allegiance of ex-Governor Al Smith, who made good on his threat "to take a walk" and vote for Landon. Referring to the New Deal in 1936, he said, "No matter how thin you slice it, it's still baloney."

The American Liberty League distributed pamphlets bearing such expressive titles as *Inflation, Expanding Bureaucracy, Dangerous Experimentation, Professors and the New Deal, Government by Busybodies,* and *You Owe Thirty-one Billion Dollars.* Critics of the American Liberty League accused its wealthy members of being "Tories" and "princes of privilege."

ROOSEVELT ROUTS LANDON

Durable Herbert Hoover, although not the official nominee, in a sense was made to run again, as in several subsequent campaigns. During the canvass of 1936, the Democratic theme was "Four Years Ago and Now," which led to "Where were you in '32?" "Remember Hoover?" was a common ploy of Democratic orators, who invariably would provoke a responsive chorus of boos. Landon, himself rich, was condemned as "the poor man's Hoover," and the Republican party was branded the party of "big money and big depression." Democratic campaign buttons urged, "Re-Elect Roosevelt: His Heart's with the People," "Four More Roosevelt Lucky Years," and "He Saved America." The President himself heard people cry out, "He saved my home" and "He gave me a job." Scrawled in chalk on the side of a freight car in Denver were the words "Roosevelt Is My Friend."

Clever Democratic campaign managers did not fail to appeal to the poor, especially "reliefers" whose checks had a curious habit of coming in bunches shortly before election day. Sickly Harry L. Hopkins, one of F.D.R.'s key administrators, is said to have advised, "Tax and tax, spend and spend, elect and elect." The authenticity of this quotation is questioned, but it preserves an anti-New Deal conception of what was taking place. One Republican button gave the brave assurance "America Cannot be Bought."

Democratic campaign strategy focused on praising the hope-giving New Deal while condemning the Republican old deals. The theme song of the party in 1936, as in 1932, was the sprightly "Happy Days Are Here Again," replayed tiresomely. Other tunes, geared specifically to this campaign, were "Things Look Rosy with Roosevelt" and "That's Why We're Voting for Roosevelt."

An on-the-job Roosevelt limited his public appearances and cleverly refused to give Landon publicity by mentioning him by name. By way of unintended reciprocation, many Republicans came to call F.D.R. contemptuously "that man in the White House." But when Roosevelt hit, he struck hard. In his acceptance speech he pilloried "the economic royalists" who had brought woe on the country. Stung by Republican charges that workers would be cheated out of their new Social Security benefits, Roosevelt delivered a fighting speech in Madison Square Garden, New York, on the eve of the election. Referring to his conservative opponents, Roosevelt cried, "They are unanimous in their hate for me—and I welcome their hatred." He continued, "I should like to have it said of my first administration that in it the forces of selfishness and of lust for power met their match. I should like to have it said of my second administration that in it these forces met their master."

On election day the country witnessed a Democratic landslide, not a "Landon-slide." Roosevelt swept to one of the most overwhelming political triumphs in American history, and the victors hailed the result as a resounding ratification of "the welfare state." F.D.R. garnered the electoral vote of every state except Maine and Vermont. The old saying "As Maine goes, so goes the nation," was turned into the quip "As Maine goes, so goes Vermont."

Roosevelt's head-turning victory was no doubt a triumph for the forgotten man, whom F.D.R. never forgot. Countless reliefers, unwilling to bite the hand that fed them, gratefully cast their ballots for "The Squire of Hyde Park," also known as "The Boss." As unhappy Al Smith declared in a speech attacking New Deal spending, "Nobody shoots at Santa Claus." Not only the poor whites but also the poor blacks supported Roosevelt. Previously the Negroes had generally voted Republican, in grateful memory of "The Great Emancipator." But times had changed. One Negro ward in Indianapolis displayed the banner message "Mr. Roosevelt, Our Saviour." The *Baltimore Afro-American* reminded black voters, "ABRAHAM LINCOLN IS NOT A CANDIDATE IN THE PRESENT CAMPAIGN." When the ballots were all counted, few voters could deny that Lincoln was "finally dead."

THE COURT-PACKING FIGHT AND AFTER

High-flying Franklin Roosevelt, buoyed by an awesome popular mandate of some kind, now prepared to get the New Deal moving again. In his acceptance speech of 1936 he had declared, "This generation of Americans has a rendezvous with destiny" ("debt," Republicans jeered). In his inaugural address of 1937 he asserted, "I see one-third of a nation ill-housed, ill-clad, and ill-nourished."

A formidable roadblock loomed in the form of the Supreme Court, often referred to as "Nine Old Men." Loaded down with aged and fossilized conservatives, it had chopped down much of the New Deal legislation that had come before it, notably in the "sick chicken" case. The learned legalists might even do the same with the epochal Social Security Act. Seeking a way out, Roosevelt hit upon an ingenious plan to "unpack" the "horse-and-buggy" Supreme Court by adding a younger Justice for every member over seventy who would not retire. The Court could thus have a maximum of fifteen members.

An overconfident Roosevelt regarded his proposal for "new blood" as "the answer to a maiden's prayer." But he sprang his bombshell message on Congress without advance notice and thus stirred up a frightful storm of opposition that raised the slogan "Keep the Supreme Court out of politics." Countless citizens, especially conservative Republicans, regarded the Court as something of a sacred cow. Critics loudly condemned the "Dictator Bill" of "Franklin Double-crossing Roosevelt," and fervently prayed, "God bless the Supreme Court." In the end, the President lost this Congressional battle, largely because the Supreme Court, no doubt aware of the impending axe, began to show increasing sympathy for New Deal legislation. The justices reversed by one vote an earlier five-to-four decision invalidating a minimum-wage law for women. "A switch in time saves nine," became the witty updating of a proverb.

"Happy days" did not dawn again, as the song had optimistically suggested, after the election of 1936. In 1937–38 came a frightening downward plunge, which produced a recession cynically known as the "Roosevelt Depression." Experts believed that some of the heavy "pump priming" had been cut back before the pump began to operate effectively. Forward progress came gradually after 1938, while people tried to lift themselves by their bootstraps with such cheery remarks as "Wasn't the Depression terrible?" or "Whew! That was a depression, wasn't it?" After all the pain and strain from 1933 to 1939 under the New Deal, Roosevelt did not manage to cure the Depression. Hitler unwittingly helped to turn the trick by precipitating a holocaust in 1939 that caused the European democracies to place huge orders for munitions in the United States. Critics said that Roosevelt "got us out of the Depression by getting us into the war."

Conservatives never ceased to assail the New Deal and all its works. Enemies especially deplored the employment of "crackpot" college professors, leftist "pinkos," and outright Communists who allegedly were trying to make America over in the image of "Rooseveltski." Hearst newspapers pointed an accusing finger at

> The Red New Deal with a Soviet seal
> Endorsed by a Moscow hand
> The strange result of an alien cult
> In a liberty-loving land.

Roosevelt was further attacked for giving ear to many bright Jewish leftists ("Jew Deal") whom he had brought into his "brain trust."

What had Roosevelt accomplished with his costly new schemes and his "Dummy Congress," from which, incidentally, he had unsuccessfully tried to "purge" uncooperative members in 1938? On unfriendly tongues, the "welfare state" became the "handout state," "planned economy" became "planned bankruptcy," and "Soak the rich" became "Soak the successful." The national motto was said to have changed from "In God We Trust" to "Government Can Do It Better," which bespoke a degree of un-Jeffersonian centralization. Cynics did not weary of complaining that the New Deal had done nothing that an earthquake could not have done better.

Viewed in perspective, Roosevelt was essentially a left-leaning middle-of-the-roader. Even liberals were critical, because the New Deal did not go far enough fast enough. F.D.R. steered a compromise course between two extremes, and he may have headed off radical socialism by a mild dose of American-grown socialism. His concern for "balancing the human budget" took priority over balancing the financial budget. "Nobody," he promised, "is going to starve."

In the atmosphere of Hoover's last days in 1933, any movement seemed better than none at all to hope-bereft Americans. Will Rogers remarked that if Roosevelt were to burn down the capitol people would say, "Well, we at least got a fire started, anyhow." F.D.R. did much better than that. In the age of authoritarians like Hitler, Mussolini, and Stalin, he avoided taking, or attempting to take, the republic down the dictatorial drain. As a liberal conservative, he helped to conserve and preserve the American way of life.

XXVIII

The New Deal
and the New Neutrality

> When you see a rattlesnake poised to strike, you do
> not wait until he has struck before you crush him.
> Franklin D. Roosevelt, fireside chat, September 11,
> 1941

ECONOMIC GOOD NEIGHBORISM

A self-confident Franklin Roosevelt foreshadowed a major phase of his administration in his first inaugural address in March 1933. "In the field of world policy," he proclaimed, "I would dedicate this nation to the policy of the good neighbor. . . ." This was the most widely publicized affirmation thus far of the "Good Neighbor Policy," although F.D.R.'s predecessors, notably Hoover, had contributed to the concept and even to its terminology. Mythologists to the contrary, the term applied to all nations, not to Latin America alone, but there it found its fullest expression.

At a meeting of the American states in Montevideo, Uruguay, in 1933, the delegation from the United States lent its support to the declaration "No State has the right to intervene in the internal or external affairs of another." Deeds followed words. The next year the Washington government released a long-protesting Cuba from the interventionist trammels of the so-called "Platt Amendment." Three months later the U.S. Marines folded their tents and ended their prolonged occupation of palm-fronded Haiti. In 1936 Roosevelt journeyed to a special Inter-American Conference for Peace at Buenos Aires, as a kind of "traveling salesman for peace." He evoked enthusiastic applause when he assured the apprehensive Latinos in a dramatic speech that foreign powers seeking "to commit acts of aggression against us will find a hemisphere wholly prepared to consult together for our mutual safety and our mutual good."

On a broader front, international finance continued to provide gnawing anxieties during these years of world depression. A conference of more than sixty nations met in London in June 1933 with the major objective of stabilizing international currencies. This was a subject which Roosevelt had previously agreed to discuss. Yet when he found that stabilization of the dollar might blight prospects of recovery from the Depression, he fired off a bombshell radio message to the London Conference while vacationing on a U.S. cruiser in the north Atlantic. "The Conference," he bluntly asserted, "was called to better and perhaps cure fundamental economic ills. It must not be diverted from that effort." This scolding ultimatum was published in America on the Fourth of July, to the accompaniment of much popular applause for what was called "a new Declaration of Independence." But the explosive message effectively torpedoed the London Conference, which seemed headed for collapse anyhow.

Red Russia meanwhile seemed to be growing pinker. Continuing depression, combined with the prospect of lucrative trade, led to protracted negotiations for a formal recognition of the U.S.S.R. The bloodstained Russian Bolsheviks had been quarantined as "moral lepers" ever since their takeover in 1917, sixteen years earlier. In the end, the Soviets agreed, among other concessions, to terminate their Communist propaganda in the United States (which they subsequently failed to do). Formal recognition was granted in November 1933.

Rock-ribbed conservatives in the United States were scandalized by the veneer of respectability given the "Bolshevik butchers," all for the sake of some Depression-curing trade that might develop (as it never did). One Congressman spoke bitterly of a betrayal for "thirty pieces of silver," while the conservative *National Republic* prophetically moaned, "Reds Win as U.S. Holds Bag" and "Profits Stained with Blood."

More important than potential commerce with Russia was the once booming international trade now crippled by the Depression. Low-tariff Democrats argued vehemently that the high Hawley-Smoot Tariff, signed by Hoover in 1930, had contributed to the sadly depressed state of international commerce. In 1934, as a part of the New Deal program, Congress passed the Trade Agreements Act, which authorized Roosevelt to raise or lower the Hawley-Smoot rates by as much as 50 percent for those nations willing to make reciprocal concessions. Again citizens heard the call for "Reciprocity," as Secretary of State Cordell Hull negotiated about twenty reciprocal pacts, many of them with Latin American nations. Such familiar watchwords again appeared as "Trade is a two-way street" and "He that does not buy, neither can he sell." The economic impact of these treaties is difficult to assess, given the abnormal conditions of depression and war, but there can be no doubt that the easing of the Hawley-Smoot barriers did much to improve international good will.

THE ERA OF THE DICTATORS

Beclouding the Roosevelt years was the menace of dictatorship. By 1929 Stalin, the bloody-handed "Sphinx of the Kremlin," had clawed his way to the top, where he felt increasingly insecure as fascist regimes arose on his flanks. In the late 1920s Benito Mussolini, the posturing, jut-jawed "Sawdust Ceasar," took over the reins in Italy. Most menacing of all was Adolf Hitler, a frustrated Austrian painter, who seized power with his brown-shirted bullies in 1933–34, and became Führer almost simultaneously with the so-called "dictatorship of Roosevelt." "Heil Hitler" became the universal, hand-raising salutation of his National Socialists (Nazis).

Hitler ended the unemployment problem in Germany, notably by building a chain of magnificent highways and by wholesale rearming in open defiance of the Treaty of Versailles. One of his chief henchmen, Hermann Goering, broadcast the message "Guns will make us powerful; butter will only make us fat." Hitler's oratorical powers before vast audiences were hypnotic. Using the "big lie" technique, he demanded "living space" for Germany and proclaimed a "Thousand Year Empire" (it lasted twelve years). He spewed out hatred of the Jews, whom he began to persecute so viciously as to cause the cry "Boycott Nazi Germany" to rise among American co-religionists and others. Under Hitler the fevered atmosphere echoed and reechoed with "Today Germany, tomorrow the world."

Germany and Italy were generally labeled "have-not nations." Even more in need of "living space" was Japan, which became a military dictatorship in the 1930s and launched out on a mad imperial quest for more territory. By 1940 these three "have-nots" were bound together in the Axis military alliance.

To discerning observers, combustibles in Europe were building up to a volcanic explosion. Yet America had turned isolationist since the "slump in idealism" after "Wilson's war" and a common reaction was "Let Europe fry in her own fat." A Middle Western farmer was quoted as saying, "I don't give a dern what happens to them fellers as long as it don't happen to me."

Signs of an impending catastrophe flashed across the eastern skies of Asia when Japanese militarists seized Manchuria in September 1931. In 1934 a flood of articles and books appeared in America exposing the arms business—those "merchants of death" who were so heavily involved in the "blood business." Some undiscerning citizens concluded that if they could only remove the profits from selling munitions, then wars would be much less likely to occur. "Take the profits out of war" was the cry that arose, and Congress was forced to act, especially after Mussolini unleashed his barefaced aggression upon primitive Ethiopia in 1935. A series of "storm cellar" Neutrality Acts passed by Congress in the 1930s—all designed to legislate the nation out of future war—placed severe restrictions on the sale or export of munitions. In this way the country attempted to legislate itself out of overseas conflicts.

Japanese militarists meanwhile had got completely out of hand when, in July 1937, they opened up a full-fledged war on China. They were still striving for "The New Order in East Asia," which involved the concept that if all the nations concerned cooperated with Nippon in developing the resources of this region, all parties would benefit. The additional Japanese cry of "Asia for the Asians" bore a resemblance to the Monroe Doctrine of 1823, with its emphasis on "America for the Americans."

Roosevelt was gravely concerned by Japan's aggressions and also by the intervention of Hitler and Mussolini in Spain's Civil War (1936–1939). In October 1937 he journeyed to Chicago, the so-called "isolationist capital of America," to deliver a sensational speech. Declaring that "war is a contagion," he pointed out that "international lawlessness" and "international anarchy" were abroad in the world. Just as a community must "quarantine" the afflicted when a contagious disease erupts, so must America find "positive endeavors to preserve peace." Such tough talk suggested an economic boycott of the aggressors, and indeed a slogan developed, "Boycott Japan—Stop Aggression." But the general reaction to the Chicago speech in isolationist America was so disapproving that Roosevelt dropped his talk of "positive endeavors."

THE END OF APPEASEMENT

Hitler had meanwhile aroused new anxieties in what came to be called "a war of nerves." After occupying the demilitarized Rhineland with his troops in 1936, he annexed by a show of force an independent but German-speaking Austria in 1938. He then opened a vehement campaign for the annexation of the Sudetenland, that is, the German-inhabited portions of neighboring Czechoslovakia. Threatening war if he did not get his way, Hitler forced a conference of the interested powers at Munich. "My patience is exhausted," he warned.

After tense hours, while Europe teetered on the brink of war, an unprepared Great Britain and France knuckled under and agreed to a lopsided compromise. Hitler carved out the portions of Czechoslovakia he demanded, while agreeing to a four-power guarantee of the remaining borders of that betrayed and mutilated little country. He declared flatly in a Berlin speech, "The Sudetenland is the last territorial claim I have to make in Europe." Less than six months later he broke his pledge and took over the remainder of Czechoslovakia, which was indisputably non-German.

After the historic sellout at Munich, Prime Minister Neville Chamberlain returned to London carrying an umbrella and optimistically announcing that he had achieved "peace for our time." General rejoicing swept Britain and France, as well as other nervous nations, over having averted a ruinous war. But events were soon to show that the two democracies had only appeased the voracious appetite of an irresponsible Hitler. "Munich" became a dirty one-word slogan, virtually synonymous with Chamberlain's "umbrella appeasement" or "surrender on the installment plan."

"Appeasement" itself was the term increasingly applied to the practice of progressively throwing the weakest occupant of the sleigh to the pursuing wolves in the hope that their hunger would be appeased and they would end the pursuit. Hitler's appetite, as events proved, was insatiable, and the word "appeasement" unfortunately came to mean any mutual adjustment, reasonable or unreasonable, with a rapacious foe. Ever since that day various drafts of desirable compromises have gone into the wastebasket lest a popular outcry against "appeasement" and "Munich" be raised by the voters at home. People often overreact to the lessons of history, rather than learning from them.

Still unappeased, Hitler began to beat the drums for the free city of Danzig and the Polish corridor, both of which had lain within German borders until 1919. The British and the French were eager to make some kind of defensive alliance with Communist Russia that would restrain Hitler. "Why die for Danzig?" was a watchword heard in the Western democracies as the passion for appeasement continued. But Stalin neatly turned the tables on the crestfallen French and British by negotiating a pact with Hitler behind their backs. Under its terms, the two dictators would divide Poland between them, as they soon did. Given this green light, the German hosts burst into Poland from the west on September 1, 1939, and Stalin came in from the rear for a conspirator's share of the loot. Britain and France reluctantly declared war on Germany after the invasion of Poland, thus honoring their public pledges of support.

In 1914, when the guns of August began to boom, Wilson had asked his fellow citizens to be neutral even in thought. In 1939 Franklin Roosevelt must have been aware of the futility of such counsel when he declared at the outset of World War II, "This nation must remain a neutral nation, but I cannot ask that every American remain neutral in thought as well."

American sympathies were overwhelmingly on the side of the Western democracies, although few citizens at this stage wanted their nation to join in the fray. Feeling secure behind their ocean moat, many people could endorse the slogan "Isn't It Great to Be an American?" while the American Legion embraced the motto "Keep Out—Keep Ready." Other citizens, particularly as the war waxed hotter, reversed a slogan of World War I when they declared, "The Yanks are not coming."

Urgently needed was a revamping of the neutrality legislation of the

1930s, which placed rigid restrictions on the shipment of arms to the embattled democracies of Western Europe. The new and hotly debated Neutrality Act of 1939, among other provisions, permitted the democracies to purchase arms on the basis of "cash and carry" or "cash on the barrelhead." American ships were forbidden to enter the danger zones, with the result that purchasers would have to transport munitions in their own ships. In this way, the United States could presumably keep out of the fighting by pursuing "storm-cellar neutrality."

Hitler's mechanized might flattened Poland in an amazing three weeks of horror. Then came a lull from September to the following spring, as Hitler shifted his fearsome striking force to the western front. This was the quiet period that bored journalists referred to as "the phony war." The tedium was somewhat relieved by Stalin's assault on tiny Finland to secure more territory with which to defend himself against his two-faced accomplice Hitler. "Brave little Finland," as it was known in America, put up an astonishing fight against powerful Russia, but in the end was flattened. Americans cheered the white-clad Finns and granted them some financial concessions, but would not involve the United States against the aggressor by sending badly needed arms. If the Western democracies, which had sent "too little too late," had gone to war with Russia over Finland, the course of the global conflict would certainly have been vastly different.

BRITAIN'S FINEST HOUR

Witticisms about the "phony war" soured overnight in the spring of 1940 when Hitler struck furiously at Norway and Denmark. He next turned against Holland, Belgium, and France, where he outflanked the supposedly impregnable steel-and-concrete defenses of the Maginot Line, routed the French Army, and narrowly missed trapping the remaining British expeditionary force. Some 300,000 Allied soldiers, mostly British, were extricated by boat and ship in the perilous "miracle of Dunkirk." Winston S. Churchill, recently made Prime Minister, rallied the British people in a series of defiant speeches, notably with the Churchillism that resolutely promised, "I have nothing to offer but blood, toil, tears, and sweat." With indomitable spirit, "the British race," so called by their leader, defiantly sang "There'll Always Be an England."

As the German hordes were about to enter Paris, Mussolini deemed it safe to declare war on France and come in for the jackal's share of the loot. Aroused by this cowardly thrust from the rear, President Roosevelt, in a speech at the University of Virginia, undiplomatically vented his wrath by saying, "The hand that held the dagger has struck it into the back of its neighbor." F.D.R.'s barb was hardly neutral, but it touched a responsive chord in America.

Britain's plight grew more desperate, especially after Hitler launched his devastating aerial "blitz" against the island's poorly defended cities.

One noteworthy result was to blast away in America much of the isolationist spirit that had found expression in the neutrality legislation of the 1930s. If Britain surrendered, leaving the British Navy in German hands, the security of the United States would be gravely jeopardized. From countless lips one heard such expressions as "Britain is fighting our fight" and "Give aid to Britain by all methods short of war." Lapel buttons also advised, "Defend U.S. by Aiding Allies" and "Help the Allies Now."

Most vocal and influential of the "Bail out Britain" organizations was the Committee to Defend America by Aiding the Allies. Its members had a large hand in the "Bundles for Britain" movement, which gathered free food as well as clothing. Posters issued under these auspices bore such messages as "Help! Defend America by Aid to Britain," "Stop This [German bombing of babies]—Help Britain—Stop Hitler," and "Help England—And It Won't Happen Here" (woman and two children in a bomb shelter). One especially striking placard carried the appeal "For America's Sake Help Britain *Now!*" It featured a tombstone with a German swastika at the top, below which appeared the names Austria, Czecho-Slovakia, Poland, Denmark, Norway, Holland, Belgium, France, Great Britain—and U.S. An arrow pointed at U.S. with the two words "After Britain."

"Aid the Allies" forces encountered strong opposition from various isolationist "peace bloc" groups, notably the America First Committee, whose most distinguished spokesman was the famed aviator Colonel Charles A. Lindbergh. (Roosevelt branded the America Firsters "Copperheads.") Favorite watchwords of these isolationists were such sentiments as "England will fight to the last American" and "Defend America first." Lindbergh stirred up a hornet's nest when he declared during an address in Iowa, "The three most important groups which are pressing this country toward war are the British, the Jewish, and the Roosevelt administration." In 1940 Colonel Lindbergh's wife Anne published her book *The Wave of the Future*, in which she wrote, "The Wave of the Future is coming and there is no fighting in it." Some isolationists still believed at this late date in the saying "You can do business with Hitler."

Battered Britain was so gravely beset by German submarines that early in September 1940, despite the laws and obligations of neutrality, Roosevelt transferred to it fifty destroyers left over from World War I. The British, for their part, granted to the United States a chain of eight base sites ranging from Newfoundland to British Guiana. American defenses could thus be erected as a "protective girdle of steel," and Roosevelt informed Congress that "this is the most important action in the reinforcement of our national defense that has been taken since the Louisiana Purchase." The "destroyer deal," so called, was bitterly denounced by isolationists and many Republicans, including the recently nominated presidential candidate Wendell Willkie. He castigated the swap as "the most arbitrary and dictatorial action ever taken by any President."

WILLKIE CHALLENGES "THE "CHAMP"

Office-deprived Republicans met in Philadelphia in late June 1940, shortly before the "blitz" known as the Battle of Britain began. Knowing full well that Roosevelt would run for an "unthinkable" third term, they cast about for a candidate who could stand up to' "The Champ," as Democrats called him. Turning aside from the most available prospects, the delegates astonished the political world by nominating Wendell Willkie amid overpowering chants of "We want Willkie" from "Willkie Amateurs" in the galleries. A tousle-haired Indiana lawyer, Willkie had until recently been a Democrat and also the high-salaried head of a giant utilities company, Commonwealth and Southern.

Democratic detractors branded this newcomer from the "power trust" as "the rich man's Roosevelt" and "the simple barefoot Wall Street lawyer." Anti-Republican campaign buttons cynically supported "Willkie for President—of Commonwealth and Southern," and urged, "Keep Roosevelt in Whitehouse—Willkie in Powerhouse." Other jibes were "We Millionaires Want Willkie" and "Willkie for the Millionaires—Roosevelt for the Millions."

Democratic politicos, burying their differences as best they could under the slogan "Love Thine Enemy," met in Chicago the next month. The issues of preparedness and of possible involvement in the European war were bound to loom large, and here Roosevelt lent a hand. He himself advised adding a phrase, "except in case of attack," to the plank denying any intention to "participate in foreign wars." Later he was less cautious.

Roosevelt, a time-tested winner, was bound to be the nominee. Following a pro-F.D.R. nominating speech, a giant amplifying system blared out, "Illinois wants Roosevelt," "America wants Roosevelt," and even "The world wants Roosevelt." An investigation revealed that the voice, coming from the electrician's office in the basement, actually belonged to Chicago's superintendent of sewers. Such lowly support added "the voice from the sewer" to the American political lexicon.

Prominent slogans in the prenomination campaign were "Draft Roosevelt for Re-election" and "America Calls." Obviously the New Deal and the third term would be the leading issues in the ensuing canvass ("No third term"), but more important to many voters was the desirability of having an experienced statesman in the Presidential chair while the Western world seemed to be falling to Naziism and fascism. "Better a third term than a third-rater" was the watchword of many Democrats, as they backed such sentiments as "Stick with Roosevelt," "Just Roosevelt," and "Repeat with Roosevelt or Repent with Willkie."

Not surprisingly, the Willkie-Roosevelt third-term campaign witnessed an enormous outpouring of slogans, most of them printed on about 80 million official and unofficial buttons. Common appeals were "We Want Willkie," "America Wants Willkie," "Willkie or Bust," "The American

Way with Willkie," and "Win with Willkie." One Democratic retort asked "Win What with Willkie?" Republicans reminded the voters of the candidate's earlier Democratic allegiance with "I am a Democrat for Willkie." An appeal to the female vote appeared in "We Women Want Willkie" and "Women's Rebellion Against Third Term." For his part, Willkie gravely affronted female voters by declaring that he would choose a new Secretary of Labor from the labor movement—"and it won't be a woman, either." This was an unsubtle slap at incumbent Frances Perkins, the first woman Cabinet member.

THE THIRD-TERMITES TRIUMPH

Much of the Republican sloganizing was aimed at the "third-termites." Various combinations produced "Eight Years Is Enough," "Strike Three F.D. You're Out," "Force Franklin at Third," and "Out! Stealing Third," which the Democrats countered with "Safe on Third." Ill-concealed eroticism appeared in "No Man Is Good Three Times." Historical precedent was invoked in "Washington Wouldn't, Grant Couldn't, Roosevelt Shouldn't." A feeble sort of joke, which became much less feeble in 1944, jibed, "No Fourth Term Either." Perhaps the sharpest response of the Democrats to all this condemnation of a third term was the revamping of an ancient proverb, "Two Good Terms Deserve Another."

Republican opposition to four more years was based more on fear of a dictatorship than on a rupturing of precedent. Among the many slogans belaboring this theme were "No Crown for Roosevelt" and "No Franklin the First." Distaste for the "My friends" fireside chats led to "My Friends but Not My Subjects," "My Friends, Good-bye," and "No More Fireside Chats." Especially vehement was the outcry "Roosevelt? No! No! 1000 Times NO!" Dislike of F.D.R. and his ruinous New Deal was summed up in "There's No Indispensable Man," "Roosevelt for Ex-President," "Perhaps Roosevelt Is All You Deserve," "No More New Deals—We Want a Square Deal," and "All I Have Left Is a Vote for Willkie."

Slogan makers for the G.O.P. were not backward about attacking Roosevelt's household, which had been much in the public eye. Among the various taunts were "No Royal Family" and "Papa, I wanna be a captain, too," which brought up the alleged impropriety of granting commissions to the President's sons. Mrs. Roosevelt, who was a vocal and visible champion of what she regarded as worthy causes, won unflattering recognition in such digs as "We don't want Eleanor either" and "Eleanor? No Soap." A slap at FDR's recreational activities came from the button, "No More Fishing Trips on Battleships."

Billboard and poster art received much attention from Willkie supporters who, evidently, had much more Wall Street money for this purpose than the anti-banker New Dealers. In these colorful displays the dictatorship theme got heavy emphasis. Featured were such thoughts as

"We Want Willkie—Third Term Means Dictatorship" and "Don't Tear Down the Statue of Liberty! Refuse Dictatorship." One billboard blared:

> In Russia—
> It's the Third International
> In Germany—
> It's the Third Reich
> In America—
> There must be
> NO THIRD TERM.

Along similar lines was the button badge:

> THINK
> Hitler *Nominated* Hitler
> Mussolini *Nominated* Mussolini
> Stalin *Nominated* Stalin
> Roosevelt *Nominated* Roosevelt
> DO YOU WANT A
> DICTATOR?

Roosevelt even became a religious issue in a huge poster warning:

> SAVE YOUR CHURCH!
> DICTATORS *HATE* RELIGION.
> VOTE STRAIGHT REPUBLICAN.

Nor did Republican political warriors spare the New Deal and all its works in outdoor advertising:

> 1932—11 million unemployed
> In 8 years—60 billion dollars spent
> 1940—Still 11 million unemployed
> That's Why
> We Want Willkie.

A large display picture of Willkie proclaimed the sentiment, presumably in his words, "It's not big business we have to fear. . . . It's big government." A common Republican slogan reflected a similar spirit: "Away with the New Deal and Its Inefficiency." One of the few effective responses by the Democrats in this flamboyant battle of the billboards was:

> Wall Street Wears a Willkie button
> America wears a Roosevelt Button.

Also

> Roosevelt's way is the American way
> America Needs Roosevelt.

Campaign songs of the old school were by now an endangered species, and those that remained were few and anemic. Aside from the shopworn "Happy Days Are Here Again," the Democrats managed to dig up

"Mister Roosevelt, Won't You Please Run Again?" At least three songs were entitled "We Want Willkie," and a fourth utilized the title "Win with Willkie." The time-honored tune "On the Banks of the Wabash" tirelessly reminded voters of the Republican candidate's Indiana birthplace.

Each of the two verbal gladiators uttered words that he later regretted. Willkie predicted that Roosevelt, if elected, would drag America into the war before April of 1941. He declared that if the Democrats kept their platform pledges of 1940 no more faithfully than those of 1932, "you better get ready to get on the transports." After the election he testified, "In moments of oratory in campaigns we all expand a bit," which newsmen translated into "mere campaign oratory." All this was especially damaging to the credibility of so high-minded a politician as Willkie.

Stung by his rival's charges of warmongering, Roosevelt let himself go in a Boston campaign speech before a cheering crowd: "I have said this before, but I shall say it again and again and again. Your boys are not going to be sent into any foreign wars." He had been urged to add "except in case of attack," but protested that it was unnecessary because obvious (and also in the Democratic platform). In point of fact, after the Japanese attacked Pearl Harbor, the war could hardly be called foreign.

As was his habit, "The Champ" handily defeated his amateurish opponent in November 1940. The "Don't swap horses" counsel of 1864 was no less valid seventy-six years later, when the voters had to choose between the known faults of F.D.R. and the unknown virtues of Wendell Willkie. Some historians have argued that the result was a clear mandate against the "two term" principle. On the contrary, the evidence indicates that Roosevelt, confronted with a grave international crisis, won in spite of the third-term issue, not because of it.

LEND-LEASING A WAR

Fearing adverse voter reactions, Roosevelt had carefully avoided hinting during the campaign that America should bail out Britain by a lend-lease program. During the month after he was safely elected, he grew bolder when he told a press conference, "The best defense of Great Britain is the best defense of the United States." In a fireside chat he declared, "We must be the great arsenal of democracy." In addressing Congress in January 1941 he sought support for the "four essential human freedoms" everywhere "in the world." He found them to be "freedom of speech and expression," "freedom to worship God," "freedom from want," and "freedom from fear."

As for aiding the Allies, chiefly Britain, Roosevelt's plan was to lend or lease military material to those nations resisting aggression. His thought was that this equipment would not be sold but could be returned or otherwise replaced when the war was over, like a borrowed garden hose. F.D.R. was striving to avoid another quarrel over Allied war debts by eliminating from the deal "the silly foolish old dollar sign."

Roosevelt's lend-lease scheme was introduced into Congress as Bill H.R. 1776, a patriotic touch deliberately contrived. The official title was "An Act Further to Promote the Defense of the United States"; the basic philosophy found expression in the slogan "Send Guns, Not Sons." "Aid the Allies" partisans enthusiastically favored the proposal, but a few criticized it as selfishly immoral: America would export weapons for its own defense so that the Allies could fight to the last Britisher or Frenchman. If the republic had a moral commitment, why not get into the fight with both feet?

Isolationists voiced vehement opposition to what they called "the blank-check bill" and this "Dictator, War, Bankruptcy Bill." One of their slogans was "Kill 1776—Not American Boys." Senator Robert Taft of Ohio scoffed, "Lending war equipment is a good deal like lending chewing gum. You don't want it back." Isolationist Senator Burton Wheeler, referring to Roosevelt's program for destroying surplus crops, branded lend-lease the "New Deal's 'triple A' foreign policy—to plow under every fourth American boy." An angry F.D.R. snapped back in a press conference, "That really is the rottenest thing that has been said in public life in my generation."

After prolonged and bitter debate, Congress voted for lend-lease by more than a two-to-one margin in March 1941. In this way the United States formally pledged itself to lend "defense articles" to those governments "whose defense the President deems vital to the defense of the United States."

Following passage of the lend-lease law, America's Depression-throttled industrial machine began to roar into high gear. The slogan of the hour became "Make America the Arsenal and Larder of Democracy," as the nation's preparedness program aimed at a war footing. U.S. defense savings bonds and stamps were floated with the appeal "Buy a Share in America." Flaming posters urged, "Keep the Home Fires Burning" and "You Are a Production Soldier—America's First Line of Defense is Here." Workers were warned by placards, "Our enemies try to upset production soldiers with cooked-up lies . . . Don't Swallow All You Hear . . . It may be poison! A well-placed *Lie* can do more damage than a bomb." Another poster showed a worker playing "God Bless America" on the "Defense Production" organ. "And it will be 'GOD HELP AMERICA' if the organ BREAKS DOWN!!"

ALL-OUT SHOOTING

An astonishing turn of events came in June 1941, when Hitler suddenly unleashed an overpowering "blitzkrieg" against Stalin, his erstwhile accomplice in the dismemberment of Poland. Misery and war make strange bedfellows, and the sins of Stalin, "The Sphinx of the Kremlin," now looked less black. After investigation, Roosevelt found the defense of the Soviet Union "vital to the defense of the United States" and started a trickle of lend-lease equipment to the Russians—"Lenin lease" said critics —that ultimately swelled to a value of some 11 billion dollars.

Snuggling ever closer to embattled Britain with lend-lease shipments, Roosevelt met secretly with Prime Minister Churchill on a British battle-ship in Newfoundland waters in August 1941. From this clandestine conference emerged a document known as the Atlantic Charter, which set forth "common principles" upon which peoples could "base their hopes for a better future for the world." Among various avowed objec-tives were self-determination, plus two of Roosevelt's "Four Freedoms" (freedom from want and fear), freedom of the seas, and also a "perma-nent system of general security," which ultimately became the United Nations.

Lurking German submarines were meanwhile torpedoing Allied ships carrying lend-lease supplies. As could have been expected, pressure mounted from "Aid the Allies" zealots for convoying such freighters with U.S. destroyers. During the debates over lend-lease in Congress, the iso-lationists had voiced fears that Roosevelt would ultimately "convoy us into war," but such objections were brushed aside. In April 1941 F.D.R. issued secret orders for American destroyers to assist the British in their convoy operations. In November he induced Congress to repeal the "crippling provisions" of the Neutrality Act of 1939 so as to permit de-fensively armed American merchant ships to enter the submarine-infested combat zones. They would be instructed to fight back against Hitler's "modern pirates." The old "storm-cellar neutrality" was thus being com-pletely thrown overboard. Ironically, some of the opposition to repeal in the House developed over the failure of Roosevelt to push proposed antistrike legislation, and the slogan of some members was "Get John L. Lewis first—then Hitler."

A clash with German submarines was inevitable, and it began in September 1941 in the Atlantic. A U-boat unsuccessfully attacked the U.S. destroyer *Greer,* which had been trailing the submarine for more than three hours and broadcasting its position to nearby British patrols. Concealing the tell-tale facts, Roosevelt went on the radio to condemn this act of "piracy" and to announce that these "rattlesnakes of the At-lantic" would henceforth be attacked in defense of a free sea. In October the U.S. destroyer *Kearny* was damaged (eleven Americans lost) and the U.S. destroyer *Reuben James* was sunk (about 100 lives lost). The United States was now involved in an undeclared naval war with Germany in the Atlantic.

An astounding stab-in-the-back eruption followed, not in the Atlantic but in the Pacific, where least expected. The Washington government, fearful of Japanese domination in the Far East and the Pacific, had at-tempted to thwart Tokyo's attempt to create a "co-prosperity sphere in Greater East Asia." American disfavor mounted, especially after the Nip-

"Give 'Em Both Barrels." Uncle Sam aroused by Japanese sneak attack at Pearl Harbor. The New Orleans *Times-Picayune*, 1941. Reproduced with permission of the New Orleans *Times-Picayune*.

ponese launched a full-scale invasion of China in what they delicately called "the China incident." Yet for many months Washington pursued a policy of partial appeasement by permitting American shippers to export to Japan mountains of scrap metal and other necessities of warfare.

Following new Japanese aggressions in French Indo-China, Washington acted decisively in July 1941. It "froze" Japanese assets in the United States and in other ways effectively stopped the outflow of war materiel to Japan, including oil and its derivatives. With limited supplies of disappearing fuel on hand, the Japanese warlords either had to knuckle under to American pressure or burst out. Driven to madness by the ticking time bomb and the dropping oil gauge, they burst out at Pearl Harbor, in the "sneak attack" on "Black Sunday," December 7, 1941.

Exploding Japanese torpedoes at Pearl Harbor almost literally sank isolationist "America Firstism." "The only thing now to do," insisted Senator Wheeler, "is to lick hell out of them." Roosevelt went before Congress to declare in solemn tones, "Yesterday, December 7, 1941—a day which will live in infamy—the United States was suddenly and deliberately attacked by naval and air forces of the Empire of Japan." He then asked for official recognition of the "state of war" which "has thus been thrust upon the United States." Congress obliged, overwhelmingly, and the nation found itself officially up to its ears in World War II.

XXIX

The War
of the Dictators

Now this is not the end. It is not even the beginning
of the end. But it is, perhaps, the end of the beginning.

> Prime Minister Churchill, November 10, 1942,
> after the Allied landing in North Africa

THE WORD WAR OF WORLD WAR II

Making the world safe for democracy may have been America's main
objective in World War I, but in World War II the cry was to make the
world safe against dictators. Patriotic citizens displayed buttons endorsing
such sentiments as "Halt Hitler," "To Hell with Hitler," "To Hell with the
Japs," and "To Hell with Hirohito." Smarting from the devastating sneak
attack at Pearl Harbor, vengeful citizens mounted a highly vocal
campaign whose battle cry was "Remember Pearl Harbor" and whose
aim was "Get Hirohito first." Other patriots, especially on the East coast,
urged "Get Hitler first." Obviously Japan would be easier to crush after
Germany was disposed of, and hence the main effort was directed at
Hitler's redoubtable "Fortress Europa."

Partial but misdirected revenge for Pearl Harbor came rather early.
About 110,000 Japanese-Americans, mostly on the Pacific coast, were
rounded up and imprisoned in "relocation centers" that were virtually
concentration camps. About two-thirds of them were American-born
citizens, but the commanding general of the Western Defense Command
insisted, "A Jap is a Jap," and a Mississippi Congressman turned an old
saying about Englishmen into "Once a Jap, always a Jap." Before the
forcible uprooting, numerous signs were posted warning, "No Japs

Wanted Here" and "No Japs Allowed." One vicious pamphlet flaunted the title *"Slap the Japs; No Jap is Fit to Associate with Human Beings."* Despite such atrocious treatment, these wronged Japanese-Americans proved to be loyal citizens, and they ultimately received limited financial recompense from the federal government that had so hysterically misjudged them.

So heavy an advantage did the democracies enjoy in population, wealth, and resources that they seemed bound to win—provided that they could gird themselves for an all-out production effort in time. President Roosevelt declared in a radio address in the third month of the war (February 23, 1942), "Never before have we had so little time in which to do so much." The year 1942 led to the popular sayings "Let's see it through in '42" and "Make America the arsenal of democracy." Songs surfaced like "Give Us the Tools," which was probably inspired by Churchill's earlier "Give us the tools and we will finish the job."

Under such pressures an entire nation enlisted "for the duration." Citizens were constantly reminded to drop "the business-as-usual attitude," and a common retort to complainers was "Don't you know there's a war on?" One colorful poster urged, "America—Open Your Eyes"; another showed a wounded Yankee machine gunner coupled with the appeal "Let's Give Him Enough on Time." Also to the point was "Go Without So They [the fighting men] Won't Have To." Aircraft production was spurred with "Say It With Flyers" and "Keep 'em Rolling, Keep 'em Flying, Keep Democracy from Dying."

As in World War I, wealthy "dollar-a-year men" came to Washington and gave cheerfully of their services. After natural rubber from East Asia was cut off at Pearl Harbor, a whole new synthetic rubber industry had to be launched under "Rubber Czar" William Jeffers. Scrap metal was needed for greatly expanded steel production, and scrap drives found support in such slogans as "Get in the Scrap," "Slap the Jap with Your Scrap," and "Cash for your Trash." Less refined was the reminder "Junk Ain't Junk No More 'Cause Junk Will Win the War."

SHORTENING THE SHORTAGES

As in 1917–18, a critical shortage of shipping had to be overcome, and the need found expression in the slogan "Ships for Victory." Riveters were egged on with posters showing a ship worker using his riveting machine alongside a machine gun. The caption read, "Give 'Em Both Barrels." A song for the times announced, "We Build 'Em, You Sail 'Em."

Official Washington was greatly concerned about losses that resulted from rumors and other indiscreet talk about ship movements. Poster captions warned, "Enemy Ears are Listening" and "Loose Lips Sink Ships." One clever song cautioned, "A Slip of the Lip Can Sink a Ship."

Slogans additionally advised, "Zip the Lip and Save a Ship," "Shut Your Traps and Beat the Japs," and "Be Smart—Act Dumb."

Laborers were urged to stay on the job. Official posters carried pointed messages: "Don't Let It [totalitarianism] Happen Here! Your Production Must Prevent It!" and "When you are A.W.O.L. [absent without leave] You're Working for the Axis." Safety was encouraged with such admonitions as "The Guy who Relaxes Helps the Axis." Despite such appeals to patriotism, some "wildcat strikes" erupted, notably among the accident-cursed United Mine Workers. As for threats to use the army, their defiant boss John L. Lewis again retorted, "You can't dig coal with bayonets." By the time the United States was fully geared for war, the Depression and unemployment were nightmares of the past. Roosevelt himself declared at a press conference late in 1943, that "Dr. New Deal" was being replaced by "Dr. Win the War."

Ration-book rationing, which America had avoided in World War I under the spell of idealism, now became imperative. Essentials such as food and gasoline were doled out, although some "gas hogs" were able to beat the system and get more than their share. Black marketeers and "meatleggers" were disturbingly common, despite the warning of an official poster, "Rationing Means a Fair Share for All of Us."

As in World War I, production and conservation of food were major concerns. One official poster warned, "Food is a Weapon, Don't Waste It! Buy Wisely—Cook Carefully—Eat it All." The Hooverizing days of World War I were brought back in "Our Food Is Fighting," "Food for Freedom," and "The Food You Save Can Help Win the War." Despite such appeals as "I Am Doing My Part—Are You?" hoarders abounded. A popular witticism ran, "I'm just stocking up before the hoarders get here."

Personalized "victory gardens" were encouraged, as in World War I, by the summons to "garden for victory." "Get Out and Dig, Dig, Dig" was the message of one song, while the sloganeers came up with "Grow More in '44." One poster caption urged, "Grow Your Own—Be Sure," which suggested both quantity and freshness. Such home-grown activity inspired the pointed pun "Weed 'em and reap."

A handmaiden of rationing was economizing. Housewives were advised to "Use It Up, Wear It Out, Make It Do or Do Without." A New York telephone company abandoned its plea "Don't write, telephone," in favor of "Use the mail whenever time permits this method of communication." Concern for the boys in uniform, popularly called G.I.s,* found vent in "Joe needs long-distance lines tonight." Other appeals encouraged more walking; one official poster bore the message "I'll Carry Mine, Too! Trucks and Tires Must Last Till Victory." The preservation of lumber was encouraged in the poster "Our Carelessness Their Secret Weapon. Prevent Forest Fires."

---

* G.I. stood for "government issue" of uniforms and other equipment.

WARRIORS OF BOTH SEXES

Slogans urging men to join the army were not especially needed; the draft (selective service) ultimately took care of most recruits. Capitalizing on the likelihood of being drafted, navy recruiters used such posters as "So Dish It out with the Navy. Choose Now While You Can" and "Join the Navy and *Free* the World." This was a clever variant of the peacetime call "Join the Navy and See the World."

Leather-necked Marines, seeking volunteers, were not backward about advertising their wares to the potential draftee. "Hit Hard and Often with the Marines" urged an official poster, which echoed the 1942 battle cry of Admiral William F. ("Bull") Halsey, "Hit Hard, Hit Fast, Hit Often."

Seabees, the construction battalions of the U.S. Navy, had a proud image of their own. Their motto was "We Build, We Fight," and their slogans were "Can Do!" and "First to Land and Last to Leave." The Seabees greeted the Marines, when they reached New Georgia in the South Pacific in September 1943, with the immortal words "The Seabees are always happy to welcome the Marines." The motto of the U.S. Army Corps of Engineers was "The difficult we do immediately. The impossible takes a little longer." With slight variations this ultimate in boasts was used by other branches of the armed services.

Women warriors, sometimes called "Victory Girls," were also urgently needed in this so-called "war for survival." One of their posters proudly announced, "I'm in this War Too." Members of the Women's Reserve of the Marine Corps were officially known as Marines, not "WAMS" or "Marinettes," although they sometimes unofficially and jocularly called themselves "Femarines," "Jungle Juliets," or "Leather Nectarines" (after the male Leathernecks). One of their poster captions read, "Be a Marine. . . . Free a Marine to Fight." Women in the navy, who "went down to the sea in slips," were officially known as WAVES, contrived from "Women Accepted for Voluntary Emergency Service." One of their posters advised, "Enlist in the Waves, Release a Man to Fight at Sea." The SPARS, whose name was derived from the U.S. Coast Guard motto "Semper Paratus" (Always Ready), were the women's branch of the Coast Guard. These volunteers were ingeniously publicized with a poster whose caption was printed on a picture of a spare tire: "Don't Be a Spare. Be a Spar."

WAACS, of the Women's Army Auxiliary Corps, used such recruiting slogans as "Speed Them [the men] Back. Join the WAAC" and "I'd Rather Be With Them—than Waiting for Them." Posters pleaded, "Back the Attack, Be a WAAC! For America is Calling" and "I Have Freed a Marine to Fight. You Can Do It Too." A throwback to World War I appeared in the song "The WAACS and WAVES Will Win the War, *Parlez Vous.*"

Women unquestionably played a significant role in winning the war, including "the new amazons" in the labor force. One song, "Rosie the

Riveter," hailed the females doing men's jobs in the shipyard, with the likelihood that Rosie's offspring would become "shipyard orphans" or juvenile delinquents. With obvious reference to the Jack and Jill of Mother Goose fame, girl lumberjacks were called "lumber jills." Song titles that told a feminized story were "We're the Janes Who Make the Planes," "The Lady at Lockheed," "Fighting on the Home Front Wins," and "The Woman behind the Man Behind the Gun."

SLOGANS AND SONGS OF VICTORY

Most of the slogans of World War II, especially those printed on buttons, seem to have been aimed at Axis foes. Included were "V for Victory,"* "Axe the Axis," "Kick 'Em in the Axis," "U.S. Will Lick Hell Out of Them," and "Exterminate the Rats." German Nazis bore the brunt of "Swat the Swastika," "Pack Up Hitler—The Yankees are Coming," and "Reserved for Hitler," with a picture of gallows on the button. Even the loud-mouthed Mussolini received some attention in "To Hell with Mussie" and "Ill Duce" (Il Duce).

The Japanese, thanks largely to the universal outcry of "Remember Pearl Harbor," appear to have been the chief victims of venom. Eye-catching slogans were "Hang Hirohito," "Let's Blast the Japs Clean off the Map," "The U.S. Will Take the Nip out of Nipponese," "Down with the Rising Sun," and "Let's Go to Tokyo." Special buttons called for "Swat the Jap," "On Your Knees You Japanese," "We'll Pay Them Back for Their Sneak Attack," "Japan Started It—U.S. Will End It," and "Moider Them Japs" (in Brooklynese). One poster noted, "For years the Japs wanted our Scrap! Save Now and Let 'Em Have it." A special group of posters, designed to win support in Latin America, carried the words "United Against Aggression," "Fight for a Free America," "Hands off the Americas," and "21 Republics—One Destiny."

Tin-pan alley, responding to the call of patriotism and a "fast buck," poured out such highly perishable musical titles as "Slap the Jap Right off the Map," "We'll Knock the Japs Right into the Laps of the Nazis," and "You're a Sap, Mr. Jap (to Make a Yankee Cranky)." In a similar vein were "We're Gonna Have to Slap the Dirty Little Jap (and Uncle Sam's the Guy Who Can Do It)," "They're Going to Be Playing Taps for the Japs," and "The Japs Haven't Got a Chinaman's Chance."

Other songs aimed at the treacherous little yellow men resorted to grim humor. Those of a more general nature carried such titles as "The Sun Will Soon Be Setting on the Land of the Rising Sun" and "We Are the Sons of the Rising Guns." Geography figured in "Goodbye, Momma, I'm Off to Yokohama" and "To Be Specific, It's Our Pacific." Pejoratively

---

* Prime Minister Churchill had often evoked cheers by defiantly holding up two spread fingers in the victory sign. Some of the Russians mistakenly interpreted this gesture as a promise of a second front.

personal were "Oh, You Little Son of an Oriental" and "When Those Little Yellow Bellies Meet the Cohens and the Kelleys."

Adolf Hitler and Benito Mussolini, largely because they were white and had not engineered a sneak attack against the United States, came off better than the Japanese in the war songs. Among them were "Put the Heat on Hitler" and "Let's Knock the Hit out of Hitler." The posturing Italian dictator got his lumps in "Bye, Bye, Benito" and "Muss up Mussolini and Tie a Can to Japan." Also barbed were "Let's Put the Axe to the Axis" and "There'll Be a Hot Time in the Town of Berlin (When the Yanks Go Marching In)."

In 1917–18 America had fought for lofty ideals: for democracy and to end wars. In 1941 the republic was forced into a war against power-mad dictatorships, and it did the dirty job that had to be done with cold efficiency. Probably for this reason the conflict was not a great singing war. Perhaps the only noteworthy song of arousal was "Praise the Lord and Pass the Ammunition," inspired by the words of a chaplain during the attack at Pearl Harbor. A more popular composition, written by Irving Berlin in 1918 but not released until 1939, was "God Bless America." A song of consecration rather than of excitation, it caught the popular mood. It may have inspired the button slogans "God Bless America—The Flag I Love" and "Thank God I am an American."

Various patriotic tunes boasted such titles as "Gee, Isn't It Great to be an American?" "Let's Put New Glory in Old Glory," and "When the Lights Go On Again All over the World." Still other compositions were primarily concerned with the embattled fighting men: "Say a Prayer for the Boys over There," "Don't Steal the Sweetheart of a Soldier," "The Army's Made a Man out of Me," and "Johnny Got a Zero." This last title did not refer to a bad report card, but to Johnny's having shot down a Zero—one of the swift and much-feared Japanese fighter planes.

Other tunes reflected other times and moods. Among them were "We Did It Before" and "I'm a Son of a Son of a Yankee Doodle Dandy." Aside from the unprintable verses of "Dirty Gertie of Bizerte" and "The Daughter of Mademoiselle from Armentières," there were not a great many risque songs. A few tunes, chiefly from movies, bore such suggestive titles as "You Can't Say No to a Soldier," "He Loved Me till the All-Clear Came," "Love Isn't Born, It's Made," "If He Can Fight Like He Can Love," "I'm Doin' It for Defense," and "The Bigger the Army and Navy Is, the Better the Loving Will Be."

Additionally, various songs commemorated the Allies, especially England. Self-revealing titles were "The White Cliffs of Dover" and "My British Buddy." Stalin, once distrusted for his war-launching pact with Hitler, took on a much better odor as an ally, especially after the highly popular movie "Mission to Moscow" pictured the ruthless dictator as a kindly, smiling, pipe-smoking, grandfatherly "Uncle Joe." Composers in America were prompted to cook up such short-lived titles as "And Still the Volga Flows," "That Russian Winter," and "You Can't Brush Off a

Russian." Especially pointed after the epochal Soviet victory at Stalingrad was "Stalin Wasn't Stallin'." Even the Latin American nations were not neglected by the song writers, as indicated by "Hands across the Border" and "Good Night, Good Neighbor."

DELIVERING DOLLARS AND AIDING ALLIES

One contribution that most adults and many minors could make to the costly war effort was to lend money to the government by buying war bonds or savings stamps. More pleas in songs, slogans, mottoes, and posters dealt with this theme than with perhaps any other. Songsmiths did their earnest bit with such monetary appeals as "Dig Down Deep," "Get aboard the Bond Wagon," and "I Paid My Income Tax Today." This must surely be the only song ever written about the income tax. A slogan also turned up on this theme: "Pay Your Taxes, Beat the Axis."

Catchwords backed the bond-buying blitz. Among the more memorable were "Get in the Scrap or Buy a Share of America" and "If You Can't Go Over, Come Across." No less pointed were "Back the Attack—Buy More than Ever Before," "Let's Go—for the Knockout Blow," "They Give Their Lives—You Lend Your Money," and "You've Done Your Bit. Now Do Your Best!" An especially appropriate gift suggestion for the Christmas season of 1942 was "A Present with a Future." Another poster appeal, appropriately illustrated and supporting war bonds, read "Save Freedom of Worship" and "Save Freedom of Speech."

Special pleas to purchasers of savings stamps urged "Keep the War News Good by Buying War Stamps and Bonds" and "Stamp Out Hitler with Defense Stamps." Realizing that small buyers made the difference in "going over the top," the Washington government requested citizens to "back the attack" by buying E bonds, the "little man's bonds." Female purchasers were exhorted in a poster caption, "Be The Woman Behind the Man Behind the Gun. Buy War Stamps Here Today."

Various drives were designed to collect books, especially for men in the service. "Books are Bullets" declared one official slogan. An arresting poster proclaimed, "Books Cannot Be Killed by Fire. . . . Books are Weapons in the War of Ideas." Special slogans for the "Victory Book Campaign" included, "Praise the Lord and Pass the New Editions."

Titles of some of the volumes published during the war were in the nature of slogans and in themselves had considerable impact. A prominent contribution was William L. White's *They Were Expendable* (1942), which honored the last-ditch American defenders of the Philippines. Wendell Willkie's *One World* (1943), an anti-isolationist book, sold more than 3 million copies. It helped to condition America's mind to accept the role of leadership in the formation and launching of the United Nations Organization. "Freedom," Willkie wrote, "is an indivisible word."

ON TO TOKYO!

Fighting against the Japanese had meanwhile been going badly. "See you in Tokyo" became a stock phrase in the armed forces that at first seemed like whistling in the dark. American and Filipino defenders of the Philippines were driven to the peninsula of Bataan, where they desperately held on as "expendables" in an effort to delay the Japanese onslaught. Finally realizing that they could expect no reinforcements from America, many of them subscribed to the cynical jingle:

> We're the battling bastards of Bataan;
> No mama, no papa, no Uncle Sam;
> No aunts, no uncles, no cousins, no nieces;
> No pills, no planes, no artillery pieces.
> . . . . And nobody gives a damn.

The heroic army nurses were called "angels of Bataan," and the brutal "Bataan death march" came after final surrender and atrociously inhumane treatment, for which General Yamashita, commanding in the area, was hanged after the war. "Remember Bataan" became a vengeful slogan, and one wartime movie flaunted the title "Back to Bataan." From this tragic experience came the words of one field sermon, "There are no atheists in fox holes."

Before the end came General MacArthur was ordered to flee the Philippines by fast boat to Australia, there to command the forces assembling to resist the feared Japanese onslaught from the north. Upon leaving his post in the Philippines he declared with unrealistic optimism, "I shall return." After reaching Australia, he further pledged, "I came through and I shall return." Several days later he ringingly proclaimed, "I shall keep a soldier's faith."

MacArthur became the first Grade A American hero of the war. He attained this status despite his association with the most humiliating surrender in the field to a foreign foe in United States history and despite the groundless charge that he had deserted his men under fire. Songs of the hour were "Here's to You MacArthur" and "Hats Off to MacArthur and Our Boys Down There."

Elsewhere in the Pacific and Southeast Asia the war had gone badly for the United States. American airmen, based in the India-Burma theater, could fly only minor quantities of supplies "over the hump" of the Himalayas to their Chinese ally, Chiang Kai-shek. The Burma campaign collapsed in 1942, with General Joseph W. ("Vinegar Joe") Stilwell blurting out, "I claim we got a hell of a beating. We got run out of Burma and it is humiliating as hell."

Gradually rising from the mud of Pearl Harbor, the navy began to hold the line and even inflict heavy defeats on the enemy. Early in 1942 a U.S. Navy pilot, Donald F. Mason, while on antisubmarine patrol, reported, with twice as many words as necessary, "Sighted sub, sank same." After the Americans worsted the Japanese in the Battle of the Coral Sea (May 1942), Lieutenant Commander Robert E. Dixon sent the message, "Scratch one flat-top (Japanese aircraft carrier)." Early in June 1942 the navy inflicted lethal losses on the Japanese during the crucial Battle of Midway, which, curiously, seems to have inspired no memorable slogan or song. In the Battle of the Solomon Islands, in November 1942, the outclassed cruiser *San Francisco* sped between two lines of Japanese warships, crippled a battleship, and polished off a cruiser and a destroyer. "We'll take the big ones first!" were the immortal words of the commander, Rear Admiral Daniel J. Callaghan.

America's ruthless submarine campaign against the Japanese merchant fleet proved so effective as to bring Japan to the verge of starvation. In commending these heroic submariners, Admiral Chester W. Nimitz declared (in the tradition of Perry at Lake Erie in 1813), "You have met the enemy and the enemy is yours." One memorable saying came out of this underseas warfare. "Take her down" was the last heroic command of the wounded Commander Howard W. Gilmore in 1943. He sacrificed his life rather than risk the delay involved in reentering his submarine from the conning tower in the face of imminent Japanese attack.

THE COLLAPSE OF TWO EMPIRES

Assaulting Hitler's Fortress Europe seemed like a well-nigh impossible dream. But the Russians, in desperate shape from the German invasion, clamored incessantly for a "second front" in France that would divert attacking Nazi manpower to the west. The Allies held out hope of a second front in 1942, then again in 1943, and finally delivered in 1944, when the prospects of success were still touch and go.

Prime Minister Churchill, remembering appalling British losses in France during World War I, dragged his feet. He much preferred some kind of diversion directed at the "soft underbelly" of Europe. Roosevelt compromised in 1942 on a smaller-scale substitute by agreeing to attack French-held North Africa. There the German "Desert Fox," Marshal Erwin Rommel, had driven eastward with his tanks from Tunis all the way across North Africa almost to the vital Suez Canal. Command of the amphibious African operation was assigned to General Dwight D. Eisenhower, who subsequently headed the gigantic D-day operation in France. American song writers responded gallantly when they contributed "The Man of the Hour Is Eisenhower" and "A Prayer for General Eisenhower and His Men." After much bitter fighting, the German forces in North Africa were destroyed in 1943, and Prime Minister Churchill could tell the American Congress, "One continent redeemed."

Success in landing on North Africa soil led to a top-level conference at Casablanca, Morocco, in January 1943. With Churchill's full agreement, Roosevelt proclaimed "Unconditional Surrender" as the policy to be adopted toward the Axis enemy. The phrase, borrowed from General

Willst Du Der Letzte Tote Des Krieges Sein? ("Do You Want to Be the Last Dead of the War?") U.S. propaganda leaflet of World War II directed at German soldiers. Hoover Institution, Stanford University.

Grant of Civil War days, rapidly became a war-aim slogan. Debate continues among historians as to whether the seductive effect of "Unconditional Surrender" was more than offset by steeling the foe to a last-ditch fight. The Nazis responded with a counterslogan, "Unconditional Resistance." Possibly Roosevelt's objective could have been better served by a softer term, perhaps "Honorable Capitulation."

Victory in North Africa lured the Allies into Sicily, where the American General Terry Allen, in the spirit of John Paul Jones, declared, "Hell, we haven't started to fight. Our artillery hasn't been overrun yet." Next came the supposedly "soft" boot of not-so-sunny Italy, which tried to drop out of the war. But the Germans would not drop out of Italy, and the Allied invaders became bogged down in a brutal, meat-grinding move northward.

Long delayed, the mammoth D-day invasion of France by the Allies came in June 1944. At the time General Eisenhower described it as a "crusade" and his later book on the European campaign was entitled *Crusade in Europe* (1948). After the Allied invaders had encountered stiff resistance and a temporary check, a breakout was achieved. The most spectacular advances were executed by General ("Blood and Guts") Patton, whose watchword was "Go forward, always go forward." Paris was liberated in August 1944, and American G.I.s reportedly served notice, "Lafayette, we are here again."

In desperation, Hitler threw his reserves into a surprise drive through the fog-shrouded forest of southeast Belgium. The 101st Airborne Division, under U.S. General Anthony C. McAuliffe, trapped at Bastogne, replied to the German demand for surrender with the single slang word "Nuts." The enemy was puzzled but got the message when the Americans continued to resist successfully. "Nuts"—meaning roughly "Go to hell"—quickly became one of America's most memorable wartime slogans.

Recovering lost ground, the Allied forces crossed the Rhine River and joined hands with the advancing Russians at the Elbe River in Germany. The days of Hitler's "Thousand Year Empire" were numbered, and, shortly after Der Führer's suicide, "Victory in Europe Day"—"V-E Day" for short—came on May 8, 1945.

Last-ditch fighting in the Pacific had meanwhile entered its final phases. Rather than attempt to capture each Japanese island stronghold, Washington adopted the policy of "leapfrogging" a number of these heavily fortified outposts, leaving them to "ripen on the vine." In November 1943 "Bloody Tarawa" or "Terrible Tarawa" was successfully assaulted and Makin Island was captured ("Makin Taken" was the terse message sent by General Ralph Smith). In October 1944 General MacArthur, after a delay of two and a half years, theatrically waded ashore in Philippine waters and declared, "People of the Philippines: I have returned! By the grace of Almighty God, our forces stand again on Philippine soil. . . . The hour of your redemption is here. . . . Rally to me."

Tiny Iwo Jima, an almost impregnable island fortress in the Pacific, was bloodily taken by American marines in February 1945. As Admiral Nimitz reported, "Uncommon valor was a common virtue." A photographer caught the historic flag raising by four of the invaders, and this dramatic picture became world-famous. The incident inspired at least two songs in America, "Stars and Stripes on Iwo Jima" and "There's a New Flag on Iwo Jima." In the same month, after MacArthur's troops captured Manila, the cry was "On to Tokyo!"

Vengeful punishment fell on Japan, in August 1945, when its "bamboo empire" collapsed under two horrendous atomic bombs—"the blasts heard 'round the world." America had won the battle of the laboratories, despite scoffing among military men about "damned professors' nonsense." President Truman, now in the White House, declared, "We have spent two billion dollars on the greatest scientific gamble in history—and won." Boundless rejoicing in America greeted V-J Day—the day of victory over Japan.

THE FOURTH-TERM ISSUE IN '44

As the scheduled presidential election of 1944 approached, much talk could be heard of postponing this diversionary domestic ordeal "for the duration." But the Constitution prevailed. Again the familiar cry was raised about not swapping horses in midstream; indeed, there were strong reasons for not replacing Roosevelt, the winning quarterback, while the war was crashing victoriously to an end. Again one heard a call for the "indispensable man."

Reelection for an unheard-of fourth term seemed less of an achievement in 1944 than reelection for a third had in 1940, despite Roosevelt's obvious ageing. In 1940 the question of breaking the hoary two-term tradition was an issue; now it was dead. F.D.R. did not seem as coy as in 1940, for he issued a statement declaring, "If the convention should nominate me for the Presidency, I shall accept. If the people elect me I shall serve." The Democrats in Chicago uproariously renominated Roosevelt in July 1944.

A ticklish problem arose in connection with the prospective renomination of the sitting Vice President, Henry A. Wallace. His ultraliberal views about the "century of the common man" had alarmed conservative politicians, all the more so since F.D.R.'s health was visibly crumbling and only "one heartbeat" was keeping Wallace out of the White House. In 1942 the left-leaning Vice President had made a speech in which he proclaimed, "The object of this war is to make sure that everybody in the world has the privilege of drinking a quart of milk a day." The dairy industry applauded, but this visionary goal was quickly twisted into "Milk for the [African] Hottentots," much to the annoyance of Wallace and the glee of conservatives. Acid-tongued Congresswoman Clare Boothe Luce declared in the House of Representatives, "Much of what Mr. Wallace calls his global thinking is, no matter how you slice it, still 'globaloney.' " In the face of this ridicule a "Ditch Wallace" movement gained such momentum that the "wild-eyed dreamer" was "dumped" in favor of Senator Harry S. Truman of Missouri, despite wild chants from the convention galleries, "We want Wallace." This cavalier discarding of the incumbent Vice President became known in political circles as "the second Missouri Compromise."

Wallace's awkward exit gave birth to an embarrassing slogan. A possible replacement, presumably favored by Roosevelt, was James F. Byrnes, a prominent war administrator. At a meeting of the Democratic leaders, one spokesman reminded the group that Roosevelt had instructed them to "clear it with Sidney." Sidney Hillman was a leading C.I.O. labor official who commanded a rich campaign chest for the support of candidates friendly to organized labor. Sidney turned thumbs down on Brynes, and subsequently Truman was chosen instead. But the slogan "Clear everything with Sidney" became a jeer that undoubtedly persuaded some citizens to vote Republican.

Cheering Republicans, meeting in Chicago, nominated "a young man in a hurry," Thomas E. Dewey. Then only forty-two years of age, he had made his reputation as a "racket-busting" district attorney who later became governor of New York. A serious rival of Willkie for the nomination four years earlier, the undersized, mustached Dewey caused Harold Ickes to quip that he looked like "the little man on top of the wedding cake." Prior to the campaign of 1940, the same Ickes had remarked that the youngish Dewey had cast "his diaper into the ring."

Conservative Republicans, distrusting Dewey's ideas of international cooperation, nominated for Vice President Governor John W. Bricker of Ohio. A handsome, white-maned isolationist, he vaguely preached "cooperation without commitments" and hence was dubbed "an honest Harding." The greater enthusiasm of the convention for the vice presidential nominee caused newsmen to jest, "The delegates loved Bricker but married Dewey." As for the head of the ticket, one Democratic political advertisement read:

> Dewey, Tom
>   On matters foreign,
> Sounds a lot like
>   Harding, Warren.

REELECTING A SICK STATESMAN

In a rich and cultivated baritone voice, Dewey waged a vigorous speaking campaign. He assailed the "twelve long years" of the "tired" and "quarrelsome old men" in Washington, and repeatedly sounded the clarion call "That's why it's time for a change"—an appeal that was shortened by sloganeers to "Time for a Change." "Dewey-eyed" Republicans feared that the country was saddled with a "lifer" who had a covetous eye on fifth and sixth terms. Clare Boothe Luce ("The Blonde Bombshell") attacked Roosevelt as the only President who ever "lied us into war because he did not have the political courage to lead us into it." As for the Roosevelt domestic program, one lapel button hailed "Dewey the Racket Buster—New Deal Buster."

Aroused Democrats, harping on Roosevelt's experienced leadership, often acted as though Hoover, not Dewey, were running again. "What were you doing in 1932?" and "Where were you in '32?" were grim reminders of Hoover and the Depression. Democrats also assailed Dewey's "me-tooism." In their view he was only claiming that he could fight the war better (at a time when victories were piling up) and deal the cards of the New Deal better (at a time when unemployment was only a memory). "Go 4th to Win the War" was a telling button slogan, as was "Three Good Terms Deserve Another." Roosevelt's personal pledge was displayed as "We Are Going To Win the War and the Peace That Follows."

Fourth-termer Roosevelt, as he had earlier announced, made no effort to barnstorm as widely as Dewey. The global war claimed his full attention, and besides he was obviously not a well man. To quiet rumors of imminent collapse, he daringly exposed himself in an open car in the chilling rain in New York City. He also delivered a smash-hit speech at a Teamsters' dinner in Washington, D.C. With cutting sarcasm he referred to Republican reports that he had dispatched a destroyer to an Aleutian island, at a cost of millions of dollars, to bring back his pet Scottie named Fala—a charge of extravagance that he said offended the dog's "Scotch soul." "These Republican leaders," he solemnly averred, "have not been content with attacks on me, on my wife, or on my sons. No, not content with that, they now include my little dog Fala. Well I don't resent attacks . . . but Fala does resent them." Uproarious laughter and acclaim greeted this speech, and prompted a furious Dewey to make some indiscreet remarks about "wisecracks" during days of "tragic sorrow."

As for songs and slogans, the "Dewey-eyed" Deweyites fell rather flat. Among them one finds "Our Yankee Dewey Dandy," "A Dewey, Dewey Day," and "We'll Do It with Dewey." A few pointed slogans cried out against the "personal dictatorship" of "One Man Rule," while asking, "Dewey or Don't We?"

Democratic posters, buttons, and badges exhibited such affirmative thoughts as "For Freedom—Four Freedoms," "We Are Going to Win This War and the Peace that Follows," and "Vote Straight Democratic: Protect America." Among the pro-Roosevelt songs were "Never Swap Horses while Crossing a Stream," "Ev'rything's Gonna Be Rosy with Roosevelt," and "Follow Through with Roosevelt."

As was his habit, Roosevelt was elected again, now for a fourth term. "The first twelve years are the hardest," he quipped. The guidance of an experienced hand was evidently wanted in winding up a victorious war, making a lasting peace, and establishing a hope-giving world organization.

XXX

Harry Truman:
The Man from Missouri

> Being a President is like riding a tiger. A man has to
> keep on riding or be swallowed.
>
> Harry S. Truman, 1956

A HABERDASHER IN THE WHITE HOUSE

Franklin Roosevelt died suddenly of a massive cerebral hemorrhage on April 12, 1945, less than three months after his fourth inauguration. His oversized mantle was then draped on a startled Vice President Truman. Previously ignored and largely unbriefed, the new leader told newsmen, "I don't know whether you fellows ever had a load of hay fall on you, but when they told me yesterday what had happened, I felt like the moon, the stars, and all the planets had fallen on me."

So spoke the Missouri farmer-haberdasher, who had come up through the notorious Pendergast political machine of Kansas City and had made a creditable record as a one-term Senator heading an investigation of scandalously wasted public money. One of the few Presidents without college training, he was dubbed "the average man's average man." He looked much like one as he peered through owlish spectacles, but Harry Truman was no average man. Decisive and "gutty," he was fully capable of making big decisions, right or wrong. The sign on his desk proclaimed, "The Buck Stops Here." Like all doers he made his mistakes—"To err is Truman" became a current quip—as does everyone who does anything. Speaker of the House Sam Rayburn reportedly credited him with being "right on all the big things, wrong on most of the little ones."

Dazed by Roosevelt's death, many Americans were talking of postponing or canceling the United Nations Conference scheduled to meet in San Francisco on April 25, 1945, to frame the United Nations Charter. But people remembered that Roosevelt had labored hard for a new organization for peace that would take the place of the defunct League of Nations. Truman's first major decision was to announce that the meeting would be held as scheduled.

After much pulling, hauling, and compromising, the Charter of the United Nations emerged in San Francisco after two months of gestation. Public opinion, remembering the Senate's rejection of the League in 1919–20, overwhelmingly favored the new pact. There were only a few mutterings by a negligible minority about "a Communist plot" and a "godless and unconstitutional" document framed by a lot of "foreigners out at San Francisco who ate up our scarce food." When formal debate opened in the Senate, Senator Tom Connally cried, with obvious reference to the rejection of the League of Nations, "Can you not still see the blood on the floor?" After rather perfunctory debate the charter was formally approved, in July 1945, by a penitent vote of eighty-nine to two.

When the war with Japan crashed to a close in August 1945, tens of thousands of homesick G.I.s were eager to return to "God's country." Not enough transports existed to bring them all back at once, and their impatience found voice in mutinous "I wanna go home" demonstrations, staged all the way from Germany to India. Pressure was brought to bear on Congressmen with the stamped warning on home-bound mail, "No boats, no votes." The clamor mounted as "Bring-Daddy-Back-Home Clubs" vented their displeasure. In the end the United States hastily demobilized a tremendous fighting machine, with the consequent creation of a power vacuum into which the Soviets began to move. Winston Churchill expressed the belief that only America's monopoly of the atomic bomb (until 1949) kept the Communists from sweeping all the way to the English Channel.

Stalin had proved to be a distrustful ally during World War II; about all he and America had in common was a Nazi foe. Seeking to enlist the Soviet Army against Japan when Hitler was crushed, Roosevelt journeyed to Yalta in the Russian Crimea early in 1945, and there entered into discussions with Stalin and Prime Minister Churchill. Concessions were made on both sides, including what was regarded as a Soviet pledge of free elections in Poland and other nations of Central Europe that were being taken over by the Moscow-directed Communists. Maddening to Polish-Americans was the agreement to permit the Soviet Union to retain about one-third of Poland—the nation whose stubborn stand against Hitler had triggered World War II. Polish spokesmen in the United States condemned the "crime of Crimea" as a "stab in the back for Poland," and branded Yalta a barefaced "betrayal."

Some of the most delicate agreements at Yalta were kept secret for many months, partly because the Russians were not yet at war with the

Japanese. Secrecy, combined with Stalin's failure to permit free elections in the Soviet satellite countries, caused countless Americans to regard the series of compromises with Stalin as a complete sellout. Yalta was widely condemned as "a second Munich," and the two words "Yalta" and "Munich" often were used thereafter as Siamese twins to thwart mutual concessions that even suggested "appeasement." American politicians were naturally eager to avoid the accusation of being "soft on communism."

ATOMIC DIPLOMACY AND THE COLD WAR

When the guns finally grew cold in 1945, a large reservoir of good will for the Soviet Union remained in the United States. Even though a distrustful ally, it had helped save American skins while saving its own. But it soon became obvious that the wartime alliance was merely a marriage of convenience, and that the interrupted ideological clash between the free world and the Communist world would be renewed. As America disarmed, the Soviets not only remained armed but cried "atomic blackmail" and "capitalistic encirclement" while they encircled their satellite neighbors and openly flouted their assurances at Yalta of free elections.

"Rattling the atomic bomb" was a repeated accusation of Communist spokesmen against Uncle Sam, and indeed the fearsome weapon proved to be an overshadowing apple of discord. In 1946 the United States offered to establish international control of atomic energy, but the Russians found the American terms, especially regarding inspection of Soviet sites, unacceptable. Bernard Baruch, speaking before representatives of the United Nations in June 1946, solemnly announced that they had come "to make a choice between the quick and the dead." If they failed, "then we have damned every man to be the slave of fear."

Few prophecies have ever proved more correct. Russia got the atomic bomb in 1949, the hydrogen bomb in 1953. From then on membership in the exclusive "nuclear club" gradually expanded, despite outcries, especially in England, of "Ban the Bomb" and "Better Red than Dead."

At Fulton, Missouri, in March 1946, ex-Prime Minister Churchill delivered a globe-shaking speech. Long a foe of communism, he solemnly declared, "From Stettin in the Baltic to Trieste in the Adriatic, an iron curtain has descended across the Continent." To stem the westward thrust of Russian communism, he boldly proposed "a fraternal association of English-speaking peoples." The reaction from those "One Worlders" who still hoped for postwar cooperation with the Russians was unfavorable, but the phrase "iron curtain" stuck. In New York pickets chanted, "Don't be a ninny for imperialist Winnie!" and also

> Winnie, Winnie, go away,
> UNO [UN] is here to stay.

Churchill's "iron curtain" speech was another giant step into the chilly waters of the "cold war"—a phrase used to describe the intense ideologi-cal warfare of the 1940s and later. The term generally referred to the diplomatic deadlocks and military confrontations short of direct blood-shed that developed between the Communist world and the capitalistic world during these postwar decades.

Tired of "babying the Soviets" and alarmed by their gains, Truman put his foot down and adopted a "Get tough with Russia" policy in 1947. Fearing that Greece and Turkey would fall to Communist infiltration, he urged Congress to appropriate $400 million to save them and to "con-tain" the Communists. At the same time he expressed the determination of the United States—a fateful avowal—to help "free peoples" resist "at-tempted subjugation" anywhere in the world. This so-called Truman Doctrine was evidently the first public avowal by a President of the "world policeman" ideal.

Appropriations for Greece and Turkey under the Truman Doctrine were small change indeed when compared with future outlays for for-eign aid. Secretary of State George C. Marshall, speaking at the Harvard commencement exercises in 1947, indicated that the United States would extend "substantial additional help" to those hungry nations of Europe that were willing to cooperate with America in pulling themselves out of the postwar chaos. Basic to the scheme was the idea that a revived Europe, capable of feeding itself, would be less likely to spawn "stomach Communists."

Most of the needy nations of Western Europe responded affirmatively to America's offer of a helping hand. Those of Central Europe, under the boot of Moscow, could not do so if they wanted to. Soviet propa-gandists assailed this "imperialist plot" by the "Knights of the Dollar" for the enslavement of Europe, while Communist satellite countries de-manded, "Yankee go home!" Even in the United States, especially among isolationists and leftists, voices rose to condemn the "Martial Plan," "Operation Rathole," and the "Share-the-American-Wealth Plan." The initial appropriation was languishing in Congress when a Communist coup in Czechoslovakia, obviously Soviet-inspired, destroyed this show-piece of democracy. An alarmed Congress struck back by passing the first Marshall aid grant of $5.3 billion in April 1948.

Response and counterresponse were the recurrent patterns of the cold war. The Truman Doctrine and the Marshall Plan came as reactions to the obvious efforts of the Soviets, by political or military means, to take over much of Europe. Then came the Kremlin's turn. In July 1948, just before the Republicans renominated Dewey for President, the Soviets cut off all land-and-water traffic between Western Germany and the city of Berlin, marooned deep in Communist-held territory. President Truman responded by inaugurating a gigantic airlift of food, coal, and other sup-plies. This "Operation Vittles" saved the city from Communist clutches, despite a number of near clashes with the Russians, and the next year the Kremlin lifted the blockade.

Truman with Money Bags and Atomic Bomb Backs Western European Statesmen. Soviet Satirical Magazine, *Kroko-
dil.*

An epochal reaction was the formation of a multination defensive pact
that came to be known as the North Atlantic Treaty Organization
(NATO). As a starter, the leading democracies of Western Europe first
banded together in a protective union. In June 1948 the United States
Senate passed the Vandenberg resolution, which indicated the willingness

of the United States to join. The resulting North Atlantic Treaty was formally signed in Washington in April 1949. The ancient no-entangling-alliance tradition went out the window when the dozen signatory nations agreed that "an armed attack against one or more of them . . . shall be considered an attack against them all." In this event, each party should take "such action as it deems necessary, including the use of armed force." The Senate approved the new pact by a lopsided vote, despite outcries from last-ditch isolationists and Communists, who branded the treaty "International Murder, Inc."

A FOUR-WAY RACE TO THE WHITE HOUSE

Victory in the upcoming presidential election of 1948 seemed like a foregone conclusion to many Republicans when their nominating convention met in Philadelphia in June of that year. High prices, high taxes, and high spending by the government—all spawned by the recent war—worried the voter. In the Congressional elections of 1946, the Republicans had gained control of both houses of Congress for the first time since 1930. Their most devastating slogans were simply "Had Enough?" and "Had Enough? Then Vote Republican." The two-word query referred, among other vexations, to the New Deal and all its works. Democrats defiantly responded with "Had Enough? Vote Republican and You'll Never Have Enough." Happily for the opposition, Truman had courageously vetoed a tax-reduction bill, which helped to fix on him the sobriquet "High-Tax Harry."

Debonair Tom Dewey, who had fallen victim to Roosevelt's barbs in 1944, was nominated again, despite Alice Roosevelt Longworth's warning, "You can't make a souffle rise twice." The Republican platform embodied a blistering attack on the New Deal, as the deceased Roosevelt was made to ride again. Popular Republican slogans featured the cautionary "Save What's Left," the optimistic "Dewey Is Due in '48," and the hackneyed "Time for a Change." In somewhat the same vein assorted Republican buttons read "Truman for Ex-President," "Back to Independence [Missouri]," "H-Club—Help Hustle Harry Home," and, with reference to recent renovations in the White House, "Truman was Screwy to Build a Porch for Dewey."

Harry S. Truman, the hand-me-down President, was disliked by many Democratic leaders, despite his "guttiness" or perhaps because of it. Many Southerners would have none of him, primarily because he had come out courageously in favor of civil rights for Negroes. A "Dump Truman" movement started in the hope of inducing General Eisenhower to run as a Democrat, but the glamorous war hero declined the opportunity to bail out the Democratic party. A popular song of 1921, "I'm Just Wild about Harry," found a reverse twist in "We're Just Mild about

Harry." Stuck with their hand-me-down President, the Democrats embarked upon the campaign in a rather despondent mood.

Outraged Southerners, like their Democratic forebears of 1860, defiantly seceded from the party as the "Lost Cause" showed new signs of life. Calling themselves "Dixiecrats," delegates from thirteen states met in Birmingham, Alabama, and there nominated Governor J. Strom Thurmond of South Carolina for President on a states'-rights ticket. One slogan of the campaign pleaded, "Save the Constitution—Thurmond for President."

A two-way split in a party usually proves fatal, but in 1948 Truman's Democrats splintered into three segments. Ultraliberal Henry A. Wallace, discarded for Vice President in favor of Truman in 1944, received the nomination of the new Progressive party in New York in July 1948. The left-leaning Wallace was especially alarmed by Truman's "Get tough with Russia" policy. His supporters numbered a nondescript collection of disenchanted New Dealers, visionary pacifists, militant progressives, well-meaning liberals, and even Communists. They chanted noisily:

> One, two, three, four,
> We don't want another war.

Wallace admirers enthusiastically advertised such sentiments as "Peace, Freedom, Abundance" and "Work with Wallace for Peace."

Out on the stump Wallace, a vigorous if misguided liberal, assailed Uncle Sam's "dollar imperialism," which was a favorite Kremlin denunciation. Drenched with broken eggs in hostile cities, this "walking omelette," as he was called, took a stance that seemed so pro-Soviet as to earn him the title "Pied Piper of the Politburo."

"Even a Chinaman could beat Truman" was a witticism as the campaign began, and Dewey exuded this overconfidence. The best-known public opinion polls, except one, had him winning in a walk. Dewey seemed smug, superior, arrogant, and evasive. He faithfully followed the ancient political dictum that when the election is in the bag, one should not tie one's hands with unnecessary commitments. He even dispensed such self-evident truisms as "Our future lies before us," thus inspiring the quip that G.O.P. meant "Grand Old Platitudes." But he was crystal clear on one point: when he got to the Presidential chair there would be just about the biggest house cleaning of Democratic officeholders in recorded history. A popular slogan urged, "Clean House with Dewey," as he promised to do.

Dewey's tour of the country by locomotive in "The Victory Special" led to the button slogan "Our Dewey Special is Due." But campaigning from rear-end platforms involves dangers. Just before a whistle-stop speech in Illinois, the observation coach from which the candidate was to speak suddenly lurched backward toward the gathering crowd. "That's the first lunatic I've had for an engineer," Dewey blurted out. "He probably ought to be shot at sunrise, but I guess we'll let him off because nobody was hurt." Among the hundreds of thousands of railroad workers there were many offended voters. "Lunatics for Truman" was written by countless fingers in the dust on the sides of numerous boxcars.

HARRY GIVES 'EM HELL

Aside from the three-way split in his party, Truman suffered from other handicaps. The New Deal had agitated the country for nearly sixteen long years, during which the Democratic party had accumulated a host of enemies. Yet the Trumanites attempted to make a virtue of this handicap, while saying "Phooey on Dewey." "Tried and True Truman" was a slogan that attempted to capitalize on the costly on-the-job training of the incumbent. As for the gains under the New Deal, including Social Security, a relevant unofficial Democratic slogan cried out, "Don't Let Them Take It Away." Another appeal for urgency was "Don't Tarry—Vote Harry." Less urgent, but still pointed, were such button appeals as "Truman Fights for Human Rights" and "60 Million People Working—Why Change?" The charge against Truman of "Communist coddling" or being "soft on communism" whether abroad or at home rang rather hollow in the light of his dramatic shift to a policy of "getting tough with Russia."

Peppery Harry Truman, especially in the early stages of the campaign, seemed to be one man alone, although actually he was not. With limited funds and relatively little public support from big names, he found his gut-fighting instincts aroused. Determined to make a whistle-stop tour of the country and display his "folksy" personality, he announced before leaving on one foray, "I'm going to give 'em hell." In all he delivered several hundred brief rear-platform speeches to increasing crowds throughout the country. In their preparation he had the help of a stable of able advisers and ghost writers. In Seattle a loud voice from the audience cried out, "Give 'em hell, Harry." He shot back, "I have never deliberately given anybody hell. I just tell the truth on the opposition—and they think it's hell." As audiences grew more enthusiastic in response to his slashing attacks, shouts arose of "Pour it on 'em, Harry!"

When stimulated by receptive audiences, "Whistle Stop" Harry was prone to exaggerate. He referred to his Republican opponents as "just a bunch of old mossbacks" who were "gluttons of privilege," all prepared "to do a hatchet job on the New Deal." He warned that if the Republicans regained power, "you will be making America an economic colony of Wall Street." As for the bloody-handed Communist dictator whom he had met at the Potsdam Conference in 1945, Truman reached the peak of naiveté. "I like Old Uncle Joe Stalin," he reportedly declared in Oregon. "Joe is a decent fellow but he is the prisoner of the Politburo. The people who run the government won't let him be as decent as he would like to be." Competent Kremlinologists could testify that the Politburo was more a prisoner of Stalin, who could be bracketed with Adolf Hitler as one of the great wholesale murderers of all time.

"Give-'em-Hell Harry" had many strings to his bow. He curried favor with organized labor by pointing to his unsuccessful veto in 1947 of the Taft-Hartley Act, known as the "slave labor law," which curbed the growing power of organized labor. He made clear that he would work for repeal of this obnoxious statute. He also reminded the farmers that the Republican Congress had "stuck a pitchfork" into their back. On the farm-aid issue he accused Republicans of resorting to the old political trick "If you can't convince 'em, confuse 'em." Much of his give-'em-hell fire was reserved for the "notorious" Republican Eightieth Congress— "the worst in history." It was a "good-for-nothing," "do-nothing" body.

Truman had already scored heavily against this "no-good Congress" by a diabolically clever political trick. After the Republicans had drawn up their platform in Philadelphia, he called the Republican Congress back into special session to enact their glittering promises into law. He knew perfectly well, as he confesses in his memoirs, that the opposition party could not or would not confer luster on his administration by passing these reforms. Some of them he was also advocating. As expected, the do-nothing Congress dithered for eleven days and did nothing of consequence. But much was accomplished in showing up what appeared to be Republican hypocrisy and in giving Truman a conspicuous whipping boy. One Democratic button read, "The Won't Do Congress Won't Do."

THE MIRACLE OF 1948

Campaign songs had fallen on evil days, and neither of the major parties offered much that was new or exciting. A favorite theme of the Truman-ites was the wordless "Missouri Waltz," which bands blared endlessly in honor of Truman and his "Show me" state of Missouri. For their part the Republicans came up with "Date in '48"—that is, a date with victory—and "What Do We Do on a Dew, Dew, Dewy Day?"

God is not always on the side of the party with the largest number of good songs, for the losing Wallaceites attracted a remarkable collection of talented folk singers. Wallace's running mate, Senator Glen Taylor of Idaho, was a vocalizing musician who could play cowboy songs on his guitar. As leftists, the so-called "Progressives" emphasized in their appeals civil rights, peace, freedom, and the rights of the "poor working stiff." One of the best songs of the protestors was "I've Got a Ballot," which would of course support Henry Wallace. Wallaceites firmly believed that both of the two major parties were rightist, and they stressed this prejudice in their theme song, "The Same Merry-Go-Round." "Truman Crusaders" for their part could sport the button "Think! Prevent Wallacitis."

Only a genius, someone quipped, could manage to lose to Harry Truman. The major public opinion polls had Dewey not only winning but winning by a wide margin. Truman sneered at the "sleeping polls," which, in his opinion, were pills designed to lull the voters to sleep. They certainly helped to lull the Republicans into a fatal state of over-confidence. The Chicago *Tribune* was so wishfully confident that it prematurely published an immortal headline, "Dewey Defeats Truman." "President" Dewey enjoyed his triumph for only a few hours, and then he realized that he had succeeded brilliantly in "snatching defeat from the jaws of victory."

"The Man from Missouri" not only won but won rather handily. Wallace carried no state, and he caused Truman by contrast to seem less of a "Communist coddler." The "Dixiecrats" under Thurmond prevailed in four states of the once solid South, but Truman's stand for civil rights earned for him a compensating Negro vote in the North. Truman had also grappled with "gut issues" like the "slave labor law" and price supports for farm products. As a former "dirt farmer" in contact with the grass roots, he played politics with consummate skill and in harmony with his earthy belief "If you don't like the heat, get out of the kitchen."

Twenty-four years later, when Truman lay dying in Independence, Missouri, shops in nearby Kansas City displayed signs saying "Give 'Em Hell Harry." Many people were still pulling for him, as they did in 1948, when the quip was current that nobody favored "The Man of Independence" "except the voters."

RED HERRINGS AND REAL REDS

Smilingly confident, Truman launched his elected administration with a "bold new program" (Point Four) to prevent backward lands from becoming Communist. Coupled with it was his "Fair Deal," especially to help impoverished Americans at home. Critics of "Deals" of any kind, old or new, branded Truman's scheme a "Fear Deal," and the new Democratic Eighty-first Congress as the "eighty-worst."

An embarrassing issue that slopped over from the months before the "miracle" election of 1948 related to Communists in the federal government, which was allegedly wormy with "security risks." The Republican-controlled "do-nothing" Eightieth Congress had undertaken probes that did not meet with Truman's full cooperation. He issued an unfortunate statement to the effect that the Communist issue was just a "red herring" to divert attention from the sins of the Republican Congress.

A prize red herring turned up in the person of Alger Hiss, formerly a prominent official in the State Department. Accused of having passed on top-secret information to the Soviets, he was brought to trial largely as a result of the red-hunting zeal of young Congressman Richard M. Nixon. Early in 1950 Hiss was found guilty of perjury in connection with these alleged dealings and sentenced to five years in prison. Truman's image as an anti-Communist received no help when his Secretary of State, Dean Acheson, a loyal friend of the accused, stated in a spirit of Christian charity, "Whatever the outcome of the appeal, I do not intend to turn my back on Alger Hiss."

Anti-Communist zealots in America became desperately alarmed over what was happening in China. The Nationalist government of that troubled nation, an ally of the United States in World War II, had fought local Communist armies with one hand while fending off Japanese invaders with the other. After the war ended, the United States continued to send financial and military aid to Chiang, whose corrupt regime rapidly lost the confidence and support of the masses. The "China Lobby" in the halls of Congress was constantly clamoring for sending good money after bad, but the complete collapse came late in 1949, when Chiang Kai-shek fled with his rump government to Formosa.

Secretary of State Dean Acheson, whom anti-Communists liked to call "The Red Dean," was asked by a group of Congressmen to predict the course of events. He replied correctly that "when a great tree falls in the forest one cannot see the extent of the damage until the dust settles." The press unfairly shortened this observation to mean that the settled policy of the administration was to "wait until the dust settles." Acheson's gaffe quickly took its place with Wilsonian "watchful waiting" in the American political lexicon.

"Who lost China?" was the damaging cry raised by conservative foes of the Truman government. Answering their own loaded question, they replied that the "soft on communism" administration had sent too few arms, which in fact were often sold or abandoned to the Communists. Some leading Republicans also charged that "pinks" or "reds" in the State Department had deliberately pursued policies designed to sell out Chiang. But informed "China watchers" concluded that Truman had not lost China, because China was never America's to lose, and that a government cannot survive that corruptly forfeits the backing of its people.

China's complete collapse provided abundant grist for the mill of red-baiting Senator Joseph R. McCarthy of Wisconsin. On February 9, 1950, he delivered a sensational speech in Wheeling, West Virginia, during which he reportedly said, "While I cannot take the time to name all of the men in the State Department who have been named [by whom?] as members of the Communist party and members of a spy ring, I have here in my hand a list of 205 that were known to the Secretary of State as being members of the Communist party and who nevertheless are still working and shaping the policy of the State Department." This was the "big lie" technique of Adolf Hitler and other prominent demagogues.

McCarthy thus launched his hysterical campaign of so-called "character assassination" which ruined the careers of many innocent people and brought great fear to the land of the free. Americans began to suspect one another more than they did the Communist adversary overseas. A favorite tactic of "McCarthyism" was "guilt by association"—that is, if a person was seen with an individual who was known to be a Communist or even suspected of being one, then he was a Communist.

"TRUMAN'S WAR" IN KOREA

McCarthyites received unexpected ammunition from the Communists in June 1950. The peace of Korea, "The Land of the Morning Calm," was shattered when Russian-built tanks of the Communist regime in North Korea crashed southward across the 38th parallel into the non-Communist Republic of Korea, a creation of the United Nations. The cold war suddenly became extremely hot.

Truman had to make an agonizing decision—and fast. He was committed by the Truman Doctrine to support the victims of Communist aggression, and he evidently feared that the UN would collapse as the old League of Nations had failed if America stood by with folded arms. He therefore decided to act. Under pressure from the White House the Security Council of the UN promptly branded North Korea the aggressor and called upon member nations "to render every assistance" in restoring peace. Under this multination authorization, which bypassed the United States Constitution, Truman threw American armed forces into Korea in what was often referred to as a "police action." Congress never declared war.

Harry Truman's "gutty" decision was widely applauded in America at the time, so great was the worry over recent Communist gains, especially in China the year earlier. Major James Jabara of Wichita, Kansas, later explained, "I fought in Korea, so I would not have to fight on Main Street in Wichita." (The same line of thought was later used to indoctrinate American soldiers in the Vietnam War.) Under the blue and white flag of the UN, General Douglas MacArthur was given supreme command, although only sixteen of some sixty member nations volunteered contingents. Uncle Sam carried the heavy end of the log in men, supplies, money, and shipping. Except for the non-UN soldiers of the Republic of South Korea (ROKS), Americans suffered by far the heaviest casualties in resisting the invasion by the "gooks."

In the early phases of the fighting the North Koreans almost drove the outmanned defenders off the southern tip of the peninsula. But a desperate MacArthur successfully executed a daring gamble when he landed an army at Inchon, far to the north, on the flank of the North Koreans. In deadly peril, they fled north across the 38th parallel with the South Koreans on their heels. After the UN rather vaguely authorized General MacArthur to join the pursuit, the five-star general rashly divided his forces in a northward thrust. His aim, as reported, was to bring the boys "home by Christmas," although he did not say which Christmas.

MacArthur's ill-advised lunge toward China gave the war a different face. The new Communist regime in Peking made clear that it would not tolerate hostile forces near its sensitive Manchurian border with North

Korea, but such warnings were brushed aside. In November 1950, the month before Christmas, "human waves" of Chinese "volunteers" ("Joe Chinks") suddenly fell on MacArthur's advanced units and drove the overextended UN forces, including the Americans, beyond the 38th parallel in a humiliating, frost-bitten retreat. The U.S. Marines took their licking manfully and unrealistically. "Retreat, hell!" exclaimed General O. P. Smith, "we're just fighting in another direction." "Retreat, Hell" became the title of a film centered on the Korean War.

SACKING A FIVE-STAR GENERAL

Conventional tactics would have dictated a bombing by the UN forces of the bases in China from which the enemy troops had come, as Mac-Arthur wished. But to bomb these "privileged sanctuaries" would widen the war with China and possibly suck in the Soviet Union, which was allied to the Chinese. From the vantage point of Washington, the Soviets, not the North Koreans or Chinese, were the main enemy. General Omar Bradley of the Joint Chiefs of Staff in Washington could properly refer to "the wrong war, at the wrong place, at the wrong time, with the wrong enemy." But the headstrong and imperious General MacArthur, smarting from defeat, attempted in various ways to shape the war to his way of thinking. His philosophy was expressed some months later in public statements: "It is fatal to enter any war without the will to win it"; "War's very object is victory, not prolonged indecision"; and "In war there is no substitute for victory."

As a military man accustomed to giving orders, MacArthur must have realized that high-level policy is made in Washington, not by the men in the field. Fed up with the general's balkiness and repeated acts of insubordination, Commander-in-Chief Truman abruptly relieved him of all his commands in April 1951. The great hero of World War II in the Pacific returned home, after an absence of fourteen years, to receive a hero's welcome. Much of the reception was a reaction against what was called the firing by "a two-bit President of a five-star general." A snowstorm of telegrams descended on Truman branding him a "pig," an "imbecile," and "a Judas." Senator McCarthy was quoted as saying, "The son-of-a-bitch ought to be impeached." Truman had indeed suffered severe provocation over a protracted period, but it seems as though he could better have shown MacArthur the door rather than kick him downstairs.

On returning triumphantly, the statuesque general was invited to address Congress. He proved to be at his melodramatic best, concluding his speech with the words of the barrack's ballad, "Old soldiers never die, they just fade away." He then promised to "fade away," although he did not do so as rapidly as his words suggested. He clearly had his eye on the Presidency, and received some trifling support at the Republican convention in 1952, as further attested by a rather lonesome button, "Back Mac."

General Matthew B. Ridgway, who succeeded MacArthur, regained essentially the line of the 38th parallel by inflicting enormous losses on the Chinese and North Koreans in "Operation Killer." But the "no-win war" in Korea grew increasingly unpopular in America, where it was bitterly known as "Truman's War." So disturbed were many patriots by the evident willingness of the UN to fight "to the last American" that there was talk about "going it alone," even with atomic bombs. Negotiations for a cease-fire were undertaken in 1951, while severe fighting continued, and in July 1953, after prolonged haggling, agreement was reached on a precarious armistice. But this was not a peace settlement.

XXXI

Eisenhower and Modern Republicanism

> The issue between the Republicans and Democrats is clearly drawn. It has been deliberately drawn by those who have been in charge of twenty years of treason.
>
> Senator Joseph R. McCarthy, 1954

"IKE" IS LIKED

As the presidential election of 1952 approached, the prospects of the Democrats were unpromising. They had occupied the seats of the mighty for nearly twenty years, and the cry of "Time for a change" gained more potency with each passing year. Truman's popularity had sunk to a new low, owing largely to the "no-win" Korean War. In addition, Republicans could point an accusing finger at "the mess in Washington." Where billions of dollars are being flung around, there are always sticky fingers, and the Democratic administration managed to acquire its share of grafters. Truman himself consorted with questionable cronies from his home state—characters known popularly as "the Missouri gang." Acid-tongued Harold L. Ickes, after resigning as Secretary of the Interior, blasted Truman with the statement "I am against government by crony."

Washington swarmed with "influence peddlers," who boasted that they had special "pull" at the White House and who also claimed a 5 percent commission on government contracts. The wives or female friends of these "5 percenters" blossomed out in expensive mink coats, thus giving point to the barb "Mink Dynasty," after the Chinese Ming Dynasty. Yet Truman, himself honest, stuck stubbornly by his old cronies. "Turn the rascals out" was the refurbished cry of office-famished Republicans, who branded Democratic policies as "plunder at home, blunder abroad."

Radiant, tooth-flashing General Dwight ("Ike") Eisenhower, victorious commander of the Allied forces in Europe, finally decided that he was a Republican and, under intense pressure, consented to run for the presidential nomination. "I Like Ike," emblazoned on placards, buttons, and neckties, was the affirmation that gave him the greatest boost. Other buttons urged "Draft Eisenhower," "The Man of the Hour is Eisenhower," and "All in Favor Say Ike." After a sharp fight in the Chicago convention, Eisenhower won the nomination over the political warhorses, who generally favored isolationist Senator Robert Taft, widely known as "Mr. Republican."

Truman, though technically eligible, wisely declared himself out of the race. He had already served almost eight troubled years, and he felt no burning desire to govern longer than any other President except Franklin Roosevelt. Further, he was now so unpopular that he had little hope of repeating "the miracle of 1948." The Democratic convention, also meeting in Chicago, finally tapped Adlai Stevenson, the witty, eloquent, and idealistic governor of Illinois. The theme song of this convention, sung lustily with emphatic claps of the hands, was "Don't Let 'Em Take It Away." It referred to prosperity for all, including the long-depressed farmer.

A NEW VICTORY FOR AN OLD GENERAL

Sparks flew when the rivals mounted the stump in the ensuing campaign. The quiet and intellectual Stevenson, dubbed an "egghead" because of his literacy and semibaldness, was handicapped by not being a household name, in contrast with his scintillating rival. He delivered a number of eloquent and literate speeches, the theme of which was "Let's Talk Sense to the American People"—an objective emphasized in his speech of acceptance. Fearing the dangers of McCarthyism, he warned, "We must take care not to burn down the barn to kill the rats." The Chicago *Tribune* branded Adlai a "cookie pusher" and "a professional bleeding heart." One of his responses was "If the Republicans stop telling lies about us, we will stop telling the truth about them." In a parody of Karl Marx, Stevenson quipped, "Eggheads of the world, unite! You have nothing to lose but your yolks."

Pro-Stevenson appeals, chiefly on buttons, declared "Adlai for Me," "All the Way with Adlai," "We're Madly for Adlai," and "We Need Adlai Badly." In a similar vein were "Hooray for Adlai," "Vote Gladly for Adlai," "I Like Stevenson," "My Favorite Son is Stevenson," and "I Like Ike but I am Going to Vote for Stevenson."

"Ike" Eisenhower, the amateur politician, came through rather well on television as he read ghost-written speeches during his "Great Crusade." He proved personable, sincere, and dignified, although Stevenson called him a "captive" of the Old Guard Republicans. Speaking in Detroit, Ike electrified the country with the pledge that if victorious "I shall go to Korea" so as "to bring the Korean War to an early and honorable end." Many voters believed that if anyone could do it, this five-star general could. President Truman offended Eisenhower by branding this grandstand play "a piece of demagoguery."

Richard M. Nixon, tapped for the Vice Presidency largely because of his red-hunting notoriety, unexpectedly proved to be a grave embarrassment to Eisenhower. Scandal struck Nixon at a time when the Republicans themselves were assailing "the mess in Washington." The news leaked out that as a Senator Nixon had been the beneficiary of a secret fund of $18,000 for political expenses—a reserve quietly established by some seventy wealthy admirers in California. Responding to pressure from party leaders, Eisenhower seriously considered throwing his running mate to the wolves and finding a substitute.

Fighting desperately for his political life, Nixon appeared on nationwide television to deliver his famous "Checkers speech." In a dramatic performance he claimed that what he had done was entirely legal and moral. Referring to his wife and taking a slap at Truman's "Mink Dynasty," he added, "I should say this—that Pat doesn't have a mink coat. But she does have a respectable Republican cloth coat, and I always tell her that she would look good in anything." He also referred to Checkers, the little black and white cocker spaniel given to Tricia, his six-year-old daughter, by a Republican well-wisher in Texas. "And you know the kids, like all kids, loved the dog, and I just want to say this right now, that regardless of what they say about it, we're going to keep it." After Nixon's "soap opera" appeal to the dog-lover voter and the cloth-coat vote, Dwight Eisenhower consented to keep Nixon on the ticket, embracing him with the words "You're my boy." Democrats retorted with "Nix on Nixon."

In the battle of the buttons, Nixon was often bracketed with "Ike." Among the better-known slogans were "Ike and Dick Sure to Click," "I Like Ike and Dick," and "Let's Clean House with Ike and Dick." But the "We Like Ike" theme, including "My Friend Ike," was clearly the favorite. Variants were "For the Love of Ike Vote Republican," "J'Aime Ike" (I Like Ike, in French), "Make the White House the Dwight House," "Vote Right with Dwight," and "Adlai Likes Ike Too." The Republican response to the Democratic "Don't let them take it away" was a refurbishing of "Had enough?" A veiled reference to Truman's Korean War came in "Peace and Prosperity" and "Peace and Power with Eisenhower."

Thanks to television and increasingly passive participation by voters, the songs of 1952 were scarce. The Democrats had the rousing "Don't Let Them Take It Away," while the talented songsmith Irving Berlin wrote a melody to, "I Like Ike." The Republicans also sang "Look Ahead, Neighbor," a title inspired by an Eisenhower speech. Such happy thoughts did not involve much brain strain for "Ike-minded" Americans, including many "Dem-Ike-crats for Eisenhower." Nor were voters much disturbed by such unfriendly button warnings as "Nix On Ike" and "NO General"; Eisenhower's nonpolitical background attracted relatively little attention.

"Ike" won in a tremendous landslide that was a tribute to his personal popularity and the liking of the people for genial war heroes. The country pulsated with prosperity, yet for one of the few times in the nation's history the masses voted against their pocketbooks. As is true of all hotly contested elections, there were numerous substantive issues, but what the Republicans deemed most persuasive was evidently summed up in their slogan "Crime, Corruption, Communism, and Korea." "Crime" stood for Truman's cronies, "Corruption" for the "Mink dynasty," "Communism" for Alger Hiss, and "Korea" for the "no-win, no-end war." The more extreme Republicans, notably Senator Joe McCarthy, sloganized their opinion of Democratic rule since 1933 in "Twenty Years of Treason."

MODERN REPUBLICANISM UNVEILED

Eisenhower's thumping victory in the "Great Crusade" raised the curtain on his attempt to introduce what came to be known as "The New Republicanism" or "Modern Republicanism." His basic philosophy, "liberal in human affairs, conservative in fiscal affairs," gave promise of a more progressive coloration for the G.O.P., especially for the conservative "dinosaur wing" of the party.

Ike's Cabinet consisted of wealthy conservatives, plus the Secretary of Labor, formerly president of the International Plumbers' Union. "Eight millionaires and a plumber" ran a current quip. The Secretary of Defense was Charles E. Wilson, former president of General Motors. Testifying before a Senate committee, he said, ". . . for many years I thought what was good for our country was good for General Motors, and vice versa." Though laughed to scorn by Democrats, this philosophy was completely in line with the familiar Republican slogan "What Helps Business Helps You." Somewhat later Wilson's foot-in-mouth disease again betrayed him when he compared unemployed workers to dogs: ". . . I've always liked bird dogs better than kennel-fed dogs . . . one who'll get out and hunt for food rather than sit on his fanny and yell." Some ex-New Dealers thought that car dealers had replaced New Dealers.

One of Eisenhower's favorite phrases was "dynamic conservatism." His concern for a balanced budget—what he called "fiscal responsibility" —amounted to almost an obsession. "Better dead than in the red," jeered Democrats, reversing the pro-Communist slogan "Better Red than Dead." In line with the reciprocal tariff policy of the New Deal, Eisenhower endeavored to promote international business in response to the appeal "Trade, Not Aid."

True to his campaign promise, "I shall go to Korea," Ike paid a visit to that war-ravaged country in December 1952, the month after his election. But "the forgotten war" ground on. In March 1953 Stalin ("The Man of Steel") died, and the Soviets launched what skeptics called a "peace offensive." Reports spread that Eisenhower had threatened to use atomic bombs to bring the Korean War to an end. The uneasy armistice that was finally signed in July 1953 was not a treaty of peace, and tens of thousands of American troops continued to remain in South Korea for decades against that day when the North Koreans might come again.

McCarthyism lost much of its bite after the anti-Communist war in Korea ended in 1953. Until that time few fellow Republicans had the backbone to challenge the chief witch hunter. One conspicuous exception was Senator Margaret Chase Smith, who in 1950 presented what became known as a "declaration of conscience." Especially pointed was her conclusion: "I don't want to see the Republican party ride to political victory on the four horsemen of calumny—fear, ignorance, bigotry, and smear."

McCarthy continued his relentless pursuit of "security risks" in government service, including "Comsymps" (Communist sympathizers) and "Radic-Libs," especially after becoming chairman of a Senate investigating subcommittee. The Senator sent his snoopers to Europe, where they examined libraries of the United States Information Agency and found a scattering of works by Communist authors. In some cases the librarians removed or burned a few books before the investigators came, thus unpleasantly recalling the literary bonfires in Hitler's Germany. Ike, consistently refusing to get into the gutter with "that guy," had hitherto steered clear of McCarthy, but speaking at Dartmouth College in 1953 he warned, "Don't join the book burners."

"Low-blow Joe" McCarthy, finally overreaching himself, exposed his essential meanness and unfairness on television while investigating alleged undesirables in the army. In June 1954 Senator Ralph Flanders spoke up and courageously declared that if McCarthy were "in the pay of the communists, he could not have done a better job for them." In December 1954 a Senate vote formally "condemned" McCarthy, who rapidly lost his influence, took heavily to drink, and died in 1957. A right-wing newspaper in Fort Worth, Texas, concluded, "Joe McCarthy was slowly tortured to death by the pimps of the Kremlin." More likely the killer was his liver.

THE ART OF BRINKMANSHIP

Stalemate war in Korea had taught the hard lesson, not fully learned, that a large and costly army of draftees was not the most effective instrument for waging war overseas. A "new look" at "conventional forces" seemed imperative, and the policy that evolved was a heavy reliance on nuclear weapons. Secretary of State John Foster Dulles, speaking in January 1954, declared, "Local defense must be reinforced by the further deterrent of massive retaliatory power." This new policy became, in the popular phrase for it, "instant" or "massive retaliation" and was sometimes even called "a bigger bang for the buck." Small conventional forces would be used to extinguish "brush-fire" or "limited wars."

Eisenhower's basic foreign policy, as reflected through Secretary Dulles, was "peaceful coexistence," or at least "coexistence," with the Soviet-dominated Communist world. Washington preached "liberation, not containment," though the administration was soon back on the old containment road of President Truman. Dulles would also "unleash" Chiang on Formosa to attack mainland China—a hopeless enterprise. He further declared in December 1953 that a weakening of policy by allies in the North Atlantic Treaty Organization would involve the United States in an "agonizing reappraisal" of its obligations.

Most spectacular of all Secretary Dulles's indiscretions was a famous interview with a correspondent for *Life* magazine, which published it early in 1956. He said that the ability to go to the "verge of war" without plunging into the war "is the necessary art." Further, "If you try to run away from it . . . you are lost." Dulles then went on to relate how the nation had recently faced up to a collision in Korea, Indochina, and Formosa. "We walked to the brink and we looked it in the face."

"Brinkmanship" became the label used by the press to describe Dulles's policy, often sneeringly. Adlai Stevenson responded, "The art of diplomacy, especially in this atomic age, must lead to peace, not war or the brink of war." As a military man, Eisenhower partially defended Dulles: "After all brinkmanship is absolutely necessary in this troubled world of ours to keep the peace. But it must be used intelligently and not recklessly."

Dulles's "brinkmanship" faced dangerous new brinks in East Asia. In 1954 the faltering French agreed at the Geneva Conference to cease fighting for colonialism in Indochina and leave the fate of a temporarily divided Vietnam to a general election in 1956. The prospects were that the Communists in North Vietnam under Ho Chi Minh would win overwhelmingly, but the election was never held, thanks largely to American support of anti-Communist South Vietnam. "Asia Firsters" in the United States condemned this "sellout" at Geneva as a "Far Eastern Munich" in which Washington had reluctantly acquiesced, at least on the surface. Partly in response to these disturbing gains of communism, Congress passed the blank-check "Formosa Resolution" early in 1955. It clothed the President with blanket authority to use the armed forces of the United States, "as he deems necessary," to protect Formosa (Taiwan) and nearby islands, obviously from Communist China.

A subsequent "Summit Conference" of the Big Four powers at Geneva in 1955, consisting of the U.S., the U.S.S.R., Britain, and France, generated the so-called "Spirit of Geneva." Eisenhower attended, radiating charm, but he got nowhere with his "open skies" proposal. His scheme was to persuade the Soviet Union to permit mutual aerial overflights so as to make certain that neither side was breaking any agreement for arms limitation. Nikita Khrushchev, the Soviet Premier, remarked that this would be like peeping into one's bedroom after the curtains were drawn. Later the next year, he remarked offhandedly to Western diplomats at a Kremlin reception, "History is on our side. We will bury you." With visions of countless shovels and graves, the free world took alarm, especially Americans. Khrushchev was at pains on several subsequent occasions to point out that he was merely referring to the nonviolent historical processes by which, in his view, communism would eventually replace capitalism.

THE VOTERS STILL LIKE IKE

Meeting in fog-girt San Francisco in the late summer of 1956, the jubilant Republicans renominated Eisenhower and Nixon on first ballots. A button-displayed message read, "America needs Eisenhower—Draft Ike in '56." Ike remained the heavy favorite despite a recent heart attack and abdominal surgery, from both of which he had made a remarkable recovery, thus giving some credence to a button accolade "The Mighty Tower—Eisenhower." "Let's Back Ike and Dick" was a theme left over from the preceding campaign, plus an updated favorite, "We Still Like Ike," which on another button was reversed to read "Ike Likes Me." From admirers in Brooklyn evidently came "I'm Wit Choo Ike."

Adlai Stevenson, who had made a gallant try four years earlier, again received first prize in Chicago, but this time only after a real fight in the primaries. The country was thus presented with two warmed-over candidates for the first time since McKinley beat Bryan in 1900. Both Ike and Adlai ran on essentially middle-of-the-road platforms, and both made a special appeal to intellectuals. "Eggheads for Stevenson," a publicized group of highbrows, were offset in some degree by a parallel list of "Eggheads for Eisenhower."

Moderation was the mood of the country, for prosperity had a soporific effect. "Only the guns are not booming" gloated the Republicans, who preened themselves, with the (shaky) Korean armistice in mind, on being "the party of peace." At the same time they accused the Democrats of "being the party of war." Democrats hotly retorted by branding the Republicans "the party of depression." In the sober light of history, neither side had a monopoly on either war or depression. Aged Herbert Hoover, as a phantom candidate, was made to run again for the fifth time since 1936. A reversible "safety pin" button for traveling salesmen proved popular: "I like Ike" appeared on one side and "All the Way with Adlai" on the other.

Recycled candidates are apt to run recycled campaigns, and 1956 was no exception. Democrats expressed grave concern over Eisenhower's fragile health and over the disquieting thought that only one damaged heart stood between "Tricky Dick" Nixon and the White House. The

Vice President's zealous campaigns against communism and Democratic "treason" were not easily forgotten. Stevenson went so far as to predict that Ike probably would not live out another term, although the ailing general lived for nearly fourteen more years, and in fact outlived his challenger. One Republican button declared "Better a Part-time President than a Full-time Phony."

Stevenson injected new issues into the campaigning when, in the interests of peace and pure air, he urged a halt to the testing of nuclear bombs. Eisenhower, true to his military mentality, branded such a proposal "incredible folly." Stevenson also advocated a volunteer army rather than one of draftees. Ironically, both ideas were subsequently embraced and implemented by Republican administrations.

A variant of the shopworn cry "Don't swap horses" appeared in the admonition "Don't change the team in the middle of the stream." Reminding voters of the silent guns and the noisy cash registers, the Republicans endorsed such slogans as "Peace and Prosperity with Eisenhower," "The Second Ike Crusade," and "For the Love of Ike [Mike], Vote Republican." An unusual appeal to women voters came in "Womanpower for Eisenhower." Rubber bumper guards carried the message "Don't Bump a Good Man Out of the White House"; imprinted hand fans proclaimed, "I Am an Eisenhower Fan"; and Little League baseball shirts assured parents, "I'm Safe [on base] with Ike."

Among Stevenson adherents an observer could still find buttons left over from 1952: "Adlai for Me," "All the Way with Adlai," "We're Madly for Adlai," and "We Need Adlai Badly." One also finds "Vote Gladly for Adlai," "Adlai Likes *Me*," and "Adlai and Estes are the Bestes," in reference to Estes Kefauver, the vice-presidential nominee. "Dollars for Democrats" may have helped to raise money.

If the Democrats were weaker than their rivals in the slogan department, they evidently had the upper hand in music. Adlai's song, "The Democratic March," borrowed its tune from "The Yellow Rose of Texas." Also popular were "Adlai's Gonna Win This Time," "Believe in Stevenson," and "Let's Go with Ad-A-Lai." One of the few Republican tunes worth mentioning was Irving Berlin's "Ike for Four More Years," an updated version of his "I Like Ike" of 1952.

In the closing weeks of the campaign a nightmarish world crisis developed in Europe and the Middle East. The Soviets—"Butchers of Budapest"—bloodily crushed rebellions in Poland and Hungary, both of which satellite countries had found encouragement in propaganda radio messages beamed in by "The Voice of America." To the rebels these delusive words of hope seemed to suggest that America would intervene in pursuance of its avowed policy of "national liberation" or "liberation of captive peoples." As if all this uproar were not enough, Egypt simultaneously nationalized the Suez Canal, thus triggering attacks by Israel, Britain, and France, with the U.S.S.R. threatening to come to the aid of Egypt. In such an explosive situation American voters preferred to have an experienced, five-starred general rather than an idealistic "egghead."

Stevenson again fought a good fight, but his criticisms and witticisms were not enough. Such was Ike's "father image" and such was the "national love affair" with him that the grinning general was returned to office by a landslide even more awesome than the first. "Any jockey would look good riding Ike," said the chairman of the Republican National Committee, but this was not true of riding Ike's unstarched coattails. The Republicans carried neither house of Congress—a phenomenon not paralleled since 1848. The voters clearly liked Ike much more than they did his party.

EISENHOWER AS A PART-TIME PRESIDENT

Eisenhower engineered no sharp break with the past as he began his second administration. After suffering a mild stroke three weeks after his election, he resorted increasingly to what Democratic critics called "golfing and goofing." His opponents made merry with "Eisen-however" and "Eisen-Hoover." The conservative wing of the Republican party showed increasing distaste for Ike's "Modern Republicanism" or "New Republicanism" (a distaste that earlier had made him seriously consider forming a third party). Yet he continued his deep concern for "fiscal integrity" and sternly opposed the damn-the-deficits attitude of the latter day New Dealers.

Eisenhower's right-hand Presidential assistant, often acting President, was Sherman Adams, former governor of New Hampshire. "Clear it with Sherm" was the crisp order that the ailing general frequently gave. But in 1958 the news leaked out that Adams had thrice interceded on behalf of a wealthy Boston industrialist who had given him expensive gifts. The Democrats, condemned under Truman for "the mess in Washington," cried for Sherman Adams's scalp. But Eisenhower replied, "I need him." No doubt he did, but the need became less compelling when the Republican party began to suffer politically, and "Sherm" had to resign.

Forcible integration of blacks into the white schools, especially in the South, suddenly became a burning issue on May 17, 1954, when the Supreme Court under Chief Justice Earl Warren ruled unanimously that the once constitutional "separate but equal" schools were now unconstitutional. "Separate educational facilities," declared the black-robed justices," are "inherently unequal." The next year the Court urged the carrying out of this decision "with all deliberate speed."

By various devices the resourceful Southerners interposed "massive resistance" against school integration. The focus of the crisis came at Little Rock, Arkansas, in 1957. White students at Central High School chanted as they marched,

> Two, four, six, eight,
> We won't integrate.

President Eisenhower, with considerable reluctance, sent federal troops to Little Rock to protect black pupils attempting to attend high school. Despite violent outcries against "military occupation," quiet was gradually restored and slow-motion integration went forward.

In the same autumn of 1957, Soviet scientists managed to shoot into orbit a small beeping satellite called "Sputnik." Eisenhower, an old general accustomed to conventional weapons, branded it a "gimmick" that should not cause "one iota" of concern. One of his special assistants dismissed it as "a silly bauble." The American people, more perceptive, were seized by "rocket fever," which sparked an overwhelming desire to "catch up with the Russians." Obviously this "bauble" was related to intercontinental missiles with nuclear payloads. One conspicuous symptom of the rocket fever was a revamping of school curricula so as to place more emphasis on subjects relating to mathematics and science.

Newer approaches were indicated when Secretary of State Dulles, on whom Eisenhower had relied heavily, died of cancer in April 1959. With both Sherman Adams and Dulles now gone, "the new Eisenhower" did less golfing and more governing. On the eve of a Summit Conference scheduled for Paris for May 1960, an American U-2 spy plane was shot down deep in the heart of Russia. After bungling denials and outright lies in Washington, Eisenhower rather naively assumed full responsibility for the embarrassing fiasco in espionage. Premier Khrushchev of the Soviet Union, assailing his "fishy friend" Ike, broke up the Summit Conference at Paris. When Eisenhower returned, he was greeted with banners proclaiming, "Thank You, Mr. President." Perhaps he was being thanked for keeping his temper, because he accomplished little else.

Cuban headaches developed for the United States in 1959 when Dr. Fidel Castro, a dark-bearded and left-leaning revolutionist, engineered the overthrow of the corrupt right-wing dictator, Fulgencio Batista. Americans suspected Castro of being a Communist, especially after he expropriated hundreds of millions of dollars in American investments as part of a program that involved land distribution. When the United States retaliated with a boycott of Cuban sugar and an embargo on exports to Cuba, Castro accused Uncle Sam of "imperialistic aggression" in place of Wall Street's "imperialistic slavery." The cries of patriotic Cubans were "Cuba sí, Yankee, no" and "Ami [American] go home." So hostile did Castro become to Eisenhower, whom Castro branded that "gangster" and "senile White House golfer," that Ike broke relations with Cuba seventeen days before the end of his administration.

Speaking solemnly on radio and television, Eisenhower delivered a memorable farewell address to the American people in January 1961. His best-remembered words related specifically to the burgeoning budget of the armed forces and their relation to the arms industry, beneficiary of tens of billions of dollars. He did not say so specifically, but he evidently feared, among other possibilities, that if the manufacturers and the military joined hands to bring pressure on Congress to vote unneeded

"What's So Lame About It?" Ike was supposed to be a Lame Duck in his second term but he showed much energy in travel. Reproduced with permission of the Philadelphia *Bulletin*.

sums, the results could be catastrophic. "In the councils of government," he said, "we must guard against the acquisition of unwarranted influence, whether sought or unsought, by the *military-industrial complex.*"

So spoke a man of war who was proud of his eight Presidential years of peace, despite some narrow escapes. His boast was that no American had died fighting under the American flag while he was President.

THE NIXON-KENNEDY CLASH OF 1960

Richard Milhous Nixon, who had served almost eight years as Vice President under Eisenhower, easily won the Republican nomination for the Presidency in 1960 at Chicago. His running mate turned out to be Senator Henry Cabot Lodge of Massachusetts, grandson of President Wilson's archfoe. Nixon himself was cordially hated by the Democrats, who resented his overkill in associating them with Communists. His numerous foes increasingly called him "Tricky Dick" or "Slippery Dick" and bitingly asked, "Would you buy a used car from this man?"

Despite partisan attacks, Nixon had performed creditably. He had traveled globally and usefully as Vice President, had served unobtrusively when Eisenhower suffered his near-fatal heart attack in September 1955, and in 1959 had stood up to Premier Khrushchev in the famous "kitchen debate" at an exhibition in Moscow. Photographs showing him pointing an aggressive finger at the Russian's pudgy midriff were standard items in the Nixon campaigns. Unimpressed, Khrushchev branded Nixon a "fumbler," a "grocery clerk," and a "lackey of imperialism." But "standing up to the Russians" was a splendid asset in these cold war years. Natural by-products of the kitchen debate were the major Republican slogans "Experience Counts: Vote Nixon-Lodge for a Better America," "Nixon and Lodge: Peace and Freedom," "They Understand What Peace Demands," and simply "Experience Counts" or "No Substitute for Experience."

When the Democrats convened in Los Angeles, Adlai Stevenson had considerable support but little stomach for becoming a three-time loser. Even so his partisans voiced the outworn slogan "We Need Adlai Badly," as well as "Two Strikes Are Not Out." Senator John F. Kennedy, a liberal young millionaire with a flashing smile, won out after a hot fight with Lyndon B. ("Landslide Lyndon")* Johnson of Texas. A clash of slogans had developed between "Back Jack" and "L.B.J. All the Way." To the surprise of most pundits, Johnson humbly accepted second place —"Half-way with L.B.J."—and joined Kennedy in his quest for a "New Frontier" that would fulfill the promise of American life and greatness. Kennedy-Johnson campaign buttons promised, "Leadership for the 60's," "On the Right Track with Jack," and "All the Way with J.F.K."

On the stump the rival candidates tackled different issues. Nixon played up Republican prosperity, which was just then suffering from a third Eisenhower recession ("inventory adjustment" on Republican tongues). Nixonites loudly claimed, "We never had it so good," while Kennedyites responded with "Nix on Nixon." A main Democratic theme was to "get America moving again," as though the country were on dead center as a result of General Eisenhower's marking time. Kennedy made much of the "missile gap" that favored Russia, although he discovered on entering the White House that the gap heavily favored the United States.

Nationwide television played a spectacular role when the two rivals clashed in four so-called "great debates." These were not all face-to-face meetings; they were hardly "great" or even debates in the Lincoln-Douglas tradition; and they did not demonstrably affect the outcome of

---

* This facetious sobriquet was born after Johnson, a candidate for the U.S. Senate, won the 1948 Democratic primary election in Texas by a mere 87 votes.

the election. But they were great in the immensity of the audiences attracted.

CATHOLICISM AND CAMPAIGN COLOR

Bigotry in the form of anti-Catholicism again showed its ugly face, for Kennedy was the first major-party presidential candidate of that faith, except for Al Smith's failure in 1928. Voters again heard the familiar stories about how the Pope would move into the White House if a Catholic were elected. At Houston, Texas, Kennedy helped to quiet apprehensions when he addressed an audience of Southern Protestant clergymen. He hoped that he would not be defeated for the reason that "40 million Americans lost their chance of being President on the day they were baptized. . . ." He also stated that "contrary to common newspaper usage, I am not the Catholic candidate for President; I am the Democratic party's candidate for President, who happens also to be a Catholic. I do not speak for my church on public matters—and the church does not speak for me."

Vice President Johnson proved to be a strong asset as a campaigner as he swept through the South stumping for Kennedy. He was especially effective in quieting fears about Catholicism in this Protestant, "Bible Belt" area. He named his train "The Corn Pone Special," and as it pulled out of the station he would shout at the whistle-stop crowd in a hog-calling voice, if the place for example was Culpeper (Virginia), "What did Dick Nixon ever do for Culpeper?"

Button makers for the Democrats countered the superior "experience" of Nixon with such calls to action as "New Leadership—Kennedy and Johnson." Voters were dosed with "America Needs Kennedy-Johnson," "Kennedy for Me," and "Senior Citizens for Kennedy." What seems to have been a slap at the Republican candidate in 1960 was "I'm for Nixon in '64." Republicans replied with such unimaginative assertions as "The Nation Needs Richard M. Nixon," "Vote Republican—The Party of Lincoln," and "Grass Rooters for Dick." More direct were the button messages: "My Pick is Dick," "Stick with Dick," and "Click with Dick."

Songs of the 1960 campaign were nothing to shout about. A tune fully identified with the young blood and new vision of the Kennedyites was "High Hopes." Nixon compositions were such rather uninspiring productions as "Nixon Is the Man for Me" and "Vote for Nixon." Campaign sound trucks appealing for his election blared forth "Here Comes Nixon," to the tune of "Merrily We Roll Along," as well as "Buckle Down with Nixon." Various mechanical devices, broadcasting "canned" music, were helping to drown out and kill off the mass singing of colorful earlier campaigns.

Kennedy triumphed in a cliff-hanging election. The vote in the Electoral College was 303 to 219, but the victor received fewer than 119,000 more votes than the vanquished out of nearly 69 million cast. Many

"Eisenhower Democrats," especially Catholics, were lured back into the Democratic fold. Scandalous irregularities, doubtless on both sides, clouded the results. Dead men tell no tales, the proverb says, but they can vote, or be made to. In Chicago the "cemetery vote" may have helped swing Illinois into the Kennedy column. But Nixon needed more than Chicago to win, and the victors naturally hailed the outcome as a mandate to push on with their wagon train to the New Frontier. "The margin is narrow," Kennedy solemnly observed, "but the responsibility is clear."

XXXII

The New Frontier
and the Great Society

> Let every nation know, whether it wishes us well or
> ill, that we shall pay any price, bear any burden,
> meet any hardship, support any friend, oppose any foe
> to assure the survival and success of liberty.
>
> John F. Kennedy, inaugural address, 1961

NEW FRONTIERSMEN ON THE POTOMAC

John F. Kennedy's energy, brains, good looks and youth captured not only national political power but also the national imagination. Americans were stirred by his rousing inaugural address, in which he proclaimed that "the torch has been passed to a new generation of Americans." He indicated that sacrifice at home and steadfastness abroad were to be twin themes of his administration, for he declared, "Let us never negotiate out of fear. But let us never fear to negotiate." He further implored all Americans to "ask not what your country can do for you, ask what you can do for your country."

Kennedy aspired to "get America moving again" after the mark-time years of Republican rule. But he found Congress highly uncooperative, especially the seniority-elevated chairmen of key committees—"rule by senility." Despite disappointments, Kennedy did manage some legislative successes, especially in creating the Peace Corps, which sent technicians and teachers to dozens of underdeveloped nations. Cynics scorned "Kennedy's Kiddie Corps," but Congress enthusiastically endorsed it. Also typical of the bold new approach to foreign aid was J.F.K.'s "Alliance for Progress"—a kind of Marshall Plan for Latin America. It proved disappointing, largely because of too little cooperation from the "good neighbor" governments to the south.

Initial appropriations for the "space race" launched a prime Kennedy program. Promising his people the moon, the President correctly predicted early in the decade that by the end of the 1960's an American astronaut would make a landing. But critics condemned Kennedy's multibillion dollar gamble as "lunar lunacy"—something "out of this world." Also significant to the money-minded was the blow struck against creeping inflation by Kennedy's temporarily successful "roll-back" of steel prices after a spectacular confrontation with the steel industry. The press quoted him as remarking that his father had always told him that all businessmen were "sons-of-bitches." In a short time anti-Kennedy buttons appeared saying, "S.O.B.—Sons of Business" and "Save Our Business."

BRINKMANSHIP IN TWO HEMISPHERES

Startling developments in the Caribbean first marred and then restored some of the luster of the Kennedy Presidency. The New Frontiersmen had the misfortune to inherit from Eisenhower plans for invading Castro's Cuba with a small band of Cuban exiles, trained and supplied by the U.S. Central Intelligence Agency. But crippling shackles on American air support doomed the bungling misadventure known as the Bay of Pigs landing. Kennedy manfully accepted blame for the fiasco, remarking ruefully, "Victory has a hundred fathers and defeat is an orphan." Republicans could disgustedly wear the button, "I Miss Ike—Hell, I Even Miss Harry."

Bolstered by his triumph at the Bay of Pigs, Castro placed Cuba on a new collision course with the United States by permitting Russian nuclear missiles to be secretly emplaced on his island, ninety miles from the shores of Florida. Kennedy, who was determined to resist any sneak violation of the Monroe Doctrine, found himself in an "eyeball to eyeball" confrontation with the Soviet Union. Soviet Premier Nikita Khrushchev played the game of "nuclear chicken" to near disaster, but finally blinked and backed down, in October 1962, in the face of an American naval "quarantine." The Soviets removed the missiles, thus countering cries of "Castro coddling" by Kennedy critics in the United States.

Checkmated during the Cuban missile crisis, the Soviets reacted by tightening their grip on East Berlin, notably when they erected the "Berlin Wall" to halt the flight of people from the East German "workers' paradise" into non-Communist West Berlin. President Kennedy, later speaking in West Berlin in the shadow of the "Wall of Shame," reaffirmed America's defense commitment by asserting, "Ich bin ein Berliner" (I am a Berliner). The implication was that he shared with these people their love of freedom.

Kennedy also inherited from Eisenhower the policy of supporting, with money and arms, the anti-Communist regime of Ngo Dinh Diem in South Vietnam. After the fall of China to the Communists in 1949,

American policy planners feared that the "domino theory" would operate. Their concept was that if China-backed North Vietnam seized South Vietnam, the rest of Indochina—Laos, Cambodia, and Thailand—would topple into the Communist camp like a row of "falling dominoes." In 1961 Kennedy arrived at the fateful decision to raise Eisenhower's 700 American advisers in South Vietnam to an eventual 16,000—a major step in the subsequent commitment of more than 500,000 troops. A slogan of the hour in Washington became "Sink or Swim with Ngo Dinh Diem."

TURMOIL AND ASSASSINATIONS

Tragic events on the world stage could not obscure the portents of domestic strife looming on the American domestic horizon. Conflicts between individual rights and national security were highlighted by a series of controversial decisions by the Supreme Court. It was often called the "Earl Warren Court" after the Chief Justice, who was accused by many critics of "Communist coddling." Landmark decisions to protect the rights of the accused also led to charges of "crook coddling," reinforced by the slogan "Handcuff Crooks, Not Cops." Many citizens were also aroused by the Court's restrictions on prayer in the public schools. They voiced the fear that the "old goats in black coats" would soon be erasing "In God We Trust" from America's money.

In their shock effect no decisions of the "Warren Court" in the Kennedy years disturbed the nation as much as the civil rights cases. Following the line set in the historic school-desegregation decision of 1954, the Court seemed to be repeating the current cry "Jim Crow—Must Go!" But the "white backlash" was widespread, and state legislatures in the South railed against "sociological" opinions, complaining that the bench had usurped legislative functions.

"Civil rights" meant rights not only for blacks but also for criminal defendants and others, including city dwellers. In its milestone "one-man, one-vote" decision the Court ruled for "reapportionment" of the state legislatures and the Congress according to population rather than geography—people rather than cows. Endless criticism of the Supreme Court culminated in a noisy but unsuccessful drive to impeach Earl Warren for "tearing down the Constitution."

School desegregation and other administration reforms to meet social and economic grievances met massive resistance. Widespread "civil disobedience" resulted in thousands of arrests and dozens of new phrases in the political vocabulary, including "sit-in," "freedom rider," and the song and slogan "We Shall Overcome!" In August 1963 several hundred thousand demonstrators peacefully participated in a massive "March on Washington," where the Reverend Martin Luther King, Jr., delivered his famous "I Have a Dream" speech near the Lincoln Memorial. Racial discrimination in the South begat violence, and during the "long hot summer" of 1963 the headlines featured murder, arson, and mayhem.

Especially shocking was the "Battle of Birmingham" between rioters and police aided by electric cattle prods and attack dogs.

As President Kennedy worried over the violent turn of the civil rights movement, the New Frontiersmen struggled with a balky Congress and a citizenry shaken by crises both at home and abroad. The vibrant young President who had written *Profiles in Courage* (this title appeared on a campaign button) was undoubtedly courageous, and he decided to venture into a hostile Texas to counteract right-wing bitterness. Portents of tragedy in Dallas could be seen in portrait-posters of Kennedy entitled "Wanted for Treason" and in "KKK" bumper stickers meaning "Kayo Kennedy Klan." The unbelievable happened when, on November 22, 1963, the President was killed by an assassin's rifle fire, and so ended the Kennedy era, which friendly writers likened to the chivalrous atmosphere of King Arthur's court at Camelot.

"Let us continue," exhorted Vice President Lyndon Johnson as he donned the mantle of the fallen President. With a remarkably smooth transfer of power the tall Texan promised a shocked nation that he would fulfill the aspirations of his predecessor. In an impressive display of political arm twisting and "flesh pressing," L.B.J. induced Congress to approve considerable parts of Kennedy's languishing program. During these "miracle months" Johnson reinforced his reputation as a back-slapping "wheeler dealer" determined to solve the nation's mounting problems. Noteworthy was the "War on Poverty," which epitomized the new President's resolve "to feed the hungry and to prepare them to be taxpayers instead of tax eaters" on welfare.

JOHNSON VERSUS GOLDWATER

After only nine months in office, Lyndon Baines Johnson easily won the presidential nomination in his own right at Atlantic City, where the Democrats convened late in August 1964. The outcome was a foregone conclusion because L.B.J. had proved that he was a "can do" president. His great goal was to secure a national "consensus" by conciliation and compromise; his favorite quotation from the Bible (Isaiah 1:18) in this context was "Come now, and let us reason together. . . ."

L.B.J.'s platform gave promise of implementing the forward-looking policies that he had already advocated in achieving what he vaguely called "The Great Society." The official Democratic pronouncement took notice of the right-wing lurch of the Republican party by emphatically declaring, "We condemn extremism, whether from the right or left, including the extreme tactics of such organizations as the Communist party, the Ku Klux Klan, and the John Birch Society." The John Birchers, as vehement right-wingers, urged taking "the U.S. out of the U.N. and the U.N. out of the U.S."

Johnson's initials lent themselves well to slogans, while suggesting the cattle business of his native state. The catch phrase, "My brand's LBJ," meant to some button makers "Let's Back Johnson." A small replica of a ten-gallon Texas hat, to be worn on lapels, bore the brand LBJ. Also popular were the campaign buttons worn four years earlier, "All the way with LBJ." Not dissimilar were "Clear the way for LBJ," "LBJ for the USA," and "USA for LBJ." "Let us continue," Johnson's plea after Kennedy's assassination, appeared on countless buttons, echoing Kennedy's inaugural "Let us begin." The feminine touch surfaced in "Ladies for Lyndon" and "Lady Bird [Mrs. Johnson] for First Lady." A lapel appeal to the heart rather than the head resulted in "Love that Lyndon."

Seeking a worthy adversary for L.B.J., the Republicans had met a month earlier in San Francisco's Cow Palace. The radical right, though a minority wing of the party, had managed to win control of the convention by clever work in those conservative states that chose delegates by conventions rather than by primaries. Outspoken Senator Barry Goldwater—a handsome, bronzed, white-haired Arizonan—won the nomination from his fanatical admirers on the first ballot.

Goldwater's chief rival was Nelson A. Rockefeller, the immensely wealthy New Yorker, who, as a moderate liberal, had lost a close primary race to Goldwater in California. The outcome in the Golden State was undoubtedly affected to some extent by the slogan, "Elect a leader, not a lover." Two years earlier, Rockefeller had divorced his wife and married a divorcee. Voters were reminded anew of the malicious gossip when a son was born to the new union only three days before the crucial primary election in California.

At the Cow Palace "Barry's boys," dubbed by critics "Stone Age Republicans," booed Rockefeller as he attempted to address the delegates. The Goldwaterites, with their ultraconservative coloration and their Western connections, thus rode contemptuously over the "Eastern Establishment." Goldwater had reportedly remarked, "We ought to saw off the Eastern seaboard and float it out to sea." The radical-right platform that emerged from the Cow Palace refused to repudiate the extreme rightists, whether John Birchers, with their "little ladies in tennis shoes," or the besheeted Ku Klux Klaners, with their "nuts and kooks." Buttons for Barry defiantly asked, "What's Wrong with Being Right?"

Barry Goldwater was an authentic conservative. He had published a widely sold paperback, *The Conscience of a Conservative* (1960), and in a speech in 1960 he had declared, "I fear Washington and centralized government more than I do Moscow." In January 1964 he had attacked the "Santa Claus" concept—"the Santa Claus of something-for-nothing and something-for-everyone." He naturally opposed Social Security. During the presidential campaign of 1964 he insisted, "A government that is big enough to give you all you want is big enough to take it all away." Such arresting thoughts appealed to his adoring followers, who reflected their sentiments in buttons declaring, "I Love Barry," "I'm Extremely Fond of Barry," and "If I Were 21 I'd Vote for Barry."

THE BURIAL OF BARRY

As a candidate, Goldwater not only attacked big government and big spending under the Democrats but also assailed "Communist coddling." One Republican button read "Goldwater for President—Victory over Communism." Barry's backers also sounded the slogan "In Your Heart You Know He's Right," which led to the scornful response "In Your Guts You Know He's Nuts." Actually, the Republican nominee freely conceded that he did not have "a first-class brain." He struck back in his acceptance speech with "I would remind you that extremism in the defense of liberty is no vice. And let me remind you also that moderation in the pursuit of justice is no virtue!"

Countless Americans, including Nelson Rockefeller, were shocked by this advocacy of extremism, with its subtle approval of lynching and other forms of vigilantism. Lyndon Johnson replied, "Extremism in the pursuit of the Presidency is an unpardonable vice. Moderation in the affairs of the nation is the highest virtue." The cleverest of the Democratic rejoinders were, "Extremism in the pursuit of vice is no virtue" and "My only vice is moderation." Referring to the many indiscreet and contradictory "Goldwaterisms," one supporter complained, "Don't quote what he says, say what he means."

Goldwater had liked red-baiting Joe McCarthy and disliked Communists, especially those in Vietnam, and as a reserve air force officer he deplored no-win wars. In 1962 he had published a book entitled *Why Not Victory?* His most costly blunder came when he "shot from the lip" and suggested that field commanders, including those in Vietnam, be given authority to use tactical and low-yield nuclear weapons at their discretion. Alarmed opponents promptly branded Goldwater a trigger-happy cowboy who would "Barry us" in a nuclear holocaust. Democrats preferred to "Bury Barry."

Such fear was a bonanza for sloganeers and button-makers. They came up with "Help Barry Stamp out Peace," together with "Hohenzollern Goldwater" (Goldwater as Kaiser), "Goldwasser für Führer" (Goldwater as Hitler), and "Defoliate Goldwater," as President Johnson was doing to the foliage in Vietnam. Some anti-Goldwater partisans took the chemical symbol for gold (Au) and combined it with that for water (H_2O), plus the election date, to produce a global blowup in this fashion:

$$Au\ H_2O + 1964 = \text{☁}.$$

Less complicated but equally suggestive was the Democratic button "Go with Goldwater," followed by a nuclear cloud. The same general thought found expression in "Hari-Kari with Barry."

One of Goldwater's chief complaints was that his Republican predecessors had been guilty of "me tooism"—that is they would carry out

Democratic programs better than the Democrats could themselves. Barry urged the voters to choose between a clear-cut right-wing program and spendthrift Democratic liberalism. "A Choice and Not an Echo" and "A Choice for a Change" were among his most effective slogans. But his critics charged that the choice was between the nineteenth and twentieth centuries, and that he was trying to repeal the twentieth century, as it were. A sardonic Democratic slogan gibed "Goldwater in 1864"—the year Lincoln was reelected.

Vietnam played into L.B.J.'s hands when, early in August 1964, North Vietnamese torpedo boats reportedly attacked two American destroyers in the Tonkin Gulf. Johnson, who had anticipated and perhaps schemed for a provocative incident, promptly launched retaliatory bombing attacks on North Vietnamese installations. American voters reacted enthusiastically to this red-blooded response, which undercut the charge of Johnson's being "soft on communism." A patriotic and duped Congress, to its later regret and with only two negative votes, passed the fateful Gulf of Tonkin Resolution. It gave blank-check authorization to the President "to take all necessary measures to repel any armed attack against the forces of the United States and to prevent further aggression." Yet L.B.J. reassured critics that he stood for a policy of "Let Asians fight Asians," and he pledged "no wider war" in Southeast Asia. Speaking in Ohio in October of 1964, he declared, in words that came back to haunt him, "But we are not about to send American boys nine or ten thousand miles away from home to do what Asian boys ought to be doing for themselves."

All was going smoothly for L.B.J. when, in the same month, a frightening scandal broke. One of Johnson's close White House aides was arrested in the nearby Y.M.C.A. on a charge of homosexuality. The inference was that this official, in a highly sensitive office, may have been vulnerable to blackmail by Soviet agents seeking top-secret information. The shocking affair quickly suggested such unflattering slogans as "Let's be gay with L.B.J." and "Either way with L.B.J.," and Johnson's stock seemed about to plummet. Luckily for him, three events in the international theater, all within forty-eight hours, eclipsed the sexual scandal: the conservative Tory government in Britain fell; Premier Khrushchev in Moscow was sacked and made an "unperson"; and the Chinese detonated their first nuclear bomb. President Johnson cleverly took advantage of Khrushchev's downfall to proclaim to a crowd, "I told him that we intend to bury no one, and we do not intend to be buried."

In keeping with the grimness of the campaign and the widespread fear of a bomb-rattling Goldwater, few songs appeared. "Hello, Lyndon" was adapted to the tune of "Hello, Dolly," from the Broadway hit show of that name. The Republicans had "Go with Goldwater," which suggested the rather empty slogan "Go-go Goldwater in '64." Aside from these two mediocre efforts one finds little campaign music worthy of mention.

Goldwater proved to be not so much a candidate as a catastrophe, for countless liberal Republicans deserted the party and voted for Johnson on election day. L.B.J. won in a landslide of prodigious proportions, while numerous Republican candidates for lesser offices were "buried with Barry." Johnson, who thus got his coveted "consensus," hailed the result as "a mandate for unity." But as the winner gradually became enmeshed in a full-scale war in Vietnam with American boys, many voters ruefully concluded that they had voted for Johnson but had got a trigger-happy Goldwater.

THE GREAT SOCIETY IN TROUBLE

Heavy Democratic majorities in the new Eighty-ninth Congress responded to Johnson's landslide victory with an avalanche of legislation reminiscent of Roosevelt's "Hundred Days Congress" of 1933. The President's "Great Society" program attacked poverty on a broad scale and was designed, in his words, to make men "more concerned with the quality of their goals than the quantity of their goods." As a result of his persuasiveness and arm twisting, the "Hip-Pocket Congress" of 1965 cooperated impressively with "Big Daddy" L.B.J. Like sausages popping out of a machine, bills for the Great Society emerged from Congress designed to cure various social ills. Conspicuous among them was legislation to turn the decaying "inner cities" into "Model Cities," as well as bills to achieve "equal opportunity" for blacks and other minorities.

Sagging political fortunes afflicted the Great Society early in 1966. Mass demonstrations by blacks led to a severe "backlash" and stinging setbacks in Congress. A bill to ban racial discrimination in housing failed to pass in the face of the outcry from many white property owners, "Your home is your castle—protect it!" Congress also refused to amend the "right to work" clause of the Taft-Hartley Act, although a new "guaranteed minimum wage" did extend new protection to millions of American workers. Deepening discontent with "crime in the streets" and with the bottomless quagmire in Vietnam added to Johnson's worries.

Alarming physical violence earmarked all of Johnson's elected term. Black militants, impatient with snaillike progress, implored their "brothers and sisters" to follow Mao Tse-tung's dictum that "power comes out of the barrel of a gun." "Black Power" advocates fought the police, whom they branded "pigs" and who in turn often overreacted with "police brutality" in upholding "law and order." The most radical left-wingers invoked the slogan "Off the Pigs," as they exhorted followers to kill ("waste") policemen. Appalling outbursts of racial rioting gutted the Watts ghetto in Los Angeles during the "long hot summer" of 1965 and Newark, New Jersey, in 1967. The assassination of Martin Luther King, Jr., in Memphis in April 1968 touched off a nationwide wave of pillage and arson, including the "second burning of Washington" in the Negro section of the capital. "Burn, baby, burn" was the ugly cry from the lips of countless rioters.

American colleges were also revolting in the late 1960s as part of the worldwide movement toward greater political awareness and participation by youth. The object of student scorn was often "The Establishment," which had failed to respond satisfactorily to the "nonnegotiable demands" presented across the "generation gap." These proposals included the recognition of "cultural identity" through "black studies" and other academic programs. Campus convulsions featured sit-ins, burnouts, window smashings, and other "trashing" of property. Youth was having its fling by flinging bricks and bottles.

Police predictably reacted with forcible evictions, tear gassing, and mass arrests—to accompanying cries of "Pigs off campus." Most ominous was the emergence of extremist student groups like the "Weathermen," an offshoot of the Students for a Democratic Society (SDS), who repeatedly resorted to bombs to back up their demands.

POSTPONING FAILURE IN VIETNAM

The fighting in Vietnam—a no-win, no-end war—was not going well for Uncle Sam, despite the massive infusion of American troops and money. Militant "hawks" opposed appeasement, urging "No more Koreas—win in Vietnam" and "Don't make Saigon our Munich." President Johnson insisted that America could not "turn tail and run" and urged soldiers in the field to "nail" that coonskin on the wall. Referring to numerous draft dodgers, one hawkish button sneered, "In their hearts, they know they're wrong—But they'd rather go to jail than fight Vietcong."

Militant "peaceniks" or "doves" opposed growing military involvement. They pressured the administration to put out peace feelers and arrange a cease-fire before the conflict escalated into a world war. "Peace or Pieces" were the sloganized alternatives. Placards carried by street demonstrators demanded "Bring the Troops Home Now" and "Make Love, Not War." Antiwar "teach-ins" often concluded with the single, simple message "Out now!"

Anti-war buttons were likewise biting. Among them one finds "Vietnam for the Vietnamese," "Bonds Buy Bombs," and "Napalm Makes Millionaires." The last-named was a reference to the brutal incendiary bombs that burned the skins of civilians and brought horrible death. A disturbing analogy was graphically arranged in this fashion on one button:

CRIMINAL INTERVENTIONS
1956 U.S.S.R.   ⟶ Hungary
1965 U.S.A.   ⟶ Vietnam

Selective Service soon became the special target of campus protests for its role in corralling the manpower to fight in Vietnam. Students burned their draft cards while thousands chanted, "Draft beer, not stu-

"We Are Winning the War." The wasteland refrain of Presidents Johnson and Ho in 1967. Paul Szep, *The Boston Globe*. Reproduced with permission of *The Boston Globe*.

dents," "Hell no, we won't go!" and "Curse this stupid war." Some responded to the slogan "Be Free—Go Canada," while others refused to pay income taxes or protested, "No Tuition—Tax War Profits."

President Johnson unwisely believed that America was strong enough to have both "guns and butter," but sentiment in the nation was shifting heavily against the war, which had become wearisome, costly, and divisive. The bloody "Tet offensive" of 1968 by the Communists rudely shattered illusions that a military victory was just around the corner. Demands to de-Americanize the war began to undercut the Johnson "game plan," which included increasing aerial bombardment. Americans everywhere were rejecting the back-breaking role of "world policeman." Bumper strips chided the President with "Lyndon's Bridges Are Falling Down" and "Johnson's Father Should Have Withdrawn Sooner."

Opposition had also arisen to administration policies of "managing the news." Spokesmen for the Pentagon and State Department were generally and routinely disbelieved, and a widening "credibility gap" emerged between L.B.J. and the public. Journalists insisted on the people's "right to know" the truth about Vietnam, especially after optimistic predictions were buried by the Tet offensive.

THE SCRAMBLE FOR JOHNSON'S CROWN

Political pundits generally agreed that President Johnson, who obviously loved power, would run for a second elective term in 1968. But no expert could be sure. Most noteworthy of the Democratic aspirants to enter the Democratic primaries was a scholarly "dove," Senator Eugene ("Clean Gene") McCarthy of Minnesota, an eloquent and outspoken foe of the Vietnam War. The younger antiwar crowd, notably college students, rallied behind his banner and with "student power" launched a campaign of door-bell ringing in the New Hampshire primary election, the first to be held. The results of this "kiddie campaign" or "children's crusade" were astonishing. McCarthy jolted the politicos by capturing most of the delegates (twenty of twenty-four) and 42 percent of the popular vote, as contrasted with 49 percent for write-in candidate Johnson. This startling evidence of Johnson's unpopularity and vulnerability caused Robert F. Kennedy, the dead President's younger brother, belatedly to toss his hat into the ring.

L.B.J. later stated that he had already decided not to run again, but in any event he needed a theatrical, face-saving gesture. This he provided, on March 31, 1968, in a nationally televised speech during which he pleaded for national unity. At the end he paused for dramatic effect, then added emphatically, "Accordingly, I shall not seek and I will not accept the nomination of my party for another term as your President." In this way he would promote unity.

Vice President Hubert Horatio Humphrey, the heir apparent, was now free to seek the nomination with L.B.J.'s blessing. Favorite slogans of his backers were "Who But Hubert?" "Hubie Baby," and "H.H.H. Fills the Prescription," with evident reference to his early career as a druggist. Obvious appeals to Latino voters appeared in "Viva Humphrey" and "H.H.H.—Si! Si! Si!"

Many pro-Republican posters or placards, on the other hand, jabbed at H.H.H., including "Keep the Country Hump-free" and, with a thrust at the President, "Why Change the Ventriloquist for the Dummy?" Humphrey's loyal support of Johnson's hawkish policies on Vietnam inspired a barbed poster reading "Hugh Bird [Hubert]: A Hawk for All Seasons." More direct were the buttons "Dump Humph" and "Dump the Hump."

Young "Bobby" Kennedy, capitalizing on his brother's name and fame, made a remarkable showing in his brief and tragic campaign, which was ended by an assassin's bullet just after a gratifying victory in the key California primary. He appealed especially to the youthful crowd that had backed McCarthy at a time when an antiwar crusade seemed hopeless. Those who still supported "Clean Gene" urged in posters to "Give the Presidency Back to the People," while sporting anti-Kennedy buttons, "Kennedy is Sex, but McCarthy is Love," and "Bobby's Not Jack."

On a different note various buttons proclaimed "McCarthy Is No Puppet," "No Malarky—Vote for McCarthy," and "McCarthy and Peace in '68."

Before his murder Kennedy's antiwar campaign had generated impressive momentum, so great was his personal magnetism and the prestige of his name. "Sock it to 'Em Bobby," was a button that caught the spirit of his crusade, as did "Vote Kennedy for Peace." An evident bid for the Latin vote could be found in "Viva Kennedy," and for the black vote in "Kennedy's White but He's Alright."

THE NEW NIXON EMERGES

Early in August 1968 the Republicans met in Miami Beach, Florida, to nominate Richard M. Nixon, heralded as "The New Nixon," on the first ballot. The "old Nixon" had developed a loser's image, but the new one, though still hawkish on the Vietnam War, favored "law and justice," which sounded less harsh than "law and order." Support for Nixon found expression in the slogans "Nixon's the One" and "Nixon's the One —Are You One Too?" Rather ironic, in the light of later developments, were the buttons "The 'I' in Nixon Stands For Integrity" and "Black Dignity—Nixon's the One." The woman vote was courted in the proud boast worn by young and pretty "Nixonettes," "I'm a Nixon Gal—Nixon for President."

Nixon surprisingly tapped as his running mate Spiro Agnew, a Greek-descended governor of Maryland. The second-spot candidate was strong on "law and order" and had considerable appeal in the color-conscious South, to which the Republicans were directing their "Southern strategy." A common response of many voters was "Spiro who?" and to ask if Spiro was a candidate or a disease, later called "Spironoia." Agnew himself modestly and correctly conceded, "I agree that Spiro Agnew is not a household name." One Democratic poster queried, "Why Rob Maryland of Its Mediocrity?" and a campaign button read, "Spiro Our Hero." Another was mathematically prophetic: "Nixon + Spiro = Zero." Actually Agnew proved to be something of an embarrassment to Nixon in this campaign, especially when he offended ethnic voters by calling Polish-Americans "Polacks" and referring to a Japanese-American reporter as a "fat Jap."

Anti-Nixon buttons, posters, and placards were especially barbed. Doubts about the "New Nixon" found vent in "Mr. Nixon: How Long Will This New Pose Last?" A variant of the used-car salesman barb appeared in "Would You Let Your Sister Marry This Man?" and in "Tricky Dick—the Human Edsel"—a reference to a Ford automobile that had spectacularly failed to make the grade financially. "Dick Is A Four Letter Word" had erotic overtones. Chronology was important in "Do It Like You Did It in '60, Dick," when Nixon lost to John Kennedy, and "Leadership for the '50's," which were eight years in the past.

THE DOOM OF THE DEMOCRATS

"The Battle of Chicago," as the Democratic convention came to be called, was fought late in August 1968. Masses of long-haired "hippies," "yippies," and other protesters poured into the Windy City to assail the barbed-wire barricades of "Fort Daley," named after the big-boss mayor of the metropolis. Flaunting Viet Cong flags, the hairy demonstrators chanted, "Stop the war," "Ho, Ho, Ho Chi Minh" (in honor of the frail George Washington of North Vietnam), and "Hey, hey, L.B.J., how many kids did you kill today?" The demonstrators baited the "pigs" (police), who lost their "cool" and pounded their night sticks on the skulls of scores of their tormentors. Hundreds of rioters were arrested and scores of the injured were hospitalized (including some police), but the only fatalities were Democratic hopes.

On the convention floor wild scenes erupted, while spectators in the galleries, many wearing black arm bands for the Vietnam dead, sang the civil rights anthem "We Shall Overcome." The antiwar McCarthyites fought bitterly for a stop-the-bombing pledge in the Democratic platform, but the majority managed to vote through the hawkish plank that they wanted. So great was the obvious division within the Democratic party, nakedly revealed to the world on television, that "United with Humphrey" posters were scrapped to avoid additional ridicule.

Further excitement was generated by the appearance of a "spoiler" third-party ticket, that of the American Independent party. Its presidential aspirant was a right-winger and racist, George C. Wallace, ex-governor of Alabama. A law-and-order man, he opposed "anarchist" demonstrations and also any enforced integration of the blacks. His cry was "Segregation now, segregation tomorrow, and segregation Forever." He enjoyed a strong grass-roots appeal with the semi-literate masses, who, in the Populist tradition, responded to such button-slogans as "Let the People Speak" and "Stand Up for America." Wallaceites did not seem to be bothered by the question often asked of third-party adherents, "Why waste your vote?"

In line with his tough stance, Wallace chose as his running mate another vice presidential embarrassment, General Curtis E. LeMay. A prominent air force officer, he was quoted as having urged that Vietnam be bombed back "into the stone age." He also complained, "We are swatting flies when we should be going after the manure pile." During the presidential campaign he "reassured" the voters by stating "The world won't come to an end if we use a nuclear weapon."

Wallace had promised to run over with his automobile any demonstrators who lay down in his path, and this indiscretion inspired a button showing Wallace and LeMay as the "Run 'Em Down" and "Blow 'Em Up" twins. A placard proposed "Drop LeMay on Hanoi," the capital of North Vietnam. To many voters the Wallace–LeMay ticket suggested Adolf Hitler, as advertised in the button "1938—Hitler-Goering, 1968—

Wallace–LeMay." Other signs told a similar story: "If you liked Hitler, You'll Love Wallace," "Wallace Über Alles," and, with an Alabama accent, "Sieg Heil Ya'll." A pro-Negro Franciscan monk carried a placard in one demonstration, "From Alabama Justice, Spare Us, Oh Lord." All such barbs made mockery of the patriotic button "Stand Up for America —Wallace–LeMay."

War in Vietnam continued to be an overshadowing issue in the campaign of 1968. Both Nixon and Humphrey favored an "honorable peace." Nixon further promised to "end the war" and "win the peace," while pledging that there would be "no more Vietnams." Disruptive disunity in the country was so obvious that one button featured "Forward Together," while a placard appeared in one of Nixon's crowds, "Bring Us Together." The candidate stressed this theme in one of his last speeches, and it took on added emphasis in the early months of his new administration.

Humphrey, as Vice President, had committed himself to Johnson's hawkish policies before the campaign, and a sense of loyalty restrained him from shifting to a "stop the bombing" position. "Get the Hump off our Backs" read one dovish placard. But late in September, Humphrey declared at Salt Lake City, "As President, I would stop the bombing of the North as an acceptable risk for peace." Lyndon Johnson later claimed that this surrender cost Humphrey the election, but the fact is that after the candidate's backdown the tide began to turn his way.

What hurt Humphrey badly during the last week of the campaign was the refusal of the American-backed government of South Vietnam, under President Thieu, to cooperate with the peace negotiators in Paris. Thieu's own bitter reply was "betrayal of an ally." The tail was so evidently wagging the dog that the sour response in America ran, "A bird in the hand is worth Thieu in the bush."

Nixon won in November 1968, in another cliffhanger: 43.4 percent of the vote to 42.7 for Humphrey. The victor's plurality, not a majority, was so close that the outcome could hardly be called a mandate for anything. In the next few weeks Lyndon Johnson closed out his long public career. He thus left the White House for his beloved ranch house in Texas, after having crucified himself politically on the cross of Vietnam.

XXXIII

The Rise and Fall of Richard Nixon

I am not a crook.

Richard Nixon, 1973

NIXON COMMANDER-IN-CHIEF

Richard Nixon rode into office in 1969 on a wave of war–weary rhetoric that featured "bring the boys home" from Vietnam. Elected as a plurality President, he attempted to forge a consensus around the "silent center" that had elected him, although his promising slogans of "Forward Together" and "Bring Us Together" never caught on. Grim problems, both domestic and foreign, bedeviled the new Chief Executive from the beginning.

Upheavals in the ghettoes, combined with a series of civil rights triumphs during the Johnson years, caused millions of Americans to yearn for coolness and caution in social reform. While minority elements continued to complain about "first-class taxes, second-class jobs," Nixon office-holders soft-pedaled desegregation through a policy of "benign neglect." Virulent organizations of the Ku Klux Klan type enjoyed a resurgence as hooded hoodlums offered their solution to desegregation by bellowing "Bus them back to Africa."

Predictably, the nation revealed a mood for "law and order" government, as promised by the Republican victor. Stone-faced John Mitchell was appointed Attorney General to oversee such federal efforts as the prosecution of the "Chicago Seven," who were charged with inciting to riot at the tempestuous Democratic convention in Chicago. Prominently displayed in strategic places was the poster plea "End the Conspiracy Against the Bill of Rights—Dump Mitchell." Although the new President pleaded for Americans to "stop shouting at one another," the Nixon years witnessed increasing dissension and polarization. But the Republicans felt certain that their man in the White House sensed the public pulse, especially that of the "great silent majority" which Nixon claimed as his chief support.

Appointments of tough-fisted figures to the courts and other agencies of government rasped the Democratic opposition. But many Americans, increasingly concerned over "crime in the streets," approved Nixon's conservative stance, which was characterized by his spokesmen as the "New Federalism."

Nixon managed to "pack" the Supreme Court with conservatives, although he here failed in pursuance of his "Southern Strategy." Two of his nominees from the South were rejected as unworthy of the high office. Yet he could take satisfaction in knowing that the new "Nixon court" was strong for "law and order," and that its fresh decisions were reversing the liberal tide of the Warren era. Increasingly the black-robed justices were rejecting "crook coddling" and favoring those who were crying "Support your local police."

Not surprisingly, the new administration gave high priority to cooling down the overheated economy. The "soaring sixties" had created an inflationary spiral that squeezed individual citizens and businesses alike. An unholy combination of unemployment, stagnation, and galloping inflation caused, according to the pundits, "stagflation."

VIETNAMIZING THE VIETNAM WAR

Overshadowing all political bickering was the overwhelming desire of the American people to see the Vietnam conflict ended. Opinions clashed sharply as to the best strategy. "Hawks" called for more military pressure, despite the fact that there were already over a half million soldiers committed, plus billions of dollars annually. "Bomb Hanoi" buttons were worn by American Legionnaires and other superpatriots. The generals stubbornly maintained that they could "see the light at the end of the tunnel," but their efforts to "win the peace" by bombing and to "save" villages by destroying them merely stiffened the resistance of the North Vietnamese. "Bring the war home" demanded a growing army of "peaceniks," who believed "It's better to pray than to slay." Some frankly endorsed a Moscow objective: "Colonialism and Imperialism Must End—Support National Liberation Movements."

Swelling opposition to the war was highlighted by street demonstrations, often riotous. A ray of hope came in 1969 with President Nixon's so-called "Guam Doctrine" or "Nixon Doctrine," under which Asians would be obliged to fight their wars without American troops. But the "doves" vented their skepticism, especially when the troop withdrawal began slowly in widely separated stages. They demanded immediate evacuation, mouthing such slogans as "No more war," "Out now," and

"Supersam get out of Vietnam." Unlike the hawks, the doves believed that a political solution would be best. "Negotiate, Don't Escalate," read a popular bumper strip displayed by "peaceniks," who fully endorsed the bumper-strip query, "What If They Gave a War and Nobody Came?" Outspoken buttons declared "Peace is Patriotic," "Our Boys Are Dying in Vain," and "Mobilization to Stop Mass Murder in Vietnam."

Futile initiatives in the diplomatic arena, despite some slow-motion troop departures, convinced opponents of the war that "Vietnamization" by "Nixonization" was merely a cover for continuing the vain American pursuit of a military victory. Cartoonists showed a bandaged Uncle Sam pleading, "I Want Out." Mass-meeting "moratoriums" and local "teach-ins" on the war attracted tens of thousands of peacefully protesting Americans of all ages. "God Is Not On Our Side," warned one placard.

Targeted for powerful protests was the Selective Service System, which was pouring thousands of reluctant young men into Southeast Asia. A chorus of demands focused on the theme "End the draft now." Campus critics chanted with considerable success, "ROTC [Reserve Officers' Training Corps] must go!" "Off ROTC," and "End campus complicity with the war." Dissatisfied with Nixon's "lottery system," installed in early 1970 to make the draft more equitable, protesters parodied medical warnings with the slogan "Caution: Military Service May Be Hazardous To Your Health." Cynical bumper strips advised, "War is Good Business—Invest Your Son" and "I Didn't Raise My Son To Be A Soldier."

Infuriating to critics was the attitude of many high government officials and citizens. These hawks questioned the patriotism of the dissenters, whose opposition allegedly gave "aid and comfort" to the enemy. Cries of "Traitors" were heard along the sidelines of several "peace marches." While proadministration citizens asked all Americans to "show your colors," equally patriotic antiadministration citizens replied, "The enemy is at home." Black students acidly reminded "whitey" that "No Viet Cong Ever Called Us Niggers." One button asked a provocative question: "Black People 10% in U.S.—22% in Vietnam. Why?"

Antiwar sentiment was spurred by sensational revelations that American soldiers had perpetrated atrocities, conspicuously in the village of My Lai. A single officer, Lieutenant W. L. Calley, Jr., was made the scapegoat for the entire sordid affair, thus creating extensive sympathy for his plight among hawks, who carried signs demanding that the army "Free Calley." By January 1970 the bloody conflict had become the longest in American history, and growing legions of marching protesters were proclaiming, "We just want to give peace a chance."

CAMBODIANIZING THE CONFLICT

Unimpressed by President Nixon's efforts to "wind down the war," much of the world community, including most of America's allies, joined in popular protest. The strain of the struggle in South Vietnam showed in repressive government actions against the press and those war-weary citizens desiring negotiations. "It's hard enough to support one government, let alone Thieu," punned one bumper strip, referring to South Vietnam's authoritarian President. Reports of totalitarian tactics, including the use of inhumane "tiger cages" for political prisoners, hastened antiwar resolve to withdraw American support completely. "What Has Thieu Done For You?" queried one poster, whose authors no doubt subscribed to the sentiment "Bid Thieu Adieu."

Frustration in military and diplomatic councils with the stubbornness of the Vietnam enemy triggered a dramatic development in April 1970. Without consulting Congress as a body, Nixon ordered American forces to invade the "sanctuaries" used by Viet Cong and North Vietnamese troops in "neutral" Cambodia. Massive waves of dissent swept America, as dovish protesters cried "No wider war" and "End imperialism."

Reacting to the Cambodian invasion, angry mobs of college students on dozens of campuses fought police and National Guard troops, chanting "Pigs off campus." A total of a half dozen students were shot and killed at Kent State University in Ohio and Jackson State College in Mississippi in the course of anti-war disturbances. While some unsympathetic citizens displayed bumper strips declaring "The Kent State Four Should Have Studied More," most Americans deplored the tragic shootings. "Remember Kent and Jackson," chorused student protest leaders, as their posters proclaimed, "Venceremos—We Shall Conquer."

Rancor generated by the Cambodian invasion deepened wounds incurred by political discussions of the war. The White House hatchet man during the ongoing debate was Vice President Spiro Agnew, who kept the press busy recording his "Agnewisms" directed at critics of the conflict. Lashing out at the news media, which he held responsible for dovish propaganda, Agnew branded the press an "effete corps of impudent snobs." As champion of the right wing, Agnew's scathing attacks on "pusillanimous pussy-footers" and "vicars of vacillation" earned him the title of "The Mouth That Roared." Some observers saw a political advantage in Agnew's serving as the White House hatchet man, perhaps foreshadowing his own campaign for President as "The Spiro of '76." Echoing Adlai Stevenson's denunciation of pessimists as "prophets of gloom and doom," Agnew reached his alliterative zenith of "Spirotechnics" by branding opponents of the administration "nattering nabobs of negativism." An approving campaign button read, "Sock It To 'Em, Spiro!"

FOREIGN AND DOMESTIC DIFFICULTIES

As hot war raged in Vietnam, President Nixon became a self-appointed emissary to world capitals in his global search for the promised "generation of peace." An initial slowing of the nuclear arms race was supposedly

"O.K., Now Let's Talk!" Nixon confronts Soviet spokesman
(Brezhnev). Charles Brooks, *The Birmingham News*. Reproduced
with permission of *The Birmingham News*.

achieved by Soviet-U.S. cooperation in the Strategic Arms Limitation
Talks (SALT), begun in 1969 and facilitated by Nixon's jet-plane diplomacy at the Kremlin. On the strength of personal relationships between
the principal leaders, the United States and the Soviet Union entered an
uneasily cooperative period of "détente," a supposed relaxation of tensions.

Shadows of nuclear incineration meanwhile fell more darkly upon
mankind. Sophisticated missiles now employed the "Multiple Independent Reentry Vehicle" (MIRV) warheads, as new cries arose of "Ban the
Bomb." American negotiators used such presumed bargaining chips as
American superiority in technology to offset the Soviet edge in "throw
weight" or rocket power. Proponents of the "Anti-Ballistic Missile

System" (ABM) warned of "nuclear blackmail" should the Communist nations gain clear superiority. Yet efforts to contain the nuclear arms race, including a nonproliferation treaty signed by many powers, were periodically sidetracked by the unwelcome entry of new nations to the exclusive and expensive "Nuclear Club."

Peaceful utilization of the new rocket technology emerged in the race into outer space. Although the Russians were the pioneers with their "Sputniks," Americans proudly hailed their own achievements, culminating in the initial conquest of the moon on July 20, 1969. Neil Armstrong, the first man on the moon, immortalized his triumph with the announcement, "One small step for man, one giant leap for mankind." But critics charged that the astronomically costly space race drained moneys needed for earthly problems, and by the mid-1970s Congress had pared the space program to a fraction of its former size.

Domestic problems often took a back seat to America's international troubles, but President Nixon sought to deal with some of them simultaneously through his legislative program called the "New American Revolution." Attempted economic medication climaxed in 1971 with the establishment of wage and price controls, repugnant to Republican philosophy but deemed necessary to fight inflation. Critics of Nixon's "New Economic Policy" displayed signs claiming, "No Inflation Without Regulation" and "Big Business Fiddles While America Burns." Distressing deficits at all levels of government signaled an era of belt tightening ahead, as observers tried to fathom the implications of "Nixonomics." The "almighty dollar" was drooping on world money markets as balanced budgets in Washington become historical curiosities.

Ominous rises in food prices heralded the end of overflowing storage silos. Widespread austerity and rationing still remained beyond the horizon, but housewives distributed leaflets at supermarkets carrying the demand "We Want Lower Food Prices, No Ifs, Ands, Or Butz." Secretary of Agriculture Earl Butz hardly endeared himself to consumers with his defense of a large grain deal with the Soviets in July 1972. As the cost of bread and meat soared at home, partially as a result of the sale, cynics referred to the "great grain steal." Prices for cattle also rose sharply as a result of shortages, and bumper strips or placards jibed, "We Got No Beef With Nixon" and "We Are Stewing over Beef."

Shocking statistics meanwhile reminded Americans that life was becoming more expendable as well as more expensive. Inspired by repeated "muggings" within sight of the capitol dome, the District of Columbia Crime Control Act was a prototype of the "law and order" approach, including "no knock" entry by the police. President Nixon embarked on a barnstorming tour in autumn 1970, during which he warned against the "rising tide of terrorism" in the nation's cities. Irritated by boisterous heckling at almost every stop, the President lashed out at "thugs and hoodlums" and "bums" opposed to the Vietnam War.

Decent Democrats, who resented Richard Nixon's slurs, charged that "dirty tricksters" in the Republican camp were trying to discredit the antiwar movement. Voters were reminded of the President's election-eve pledge, barely two years earlier, that he would "bring us together." Instead, war critics were threatened with arrest and such harassments as income tax audits. Blacks and other minorities continued to suffer from the "benign neglect" of the administration toward home-front problems while Nixon pursued his objectives in foreign policy.

Most dramatic of the achievements in foreign policy during the Nixon years was the partial lifting of the "bamboo curtain" sheltering mainland China. After the way was smoothed by "ping-pong diplomacy" or exchange visits by rival table-tennis teams, President Nixon traveled to Peking early in 1972. Russia and China had split over ideological differences, and balance-of-power strategy dictated that the President of the United States should be sipping toasts with the Premier of Communist China. Nixon had been a card-carrying anti-Communist throughout his political career, and his spectacular flipflop dismayed conservatives and even led to an ironically premature and ineffective cry of "Impeach Nixon" from a few critics.

One reason for Nixon's opening of informal relations with Red China seems to have been the expectation that Peking would exert pressure on neighboring North Vietnam to agree to some kind of peace settlement. But such hopes were dashed as increasing waves of antiwar discontent swept America. The opening of negotiations with the contending Vietnamese in Paris resulted in discouraging procedural delays, which prompted antiwar protesters to chant, "Save lives, not faces." Massive new assaults by the North Vietnamese forces in the spring of 1972 caused Nixon to retaliate with blistering air attacks on the cities and harbors of North Vietnam. Administration supporters took up the now familiar threat to "bomb them back into the stone age," while despairing youths chanted "Brahms, not Bombs," and "Make wine, not war."

McGOVERN CHALLENGES NIXON

Vexatious Vietnam proved to be the burning issue in the 1972 presidential primaries. Senators Humphrey and Muskie divided the liberal vote and thus enabled a little-known liberal, Senator George McGovern of South Dakota—"Senator Who?"—to win significant victories on the Democratic ticket. After receiving the nomination in Miami Beach, he delivered a fiery acceptance speech to the convention in which he issued the clarion call "Come home, America," which soon became a leading slogan in the campaign. As the earnest and indefatigable "Prairie Populist," McGovern enlisted a diverse following including liberals and minorities but managed to alienate the conservative backbone of his party.

Panic struck the Democratic camp almost immediately when the news leaked out that Senator Thomas Eagleton of Missouri, tapped as McGovern's running mate, had previously undergone psychiatric treatment.

Yet McGovern declared himself behind Eagleton "1,000 percent." As misgivings mounted, McGovern dumped his nominee in about a week and replaced him with a brother-in-law of the late John Kennedy, Sargent Shriver. The demoralized Democrats recovered what ground they could with the slogan "Let George and Sarge Take Charge." Right-wing Republicans, painfully remembering the charges of extremism hurled at Barry Goldwater in 1964, countered by naming McGovern "The Goldwater of the Left."

Undaunted Democrats replied with such diverse slogans and buttons as "Make America Happen Again," "Peace, Jobs, and McGovern," and "If You Work for a Living, How in Hell Can You Vote for Nixon?" More frivolous was "Kiss Me—I'm for McGovern," presumably displayed by pretty girls.

Republican stalwarts, meeting also in Miami Beach, enthusiastically renominated Nixon and Agnew, chanting "Four more years, four more years." McGovern was pilloried for his "crackpot" welfare schemes and his alleged intention to make America a "second-class power" through slashes in defense spending. As for Vietnam, a "peace with surrender" was ruled out as cheering delegates, sensing the possible landslide proportions of the expected victory, wore buttons and carried signs proclaiming, "Nixon Now More Than Ever" and "Reelect the President." "Four More Years," the theme of a campaign song written for Dwight Eisenhower in 1956, was resurrected. Clever bumper strips declared, "The Nation Needs Fixin' with Nixon" and "Stand Pat with Nixon," a pun involving the President's wife Patricia.

Democratic strategists sought to revive the "Tricky Dick" image. The old barb "Would You Buy a Used Car from This Man?" was now changed to "Would You Buy a Used War from This Man?" The Watergate affair occurred in June, 1972, when Republican agents, seeking political information, botched their burglary of the Democratic national headquarters in Washington. McGovern tried to capitalize on the incident but dropped it when the voters showed little interest. At that point no one knew just how ironic was the popular Republican campaign slogan and song "Nixon's the One!"—though an evil twist was given this affirmation on a button which also showed a woman in an advanced state of pregnancy.

Nixon subsequently remarked that "the election was over the day he [McGovern] was nominated." Despite McGovern's reputation for candor and credibility, the "Crazy Tom" Eagleton fiasco had seriously damaged the image of decisiveness that McGovern hoped to cultivate. Republicans cuttingly remarked that "Will Rogers never met McGovern," alluding to the humorist's observation in 1930, "I never met a man I didn't like."

Enthusiastic McGovernite backers did not concede that the cause was lost, despite a dismal showing in the public opinion polls. Opposition to the President found expression in such slogans as "Nixon is Through in '72," "No Nixon—Now or Ever," and the hackneyed "Nix on Nixon." An added thrust was "We Don't Want Agnew Either." Many buttons, bumper strips, and placards featured the President's well-earned reputation for hawkishness, as in "Nixon the Mad Bomber," "Drop Nixon from a B-52," and "The Blood is on Your Hands."

Voters recalled Nixon's claim in 1968 of a closely guarded blueprint for ending American involvement in Vietnam. They now asked cynically, four years later and with war still raging, "What happened to the secret plan?" An ironical Democratic button quoted from a Nixon campaign speech in October 1968: "Those who have had a chance for four years and could not produce peace, should not be given another chance." Nixon eventually kept the war going three days more than four years—longer by some four months than America's formal participation in World War II.

PEACE WITHOUT HONOR

News of progress at the Paris peace talks late in 1972 gave promise of ending the Vietnam War and rallied a host of voters behind President Nixon. Less than two weeks before the balloting, Secretary of State Henry A. Kissinger returned from France and prematurely announced that "peace is at hand," although unsigned and unwon. Suspicious Americans reacted with "No more Munichs." Yet Nixon won by an overwhelming landslide, which masked the light turnout and voter apathy.

Claiming a resounding mandate, the reelected President chose to highlight the theme of self-help in his second inaugural address. He urged citizens to ask "not just what will government do for me, but what can I do for myself." Justifying his legislative program by his presumed mandate, Nixon pressed in early 1973 for economic reforms. The "Nixon Court," often by one-vote majorities, continued to hand down "strict constructionist" decisions that interpreted the Constitution conservatively. Racially, the cities were relatively quiescent, as the ardor of earlier civil rights zealots faded. But militants were still proclaiming, "All power to the people," while less strident voices complained that "Nixon doesn't care." Various civic organizations tried to encourage racial peace with such slogans as "Good neighbors come in all colors."

Beclouding the domestic scene was the turmoil caused by the Vietnam War and the increasing political polarization of the citizenry. The skittish dove of peace took flight after the election, and in response to North Vietnamese escalations Nixon, "the mad bomber," launched a furious aerial attack known as the twelve-day "Christmas blitz." Spokesmen for the Defense Department explained that many of the forays were "protective reaction raids" against antiaircraft batteries. But the relentless pounding drove the North Vietnamese back to the Paris conference table and a so-called "cease-fire" was finally signed in January 1973. Antiwar protesters in America tried to maintain momentum toward a negotiated settlement with such slogans as "Escalate Peace!" and "Rice, not Rifles!"

North Vietnamese troops were allowed to remain in much of South Vietnam by the terms of the "Paris Accords," but all American armed forces were to withdraw. The President, interpreting retreat as no defeat, hailed the face-saving agreement as "peace with honor" while others complained that he had brought neither peace nor honor. Especially gratifying to Nixon was the enemy's pledge to return some 560 American prisoners of war (POWs) whose cause he had strongly championed. Bumper strips reminded Americans that "POWs Never Have a Nice Day" and pleaded, "Don't Let Them Be Forgotten." When they finally returned, some of the grateful American ex-prisoners exhibited signs reading, "God Bless America and Nixon." All returnees were included in the poster appeal "Don't Forget, Hire a Vet."

WATERGATE WOES

Watergate drowned Richard Nixon's hopes of completing his Presidency in glory and instead washed him out of office in unprecedented disgrace. The bungled Watergate burglary, which the White House news secretary dismissed as a "third-rate affair," eventually unraveled a long skein of Republican and Nixonian misdeeds. The "bugging" burglars arrested inside the Democratic headquarters in June 1972 proved to be agents for "CREEP," the Committee for the Re-Election of the President. Republican campaigns involving "dirty tricks"—secretive, unethical, and unlawful—were subsequently shown to have damaged various Democratic candidates. Televised Watergate hearings, conducted by a Senate committee in 1973 and 1974, exposed even more of the iceberg. A dramatic revelation came with the disclosure that President Nixon had "bugged" visitors to the Oval Office with special recording equipment.

Stung by criticism and claiming innocence, Nixon was forced by public pressures to appoint a "Special Prosecutor" to probe the Watergate mess. Investigations revealed a catalogue of official malfeasance, including the existence of a White House "plumber's unit" of ex-CIA agents whose task was to plug leaks of confidential information. When the probe of White House corruption got too close for comfort, Nixon fired the Special Prosecutor and also accepted the resignations of the Attorney General and his deputy in the startling "Saturday Night Massacre," October 20, 1973.

Public outcries deluged Washington in the form of telegrams, letters, and telephone calls. Unfriendly editorials demanded Nixon's removal, while street demonstrators insisted, "Resignation or impeachment," "Throw the bums out," and "Impeachment now more than ever." Automobile bumper strips demanded, "Honk for Impeachment," "Nixon Go Home" and "Impeachment with Honor." Paraphrasing a Goldwater slogan of 1964, critics claimed of Nixon, "In your heart you know he knows." By the autumn of 1973 the President was obviously in deep trouble; many citizens were supporting the sentiment "Down with King Richard!"

Headaches for the White House were compounded by the forced resignation of Vice President Spiro Agnew. Involved in bribes or "kickbacks" while governor of Maryland and even as Vice President, he "plea-bargained" a "no-contest" response to lesser charges of income tax evasion, and was hustled out of office in October 1973. Americans afflicted with "Spironoia" admitted their satisfaction; loyal supporters demanded, "Keep our Veep." Foes of the President added a twist to an earlier slogan: "Nixon's the One—Not Agnew."

Nixon was now obligated by the Twenty-fifth Amendment to nominate a successor as Vice President, and chose Gerald ("Jerry") Rudolph Ford, the House Minority Leader. A former football star and a twelve-term Republican Congressman, Ford presented such a "straight" image and impeccable record as to prompt the press to hail him as "Mr. Clean." He was wont to say with becoming modesty, "I am a Ford, Not a Lincoln."

THE NEW ISOLATIONISM

While the nation was "wallowing in Watergate," Uncle Sam still managed to keep in the global eye. New disclosures about Nixon's unauthorized bombing of Cambodia proved that he was continuing the aerial blitz even after the cease-fire in Vietnam. Placards demanding "Stop the Bombing Lord," "U.S. Out of Cambodia," and "No More War" sprouted in front of the executive mansion. In the teeth of dogged opposition from the White House, Congress finally managed to end the blitz in Cambodia and to place severe paper restraints on future "Presidential wars."

Menacing rumbles in the Middle East threatened new burdens for the United States. The Arab-Israeli conflict erupted anew in October 1973, when the Jewish state was caught off guard as Egyptian and Syrian forces unleashed surprise attacks in the so-called "Yom Kippur War." Mortified by the spectacular successes of Israel in the "Six-Day War" of 1967, Arab armies sought to regain their pride as well as lost territory. Surrounded by hostile neighbors, Israel battled desperately with heavy losses of men and equipment. Supporters in the United States, vowing that "their fight is our fight" and crying "Let Israel live," pressed for action in resupplying the tiny democracy. Nixon responded with gigantic airlifts of arms which helped to turn the tide in favor of Israel and to bring an uneasy cease-fire. Official Washington ignored signs waved by Arab demonstrators in New York demanding, "Defeat U.S. Zionist Aggression."

In retaliation for America's support of their foe, the Arab states clamped an embargo on oil shipments to the friends of Israel in October 1973. Long predicted, the "energy crisis" hit with devastating impact. To save fuel, daylight-saving time was imposed in the dark winter months, during which it was dubbed "daylight disaster time."

Arab "blackmail," which deprived gas-guzzling cars of their accustomed rich diet, created long lines and short tempers at the fuel pumps. "We need gas, not hot air," shouted a crowd outside the White House in dissatisfaction with stalemated administration efforts to resolve the crisis. Motorists were urged to conserve gasoline and form car pools with such slogans as "Don't be Fuelish" and "If You Can't Fuel It, Pool It." Finally, after five months of preoccupation with the "politics of petroleum," the oil embargo was lifted, in March 1974. But no one could safely say that the oil barons of the Middle East might not impose it again.

Opportunities for Arab diplomatic gains flowered as the Western democracies cowered before the "oligarchs of oil." Israel was increasingly isolated as the Arab guerrilla groups known as the "Palestine Liberation Organization" (PLO) capitalized on Arab political momentum. At the United Nations in New York the gun-toting leader of the Palestinian terrorists was uproariously welcomed by the General Assembly. Outside, Jewish-Americans carried signs warning, "The Stink of Munich is in the Air, and it Reeks of Arab Oil." Other placards declared, "The United Nations is Not a Gas Station" and "Death takes a seat at the U.N." Young Jewish militants vowed, "Never again!" in reference to the horrors of Hitler's genocidal holocaust—the "final solution" of the "Jewish problem."

Muddle in the Middle East was further complicated by the unwillingness of the Soviet Union to permit Jewish nationals to emigrate to Israel without paying substantial sums for their education. Before the Russian consulate in San Francisco Jewish demonstrators waved signs declaring, "Ransom No! Let My People Go!" Efforts by the Washington government to wring concessions from Moscow in return for economic favors proved generally unsuccessful.

IMPEACHMENT WITH HONOR

Double-digit inflation spurred by the energy crisis failed to crowd "impeachment politics" from center stage, as continuing inquiry revealed the sordid "Watergate" story in demoralizing detail. Nixon's henchmen had maintained "enemies lists" and had harassed opponents by using the FBI and Internal Revenue Service. In the name of "national security" numerous illegal wiretaps and breakins had occurred. The slimy sea of corruption engulfed a score or so of large corporations that had made illegal campaign contributions, more accurately called "extortion" or "blackmail." The payment of "hush money" and other attempts to obstruct the Watergate probe led anti-Nixonites to demand, "Four more years—two off for good behavior," and "Finish the turkey by Thanksgiving."

Democrats delighted in the deterioration of the Republican administration while partially concealing their partisan satisfaction. "Don't blame me, I voted for McGovern," crowed one bumper strip, and others pleaded, "Come Home Democrat" and "Don't Mourn, Organize," as the

"Watergate follies" increased the political prospects of the loyal opposition. Impeachment and removal were increasingly recognized as the only solution that could restore faith in the moral majesty of the Presidency. Some Americans wanted more than Nixon's removal from office, as suggested when they rewrote the song title "Hail to the Chief" as "Jail to the Chief!"

"Don't give up the tapes," was Nixon's unannounced motto as he battled the courts, under the plea of "executive privilege," to retain his incriminating records of "bugged" White House conversations. The suspicion was strong that he had committed the crime of obstructing justice in falsely editing or erasing the record. Increasingly, the public outcry made clear that the nation would not condone unlawful conduct by the President, even in "the national interest" or for "national security," as interpreted by Nixon.

Bumper strips and placards urged "Impeachment with Honor," "Honk If You Think He's Guilty," and "Impeach Nixon Now more than Ever." Nixon's backers, sneering at the Democratic heir apparent Senator Ted Kennedy, cynically called "The Hero of Chappaquiddick," rejoined, "Nobody drowned at Watergate." The reference was to the mysterious drowning of a young woman at Chappaquiddick, Massachusetts, in an auto accident involving Senator Kennedy.

President Nixon, after submitting only severely "sanitized" tapes to Congress and withholding others, was finally forced to disgorge, following a decision of the Supreme Court in July 1974. The "smoking pistol" that the advocates of impeachment needed came to light when a White House tape, recorded June 23, 1972, revealed that Nixon had instructed the Central Intelligence Agency to prevent the Federal Bureau of Investigation from continuing its probe of the Watergate scandal—a criminal obstruction of justice. Forestalling inevitable impeachment, Nixon announced his formal resignation in a televised speech August 8, 1974. He admitted error but not wrongdoing. His "judgments" could be faulted, he conceded, but they were made "in what I believed at the time to be the best interests of the nation."

Skeptics voiced disbelief, especially over Nixon's claim in his farewell address that he was being forced to leave office not for unlawful conduct, but because, like a British Prime Minister, he had lost his "political base in Congress." Sign wavers at rallies reminded the nation that "Capone got 10 Years" and proposed that the popular Nixon slogan "Four More Years" be changed to "Five to Life." Ironically, the departure of the tape-entangled President helped to redeem his campaign slogan of 1968, "Bring Us Together."

A FORD FROM MICHIGAN

Gerald R. Ford, an accidental and nonelected Vice President and then an accidental nonelected President, projected the image of a "good guy"

—an "earnest mediocrity," remarked foreign observers. But his brief "honeymoon" with Congress ended abruptly when, after one month, he granted Nixon a full pardon for any illegal acts he might have committed as President. Countless Americans believed that Nixon had made a "buddy system" deal with Ford before naming him for the Vice Presidency. Others complained of "Ford's double standard" which put Nixon associates in jail but not the master criminal himself. "We want a trial" was the clamor that rose from frustrated critics, but Ford felt that such a prosecution would further divide the nation and perpetuate the emphasis on Presidential wrongdoing. The new President was also suspected of trying to dispose quickly of the entire scandal so that the Republican party might face the elections of 1976 cleansed of Watergate. "There's a Ford in your future," he was accused of thinking, as the popularity of the man from Grand Rapids rapidly shrank. A bumper strip read "Ford Is Nixon's Revenge," while another urged, "Don't Vote: You'll Encourage Them."

A semblance of tranquility returned with a lessening of political tensions, but the darkening clouds of inflation, recession, and unemployment haunted the economy. "Be a Pricefighter" urged one bumper strip. A Ford-sponsored campaign to "Whip Inflation Now" (WIN), complete with bright red and white "WIN" buttons, never got off the ground. One White House staffer, wearing his button upside down, warned that his "NIM" stood for "No Immediate Miracles."

Overseas, resistance by U.S.-financed South Vietnam collapsed in the spring of 1975, to the accompaniment of charges at home and in Southeast Asia of "betrayal of an ally." The few remaining American civilians were hastily flown out, along with about 150,000 Vietnamese refugees, mainly "loyal" government workers and those closely associated with the Americans. President Ford stated that a "bloodbath" would occur if these Vietnamese were not rescued from the approaching enemy armies. But many Americans, especially the unemployed, resented having to shoulder additional burdens for Vietnam. Marchers brandished signs asking, "Would They Do This For Us?" and crying, "Gooks Go Home." Other unfriendly complaints were "Charity Begins at Home" and "Only Ford Wants Them." One bumper strip forecast, "Now Our Money, Next Our Jobs, Then Our Country"; another queried, "How Many Vietnamese Fought in our Civil War?"

Yet President Ford spoke for millions in extending the open arms which America has traditionally offered to the poor and oppressed seeking refuge. In the spirit of the words on the Statue of Liberty that had welcomed millions of immigrants—"those huddled masses, yearning to breathe free"—the nation generously offered a compassionate hand.

Mighty America, seemingly a pitiable giant, thus lost the last phase of the Vietnam War—or rather its protégé did. Nixon's stalemate "peace with honor" in 1973 had become peace with horror in 1975. The nation's image as world policeman and world nursemaid had suffered a humiliating blow. Much water would have to flow down the Mekong River before the peoples of the free world could repose their former faith in the willingness and ability of the United States to honor its solemn commitments, including those made unwisely. Cynics were heard to say that America's enmity was unpleasant but its friendship was fatal. Such were the bitter fruits of supporting an authoritarian regime that lacked the whole-hearted support of its own people.

XXXIV

America
in the Crucible

We must learn to live together as brothers or perish together as fools.

Martin Luther King, Jr., 1964

POPULATION EXPLOSION

Beyond doubt the first three decades after World War II were yeasty ones for America and the rest of the world. Political, diplomatic, and military events—such as assassinations, corruption, wars, and the nuclear arms race—dominated headlines. Especially alarming was the proliferating population that strained global capacities and threatened "people pollution." The unlimited procreative powers of a world possessing only limited material resources gave point to the slogan "The Population Bomb—Everybody's Baby." Faced with the frightening prospect of some 25 billion people on earth by 2075, proponents of "zero population growth," saying "Two are enough," distributed a stream of propaganda calling upon humans to "Cork the Stork" and "Stop Heir Pollution."

Looming mass starvation could theoretically be offset in some degree by the practice of family planning or birth control, especially in the less industrialized, "underdeveloped" nations. Vocal proponents of social action in the United States urged women to take "The Pill" and practice "planned parenthood." Liberal abortion laws also helped to check the "baby boom" as "liberated women" proclaimed, "Love is beautiful, over-population isn't." Minority groups, equating more bodies with increased political power, demanded "the right to breed" and "the right to be born," as crowded ghettoes in the industrial Northeast rang with protests against "whitey's genocide." Mexican-American "Chicanos" and other "Third World" peoples often opposed population control because of religious traditions.

Equally dramatic were population shifts, resulting in the growth of sprawling "suburbia." Most Americans lived in large metropolitan areas that included cities surrounded by a necklace of "bedroom communities," from which commuters traveled to work along snarled highways. Planners foresaw that the "urban slopover" would eventually link such once distant sites as Boston and Washington in large, continuous cities—"Boswash."

Suburban sprawl naturally troubled observers of the changing scene. The upper middle class, a strong tax base, was deserting the central areas in a "white flight," leaving the "inner cities" with their deteriorating schools and violent crime "black, brown, and broke." The ghettoized centers, including the nation's capital, became cesspools of fear, hopelessness, and racial anger.

President Johnson's "War on Poverty" tried to battle some of these severe afflictions, but in the end poverty won. The billions poured into urban renewal often meant black removal, while ambitious plans to build "Model Cities" ran afoul of community rivalries that all too often ended in costly failures.

TRANSPORTATION TROUBLES

Automobiles multiplied faster than people, as Americans continued their love affair with the careening death traps. Improved designs of highways and motor vehicles at least reduced the risk of injury. Safety-minded citizens responded to seat-belt campaigns urging car riders to "Buckle Up and Live" and adding "It's a Nice Way to Say I Love You." Billboard warnings reminded drivers to "Watch Out for the Other Guy" and to "Drive Defensively," which supplemented a slogan of the 1930s, "Rely on Your Brakes Instead of Your Horn." The National Safety Council featured the personalized slogan "The Life You Save May Be Your Own."

By a curious quirk of fate, the fuel crisis in the 1970s dampened both the speed and use of the gas-guzzling automobile, but tens of thousands of Americans still became statistics in the deplorable highway carnage. Crusaders for safety, notably Ralph Nader, implored motorists to remember that "Speed Kills," but many citizens regarded such campaigns for lower speed limits and "crashworthy" cars as too little and too late.

Travelers impatient with old-fashioned land travel streamed to the nation's airports to be hurtled through the air in "jumbo jets" of elephantine proportions. Responding to such tasteless Madison Avenue appeals as "Fly Me" and "We Really Move Our Tail for You," the huge airships carried as many as 300 passengers from sea to shining sea at speeds unimagined by the Wright brothers.

Spectacular growth in the air industry further sidetracked the ailing railroads. Interminable troubles plagued the once proud lines, forcing some into bankruptcy and others into a quasi-government corporation, Amtrak, whose aged equipment earned the complaint of "cattle cars." Songs which immortalized the iron monster, like "Chattanooga Choo-Choo" and "Take the 'A' Train," vanished along with dozens of railroads into the junkyard of history.

AMERICA THE BLIGHTED

Uncontrolled growth of cities, factories, and fume-spewing automobiles and airplanes threatened America with polluting "smog" and "uglification." The garbage in the air and water and on the earth mocked the slogans "Keep America Green" and "Keep America Beautiful." Once-clean cities were beginning to choke in their own leavings. Ardent conservationists, in the spirit of Teddy Roosevelt, were turning their attention to saving the landscape with campaigns of "Don't be a Litterbug" and "Every Litter Bit Hurts."

Political pressures were increasing to "police the polluters," as government responded with stiff fines for the "pollutocrats" responsible for oil slicks, belching smokestacks, and liquid industrial waste. A popular song of the mid-1960s, "My Dirty Stream," held out hope for pure water someday in the Hudson River. "Woody the Owl," hatched by the U.S. Forest Service, urged citizens to "Give a Hoot, Don't Pollute!" But tougher standards for factories would have to be established, at a cost of billions of dollars, before the rivers ran clear and some of the nation's largest cesspools became lakes again. Bumper strips declared, "Earth: No Deposit, No Return," "Earth—Love It or Leave It," and "Pollution Stinks." Verdant Oregon, looking southward in alarm, supported the theme "Don't Californicate Us."

Alarmingly, the republic's resources were being rapidly depleted. Once a "have" nation with abundant natural resources, America was becoming a "have-not" nation, and the slogan "Recycle for Survival" was gaining pertinence. A growing energy crisis assumed paralyzing proportions in 1973 as the nation was gripped by the Arab oil boycott; "They've got us over a barrel" was one grim response.

Noxious exhausts and dwindling resources made life difficult not only for human beings but also for plants and animals. Forests were being attacked by industrial smoke, while water life was being choked to death by the dumping of raw sewage. Precious timber reserves were being devastated. Environmentalists were often condemned as holding the nation back from self-sufficiency in energy, as when they opposed strip mining in Appalachia and pipelines in Alaska. A cynical anticonservation bumper strip in Alaska jibed, "Let the Bastards Freeze in the Dark." A much-needed campaign to reduce "noise pollution" invited another irreverent request, "If You're for Noise Abatement, Honk!"

"The Thinker." Ray Osrin, the Cleveland *Plain Dealer*. Reproduced with permission of the *Plain Dealer*.

Moonscape countrysides, the result of strip mining, paralleled the urban landscape, which was suffocating under blankets of concrete known as "asphalt jungles." A popular song, in the spirit of Cole Porter's "Don't Fence Me In," moralized "This Land Is Your Land" in an effort to arouse the public against despoiling the environment. A popular hit about "ticky-tacky" houses decried look-alike residential areas. Consumer organizations warned that Americans would have to live with the "abundance of scarcity." Yet simple pleas to "Save our Seashore" and to "Think Green" met political and economic resistance. A popular and pathetic automobile bumper strip queried, "Have You Thanked a Green Plant Today?" Environmentalists who opposed nuclear power stations pleaded, "Don't Grow Nuclear Plants."

Escalating threats to the external environment were matched by internal dangers as well. Human resources were being decimated by heart disease, cancer, and alcoholism, as the costs of medical care rose shockingly. Medically backed campaigns appealed to Americans to "Fight Cancer with a Checkup and a Check" and to "Give So More Will Live." For a time President Kennedy's emphasis on physical fitness, including fifty-mile hikes, stimulated interest in "Alcoholics Anonymous," "Weight-Watchers" clubs, and "organic natural foods," allegedly grown without pesticides.

Such large-scale efforts to combat the "soft life" were generally unsuccessful. Americans were typically complacent or defiant, especially about the dangers of cigarette smoking. The official admonition "Warning: The Surgeon General Has Determined That Cigarette Smoking Is Dangerous to Your Health" was printed in magazine advertisements and on the packages themselves. Yet sales increased. One slogan maker noted that "Cancer Cures Smoking," while tuberculosis associations pleaded with the public to give up smoking as "a matter of life and breath." The concern of non-smokers over the dangers of second-hand smoke led to the posting of such signs as "Thank You for Not Smoking" and "Yes, I Mind If You Smoke." Many addicts resented such encroachments on their "rights," and they were met with the retort, "Your Right to Smoke Ends Where My Nose Begins."

REVOLTING YOUTH

Young people—"The Now Generation"—captured the headlines of fad and fashion in the 1960s, notably after the inauguration of John F. Kennedy as the youngest elected President in U.S. history. Overwhelmed by the results of the maturing "baby boom" of the post-World War II period, colleges and schools became centers of political, social, and cultural rebellion, much of which was imitated by adult admirers. Uncouth "counterculture" characters with long hair and bare feet generally disdained "The Establishment," as indicated by the popular slogan "Trust No One over Thirty." A celebrated song of individualistic student protest in the 1960s bore the title "I'm Gonna Say It Now."

Ear-splitting music pounded home the theme "Do your own thing" to the hairy "hippies," who divided the world into "straights" and "freaks." Some of the most alienated young people were "punks" and "dropouts" who had been "passed through" or had passed out of school on their way to lifetime careers as delinquents, functional illiterates, and welfare recipients. Free food stamps helped to support much free love.

Mind-blasting drugs, both "hard" and otherwise, darkened the brighter aspects of the youth movement, especially in the 1960s. An epidemic of narcotic abuse inflated the crime rate, as "pushers" and "users" appeared in city ghettoes as well as in suburban schoolyards. Singers crooned thinly disguised paeans to "Maryjane" (marijuana). The "Flower Children" of happier days in San Francisco's Haight-Ashbury district were drowned in a wave of antisocial behavior that found expression in the advice of drug-user Dr. Timothy Leary, to "turn on, tune in, and drop out."

To its credit, the youthful rebellion also manifested itself in constructive achievement. Thousands of college students volunteered for Kennedy's Peace Corps to "help other nations build their nations." At home, expanding student awareness in the 1960s elbowed aside the "apathetic fifties." Young reformers railed against social injustice, while "rock and roll" singers ungrammatically implored youth to "tell it like it is." The more seriously motivated leaders asked young people to "give a damn" and not to be polarized by the "generation gap."

Ranking first among the burning political interest of students throughout the Johnson and Nixon years was the antiwar movement, in which "New Left" radicals mounted street protests against the escalating conflict in Vietnam. The thousands of people who marched and chanted in antiwar parades were mostly young. And when Presidents Johnson and Nixon conducted their war on war protesters, conservative Americans joined in with the widely distributed bumper strip "America: Love It or Leave It!" A youthful retort was "Change It or Lose It!"

Sexual and moral attitudes were clearly being revolutionized by rebellious youth. Some of their behavior, which parents once thought "permissive" in young people, was subsequently aped by older folks. Young women and matrons alike "made the scene" in miniskirts and peek-a-boo dresses, as the "new morality" spread like wildfire. "Yes On All Propositions," was a bumper strip that burlesqued election-time advertising.

Venereal disease reached epidemic proportions as many people discovered that "Free Love Isn't" and health agencies pleaded with young people to "Fight Love Pollution." The pornography industry, promoted by so-called "merchants of Venus," spewed a constant stream of salacious material. Purveyors of "smut," especially through cheap paperbacks, "girlie magazines," and "adult movies," argued that "Nude Is Not Lewd" and that "Sex Has No Calories." "Banned in [puritanical] Boston," a label once used to promote prurient literature, no longer had much meaning.

CRIME AND CHRISTIANITY

Sinister forces were meanwhile conspiring to drag a prosperous nation down the road to violence and degeneracy. The crime rate became the most alarming statistic, as increasing numbers of citizens fell victim to the "mugger," the "pusher," and the drug addict or "hophead" trying to "score." They were joined by the housebreaker, the rapist, and the hold-up man, with his cheap revolver known as "the Saturday night special." Syndicated crime, portrayed by Hollywood films as the "Mafia," raked in an annual "take" of billions as its underground tentacles enfolded even legitimate businesses. But many citizens shrugged off all interference with the comment "I don't want to get involved." A "sick joke" appeared on bumpers: "Stamp Out Rape—Say Yes."

Untold riches were at stake in the crime business, especially in the narcotics traffic, where men murdered for a few ounces of "horse" (heroin) or "coke" (cocaine). Gang rivalries resulted in "rubouts" reminiscent of the gangster executions by "hit men" in the 1920s. By the mid-1970s the crime bill for the nation reached an estimated $50 billion annually—a cynical rebuke to America's Pollyanna belief that "crime doesn't pay."

International crime also threatened. A few Americans became involved in political terrorism overseas or vented their frustrations by "hijacking" or "skyjacking" airplanes to Cuba. Scores of young men and women were interned in foreign prisons in drug crackdowns, after having ignored the U.S. Customs Service slogan warning, "There's No Hope with Dope."

To combat rising crime, citizens embarked on "law and order" drives seeking tougher punishment and an end to "crook coddling." President Nixon made "crime in the streets" a major campaign issue in 1972. When "hard-liners" endorsed his stand with the slogan "Support Your Local Police," hippies responded with "Support Your Local Fuzz"—their generally unfriendly name for the police.

Vitriolic attacks from the right wing against antigun legislation gave an emotional charge to the "law and order" campaigns. Lobbyists against restrictive regulations parroted a potent watchword, "If Guns Are Outlawed Only Outlaws Will Have Guns," which overlooked the simple fact that the police would remain armed. Similarly specious slogans were "Guns Don't Kill People, People Kill People," "The West Wasn't Won with a Registered Gun," and "Register Communists—Not Firearms." Opponents of gun control found no comfort in the bumper sticker "You Need a Bullet Like You Need a Hole in the Head."

Many Americans were understandably wary of any apparent movement toward a "police state." Cries of "Police brutality" and "Handcuff the cops" greeted the attempts of lawmakers to combat crime with force. On the other hand, some citizens complained that criminals often received more consideration than their victims, especially the raped, and "vigilante justice" was occasionally meted out by outraged citizens. Resentful officers of the law bumper-stripped their cars with "If You Don't Like Police, Call a Hippie for Help."

Capital punishment proved to be perhaps the most hotly debated facet of the crime problem. The U.S. Supreme Court temporarily halted all executions in the early 1970s by invoking the Eighth Amendment prohibition against "cruel and unusual punishment." Many states legislated more "democratic" procedures to avoid the employment of the ultimate penalty primarily against the poor, friendless, and the non-white. Critics continued to protest, "Death is so final" and to invoke the

Biblical "Thou shalt not kill." Often there was a scandalous discrepancy between "blue collar justice" and "white collar justice."

Many nerve-frayed Americans sought solace from the increasing strains of crime and nuclear tension in religion. Church membership generally rose in the decades after World War II. Yet paradoxically the role of religion in millions of lives was declining markedly as material pursuits and the currents of liberalism steadily eroded traditional allegiances. A natural result was the "God Is Dead" movement during the mid-1960s; it was countered by "God May Be Dead but the Devil Isn't." Painted roadside signs declaring, "Jesus Saves" often invited such crudely lettered additions as "But We Spend!"

Surprisingly, many young people were "turned on" by the emergence of a strong fundamentalist current toward the close of the 1960s. One by-product was the "Jesus Freaks," many of them nomadic types. Bumper strips on beat-up vans or "rolling bedrooms" advised, "Have a Nice Forever," "Find Help Fast in the Bible Pages," and "Honk If You Love Jesus!"

Advocate-in-chief of the "old-time religion" and "ecumenical movements" was the world-renowned evangelist, Billy Graham. Huge rallies in stadiums featured thousands of "sinners" making their "decisions for Christ" before Graham, who once defined his role by saying, "I just want to lobby for God." Graham preached, "There is so much hell in the country because there is not more hell in the pulpit."

ECONOMIC CROSSCURRENTS

Ordinary citizens, pinched by rising taxes, galloping inflation, and "tight money" at high interest rates, were buffeted during the mid-1970s by the harsh winds of a major economic "downturn." Most Americans blamed a spendthrift government and the large "multinational" corporations, especially those with "oil depletion allowances" and other escape hatches to frustrate the tax collector. Meanwhile, the national debt continued snowballing toward the $1 trillion mark, as squandering citizens with credit cards bought on the installment plan in response to the invitation to "Charge It—and Feel Like a King." "Moonlighting," working at several jobs to make ends meet, became a virtual necessity for millions.

Spending by Washington skyrocketed to about $400 billion a year in the 1970s and accounted for much of the economic dilemma. The largest portions of the "federal pie" went to defense, and hence strengthened the "military-industrial complex" against which President Eisenhower had far-sightedly warned in his farewell address. Other interest groups competed for the "revenue-sharing" funds allocated by the federal government to the cities and states. "We want our share," proclaimed local officials, but tax money sent to Washington did not come back without shrinking.

Some farmers, especially those in the large operations "agribusiness," were flourishing. Most producers were concerned with a fickle agricultural market, on the one hand, and the continuance of Congressional "price supports," on the other. Non-farming farmers were even being paid not to grow crops that would increase the surpluses. But prices in the supermarkets escalated into double-digit inflation by the early 1970s, and harried housewives marching in front of stores bore signs reading, "We Can't Afford To Eat."

On the other side of the coin, economic growth created both opportunities and problems for America's labor force. Powerful labor unions were securing higher wages and fringe benefits, including "profit-sharing plans" and "the guaranteed annual wage" in some industries. In a few large cities street sweepers earned better wages than many college professors. But political and economic power in the hands of unions was all too often abused, and several tough-fisted bosses went to prison. "Get Jimmy Hoffa"—the Teamsters' Union boss—was the successful goal of the federal prosecutors in 1967. Teamsters displayed "Nixon Free Hoffa" buttons, and the President obliged in 1971 with a pardon on the eve of his campaign for reelection, presumably with an eye on the labor vote.

Spiraling inflation, among other causes, often resulted in paralyzing strikes, "slowdowns," or "sickouts," even by school teachers and police and fire departments. Employers repeatedly reacted with lockouts and efforts to eliminate "featherbedding"—that is, the practice of maintaining superfluous jobs. Posters advised workers, "You Are Entitled To A Guaranteed Minimum Wage."

Blue-collar and white-collar workers, for their part, faced special problems. Migrant farm workers in California, largely Mexican, fought to establish unions of their choice by distributing leaflets at supermarket entrances requesting customers to "Boycott Lettuce" and "Don't Eat Grapes!" Professional groups, especially teachers, increasingly deplored inadequate salaries and difficult conditions of employment ranging from student rowdyism and "teenage tyranny" to overcrowded classrooms. In protest, teachers were going out on strikes in increasing numbers, and were consequently accused of "cutting classes" or "playing hookey" on a larger scale than their students.

CULTURAL CURRENTS

Material well-being also brought rewards in expanded opportunities for leisure. Some Americans responded to the call "Think skiing" by rushing to the icy runways. Millions of others sat before the television "boob tube" to watch everything from coronations and "space shots" to mindless "soap operas" and "sitcoms" (situation comedies). An entire generation of children, beginning in the 1950s, grew up on a six-hour-a-day diet of the "idiot box," watching orgies of violence and "reruns of reruns." Parents did not seem to be properly aware that perceptive critics had labeled television a "vast wasteland" that interfered with the development of reading skills.

Among moguls of music were sideburned youths who parlayed the "rock and roll" craze of the 1960s into a $2 billion business in records, tapes, and "stereo" equipment. Lyrics like "I want to hold your hand" sent caterwauling hordes of pubescent youth into a gyrating frenzy with dances like the "Twist," "Swim," and "Mashed Potato." Troubadours of the counterculture intoned their songs of unrequited love, social protest, and general dissatisfaction with the "rat race."

The visual arts also enjoyed boom times in these postwar years, especially in the gallery sales of "billboard art" and in the "paint-by-number kits" sold in stores. Millions of eager viewers thronged the museums to admire major exhibits. American architecture soared in the postwar decades, though some urban dwellers protested against "Manhattanization of the skyline." Innovators like the controversial Frank Lloyd Wright, about whom critics commented, "He was more frank than right," challenged conventional construction practices and materials with spectacular futuristic edifices. "Form and function are one" was his watchword.

Concurrently, the printed word continued to play a vital role, despite competition from the electronic media. But American newspapers went into a general decline, at least numerically, and many urban centers became "one-newspaper towns." Even New York City dropped to three daily papers, one of them, *The Times*, still proudly bearing its motto "All the News That's Fit to Print." The costs of automation, combined with increasing public dependence on television-style "eyewitness news," proved too burdensome for most newspapers.

EMERGING MINORITIES

Explosive civil rights movements broke into the headlines in the 1960's and 1970's. In general they were attempts by underprivileged Americans to gain for themselves, especially in political and social life, the rights and privileges enjoyed by the white middle-class majority. "Black Power" militants raised the banner of "Power to the People!" as they took advantage of "affirmative action" regulations by the federal government to secure more jobs and better ones. One slogan called for "Black Control of the Black Community." Yet an official legislative end to "Jim Crow" segregation in America did not guarantee the end of discrimination, thus reaffirming the old truism "You can't legislate morality." White racists, who longed to keep the Negro "in his place," resented the push toward equality. One cruel thrust urged, "Be tolerant—take a nigger to lunch." A half-humorous but perceptive response was, "Patience is the watchword in dealing with white folks."

Many concerned whites, as well as some blacks, resented having "big brother" in Washington, D.C., interfere in racial disputes. "Fair housing," plus "equal opportunity" programs in education and employment, sought to remove the racial character of previous abuses. Probably the most inflammatory issue of the late 1960s and early 1970s was "busing," designed to promote court-ordered integration. Many white parents opposed using small children as "freedom riders," and the elders marched militantly in parades chanting, "Two, four, six, eight—we won't integrate!"

Black leaders naturally deplored the violence that often resulted from racial confrontations. Martin Luther King, Jr., shot down in his prime by an assassin's weapon shortly before Senator Robert Kennedy met a similar fate in 1968, was the premier spokesman for his race. But King's vision of peaceful change met opposition from extremists on both sides, including "White Power" rednecks and black militants. The latter promised they would make the cities "Burn, baby, burn," as they did on a number of occasions, notably after the violent murder of the nonviolent Doctor King, winner of the Nobel Peace Prize.

Polarization of the electorate over racial issues, especially in regard to housing and education, helped to create a "white backlash." Critics angrily charged that higher levels of racial equality had been purchased at the expense of higher standards of excellence. Caucasian candidates for office in both Southern and Northern elections appealed to white voters with such slogans as "Your Home Is Your Castle, Protect It!"

Admittedly the "benign neglect" of the Nixon administration hindered some progress, yet in general the blacks could point to impressive changes, including a move toward "Black Capitalism." In education, "compensatory programs" drew more minorities into higher education, while "ethnic study" curricula were developed for public school children. The prideful slogan "Black is Beautiful" was used by blacks to reinforce young people's appreciation of their own subculture, which featured "soul food" and "soul music." The United Negro College Fund, seeking help especially for the impoverished black educational institutions in the South, pleaded "A mind is a terrible thing to waste."

Other minorities also demanded attention in their efforts to capitalize on "ethnic power." Spanish-surnamed populations, ranging from California to New York, voiced their own versions of the "We Shall Overcome" theme of the 1960s. Italian-Americans fought the stereotype of the Chicago gangster popularized by the movies. Jewish and Catholic politicians found their election prospects improved by a decline in the most virulent types of religious bigotry.

Native Americans, as the Indians call themselves, also experienced increased political consciousness during the 1960s and early 1970s, but they had perhaps the longest road to travel of any emerging minority, for they were being ignored to death. Serious deficiencies in housing, medical care, education, and employment still afflict the "original Americans." Militant Indians staged "occupations" of Alcatraz Island in San Francisco Bay and Wounded Knee, South Dakota, thus dramatizing their plight. The "Great White Father" in Washington, D.C., was reminded that "Custer Had It Coming" and "Custer Died for Your Sins," as automobile bumper strips alleged. Tribal identity was slowly slipping away, for about one-half of the Indian population had moved off the reservations, nursing their bitter memories of "the trail of broken treaties."

A more numerous minority were the millions of homosexuals who, in the early 1970s, began to "come out of the closet" and "go public" in large numbers. Despite continuing ridicule and social ostracism, "Gays" claimed that most people of their persuasion were simply afraid to speak out. Insisting on "the right to be different," males and females alike chanted as they marched, "Two, four, six, eight, we don't overpopulate," "Less population, more deviation," and "Ho-ho-ho-mosexual." Other advocates of "Gay Power" made known such views as "Gay is good" and urged, "Let gays live," "Full rights for gays," "Employ a homosexual citizen," and "Government has no place in the bedroom."

WOMEN ON THE WARPATH

Women, although a slight majority in numbers, emerged as a "minority group" with political "clout" in the first half of the 1970s. "Women's liberation" movements in America featured "bra burners," "bralessness," and the demand for "equal pay for equal work." Many former college coeds, now housewives, were enthusiastically endorsing the slogan "Women's Brains Are Valuable—Don't Waste Them." On the other hand, many "male chauvinist pigs," while admitting female equality in some areas, frowned upon the growing legions of "libbers," as the "liberationists" were called. Most males were evidently inclined to believe that the chief role of females was to bear and care for children. A few women traditionalists, disapproving of militant feminism, boldly paraded as "MOMS"—"Men Our Masters."

Rejecting the traditional role of "house spouse," many women fought "sex discrimination" in employment and finally secured "feminist" legislation in a number of states. "Woman Power: It's Much Too Good To Waste" proved to be an effective slogan. Progress in the political arena was hastened by the election of more female "Congresspersons," as the "nonsexists" put it. While men sneered, "Support women's lib—take a broad to lunch," feminists retorted, "A woman's place is in the House—and Senate." Increasingly, the housewife was seeking gainful employment while the employed "house husband" was required to share the housework and child care. "Give Your Wife Equality for Xmas" urged one bumper sticker.

"Woman Power" also manifested itself in a flood of proabortion legislation, capped by a landmark Supreme Court decision in 1973. Hailing the right to abortion as a "new birth of freedom," women demanded an end to "sexist" control over their bodies with such slogans as "Every Child a Wanted Child, Every Mother a Willing Mother." Street demonstrations featured females crying, "Women unite, abortion is our right." Antiabortionists, heavily Roman Catholic, defended the unborn child's "right to life" with such slogans as "unborn babies are people."

A major goal of the "libbers" was ratification of the proposed 27th Amendment—the so-called Equal Rights Amendment (ERA). Submitted to the states by Congress in 1972, it was designed to confer equality on women, including the "right" to be drafted into the armed services. Some women opposed the amendment because of its drawbacks; many others favored it in spite of them, including the National Organization for Women—NOW. At a Philadelphia rally women chanted "equal rights, equal rights, ratify the E.R.A.," which presumably would usher in a new ERA. Elsewhere, antifeminist females were reluctant to surrender their special privileges for so-called equality. Unwilling to have second-class manhood forced on American women, they displayed such placards as "Women Who Want to be Women," "The League of Housewives," and "Look Out! They're Planning to Draft Your Daughter."

Amid all this uproar America was continuing to grow and with growth inevitably came change, much of it not to the liking of many citizens. With added new world responsibilities pressing and with nuclear incineration possible, the boastful query of the 1940s, "Isn't it great to be an American?" had lost much of its appeal. "I'm proud to be an American" was a slogan of the 1970s more in tune with the spirit of the times.

XXXV

The Magic
of Words

All words are pegs to hang ideas on.
                        Henry Ward Beecher, *c.* 1870

Public officials, such as Presidents and Secretaries of State, can now speak most effectively for America to Americans through the electronic media. But such person-to-person communication involves only a few active participants addressing as many as tens of millions of passive listeners. Likewise newspaper editors, columnists, and commentators, especially those using radio and television, can also reach the masses directly. But again the number of such spokesmen is small and their listeners are not actively involved, except through such limited media as telephonic "talk shows."

How can the workaday American speak directly to considerable numbers of fellow citizens who are not immediate neighbors? One approach is through letters to the editor, but many of these are not published, and the remainder are often ignored, especially by the sports-minded reader. Citizens may also express their views through a public opinion poll, but this is only a small and carefully refined sample of respondents ranging from a few hundred to several thousand adults. Millions of Americans have never even seen a pollster.

Authors with gifted pens (or typewriters) can write books and articles, but here again only an articulate few can make such contributions. The woods are full of frustrated writers, some of whom could paper their walls with rejection slips.

Qualified citizens may theoretically express their views at the balloting booth, either in local or national elections or both. But voters are usually asked to record their approval or disapproval of little-known or unknown candidates, rather than of issues. Too often the citizenry are presented with a list of strange names or a choice between two evils, especially for the Presidency. Even where one is asked to vote on propositions, whether state or local, the voter is routinely confronted with accepting the ills he dimly perceives or those yet unrevealed.

Slogans or catch phrases are about the only medium through which large numbers of ordinary citizens can express their views personally and repeatedly for or against given candidates or propositions. This fact may account for the spontaneity of many slogans; their authors are usually difficult to trace. Among the most effective vehicles for these capsuled opinions are buttons, banners, ribbons, placards, campaign songs, and, in recent decades, bumper strips or stickers. Increasing traffic jams, in the never-ending battle of the bumpers, generate large numbers of captive readers.

Beginning in the 1890's, the pin-back (pin-on) celluloid button became perhaps the most popular device for disseminating slogans. In the presidential campaigns of the present century they have been struck off by the tens of millions, mostly for free distribution by the managers of political parties or for sale by manufacturers of buttons. Presumably the official sources endorse what they publish and the private agencies, with profits in view, offer sentiments that they believe are shared by a considerable number of prospective purchasers. Citizens who wear such messages obviously support the views proclaimed or the candidate touted. Pin-on buttons have been called one of the last refuges of the politically timid: the wearers can register their support of an issue, such as "No Third Term" or "Impeachment Now," without making themselves offensively conspicuous or ridiculous.

The impact of such catch phrases is impossible to measure with precision but it obviously exists. "Rum, Romanism, and Rebellion" almost certainly cost James G. Blaine the presidency in 1884. The Wilson-Hughes presidential contest of 1916 was so breathtakingly close that one potent slogan, "He Kept Us Out of War," undoubtedly accounted for at least the margin of victory.

Hundreds of other but less effective catch phrases have survived, and they are of value historically as visible evidence of what many contemporaries thought were the salient issues. For example, "United We Stand" and a flood of other slogans spawned by the Civil War impress one anew with their suggested devotion to the ideal of union. At the same time one cannot fail to appreciate the determination of the South to fight for what it honestly believed to be its rights.

Yet slogans are not an unmixed blessing, important though they may be as expressions of popular sentiment, political partisanship, and pressure-group objectives. Catch phrases are undoubtedly foes of sober reasoning; they implant the comfortable but illusory feeling that the user is thinking when only mouthing. Some wit has pointedly observed that slogans are "the good old American substitute for the facts." Wendell Willkie remarked in the late 1930's that "A good catchword can obscure analysis for fifty years." Bertrand Russell, the British philosopher who backed "Ban the Bomb," declared, "Most people would rather die than think. In fact, some do."

Catch phrases are almost invariably one-sided, with little or no room for qualifiers or argument. They often contain untruths or half truths, such as "Guns don't kill people; people kill people." Some slogans not only serve as drugs for the brain but also as opiates for the conscience, notably when "Remember Pearl Harbor" rendered more righteous the dropping of two atomic bombs on Japan.

Slogans also encourage voters to think with their lungs, as with the "Sixteen to One" of 1896, when the complex silver-gold issue was furiously debated. Some contemporaries, to judge from faded lapel buttons, must have thought that something disastrous was about to happen at sixteen minutes to one o'clock—perhaps the end of the world. Finally, slogans prompt people to "think" with wisecracks, as in the anti-Goldwater slogan of 1964, "In Your Guts You Know He's Nuts."

Yet if sloganeering is not a perfect technique, neither is democracy, of which it is a prominent part. As voices of America, catch phrases usually express, reflect, or even stimulate public sentiment, sometimes even thinking. Dr. Samuel I. Hayakawa, the semanticist, has called slogans "essential shortcuts to a consensus." If a democracy is to endure without an explosion, what the people believe or feel has to come out in some way for the guidance of their government. One of the most perceptive foreign critics of the American scene, Sir Denis W. Brogan, wrote that "the evocative power of verbal symbols must not be despised, for these are and have been one of the chief means of uniting the United States and keeping it united."

Slogans have the additional merit of helping Americans to recall a colorful dimension of their history, however hazily. A Gallup poll in 1975, to the shame of the nation's costly school system, revealed that nearly three Americans in ten do not know the significance of the year 1776. It is better to "Remember the Alamo," "Remember the *Maine*," and "Remember Pearl Harbor"—among other famous war cries that have aroused America—than to remember nothing at all. The importance and centrality of some of these slogans is best realized only in perspective. If a people cannot recall where they have been as a nation, even vaguely, they have lost their way. They have also lost one of the priceless attributes that enrich their national heritage.

As the United States embarked upon its bicentennial year, many observers sensed a new spirit of dedication to the ideals of the Founding Fathers, as well as a deepened appreciation of the nation's heritage. Concerned citizens continued to express their feelings in strong and colorful language, as they had often done since colonial days. One nationally syndicated journalist inaugurated a contest to bring out a slogan that would best encapsulate the renewed sense of national pride. To his astonishment, his appeal elicited more than a million entries, most of them unashamedly patriotic, such as "Freedom's Way—for the U.S.A." and "America—the Possible Dream." As long as the Bill of Rights continues to guarantee the precious privileges of free speech and a free press, the world will continue to hear the myriad voices of America.

Bibliography

Much of the material incorporated in his book comes from a fifty-year hobby that involved collecting memorable phrases or sayings while reading newspapers, magazines, and books. A complete listing of all such sources would soon become unmanageable, and hence the references listed below represent a severe distillation.

Much of the basic research was conducted in the Library of Congress, particularly in the enormous collection of broadsides and other leaflets; in the sheet-music campaign songs; in the extensive collection of songsters; and in the leaflet songs and imprinted envelopes, notably for the Civil War years.

The remarkable collections of colored posters for World War I and World War II in the Hoover Institution, Stanford University, proved richly rewarding. Those of the Library of Congress for World War II were also useful.

Materials relating to campaign songs and slogans in the Huntington Library, San Marino, California, were likewise utilized.

As for campaign buttons, I have been privileged to examine two extraordinary private collections, that of John Stanton of the *Palo Alto Times* and that of Joseph Kokes, of San Jose, California. Many of these appear photographically in the button books of Ted Hake listed below.

The annual *Readers' Guide to Periodical Literature*, published for as early as 1890, lists hundreds of articles on various kinds of campaigns, especially as they relate to slogans, banners, pins, posters, medals, buttons, and songs. Many of these articles are accompanied by revealing photographs of posters and other pictorial material. The periodical items were systematically examined for this study.

GENERAL WORKS

Edward Channing, *A History of the United States,* 6 vols., New York, 1905–1925.

Henry S. Commager and R. B. Morris, eds., *The New American Nation Series,* New York, 1954–.

John B. McMaster, *A History of the People of the United States from the Revolution to the Civil War,* 8 vols., New York, 1883–1913.

E. P. Oberholtzer, *A History of the United States since the Civil War,* 5 vols., New York, 1917–1937.

J. F. Rhodes, *History of the United States from the Compromise of 1850,* 7 vols., New York, 1893–1906.

Arthur M. Schlesinger and D. R. Fox, eds., *A History of American Life,* 13 vols., New York, 1927–1948.

Arthur M. Schlesinger, Jr., ed., *History of U.S. Political Parties,* 4 vols., New York, 1973.

Arthur M. Schlesinger, Jr., and F. L. Israel, eds., *History of American Presidential Elections, 1789–1968,* 4 vols., New York, 1971.

Mark Sullivan, *Our Times,* 6 vols., New York, 1926–1935.

SPECIAL STUDIES

Frederick L. Allen, *Only Yesterday: An Informal History of the Nineteen-Twenties,* New York, 1931.

Frederick L. Allen, *Since Yesterday,* New York, 1940.

Carleton Beals, *Brass-Knuckle Crusade: The Great Know-Nothing Conspiracy: 1820–1860,* New York, 1960.

Roy A. Billington, *The Protestant Crusade, 1800–1860,* New York, 1938.

Wayne S. Cole, *America First: The Battle Against Intervention, 1940–41,* Madison, Wisconsin, 1953.

Louis Filler, *The Crusade Against Slavery, 1830–1860,* New York, 1960.

J. C. Furnas, *The Life and Times of the Late Demon Rum,* New York, 1965.

Charles D. Hazen, *The French Revolution as Seen by the Americans of the Eighteenth Century,* Washington, D. C., 1896.

Walter Johnson, *The Battle Against Isolation,* Chicago, 1944.

Aileen Kraditor, *The Ideas of the Woman Suffrage Movement, 1890–1920,* New York, 1965.

Richard R. Lingeman, *Don't You Know There's a War On? The American Home Front, 1941–1945,* New York, 1971.

James R. Mock and Cedric Larson, *Words That Won the War: The Story of the Committee on Public Information, 1917–1919,* Princeton, 1939.

George E. Mowry, *Theodore Roosevelt and the Progressive Movement,* Madison, Wisconsin, 1946.

Andrew Sinclair, *Prohibition: The Era of Excess,* Boston, 1962.

Moses Coit Tyler, *Literary History of the American Revolution, 1763–1783,* 2 vols., New York, 1897.

Elizabeth B. White, *American Opinion of France: From Lafayette to Pioncaré,* New York, 1927.

Carl Wittke, *The Irish in America,* Baton Rouge, Louisiana, 1956.

PRESIDENTIAL ELECTION MONOGRAPHS

Wesley M. Bagby, *The Road to Normalcy: The Presidential Campaign and Election of 1920*, Baltimore, 1962.

Charles H. Coleman, *The Election of 1868*, New York, 1933.

Emerson D. Fite, *Presidential Election of 1860*, New York, 1911.

Samuel R. Gammon, Jr., *The Presidential Election of 1832*, Baltimore, 1922.

Paul Glad, *The Trumpet Soundeth: William Jennings Bryan and His Democracy, 1896–1912*, Lincoln, Nebraska, 1960.

Robert G. Gunderson, *The Log Cabin Campaign*, Lexington, Kentucky, 1957.

Stanley L. Jones, *The Presidential Election of 1896*, Madison, Wisconsin, 1964.

George H. Knoles, *The Presidential Campaign and Election of 1892*, Stanford, 1942.

Herbert S. Parmet and Marie B. Hecht, *Never Again: A President Runs for a Third Term*, New York, 1968.

Roy V. Peel and Thomas C. Donnelly, *The 1928 Campaign: An Analysis*, New York, 1931.

Roy V. Peel and Thomas C. Donnelly, *The 1932 Campaign: An Analysis*, New York, 1935.

Robert V. Remini, *The Election of Andrew Jackson*, Philadelphia, 1963.

Earle D. Ross, *Liberal Republican Movement*, New York, 1919.

Irwin Ross, *The Loneliest Campaign: The Truman Victory of 1948*, New York, 1968.

Karl M. Schmidt, *Henry A. Wallace: Quixotic Crusade, 1948*, Syracuse, New York, 1960.

Theodore White, *The Making of the President, 1960*, New York, 1961.

Theodore White, *The Making of the President, 1964*, New York, 1965.

Theodore White, *The Making of the President, 1968*, New York, 1969.

Theodore White, *The Making of the President, 1972*, New York, 1973.

MEMORABLE SAYINGS

John Bartlett, *Familiar Quotations*, 14th ed., Boston, 1968.

Bruce Bohle, ed., *The Home Book of American Quotations*, New York, 1967.

Paul F. Boller, Jr., *Quotesmanship*, Dallas, 1967.

Constance Bridges, ed., *Great Thoughts of Great Americans*, New York, 1951.

Barnaby Conrad, *Famous Last Words*, New York, 1961.

Clifton Fadiman, *The American Treasury, 1455–1955*, New York, 1955.

Walter Fogg, *One Thousand Sayings of History*, New York, 1929.

Arthur T. Hadley, *Power's Human Face*, New York, 1965.

Robert D. Heinl, Jr., *Dictionary of Military and Naval Quotations*, Annapolis, Md., 1966.

David Kin, ed., *Dictionary of American Maxims*, New York, 1955.

Charles N. Lurie, *Putnam's Everyday Sayings*, New York, 1928.

Mitford M. Mathews, ed., *A Dictionary of Americanisms on Historical Principles*, 2 vols., Chicago, 1951.

H. L. Mencken, *The American Language*, New York, 1942.

H. L. Mencken, ed., *A New Dictionary of Quotations*, New York, 1942.

George Seldes, ed., *The Great Quotations*, New York, 1960.

James B. Simpson, comp., *Contemporary Quotations*, New York, 1964.

Burton E. Stevenson, ed., *Poems of American History*, Boston, 1908.

A. Marjorie Taylor, *The Language of World War II*, revised ed., New York, 1948.

Richard H. Thornton, *An American Glossary*, 2 vols., Philadelphia, 1912; revised vol. III (by Louise Hanley), Madison, Wis., 1939.

PRESIDENTIAL QUOTATIONS

Bill Adler, ed., *The Kennedy Wit*, New York, 1964.

Edward Boykin, ed., *State of the Union*, New York, 1963.

David C. Coyle, *Ordeal of the Presidency*, Washington, 1960.

Louis Filler, ed., *The President Speaks*, New York, 1964.

Gerald Gardner, ed., *The Quotable Mr. Kennedy*, New York, 1963.

Caroline T. Harnsberger, ed., *Treasury of Presidential Quotations*, Chicago, 1964.

Albert B. Hart and H. R. Ferleger, eds., *Theodore Roosevelt Encyclopedia*, New York, 1941.

Frances S. Leighton, ed., *The Johnson Wit*, New York, 1965.

Maxwell Meyersohn, ed., *The Wit and Wisdom of Franklin D. Roosevelt*, Boston, 1950.

Maxwell Meyersohn, ed., *Memorable Quotations of John F. Kennedy*, New York, 1965.

Merle Miller, *Plain Speaking: An Oral Biography of Harry S. Truman*, New York, 1973.

Saul K. Padover, ed., *Thomas Jefferson on Democracy*, New York, 1939.

Archer H. Shaw, ed., *The Lincoln Encyclopedia*, New York, 1950.

Arthur B. Tourtellot, *The Presidents on the Presidency*, Garden City, N.Y., 1964.

SLOGANS

Frank C. Bray, *Headlines in American History*, New York, 1937.

Everit Brown and Albert Strauss, *A Dictionary of American Politics*, New York, 1907.

Robert Lawson, *Watchwords of Liberty*, New York, 1957.

Edwin V. Mitchell, *An Encyclopedia of American Politics*, Garden City, N.Y., 1946.

Valerie Noble, ed., *The Effective Echo: A Dictionary of* [13,000] *Advertising Slogans*, New York, 1970.

William Safire, *The New Language of Politics*, revised ed., New York, 1972. The best single collection of slogans and catch phrases.

George E. Shankle, *American Mottoes and Slogans*, New York, 1941.

Edward C. Smith and Arnold J. Zurcher, *Dictionary of American Politics*, New York, 1968.

Hans Sperber and Travis Trittschuh, *American Political Terms*, Detroit, 1962.

George W. Stimpson, *A Book about a Thousand Things*, New York, 1946.

George W. Stimpson, *A Book about American Politics*, New York, 1952.

William Sunners, *American Slogans* [advertising], New York, 1949.

Henry F. Woods, *American Sayings: Famous Phrases, Slogans, and Aphorisms,* New York, 1945.

CAMPAIGN BUTTONS

J. Doyle DeWitt, comp., *A Century of Campaign Buttons, 1789–1889,* Hartford, Conn., 1958. The bible of collectors.

Ted Hake, *The Button Book,* New York, 1972.

Ted Hake, *Encyclopedia of Political Buttons: United States, 1896–1972,* New York, 1974.

Sally C. Luscomb, *The Collector's Encyclopedia of Buttons,* New York, 1967.

Dale E. Wagner, *A Concise History of American Campaign Graphics, 1789–1972,* Washington, D. C., 1972.

SONGS

American War Songs, Ann Arbor, Mich., 1971. Compiled for Colonial Dames of America.

Louis A. Banks, *Immortal Songs of Camp and Field,* Cleveland, 1898.

Kenneth A. Bernard, *Lincoln and the Music of the Civil War,* Caldwell, Idaho, 1966.

Margaret B. Boni, ed., *The Fireside Book of Favorite American Songs,* New York, 1952.

Gilbert Chase, *America's Music,* revised ed., New York, 1966.

Joseph M. Clary, comp., *Our Nation's History and Song,* Chicago, 1896.

Edward A. Dolph, *"Sound Off!" Soldier Songs from Yankee Doodle to Parley Voo,* New York, 1929.

David Ewen, ed., *American Popular Songs,* New York, 1966.

Richard B. Harwell, ed., *Songs of the Confederacy,* New York, 1951.

J. T. Howard, *Our American Music,* revised ed., New York, 1946.

The Burl Ives Sing-Along Song Book: A Treasury of American Folk Songs and Ballads, New York, 1963.

Maymie R. Krythe, *Sampler of American Songs,* New York, 1969.

Vera B. Lawrence, *Music for Patriots, Politicians, and Presidents,* New York, 1975.

Ruth and Norman Lloyd, *The American Heritage Songbook,* New York, 1969.

John A. Lomax and Alan Lomax, *American Ballads and Folk Songs,* New York, 1934.

John A. Lomax and Alan Lomax, *Our Singing Country,* New York, 1941.

Frank Luther, *Americans and Their Songs,* New York, 1942.

Carl Sandburg, *The American Songbag,* New York, 1927.

Irwin Silber, *Songs America Voted By,* Harrisburg, Pa., 1971. The best collection of campaign songs.

Wanda Willson Whitman, *Songs That Changed the World,* New York, 1969.

Index

DATE DUE

PRINTED IN U.S.A.